Price for
Ethical Clothing

The Ethical Environment

We have discussed the two major themes, (1) creativity and change and (2) the emergence of a global society, that we will develop throughout the course of this book; you should look for both case studies and larger vignettes developing these themes in each chapter. We also want to introduce several subthemes that we will group under the title, "The Ethical Environment." These include personal integrity, a cultural mindset, social responsibility, and global sustainability. Although much of what we discuss in this book will involve the work that leaders and managers do within the organization, it's important to realize that such work takes place in a larger social environment that shapes the values that those in the organization pursue. No one is immune to these influences, and, indeed, each one of us has a responsibility to be attentive to the ethics and values of the society in which we live. Sometimes we accept those values readily, yet at other times we resist those values and try to modify or replace them. But the ethical dialogue that occurs with respect to these values importantly shapes our behavior in organizations and defines our role in society. For that reason, it is important for us to examine these four subthemes at the beginning. Then, as we go through the text, we will note where these subthemes arise.

Personal Integrity

Most of today's la...

> ### Exercise 1.1 Ethical Dilemmas in Cross-Cultural Work

Working in different cultures also involves confronting different ethical norms including norms related to business transactions. Imagine that you are working in another country trying to get a new plant built for your firm, but you are having difficulty working your way through complex regulations. A representative of a government agency in that country suggests that you have lunch together and talk more informally about some issues that need to be resolved. In the discussion, he makes it clear that for $5,000 he can make all of those issues go away. What would be the appropriate course of action in a case like this? Currell and Bradley, authors of the article from which this case was adapted, pull no punches in their assessment of what should be done:

Organizations must insist on a swift response to complaints, unbiased investigations, and "public hangings" of offenders, and they should praise employees who have the courage to call out wrongdoing. These actions are critical to employees' perceptions of organizational justice, and they can help head off or mitigate the damage from bribery offenses.[68]

Do you agree with this judgment? If not, how would you frame an ethical solution?

TAKE ACTION With Complete Ethics Integration That Fully Aligns With AACSB

Chapter 1 lays the ethics foundation, and ethics is continually integrated throughout the text in context.

Consistent themes related to ethics include personal integrity, a cultural mindset, social responsibility, and global sustainability.

"This textbook seems designed to prepare thoughtful and creative managers who are alert to ethical nuances and the impact of globalization on organizational decision making."

—Hindy Schachter, New Jersey Institute of Technology

TAKE ACTION With a Focus on Creativity and Change

The 2010 IBM Global CEO Study concluded that the single most important attribute of future leaders will be creativity.

A full chapter on creativity and Creativity and Change features illustrate how organizations react to change creatively and introduce techniques for enhancing creativity.

"The toolbox for creativity and innovation is very practical."

—Bing Ran, Pennsylvania State University Harrisburg

CREATIVITY AND CHANGE — A CULTURE OF RESPONSIBILITY

Suzanne Fallender, Director of Corporate Social Responsibility, Strategy and Communications at Intel, was interviewed by Robert Denhardt of the University of Southern California in the Spring of 2013.

Q How do you define Corporate Social Responsibility? And how long has Intel engaged in CSR?

A I define CSR as a management approach—CSR is about looking at the full range of environmental, social, and governance impacts related to your business and effectively managing the risks and taking advantage of the opportunities that arise. Intel's history of CSR goes back to the company's founding. Intel co-founder Gordon Moore has long been a strong advocate of environmental stewardship, and he instilled a commitment to the environment that continues today. When I reflect on how Intel's commitment to and actions around CSR have evolved, I believe the main development has been one of integration. Particularly over the past five years—we have continued to embed CSR even further into the company's culture and governance structures. We have integrated CSR directly into our new vision and strategy, developed programs to engage our employees on CSR issues, and even linked a portion of every employee's compensation (from front line employees up to the CEO) to CSR factors.

Q What are the factors that have gone into the most successful CSR efforts?

A There are many different examples—at large and small companies. I think the keys to success are integration, collaboration, and scale and sustainability.

- *Integration:* Successful companies have taken steps to effectively integrate CSR into their business—it's not just done by a separate CSR department—they have engaged multiple parts of the business (such as supply chain, finance, IT) and have the support of senior management.

- *Collaboration:* On collaboration, success stories involve companies working with multiple partners (sometimes including other companies)—but forming partnerships with NGOs, governments, and development agencies to develop solutions that meet the needs of multiple stakeholders.

- *Scale and Sustainability:* Successful initiatives are ones that have a longer time horizon—they are not one-off projects or programs that are announced for a PR benefit. They have a plan for sustained investment and how the impact will be scaled.

Q One important element of CSR is environmental sustainability. How would you describe Intel's performance in this area?

A Intel's approach to environmental sustainability covers three main areas: reducing the impact of our manufacturing operations, improving the energy efficiency of our products, and applying our technology to help solve global challenges. In terms of products, we estimate that Intel technology will enable the billion PCs and servers installed between 2007 and 2014 to consume half the energy and deliver 17 times the computing capacity of the first billion PCs and servers (installed between 1980 and 2007).

Q But CSR is more than environmental sustainability. How would you describe your other efforts to create a culture of social responsibility and community engagement?

A In terms of social responsibility, Intel has also adopted a comprehensive approach to transforming educational access and quality through technology. We believe our approach benefits not only society but also our business since our future success rests on the availability of skilled workers, a healthy technology ecosystem, and knowledgeable customers.

TAKE ACTION With Compelling Cases That Begin and End Chapters

Relatable cases of varying lengths provide real-world examples.

A Case Study: Happiness at Work

For years, scholars and businesspeople have known that employee engagement was positively correlated with the organization's productivity; indeed, research shows that engaged groups of employees are more than 25% more productive. Engagement means that people want to come to work, they feel emotionally connected with others at the workplace, and they find their work both challenging and meaningful. But is that all there is?

Some executives today are saying "no," and, taking a page from Zappo's playbook, are trying to extend beyond engagement to something called happiness. (It's an old term, but you may have heard of it.) For example, Russ Lidstone, CEO of Havas Worldwide, an advertising firm, is trying to build a more resilient and more creative workforce through efforts to enhance his employees' happiness.

The idea is related to the positive psychology approach (see Chapter 1), an approach that suggests that instead of trying to fix problems (which only continue to pop up), managers and leaders should focus on the positive aspects of what's happening in their organizations and build on their strengths.

Case Study 5.1 SOS in DHS: A Problem of Motivation

About 18 months ago, Jess Johnson was appointed to direct a newly created unit in the state's Department of Human Services (DHS). Shortly thereafter, she interviewed and hired six new employees to staff the unit. The name of the unit is Service Outreach for Seniors (SOS). Its purpose is to coordinate services for the vulnerable elderly. This is Jess's first supervisory position.

Susan Jones and Bob Martin were two of the new employees Jess hired. Initially, both were very productive, enthusiastic, and industrious. Bob had taken the initiative to work closely with several prominent private service providers to ensure their cooperation and involvement in the new program. Susan had done a terrific job of producing publications and other materials describing the goals of the unit and [...]

since thi[...]
both Su[...]
employe[...]

Within t[...]
Jess con[...]
lunches[...]
Bob de[...]
for his v[...]
at least[...]
directly[...]
takes th[...]
ees who[...]
critical i[...]
and to c[...]

Susan,[...]
ative" i[...]

Jess (or anyone) on important policy matters before speaking to external groups and individuals. On several occasions, she has promised things to representatives of organizations and to elected officials that the SOS program simply could not deliver. On other occasions, she has misrepresented her role as a staff member, instead leaving the impression that she was directing the unit. This has embarrassed Jess and her supervisors more than once. Despite Susan's apparent desire to be "in the limelight" in the political and community arena, she has developed an open disdain for the regular workload in her area. She routinely misses deadlines and fails to complete important paperwork.

Jess has met with Bob and Susan separately to discuss her dissatisfaction with their performance. Being a matter-of-fact person, Jess simply told them that their [...]

GLOBAL SOCIETY

GLOBAL AMBASSADORS MENTOR EMERGING WOMEN LEADERS ACROSS THE GLOBE

"In today's ever-changing world, where global challenges necessitate strong leadership, the need for training and mentoring for women leaders has never been so acute" says Justine Metz, an executive at the Global Ambassadors program, a partnership between the Bank of America and Vital Voices,[46] an NGO that invests in unleashing the potential of women worldwide.[47] The role of women in economic development around the world has been emphasized by the United Nations and other global organizations such as the World Economic Forum.[48] However, while women make up 50% of the world's population, many do not get the education, training, and support they need and face considerable discrimination that prevents them from contributing fully to their communities. Programs such as Global Ambassadors recognize the importance of developing global leadership and allow emerging leaders to benefit from the experience of established leaders.

The program's mentors come from a variety of industries, including banking and entertainment, and are dedicated to helping their mentees grow while they themselves learn about global challenges. Candace Browning, head of Global Research Bank of America Merrill Lynch and one of the program's mentors, believes that "mentorship is critical to helping women drive change across economic, political and social channels."[49] Another mentor in the program, Wendy Luhabe, cofounder of Women Investment

Portfolio Holding in South Africa, is inspired by the program's mission to build bridges between new and emerging leaders. She says: "At its basic level, leadership is developing the capacity to transform our own lives and circumstances, and as our confidence grows we extend that capacity to our broader sphere of influence."[50] A third mentor, Ann Veneman, former Executive Director of UNICEF and former U.S. Secretary of Agriculture, believes the program can have long-lasting impact: "Good mentors can help create good leaders, and good leaders become mentors for the next generation," and she tells young leaders to "take advantage of opportunities that may come your way. It is not always easy to start on a new path, but it can lead to incredible opportunities to make a difference."[51] Susan Chambers, Wal-Mart People Division Executive Vice President, who mentors Smita Mankad, managing director of Artisans Micro Finance, says she helps her mentee focus so that she can continue to do "good" and do it well and, as a result, help other people by providing economic opportunity.[52] Cooperative efforts such as the Global Ambassador program exemplify the importance of developing global leadership and the role of one-on-one mentoring in the process.

1. Why should business get involved in programs such as Global Ambassadors?

2. Should business get involved in social and cultural issues?

TAKE ACTION With Culture and Diversity Coverage

Today's organizations function in a global environment where culture plays a central role. Chapter 2: Culture and Diversity explains the foundational importance of developing a cultural mindset.

AACSB International considers global and cultural forces and diversity as among the key challenges managers will face in the future.

A Global Society feature illustrates how globalization influences organizational behavior and includes discussion questions to promote critical thinking.

"By far the best material on culture I have ever seen in an organizational behavior text."

—Cynthia Nicola, Carlow University

TAKE ACTION With Abundant Critical Thinking and Skill Development Exercises

What Would You Do? features present hypothetical scenarios that require students to immediately interact with a chapter concept and connect it to their own behavior.

What Do You Think? features challenge students to exercise critical thinking.

What Would You Do?

▶ You feel that your team has become complacent and uncreative. The members are just too cozy and comfortable. So you take action. You pick several of the most complacent members and pair them with aggressive go-getters that you know will push them. You hear that conflict is intense and stressful. Should you intervene?

What Do You Think?

▶ You are hiring a new employee for a management position in your organization. There are two candidates and they seem exactly even in all regards—except one is a liberal arts major and the other is a business major. Again, all else being equal, who would you hire? And—the big question—why?

"'What Would You Do' sections are quite appealing and engaging for students and are not in my current text."

—Filiz Tabak, Towson University

"This text offers a brilliant combination of creativity and innovation, along with real-world illustrations that will equip any student for today's diverse workforce. Full of case studies, exercises, and self-assessments, it is a treasure trove of insights."

—Kenyatta McCurty, Amridge University

"A refreshing approach to the study of organizational behavior."

—Rudy Soliz, Houston Community College

TAKE ACTION With SAGE's Comprehensive Instructor Resources

Give Your Students the SAGE edge

SAGE edge for Instructors supports your teaching by making it easy to integrate quality content and create a rich learning environment for students.

SAGE edge provides comprehensive and chapter-specific multimedia online resources at edge.sagepub.com/nahavandi

Instructors Receive Full Access to the Password-Protected Instructor Teaching Site

- **Test Bank in Word and Respondus**
- **PowerPoint**
- **Video Resources**
- **Audio Resources**
- **Chapter Lecture Notes**
- **Chapter Objectives**
- **Sample Syllabi**
- **Discussion Questions**
- **Ideas for Classroom Activities**
- **ENGAGING Experiential Exercises**
- **SAGE Journal Articles**
- **Common Course Cartridges for Course Management Systems**
- **SAGE Handbook and Reference Links**
- **Real-World Research Articles From *Pacific Standard Magazine***

TAKE ACTION With SAGE's Comprehensive Student Resources

Students Can Sharpen Their Skills With SAGE edge

SAGE edge for Students provides a personalized approach to help you accomplish your coursework goals in an easy-to-use learning environment.

SAGE edge provides comprehensive multimedia online resources at edge.sagepub.com/nahavandi

Students Benefit From the NO Passcode Required, NO Additional Cost, Open-Access Student Study Site

- Mobile-friendly eFlashcards
- Mobile-friendly Self-Quizzes
- Study Questions
- Web Exercises
- Video Resources
- Audio Resources
- Additional Web Resources
- Chapter Outlines
- SAGE Journal Articles
- Real-World Research Articles From *Pacific Standard Magazine*
- SAGE Reference Articles

TAKE ACTION With SAGE's
Multimedia-Rich INTERACTIVE eBook

Improves Student Performance—Fully Searchable, Fully Assignable

This dynamic new Interactive eBook version of Organizational Behavior is ideal for students in online and traditional courses who prefer a more contemporary, multimedia–integrated presentation for learning. Fully searchable, it provides students with integrated links to engaging video and audio as well as access to complete academic and professional articles, all from the same pages found in the printed text. Students will also have immediate access to study tools such as highlighting, bookmarking, note–taking, and more!

BUNDLE: Nahavandi: Organizational Behavior + Interactive eBook	9781483345819	$120.00

"The action-oriented/practical, experiential approach is key since my professional students want to see the immediate application to their real organizational world. I would adopt the Interactive eBook."

—Cynthia Roman, Marymount University

TAKE ACTION With SAGE's Price ADVANTAGE

▶ **SAGE provides students a great value at a price**

30%–40% less

than the average new text.

"The SAGE value price is a huge benefit, and not having to worry about passwords is priceless."

—Students everywhere responding to SAGE's value and password-free study site

ORGANIZATIONAL BEHAVIOR

ORGANIZATIONAL
BEHAVIOR

AFSANEH NAHAVANDI
University of San Diego

ROBERT B. DENHARDT
University of Southern California

JANET V. DENHARDT
University of Southern California

MARIA P. ARISTIGUETA
University of Delaware

Los Angeles | London | New Delhi
Singapore | Washington DC

Los Angeles | London | New Delhi
Singapore | Washington DC

FOR INFORMATION:

SAGE Publications, Inc.
2455 Teller Road
Thousand Oaks, California 91320
E-mail: order@sagepub.com

SAGE Publications Ltd.
1 Oliver's Yard
55 City Road
London EC1Y 1SP
United Kingdom

SAGE Publications India Pvt. Ltd.
B 1/I 1 Mohan Cooperative Industrial Area
Mathura Road, New Delhi 110 044
India

SAGE Publications Asia-Pacific Pte. Ltd.
3 Church Street
#10-04 Samsung Hub
Singapore 049483

Printed in Canada.

Library of Congress Cataloging-in-Publication Data

Nahavandi, Afsaneh.

Organizational behavior / Afsaneh Nahavandi, University of San Diego, Robert B. Denhardt, University of Southern California, Janet V. Denhardt, University of Southern California, Maria P. Aristigueta, University of Delaware.

pages cm

ISBN 978-1-4522-7860-5 (hardcover)

1. Organizational behavior. I. Title.
HD58.7.N338 2015
302.3'5—dc23   2013032049

Acquisitions Editor: Patricia Quinlin
Associate Editor: Maggie Stanley
Digital Content Editor: Katie Guarino
Editorial Assistant: Dori Zweig
Production Editor: Jane Haenel
Copy Editor: Kristin Bergstad
Typesetter: C&M Digitals (P) Ltd.
Proofreader: Susan Schon
Indexer: Terri Corry
Designer: Scott Van Atta
Marketing Manager: Liz Thornton

This book is printed on acid-free paper.

14 15 16 17 18 10 9 8 7 6 5 4 3 2 1

Brief Contents

Detailed Contents

Preface

Failure is simply the opportunity to begin again, this time more intelligently.

—*Henry Ford*

The greatest danger in times of turbulence is not the turbulence; it is to act with yesterday's logic.

—*Peter Drucker*

Our Approach: Knowledge and Action

We believe organizational behavior is not *just* a field of *study*. Organizational behavior is a *practical* discipline that enables us to act effectively and responsibly. Our text provides an *action orientation* that demonstrates how organizational behavior is a way of thinking and acting that is of critical importance to leaders, to managers, to their employees, and to their customers.

This book is about helping students understand, manage, and change their own behavior, as well as influence the behavior of others. We believe that the ability to lead and manage effectively requires knowledge, creativity, and practice. No matter what organizational setting students encounter, there are certain skills they will need to address the "people" challenges they will face. Questions of motivation, power and authority, communications, group dynamics, and leadership arise in organizations large and small and in all sectors. Whether managing the corner store, a large manufacturing firm, a major league baseball team, a nonprofit foundation, a city department, or a day spa, questions about managing people may be the most important ones future leaders face.

Many organizational behavior texts focus on the *study* of organizational behavior rather than the *practical application* of these lessons, that is, how you can more effectively manage human behavior in real-world circumstances. This book has a distinctive "action orientation" that is reflected in our pedagogy. The book is designed with three concepts in mind:

1. The importance of understanding the behavior, motivations, and actions of *individuals* in organizations

2. A focus on building the knowledge, self-awareness, and skills appropriate and necessary for leadership and organizational change

3. An emphasis on students learning not only from readings and discussions but also from their own *experiences*

We are not only concerned with students learning *about* organizational behavior; we also want them to be able to acquire practical skills and develop habits of mind that will support continued learning from their experiences. To develop the capacity for action, a different style of learning is necessary, something that goes beyond just reading about a topic. Learning the practical skills to support effective and responsible action requires not only discussing new material but also improving students' capacity to act in pursuit of ideas.

Target Audience

Organizational Behavior is a core text for organizational behavior courses in schools of business as well as in public administration, nonprofit management, educational administration, and health care management. While the text is primarily oriented toward undergraduates, it is also suitable for graduate-level courses. The book covers all the topics in organizational behavior and the all-important "people skills," but does so with a practical focus on how students, as future managers and leaders, can think and act creatively to motivate employees, address change, and overcome challenges in today's interconnected global society.

Our Goals

Our intent is to provide lessons and perspectives that will enhance students' understanding of their own behavior and their ability to influence the behavior of others. To that end, this book examines the knowledge and skills acquired by the most successful leaders and managers, draws from the research and observations of scholars from various fields, and provides opportunities for students to develop both the skills and the habits of mind that will allow them to learn now and to continue to learn throughout their careers. Accordingly, the goals of this book are as follows:

1. To explore some of the most contemporary approaches to leading and managing people

2. To understand the importance and impact of the global context and of culture on people and organizations

3. To examine the factors that affect human behavior in organizations

4. To understand human behavior from multiple levels: individual, group, and organizational

5. To develop critical management and leadership skills and provide students with the capacity to act effectively and responsibly given the stress, complexity, and uncertainty of the "real world"

The book is organized into four parts titled Introduction, Individual Behavior and Characteristics, Group and Team Processes, and Organizational Context. Note that in contrast to other texts that discuss the individual, the group, and the organization, we emphasize the interaction between these levels. For example, the topic of emotions is introduced in Chapter 3, then revisited in Chapters 8 and 11.

Themes

To be effective, leaders and managers must understand their global and cultural contexts and their impact on people and organizations. They must use their knowledge, skills, and creativity to motivate others, function well in groups and teams, communicate clearly, manage conflict, and navigate change successfully. They must cope with their own and their employees' stress, be self-reflective and open to learning and growth, and maintain their commitment to their work in spite of sometimes unreachable goals and limited resources.

We present organizational behavior topics by weaving four themes throughout the chapters and integrate them in cases, examples, exercises, self-assessments, and application-oriented questions.

Global and Cultural Perspective

Organizations today function in a global environment where culture plays a central role. AACSB International, the business school accrediting body, considers global and cultural forces and cultural diversity among the key challenges managers will face in the future. Whether working across national boundaries or with diverse populations within a country, today's managers and leaders must have an appreciation and understanding of the importance and impact of culture. Chapter 1 introduces students to the concept of globalization, explaining how our global society affects individual engagements, social relationships, and social institutions. Chapter 2 focuses on workplace diversity, explaining how culture, ethnicity, gender, and age influence behavior in organizations.

Creativity and Change

The complexity, interconnectedness, and dynamic nature of today's organizations requires managers and leaders who can think and act creatively to navigate the ever-changing organizational landscape. The 2010 IBM Global CEO Study, based on face-to-face interviews with 1,541 CEOs, general managers, and senior public sector leaders around the world, concluded that the *single most important* attribute of future leaders will be creativity. "Creative leaders invite disruptive innovation, encourage others to drop outdated approaches and take balanced risks. They are open-minded and inventive in expanding their management and communication styles, particularly to engage with a new generation of employees, partners, and customers." Chapter 7 helps students understand the creative process and common impediments to creativity as well as how to overcome those challenges, and introduces techniques for enhancing their own and their employees' creativity. Creativity and Change boxes illustrate how organizations around the globe react to change creatively.

Thinking and Acting Ethically

Integrity and acting in an ethical manner are essential to effective leadership and the survival of our organizations. Chapter 1 frames organizational behavior using an ethical context. Ethics is then incorporated in subsequent chapters, showing students how ethics relates to topics such as decision making, teams, negotiation, leadership, and managing change.

Positive Psychology and Strength-Based Approach

We wrote this text with a strong emphasis on positive psychology. We believe that effective managers must be aware of their values and their strengths. We focus on teaching students to build self-awareness and the importance of investing in followers' and employees' strengths rather than weaknesses as a way to enhance individual and organizational success and create even more positive conditions. The importance of positive psychology and self-awareness are introduced in Chapters 1 and 2, then echoed in the following chapters.

Action-Orientation

In each chapter, we present a review of the relevant material related to each of the topics, and we provide some specific and immediate ideas and tools that will help students aspire to be managers and leaders. The presentation of various topics in this ordered and pedagogically sound manner engages students immediately in the material as a personal concern, acquaints them with the relevant and important thinking on the topic, gives them immediate and practical guidelines for action, and then leads them through case analysis, critical thinking questions, and exercises to test and improve their skills and abilities.

To achieve our goals, we present a solid foundation of ideas as well as real-world illustrations and applications that will help students develop their own personal, interpersonal, and institutional skills in areas such as motivation, creativity, decision making, communication, and group dynamics—what we have called the people or process skills.

Real-World Illustrations

- Chapter-Opening Cases begin each chapter to set the stage for the material covered in the chapter. They provide students with an example of an organization that faces the challenges discussed in the chapter and allow them to see how the material they will read can be applied.

- Chapter-Concluding Cases put students in the driver's seat and allow them to respond to an organizational behavior challenge.

- Global Society vignettes illustrate organizational behavior concepts in an international context. Discussion questions urge students to deepen their understanding of globalization and culture.

- Creativity and Change vignettes spotlight organizations that are responding creatively to change. Discussion questions help students take their understanding to the next level.

Applications

- Self-Assessments are interspersed throughout the chapters to allow students to gain awareness of their values, personal characteristics, and strengths.

- What Would You Do? boxes present hypothetical scenarios that require students to immediately interact with a chapter concept and connect it to their own behavior.

- **What Do You Think?** boxes challenge students to exercise critical thinking in making judgments about significant issues. These questions help students think like future managers by presenting them with issues commonly facing those in business, in public, and in nonprofit organizations, especially judgments concerning ethical issues.

- **Applications for Managers** end each chapter with a list of specific action recommendations that help students tie the information provided in the chapter to managerial action.

- **Exercises** help students apply chapter concepts and develop their skills.

We believe the above tools provide information as well as opportunities for students to enhance their management and leadership skills and broaden their perspectives.

Our goal is to provide substantive insights that will prepare students to be effective managers, feel more competent and confident in their interactions with people, lead others in their work to achieve a better world, and gain greater satisfaction and joy from the career they have chosen.

$SAGE edge™

edge.sagepub.com/nahavandi

SAGE edge offers a robust online environment featuring an impressive array of tools and resources for review, study, and further exploration, keeping both instructors and students on the cutting edge of teaching and learning. SAGE edge content is open access and available on demand. Learning and teaching has never been easier!

SAGE edge for students provides a personalized approach to help students accomplish their coursework goals in an easy-to-use learning environment.

- Mobile-friendly **eFlashcards** strengthen understanding of key terms and concepts

- Mobile-friendly practice **quizzes** allow for independent assessment by students of their mastery of course material

- A customized online **action plan** includes tips and feedback on progress through the course and materials, which allows students to individualize their learning experience

- **Study questions** provide students with further review and great prompts to practice their knowledge

- **Multimedia content** includes links to video, audio, and web-based content that appeal to students with **different learning styles**

- Interactive exercises and meaningful web links facilitate student use of internet resources, further exploration of topics, and responses to critical thinking questions

- EXCLUSIVE! Access to full-text SAGE journal, encyclopedia, and handbook articles that have been carefully selected to support and expand on the concepts presented in each chapter

SAGE edge for instructors supports teaching by making it easy to integrate quality content and create a rich learning environment for students.

- **Test banks** provide a diverse range of pre-written options as well as the opportunity to edit any question and/or insert personalized questions to effectively assess students' progress and understanding

- **Sample course syllabi** for semester and quarter courses provide suggested models for structuring one's course

- Editable, chapter-specific **PowerPoint®** slides offer complete flexibility for creating a multimedia presentation for the course

- EXCLUSIVE! Access to full-text **SAGE journal, encyclopedia, and handbook articles** support and expand on the concepts presented in each chapter to encourage students to think critically

- **Multimedia content** includes links to video, audio, and web-based content that appeal to students with different learning styles

- **Lecture notes** summarize key concepts by chapter to ease preparation for lectures and class discussions

- **Chapter objectives** are provided for each chapter to guide instructors as they assess their students

- **Discussion questions** are designed to spark conversation of concepts covered in the book

- **Class activities** give instructors tools to engage students with fun and interesting activities and experiential exercises

- A **course cartridge** provides easy LMS integration

Acknowledgments

We thank our many friends and colleagues at the University of Southern California, Arizona State University, and the University of Delaware who contributed to this book and provided special knowledge and insight. We also thank a group of dedicated practitioners who helped substantially enhance our understanding of how to most effectively manage and positively influence behavior in organizations. We dedicate this book to both groups!

We'd also like to thank the following reviewers who provided valuable insights and critiques during the development of this text:

Derek D. Bardell, Delgado Community College

Carl Blencke, University of Central Florida

Ralph R. Braithwaite, University of Hartford

Serena C. Brenneman, University of Arkansas

Bill Carnes, Metropolitan State College of Denver

Maryalice Citera, State University of New York at New Paltz

Nicole L. Cundiff, University of Alaska Fairbanks

Diane Denslow, University of North Florida

Aimee Dars Ellis, Ithaca College

Gerald G. GeRue, Rock Valley College

Bruce Gillies, California Lutheran University

Karen N. Gleason, Viterbo University

Lynn Godkin, Lamar University

Marvin Gordon, University of Illinois at Chicago

Paul Govekar, Ohio Northern University

Melissa Gruys, Wright State University

Michael A. Guerra, Lincoln University

Nell Tabor Hartley, Robert Morris University

James Jeremiah, Ashford University

James Katzenstein, California State University, Dominguez Hills

Aleksey Kolpakav, Indiana University

Cayce Lawrence, Christian Brothers University

Edward F. Lisoski, Angelo State University

Gypsi Luck, California State University, San Bernardino

Kenyetta McCurty, Amridge University

Rakesh Mittal, New Mexico State University

Dan Morrell, Middle Tennessee State University

Cynthia Busin Nicola, Carlow University

Patricia K. O'Connell, Lourdes University

Deborah Olson, University of LaVerne

Floyd Ormsbee, Clarkson University

John Overby, The University of Tennessee at Martin

Michael Palanski, Rochester Institute of Technology

Kannan Ramanathan, University of Texas at Dallas

Hindy Lauer Schachter, New Jersey Institute of Technology

Andrea Smith-Hunter, Siena College

Rudy Soliz, Houston Community College

Martha C. Spears, Winthrop University

Lisa Stamatelos, Pace University

Joe Stauffer, The University of Texas of the Permian Basin

David L. Sturges, University of Texas-Pan American

Marjolijn van der Velde, Davenport University

J. Lee Whittington, University of Dallas

Shirley A. Wilson, Bryant University

Marilyn Young, The University of Texas at Tyler

About the Authors

Afsaneh Nahavandi is Professor and Chair of the Leadership Studies department at the University of San Diego and Professor Emeritus at Arizona State University. Previously, she was Associate Dean of the College of Public Programs and Professor of Public Administration at Arizona State University, as well as the Director of the MBA Program and Professor of Management at Arizona State University West campus. Her teaching and research interests include organizational behavior, leadership, culture and diversity, and ethics. She is author of a top leadership text, *The Art and Science of Leadership* (6th edition) (2012). She is also the author of numerous journal articles and other works, including *Ancient Leadership Wisdom* (2012), *Organizational Behavior: The Person-Organization Fit* (1999), and *Organizational Culture in the Management of Mergers* (1993).

Robert B. Denhardt is Professor and Director of Leadership Programs in the Sol Price School of Public Policy at the University of Southern California, Regents Professor Emeritus in the School of Public Affairs at Arizona State University, and Distinguished Visiting Scholar at the University of Delaware. Dr. Denhardt is a past president of the American Society for Public Administration and a member of the National Academy of Public Administration. Dr. Denhardt has published 22 books, including *Managing Human Behavior in Public and Nonprofit Organizations*, *The Dance of Leadership*, *Theories of Public Organization*, *Public Administration: An Action Orientation*, *In the Shadow of Organization*, and *The Pursuit of Significance*.

Janet V. Denhardt is the Chester A. Newland Professor of Public Administration and Director of the Price School Sacramento in the Sol Price School of Public Policy at the University of Southern California. She is a member of the National Academy of Public Administration and her teaching and research interests focus on organization theory, organizational behavior, and leadership. She has authored numerous books including *Managing Human Behavior in Public and Nonprofit Organizations*, *The Dance of Leadership*, *The New Public Service*, and *Street-Level Leadership: Discretion and Legitimacy in Front-Line Public Service*. Prior to joining the faculty at the University of Southern California, Dr. Denhardt taught at Arizona State University and at Eastern Washington University, and she has served in a variety of administrative and consulting positions.

 Maria P. Aristigueta is the Charles P. Messick Professor, Director of the School of Public Policy and Administration, and Policy Fellow in the Institute of Public Administration at the University of Delaware. Her teaching and research interests are primarily in the areas of public sector management and include performance measurement, strategic planning, civil society, and organizational behavior. She is a coauthor of *Managing Human Behavior in Public and Nonprofit Organizations* (3rd edition), author of *Managing for Results in State Government* and *Managing Behavior in Public and Non-Profit Organizations*, and coeditor of the *International Handbook of Practice-Based Performance Management*.

INTRODUCTION ◀

1

Introduction to Organizational Behavior

History, Trends, and Ethics

LEARNING OUTCOMES

After studying this chapter, you should be able to:

1. Explain what organizational behavior is and why it is relevant to your career

2. Compare the differences between leaders and managers and the roles each play

3. Summarize the contributions leaders and managers make to their organizations

4. Trace the development of the field of organizational behavior in study and practice

5. Explain why understanding creativity and change in a global society is so important to future organizations

6. Describe how personal integrity, a cultural mindset, social responsibility, and global sustainability affect the way leaders and managers act

Turning Around a Bank ▶

Consider the following case. In your 21 years with a well-established European banking institution, you have earned a reputation as a turnaround specialist, someone who can come into a difficult situation and move the organization in a positive direction. Because of this reputation, you have just been appointed as the head of the company's corporate and investment banking unit. The previous manager left in a storm of controversy following an in-house investigation showing an abysmal track record, one that significantly contributed to the larger bank's fourth quarter losses. The investigation leading to your appointment was initiated after a popular television "newsmagazine" highlighted how much more effective other companies were in maintaining client trading, even in the face of Europe's deepening debt crisis.

Understandably, the workers in your division are disheartened. Turnover and absenteeism are high. Workers report feeling unfairly criticized and point to the lack of necessary resources to effectively do their jobs. Yet, as you talk with these individuals, you find that they are bright, committed, and hardworking. The truth is, forces outside their control have contributed to the crisis, and some of the criticism does seem unwarranted. You believe that you can work with these people to build a stronger, more service-oriented division. But it's going to take special skills—and more than a little luck!

Others were interested in the behavior of commodities, while I was interested in the behavior of people.

—Peter Drucker, Management Theorist

> *I believe the real difference between success and failure in a corporation can be very often traced to the question of how well the organization brings out the great energies and talents of its people.*
>
> — *Thomas J. Watson, CEO of IBM*
>
> *People don't quit their jobs, they quit their bosses.*
>
> — *Anonymous*

This case raises many important questions that help us define organizational behavior. Think about them from a practical standpoint: What are the most important issues here? Are they technical issues or are they people issues? Well, the truth is that there are probably some of both, but there is no question that in most situations, including this one, the human issues are central. Knowing that, you must then decide whether you will respond by dealing with one person at a time, by trying to work with groups, or by seeking some system-wide intervention. Obviously, there is some overlap among these three levels, but each becomes a lens through which we see, interpret, and respond to the specific circumstances that we confront.

As we change the lenses through which we see a given situation, our definition of the problems that the situation entails and the possible solutions to those problems also change. For example, if you focus on individual behavior, then you might think of the problem as one of employee motivation, the failure of employees to communicate effectively with customers, or employees' lack of understanding the broader purposes and goals of the division and the larger organization. As a result, you might meet and talk with employees; try to understand their needs, desires, and motivations; work with them to set individual and group goals; and seek their input on policy and operational changes that would improve outcomes.

Looking through the group lens, you might ask whether existing work groups are functioning effectively. Do employees feel like they are part of a team or do they feel alienated from their coworkers and supervisors? Is the culture of existing groups or teams conducive to achieving division goals? You might form task forces of employees to address particular problems, or you might reconfigure work teams to address certain types of cases.

If you focus on the organizational level, you might ask whether the department is structured appropriately to accomplish its tasks. Are management systems, such as goal setting and performance measurement, in place? Is management information available to guide decision making? Are organizational communications clear, and are policies documented and disseminated? Are the reporting and coordination methods appropriate? Here you might create new structures or mechanisms for communications throughout the organization. All of these questions fall in the domain of organizational behavior—and are absolutely essential to successfully dealing with the issues that arise in today's organizations.

A Facebook employee walks past a sign at Facebook headquarters in Menlo Park, California. In 2013, Facebook was ranked as the best place to work by Glassdoor's Employees' Choice Awards. Studies indicate that companies where employees are happy also tend to perform well financially, demonstrating the link between individual factors (employees' happiness) and organizational factors (financial success).

What Is Organizational Behavior?

Fundamentals of
Organizational
Behavior

Organizational behavior is the study and practice of how to manage individual and group behavior in business, government, and nonprofit settings. Accordingly, the field provides critically important and highly useful perspectives on motivation, leadership, communications, groups, power and politics, culture, and other matters that directly concern individual and group behavior. It also speaks to organizational issues and even community issues, but it does so through the lens of individual and group behavior.

Individual, Group, and Organizational Levels of Analysis

To give you a complete picture of the field of organizational behavior, let's look at the four perspectives or levels as shown in Figure 1.1. The first level studies the individual. It is the smallest possible level of analysis in organizations and includes topics such as individual differences, perception, motivation, and learning. The second level is the small group. Groups can be as small as two people or can be much larger, depending on the group's goal and tasks. The study of groups and teams in organizational behavior includes issues of group size and composition, cohesion, trust, team building, and decision making.

The third level of analysis in organizational behavior is concerned with the larger groups, such as departments, and with organizational processes. It includes issues such as the design and structure of organizations, organizational culture, power and politics, and change. Managers must understand their organizations at all three levels of analysis to meet the daily challenges they face. Organizational behavior then can be seen as resulting from the exchanges among these levels. (Note that the three major sections of the book emphasize the *interaction* among these layers.)

Social, Economic, and Ethical Context

In our view, leaders and managers today must consider a fourth level of analysis—that which concerns the social, economic, and ethical context in which they act. As we will see later in this chapter, today's society is becoming increasingly a global society, marked by networks and lines of communication unheard of only a few years ago. Consider the case of Kentucky Fried Chicken moving into China in a dramatic way, aiming at opening a new outlet every day for a total of 15,000 restaurants. Think of the issues involved. Should they adapt their offerings to the local market or should they completely revamp their business model—and their menu? And what about the people questions that are raised in working in a country with different traditions of leadership, communications, and a variety of other areas?

FIGURE 1.1 LEVELS OF ANALYSIS IN ORGANIZATIONAL BEHAVIOR

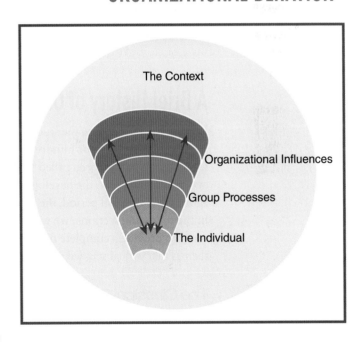

The Context

Organizational Influences

Group Processes

The Individual

Organizational behavior: the study and practice of how to manage individual and group behavior in business, government, and nonprofit settings

THE TELLER DILEMMA

Tanya R. Li has been promoted to director of the Bank at the Urban Center. The customers serviced by the bank are racially and ethnically diverse. The white tellers are in the minority and feel isolated. The tellers of color feel that the white tellers do not understand the customers. In addition, James, a veteran teller, has been discovered to have a criminal record prior to employment at the bank. Headquarters has a policy that does not allow anyone with a criminal record to work in direct contact with money, but the supervisor who hired James was not aware of the policy.

Tanya has identified three problems: (1) how can she make the tellers gain better understanding of each other's cultures? (2) How can she help the tellers gain better understanding of the customers' culture? (3) How does she deal with James, whose performance has been stellar since he joined the bank 15 years ago?

Before trying to advise Tanya on how to proceed, consider these questions:

1. What knowledge, skills, and abilities in organizational behavior would Tanya need to possess in order to deal with this situation?

2. Which of these capacities do you already have?

3. Which of these capacities do you need to acquire or improve upon?

Please come back to this case after studying this chapter to see how your answers differ.

A Brief History of Organizational Behavior

Let's look briefly at how the study of human behavior in organizations has addressed these questions. Although for hundreds of years, historians and philosophers have discussed leadership, what has been called "the management century"[1] began about a hundred years ago. From that point, the development of organizational behavior can be divided into categories: the classical period, the humanistic period, and modern organizational behavior. In the following sections, we will examine representative works in each area. Our intent is not to provide a complete overview of work in each period but just to suggest the main themes that were discussed in each.

Leadership: occurs where one or more members of a group or organization stimulate others to more clearly recognize their previously latent needs, desires, and potentialities and to work together toward their fulfillment

The Classical Period

Most managers and writers on management in the early 20th century focused on simply controlling workers and manipulating their environment so as to maximize efficiency and productivity. From the perspective of early management experts, people were primarily viewed as extensions of their tools and machines. For example, employee motivation, if it was considered at all, was based on patterns of compensation (rewards), but also on the fear of physical or economic abuse (punishment). It was assumed that workers found work to be unpleasant and therefore had to be motivated, mostly by money, to contribute to the organization. It also was assumed that workers would do what they were told because they would be punished or fired if they did not.

Frederick Taylor, best known as the father of scientific management, is representative of these traditional perspectives on human behavior.[2] Taylor's overall purpose was to make workers, who he assumed to be naturally lazy, more productive. Using the analogy of a baseball team, Taylor argued that you have to recognize the "utter impossibility of winning . . . unless every man on the team obeys the signals or orders of the coach and obeys them at once when the coach give those orders."[3]

There were a few early voices that were more humanistic, people such as Hugo Muntsberg[4] who urged greater attention to the psychology of workers, and Mary Parker Follett, who argued that dynamic administration must be grounded in "our cognition of the motivating desires of the individual and of the group."[5] But such work was largely considered outside the mainstream until the Hawthorne studies, published during the 1930s, pointed the way toward a greater acceptance of the importance of social factors at work.[6]

In 1927, a group of researchers led by Elton Mayo and F. J. Roethlisberger from Harvard University embarked on a study of worker productivity in the Hawthorne Works of the Western Electric Company in Chicago.

The Humanistic Period

In 1927, a group of researchers led by Elton Mayo and F. J. Roethlisberger from Harvard University embarked on a study of worker productivity in the Hawthorne Works of the Western Electric Company in Chicago. The findings from this research ultimately would signal a fundamental shift in how employee behavior was to be understood. Actually, a series of early experiments to measure the effects of lighting on efficiency found no direct relationship between changes in illumination and worker efficiency. In fact, short of literally making it so dark that the workers could not see, every change that the researchers implemented seemed to increase productivity.

After observing, consulting, and interviewing this group of employees for 5 years, however, the researchers arrived at two conclusions that would profoundly change research on worker behavior. First, they found that people change their behavior when they know they are being observed (the so-called **Hawthorne effect**). Second, they concluded that human relationships (including a relationship with the researchers) influenced the behavior of workers and, consequently, that new ideas were needed to explain worker behavior. The Hawthorne experiments showed that human behavior and motivation are complex, and are influenced by attitudes and feelings, the meaning that people assign to their work, and their relationships at work.

Research conducted over the subsequent few decades confirmed the Hawthorne findings and resulted in a more sophisticated understanding of the relationship between people and organizations. The importance of human cooperation in organizations was emphasized in executive-turned-writer Chester Barnard's definition of a **formal organization** as "a system of consciously coordinated activities or forces of two or more persons."[7] For Barnard, the participation of the individual was necessary for cooperation, and indeed, he viewed the need to build cooperation among organizational subunits as the crucial function of the manager.

Scientific management: the application of scientific techniques to work processes, as advocated by Frederick Taylor

Hawthorne effect: the finding that people change their behavior when they know they are being observed

Formal organization: a system of consciously coordinated activities or forces of two or more persons

FIGURE 1.2 THE SOCIAL SCIENCES THAT CONTRIBUTE TO OB

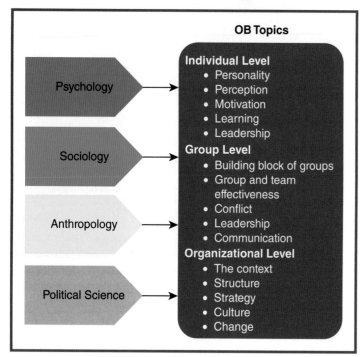

In *The Human Side of the Enterprise,* McGregor[8] discussed the now familiar Theory X and Theory Y, arguing that traditional command-and-control approaches, Theory X—based on assumptions of people as lazy, uninvolved, and motivated solely by money— actually caused people to behave in a manner consistent with those expectations. His alternative, Theory Y, suggested a much more optimistic and humanistic view of people, emphasizing the inherent worth of individuals in organizations. Similarly, Abraham Maslow[9] proposed his well-known hierarchy of needs as a way of understanding the complexity of human beings' motivations and desires.

Meanwhile, the famous German sociologist, Max Weber, writing a hundred years ago, first laid out the principles that govern hierarchical organizations and the way in which individuals exercise power and control within a **bureaucracy,** exhibiting hierarchy, division of labor, impersonal rules, and top-down authority.[10] Hierarchy refers to a top-down system of control in which different groups report to a single individual who then reports to another and so on up the ladder.

Modern Organizational Behavior

Theory X: the traditional command-and-control approach based on assumptions of people as lazy, uninvolved, and motivated solely by money

Theory Y: more humanistic form of management based on assumptions of people as active and involved in their work

Bureaucracy: a form of organization exhibiting hierarchy, division of labor, impersonal rules, and top-down authority (Weber, 1947)

Modern organizational behavior has relied heavily on work from many different social sciences (see Figure 1.2). Sociologists, such as Max Weber, contributed to the study of bureaucracy and group decision making. Anthropologists, exploring the role of culture in society, offered important insights into organizational culture. Finally, political scientists contributed to our understanding of organizational behavior by focusing on democratic governance, power, leadership, and strategy.

In the past few decades, management theorists, primarily those studying business organizations, have made important contributions to our understanding of organizational behavior and management, often working from a social psychology perspective. For example, Peter Drucker[11] studied the limitations of traditional command-and-control models of organization in stimulating worker productivity, especially in areas in which knowledge workers are especially important. Margaret Wheatley[12] extended this notion by encouraging managers and workers in times of uncertainty and chaos to embrace resilience, adaptation, and creativity, while Peter Senge[13] led the exploration of learning organizations and Edgar Schein[14] defined the contemporary version of organizational culture. In a related vein, Tom Peters and Robert Waterman[15] established the role of executives in all sectors striving for excellence in a strategic fashion, a theme recently echoed by Jim Collins[16] in his books *Good to Great* (2001) and *Great by Choice* (2011).

Current Trends in Organizational Behavior

Positive Organizational Behavior

A recent and compelling emphasis in the social psychology of organizational behavior is termed "positive organizational scholarship," the study, or "**positive organizational behavior**," the practical outcome. Positive organizational scholarship traces its beginnings to the late 1990s, when Martin Seligman, president of the American Psychological Association, argued that his field had too long focused on illness or pathology and proposed as an alternative, what he called positive psychology.[17] Instead of concentrating on what was wrong with people, that is, their deficiencies, positive psychology focused on positive experiences, such as happiness, pleasure, and joy, and how human beings could use their talents to create positive institutions that would, in turn, promote even more positive conditions.

Recent studies have shown that emphasizing the positive strengths of those in groups and organizations—such elements as happiness, meaningfulness, and effectiveness—actually creates even more positive results. This finding is closely related to the strength-based approach we emphasize in this book—that building on strengths rather than trying to correct weakness may in the long run be far more successful in building individual and original capabilities.

Organizational scholars soon began to explore how this new approach to psychology might be reflected in studies of organizational behavior.[18] Fred Luthans, working with the Gallup organization, proposed that organizational behavior should give more attention to such ideas as confidence, hope, and resiliency.[19] Similarly, others argued for a greater emphasis on human strength, resilience, and vitality and the creation of settings characterized by appreciation, collaboration, fulfillment, abundance, and human well-being.[20]

For example, "Imagine a world in which almost all organizations are typified by greed, selfishness, manipulation, secrecy, and a single-minded focus on winning. Wealth creation is the key indicator of success."[21] Individuals in those organizations would be characterized by distrust and anxiety, and social relations would be strained. Researchers looking into such organizations would emphasize such topics as problem solving, resistance, and competition. In contrast, "imagine another world in which almost all organizations are typified by appreciation, collaboration, virtuousness, vitality, and meaningfulness. Creating abundance and human well-being are key indicators of success."[22] Individuals in those organizations would be characterized by trustworthiness, humility, and positive energy, and researchers would emphasize excellence and extraordinary performance. Positive organizational behavior does not dismiss the first view, which has a clear basis in reality, but emphasizes the second; it seeks, as the old, old song says, to "accentuate the positive."

This approach is closely related to what we might call a *strength-based* approach to personal and organizational development. Instead of focusing on deficiencies—either those of the individual or of the organization—this approach builds on their strengths. (A parallel strength-based approach is often used in community development—the focus is not on what's wrong with a community, but what is right and what can be built upon.) We will emphasize a strength-based approach to organizational behavior in this book.

Positive organizational behavior: an approach to organizational behavior based on positive psychology and emphasizing strengths rather than weaknesses

Neuroscience and Organizational Behavior

We should note one other contemporary approach to the study of organizational behavior. New developments in the way the brain affects behavior, called neuroscience, or more informally *brain science*, suggest that the physiology of the human brain is directly connected to human behavior, including organizational behavior. For example, stress affects everyone, but the structure of the brain means that certain people are less affected by stress than others. Brain science may eventually be able to tell us, from a physical standpoint, which individuals are likely to be most resilient and why. Brain research has also shown that our brains are highly flexible and adaptable, which means that learning can take place not just in our early years but throughout our lives.[23]

What Would You Do?

▶ How do you balance these sensitivities? One of your employees is concerned that her salary is well below that of those who have the same experience that she has. Another is clearly motivated by doing meaningful work and being recognized for that work. Your initial response is to try to give the first employee a raise and more frequently compliment the second. But then, in terms of productivity, he's every bit as deserving of a raise as she is. What would you do?

A similar argument is developed in a popular and highly readable book by New York Times columnist David Brooks, called *The Social Animal*.[24] Drawing on recent work in neuroscience as well as psychology, Brooks contends that our conscious or rational mind often receives credit for thinking through options and guiding our actions, when in fact the unconscious mind, the world of emotions, intuitions, and deep-seated longings, tends to play a much more significant role. Brooks concludes that we are not rational animals but, first and foremost, social animals. Daniel Goleman, writing in *Social Intelligence*, comes to the same conclusion. Basing his work on recent advances in neuroscience, Goleman identifies a human predisposition to be aware of and sensitive to other human beings.[25] One emerging theme in brain studies is that human behavior is never purely rational; the emotions play a central role in all aspects of organizational behavior. As we will see, that can often be a very good thing.

People Skills in Management

Let's turn toward the more specific challenges you will face as a manager, challenges that are quite different from those of only a few decades ago. The complex and interconnected world that today's organizations face requires new skills and approaches in management and leadership. Increasingly, we are learning that the top-down leadership and bureaucratic management models, based on manufacturing rather than knowledge work, are a relic of the 20th century.[26] Top-down management is not only inconsistent with today's open and interconnected world, it is simply too slow to respond to events that occur at "warp-speed." Instead, we are seeing the emergence of leadership and management approaches that emphasize openness and engagement, resilience and adaptability, and, most of all, creativity.

Differentiating Between Managers and Leaders

We might begin by thinking about whether there are differences between managers and leaders. Abraham Zaleznik's[27] classic discussion of this topic continues to be relevant. Zaleznik begins by noting that a managerial culture emphasizes rationality and control. Managers are concerned with problem solving and getting people to operate efficiently throughout the organization. Leaders, on the other hand, are not bound to structure nor to existing goals; indeed, they accept chaos, suspense, and risk. Ultimately, they seek to shape the future, even if that means moving in completely new and unexpected directions.

Although the differences between managers and leaders may initially seem distinct, most organizational behavior scholars today, as well as their counterparts in the real world, would agree with Harvard professor John Kotter that management and leadership are not opposing forces in organizations but are complementary to one another. Indeed, Kotter argues that you can't have one without the other.[28] That is, managers need strong leaders in order for them to succeed, and leaders need strong managers in order for them to succeed. Managers tend to promote stability in the organization, while leaders often press for change. But both forces may be essential as businesses and other organizations face increasingly turbulent, indeed chaotic circumstances.

What Do You Think?

▶ Make a list of those skills or abilities or qualities you associate with managers and those you associate with leaders. Or you might ask what do managers do—and what do leaders do. See if you can build a chart with management on one side and leadership on the other. What do you think?

What Managers Do

Let's look at the job of the manager. That is, what do you need to know, and what do you need to be able to do to act effectively and responsibly in the organizations of which you are or will be a part? You have probably already seen lists of management functions such as planning, organizing, staffing, directing, coordinating, reporting, and budgeting. Elaborating these ideas, Peter Drucker suggested that the first task of management is to set objectives, to establish the goals of the group or organization and offer ways to meet those goals (see Table 1.1). Second, the manager organizes the tasks, saying who will do what and when. Third, the manager motivates and communicates, encouraging others to accomplish their work and engage with others. Fourth, the manager assesses performance, that is, the manager devises ways in which to measure the performance of the organization against the organization's goals and objectives. Fifth, the manager develops people. Especially in a time in which what Drucker calls **knowledge workers** (those whose primary contribution to the organization is not physical but mental) are the primary assets of most organizations, the development of their skills and abilities is paramount.

What Managers Do

TABLE 1.1 WHAT DO MANAGERS DO?

1. Set objectives
2. Organize tasks
3. Motivate and communicate
4. Monitor and measure
5. Develop people

In the late 1960s, Henry Mintzberg conducted a classic set of "structured observations" of five executives in medium to large organizations, spending a full week with each and recording in detail their activities. He concluded that traditional terms such as planning and decision making fail to capture the complexity of managerial work; they fail to show what managers actually do. In Mintzberg's view, the work of managers had six characteristics,[29] summarized in Table 1.2.

Mintzberg's research shows that the daily work of managers is characterized by a large number of activities that occur at a fast pace and are not always predictable. Additionally, managers spend a considerable amount of time communicating and interacting with other people. In addition to his examination of what managers did, Mintzberg also studied the behavior of those managers, concluding that all of their activities were found to involve one or more of three basic behaviors: interpersonal contact, the processing of information, and the making of decisions. Mintzberg

What Do You Think?

▶ Mintzberg's study took place more than 40 years ago. To what extent has the role of the manager changed? What about the effect of modern information technology? How has the complexity that managers face changed?[30]

Knowledge workers: those whose primary contribution to the organization is not physical but mental

TABLE 1.2 CHARACTERISTICS OF MANAGERS' JOBS

Characteristic	Description
1. A lot of work at unrelenting pace	Despite the appearance of boundaries to the manager's day, that day is typically filled with activity and can be both physically and mentally taxing.
2. Variety, fragmentation, and brevity	There is no order to the manager's day; interruptions and moving from topic to topic are quite typical.
3. Current, specific, and ad hoc issues	There is little time for reflective planning, and managers prefer live, concrete situations. They demonstrate a strong action orientation.
4. Managers are between their organization and a network of contacts	Much of managers' communication is horizontal, and often involves communications with people outside the organization itself.
5. Use of verbal media	Though managers have many ways to communicate, there seems to be a preference for verbal communication.
6. Some control over schedule	Though there are many pressures pushing and pulling managers, they have the capacity to control their schedules so as to emphasize what they feel is most important.

Source: Based on Mintzberg, H. (1971). Managerial work: Analysis from observation. *Management Science, 18*(2), B97–B110.

then described 10 managerial roles, all of which will sound familiar to those who study management (see Figure 1.3).

The question of what managers do leads directly to two other questions that we address throughout the book:

1. What values, attitudes, and beliefs underlie managerial work?

2. What specific skills are needed by managers at different levels?

These are key questions in becoming an effective manager. Scholars have suggested that managers must not only act, but also reflect on their actions: "Action without reflection is thoughtless; reflection without action is passive."[31] They further suggest that the key to management is collaboration and that managers must focus on reality and maintain a worldly mindset that is rational and analytical.[32] Table 1.3 summarizes the five key mindsets.

FIGURE 1.3 MANAGERIAL ROLES

Interpersonal	Informational	Decision Making
• Figurehead	• Disseminator	• **Negotiator**
• Liaison	• Spokesperson	• **Entrepreneur**
• Leader	• Monitor	• **Disturbance Handler**
		• **Resource Allocator**

TABLE 1.3 THE FIVE MANAGERIAL MINDSETS

Effective Management Mindset	
Mindset	**Task**
1. Reflective Mindset	Managing Self
2. Action Mindset	Managing Change
3. Collaborative Mindset	Managing Relationships
4. Worldly Mindset	Managing Context
5. Analytical Mindset	Managing Organizations

Source: Based on Gosling, J., & Mintzberg, H. (2003, November). The five minds of the manager. *Harvard Business Review,* pp. 54–63.

The second question we raised above was what skills are needed for managers at different levels in the organization. This question was addressed in a classic study conducted by the U.S. Office of Personnel Management (OPM) that sought to identify the skills that are critical to managerial success. Based on information collected from a large number of highly effective managers and executives, the researchers developed two categories of competencies: one focusing on management functions (or the "what" of management) and one focusing on effectiveness (or the "how" of management). Those competencies are presented in Table 1.4.

The first thing we notice when we look at Table 1.4 is how many of these competencies require effective skills in organizational behavior. Certainly, interpreting and communicating, guiding and leading, supervising and promoting performance, and flexibility and adaptation are all organizational behavior skills. But a second look reveals how integral the skills in organizational behavior are to virtually every aspect of managerial competence. Look at the list and see whether you see any elements that do not require, or at least could not be strengthened by an ability to effectively influence, manage, motivate, and lead people.

What Leaders Do

Among other things, the leader is expected to

1. encourage the development of goals and performance objectives;

2. communicate effectively both with the organization and with external constituencies;

3. encourage the highest level of creativity and innovation in the group or organization;

4. design opportunities for other participants in the organization to involve themselves in decisions made by the group;

5. carefully assess the progress of the group or organization and make sure that everything is on track; and

6. develop and exemplify the highest moral and ethical standards.

Leaders have another key function and that is the creation and maintenance of an organizational culture.[33] Organizations often come to mirror their leaders' personalities. Consider how Starbucks, the global provider of gourmet coffee, reflects the dreams and fears of its founder, Howard Schultz. Schultz is the son of a construction worker who lost his job as a result of a work injury, which had a devastating impact on him and his family.

Leadership

Essence of Leadership

TABLE 1.4 MANAGEMENT FUNCTIONS

Management Functions: The What		Management Functions: The How	
External Awareness:	Identifying key agency politics and priorities and/or external issues and trends likely to affect the work unit	Broad perspective:	Ability to see the big picture and to balance long- and short-term considerations
Interpretation:	Keeping subordinates informed about key agency and work unit policies, priorities, issues, and trends and about how these are to be incorporated into the unit	Strategic view:	Ability to collect and analyze information and to anticipate and make judgments
Representation:	Presenting, explaining, selling, and defending the work unit's activities to the supervisor in the agency and to persons and groups outside of the agency	Environmental sensitivity:	Awareness of the agency in relation to its environment
Coordination:	Performing liaison functions and integrating the work of various units within the organization and interacting with other organizations	Leadership:	Individual and group leadership and willingness to lead, manage, and accept responsibility
Planning:	Developing long-term goals, objectives, and priorities and deciding on actions	Flexibility:	Openness to new information, change, and innovation as well as to tolerance for stress and ambiguity
Guidance:	Converting plans to action by establishing schedules and standards	Action orientation:	Independence, pro-activity, calculated risk taking, problem solving, and decisiveness
Budgeting:	Preparing, justifying, and administering the budget	Results focus:	Concern with goal achievement
Managing materials:	Making sure that the needed supplies, equipment, and facilities are available	Communication:	Effective speaking, writing, and listening
Personnel management:	Projecting needs and recruiting, selecting, appraising, and retaining employees	Technical competence:	Specialized expertise in agency programs and operations
Supervision:	Providing guidance and oversight while working to promote and recognize performance		
Monitoring:	Staying up-to-date on the status of activities, Identifying problems, and taking corrective action		
Evaluation:	Assessing how well program goals are met and identifying ways in which to improve		

Source: Flanders, L. R., & Utterback, D. (1985). The management excellence inventory. *Public Administration Review, 45*(3), 403–410.

One of the key elements of Schultz's vision for Starbucks is to offer employees a fair workplace with full benefits.[34] David Neeleman, former CEO of JetBlue, has a passion for customer service and high quality; the airline he founded reflects those values.[35] Figure 1.4 summarizes the leader's functions in shaping the culture of the organization.

Influence of Managers

We know now that managers and leaders perform many different roles and functions in organizations, but do these actions make a difference in the productivity of the organization? Certainly that has been the prevailing wisdom in management and organizational behavior for some time.[36] Recently, the Gallup organization, better known for its broad social and political public opinion surveys, has been measuring management practices and their effect on productivity. This research has shown that employees who are engaged in their work essentially doubled their odds of success when compared to those who are less engaged. Moreover, employee engagement clearly made a difference in terms of productivity, quality, and customer service.[37] The survey investigated how employees become engaged and found that managers using positive leadership behaviors such as a strengths-based approach, maintaining a positive perspective when difficulties arise, and providing frequent recognition and encouragement were a key factor in employee engagement. Another extensive study, this one of school districts, found that managerial quality was related to ten of eleven performance indicators, covering a wide range of organizational goals from school attendance and student success on standardized tests.[38] These findings indicate that good management and good leadership clearly make a difference.

What exactly is a good boss worth? A recent research study by the National Bureau of Economic Research looked at 23,878 workers, matched to 1,940 bosses, at a very large technology service company between 2006 and 2010. The study found that removing a poorly performing manager and replacing him or her with a top performing manager is roughly equal, in terms of productivity, to adding an extra person to the team.[39] The top-performing manager is like the star athlete who makes everyone around him or her look better.

Many organizational cultures reflect the personal experiences of their founders or chief operating officers. Howard Schultz, CEO of Starbucks Coffee, emphasizes a workplace culture that features fair wages and benefits for all his employees. In part, that culture reflects Schultz's own personal history. His father was laid off because of a work injury with devastating consequences for his family.

FIGURE 1.4 LEADER'S FUNCTIONS IN SHAPING ORGANIZATIONAL CULTURE

Managers and
Leaders

Researchers have also looked at the other side of the coin—how does poor management affect the work of the organization? There's an old adage that people don't quit their jobs, they quit their bosses. Studies have shown that old adage to be true. In study after study, when asked what one factor determines their satisfaction, engagement, and commitment, employees point to the quality of their immediate supervisor. According to a 2005 study, when employees were asked what factor most negatively impacted their productivity, 58% cited poor management, a figure 20 points above the second leading negative impact, lacking motivation.[40] Another recent study of 2,865 leaders in a large financial services company that used feedback from employees, other managers, and their associates—a method called 360 degree feedback—shows a direct correlation between levels of employee engagement and the effectiveness of their supervisors (see Figure 1.5). Good leadership is associated with happy, engaged, and committed employees.[41] Clearly, managers and leaders make a difference and if you have the skills and abilities to manage and lead effectively you will likely have more productive and satisfied employees and be much more successful in your career (Figure 1.6). Obviously, this is a compelling reason to learn the ins and outs of organizational behavior.

Creativity and Change in a Global Society

Many books like this one have subtitles or stated emphases that are relatively meaningless. We take our emphasis—*Creativity and Change in a Global Society*—very seriously. We strongly believe that the world in which we live is placing special demands on organizations of all types. The complexity of the world; the interconnectedness of business, government, and society; and the rapidity of social and technological change all present new challenges to today's organizations. Those organizations are expected to meet customer demands; they are expected to be attentive to their place in the market and to the economic consequences of every move they make; and they are expected to be good citizens, contributing to the overall betterment of society. Moreover, they are being asked to do all of these things in a world that is constantly changing, creating situations in which a premium is placed on the agility of organizations, their capacity to deal with problems that are both fast moving and complex, and their willingness to be creative and innovative. And, of course, there is no force impinging more strongly on our organizations than the fact that we are living in a highly connected global society. For this reason, we emphasize creativity and change in a global society.

4 P's of Creativity

Creativity and Change

The 2010 IBM Global CEO Study, based on face-to-face interviews with 1,541 CEOs, general managers, and senior public sector leaders around the world, concluded that global complexity will only increase in the future and that more effective management and leadership will be needed to steer tomorrow's organizations through a more complex world. The study found that the biggest challenge facing those in private and public enterprises in the future will be the accelerating pace and complexity of a global society operating as a massively interconnected system.

Even more important, the study connected creativity and effectiveness. According to those surveyed, in order to cope with global complexity, future leaders will need to place a strong emphasis on creativity. When asked to name the *single most important attribute*

FIGURE 1.5 FACTORS THAT AFFECT PRODUCTIVITY

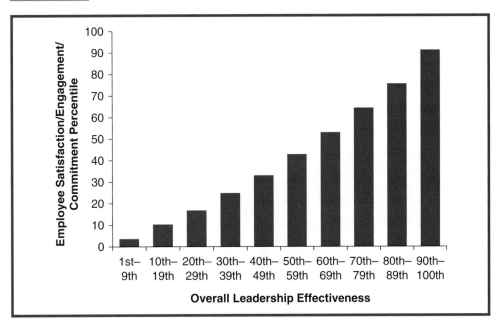

Source: Zenger, J., & Folkman, J. (2012, July 6). How damaging is a bad boss, exactly? *Harvard Business Review Blog.*

for leaders in the next five years, 60% of the respondents to the survey listed creativity; 52% listed integrity; and 35% listed global thinking. What is it about creative leaders that enables them to respond to the complexity of the modern environment? "Creative leaders invite disruptive innovation, encourage others to drop outdated approaches and take balanced risks. They are open-minded and inventive in expanding their management and communication styles, particularly to engage with a new generation of employees, partners, and customers."[42] Moreover, the best leaders see creativity occurring throughout the organization rather than being captured at one level or in one department. Creative leaders and managers are needed not just at the top and not just in the creativity "department."

Sarcasm Boosts
Creativity

Creative managers and leaders seek organizational cultures that allow a great deal of empowerment and engagement on the part of employees. Employees are encouraged to seek innovative solutions to problems facing the organization and are given the autonomy to pursue possible avenues for new ideas. One manager told us that, when an employee brings a good idea to him, even if he knows a better solution to the problem, he will accept the employee's recommendation, because it's more important to encourage employees to bring ideas forward than to play with those ideas at the margin. Ralph Kerle, a creativity consultant in Australia, thinks that there are four attributes that are most important for creative leaders—empowerment, enjoyment, enlightenment, and courage—and the greatest of these is empowerment. Creative people, he points out, are likely to prefer organizational structures and cultures that are characterized by high levels of autonomy and opportunity. The fact that these same structures also may be riskier is of less importance than achieving creative outcomes.[43]

FIGURE 1.6 WHAT DOES IT TAKE TO
BECOME A BETTER LEADER?

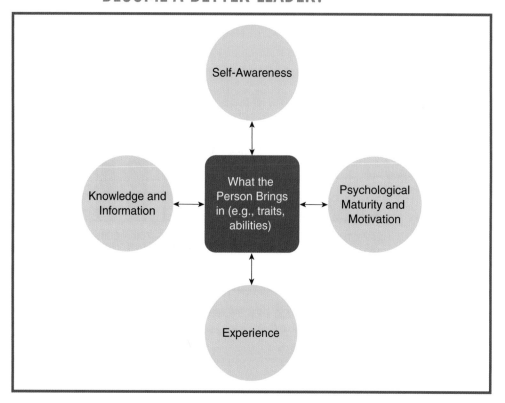

A Global Society

There is no question that we are living in an increasingly global society. We are all acutely aware of **globalization**, the extent to which cultures, societies, and economies are interconnected and integrated. Globalization is a reality in terms of individual engagements, social relationships, and social institutions, all of which have become more extended, more complex, and more diverse. Decreased travel times enable people to move around the world quickly and (for the most part) comfortably. Increased access to the web further puts people in contact with others throughout the world. Access to global 24/7 news channels such as CNN, BBC, France 24, and Al Jazeera further reinforce global interconnectedness. But we should note that the benefits of increased travel and expanded access to information are not evenly distributed. By some estimates, access to the web is highest in North America with over 79% penetration, to 68% in Oceana/Australia, and at its lowest in Africa with 16%.[44] Moreover, Internet penetration is growing rapidly all over the world (see Figure 1.7).

Globalization

There are three intricately related phenomena that define our global society today. The first of these is *globalization* itself, the extension of political, social, and economic relationships around the globe. Second and very closely related to globalization is *complexity*, in some ways a byproduct of globalization and in some ways a separately developing phenomenon. Third is *connectedness*, the capacity for groups and organizations around the world to connect with one another and, indeed, the necessity that they do so. We will briefly examine each of these elements.

We have seen the impact of globalization on our individual lives, but globalization has had an even greater impact in the economic realm. If you work in business, your competitors,

Globalization:
the extent to which
cultures, societies,
and economies are
interconnected and
integrated

FIGURE 1.7 WORLD INTERNET PENETRATION RATES BY GEOGRAPHIC REGIONS, JUNE 2012

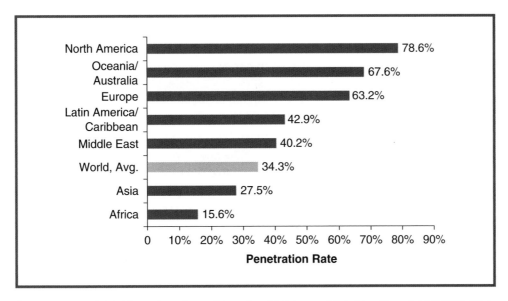

Source: Internet World Stats, http://www.internetworldstats.com/stats.htm. Copyright © 2012, Miniwatts Marketing Group. *Note:* Penetration rates are based on a world population of 7,017,846,922 and 2,405,518,376 estimated Internet users on June 30, 2012.

your suppliers, and your customers are now global. If you are in government or a nonprofit organization, globalization impacts you through your connection with people from different cultures, through the availability of services across the globe, and through the constant exchange of information. We recognize that globalization is a reality; however, we don't always understand what we see and hear nor do we correctly interpret the information. We need greater clarity about how to understand this new phenomenon and how to navigate globalization. It's here to stay.

Several writers have drawn a distinction between "stable" situations and "liquid" situations, or between "stability" and "liquidity." For many years, societies around the world remained fairly stable, in the sense that people stayed in one area, the flow of information among societies was restricted, and the tools and artifacts of the society tended to be used where they were produced. In some cases, there were physical barriers such as mountains or rivers that restricted travel; in other cases, social and political institutions put limits on movement. And, of course, there were no airlines, cell phones, or Internet connections to bring people together.

There is, however, abundant evidence that many parts of the world and many aspects of society and culture are being "liquefied." Certainly modern technology plays a strong role in transmitting information from place to place and, indeed, moving people from place to place. Consequently, institutional structures seem to be melting into liquid form and the constraints of time and space become increasingly irrelevant, as, for example, international banking transactions occur in microseconds without actual resources being transmitted from one place to the other. As philosopher Zygmunt Bauman has argued, we live in an increasingly liquid society, what he calls **liquid modernity**.[45]

Liquid modernity:
the tendency for modern societies to exhibit more liquid or fluid tendencies

GLOBAL AMBASSADORS MENTOR EMERGING WOMEN LEADERS ACROSS THE GLOBE

"In today's ever-changing world, where global challenges necessitate strong leadership, the need for training and mentoring for women leaders has never been so acute" says Justine Metz, an executive at the Global Ambassadors program, a partnership between the Bank of America and Vital Voices,[46] an NGO that invests in unleashing the potential of women worldwide.[47] The role of women in economic development around the world has been emphasized by the United Nations and other global organizations such as the World Economic Forum.[48] However, while women make up 50% of the world's population, many do not get the education, training, and support they need and face considerable discrimination that prevents them from contributing fully to their communities. Programs such as Global Ambassadors recognize the importance of developing global leadership and allow emerging leaders to benefit from the experience of established leaders.

The program's mentors come from a variety of industries, including banking and entertainment, and are dedicated to helping their mentees grow while they themselves learn about global challenges. Candace Browning, head of Global Research Bank of America Merrill Lynch and one of the program's mentors, believes that "mentorship is critical to helping women drive change across economic, political and social channels."[49] Another mentor in the program, Wendy Luhabe, cofounder of Women Investment

Portfolio Holding in South Africa, is inspired by the program's mission to build bridges between new and emerging leaders. She says: "At its basic level, leadership is developing the capacity to transform our own lives and circumstances, and as our confidence grows we extend that capacity to our broader sphere of influence."[50] A third mentor, Ann Veneman, former Executive Director of UNICEF and former U.S. Secretary of Agriculture, believes the program can have long-lasting impact: "Good mentors can help create good leaders, and good leaders become mentors for the next generation," and she tells young leaders to "take advantage of opportunities that may come your way. It is not always easy to start on a new path, but it can lead to incredible opportunities to make a difference."[51] Susan Chambers, Wal-Mart People Division Executive Vice President, who mentors Smita Mankad, managing director of Artisans Micro Finance, says she helps her mentee focus so that she can continue to do "good" and do it well and, as a result, help other people by providing economic opportunity.[52] Cooperative efforts such as the Global Ambassador program exemplify the importance of developing global leadership and the role of one-on-one mentoring in the process.

1. Why should business get involved in programs such as Global Ambassadors?

2. Should business get involved in social and cultural issues?

Complexity

Closely related to the issue of globalization is the increasing complexity of doing business in a world marked by turbulence, ambiguity, and surprise. The uncertainties of the social, political, and economic worlds are vexing to those in business, those in the public sector, and citizens generally. Over the last couple of decades, change has been seen as the most difficult factor to overcome in achieving organizational success. Indeed, many have commented that we have moved from a society largely stable with occasional interruptions of change, to one that is marked by constant change with occasional interruptions of stability. Certainly changing technologies have dramatically altered the social, political, and economic landscape, but change has come about in other ways as well. There are the changing demands of customers and citizens, with new preferences being registered daily. There are the changes brought about by the almost instantaneous flow of news and information from around the world. In general, leaders and managers in all sectors recognize that the most significant difference in their lives today as compared with when they started their work is the pace at which they are required to work—and the pace at which they must require their organizations to work.

This difference was also documented in the IBM 2010 Global Leaders Study we mentioned earlier. Again, the study paints a picture of increasing complexity in the way that businesses and governments are required to act. The respondents suggested that the new global society is more turbulent, uncertain, and chaotic than ever before—and they expected that these new complexities will not only continue through the coming decades, but they will accelerate. Under these circumstances, the changes that are required to adapt are not simply incremental, but transformational. Those who were interviewed expected that change and complexity would become even more dramatic over the next years and next decades, and, as we recall from our earlier discussion, creative responses would be required to meet these challenges. Interestingly, many companies have adapted well to these new circumstances and benefited financially from them. These standout companies have devised ways to organize and simplify their operations to the benefit of those inside as well as external partners and customers. In describing their work, words like *agility, dexterity, speed, flexibility, adaptability*, and *resilience* are mentioned over and over—words that will need to describe *your* work.

Connectedness

Obviously, the new global society has been made possible by technological advances, especially in the area of communications. The Internet has opened new opportunities for instantaneous connections across long distances. Employees, customers, and partners are connected in new ways and the interaction between businesses or public organizations and their customers or citizens has changed dramatically. One notable aspect of this change has been the rise of social media and its importance in both local and global affairs. You only need to be reminded of the Arab Spring uprisings to recognize the importance of social media in the political sphere. Similarly, most businesses today are exploring new ways to interact with customers through social media and distributed commerce.

Another IBM study, this one taking place in 2012 and based on interviews with some 1,700 executives in the private and public sector, explored this newly connected world and how companies, especially high-performing organizations, have responded.[53] Over the past decade, executives and managers have been buffeted by economic challenges, many of which

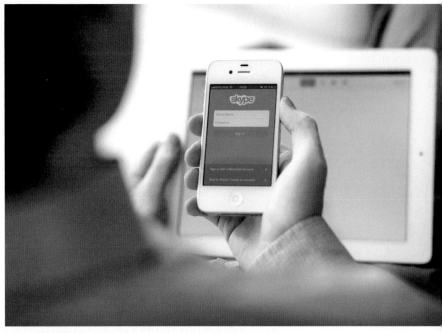

One of the obvious features of the emerging global society is the way so many things are interconnected. A transaction made in one part of the world instantly affects business in many other parts of the world. This interconnectedness creates great opportunities for business but also presents challenges in terms of greater complexity and the difficulty of coordinating events in time.

are not confined to national boundaries but are felt around the globe. For example, recall the disruption in various parts of the world caused by the European financial crisis. It's not surprising, then, that the executives interviewed for the IBM study listed technology (including such areas as information technology, biotechnology, and nanotechnology) as the number one force likely to impact their work over the coming 3 to 5 years. This was a change from previous studies that had shown market factors as the most significant force. (We might note that people skills have fairly steadily remained in the number two position over all the years—and those are the skills that we will focus on in this book.)

Although connectedness is part of the problem for companies and governments, it also can be part of the solution. These new connections affect the relationship between, say, a business and its customers and suppliers, but, at the same time, the connected world opens opportunities for organizations to restructure and reshape their internal operations, typically in the direction of more open and innovative practices. For example, a variety of new applications are aimed at facilitating group collaboration, even if everyone in the group is not "in the room." These range from contextual, real-time conferencing integrating video, audio, and instant messaging (IM), to software applications such as Basecamp that make asynchronous collaboration possible across vast distances and with many partners involved. And, of course, there are Tweets, Facebook updates, Google+ shares, LinkedIn updates, Pinterest pins, and Instagram uploads. All of these applications hold the possibility for making organizations more open, more collaborative, and more creative—all characteristics of a flexible and adaptive organization, exactly the type that is required to deal with a global complexity and fluidity.

The Ethical Environment

Price for
Ethical Clothing

We have discussed the two major themes, (1) creativity and change and (2) the emergence of a global society, that we will develop throughout the course of this book; you should look for both case studies and larger vignettes developing these themes in each chapter. We also want to introduce several subthemes that we will group under the title, "The Ethical Environment." These include personal integrity, a cultural mindset, social responsibility, and global sustainability. Although much of what we discuss in this book will involve the work that leaders and managers do within the organization, it's important to realize that such work takes place in a larger social environment that shapes the values that those in the organization pursue. No one is immune to these influences, and, indeed, each one of us has a responsibility to be attentive to the ethics and values of the society in which we live. Sometimes we accept those values readily, yet at other times we resist those values and try to modify or replace them. But the ethical dialogue that occurs with respect to these values importantly shapes our behavior in organizations and defines our role in society. For that reason, it is important for us to examine these four subthemes at the beginning. Then, as we go through the text, we will note where these subthemes arise.

Personal Integrity

Human Values and
Corporate Actions

Most of today's leaders would agree with Mountain Equipment CEO Peter Robinson when he says, "Ethics is the new competitive environment."[54] Similarly, when employees are asked what are the most important characteristics they desire from their leaders, honesty and integrity always rank at the top of the list. It's only natural that we would expect the same sense of values from our leaders that we expect of people throughout society—that they tell the truth, that they don't do violence to others, that they don't steal, that they keep promises, and so forth. But, as we know, matters of integrity within large organizations are often more complicated and potentially more damaging than these simple statements of ethical norms might make it appear.

The recent cases of Enron, Tyco, and Arthur Andersen, for example, show that integrity within the world of business is a principle often violated, sometimes accidentally, but often with malicious intent. In many cases, a manager will make a business decision without even taking the ethical implications into account—and consequently act in an unethical way without even realizing it.[55] Rushworth Kidder, founder of the Institute for Global Ethics, has written, "What is needed is a capacity to recognize the nature of moral challenges and respond with a well-tuned conscience, a lively perception of the difference between right and wrong and an ability to choose the right and live by it. What is needed is ethical fitness."[56]

A Cultural Mindset

Today's global organizations require a way of thinking that puts culture and its diversity at the forefront. The idea of **diversity** has traditionally focused rather narrowly on requiring equal opportunity in hiring and promotion practices. Indeed, there is a large body of legislation and judicial rulings that regulate what companies and government agencies can or cannot do with respect to these areas. Diversity today, however, has taken on new meanings, as leaders and managers have come to realize that taking culture into consideration in the workplace is not only the right thing to do, it also aids creativity and productivity. Having men and women, people from different cultural backgrounds and countries, gays and straights, people with both special talents and disabilities, and people of all ages working together ensures that different viewpoints are brought to discussions about management practices, product design, sales and marketing, and a host of other topics. Successfully managing such diverse organizations requires a cultural mindset that values and encourages diversity and considers it a competitive advantage, not just something you have to do. "The leadership challenge of facilitating appropriate responses to diversity is a business objective that must be met to ensure effective organizational outcomes in both domestic and foreign markets."[57]

This man is looking at a rice egg sandwich in a McDonald's in Jakarta, the capital and largest city in Indonesia. Companies like McDonald's are rapidly moving into new markets but finding it necessary to adjust their products to fit the local culture.

Globalization has extended the notion of diversity beyond demographic categories, such as age, race, and gender, and opened new questions about cultural diversity. Consider the case of McDonald's, the quintessential American company with a global reach. The Golden Arches' burgers are appreciated all over the world, from the fanciest shopping districts in Paris to the busy streets in China and India. Although the basic menu of its restaurants is focused on hamburgers, the company has adjusted its products, its restaurants, and its management practices to respond to the needs of its global customers. McDonald's serves wine in France, and some burgers are meatless in India where almost 50% of the population is vegetarian and cows are considered sacred by many.[58]

Social Responsibility

Over the last several decades, there has been an increasing interest in the commitments that public, private, and nonprofit organizations have to meet social needs. This concern is known as **corporate social responsibility** (or CSR) and it refers to companies going beyond their bottom line and economic interests to engage in activities that promote social well-being and environmental sustainability. Tayla Bosch, senior director for social values at Western Union, reports

Diversity: achieving a workforce generally reflective of the social environment surrounding the organization, with special attention to race, gender, sexual orientation, and so on, as well as cultural differences

Corporate social responsibility: companies going beyond their bottom-line economic interests and engaging in activities that promote social well-being and environmental sustainability

CREATIVITY AND CHANGE

DO WELL, DO GOOD, OR DO BOTH?

Many have argued that companies can "do well" and "do good" at the same time, that is, the economic and social goals of companies are not at odds but in fact complement and reinforce one another. Certainly companies like COSTCO, well-known for their treatment of employees and passing on savings to customers, hold this view. Harvard Business professor and author Rosabeth Moss Kanter is also one who has taken this position, though with a slight variation. She argues that there is not a strict dichotomy between doing well and doing good, that it is not an either/or question. Rather, she contends that profitability and social good are both desirable ends for business, and companies should both seek to improve the bottom line and to provide benefit to society. Indeed, she argues, the most progressive companies will find a way to build synergies between the two and build those synergies into corporate strategy.[59]

The idea of increasing social responsibility raises broader questions about the role of business in society. The basic question is whether an economic system that places primary value on the corporate bottom line can serve the needs of the future. Gary Hamel, management expert and visiting professor at the London School of Economics, has recently argued forcefully against this point. "Millions of consumers and citizens," he writes, "are already convinced of a fact that many corporate chieftains are still reluctant to admit: the legacy model of economic production that has driven the 'modern' economy over the last hundred years is on its last legs. Like a piece of clapped out engine, it's held together with bailing wire and duct tape, frequently breaks down and befouls the air with noxious fumes."[60]

Many executives cling to the idea that business is only for making money and that a focus on short-term economic benefits, one that disregards long-term social and environmental consequences, is the appropriate way to judge success in business. Hamel counters, "we long for a kinder, gentler sort of capitalism—one that views us as more than mere 'consumers,'" one that understands the difference between maximizing consumption and maximizing happiness, one that doesn't sacrifice the future for the present and regards our planet as sacred.[61]

This view is echoed by the founders of Generation Investment Management:

> Some of the ways in which [capitalism] is now practised do not incorporate sufficient regard for its impact on people, society and the planet. Capitalism in its current form is creating and fostering numerous challenges, not least short-termism, over-reliance on GDP growth as a primary metric of prosperity, rising inequality, increasing volatility in the global financial market, and growing contributions to the climate crisis.[62]

While this debate is far from concluded, it is important to understand that these questions form part of the ethical environment of organizational behavior. At some point you will have to take a position on these important ethical issues.

1. Are there inevitable trade-offs between a focus on profits versus corporate social responsibility?

2. How can both be increased at the same time?

that her company is trying to create broad financial literacy and promote economic opportunity. She describes the path of corporate social responsibility as moving from "philanthropy (just giving money away) to cause marketing (aligning your company with a social issue) to corporate responsibility (changing the way a company operates internally). Now . . . We're in a stage of shared value, where companies seek to have social impact and business return simultaneously."[63] As you can imagine, corporate social responsibility raises interesting questions for businesses, many of which were, and many of which still are primarily concerned with return on shareholder investment. Would corporate partners, shareholders, or potential investors approve of an activity that might be seen as taking away from company profits? Or, on the other hand, can a case be made that corporate social responsibility actually contributes to the bottom line? Or, does it

Ethical Business Culture

really matter—is corporate social responsibility simply the right thing to do? Finally, corporate social responsibility raises fundamental questions about the future role of business and society.[64] Recent studies also show that a growing number of companies are recognizing the importance of sustainability as a core strategy in order to be competitive. One study compared companies that adopted environmental and social policies with companies that didn't. High sustainability companies outperformed their competitors over an 18-year period, in terms of both market and accounting criteria, such as return on assets. These companies also had a stock market performance that was 4.8% higher than the low sustainability companies.[65]

Given findings like these, we can certainly expect many more firms to incorporate sustainable practices into their operations. But again, you might argue that sustainability is not only good business, it's simply the right thing to do.

EPA administrator Lisa Jackson tours the main Ben & Jerry's ice cream factory in Waterbury, Vermont, to view new pollution control devices in use at the plant on Friday, August 24, 2012. Many companies like Ben & Jerry's are stressing the importance of environmental sensitivity.

Global Sustainability

Sustainability basically means meeting the needs of the present generation in a way that doesn't compromise the capacity of future generations to meet their needs. Obviously, doing so has become more problematic as we have come to recognize that the population of the planet will grow dramatically over the coming years while the resources available to sustain that population will remain stable at best. There are new concerns, including the decline of natural ecosystems, climate change, water quality and scarcity, the fragility of food and food systems, the accumulation of waste, and the restructuring of transportation systems. All of these represent issues that must be addressed by both public and private action, as do such current policy concerns as sustainable development, environmental justice, land and urbanization, changing materials and technology—to name just a few. Leaders and managers in business and the public sector must keep the idea of sustainability in mind as they create new products, services, and infrastructures, for example, through building green wherever possible. But they must also recognize the importance of building viable and sustainable social and economic systems. And both private and public managers must engage in transformational stewardship of the people, places, and planet with which they are entrusted or for which they are responsible as leaders. The idea of sustainability requires an expansive view of social responsibility that extends beyond self-interest, geographically and even generationally. This ethic of stewardship must characterize the work of individual managers but also be taken to scale on a local, national, and planetary basis.

Taking on such major challenges as these, requires strong and creative action. Coca-Cola, for instance, has worked with its bottling partners to create lighter-weight packaging, cutting greenhouse gas emissions, and generating savings in the tens of millions of dollars. It has also made a commitment, in cooperation with its bottlers and with several nongovernmental organizations, to "water neutrality"—an initiative that will reduce environmental impact by replenishing watersheds to the full extent of the water the company removes.[66] But sustainability is an issue that cuts across national boundaries and will require a global commitment. Marvin Odum, president of Shell Oil Co., comments, "When I look at an investment proposal now, it still covers the technical issues, of course. It certainly covers the financial issues. But fully half of that proposal deals with the nontechnical risk: social performance and sustainability issues."[67]

Goodness
From Within

Kellogg CEO
Challenged

Women Need
Global Spotlight

Sustainability:
meeting the needs of the present generation in a way that doesn't compromise the capacity of future generations to meet their needs

▶ Summary: Learning Organizational Behavior

In this first chapter, we described organizational behavior as the study of how to manage individual and group behavior within business, government, and nonprofit settings, but we also emphasized the importance of learning to *act* effectively and responsibly within those organizations. We also introduced the field of organizational behavior, noting some historical highlights and bringing us up to the most contemporary work in positive psychology and behavioral neuroscience. We examined both the roles and responsibilities of leaders and managers, and discussed the importance of leadership extending throughout organizations. We then turned to the central themes of this book—creativity and change in a global society. After introducing each of these themes, we turned to four subthemes that we grouped as comprising the ethical environment of organizational behavior. These four subthemes are personal integrity, group diversity, social responsibility, and global sustainability.

▶ Key Terms

Bureaucracy   8

Corporate social responsibility   23

Diversity   23

Formal organization   7

Globalization   18

Hawthorne effect   7

Knowledge workers   11

Leadership   6

Liquid modernity   19

Organizational behavior   5

Positive organizational behavior   9

Scientific management   7

Sustainability   25

Theory X   8

Theory Y   8

▶ Exercise 1.1   Ethical Dilemmas in Cross-Cultural Work

Working in different cultures also involves confronting different ethical norms including norms related to business transactions. Imagine that you are working in another country trying to get a new plant built for your firm, but you are having difficulty working your way through complex regulations. A representative of a government agency in that country suggests that you have lunch together and talk more informally about some issues that need to be resolved. In the discussion, he makes it clear that for $5,000 he can make all of those issues go away. What would be the appropriate course of action in a case like this? Currell and Bradley, authors of the article from which this case was adapted, pull no punches in their assessment of what should be done:

> Organizations must insist on a swift response to complaints, unbiased investigations, and "public hangings" of offenders, and they should praise employees who have the courage to call out wrongdoing. These actions are critical to employees' perceptions of organizational justice, and they can help head off or mitigate the damage from bribery offenses.[68]

Do you agree with this judgment? If not, how would you frame an ethical solution?

▶ Exercise 1.2   Shadowing a Manager

We discussed how several scholars attempted to describe what managers do and, in turn, what skills, knowledge, and abilities they must acquire. Arrange to shadow a manager in your local community for at least a day. Focus your observations on the categories Mintzberg discusses in his 1960 article. But look also for deviations from his conclusions. Take detailed notes for reporting to the class.

► Case 1.1 Coaching the Green Team

You have just been named coach of a mixed boys' and girls' soccer team of 5-year-olds, which the players have affectionately named "The Green Team," an obvious reference to their blue uniforms. Most of the game consists of "scrums," where all the players gather closely around the ball and try to kick the ball but usually wind up kicking each other. Every now and then, however, the ball breaks free and your "star" player, whose name is Cari, steers it down the field in a complete breakaway and scores. (All the while the parents of those on the Green Team are chanting "CARI! CARI! CARI!") You soon despair of teaching the kids much about soccer, but it occurs to you that they could learn some important lessons about teamwork, communication, decision making,

motivation, leadership, and the like, and you set this as your goal. When you tell a friend about your decision, she remarks that if you can teach these behavioral skills to the Green Team, perhaps you could then come and teach them to the management team at her office—which is probably as much in need of these same skills as the soccer kids.

Answer these questions:

1. Have you ever been in a group or organization that didn't have problems with these issues? Don't they seem pervasive—whatever task you are trying to perform?

2. Wouldn't it be helpful to know more about these skills as you develop in your career?

⑤SAGE edge™

Sharpen your skills with SAGE edge at edge.sagepub.com/nahavandi

SAGE edge for students provides a personalized approach to help you accomplish your coursework goals in an easy-to-use learning environment.

► Endnotes

1. Kiechell, W., III. (2012, November). The management century. *Harvard Business Review,* pp. 62–75.

2. Taylor, F. (1911). *Principles of scientific management.* New York, NY: Norton.

3. Taylor, F. (1997). Scientific management. In Shafritz, J., & Hyede, A. (Eds.), *Classics of public administration* (4th ed.). Orlando, FL: Harcourt Brace, p. 32. (Original work published 1912)

4. Muntsberg, H. (1913). *Psychology and industrial efficiency.* Boston, MA: Houghton Mifflin.

5. Metcalf, H. C., & Urwick, L. (Eds.). (1940). *Dynamic administration: The collected papers of Mary Parker Follett.* New York, NY: Harper & Row, p. 9.

6. Roethlisberger, F. J., & Dickson, W. (1939). *Management and the worker.* Cambridge, MA: Harvard University Press.

7. Barnard, C. (1948). *The function of the executive.* Cambridge, MA: Harvard University Press, p. 81.

8. McGregor, D. (1960). *The human side of the enterprise.* New York, NY: McGraw-Hill.

9. Maslow, A. H. (1962). *Toward a psychology of being.* Princeton, NJ: Von Nostrand.

10. Weber, M. (1947). *The theory of social and economic organization* (A. M. Henderson & T. Parsons, trans.). New York, NY: Oxford University Press.

11. Drucker, P. (1967). *The effective executive*. New York, NY: Harper & Row.

12. Wheatley, M. (2006). *Leadership and the new science*. San Francisco, CA: Berrett-Koehler.

13. Senge, P. (1990). *The fifth discipline: The art and practice of the learning organization*. Garden City, NY: Doubleday.

14. Schein, E. H. (1985). *Organizational culture and leadership*. San Francisco, CA: Jossey-Bass.

15. Peters, T. J., & Waterman, R. H. (1982). *In search of excellence*. New York, NY: Harper & Row.

16. Collins, J. C. (2001). *Good to great*. New York, NY: HarperBusiness; and Collins, J. C., & Hansen, M. T. (2011). *Great by choice*. New York, NY: HarperCollins.

17. Seligman, M. E. P. (2002). *Authentic happiness: Using the new positive psychology to realize your potential for lasting fulfillment*. New York, NY: Free Press.

18. Cameron, K. S., Dutton, J. E., & Quinn, R. E. (2003a). *Positive organizational scholarship: Foundations of a new discipline*. San Francisco, CA: Berrett-Koehler; and Nelson, D. A., & Cooper, C. L. (2007). *Positive organizational behavior*. Thousand Oaks, CA: Sage.

19. Luthans, F. (2002). The need for and meaning of positive organizational behavior. *Journal of Organizational Behavior, 23*(6), 695–706.

20. Cameron, K. S., Dutton, J. E., & Quinn, R. E. (2003b). An introduction to positive organizational scholarship. In K. S. Cameron, J. E. Dutton, & R. E. Quinn (Eds.), *Positive organizational scholarship: Foundations of a new discipline* (pp. 3–13). San Francisco, CA: Berrett-Koehler.

21. Cameron et al., 2003b, p. 3.

22. Cameron et al., 2003b, p. 3.

23. Williams, R. (2009). Wired for success. *Psychology Today*, September 13. Retrieved from http://www.psychologytoday.com/blog/wired-success/200909/management-rewired-what-can-brain-science-tell-us-about-leadership on September 11, 2013.

24. Brooks, D. (2011). *The social animal*. New York, NY: Random House.

25. Goleman, D. (2006). *Social intelligence*. New York, NY: Bantam Books.

26. Uhl-Bien, M., Marion, R., McKelvey, B. (2007). Complexity leadership theory. *The Leadership Quarterly, 18*(4), 296–318.

27. Zaleznik, A. (1977, May–June). Managers and leaders: Are they different? *Harvard Business Review*, pp. 67–78.

28. Kotter, J. P. (2001). What leaders really do. *Harvard Business Review, 79*(11), 85–98.

29. Mintzberg, H. (1971). Managerial work: Analysis from observation. *Management Science, 18*(2), B97–B110.

30. For one CEO's view, see Kahan, S. (2009). The changing role of leaders and managers today. *Fast Company*, September 7. Retrieved from http://www.fastcompany.com/1350353/changing-role-leaders-and-managers-today-are-you-keeping on September 11, 2013.

31. Gosling, J., & Mintzberg, H. (2003, November). The five minds of the manager. *Harvard Business Review*, p. 56.

32. Gosling & Mintzberg, 2003, p. 56.

33. Nahavandi, A. (2012). *The art and science of leadership*. Upper Saddle River, NJ: Prentice Hall; and Schein, E. H. (2004). *Organizational culture and leadership*. San Francisco, CA: Jossey-Bass.

34. George, B. (2007). *True north*. San Francisco, CA: Jossey-Bass.

35. Tuggle, K. (2007). Marathon man. *Fast Company*, February, p. 54.

36. Pfeffer, J. (1998). Seven practices of successful organizations. *California Management Review, 40*(2), 96; see also Zaccaro, S. J., & Klimoski, R. J. (2001). *The nature of organizational leadership: Understanding the performance*

imperatives confronting today's leaders. Jossey-Bass Business and Management Series. San Francisco, CA: Jossey-Bass.

37. Asplund, J., & Blacksmith, N. (n.d.). The secret of higher performance. *Gallup Business Journal.* Retrieved from http://businessjournal.gallup.com/content/147383/Secret-Higher-Performance.aspx#1 on September 11, 2013.

38. Meier, K. J., & O'Toole, L. J. (2002). Public management and organizational performance: The effect of managerial quality. *Journal of Policy Analysis and Management, 21*(4), 629–643.

39. McGregor, J. (2012). What's a great boss worth? *Washington Post on Leadership,* August 13. Retrieved from http://www.washingtonpost.com/blogs/post-leadership/post/whats-a-great-boss-worth/2002/08/23/bc50c360-ed3a-11e1-9ddc-340d5efble9c_blog.html on September 10, 2013.

40. Malveaux, J. (2005, January 28). *Poor management responsible for negative impact on productivity.* Retrieved from http://www.shrm.org/about/pressroom/PressReleases/Pages/CMS_011140.aspx on September 11, 2013.

41. Zenger, J., & Folkman, J. (2012). How damaging is a bad boss, exactly? *Harvard Business Review,* HBR Blog Network, July 16. Retrieved from http://blogs.hbr.org/cs/2012/07/how-damaging-is-a-bad-boss-exa.html on December 10, 2012.

42. IBM. (2010). *Capitalizing on complexity* (p. 12). Somers, NY: IBM. Retrieved from ftp://public.dhe.ibm.com/common/ssi/pm/x/n/gbe03297usen/gbe03297/USEN.PDF on December 11, 2012.

43. Quoted in Lombardo, B. J., & Roddy, D. J. (2011). *Cultivating organizational creativity in an age of complexity* (pp. 9–10). Somer, NY: IBM. Retrieved from http://public.dhe.ibm.com/common/ssi/ecm/en/gbe03418usen/GBE03418USEN.PDF on September 12, 2013.

44. Internet World Stats. (2012). Available at http://www.internetworldstats.com/stats.htm

45. Bauman, Z. (2000). *Liquid modernity.* Malden, MA: Wiley.

46. Vitalvoices. (2012). Retrieved from http://www.vitalvoices.org/about-us/about on September 12, 2013.

47. Global Ambassadors. (2012). Retrieved from http://globalambassadors.vitalvoices.org/about.php on September 12, 2013.

48. UN News Centre. (2010, July 2). *High-level UN forum stresses role of women in advancing global development.* Retrieved from http://www.un.org/apps/news/story.asp?NewsID=35233&Cr=ecosoc&Cr1#.UMYWRKVnSc8 on December 10, 2012.

49. Kanani, R. (2012a). Bank of America tackles women's leadership in the developing world. *Forbes,* July 23. Retrieved from http://www.forbes.com/sites/rahimkanani/2012/07/23/bank-of-america-tackles-womens-leadership-in-the-developing-world/ on September 12, 2013.

50. Kanani, R. (2012b). Wendy Luhabe of South Africa on the importance of mentorship. *Forbes,* July 25. Retrieved from http://www.forbes.com/sites/rahimkanani/2012/07/25/wendy-luhabe-of-south-africa-on-the-importance-of-mentorship/ on September 12, 2013.

51. Kanani, R. (2012c). Ann Veneman on women's leadership and mentorship in the developing world. *Forbes,* July 23. Retrieved from http://www.forbes.com/sites/rahimkanani/2012/07/23/ann-veneman-on-womens-leadership-and-mentorship-in-the-developing-world/ on September 12, 2013.

52. Global Ambassador—India [Video]. (2012). Susan Chambers and Smita Mankad. Retrieved from http://www.youtube.com/watch?v=HxmUev8ETc8 on September 12, 2013.

53. IBM. (2012). *Leading through connections.* Somers, NY: IBM. Retrieved from http://public.dhe.ibm.com/common/ssi/ecm/en/gbe03485sen/GBE03485USEN.PDF on December 10, 2012.

54. Interpraxis. (2012). *Quotes on corporate social responsibility.* Retrieved from http://www.interpraxis.com/quotes.htm on September 12, 2013.

55. Banaji, M. R., Brazerman, M. H., & Chugh, D. (2003). How (un)ethical are you? *Harvard Business Review,* reprint, 1–10. Retrieved from https://hrb.org/download/how-unethical-are-you/R0312D-PDF-ENG/R0312D-PDF-ENG.PDF; and Brazerman, M. H., & Tenbrunsel, A. E. (2011). Ethical breakdowns. *Harvard Business Review,* reprint, 1–9.

56. Kidder, quoted in Rossey, G. L. (2011). Five questions for addressing ethical dilemmas. *Strategy and Leadership, 39*(6), 37.

57. Combs, G. M. (2002). Meeting the leadership challenge of a diverse and pluralistic workplace: Implications of self-efficiency for diversity training. *Journal of Leadership Studies.* Retrieved from http://www.accessmylibrary.com/article-1G1-88609137/meeting-leadership-challenge-diverse.html on September 12, 2013.

58. Fulton, A. (2012, September 4). McDonald's goes vegetarian—in India. *National Public Radio.* Retrieved from http://www.npr.org/blogs/thesalt/2012/09/04/160543754/mcdonalds-goes-vegetarian-in-india on October 18, 2012.

59. Kantor, R. M. (2010). How to do well and do good. *Sloan Management Review,* September. Retrieved from http://sloanreview.mit.edu/the-magazine/2010-fall/52118/how-to-do-well-and-do-good/ on September 11, 2013.

60. Hamel, G. (2010). Capitalism is dead. Long live capitalism. *Wall Street Journal,* September 21. Retrieved from http://blogs.wsj.com/management/2010/09/21/capitalism-is-dead-long-live-capitalism/ on September 11, 2013.

61. Harvey, F. (2012). Al Gore: How to modify capitalism to take a greener long view. *The Guardian,* February 16. Retrieved from http://www.guardian.co.uk/environment/2012/feb/16/al-gore-quarterly-reporting on September 11, 2013.

62. Harvey, 2012.

63. Bosch, K. (2012). The rise of shared value [Video]. *Co-Exist.* Retrieved from http://www.fastcoexist.com/1680445/the-rise-of-shared-value on September 11, 2013.

64. Vallaster, C., Lindgren, A., & Maon, F. (2012). Strategically leveraging corporate social responsibility. *California Management Review, 54*(3), 34–60.

65. Eccles, R. G., Perkins, J. M., & Serafeim, G. (2012). How to become a sustainable company. *Sloan Management Review.* Retrieved from http://sloanreview.mit.edu/the-magazine/2012-summer/53415/how-to-become-a-sustainable-company/ on September 11, 2013.

66. Luban, D. A., & Esty, D. C. (2010, May). The sustainability imperative. *Harvard Business Review,* reprint, p. 6.

67. Odum, M. (2011). Interview by M. S. Hopkins [Web based recording]. From "trust me" to "show me." *Sloan Management Review.* Retrieved from http://sloanreview.mit.edu/the-magazine/2011-spring/52317/moving-sustainability-at-shell-oil-from-priority-to-core-value/ on September 12, 2013.

68. Currell, D., & Bradley, T. D. (2012, September). Greased palms, giant headaches. *Harvard Business Review,* p. 4.

INDIVIDUAL BEHAVIOR AND CHARACTERISTICS

PART

2

2 Culture and Diversity

Developing a Cultural Mindset

Sodexo: Committed to Diversity Management ▶

What does it take for a company to be ranked as one of the best for managing a diverse workforce? Sodexo, the $20 billion food services and facility management company and one of the world's largest employers, can provide the answer.[1] Sodexo keeps diversity in the forefront of its activities through a strong commitment from the top leadership, a managerial reward system based partially on achieving diversity objectives, extensive diversity training and mentoring, and numerous diversity-focused partnerships and relationships including cooperation with historically Black colleges and universities.[2] A high touch culture with an orientation toward action is responsible for the implementation of various diversity initiatives says Betsy Silva Hernandez, senior director for corporate diversity and inclusion.

A diversity leadership council, in place since 2002, and the recently added committee of operation leaders, are tasked with implementation and oversight of various policies through managers and employee groups.[3] The company president and CEO, George Chavel, says: "Our diversity expertise helps us be more agile and responsive to customers and differentiates us from our competitors, and therefore directly contributes to our long-term business success."[4] Rohini Anand, Sodexo's chief diversity officer, who gets much of the credit for the company's achievements in this area, believes that diversity is a key to the company's success and at the core of what they do. "Sodexo considers diversity and inclusion a business imperative as well as a social and ethical responsibility grounded in core values of team spirit, service spirit, and spirit of progress."[5]

Keeping diversity at the forefront of their mission and their management practices has paid off. In addition to many awards and recognition from groups such as DiversityInc and Catalyst, the numbers speak for themselves. Over 12% of the company's executives are Black and the overall number of minorities and women in management increased by 15% and 8%, respectively, in just 5 years.[6] On a 2012 company survey, 83% of employees

Preservation of one's own culture does not require contempt or disrespect for other cultures.

—Cesar Chavez

indicated that they felt valued for the differences they bring to the workplace, an impressive 16-point improvement from 2006.[7] Additionally, close to 90% of Sodexo managers participate in various employee resource groups that are instrumental in implementing diversity initiatives.[8] These accomplishments are particularly noteworthy given that just a few years back, in 2006, the company settled an $80 million discrimination class-action lawsuit.[9] Those days are long gone and Sodexo now considers diversity not only a good business practice, but simply the right thing to do.

Sodexo has made a conscious choice to capitalize on the many cultures and groups within society and build on that diversity to strengthen its workforce and address and expand its markets. In our global world, and particularly in countries such as the United States where many cultures are represented, cultural diversity is a fact of life. If you ask people about their cultural background and identity, they are likely to tell you which country they are from, where they grew up, or where their parents come from. For most people culture is equated with nationality or ethnicity. One is American, Chinese, Egyptian, Brazilian, African American, Asian, or some combination of different nations and ethnicities. People may also identify with a particular region within a country, such as the Northeastern United States or Southern France. Unless probed further, few people will mention their gender, religious background, sexual orientation, hobbies, or profession. However, all of these elements as well as many others make up someone's cultural background and identity. Our cultural identity is complex and has a pervasive and strong impact on how we think and behave. Therefore understanding culture is a critical component of developing the self-awareness necessary to effective leadership and can help us become more successful in interacting with others and in managing our teams and organizations in an increasingly diverse, interconnected, and global world. This chapter discusses the importance of understanding culture and diversity in today's global organizations and introduces the concept of cultural mindset as a way of respecting and capitalizing on cultural diversity.

What Is Culture and Why Does It Matter?

Recent Diversity
Training

Why should global leaders understand culture? Why is it so important? Whether you live and work in the United States or any other country in the world, you are likely to face a global world where you interact with people from many different countries and cultures. Because culture impacts how we think and act, we are well advised to understand culture and its impact. Examples of blunders related to lack of cultural knowledge abound.[10] Companies use the wrong names and fail to sell their goods; leaders make an inappropriate gesture and offend their negotiation partners from another culture; employees misinterpret their leader's openness and desire for team decision making as a weakness; managers overlook outstanding job applicants because of preconceived cultural beliefs; compliments are seen as sexual harassment; firms fail to capitalize on a growth opportunity because they overlook a different market. On a personal level, such

SELF-ASSESSMENT 2.1

DO YOU HAVE A CULTURAL MINDSET?

For each of the following items, please use the scale below to indicate your answer.

		Strongly disagree	Disagree	Agree	Strongly agree
1.	I know a lot about my own culture.	1	2	3	4
2.	I don't think much about how my culture impacts me.	1	2	3	4
3.	I can tell how my cultural background influences how I think and what I do.	1	2	3	4
4.	I enjoy asking people about their culture.	1	2	3	4
5.	I seek out various cultural experiences any chance I can (e.g., food, travel, festivals, music).	1	2	3	4
6.	I know a lot about how cultural differences impact the thinking and behavior of those I work with.	1	2	3	4
7.	I like sharing my culture and its customs and beliefs with those who don't know it.	1	2	3	4
8.	I often include culture as one of the factors I consider when I think about solving problems either in my personal or professional life.	1	2	3	4
9.	I am comfortable with people who are from different cultures.	1	2	3	4
10.	When people around me speak a different language, it often makes me uncomfortable.	1	2	3	4
11.	I think people are the same, no matter where they are from.	1	2	3	4
12.	Although I am from _____ (state your country), I often think of myself as a citizen of the world.	1	2	3	4
13.	People may have different views, but I believe that in the end, there is always a right way and wrong way.	1	2	3	4
14.	I am good at adjusting my behavior to different situations.	1	2	3	4
15.	My own and other people's cultural background is important to me.	1	2	3	4

Scoring: Reverse the scoring for items 2, 10, 11, 13 (1 = 4; 2 = 3; 3= 2; 4 =1). Then add up your scores for all questions.

Total: _____

The range of scores is 15 to 60. A score in the upper third (60 to 45) indicates strong cultural mindfulness. A score in the bottom third (30 to 15) shows little awareness of culture. Review each of your responses and the material about diversity and cultural mindset in this chapter to identify your areas of strength and weakness and decide what you can do to strengthen your cultural awareness and ability to work across diverse cultures.

Source: Adapted with permission from Nahavandi, A. (2012). *The Art and Science of Leadership* (6th ed.) New York, NY: Pearson–Prentice Hall.

mistakes and misinterpretations may embarrass people and prevent them from establishing effective relationships; the impact is limited to one individual and the missed opportunities. On an organizational level, cultural misunderstandings can have considerable impact not only on the individuals involved, but also on whole organizations and even whole countries. Not understanding culture can have dire individual, organizational, political, and economic consequences.

Consider the simple images in Figure 2.1. What do they mean to you? If you speak a language that is written from left to right, the pictures will tell you that the washing machine will clean your pile of dirty clothes. However, if you speak a language written from right to left, the meaning changes drastically! Such a simple mistake can have dire consequences if you are marketing a washing machine in the Middle East.

Defining Culture

Unable to Befriend

Culture: a set of beliefs and values shared by members of a given group

Culture is a set of beliefs and values shared by members of a given group. These beliefs and values lead to patterns of behavior that are acquired and transmitted from one member to another.[11] These beliefs, values, and behaviors make a group unique and set it apart from others. As such, culture creates differences among people and groups. Culture also shapes how people view the world. From simple greeting rituals to what we expect of our leaders, to how we raise our children, and what we consider appropriate behavior in organizations, many of our actions and thoughts are influenced by our culture. Culture both provides the framework or the lens that allows us to perceive and understand events, and through that lens, makes us focus on certain things and tells us what matters and what does not. For example, recent research shows that American education highlights themes of individualism and self-direction and achievement, while Japanese education focuses on conformity and group harmony.[12] Each culture focuses on values that it considers important in the education of its children.

FIGURE 2.1 WHAT IS WRONG WITH THIS PICTURE?

In organizational settings, research indicates many cultural differences in factors such as organizational commitment, turnover, the type of role model people respond to best, leadership ideals, and nonverbal behaviors.[13] Ignoring culture, either consciously or because of lack of knowledge, will more than likely lead to missteps if not blunders. Therefore, cultural understanding can distinctly enhance both individual and organizational effectiveness.

Characteristics of Culture

Culture is handed down from one generation to the next and has *permanence*. While cultures do change and evolve, they do so slowly. Older and more experienced members show and tell younger and newer members what is important and valuable and how to do things. Younger and newer members are taught what the culture is, what they should believe and value, and how they should act. Partly because culture is transferred and handed down from one person to another, cultural beliefs are *hard to change*. We carry the culture we were taught by our parents with us even if we leave our home country and live and work in a different cultural environment. For example, the belief in arranged marriages, which is shared by many cultures around the world, does not change when people move to a Western country where such marriages are not the norm. A case in point are Indian families who have established themselves successfully in Great Britain, the United States, and other parts of the world, but often still rely on family and social contacts to find a mate for their children. Similarly, most immigrants continue to celebrate their holidays and teach their kids the specific values that make their culture unique. Culture is therefore stable over time and slow to change.

Hand gestures have different meanings in different cultures. For example, while the "thumbs up" gesture indicates approval in some cultures (e.g., the United States), the gesture can also be interpreted as offensive or insulting in other cultures (e.g., Iran). Misunderstanding cultural context can have unintended consequences in organizational behavior.

In spite of its permanence and the fact that cultures resist attempts at change, another key characteristic of culture is that it is *dynamic*. It evolves as people adapt to their environment and adjust their beliefs to address new situations and challenges. The same Indian families who believe in arranged marriages, have altered the way such marriages are handled when they live in the West. Rather than an agreement among parents and elders, the children are now involved in those decisions. The cultural value of arranged marriages survives, but has been modified and modernized. This modification is an example of how culture changes slowly over time and integrates new beliefs, values, and behaviors. In another example, while in many cultures women are still expected to stay home and take care of their families, the role of women has evolved, even in traditional societies. Girls in Saudi Arabia go to school and continue on to college. The country even introduced its first-ever female athlete in the 2012 London

What Do You Think?

▶ Take a minute to think about the last time you interacted with someone from a different culture. Did cultural differences affect your interaction? How so? What do you think?

Indira Gandhi was India's first and only female prime minister, an unexpected event in a culture where gender roles are highly defined. However, since her election, women have taken an increasingly active role in politics.

TABLE 2.1 CHARACTERISTICS OF CULTURE

- Shared by group members
- Transferred from one member to another
- Affects thinking and behavior
- Stable and dynamic

Olympics. Similarly, women in India have taken an active role in political life starting with the election of Indira Gandhi as prime minister in the 1960s, and they play a crucial role in many business organizations while still retaining highly traditional roles in society. Argentina, a country with a strong value for male dominance, elected Eva Perón as Vice President in the 1950s. French laws that, up to the middle of the 20th century, did not allow women to open bank accounts without their husband's permission, have changed as a result of the social and cultural evolution. Women in the United are allowed to be members of country clubs in their own right, something that was unheard of even in the middle of the 20th century. While cultural change is almost always slow and evolutionary, rather than fast and revolutionary, it does take place. Therefore, cultures are both stable and dynamic. The key characteristics of culture are summarized in Table 2.1.

Three Levels of Culture

Culture exists at *three levels* presented in Figure 2.2. (The definition and characteristics of culture we presented above apply to all three levels.) The first level of culture is national culture, the set of values and beliefs shared by people within a nation. Because national culture addresses many different aspects of life, it has a strong and pervasive influence on people's behavior, both in everyday activities and in organizations. In addition to an overall national culture, there may be ethnic and other cultural groups within each nation. Although these groups share national cultural values, they also have their own unique culture. These ethnic or group cultures form the second level of culture. Some nations and cultures, such as the United States, Canada, and Indonesia, include many such subcultures; others such as Japan do not. National cultures that have many different subcultures are heterogeneous; those that have only a few subcultures are homogeneous.

People within ethnic and other subgroups share worldviews, norms, values, beliefs, and behavior that differentiate them from others and make them unique. Such groups can be based on ethnicity and race such as African Americans, Native Americans, or Asian Americans within the United States, or on cultural groupings such as Hispanics, or on yet other factors such as gender or geographic location. For example, as you will learn in this chapter, gender affects behavior in organizations in a variety of ways. In particular, widely

National culture: the first level of culture; a set of values and beliefs shared by people within a nation

Ethnic or group culture: the second level of culture; a set of values and beliefs shared by people within a group

Heterogeneous cultures: include many different cultural groups

Homogeneous cultures: include one or few cultural groups

FIGURE 2.2 THE THREE LEVELS OF CULTURE

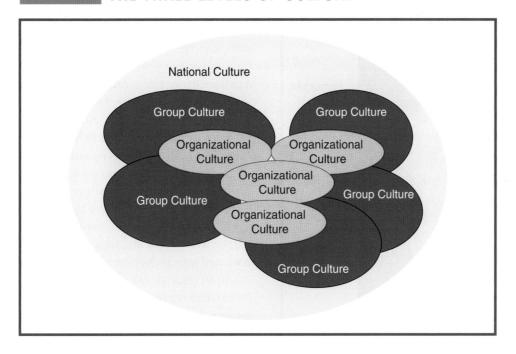

Equal Common
Culture

held gender stereotypes affect our views of leadership and create significant differences in power and authority between men and women.[14]

Furthermore, people who belong to different groups often have different experiences within organizations, not always because of their actual cultural differences, but because others may perceive them differently.

Cultural diversity then refers to differences at the national level as well as the differences in race, gender, ethnicity, language, religion, sexual orientation, generations, physical ability, social background, and even things such as marital status and educational background. The world is a mosaic of individuals and groups with varying backgrounds, experiences, working styles, abilities, perceptions, values, and beliefs. Cultural diversity refers to that variety of human culture at all levels.

The third level of culture is **organizational culture**—the set of values, norms, and beliefs shared by members of an organization.[15] Given time, all organizations develop a unique culture or character whereby employees share common values and beliefs about work-related issues. The influence of organizational culture is generally limited to work-related values and behaviors. However, organizational culture is strongly influenced by both national culture and cultural diversity. This chapter will focus on national and cultural diversity; the topic of organizational culture will be discussed in Chapter 15.

The Cultural Iceberg: What We Know and What We Don't Know

A common view of culture is that what we see and can observe is only a small part of what culture is. This model is commonly known as the **iceberg** view of culture.[16] Just as

Cultural diversity: refers to such differences at the national level as well as the differences in race, ethnicity, language, religion, gender, or generations among various groups within a community or nation

Organizational culture: the set of values, norms, and beliefs shared by members of an organization

Cultural iceberg: what we see and can observe from culture is only a small part of what culture is

FIGURE 2.3 CULTURAL ICEBERG

- Visible culture
- Water line
- Hidden culture

- Behaviors
- Expressed values
- Basic assumptions
- Deep values

an iceberg has roughly nine tenths of its mass hidden under water, a good portion of culture is hidden from view, especially to outsiders. You cannot judge the shape of an iceberg from the visible portion; similarly, the nature and depth of the values of a culture cannot be ascertained by simply looking at the visible behaviors (see Figure 2.3). Casual contact with other cultures provides access to the visible behaviors and expressed values. However, understanding any culture requires access to the hidden portions, the core of culture that may be hard even for people from that culture to clearly express. Some values are so much part of who people are, they are unarticulated and sometimes even unconscious. For example, research has found that there are differences regarding how often men and women smile and that different cultures also perceive and interpret the meaning of smiling differently.[17] However, when and how we smile is not something that people think of as culturally based. Many similar behaviors are almost automatic and their cultural roots unconscious. Understanding culture requires observation of the visible parts and exploration of the hidden parts of the cultural iceberg.

Observable components of culture are visible to insiders and outsiders. They are cultural elements such as language and nonverbal behavior, art, greeting rituals, and so forth. Rituals are prescribed ceremonies that members perform at certain times. The other aspects are not easily observable, though some members may be aware of them and can describe them. In addition, culture also includes basic assumptions that are often unstated and hard to observe.[18] These assumptions are at the root of values and behaviors shared by group members and deal with general philosophical issues that are not always directly related to business.

Culturally Diverse Environment

Sophisticated Stereotypes

Throughout this chapter we will discuss culture and its impact on people and organizations. We will explore how different countries and groups have different cultures and how people within these groups think and behave in certain ways. In that process, we are grouping people in broad categories. We'll discuss how the people in the United States, France, or China have certain values; how women have different management styles; how minorities and women may face challenges in the workplace; and how generations differ in terms of their motivation and needs. The information we provide is based on extensive research, but not everyone in each of these groups necessarily behaves the same way. At some level, we are *stereotyping* people. However, because our discussions are based on reliable and valid research, rather than personal experience or opinion, as stereotypes often are, we are relying on **sophisticated stereotypes**.[19] These are generalizations based on research. While they have validity and can be used to make better decisions, you should be aware that culture is just one factor among many that impact how people behave. Understanding culture is essential but not sufficient in managing well.

Sophisticated stereotypes: generalizations about people based on valid and reliable research rather than opinion or personal experience

Diversity in Today's Workplace

Many countries around the world include groups with different cultural backgrounds. As we defined earlier, this group diversity is referred to as cultural diversity. Some countries are culturally diverse; others are less so. For example, Malaysia's 25-million population is highly diverse and consists of Malays, Chinese, Indians, Arabs, Sinhalese, Eurasians, and Europeans, with the Muslim, Buddhist, Daoist, Hindu, Christian, Sikh, and Shamanistic religions all practiced.[20] Similarly, although the majority of Singapore's population of more than 4 million is Chinese, it also includes Malays, Indians, and Eurasians. As a result, the country has four official languages: English, Malay, Mandarin, and Tamil.[21] Nigeria, Africa's most populous nation, includes over 250 different ethnic groups.[22] The United States is also a culturally diverse country (see Figure 2.4). To help your organization be effective, you must understand culture and be able to apply diversity concepts where appropriate.

Diversity in Everyday Discourse

FIGURE 2.4 DIVERSITY IN THE U.S. POPULATION

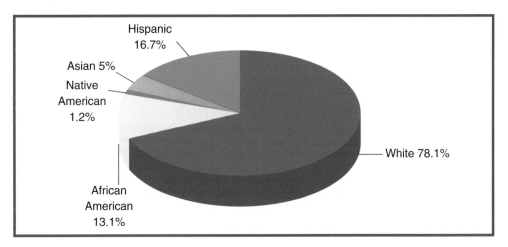

Hispanic 16.7%
Asian 5%
Native American 1.2%
White 78.1%
African American 13.1%

Source: United States Census Bureau. (2013). Available from http://quickfacts.census.gov/qfd/states/00000.html on May 30, 2013.

Primary and Secondary Dimensions of Diversity

Cultural diversity may consist of a number of primary factors such as gender, ethnicity, and age and other secondary factors such as income, education, and membership in various groups (Figure 2.5). The **primary dimensions of diversity** are the visible and stable aspects of a person. The **secondary dimensions of diversity** are less visible or more dynamic. For example, your ethnicity and age are stable and often visible while your marital status and religion can change. Group culture can affect people in two important ways. First, an individual's work and management style may vary based on her group membership. For example, women managers have been found to be more participative in their leadership style.[23] Second, membership in some groups impacts how others view the members and therefore how they may react to them.

Table 2.2 highlights some of the ethnic and demographic changes and trends in the United States. Major demographic trends in the United States indicate that the number of minorities—individuals from a non-European and non-Caucasian background—is increasing in the U.S. population. Similarly, women are also fast becoming close to half of the workforce. The presence of what some call "nontraditional" workers in organizations that were homogeneous, mostly male and mostly Caucasian, is creating both opportunities and challenges for managers.

Primary dimensions of diversity: the visible and stable aspects of a group or person

Secondary dimensions of diversity: the less visible or more dynamic aspects of a group or person

FIGURE 2.5 DIMENSIONS OF DIVERSITY

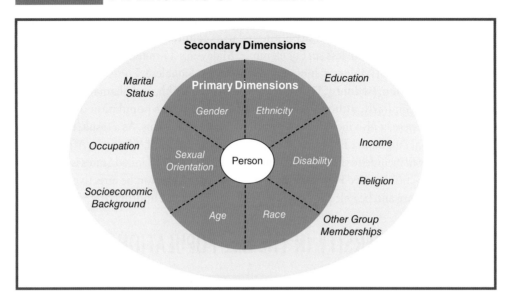

TABLE 2.2 U.S. DEMOGRAPHIC HIGHLIGHTS AND TRENDS

- In 2007, 20.3% of the U.S population spoke a language other than English at home compared to 13% in 2000.
- More than half of the U.S. workforce consists of women and minorities.
- By 2016, minorities will make up one third of the U.S. population.
- By 2025, the percentage of European Americans in the population will drop from 72% in 2000 to 62%.
- By 2025, Hispanics are estimated to be 21% of the population, outnumbering African Americans, who will make up 13% of the population.
- By 2050, the Hispanic population of the United States will grow to 30.25%.
- By 2025, the average age will be close to 40, as opposed to under 35 in 2000.
- By 2025, more than 50% of the population of Hawaii, California, New Mexico, and Texas will be from a minority group.
- By 2050, the average U.S. resident will be from a non-European background.
- By 2050, only about 62% of the entrants into the labor force will be white, with half that number being women.

Source: U.S. Bureau of Labor Statistics. (2013). Available from http://www.bls.gov/emp/ep_table_303.htm; Census Bureau, Census 2010 at www.census.gov/population

Houston's
Diverse Future

Benefits and Challenges of Workplace Diversity

"Business is at its core about relationships. I think diversity work takes away barriers that interfere with relationship building," says Ted Childs, who used to be IBM's president of global workforce diversity.[24] He believes that: "You're going to have to sell to people who are different from you, and buy from people who are different from you, and manage people who are different from you. . . . This is how we do business. If it's not your destination, you should get off the plane now."[25] As stated by Childs, cultural diversity is not an option or a choice; it is a reality in today's global world. Some organizations such as Sodexo (in our opening case) and Deloitte (later in the chapter), or Procter & Gamble have successfully embraced diversity and made it the core of their organization. At the end of this chapter, we will review various methods that can help make an organization culturally diverse.

For now, let's consider the impact of diversity. Research indicates that diverse membership in groups contributes to higher creativity, increased flexibility, and better problem solving, especially for complex problems.[26] Talking about the 2008 financial crisis and how the lack of diversity in the financial industry may have contributed to it, Christine Lagarde, former French finance minister and head of the International Monetary Fund (IMF) said: "If Lehman Brothers had been 'Lehman Sisters,' today's economic crisis clearly would look quite different."[27] Diverse organizations, if managed well, can take advantage of markets and opportunities that they would otherwise miss.

However, diversity can also pose some challenges and conflict among members of an organization. Members of groups with similar background and orientations can achieve higher cohesion, like each other more, and often can reach decisions more quickly.[28] Research in psychology indicates that we get along more readily with people who are similar to us. On the other hand, diverse perspectives have been found to be key when facing complex situations.[29] Diversity can also be particularly helpful when groups are facing challenging ethical decisions.[30] For example, the inclusion of women in groups has been shown to help in processing and managing complex information.[31]

These research findings have been part of the impetus for recommendations to increase diversity in organizations, and especially to increase diversity in the leadership of public and business organizations.[32]

Legal Considerations

Diversity also has legal implications for organizations and some have had to adjust their human resource practices as a result of policy changes in the United States. **Discrimination** refers to organizations making personnel decisions based on factors unrelated to the job or to a person's performance. In the United States, specific legislation called **equal employment opportunity (EEO)** forbids discrimination on the basis of race, ethnicity, national origin, sex, religion, age, disability, political beliefs, and marital or familial status.[33] These categories are referred to as protected groups. The goal of EEO is to be proactive and encourage diversity in the workplace. In 2012, the EEO Commission (EEOC) received 99,412 private sector workplace discrimination charges. These included retaliation (37%), race (33%), and sex discrimination (31%).[34] **Affirmative Action**, in comparison, aims at correcting past injustice and imbalance through direct action aimed at increasing the number of members of minority groups or women. While people typically associate Affirmative Action with quotas, the latter are illegal and have never been part of the legislation.

What Do You Think?

▶ To achieve cultural diversity, some organizations set specific targets for how many women and minorities should be hired. Some people believe that such targets are necessary to correct historical trends; others think they are unfair. What do you think?

Does Diversity Pay?

Discrimination: organizations making personnel decisions based on other than job-relevant factors or performance

Equal employment opportunity (EEO): forbids discrimination on the basis of race, color, national origin, sex, religion, age, disability, political beliefs, and marital or familial status; the goal of EEO is to be proactive and encourage diversity in the workplace

Affirmative Action: aims at correcting past injustice and imbalance through direct action aimed at increasing the number of members of minority groups or women

Many people believe that unique cultures within a country or organization are valuable and should be preserved. Recognition and preservation of cultural differences is at the heart of the concept of cultural diversity. Having leaders and employees with diverse worldviews, different approaches to problem solving, and distinct styles is one way businesses can address the complex issues they face in an increasingly global world. Effective managers not only follow the law and do not discriminate against protected groups, but go beyond and act proactively to create inclusive organizations where differences that are not addressed in EEO, for example sexual orientation, are also considered and celebrated. Several companies such as Citibank and Procter & Gamble put this belief into practice: Over half of the senior managers of these two U.S. companies are non-Americans. Years ago, the legendary chairman of Procter & Gamble, John Pepper, declared that whatever the U.S. laws governing diversity, his company would continue to promote it because of the benefits to the company.

Gender Diversity

Breaking the Glass Ceiling

A recent and much publicized article titled "Why Women Still Can't Have It All" reignited the debate over whether women can achieve the same success as men and how they can balance their personal and work life.[35] In the article, Anne Marie Slaughter, dean of Princeton University's Woodrow Wilson School of Public and International Affairs, who quit her job as director of policy planning in the U.S. State Department, states: "I still strongly believe that women can 'have it all' (and that men can too). I believe that we can 'have it all at the same time.' But not today, not with the way America's economy and society are currently structured."[36] While many disagree with her assertions, there is strong consensus that women, like minorities, face challenges in the workplace.

Since the 1960s, women have entered organizations and continue to do so at a very high rate. However, while they are close to 50% of the workforce, they still face major challenges.

Current State

Women make up 47% of the general workforce in the United States, with a clear majority of women being part of the labor force; however, they hold only 10% of the executive positions in the United States.[37] Table 2.3 presents a summary of gender-related statistics. Similar trends exist all over the world. For example, in Canada women comprise almost 47% of the labor force, close to 45% in China, over 50% in Russia.[38] The number of women in leadership positions is highest in Scandinavian countries where, for example, women hold 23% of the board seats in Sweden.[39] In spite of the growing number of women in organizations, there still are considerable challenges.

In the United States, women's income continues to lag behind that of men at about 77% of men's income.[40] In 2011, women held only 16% of corporate officer positions.[41] As of 2013, there were only 20 female CEOs in the *Fortune* 500 (4%) in the United States and another 25 in the next 500 companies (5%).[42] It is estimated that if the current trends continue, by 2016 maybe 6% of top leadership positions will be held by women.[43] The salary gap between men and women is further evidence of the challenges women face.

TABLE 2.3 **WOMEN IN TODAY'S U.S. WORKPLACE**
• Women make up 47% of the labor force
• Women hold 10% of leadership positions
• Women hold 15.2% of corporate officer positions
• 3% of *Fortune* 500 companies are headed by women
• Women's income is approximately 77% of that of men's
• 4% of U.S. *Fortune* 500 CEOs are women
• Only 2 of the top 100 highest paid CEOs are women

According to *Forbes*, only 2 of the 100 highest paid executives in the United States in 2012 were women, ranking number 40 and 88.[44]

An even more disturbing issue is that even when women are in leadership positions, they have less decision-making power, less authority, and less access to the highly responsible and challenging assignments than their male counterparts.[45] Another alarming development for women is that despite consistent gains in achieving equality with men in the workplace, a series of surveys conducted since 1972 indicate that, overall, women are unhappier than they were previously, and they get less happy as they age, a finding that is reversed for men.[46] The primary explanation provided is that women feel rushed and stressed much more than before and more than men, and that they feel drained rather than fulfilled. All the progress that women have made was assumed to make them happier. The opposite may be the case.

Reconsidering Gender Stereotypes

Challenges

What obstacles do women face and what explains the challenges they face? Many factors have been considered and researched.[47] Table 2.4 presents the various reasons that have been suggested.

TABLE 2.4 SUGGESTED REASONS FOR GENDER INEQUALITY

Issue	Do They Contribute to Inequality?
Gender differences in style and effectiveness	There are some gender differences, but if anything, women appear to have a style that is recommended in today's organizations
Challenges in balancing work-life	Women still carry a heavy burden of childcare and household work
Women are less committed to their career	Women leave more often to have a family and have a nonlinear career, but they come back after a short break
Women have less education and experience	Equal or higher percentages of women compared to men have been getting education in all but the sciences and they have been in various positions in organizations for over 50 years
Persistent stereotypes	Continued gender stereotypes held by organizational leaders and structural barriers due to traditional practices negatively impacts women's success in organizations
Discrimination	Either intentionally or unwittingly, women face discrimination in the workplace

Work-Life Balance. In spite of the fact that women have a strong presence in organizations, including in managerial positions, traditional gender views and stereotypes continue to create obstacles to their success in organizations. Cinta Putra, CEO of National Notification Network, believes: "The greatest challenge has been balancing all the demands of being a woman, a parent, a wife, a sister, a daughter, a friend, *and* a CEO."[48] Similarly, Sheryl Sandberg, COO of Facebook and author of the best-selling book, *Lean In*, believes that the disequilibrium in household responsibilities is a basic reason for women's lack of progress.[49] Although there have been some changes over the past few years, research indicates that women still continue to carry most of the burden for childcare and household work

Ursula Burns, CEO of Xerox, is one of the very few female CEOs of a Fortune 500 company. Although the lack of female CEOs is a complex issue, some attribute the gender disparity to work-life balance.

and that, as a result, mothers are less employed than other women, where fathers work more than other men.[50]

In spite of this, women are highly committed to both their education and their work. They are earning 59% of the undergraduate college degrees, 61% of the master's degrees, and 51% of MBAs.[51] Recent research indicates that although more professional women than men do take a break from work when they start a family (16% for women vs. 2% for men), over 90% of them try to get back in after about 2 years, further contradicting the idea that women have less commitment to their careers than men.[52] Some women executives have even suggested that motherhood provides women with skills that can be helpful in taking on organizational leadership roles. Gerry Laybourne, founder of the TV network Oxygen, states, "You learn about customer service from your 2-year-old (they are more demanding than any customer can be). You also learn patience, management skills, diversionary tactics, and 5-year planning."[53]

Stereotypes and Discrimination. While there may be some differences in management and leadership styles between men and women, such differences, if anything, should help women rather than hurt them.[54] Women have been found to be more cooperative, team oriented, and more change oriented (you will learn about this transformational leadership style in Chapter 12).[55] Management guru Tom Peters believes that the success of the new economy depends on the collaborative style that women leaders use instead of the command-and-control style that male leaders have traditionally used.[56]

That leaves one major explanation for the challenges women face: continued stereotypes and the resulting discrimination prevent them from achieving their potential. Both men and women continue to hold traditional stereotypes about what roles women should and can play in organizations. Facebook's Sandberg suggests that women sometimes sabotage their own career.[57] She finds that many of the young women she targets for challenging positions take themselves out of the running because they think having a family, which is in their future plans, will not allow them to continue working as hard, so they slow down too early. Women are not alone in this type of stereotypical thinking. Research suggests that bosses' perception of potential conflict between family and work affects their decision to promote women.[58] In this case, as in some others, perception appears to play a bigger role than reality.

Glass ceiling:
invisible barriers and obstacles that prevent individuals from moving to the highest levels of organizations

Stereotypes and tradition then lead to intentional and unintentional discriminatory practices. Women face the so-called **glass ceiling**—invisible barriers and obstacles that prevent them from moving to the highest levels of organizations.[59] Some have suggested that men are fast-tracked to leadership positions through a "glass elevator," and a recent review suggests the presence of a "glass cliff," whereby successful women are appointed to precarious leadership positions with little chance of success, thereby exposing them to yet another form of discrimination.[60]

Sexual harassment:
unwelcome sexual advances, requests for sexual favors, and other verbal or physical conduct of a sexual nature that tends to create a hostile or offensive work environment

Sexual Harassment. **Sexual harassment**, which is defined as unwelcome sexual advances, requests for sexual favors, and other verbal or physical conduct of a sexual nature that tends to create a hostile or offensive work environment, is considered workplace discrimination. According to the U.S. Equal Employment Opportunity Commission (EEOC), sexual harassment claims were by far the largest portion of sex discrimination claims in 2012.[61]

DELOITTE BUILDS DIVERSITY

Deloitte, one of the Big Four accounting firms with global reach, has 4,500 partners and other top executives. Ninety-two percent of them are white despite many years of efforts to build diversity in the company.[62] This statistic is on CEO Barry Salzberg's mind. He is focused on making his company a more diverse place and on opening up doors for the talent that Deloitte needs to recruit and retain in order to succeed. One of the steps the company has taken is to recruit from community colleges rather than only top notch universities, a practice that is typical for large global companies. Salzberg states: "Targeting these schools offers us a unique opportunity to reach another distinct population of diverse top talent."[63] In addition, Deloitte has implemented an innovative program called Mass Career Customization that provides every employee, not just women and minorities, the opportunity to develop his or her own unique path. The program grew out of a women's initiative within the company but now applies to all employees. "Mass career customization provides a framework in which every employee, in conjunction with his or her manager, can tailor his or her respective career path within Deloitte over time."[64] The program allows employees to create a better fit between their life and career and provides multiple paths to the top of the organization, thereby addressing one of the primary challenges that women face in balancing work and life.

Deloitte's efforts have not gone unnoticed. The company was named by Business Week as the number one company for starting a career and got high marks in the Shriver Report, a report that describes the status of women in the United States, as a model employer.[65] The report gives Deloitte high marks for being "an excellent example of an employer that has taken an aggressive leadership position in protean career approaches, providing career-life integration programs that allow both the organization and its workforce—women and men—to reach their goals."[66] Cathy Benko, Vice Chairman and chief talent officer at Deloitte believes that: "Through our own journey to retain and advance women, we know that what is good for women is good for all our people."[67]

1. What impact does each level of culture have on how Deloitte manages diversity?

2. What impact do diversity initiatives have on the organization?

Other more subtle forms of discrimination include the fact that although they are in mid-management positions, women and minorities are often not mentored by the right people, at the right time, a factor that is critical to success in any organization. Men are also made team leaders more often than women are (46% vs. 34%), they get more budgetary authority (44% vs. 31%), and they have increased responsibilities (89% vs. 83%).[68] Furthermore, women and minorities are often not exposed to the type of positions or experiences that are essential to achieving high-level leadership. For example, women and minorities may not be encouraged to take on international assignments or are kept in staff rather than line positions and therefore may lack essential operational experience. Finally, subtle social and organizational culture factors, such as going to lunch with the "right" group, playing sports, being members of certain clubs, and exclusion from informal socializing and the "good old boys" network, can contribute to the lack of proportional representation of women and minorities in leadership ranks.

The common theme in all these situations is the presence of invisible barriers that discriminate against women and minorities based on their group membership and prevent them from achieving their full potential.

Values Across
Generations

Generational Diversity

Futurist Andrew Zolli believes that: "Our leaders, as a rule, completely miss the boat on demographics and how it informs their own organizations, customers, and constituencies."[69] One demographic with important implications for management in the coming years has to do with generational differences.

Current State

The U.S. population is shaped like what is called an hourglass, with the largest percentage of the population being older baby boomers (born between the late 1940s and the 1960s) at the top, and the millennial generation (born after the mid-1980s) at the bottom, with the generation Xers (born between the 1970s and 1980s) pinched in the middle.[70] This hourglass has considerable implications for managers and the factors they must consider. Older employees and managers have values regarding work that may differ from those of younger people joining the workforce. Additionally, employees attain increased levels of education today, and the younger generation is entering the workplace with expectations of participation and autonomy, and worries about balancing life and work and expectations of work-life balance.[71] These generational value differences cause conflict that can be managed better with cultural awareness and understanding. Some researchers suggest that "At no previous time in our history have so many in such different generations with such diversity been asked to work together shoulder to shoulder, side-by-side, cubicle to cubicle."[72] Even in culturally homogeneous countries such as Japan or Greece, demographic factors impact how people work and to what extent they need to understand culture and its impact.

Different generations bring with them different values and ambitions, based on their different experiences growing up, a distinctive way of viewing the world. These views can be divisive (see Table 2.5). By some reports, 70% of older employees are dismissive of younger workers' abilities, while 50% of younger employees are dismissive of the abilities of their older coworkers.[73] Obviously, this is a situation in which conflict is likely to occur. The diverse orientations that each generation brings to the workplace mean that effective managers need to manage each group differently and be aware of the potential conflict among the groups.

Challenges

Because the circumstances in which each group grew up were different from those of the other groups, each seems to have particular tendencies or generational personalities that distinguish them from the others. The clash of these generations in the workplace can be disruptive, but the most effective leaders and managers will understand the differences and manage accordingly.

What are the most significant differences and how can they be managed? First, there are differences according to one's place in the workforce. For example, according to one study, "Mature workers are least likely to describe themselves as ambitious, but most likely … to consider themselves reliable, hard working, confident, optimistic, sociable, spiritual or religious, high achieving, and—breaking a stereotype—open to new ideas."[74] Many of these workers expect to level off their contributions nearing retirement through part-time work and job sharing. On the other hand, these workers still have a great deal of knowledge and the capacity to learn new things. Consequently, managers interested in maintaining a highly productive workforce will seek to engage these workers and implement flexible strategies through which they can stay engaged and eventually transition to retirement.

Generational
Diversity

TABLE 2.5 GENERATION-BASED VALUE DIFFERENCES IN THE UNITED STATES

Generation	Key Social and Historical Influences	Dominant Value System
The Traditionalists; *GI generation*, 60+ (born 1940s or before)	Raised by Depression-era parents in post-Depression period or around WW II; Big Band music	Hard work; frugality; patriotism; Protestant work ethic; respect for authority
Baby Boomers, 50–65 (born between late 1940s and 1960s)	Raised by WW II parents; grew up during Korean and Vietnam wars; Kennedy assassination; moon landing; rock & roll and Woodstock; cold war energy crisis	Nonconformity; idealism; self-focus; distrust of establishment; happiness and peace; optimism; involvement
Baby Busters, 40–50 (born between the 1960s and 1970s)	Raised by the early hippies; post Vietnam era; Watergate; the Beatles, Grateful Dead, Jimmy Hendrix	The Yuppies; "me" generation; ambitious; material comfort; success driven; stressed out
Generation Xers, 30–40 (born between 1970s and 1980s)	Peaceful era; fall of communism; Iran hostage crisis; recession and economic changes; Bill Clinton; AIDS; MTV; The Eagles, Michael Jackson	Enjoyment of life; jaded; latchkey kids; single-parent family; desire for autonomy and flexibility; self-reliance; spirituality; diversity; balance work and personal life
Millennials or *Nexters,* under 30 (born after the mid-1980s)	A lot of parental focus; Oklahoma bombings; 9/11 World Trade Center attack; school shootings; globalization; threat of terrorism; first Black president; Internet and media; tech savvy; Lady Gaga; Kanye West	Flexibility; choice; socially conscious; meaningful experiences and work; diversity; achievement; tolerance and openness

Sources: Partially based on Hira, N. A. (2007, May 28). You raised them, now manage them. *Fortune*, 38–43; Massey, M. E. (1986). The past: What you are is where you were when (videorecording). Schaumberg, IL: VideoPublishing House; Cherrington, D. J., Condies, S. J., England, J. L. (1979, September). Age and work values. *Academy of Management Journal,* 617–623; Taylor, P., & Morin, R. (2009). Forty years after Woodstock: A gentler generation gap. *Pew Research Center: Social and Demographic Trends*. http://pewsocialtrends.org/pubs/739/woodstock-gentler-generation-gap-music-by-age (accessed February 21, 2010).

Midcareer workers find themselves in a career bottleneck in which too many people are competing for too few positions, especially positions of leadership. They also find themselves sandwiched between children and parents, often at the same time when their own work responsibilities are heaviest. This group, more than others, struggles to maintain the necessary skills needed for their jobs and many become disillusioned with their prospects for the future.[75] The resulting crisis of confidence that characterizes many of these employees can be damaging not only to them personally but also to the organization. Managers wishing to effectively engage this group must find a way to rekindle their passion for work and provide them with opportunities for personal and professional development that are satisfying and indeed exciting.

Work-Life Balance

Frank Brincho, 93, greets a customer at the Wal-Mart store in Foothill Ranch, California. Brincho has been a greeter at the store for 10 years. Understanding generational differences is key to effective management.

Younger workers grew up with technology and constitute a far more diverse demographic. They also were the first latchkey generation and consequently they are highly independent and networked. They expect greater flexibility in their work assignments; they place a greater emphasis on social interactions within the workplace; and especially appreciate opportunities to learn and grow and to contribute. At the same time, they are more likely than other groups to break the rules, especially those that they see as being especially restrictive, and they are the most likely to move quickly from one job to another. Managers wishing to connect with this group should be especially attentive to quickly incorporating them into the organization, providing flexible work assignments and extensive learning opportunities, and maintaining contact with employees who leave, but may someday return.

Managing Different Generations

One implication for managers is how to motivate employees from each generational group. For example, each group has a distinctive orientation toward career goals that may affect communication. The traditionalists expected to be working with one company or at least in one field throughout their careers, and hope to leave a legacy based on that work. Baby boomers, on the other hand, seek excellence in their careers and want to make the most of what remains in their work life. Generation Xers are more interested in establishing careers rather than working with one organization; they value a diverse portfolio of experiences. Millennials are centered around establishing parallel careers, enjoying a variety of employment opportunities while balancing career challenges with other experiences.

As a manager, you need to take into account the generations that are involved in your organization. For example, the traditionalists expect relatively little feedback and assume that "no news is good news." The millennials, on the other hand, expect instantaneous feedback, often targeted to specific work that they are doing and conveyed technologically. The baby boomers and the Generation Xers fall somewhere between. Similarly, there are differences in the formality that is expected in terms of organizational communications and it's no wonder that the younger groups often react to communications they receive from older coworkers by saying "lighten up." In these situations and many others, the best advice may be to recognize that each generation may have to bend a little in working with others.

Several recent books have given special attention to managing the millennials. Lancaster and Stillman,[76] for example, pointed out that millennials typically see themselves as highly valuable and expect appropriate recognition and promotions, often in a way that others don't see as appropriate. Similarly, millennials have high expectations for work that they find meaningful, but this view can sometimes cause communication problems with others. Millennials have grown up with information technology that provides not only quick access to information, but also a variety of social networking possibilities that other generations are just catching on to. Finally, there's the matter of collaboration. As they have grown up, "Millennials have been given the floor to express their opinions. It shouldn't surprise employers that Millennials are going to show up on the job expecting to have a voice. Giving orders is out; candid conversations and give-and-take negotiations are in."

Many of these same lessons apply interestingly to the way in which different generations approach and react to leadership. Bennis and Thomas[77] have explored this topic in their book, *Geeks and Geezers*. They found that since younger leaders and older leaders grew up in quite different eras, their formative experiences with respect to leadership vary accordingly. The different generations had different cultural experiences, they had different models for leadership, and they had different resources available to them. One of the most dramatic differences, as we would expect, was that "geezers" grew up in an analog era, characterized by linearity, command and control, mechanical systems, and specialization. "Geeks," on the other hand, grew up in a digital world, characterized by nonlinearity, management through creativity and empowerment, an emphasis on living systems, and a commitment to generalist models. Consequently, geeks tend to have more ambitious goals, such as changing the world, than geezers, whose initial goals were just to make a living. Geeks also are more concerned with balance in their work and personal lives than geezers. But geeks also have a greater capacity for realistically dealing with change. These tendencies, along with other multigenerational differences, are significant for leadership. For example, how does a geek lead a group of geezers? Or vice versa?

Obviously, these questions get even more difficult when you consider generational differences in a cross-cultural context. That is, it is important to consider not only how millennials interact with others within a single organization or culture, but how they interact with others, including other millennials, across cultures. As we noted earlier, globalization has potential benefits in that it increases opportunities for exchange, but it can also highlight differences that may be difficult to overcome. The activities of millennials seem to reflect these conflicting tendencies, at times appearing to value the increasing liquidity of cross-cultural transactions and welcoming the risk and challenge often associated with new ventures, but at times also seeking conformity and stability. "This is the central cross-cultural challenge for the Millennials—learning to work together across boundaries in order to solve complex global problems. A global perspective on leadership calls on Millennials to transcend local norms in order to develop transnational agendas."[78]

National Culture

So far we have discussed cultural diversity within a country and based on group cultures such as gender or age. Another component of diversity is an individual's national culture. National culture has an even more pervasive impact on the individual than group culture does, and countries such as the United States include individuals from many different national cultural backgrounds. In addition, because today's organizations are almost inevitably global, being able to understand and work across cultures is essential to effective management.

How can managers learn about national culture? Certainly they can visit and study many different cultures. Many companies will send their managers and employees around the world to learn about the language, norms, and religions of countries where they do business. Another way is for leaders to learn

What Would You Do?

▶ The leadership of organizations continues to be primarily male and white, even in the case of Western countries. As a leader, what would you do to change this trend?

about classifications of national cultures, gleaned from research results, particularly as they apply to a nation's business organizations. Each country and region in the world has developed a particular organizational management style largely based on national culture. This is called the **national organizational heritage**.[79] These form the basis of what we have already defined as sophisticated stereotypes and can be helpful in your understanding of national cultural differences.

Hall's Cultural Context Framework

One of the simplest models for understanding culture divides communication styles into two groups: **high context and low context**.[80] In this model, *context* refers to the environment and the information that provide the background for interaction and communication. Members of high-context cultures rely heavily on the context, nonverbal cues, and situational factors, to communicate with others and understand the world around them. They use personal relationships to establish communication. Members of low-context cultures focus on explicit, specific verbal and written messages to understand people and situations.[81]

For example, Japan, Saudi Arabia, Greece, Italy, Vietnam, Korea, and China are all high-context cultures, where subtle body posture, tone of voice, detailed rituals, and a person's title and status convey strong messages that determine behavior and its interpretation (Figure 2.6). In these cultures, communication does not always need to be explicit and specific, and trust is viewed as more important than written communication or legal contracts. In low-context cultures, such as those of Germany, Scandinavia, Switzerland, the United States, Great Britain, and Canada, people pay attention to the verbal message. What is said or written is more important than nonverbal messages or the situation. People are, therefore, specific and clear in their communication with others.

The difference between high and low context can explain many cross-cultural communication problems that leaders face when they interact with those of a culture different from their own. The low-context European and North American leaders may get frustrated

National organizational heritage: a particular organizational management style largely based on national culture

High-context culture: a culture in which people rely heavily on nonverbal cues and situational factors to communicate with each other and understand situations

Low-context culture: a culture in which people rely on explicit, specific cues such as verbal or written messages to communicate with each other and understand situations

FIGURE 2.6 HIGH- AND LOW-CONTEXT CULTURES

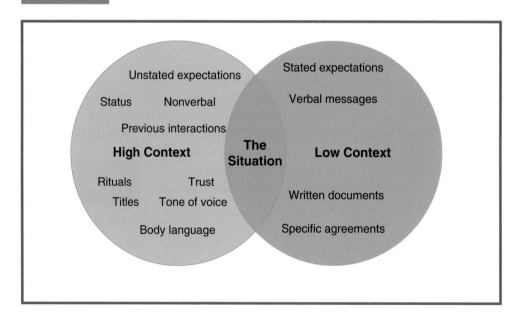

with their high-context Asian or Middle Eastern partners' lack of preciseness. Similarly, high-context leaders might be offended by their low-context followers' directness, which they may interpret as rudeness, lack of respect, and a challenge to their authority. The cultural context model can help leaders understand some important national culture differences and their effects on communication style and organizational behavior.

Hofstede's Five Cultural Dimensions

Researcher Geert Hofstede developed one of the often-cited classifications of culture, known as Hofstede's dimensions.[82] He originally conducted more than 100,000 surveys of IBM employees in over 40 countries,[83] then used the results to develop five basic cultural dimensions: *individualism, power distance, uncertainty avoidance, masculinity, and time orientation* (Table 2.6). According to Hofstede, the combination of these five dimensions lends each national culture its distinctiveness and unique character.

TABLE 2.6 HOFSTEDE'S FIVE CULTURAL DIMENSIONS

Individualism	The extent to which individuals or closely knit social structures, such as the extended family, are the basis for social systems. Individualism leads to reliance on self and focus on individual achievement.
Power distance	The extent to which people accept unequal distribution of power. In higher power-distance cultures, there is a wider gap between the powerful and the powerless.
Uncertainty avoidance	The extent to which the culture tolerates ambiguity and uncertainty. High uncertainty avoidance leads to low tolerance for uncertainty and a search for absolute truths.
Masculinity	The extent to which assertiveness and independence from others is valued. High masculinity leads to high sex-role differentiation, focus on independence, ambition, and material goods.
Time orientation	The extent to which people focus on past, present, or future. Present orientation leads to a focus on short-term performance.

Sources: Hofstede, G. (1992). *Culture and organizations*. London: McGraw-Hill; Hofstede, G. (1996). An American in Paris: The influence of nationality on organization theories. *Organization Studies, 17,* 525–537; Hofstede, G. (2001). *Culture's consequences: Comparing values, behaviors, institutions, and organizations across nations*. Thousand Oaks, CA: Sage; and Hofstede, G., & Hofstede, G. J. (2005). *Culture and organizations: Software of the mind*. New York, NY: McGraw-Hill.

For example, when compared with other nations, the United States is highest in individualism (closely followed by Australia), below average on power distance and uncertainty avoidance, above average on masculinity, and has a moderate to short-term time orientation. These scores indicate that the United States is a somewhat egalitarian culture in which uncertainty and ambiguity are well tolerated; a high value is placed on individual achievements, assertiveness, performance, and independence; sex roles are relatively well defined; and organizations look for quick results with a focus on the present. Japan, on the other hand, tends to be considerably lower in individualism than the United States, higher in power distance, masculinity (one of the highest scores), and uncertainty avoidance, and with a long-term orientation. These rankings are consistent with the popular image of Japan as a country in which social structures such as family and organizations are important, their power and obedience to them tend to be absolute, risk and uncertainty are averted, gender roles are highly differentiated, and high value is placed on achievement.

Hofstede's Dimensions of Culture

Greeting rituals vary greatly from one culture to another. A firm handshake with direct eye contact is standard greeting practice in most Western countries. In some East Asian cultures, however, a bow is the appropriate form of greeting.

GLOBE: Global Leadership and Organizational Behavior Effectiveness; cross-cultural differences and leadership study conducted in 62 countries

Managers can use the cultural dimensions to understand and predict organizational and management styles. For example, in countries with a collectivist culture, such as Japan and Sweden, team efforts are generally more easily implemented than in individualist cultures. Similarly, a participative management style—one in which leaders delegate decision making to employees— may be hard to implement in cultures with high power distance, such as Malaysia or the Philippines, even though both countries value collectivism. Hofstede's dimensions provide leaders with general information about five cultural dimensions. They are a good starting point for learning about other cultures, but should not be used as the sole means of understanding the organizational behavior.

Global Leadership and Organizational Behavior Effectiveness—GLOBE

One of the most exciting and extensive research projects about cross-cultural differences and leadership was conducted by a group of researchers in 62 countries.[84] The model is comprehensive and highly useful in understanding leadership and culture. GLOBE examines culture using nine dimensions, predicting their impact on leadership and organizational processes (see Table 2.7 for a description of the dimensions). Although some of the dimensions proposed by the GLOBE researchers are similar to those presented by Hofstede, others are unique and refine our understanding of culture. As with previous research, GLOBE assumes that culture affects what leaders do and how organizations are structured and managed. Based on their findings, the United States is among the highest in assertiveness and performance orientation and falls in the middle in all the other dimensions.[85] Spaniards and Germans are the most assertive and direct, while Germans also avoid uncertainty and are the lowest in valuing generosity and caring. Austrians and the Swiss, like Germans, require clear communication and will rely on rules and procedures to determine their behaviors. Russians and Italians invest the least in the future and are least likely to focus on performance and excellence. Furthermore, like the Greeks, Russians do not require much structure and can tolerate uncertainty to a greater extent than some Germanic Europeans. While differing in gender egalitarianism, the Swedes and Japanese are among the least assertive and direct. In countries with high power distance, such as Thailand and Russia, communication is often directed one way, from the leader to followers, with little expectation of feedback. Finally, in cultures that value kindness and generosity, such as the Philippines or Egypt, leaders are likely to avoid conflict and act in a caring but paternalistic manner.[86]

TABLE 2.7 GLOBE DIMENSIONS

Dimension	Description	Country Rankings
Power distance	The degree to which power is distributed equally	High: Russia, Spain, Thailand Moderate: England, U.S.A., Brazil Low: Denmark, Israel, Costa Rica
Uncertainty avoidance	The extent to which a culture relies on social norms and rules to reduce unpredictability (high score indicates high tolerance for uncertainty)	High: Denmark, Germany, Sweden Moderate: Israel, U.S.A., Mexico Low: Russia, Greece, Venezuela
Humane orientation	The degree to which a culture values fairness, generosity, caring, and kindness	High: Indonesia, Egypt, Philippines Moderate: Hong Kong, Sweden, U.S.A. Low: Germany, Singapore, France
Collectivism I (institutional)	The degree to which a culture values and practices collective action and collective distribution of resources	High: Denmark, Singapore, Japan Moderate: U.S.A., Egypt, Indonesia Low: Greece, Germany, Italy
Collectivism II (in-group)	The degree to which individuals express pride and cohesion in their family or organizations	High: Egypt, China, Iran Moderate: Japan, Israel, Italy Low: Denmark, Finland, Sweden
Assertiveness	The degree to which individuals are assertive, direct, and confrontational	High: U.S.A., Germany Moderate: France, Philippines Low: Sweden, Japan, Kuwait
Gender egalitarianism	The extent of gender differentiation (high score indicates more differentiation)	High: South Korea, Egypt, India Moderate: Italy, The Netherlands Low: Sweden, Poland
Future orientation	The extent to which a culture invests in the future rather than in the present or past	High: Denmark, Singapore Moderate: Australia, India Low: Russia, Italy
Performance orientation	The degree to which a culture values and encourages performance and excellence	High: U.S.A., Taiwan, Singapore Moderate: Sweden, England, Japan Low: Russia, Venezuela, Italy

Sources: Based on House, R. J., Hanges, P. J., Javidan, M., Dorfman, P. W., & Gupta, V. (2004). *Culture, leadership and organizations: The GLOBE study of 62 countries.* Thousand Oaks, CA: Sage; House, R. J., Javidan, M., Hanges, P., & Dorfman, P. (2002). Understanding cultures and implicit leadership theories across the globe: An introduction to project GLOBE. *Journal of World Business, 37:* 3–10; Javidan, M., & House, R. J. (2001). Cultural acumen for the global manager: Lessons from project GLOBE. *Organizational Dynamics, 29:* 289–305.

GLOBE identifies several categories of leader behavior that are either universally desirable, undesirable, or whose desirability is contingent on the culture.[87] For example, charismatic/value-based leadership is generally desirable across most cultures. Similarly, team-based leadership is believed to contribute to outstanding leadership in many cultures. Although participative leadership is generally seen as positive, its effectiveness depends on the culture. Autonomous leaders are desirable in some cultures but not in all, and being self-protective is seen as impeding effective leadership in most cultures. Even some behaviors that are somewhat universal reflect cultural differences. For example, Americans and the British highly value charisma whereas Middle Easterners place less importance on this behavior from their leader. Nordic cultures are less favorable toward self-protective leadership behaviors whereas Southern Asians accept it more readily.

The models of culture presented in this section provide different ways of understanding national and organizational culture. While the models are useful, they can also be misapplied if used to stereotype national or organizational cultures. Where Hall and Hofstede focus primarily on national culture, GLOBE has one of the most comprehensive models available with a strong focus on leadership characteristics across cultures.

Culture and Individual Behavior

How many different cultures do you belong to? Which ones are most important to you? Are there some that define you more than others? To what extent do they each influence your thinking and behavior? How much of what you think and what you do is related to your culture and to what extent are your thoughts and behaviors the result of your unique personality? Are you a typical representative of your culture or nation? If not, what makes you unique? These are all questions that one must consider when contemplating the power of culture in influencing individual behavior. Who we are, what we believe, and how we behave are, to some extent, but not entirely, the result of our cultural backgrounds. Figure 2.7 presents some of the key factors that impact how people think and behave. Clearly culture is only one factor, and often related to others. For example, culture is closely related to family and environment, or even the organization in which people work.

As one of the factors that determine who we are and how we behave, culture impacts our values, beliefs, attitudes, and behaviors. Values are what people believe *should* be; they are preferred states. We are conscious of many of our values and not aware of others. Some of our values represent what we believe we should do and how we should behave. Honesty, hard work, respect for elders are examples of such values; they are the means to an end. Other values that we hold indicate where we would like to end and what we would like to achieve. Happiness, spiritual enlightenment, or wealth are examples of these. Both types of values are influenced by one's culture. How much one values financial achievement is to some extent a product of one's culture. For example, while Western countries and most other nations measure their Gross National Product (GNP), an indicator of the importance of material goods, the Bhutanese, a people who live in a small South Asian country, calculate their Gross National Happiness (GNH) index.[88] The GNH, more than the GNP, is considered to be a holistic measure of the success of their nation, a reflection of the cultural value placed on happiness over material achievement.

As opposed to values, which are the "shoulds," beliefs are how things are. For example, in some countries where power distance is high, bosses are believed and expected to have the answers. Employees, even if not happy about decisions, believe that the boss is always right. Another individual factor that is impacted by culture is our attitudes. They are the specific views we have about people, objects, or situations. For example, your attitude about the importance of work is influenced by your culture. People from the United States are often considered to place a high value on work; they "live to work." Europeans, for example, the French or the Italians, have a different attitude toward their work; they "work to live." These two cultural attitudes lead to different work schedules and vacation habits and recreation norms for each nation; all factors that leaders must take into account.

Finally, our values, beliefs, and attitudes impact how we behave. The terminal value of wealth and material goods impacts beliefs about working hard, which leads to a positive view of work, and contributes to actually working hard. The example of the United States fits well here. Material achievement, a terminal value, is generally considered worthwhile; there is an accepted belief in working hard that translates into a specific attitude about the appropriateness of long work hours, few vacations, and, some suggest, a productive and entrepreneurial economy. Another example is the Chinese value of filial loyalty and obedience. It is considered appropriate for children to obey their parents and other elders and for employees to comply with their supervisors. Obedience is a central component of social order. As a result of this value, the Chinese believe that those who are older and in positions of authority have more knowledge and wisdom. From this belief follows the attitude that employees must respect their supervisors and their decisions. Finally, the attitude leads to a behavior of working toward goals identified by a leader with little challenge of their decisions.

In addition to being related to one's upbringing and environment, culture has a direct impact on the individual through values, beliefs, attitudes, and behavior. It is therefore essential for understanding people that we learn about and understand culture.

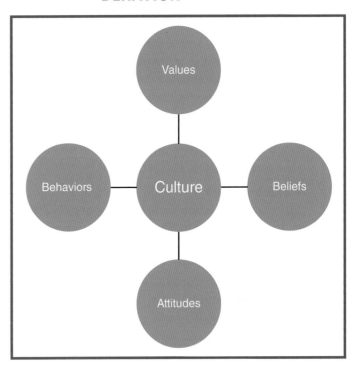

FIGURE 2.7 CULTURE AND INDIVIDUAL BEHAVIOR

Developing
Intercultural
Sensitivity

Developing a Cultural Mindset

Culture and cultural diversity play a key role in the success of organizations. On an individual basis, learning to interact successfully with many cultures can expand one's perspective and open up many opportunities. On an organizational basis, being able to manage across cultures is imperative. The key to success in intercultural contact and interaction is cultivating a **multicultural mindset**, a way of thinking and outlook where culture is taken into consideration in deliberations, decisions, and behaviors. For many years, organizations have emphasized the concept of cultural and linguistic competence, a set of behaviors, attitudes,

Multicultural
mindset: a way of
thinking where culture is
taken into consideration
in deliberations,
decisions, and behaviors

CREATIVITY AND CHANGE

RESPONDING TO CULTURAL DIFFERENCES

Angela Blanchard is President and CEO of Neighborhood Centers in Houston, Texas, an advocacy and service delivery nonprofit "bringing resources, education, and connection" to Houston's neighborhoods and serving over 400,000 people a year. She was recently featured in Fast Company's article on "Generation Flux," and was interviewed for this book by Robert Denhardt.

Angela Blanchard grew up in a poor and struggling Cajun family and is now the head of one of the leading nonprofits in the country. Much of her success is attributable to her sensitivity to the cultural backgrounds and the needs of others, from hurricane evacuees, to undocumented immigrants, to those in impoverished communities, to major funders leading the top corporations in Houston and beyond.

Over the years, Blanchard has come to approach community and neighborhood development through a strength-based approach, that is, "a community should be defined by its strengths, resources, achievements, and hopes—not its degree of 'brokenness.'" Such an approach carries with it an implicit understanding of and respect for different cultures.

For instance, Neighborhood Centers works with undocumented immigrants to help them find their way through the maze of bureaucracy they often encounter. One Muslim woman came forward, covered with a scarf, as her culture prescribed. When she was told that in order to meet a deadline, she would have to have a picture taken, she and her husband were indignant, because that meant she would have to uncover her face in public. But the Neighborhood Center manager stepped forward with a respectful question: "How can we make this work for you?"

The result was that the picture was taken in the ladies restroom, printed then folded so it would not be revealed to anyone—and the problem was solved. Blanchard commented that "we have to have a great deal of standardization on those forms, but we also need to be able to say, how can we make this work for you?"

The same respect for cultural differences has marked Blanchard's approach to the immigration issue, a particularly contentious issue in a place that Blanchard describes as "a red state, a red county, and a sorta blue city." Her approach has been to emphasize what she calls the BIG WE. She points out that 70% of the population of the area has come from somewhere else. "They crossed rivers, they crossed mountains, they crossed borders–all in pursuit of a better life. That's why we're here–and that's what we have in common." So where differences arise, Blanchard points out, it's important to go back to the why question—why are we here. And the answer is the BIG WE. We are all interested in an opportunity for a better life. We may differ on the what and how, but the why question can always anchor the discussion. Following this view, Blanchard has been recognized for her contributions to building a positive dialogue on immigration issues in Houston and beyond.

To be able to comprehend and respond to rapidly unfolding events—whether immigration or an influx of refugees from Hurricane Katrina—Neighborhood Centers has developed the capacity of being flexible but also consistent. Blanchard points out that there are certain processes that have to be routine so that they work consistently—like issuing the payroll. But the organization must also develop a capacity for flexibility so as to adapt to changing circumstances and emerging needs. Blanchard says, "If we're moving along a path and someone sees something that will move us in a better direction in terms of why we're here, I want them to speak up—and we'll listen."

1. How do you think Angela Blanchard developed her capacity to work with different cultures?

2. Part of Blanchard's job seems to be to translate cultures—from impoverished community residents who are in need of help to corporate executives who might fund specific projects. What's needed to be able to do this kind of translation?

3. Blanchard seems to have done a remarkable job in reorienting the area's discussion of immigration. What do you think might contribute to such a dramatic cultural change around this issue—or another one?

and policies that are integrated to help deal with cross-cultural situations.[89] The Georgetown National Center for Cultural Competence suggests that it includes awareness, attitudes, knowledge, and skills.[90] This competence is essential for today's managers.

The cultural mindset includes the concept of competence and moves beyond it by focusing on a new of way of thinking. In order for organizations to truly become diverse and multicultural, managers must think about culture, not simply act. While it is almost impossible for anyone to acquire in-depth knowledge about all the cultures he or she might encounter, or to learn all the necessary behaviors, it is possible to have a cultural mindset that allows one to understand cultural differences and their impact on behavior, and to take that knowledge into consideration when interacting with or leading others. That cultural mindset then allows for the development of appropriate skills and competencies.

Cultural Mindset Components

A cultural mindset is a way of thinking that allows the individual to be aware of and open to culture and how it impacts our own and others' thinking and behaviors. It involves both how one thinks and how one acts (see Figure 2.8). It starts with attentiveness to your own culture and how it influences how you perceive the world and what you do (Table 2.8 presents the components of a cultural mindset). Awareness of the role of culture is essential because culture is stable and hard to change and because some of the assumptions are not fully conscious. In addition to self-awareness, a cultural mindset requires knowing how culture may impact others. It further involves a degree of curiosity and inquisitiveness about how and why other people do what they do and appreciation and respect for differences. A culturally mindful person knows that the visible parts of culture are only a small part and seeks to uncover the hidden parts. He looks for cultural indicators, signs, and symbols that make people unique and values the diversity and potential strength culture can bring to interpersonal or organizational settings.

Another component of a cultural mindset is the willingness to share your culture and learn from those who are different. A culturally mindful manager sees herself as part of the world and uses the knowledge she acquires to improve her decisions and her effectiveness. While a cultural mindset is first a way of thinking, how we think influences what we do; so it also becomes a way of acting. A manager with a cultural mindset is proactive in addressing cultural issues and challenges rather than either not addressing them or only reacting to them. For example, when a team with members from different cultures is formed, one of the issues that the culturally mindful manager includes in team training is knowledge of cultural factors and how to address cultural conflicts. The culturally mindful manager is one who acquires skills and competencies in working with other cultures. Finally, a cultural

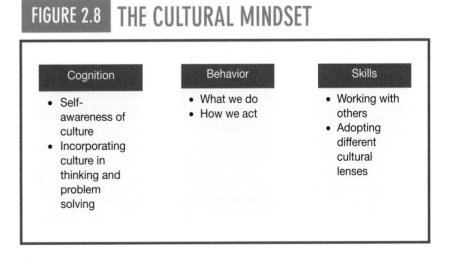

FIGURE 2.8 **THE CULTURAL MINDSET**

Cognition	Behavior	Skills
• Self-awareness of culture • Incorporating culture in thinking and problem solving	• What we do • How we act	• Working with others • Adopting different cultural lenses

TABLE 2.8	COMPONENTS OF A CULTURAL MINDSET

- Self-awareness of own culture and behavior
- Attentiveness to cultural indicators
- Curiosity about own and others' culture
- Willingness to share own culture and learn about others
- Seeing self as part of a diverse world
- Proactive in considering culture in decisions
- Willing to acquire skills and competencies
- Able to adopt multiple cultural lenses

mindset allows managers to capitalize on the potential benefits of a multicultural workforce. Knowledge of other cultures opens many opportunities for new ideas, products, and services and the different cultural perspectives can provide novel approaches to problem solving. Thinking about culture, keeping it mind, and using it in your daily interactions and in addressing challenges are all part of a cultural mindset.

The Cultural Mindset in Organizations

A cultural mindset allows for a multicultural approach, which aims at inclusiveness, social justice, affirmation, mutual respect, and harmony in a pluralistic world. Rather than being viewed as an issue of quotas and percentages, diversity and multiculturalism refer to building a culture of openness and inclusiveness. The benefits of building a multicultural organization with a cultural mindset go beyond women and other minority groups; they extend to all employees. A Gallup survey suggests that organizations where diversity is valued have the most satisfied employees and better retention.[91]

Managers play a critical role in encouraging a cultural mindset in organizations and in creating a multicultural organization (see Figure 2.9). Through their words and actions, they demonstrate the value of maintaining a multicultural organization where discrimination is not tolerated and where cultural differences are fully considered as part of all decision making. Ed Zander, former CEO of Motorola, once stated, "Business and diversity are one and the same. Business means diversity, and diversity means business."[92] Similarly, Barry Salzberg, CEO of Deloitte, is focused on increasing diversity in his organization. The Gallup survey linking diversity to satisfaction further indicates that organizational leaders' commitment to diversity is linked to overall employee satisfaction. Leaders influence the culture and organizational processes that determine how decisions are made, how others behave, and what is accepted and tolerated and what is not. Managers are not only decision makers, but also exercise considerable influence through formal and informal communication, role modeling, and other powerful means. The message they send through words and actions about the role of women and minorities and the importance of multiculturalism in an organization is one of the most important factors.

Frustration of Diversity

Changing the culture of an organization to address discriminatory practices, behaviors, and symbols is another powerful tool. Changing culture is one of the most difficult and lengthy processes any organization can undertake (you will learn about change in Chapter 15). Without a cultural change to address informal discriminatory practices and attitudes, however, other improvements are not likely to be as effective. The presence of diverse role models throughout an organization is another part of the solution to providing leadership opportunities for women and minorities. By having diverse people in leadership positions, an organization "walks the talk" and can demonstrate its commitment to diversity. For example, Toyota U.S.A. has had a program called "diversity champion" since the late 1990s. Employees nominate other talented and high-potential employees to receive intensive diversity management training and return to their work units with a "champion" badge and a mission to help implement changes to make the workplace more inclusive and emphasize commonalities.[93] Another step toward changing culture is providing support groups for various diverse groups. In our opening case, Sodexo provided an example of how such groups are used to implement diversity policies. Similarly, the Chubb Group, one of the largest insurance companies in the United States, has put in place networks for various employees. The company supports employee networks for working parents and young people, as well as more traditional diverse groups such as gays and lesbians, people with disabilities, Latinos, and women. Donna Grif-

FIGURE 2.9 FACTORS IN BECOMING A MULTICULTURAL ORGANIZATION

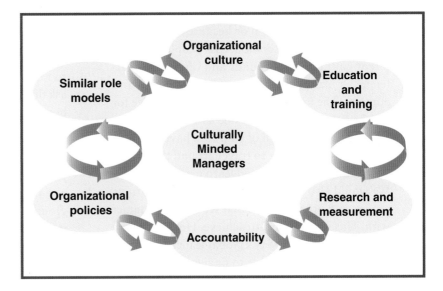

fin, the company's diversity officer, believes these groups provide a positive image for the organization, help attract diverse talent, and affect the bottom line positively.[94]

Training and education can help people become aware of their biases, understand their own and others' cultural point of view, and better accept differences. When the consulting firm of Bain & Company transfers its consultants from one part of the world to another, it not only provides them with information about living in the new country, but also arms them with cultural knowledge specific to the country to allow them to function more effectively.[95] Other companies such as Procter & Gamble (P&G) value and encourage the development of cultural knowledge in their employees and leaders. Because their employees are as likely to work with someone from their own culture as with someone from a different culture, P&G immerses its employees in international assignments.

The case of Deloitte in the Global Society case study is an example of how organizations need to change their existing policies and implement creative new systems to support the development of their employees. Many organizational policies such as those on family leave can hinder people's chances of advancement. Similarly, traditional performance evaluation criteria, which emphasize the stereotypical male and Western characteristics associated with leaders as the basis for success, may undermine the ability of people who have other diverse characteristics and skills to rise to leadership positions. Finally, successful change requires careful measurement and monitoring. Organizations must have baseline information about the hard facts about the actual numbers of women and minorities in leadership and about the softer data related to satisfaction, attitudes, and the less-visible obstacles that may be in place. Keeping track of changes and holding decision makers accountable are essential to solidifying any improvement that may take place. For example, another indicator of Toyota's commitment to a diverse and inclusive workforce is its quick action after one of its top executives was accused of sexual harassment. Not only did the executive leave his position, but the company also created a task force to enhance training of its executives and put in place better procedures for responding to allegations and complaints.

► Summary and Applications for Managers

Understanding and working with different cultures and building diversity have become essential parts of every manager's job. Either because of cultural diversity within a nation or because of increasing globalization, we all come across people from different cultural backgrounds and often face challenges in making those interactions fruitful and effective. The impact of culture is too pervasive for it to be either ignored or treated as an afterthought. In an ideal world, each of us would have the time, resources, and ability to travel around the world, study different cultures, and learn many languages. We would also explore the cultures of the various groups and organizations that we come in contact with. This ideal is hard to achieve. However, there are other ways for today's global leaders to understand culture and be able to navigate in a diverse world and in diverse organizations.

1. *Develop awareness of your own cultural background.* The first step in having a cultural mindset is to know yourself. By understanding and being aware of your own culture, or cultures, you can know how they influence how you think and what you do.

2. *Make a conscious effort to consider culture in your daily life.* Cultural elements are all around you, in your personal and organizational life. Pay attention to them; become aware of their presence and their impact. This step can involve interpersonal events as well as other cultural events such a food, music, and art.

3. *Be mindful that national and group cultures are pervasive and often hard to change.* People may not be aware of the impact culture has on them and may not know why they think a certain way or value certain things. If culture plays a role, it is often hard, if not impossible to change. Knowing the power of culture can provide you with insight that can make you a more effective leader.

4. *Ask questions.* People like to talk about their culture and share it with others. They are likely to respond well and share information if you ask them about their culture or more specifically how their culture impacts them, what they do, and how they think.

5. *Share your culture with others.* In both your personal and organizational life, don't be shy about talking about your own cultural background, how it influences you, and about sharing your beliefs and values with others. Your actions will indicate that you care about culture and pay attention to it and encourage others to do the same.

6. *Learn another language.* If you get a chance, take a course to learn another language. Language is a key element of culture and shapes how people think, so by learning a new language you expand your own perspectives and horizons.

7. *Travel to new places.* Whenever you get a chance, travel to new places, especially if they are outside your own country. Nothing replaces face-to-face interaction with people from other cultures.

8. *Respect your own and others' cultures.* You can respect your own cultural values while at the same time respecting those of others. Liking your own culture does not mean devaluing that of others. Cultural diversity means understanding and valuing all the various groups that you work with.

► Key Terms

Affirmative action 43	Discrimination 43	Ethnic or group culture 38	Heterogeneous cultures 38
Culture 36	Equal employment opportunity (EEO) 43	Glass ceiling 46	High-context culture 52
Cultural diversity 39		GLOBE 54	
Cultural iceberg 39			

▶ Exercise 2.1 World Map

On a blank sheet of paper, draw a map of the world that includes all seven continents (or as many as you can remember).

1. How many continents did you place correctly (generally correct location)?

2. Where did you start your map? What's the first place you drew?

3. What continent is in the center? Why?

4. What does your map tell you about your knowledge of the world?

▶ Exercise 2.2 What Is Your Primary Cultural Background?

Identify the culture that you consider to be your primary cultural background (recognizing that many are from multiple backgrounds).

1. What do you think makes that culture unique?

2. What are some of its key teachings about what is important? What is right?

3. How did you learn these?

4. How much do you agree with them? Why or why not?

5. How often do you share these cultural elements with others?

6. How much of your behavior do you think is influenced by that culture?

▶ Case 2.1 The Trouble With JB

Jean Baptiste Honoré was very proud and excited about his new job. After finishing his BA in accounting and graduating with honors, he had landed the perfect job with a small accounting firm just a few miles from his family home. The pay was great, the benefits excellent, and the firm was offering support for the CPA exam and a bonus for every stage he passed. His supervisor had told him about working in several teams and departments and the opportunity to learn different areas of accounting. He could not ask for more.

His parents had immigrated to the United States after fleeing Haiti in the 1970s. They had faced considerable hardship, worked at many menial jobs to put their only son through college while also helping support a large extended family in Haiti. Jean Baptiste felt the weight of his community and family on his shoulders and he was ecstatic that he would finally be able to fully contribute to his family. Life in the United States had not been easy, but it was much better than what the family would have faced back home. Jean Baptiste had often felt that he did not fit in, although his family lived in a diverse neighborhood in Baltimore. While in college, he had joined a Black student association and tried an international student group where he got to speak French, a language he had learned at home, but neither felt quite right. The other students often appeared childish to him. He had felt most at home in the accounting "nerd" club, where his excellent study habits and great accounting skills had made him a favorite teammate for projects.

Although Jean Baptiste was one of only a handful of minority employees at the company, he had felt welcome during the interviews. His boss and the senior partners appeared very eager to bring him on. The people there seemed to have a lot in common with him: they were young, good at their jobs, liked accounting, and all wanted to make a good impression. He was working with a group of five other new hires, three women and two other men. All three women were Caucasian, as was one of the other men. The final member of the new group was Asian, part Vietnamese and part Chinese. They seem to be comfortable with one another during orientation and the training meetings and as each started working in different departments within the firm.

Right from the start, JB, as he came to be called—his name was too hard and too long his manager told him—was put on several projects that were right up his alley. He was pleased that he was starting with easy projects so that he could demonstrate how well prepared he was. He was also happy that he was working with minority clients who quickly came to rely on him. Their business was pretty routine, but JB was happy to be able to contribute to people from his own neighborhood that he often got to visit since a lot of his work was done off-site with the clients. He was initially fine with the arrangement and he made sure not to bother his supervisor but to give him regular updates. He did not hear much from his supervisor, Dennis Hampton, except for an occasional "great job" and "we are so glad you have joined us" in e-mails when he sent in reports.

After four months, the work started to become boring. Doing taxes, some HR stuff, and helping small business-owners with their books was fine, but it got old. Jean Baptiste was applying what he had learned, but there was little challenge, and for the most part, he felt like he was a bookkeeper, not an accountant. His schedule was very busy though, and he had more clients than everyone else, which was great, because he actually got some bonuses, but it did not leave him enough time to prepare for the CPA exams. Everyone at the company was friendly and nice enough. The atmosphere was relaxed and few people wore suits or ties, something Jean Baptiste found a bit strange. He was used to dressing up formally and he thought some of his colleagues looked a bit sloppy. As one of the few minorities in the firm, he certainly did not want to make a bad impression. He also thought his clients expected him to look like the professional that he was. Jean Baptiste was beginning to feel less and less part of the team or the organization. The others went to lunch and hung out after work; they often talked about things that were going on in the office that he knew nothing about, and they already knew the senior partners well.

He started asking Dennis for new projects and about getting some help with the heavy workload and was told that new assignments would come soon, but that they needed him where he was. Dennis also jokingly asked him: "So how can you get new projects if you already feel overwhelmed? Which one is it? Too much or too little?" Jean Baptiste was taken aback. The rest of the people who had started with him had already each worked in at least two groups and two of them had already taken part of the CPA exam. He knew that they had fewer clients to handle, so he pushed back gently and told Dennis that he was looking for new projects to broaden his experience, not more of the same. A few days later, Dennis sent him an e-mail with "Congratulations" in the subject line. He informed Jean Baptiste that he was able to give him new projects that he asked for and assigned him to the board of two nonprofit organizations that were important clients of the firm to replace one of the partners. Not exactly what Jean Baptiste had asked for, but he thought it was a great honor that they trusted him so much, until he found out that both organizations were small minority-run community groups.

Jean Baptiste's six-month review was "just fine." Dennis told him he was doing great and helping the firm with an area that they needed badly. He just needed to be patient and not to push so hard; he needed to work on being a better team player. Four out of the five other people who had started with him passed the CPA and got a substantial raise. Two weeks later, Jean Baptiste accepted a job with a large accounting firm and gave his notice. Dennis was very surprised and felt betrayed.

1. Define the problem in this case.

2. Apply a cultural lens, at both the national and group levels, to explain what each of the people may be experiencing.

3. What do you think Jean-Baptiste and Dennis's motives are?

4. What did each do wrong? What could they have done differently?

⑤SAGE edge™

Sharpen your skills with SAGE edge at edge.sagepub.com/nahavandi

SAGE edge for students provides a personalized approach to help you accomplish your coursework goals in an easy-to-use learning environment.

▶ Endnotes

1. Reed, W. (2013). Diversity turnaround at Sodexo. *Louisiana Weekly,* March 4. Retrieved from http://www.louisianaweekly.com/diversity-turnaround-at-sodexo/ on June 18, 2013.

2. *Sodexo: No. 1 in the DiversityInc top 50.* (2012). Retrieved from http://www.diversityinc.com/sodexo/ on June 18, 2013.

3. Inside diversity structure at Sodexo, Johnson & Johnson, and Rockwell Automation. (2013). *Diversity Best Practices,* January 29. Retrieved from http://www.diversitybestpractices.com/news-articles/inside-diversity-structure-sodexo-johnson-johnson-and-rockwell-automation on June 18, 2013.

4. Sodexo ranked number one company for diversity by DiversityInc. (2010). *PRNewswire,* March 10. Retrieved from http://www.prnewswire.com/news-releases/sodexo-ranked-number-one-company-for-diversity-by-diversityinc-87219747.html on June 18, 2013.

5. Reed, 2013.

6. Sodexo ranked number one, 2010.

7. Sodexo Inc. 2012. *3BL Media,* October 23. Retrieved from http://3blmedia.com/News/CSR/Sodexo's-2012-Diversity-and-Inclusion-Annual-Report-Highlights-Efforts-Established-Company on June 18, 2013.

8. Inside diversity structure, 2013.

9. Reed, 2013.

10. Ricks, D. A. (2006). *Blunders in international business.* Malden, MA: Blackwell.

11. Kroeber, A. L., & Kluckhohn, C. (1952). *Culture: A critical review of concepts and definitions.* New York, NY: Vintage Books.

12. Imada, T. (2010). Cultural narratives of individualism and collectivism: A content analysis of textbook stories in the United States and Japan. *Journal of Cross-Cultural Psychology, 43*(4), 576–591.

13. For a general article on the impact of culture, see Triandis, H. C. (2004). The many dimensions of culture. *The Academy of Management Executive, 18*(1), 88–93; also Hall, T. C., & Hall, M. R. (1990). *Understanding cultural differences.* London: Nicholas Brealy. For research on turnover and role models see Chen, X. Z. (2000). Employee demography, organizational commitment, and turnover intentions in China: Do cultural differences matter? *Human Relations, 53*(6), 869–887; Lockwood, P., Marshall, T. C., & Sadler, P. (2005). Promoting success or preventing failure: Cultural differences in motivation by positive and negative role models. *Personality and Social Psychology Bulletin, 31*(3), 379–392; and House, R. J., Hanges, P. J., Javidan, M., Dorfman, P. W., & Gupta, V. (2004). *Culture, leadership and organizations: The GLOBE study of 62 countries.* Thousand Oaks, CA: Sage.

14. Eagly, A. H., & Carli, L. L. (2004). Women and men as leaders. In J. Antonakis, A. T. Cianciolo, & R. J. Sternberg (Eds.), *The nature of leadership* (pp. 279–301). Thousand Oaks, CA: Sage.

15. Schein, E. H. (2004). *Organizational culture and leadership.* San Francisco, CA: Jossey-Bass.

16. Schneider, S. C. (1997). *Managing across cultures.* Upper Saddle River, NJ: Prentice Hall.

17. LaFrance, M., Hecht, M. A., & Paluck, E. L. (2003). The contingent smile: A meta-analysis of sex differences in smiling. *Psychological Bulletin, 129*(2), 305–334; and Masuda, T., Ellsworth, P. C., Mesquita, B., Leu, J., Tanida, S., & Van de Veerdonk, E. (2008). Placing the face in context: Cultural differences in the perception of facial emotion. *Journal of Personality and Social Psychology, 94*(3), 365–381.

18. Schein, 2004.

19. Osland, J. S., Bird, A., Delano, J., & Jacob, M. (2000). Beyond sophisticated stereotyping: Culture sensemaking in context. *Academy of Management Executive, 14*(1), 65–79.

20. *World fact book: Malaysia.* (2013). Retrieved from https://www.cia.gov/library/publications/the-world-factbook/geos/my.html on June 13, 2013.

21. *World fact book: Singapore*, 2013. Retrieved from https://www.cia.gov/library/publications/the-world-factbook/geos/sn.html on June 13, 2013.

22. *World fact book: Nigeria.* (2013). Retrieved from https://www.cia.gov/library/publications/the-world-factbook/geos/ni.html on June 13, 2013.

23. Eagly & Carli, 2004.

24. Childs, T. (2013). *Workforce diversity: The bridge between the workplace and the marketplace.* Retrieved from http://www.tedchilds.com/experience.html on May 30, 2013.

25. Swan, K. (2000, July). Difference is power. *Fast Company*, pp. 258–266.

26. For examples of some research studies on the benefits of diverse group membership see Rink, F., & Ellemers, N. (2010). Benefiting from deep-level diversity: How congruence between knowledge and decision rules improves team decision making and team perceptions. *Group Processes and Intergroup Relations, 13*(3), 345-359; Esser, J. K. (1998). Alive and well after 25 years: A review of groupthink research. *Organizational Behavior and Human Decision Processes, 73*(2/3), 116–141; Morehead, G., Neck, C., & West, M. (1998). The tendency toward defective decision making within self-managing teams: The relevance of groupthink for the 21st century. *Organizational Behavior and Human Decision Processes, 73*(2/3), 327–351; and, e.g., Finklestein, S., & Hambrick, D. C. (1996). *Strategic leadership: Top executives and their effects on organizations.* St. Paul, MN: West Publishing.

27. Lagarde, C. (2010). Women, power, and the challenge of financial crisis. *The New York Times*, May 10. Retrieved from http://www.nytimes.com/2010/05/11/opinion/11iht-edlagarde.html?_r=1 on June 20, 2013.

28. See research by Dunlop, W. L., & Beauchamp, M. R. (2011). Does similarity make a difference? Predicting cohesion and attendance behaviors within exercise group settings. *Group Dynamics: Theory, Research, and Practice, 15*(3), 258–266; Civettini, N. H. W. (2007). Similarity and group performance. *Social Psychology Quarterly, 70*(3), 262–271; and Glaman, J. M., Jones, A. P., & Rozelle, R. M. (1996). The effects of co-worker similarity on the emergence of affect in work teams. *Group and Organizational Studies, 21*(2), 192.

29. Mello, A. S., & Ruckes, M. E. (2006). Team composition, *Journal of Business, 79*(3), 1019–1039.

30. Kujala, J., & Pietilainen, T. (2007). Developing moral principles and scenarios in the light of diversity: An extension to the multidimensional ethics scale. *Journal of Business Ethics, 70*(2), 141–150.

31. Fenwick, G. D., & Neal, D. J. (2002). Effect of gender composition on group performance. *Gender, Work, & Organization, 8*(2), 205–225.

32. Combs, G. M., & Luthans, F. (2007). Diversity training: Analysis of the impact of self-efficacy. *Human Resource Development Quarterly, 18*(1), 91–120; Cox, T. H. (2000). *Creating the multicultural organization: A strategy for capturing the power of diversity.* San Francisco, CA: Jossey-Bass; and Dass, P., & Parker, D. (1996). Diversity, a strategic issue. In E. E.

Kossek & S. A. Lobel (Eds.), *Managing diversity: Human resource strategies for transforming the workplace.* Cambridge, MA: Blackwell Business.

33. See the text of the legislation, available at http://definitions.uslegal.com/e/equal-employment-opportunity-act/

34. EEOC Press release. (2013). *US Equal Employment Opportunity Commission,* January 18. Retrieved from http://www.eeoc.gov/eeoc/newsroom/release/1–28–13.cfm on June 21, 2013.

35. Slaughter, A. M. (2012). Why women still can't have it all. *The Atlantic,* July/August. Retrieved from http://www.theatlantic.com/magazine/archive/2012/07/why-women-still-cant-have-it-all/309020/ on June 19, 2013.

36. Slaughter, 2012.

37. Women in the labor force: A databook. (2013). *Bureau of Labor Statistics,* February. Retrieved from http://www.bls.gov/cps/wlf-databook-2012.pdf on June 24, 2013.

38. Women in the labor force, 2013.

39. Amble, B. (2006). Women still rare in Europe's boardrooms. *Management Issues,* June 20. Retrieved from http://www.management-issues.com/2006/8/24/research/women-still-rare-in-europes-boardrooms.asp on June 19, 2007.

40. Drum, K. (2012). Digging into the pay gap. *Mother Jones,* May 3. Retrieved from http://www.motherjones.com/kevin-drum/2012/05/digging-pay-gap on June 19, 2013.

41. Fulfilling the promise. (2012). *Statement by the Policy and Impact Committee of the Committee for Economic Development.* Retrieved from http://www.fwa.org/pdf/CED_WomenAdvancementonCorporateBoards.pdf on June 19, 2013.

42. Women CEOs in the Fortune 1000. (2013). *Catalyst–knowledge center,* June 18. Retrieved from http://www.catalyst.org/knowledge/women-ceos-fortune-1000 on June 19, 2013.

43. Helfat, C. E., Harris, D., & Wolfson, P. J. (2006). The pipeline to the top: Women and men in the top executive rank of U.S. corporations. *Academy of Management Perspectives, 20*(4), 42–64.

44. America's highest paid chief executives. (2012). *Forbes.* Retrieved from http://www.forbes.com/lists/2012/12/ceo-compensation-12_rank.html on June 19, 2013.

45. Smith, P. B. (2002). Culture's consequences: Something old and something new. *Human Relations, 55,* 119–135.

46. Buckingham, M. (2009). Why are women unhappier than they were 40 years ago? *Business Week,* October 16. Retrieved from http://www.businessweek.com/managing/content/oct2009/ca20091016_302039.htm?chan=careers_special+report+—+women+_and+leadership_special+report+-+women+and+_leadership on January 18, 2010.

47. For a thorough analysis of the possible reason for inequality of men and women in the workplace see Eagly & Carli, 2004.

48. Bisoux, T. (2008, January–February). The instant messenger. *BizEd,* pp, 16–20.

49. Seller, P. (2009). 40 under 40: Where are the women? *Fortune-Postcards.* Retrieved from http://postcards.blogs.fortune.cnn.com/2009/10/26/40-under-40-where-are-the-women/ on August 6, 2013.

50. Bianchi, S. M. (2000). Maternal employment and time with children: Dramatic change or surprising continuity? *Demography, 37,* 401–414; and Kaufman, G., & Uhlenberg, P. (2000). The influence of parenthood on the work effort of married men and women. *Social Forces, 78,* 931–949.

51. For some research see Eagly & Carli, 2004, and Buckingham, 2009.

52. Search for women. (2006). *Executive MBA Council.* Retrieved from http:www.emba.org/exchange/expanded_web_may_2006/feature_1.html#the_world_looks on January 12, 2010); also, Hewlett, S. A. (2007). *Off-ramps and on-ramps.* Boston, MA: Harvard Business School Press.

53. See Grzelakowski, M. (2005). *Mother leads best.* Chicago, IL: Dearborn Trade Publishing; for an interview with Laybourne see *Startup Nation,* May 7. Retrieved from http://www

.startupnation.com/pages/radio/RD_May7_2005_GerryLaybourne.asp on June 27, 2007.

54. For some research on gender differences in style of management and communication, see Su, R., Rounds, J., & Armstrong, P. I. (2009). Men and things, women and people: A meta-analysis of sex differences in interests. *Psychological Bulletin, 135*(6), 859–884; for communication styles see Tannen, D. (Ed.). (1993). *Gender and conversational interaction.* Oxford, UK: Oxford University Press; for research related to negotiation styles see Amanatullah, E. T., & Morris, M. W. (2010). Negotiating gender roles: Gender differences in assertive negotiating are mediated by women's fear of backlash and attenuated when negotiating on behalf of others. *Journal of Personality and Social Psychology, 98*(1), 256–267.

55. Eagly, A. H., Johannesen-Schmidt, M. C., & van Engen, M. (2003). Transformational, transactional, and laissez-faire leadership styles: A meta-analysis comparing women and men. *Psychological Bulletin, 95,* 569–591.

56. Reingold, J. (2003, October). Still angry after all these years. *Fast Company,* pp. 89–94.

57. Sandberg, S. (2013). *Lean in: Women, work and the will to lead.* New York, NY: Knopf.

58. Hoobler, J. M., Wayne, S. J., & Lemmon, G. (2009). Bosses' perception of family–work conflict and women's promotability: Glass ceiling effects. *Academy of Management Journal, 52,* 939–957.

59. Arfken, D. E., Bellar, S. L., & Helms, M. M. (2004). The ultimate glass ceiling revisited: The presence of women on corporate boards. *Journal of Business Ethics, 50,* 177–186.

60. Maune, D. J. (1999). The glass ceiling and the glass escalator: Occupational segregation and race and sex differences in managerial promotions. *Work and Occupations, 26,* 483–509.

61. EEOC Press release. (2013). *US Equal Employment Opportunity Commission,* January 18. Retrieved from http://www.eeoc.gov/eeoc/newsroom/release/1-28-13.cfm on June 21, 2013.

62. Crockett, R. O. (2009). Deloitte's diversity push. *Business Week,* October 2. Retrieved from http://www.businessweek.com/managing/content/oct2009/ca2009102_173180.htm on January 18, 2010.

63. Crockett, 2009.

64. Deloitte. (2010). Retrieved from http://careers.deloitte.com/united-states/students/culture_benefits.aspx?CountryContentID=13709 on January 18, 2010.

65. See Gerdes, L., & Lavelle, L. (2009). Best place to launch a career. *Business Week.* Retrieved from http://bwnt.businessweek.com/interactive_reports/career_launch_2009/ on January 18, 2010; and the *Shriver report: A woman's nation changes everything.* (2009). Retrieved from http://awomansnation.com on January 18, 2010.

66. Deloitte-Shriver report. (2009). Deloitte recognized for its strategies to adapt to the evolving workforce. Retrieved from http://www.deloitte.com/view/en_US/us/press/Press-Releases/press-release/5e6c7475aa455210VgnVCM200000bb42f00aRCRD.htm on January 18, 2010.

67. Model employer. (2009). Retrieved from http://www.deloitte.com/view/en_US/us/About/Womens-Initiative/article/c7aa98bbcf084210VgnVCM100000ba42f00aRCRD.htm on January 18, 2010.

68. Search for women, 2006.

69. Zolli, A. (2006). Demographics: The population hourglass. *Fast Company,* March. Retrieved from http://www.fastcompany.com/56218/demographics-population-hourglass on June 19, 2013.

70. Zolli, 2006.

71. Bryner, J. (2010). Big generation gap in work attitudes revealed. *Live Science,* March 10. Retrieved from http://www.livescience.com/6195-big-generation-gaps-work-attitudes-revealed.html on June 19, 2013; and Mielach, D. (2012). Gen Y seeks work-life balance above all else. *Business News,* March 30. Retrieved from http://www.businessnewsdaily.com/2278-generational-employee-differences.html on June 19, 2013.

72. Zemke, R., Raines, C., & Filipczak, B. (2000). *Generations at work: Managing the clash of veterans,*

boomers, Xers, and nexters in your workplace (pp. 9–10). New York, NY: AMACOM.

73. Espinoza, C. M., Ukleja, M., & Rusch, C. (2010). *Managing the millennials: Discover the core competencies for managing today's workforce*. Hoboken, NJ: Wiley, p. 11.

74. Dychtwald, K., Erickson, T. J., & Morison, R. (2006). *Workforce crisis: How to beat the coming shortage of skills and talent*. Boston, MA: Harvard Business School Press, p. 40.

75. Dychtwald, Erickson, & Morison, 2006, p. 68.

76. Lancaster, L. C., & Stillman, D. (2010). *The M-factor: How the millennial generation is rocking the workplace*. New York, NY: Harper Business, p. 38.

77. Bennis, W. G., & Thomas, R. J. (2002). *Geeks & geezers: How era, values, and defining moments shape leaders*. Boston, MA: Harvard Business School Press.

78. Bennis & Thomas, 2002.

79. Bartlett, C. A., & Ghoshal, S. (1989). *Managing across borders: The transnational solution*. Boston, MA: Harvard Business School Press; and Bartlett, C. A., & Ghoshal, S. (1992). Managing across borders: New organizational responses. *Sloan Management Review, 28*(9), 3–13.

80. Hall, E. T. (1976). *Beyond culture*. Garden City, NY: Anchor Press, Doubleday; and Hall, E. T., & Hall, M. R. (1990). *Understanding cultural differences*. London: Nicholas Brealy.

81. Munter, M. (1993, May–June). Cross-cultural communication for managers. *Business Horizons, 36*, 69–78.

82. Hofstede, G. (1992). *Culture and organizations*. London: McGraw-Hill; Hofstede, G. (1996). An American in Paris: The influence of nationality on organization theories. *Organization Studies, 17*, 525–537; Hofstede, G. (2001). *Culture's consequences: Comparing values, behaviors, institutions, and organizations across organizations*. Thousand Oaks, CA: Sage; and Hofstede, G., & Hofstede, G. J. (2005). *Culture and organizations: Software of the mind*. New York, NY: McGraw-Hill.

83. Hofstede, 1996.

84. House et al., 2004.

85. Javidan, M., & House, R. J. (2001). Cultural acumen for the global manager: Lessons from project GLOBE. *Organizational Dynamics, 29*, 289–305.

86. Javidan & House, 2001.

87. House et al., 2004.

88. *Gross National Happiness*. (2013). Retrieved from http://www.grossnationalhappiness.com on June 21, 2013.

89. Cross, T. L., Bazron, B. J., Dennis, K. W., & Isaacs, M. R. (1989). *Towards a culturally competent system of care: A monograph on effective services for minority children who are severely emotionally disturbed: Volume 1*. Retrieved from http://minorityhealth.hhs.gov/templates/browse.aspx?lvl=2&lvlID=11 on June 21, 2013.

90. Georgetown National Center for Cultural Competence. (2013). Retrieved from http://www11.georgetown.edu/research/gucchd/nccc/foundations/frameworks.html#ccprinciples on June 21, 2013.

91. Wilson, D. C. (2006). When equal opportunity knocks. *Gallup Management Journal*, April 16. Retrieved from http://businessjournal.gallup.com/content/22378/When-Equal-Opportunity-Knocks.aspx on September 12, 2013.

92. Winters, M. F. (2007, April 14). CEOs who get it. *Leadership Excellence, 24*(4), 7.

93. Wiscombe, J. (2007). Toyota: Driving diversity. *Workforce Management*, January. Retrieved from http://www.workforce.com/section/09/feature/24/62/58/index.html on July 6, 2007.

94. Solomon, N. (2010). In-house resource groups can help and harm. *NPR-Morning Edition*, January 13. Retrieved from http:www.npr.orgtemplatesstorystory.php?storyId122516577 on January 18, 2010.

95. Holland, K. (2007). How diversity makes a team click. *New York Times*, April 22. Retrieved from http://select.nytimes.com/search/restricted/article?res=F20D10FD3D5A0C718EDDAD0894DF404482 on June 27, 2007.

3

Self-Awareness, Personality, Emotions, and Values

LEARNING OUTCOMES

After studying this chapter, you should be able to:

1. Illustrate individual differences, identify their determinants, and explain their effects on behavior

2. Evaluate the importance of self-knowledge and self-awareness in becoming an effective manager

3. Consider the role of skills and abilities, particularly emotional intelligence, in management and leadership

4. Compare and contrast various personality traits that influence work-related behavior

5. Evaluate the importance of values in organizational behavior

6. Adopt new skills in self-awareness, self-reflection, and self-critique

7. Evaluate your own path to self-awareness

The Evolution of Jeffrey Katzenberg ▶

Jeffrey Katzenberg recently extended his contract as CEO of DreamWorks Animation to 2017 with an annual base salary of $2.5 million. Since its foundation in 1994, the studio has produced hits such as the Shrek movies, Puss in Boots, and Kung Fu Panda, with the latter two grossing $1.2 billion globally.[1] Katzenberg partnered with Steven Spielberg and David Geffen to start the company after he was unceremoniously fired from Disney in 1994. His career includes serving as president of Paramount Studios and chairman of the Walt Disney Studios. However, in spite of his amazing talent and continued success, Katzenberg had a reputation for being demanding, sometimes unreasonable, and having very public outbursts of anger, lashing out at colleagues and Hollywood stars. A Disney official described him: "He was a screamer, and he was a shredder and a very tough force to be reckoned with."[2] He was reputed to have greeted an employee at 6:30 in the morning with "Good afternoon." He joked about telling people: "If you don't come to work on Saturday, don't bother showing up on Sunday."[3]

Over the years, Katzenberg has undergone considerable transformation in his approach to leadership. While the tremendous work ethic remains, Katzenberg has changed, according to Katzenberg himself, because of his firing in 1994: "Getting fired when you're doing your best work can wake you up pretty well. It's called a swift kick in the butt. But I learned from that experience that change is good. You know the saying, 'What doesn't kill you makes you stronger?' Well, I'm an optimist. My attitude is when one door closes, another opens."[4] He has learned to temper his impatience because he understands the effect it has on his employees. To moderate his extreme drive and impatience, he uses what he calls a "five second tape delay" to "self-edit" before he expresses his opinion. He is also more aware that others may not want to work at the same pace he does:

He who knows about others may be learned; but he who knows himself is more intelligent.

—Lao-tzu

> *To do . . . things well, you'll need to cultivate a deep understanding of yourself—not only what your strengths and weaknesses are but also how you learn, how you work with others, what your values are, and where you can make the greatest contribution. Because only when you operate from strengths can you achieve true excellence.*
>
> *—Peter Drucker*
>
> *By far the most important thing in leadership is to have a brutally honest understanding of who you are.*
>
> *—Dr. Jim Yong Kim, President of the World Bank*

Something that I was kind of oblivious to for a long period of time is that I ended up setting a pace for everyone else, and they assumed if the boss is working 24/7, then we all must work 24/7. That's not such a good thing because not everyone loves it as much as I do, and it's not actually how you get the best out of people.[5]

Katzenberg's biggest leadership lesson is to cultivate his followers: "I started to realize that if I wanted to stay surrounded by great people, I had to get out of their way and create the room and make sure they started to get the recognition and the credit and everything that goes with it. Honestly, it allowed me to stay around longer."[6] He further states: "The thing that I have learned, and I only wish that I knew it twenty-five or thirty years ago, which is to honor and celebrate, recognize and reward your employees and their work—is a fantastic business strategy. If they love their work, they love coming to work, they will strive to do great work and you'll succeed."[7]

We are all familiar with the ancient Greek admonition to "know thyself." This time-honored advice still has a great deal of currency. Knowing yourself and being reflective about your own behavior is essential to realizing your potential as a leader and having positive relationships with others. As you face the challenge of understanding and managing individual differences in others, you also need to be self-aware and understand your own needs, motivations, strengths, and weaknesses.

Identical Twins
Are Different

Knowledge of ourselves not only is valuable from a personal standpoint but also is critical to success and satisfaction in our work lives. Effective leaders know how to analyze their own and others' behaviors in organizational settings and use that information to make themselves and their employees more productive. Today, leaders at all levels of organizations are often asked to work with diverse groups inside and outside of their organizations. Everyone is under pressure to be more productive, to do more with less, and to serve customers better. These changes sweeping businesses and other organizations have created considerable ambiguity, confusion, and stress. Your understanding of yourself will greatly enhance your ability to deal with these difficult times and both you and your organization will benefit.

Keep in mind that self-awareness is a lifelong journey. We are each unique in our values, beliefs, preferences, and behaviors. You may be outgoing and seek the company of others, whereas your brother or sister may be reserved and prefer quiet evenings at home. Some of us are intense and engage in a whirlwind of activities; others are relaxed and focus on a few specific tasks. The challenge of a new job that inspires one person may dishearten another. The skills that are easy for one person to learn pose a challenge for another. What makes us different from one another?

LIFE EXPERIENCES

Though attaining self-knowledge is an ongoing lifelong process, the following are some exercises designed to help you reflect on the experiences, values, and perspectives that have shaped who you are. Obviously, the culture in which we live, our life experiences, and our interactions with others affect our self-concepts and our views of the world. What events and relationships have influenced you? Make some notes in response to the following:

- What world or national events have taken place during your lifetime?
- Which of these influenced your life most dramatically?
- How was your life influenced by those events?

Examples might include 9/11 and the mortgage crisis. More positive influences might have come from an admired leader or public figure or from travel.

- Are there local events that have been particularly influential in your life?
- Were there cultural opportunities or political events in your hometown that were particularly influential?

Examples might include activities in a local theater, library, sports team, or government.

- What were your most important educational experiences?
- Which personal relationships influenced you the most?
- What roles have these individuals played in your life?

Examples might include relationships with grandparents, parents, teachers, siblings, spouses, or children.

Your Lifeline

On the chart below, plot the major events and relationships of your life and then draw your lifeline. On the horizontal axis, fill in the years beginning with your birth and ending with the current year. On the vertical axis, use a 5-point scale with 0 as the midpoint (5, 4, 3, 2, 1, 0, –1, –2, –3, –4, –5) to represent the level of significance of each event or relationship and whether it had a positive or negative impact. This timeline should represent people and events that have had an impact in formulating your values, your style, and your orientation to life. This information might help you later in answering questions regarding your motivation for change and capacity for decision making.

Lifeline of Experiences and Relationships

```
5
4
3
2
1
```

(Continued)

(Continued)

0				
−1				
−2				
−3				
−4				
−5				
Birth	Childhood	Adolescence	Young Adult	Now

Understanding Individual Differences

Every person is unique because of a combination of many factors, including demographic, physical, psychological, and behavioral differences. These are at the core of who you are. Figure 3.1 presents a framework for organizing individual differences and their complex components.

The interactionist view of individual differences, as shown in Figure 3.1, suggests that heredity and the environment interact, and that both influence the development of individual differences. This view is widely accepted, though many experts debate the relative

Individual
Differences

FIGURE 3.1 INDIVIDUAL DIFFERENCES FRAMEWORK

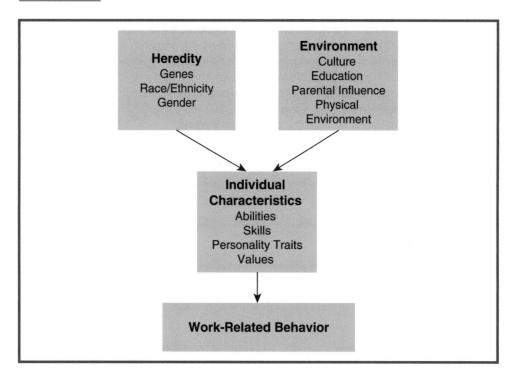

Interactionist view:
suggests that heredity
and the environment
interact to influence
the development of
individual differences

influence of each factor and recent research indicates that heredity may play an especially powerful role.

Heredity consists of an individual's gene pool, gender, race, and ethnic background. It has an early, and some suggest indelible influence on personality. For example, studies done with identical twins find that even when raised apart, the twins are more similar to each other than to their adoptive family members.[8] Though genetic studies establish a link between heredity and some personality traits, research also shows that the environment strongly affects us. Influences include physical location, parents, culture, religion, education, and friends. A child born and raised in a poor remote farm in Appalachia will think and behave differently from one born and raised in a wealthy area of Silicon Valley in Northern California. Similarly, a female child growing up in Japan is likely to differ from one raised in Sweden.

Life experiences influence our perception and view of the world. These children from a rural Indian village are likely to think and behave differently than children who grow up in an urban Indian city.

Environmental and social conditions can reinforce genetic patterns to influence a person's personality, as can cultural factors, the educational system, and parental upbringing. For instance, in the United States, the genetic traits typically associated with being male are further reinforced by social norms that encourage boys to be competitive and not show their emotions. Similarly, although female babies tend to develop language skills earlier than males, parents who speak more to their girls and schools that expect them to be proficient in language further reinforce their verbal skills.

Consider the recent research about happiness and contentment.[9] It appears that being optimistic or pessimistic may have a genetic component that we cannot control or change easily. That outlook, in turn, plays a key role in whether someone has a happy disposition. However, about half of how happy we are is determined by what we think and how we behave. Having *positive* emotions, being *engaged* in our activities, having positive *relationships*, doing things that have *meaning*, and finally *achievement* or accomplishment—PERMA for short—all things that are related to opportunity and the environment, determine the other half.[10] How we feel and what we do, indeed who we are, results from an interaction between our heredity and our environment.

As shown in Figure 3.1, three major individual difference characteristics can affect leadership and management behaviors and styles: abilities and skills, personality traits, and values. **Skills** are acquired talents that a person develops related to specific tasks. **Abilities**, also called aptitude, are natural talents to do something mental or physical. Intelligence, for example, is considered to be an ability. Abilities are relatively stable over time, while skills change with training and experience and from one task to another. You cannot train people to develop an ability or aptitude, but you can train them to learn new skills. The

Neuroscientist Discovers Keys

Skills: acquired talents that a person develops related to specific tasks

Abilities: natural talents to do something mental or physical

goal in many organizations is to recruit and hire employees who have certain abilities and fit the job requirement, then help them acquire needed skills.

Personality refers to a set of psychological characteristics that make each person unique. It is stable and tends to stay the same over time and across situations, although it is not rigid and it does evolve gradually. While personality refers to character and temperament, **values** are stable long-lasting beliefs and preferences about what is worthwhile and desirable. Like personality traits, values guide your behavior and are influenced by a combination of biological and environmental factors. For example, if you hold the value "honesty is the best policy," you will attempt to behave fairly and honorably and show integrity in your words and actions. Like personality, values are shaped early in life and are resistant to change. Values are also influenced heavily by one's culture.

Influence of Individual Differences: Behavioral Range

Although our individual differences affect how we think and behave, they do not dictate what we do. A useful approach is to consider a variety of individual differences that explain a person's behavior rather than focus on any one trait. Ideally, to understand who we are and what makes us unique, we would consider all possible aspects of personality, values, attitudes, demographic factors, abilities, and skills. Additionally, situations influence what we do: When the situation provides us with clear cues regarding what is expected of us, most of us simply behave accordingly, regardless of our individual differences.[11] However, when situations provide little guidance, we are more likely to behave based on our individual traits and values. For example, if you work in an organization with a strong culture that provides detailed and clear rules of behavior, you are less likely to express your individuality. In contrast, if you work in an organization that is loosely structured, you are more likely to show your own preferences.

Although individual characteristics tend to be stable, that stability does not mean that people cannot behave in ways that are inconsistent with their personality, values, and attitudes. Our individual characteristics provide a behavioral zone or a range of behaviors that come naturally and feel comfortable because they reflect who we are (see Figure 3.2). But, as we have said, the situation may demand that we change our behavior. Of course, behaving outside of our normal behavioral zone is challenging, takes practice, and in some cases might not be possible. But, in the end, we learn and grow by moving out of our comfort zones to activities that challenge us, stimulate us, and push us to our limits.

A related question is how we respond to emotional challenges.[12] The term **emotional challenge** refers to any real or perceived threat to our security, self-image, or sense of self-worth that stimulates our instinctive self-protective tendencies to either withdraw or become aggressive. Interestingly, when facing emotional challenges most of us try to change or control other people's behavior. However, the truth is that we can control only one person—ourselves. If we can enhance our understanding of ourselves and how our personality, abilities, and values influence our behavior, if we can gain insight into how our attitudes and behaviors affect others, and if we can accept that how we view the world is not necessarily how others view the world, then we can build our capacity to handle emotional challenges and to maintain positive and productive relationships.

Personality: a set of psychological characteristics that makes each person unique

Values: stable long-lasting beliefs and preferences about what is worthwhile and desirable

Emotional challenge: any real or perceived threat to our security, self-image, or sense of self-worth

FIGURE 3.2 BEHAVIORAL RANGE

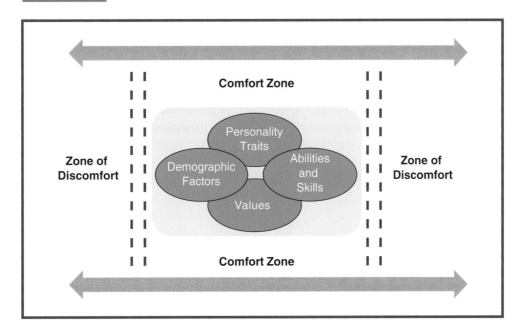

Why Is Self-Awareness Important?

There is very strong agreement that the one defining characteristic of virtually every great entrepreneur, manager, and leader is self-awareness. Anthony Tjan, managing partner and founder of the venture capital Cue Ba, believes that "Without self-awareness, you cannot understand your strengths and weaknesses, your 'super powers' versus your 'kryptonite.'"[13] He refers to the trinity of self-awareness as know thyself, improve thyself, and complement thyself by adding others with different skills to your team. The latter is important because it is impossible for one person to have all of the traits necessary for business success. In order to be most effective, you must surround yourself with people who complement your traits and balance your strengths and weaknesses. That can be done only if you have a strong awareness of who you are and what you do well.

One way of thinking about developing self-awareness is to focus on skills development.[14] Consider the way people learn any skill such as sports, art, music, or management. They must first have an intellectual understanding of the task—cognitive knowledge. But cognitive understanding alone is not enough. People also must develop the *behavioral skills* needed to accomplish these

Skill development is a key aspect of strengthening your self-awareness. Pictured here is David Henderson who joined Toastmasters to work on his speaking skills and eventually went on to win the Toastmasters World Championship of Public Speaking, the world's largest speech contest, in 2010, surpassing more than 30,000 contestants from more than 100 countries.

technical moves on every occasion. For the athlete or artist, this requires extensive practice or rehearsal. The same is true of leaders, although in their case the most important skills are not swinging a bat or mixing colors but, rather, becoming effective in terms of interpersonal skills. For leaders, these skills are developed through watching and modeling others—through workshops, simulations, case studies, and (most important) experience.

But even those who fully understand their discipline and have acquired the necessary behavioral and technical skills through practice and experience might not always follow the correct course of action. For example, most modern managers know the importance of involving employees in organizational change. Even managers who have done so effectively in the past might—under conditions of complexity, uncertainty, and stress—fail to consult and involve others. Something beyond cognitive knowledge and behavioral practice is needed, something we might think of as maturity, self-esteem, or self-confidence.

Skills and Abilities

Skills

The skills that are most relevant to managers are divided into three categories: technical, interpersonal, and conceptual (Table 3.1). As leaders and managers move up in their organization, they rely less on technical skills and increasingly on interpersonal and conceptual skills. Company CEOs, school principals, or hospital administrators do not need to be able to perform various jobs in detail. They, however, should be able to negotiate successfully and effectively and manage interpersonal relationships inside and outside the organization. Furthermore, top executives more than lower-level leaders and managers need to read and analyze their internal and external environments and make strategic decisions that require considerable problem-solving skills. It is important to know that although skills can be learned and can affect a person's behavior, there tends to be a lag time between learning a skill and translating it into actual behavior.[15]

Abilities

Skills alone are not enough for success. In order to succeed, certain abilities are also required. Examine the situation of someone with technical and professional expertise getting promoted to a managerial job. Often this is a prescription for failure because the person is being moved to a new job—management—for which he or she is poorly trained and underequipped. Often it is attributable to a lack of understanding of the individual's own emotions and an inability to appreciate the emotions of the people with whom he or she works.[16]

Technical skills: knowledge of job processes, methods, tools, and techniques

Interpersonal skills: knowledge of interpersonal relationships including communication, conflict management

Conceptual skills: knowledge of problem solving, logical thinking, decision making, creativity, and reasoning in general

TABLE 3.1 MANAGERIAL SKILLS

Skills Category	Description
Technical skills	Knowledge of the job processes, methods, tools, and techniques
Interpersonal skills	Knowledge of interpersonal relationships including communication, conflict management, negotiation, and team building
Conceptual skills	Knowledge of problem solving, logical thinking, decision making, creativity, and reasoning in general

CREATIVITY AND CHANGE

THE MUSICAL INSTRUMENT MUSEUM

In April 2010, the Musical Instrument Museum (MIM) opened in Phoenix, Arizona. MIM has a collection of some 15,000 musical instruments from countries all over the world, and displays about a third of that number at any one time. MIM was originally conceived by Bob Ulrich, who served as CEO of Target from 1987 to 2008. Under his leadership, Target grew from a small Midwestern discount operation to a major national company known for its innovations, success, and philanthropy.

The idea for MIM came to Ulrich during a visit to Brussels. Ulrich and a friend had visited the Musical Instrument Museum in Brussels—yes, the same name. Later in the evening they were sitting in an outdoor café having a beer and a cigar and discussing art and museums. Ulrich mentioned that he was thinking about buying a major Impressionist painting, which he would eventually donate to the Minneapolis Institute of the Arts. His friend remarked, "For what you would pay for that you could buy an entire museum."

From there the conversation turned to the question of what kind of museum would be worth supporting and the idea of a MIM was born. When Ulrich returned home, he convened a curatorial council representing museums that had instrument collections to get their ideas, and then he began recruiting a director, Bill DeWalt, an anthropologist who was at the time running the Carnegie Museum of Natural History in Pittsburgh, Pennsylvania.

According to DeWalt, from the outset the project has been about bringing together people with different personalities and outlooks. DeWalt commented that creativity comes about when leadership resides in a team of people who may be quite different but who can work back and forth together. For instance, he said, Ulrich and he were off the ends of the spectrum on many dimensions. Ulrich has a motto that "Speed is life," a motto he even used on Target's corporate jets, while DeWalt described himself as more thoughtful and

analytical. Yet sharing the vision of a museum devoted to instruments and music of every country in the world, Ulrich and DeWalt and a few others formed the creative team that would develop the MIM in record time.

After DeWalt was hired, there were three major things to do: (1) to preview other collections and begin to acquire instruments from around the world, (2) to create a building that would house the collections, and (3) to put together a team of people to staff the organization.

A team of ethnomusicologists and consultants who were experts in particular parts of the world were enlisted to identify instruments worth considering and then acquiring.

A choice was made to build the museum in Phoenix, a choice based on the city's large population, its strong cultural institutions, its huge convention population, and its attractiveness to international visitors going to the Grand Canyon. Target Corporation lead designer Rich Vardar and his old firm RSP Architects designed the building, which marvelously captures the feel of its desert setting, the gracefulness of musical instruments, and the flow of music itself.

Staffing the museum also required bringing together different people with different skills and backgrounds who could work well together. Just putting together one exhibit, for example, requires designers, graphics people, multimedia experts, curators, writers, conservators (the people who take care of the instruments), and many others. According to DeWalt, what you need are people who are comfortable working creatively with others from very different backgrounds.

Uniquely, the instruments are not put in cases. Ulrich wanted people to get close to the instruments and see around them and not simply see the glass protecting the instruments. The combination of these efforts has resulted in a huge collection of instruments from all around the world, housed in a spacious building architecturally consistent with its location and the musicality

(Continued)

of the collection, and staffed by a diverse team of creative artists and technicians.

1. Urlich and DeWalt are quite different types of people. Explain how people who are so different can work effectively together.

2. Part of the answer to question one is that DeWalt recognized the differences and the advantages of each. How can you pick up clues to how others are

different from you and make good decisions about how to approach them and use their talents?

3. To stage a single exhibit requires people of many different backgrounds and skill sets, including artists and technicians. How can you help members of such groups to work effectively together?

Source: This vignette is based on an interview with Bill DeWalt by Robert Denhardt.

Alleviating
Emotional Labor

Emotional
Intelligence

Emotional intelligence: the social and interpersonal aspect of intelligence

Intelligence is one of the most often used characteristics to describe leaders and is often included in discussions of leadership.[17] It is clear that the complex task of managing others requires a person with a cognitive ability to remember, collect and integrate information, analyze problems, develop solutions, and evaluate alternatives, all of which are related to traditional definitions of intelligence. For most people, intelligence is a factor in leadership; however, a direct connection between intelligence and effectiveness is far from clear, as is the case for the relationship between intelligence and success in other areas.[18]

Consider Scott Rudin, producer of hit movies such as *True Grit, The Social Network, It's Complicated,* and *No Country for Old Men,* and the only producer who has won Emmy, Grammy, Tony, and Oscar awards for his work. There is no question that he is intelligent and successful. Some of the people who work with him consider Rudin to be "one of the smartest and most clever and witty guys I have ever met."[19] However, Rudin is also known for his fiery outbursts, throwing phones and office supplies, outrageous demands, and on-the-spot firing and re-hiring of assistants—by some accounts 250 in a 5-year period.[20] He has been ranked as one of the worst bosses in New York City.[21] As one of Rudin's ex-assistants states, "I think the people that work there—most of them hate him. Nobody likes him. Everybody's miserable."[22] While Rudin is undeniably intelligent in the traditional sense of the word, he lacks what is known as emotional intelligence.

FIGURE 3.3 EMOTIONAL INTELLIGENCE

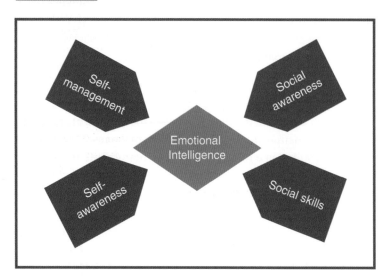

Emotions

Emotional Intelligence

Emotional intelligence describes the social and interpersonal aspect of intelligence. Although intelligence generally is defined in terms of mental and cognitive abilities, the ability to relate interpersonally, interact well with followers, satisfy their emotional needs, and motivate and inspire them is key to effective leadership and management. The four components of Emotional Intelligence are presented in Figure 3.3.

Self-management is the ability to control or redirect disruptive impulses and moods and regulate your own behavior, coupled with an ability to pursue goals with energy and persistence. Self-management includes self-control, trustworthiness, integrity, initiative, adaptability and comfort with ambiguity, openness to change, and a strong desire to achieve.

Self-awareness is the ability to recognize and understand your moods, emotions, and drives as well as their effect on others. Self-awareness is comprised of three elements—emotional awareness, accurate self-assessment, and self-confidence. Individuals with a high degree of self-awareness understand the emotions they are feeling and why, they recognize the links between their feelings and what they think and say, they recognize how their feelings affect their performance, and they have a guiding awareness of values and goals.[23] In other words, self-awareness is the ability to understand what one is feeling and how to direct those feelings.[24]

Social awareness is the ability to understand the emotional makeup of other people and skills in treating people according to their emotional reaction. This is linked to empathy for others, expertise in building and retaining talent, organizational awareness, cross-cultural sensitivity, valuing diversity, and service to stakeholders.

Finally, **social skills** involve proficiency in managing relationships and building networks to get the desired result from others, reach personal goals, build rapport, and find common ground. Social skills include leadership, effectiveness in leading change, conflict management, influence/communication, and expertise in building and leading teams. All of these competencies are discussed in this book.

Ken Chenault, Chairman and CEO of American Express, is a good example of a socially intelligent leader.

Ken Chenault, Chairman and CEO of American Express (AmEx), provides a good example of a socially intelligent leader. He relies on his ability to show empathy and express his emotions to win his employees' trust and build cohesion. Those who know him say he is understated, modest, and unassuming, with quiet warmth and a style that makes people want to be on his team.[25] His social and interpersonal skills are evident in his emphasis on communication: "You've got to communicate constantly."[26] He also believes that self-awareness and knowing what you stand for are essential to leadership: "If you are not clear on who you are, on what it is you stand for, and if you don't have strong values, you are going to run your career off a cliff."[27]

Emotions in the Workplace

Feelings and emotions are at the core of the human experience. The workplace brings out a wide variety of emotions in all of us. When they are positive, such as in the satisfaction we get from our jobs, they become some of the most gratifying experiences of our lifetimes. Likewise, when they are negative, such as the stress that our job may be causing, they can represent some of our most upsetting experiences (see Table 3.2).

Self-management: ability to control or redirect disruptive impulses and moods and regulate your own behavior

Self-awareness: ability to recognize and understand your moods, emotions, and drives as well as their effect on others

Social skills: proficiency in managing relationships and building networks

Emotional Labor Study

TABLE 3.2 EMOTIONS IN THE WORKPLACE

Categories of Emotions	Examples of Emotions
Nasty emotions	Anger, envy, and jealousy
Existential emotions	Anxiety, guilt, and shame
Emotions provoked by unfavorable life conditions	Relief, hope, sadness, and depression
Emotions provoked by favorable life conditions	Happiness, pride, and love
Empathetic emotions	Gratitude and compassion

Emotional labor: the act of expressing organizationally desired emotions during service transactions

Waiting tables in a restaurant is a position that often requires emotional labor as employees strive to serve customers and provide a pleasant dining experience. What are some other occupations that require emotional labor?

Emotional dissonance: projecting one emotion while feeling another

Feelings: indicators of our implicit or unconscious judgments of the significance of events

Emotions: provide information about our reactions to situations and reveal our needs, concerns, and motives

Emotional labor emerged from studies in service jobs; think of the first responder at the scene of an accident or the nurse caring for patients in a hospital. However, emotional labor is relevant to almost any job because employees expect their manager to be courteous and not hostile to others. Emotional labor is generally defined as the act of expressing organizationally desired emotions during service transactions.[28] The challenge arises when employees have to project one emotion while feeling another, something that is called **emotional dissonance**, and which can take a heavy toll on the individual.[29]

Individuals not only try to interpret the emotions of other people, but also their own emotions. Our **feelings** are indicators of our implicit or unconscious judgments of the significance of events. Our own **emotions** give us information about our reactions to situations that we might not otherwise be aware of, and they reveal to us our needs, concerns, and motives. Our emotions tell us when things feel incomplete, and they imply the need for action. Sometimes unknown to an individual, the action implied is one that will have a chance of returning the individual from a crisis state to a neutral or normal state.

Lazarus and Lazarus offer five categories of emotions.[30] The first is what they call the "nasty" emotions, which include anger, envy, and jealousy. Who among us can say they have never experienced any one of the nasty emotions in our own work lives? The second is what is referred to as the existential emotions, including anxiety, guilt, and shame. The research on job stress and coping mechanisms (discussed in Chapter 6) demonstrates the saliency of these work-related emotions. The third category is emotions provoked by unfavorable life conditions, including relief, hope, sadness, and depression. The fourth category is emotions provoked by favorable life conditions, including happiness, pride, and love. Lastly, there are the empathetic emotions, including gratitude and compassion. You may want to explore all of these categories as you work on your timeline in this chapter.

EMOTIONAL INTELLIGENCE

Instructions: Ask yourself how often you respond in a healthy way when severely disappointed, verbally attacked, or treated unfairly by analyzing these attitudes and behaviors:

1. When I am upset, I respond rationally, so that I can remain analytical and solve the problem or otherwise make the best of the situation.

2. I reject the harm than can result from reacting emotionally when I am upset and getting angry or feeling battered.

3. When verbally attacked, I allow for the likelihood that the attackers might never have learned how to respond when their needs aren't met.

4. When verbally attacked, I allow for the probability that the attack is prompted by pain or fear.

5. When verbally attacked, I keep my role as a manager separate from my identity as a person.

6. I resist the temptation to feel entitled to better treatment and to lose emotional control.

7. I understand that victims of my outbursts will remember my accusatory statements and name-calling long after I have calmed down.

8. I accept that others cannot make me angry without my full cooperation. In other words, I control my anger.

9. When I get angry, I talk about my feelings to calm myself down, rather than focus on what the other person did.

Interpreting Results

The first two behaviors lay a firm foundation for emotional intelligence. Behaviors 3 through 5 are proven strategies for staying in control when under attack. Regardless of the root of your anger, deal with it as suggested in points 6 through 9.

These prescriptions will take practice, and it will help to have a positive role model share how he or she deals with these difficult situations.

Source: Adapted from Deep, S., & Sussman, L. (2000). *Act on it! Solving 101 of the toughest management challenges* (p. 33). Cambridge, MA: Perseus Publishing. Reprinted with permission.

Personality Traits

What Are Emotions?

A number of personality traits affect work-related behaviors. The challenge for managers is not only to develop self-awareness regarding their own traits, but also to understand what their employees' wants and needs may be. This is difficult, of course, because every employee is unique to begin with, and each learns new behaviors at a different speed and with varying amounts of ease.

Myers-Briggs Type Inventory (MBTI)

Psychologist Carl Jung described several aspects of the human psyche based on the way in which we take in and process information (see the Myers-Briggs Type Inventory, used

Outbursts at Work

to assess an individual's Jungian personality types, in Figure 3.4).[31] For example, information may be acquired through our senses or through our intuition. Information then is processed through rational processes or through feelings. Jung's framework also includes our orientation to the external world (extroverts) and those oriented toward the internal world (introverts) as well as two modes of decision making, one relying on perception and the other relying on judgment. Over time, individuals become more dependent on one way of collecting and processing information than on other ways. They also come to depend on one orientation to the external world and on one decision-making style. That is not to say that one way is better than another way, and indeed, we all possess all of these capacities to some degree. But over time, we become more comfortable with one approach and come to rely on that approach. Our preferences are then reflected in our personalities.

Those who rely on "sensing" are likely to focus on specific data and what is immediately present; those who rely on "intuition" are more likely to focus on the future, to see the potential in a situation, and to be highly creative. Imagine two people looking in the window of a house they are thinking about buying. One (the sensing type) might see all the flaws—torn carpets, peeling paint, and so on. The other (the intuitive type) might think in terms of possibilities (e.g., "We could do great things with this house"). Two people can look at the same situation and see it in completely different ways (see Figure 3.4).

The different types reinforce and need one another.[32] The sensing type needs an intuitive to generate possibilities, to supply ingenuity, to deal with complexity, and to furnish new ideas. Intuitives add a long-range perspective and spark things that seem impossible. The intuitive needs a sensing type to bring facts to inspect, to attend to detail, to inject patience, and

Emotional
Intelligence
and Heart

Individuation
and Archetypes

FIGURE 3.4 FOUR MBTI GROUPINGS

Artisans (SP) – Tend to Be	**Guardians (SJ)** – Tend to Be
Playful	Responsible
Optimistic	Helpful
Sensual	Hardworking
Unconventional	Sociable
Daring	Loyal
Impulsive	Stable
Excitable	Traditional
Adaptable	Law-abiding
Rationals (NT) – Tend to Be	**Idealists (NF)** – Tend to Be
Pragmatic	Enthusiastic
Skeptical	Romantic
Analytical	Intuitive
Independent	Kind-hearted
Strong-willed	Intense
Logical	Authentic
Even-tempered	Symbolic
Curious	Inspiring

Source: From Keirsey, D. W. (1998). *Please understand me II*. Del Mar, CA: Prometheus Nemesis Books. Used with permission.

SP = sensation, perceiver; SJ = sensation, judging; NT = intuitive, thinker; NF = intuitive, feeler

to notice what needs attention. The thinker needs a feeling type to persuade and conciliate feelings, to arouse enthusiasm and to sell or advertise, and to teach and forecast. The feeling type needs a thinker to analyze and organize, to predict flaws in advance, to introduce fact and logic, to hold to a policy, and to stand firm against opposition.[33]

Knowing your preferences and those of others you work with is very helpful information. Some people will adapt to some tasks naturally, while those at the other end of the spectrum will have to make a much more conscious effort. While the MBTI is one of the most widely used personality measures in organizations, results from research about its validity are mixed. But as a rough guide to personality preferences, it can be extraordinarily helpful.

Big Five Personality Traits

Over the past several decades, psychologists and human resource management researchers have condensed countless personality traits into a list of five major personality dimensions known as the Big Five. While these dimensions are not as widely used as the MBTI, they are supported by a considerable body of research.[34] Table 3.3 summarizes the five dimensions. Several of the dimensions are related to work-relevant behaviors such as academic and career success, and performance on global assignments. Among the dimensions, conscientiousness is the most strongly correlated to job performance. People who are dependable, organized, and hard-working tend to be better employees because they are more likely to show up on time, make their deadlines, and work hard.

What Would You Do?

▶ One of your employees is technically well qualified and has an impressive educational background. She has been with the department for 6 years and her promotions and raises have been lower than average. Her technical work is excellent and she works well alone. However, her coworkers often complain that she is not a team player, tends to be insensitive to others, and generally does not appear very concerned about what others do and how they feel. She is confused about why she is not progressing well. What would you do? How would you explain to her the cause of the problem?

Knowledgeable
Personality

TABLE 3.3 THE BIG FIVE DIMENSIONS

Personality Dimensions	Description
Conscientiousness	Degree to which a person is dependable, responsible, organized, and forward looking (plans ahead)
Extraversion/introversion	Degree to which a person is sociable, talkative, assertive, active, and ambitious
Openness to experience	Degree to which a person is imaginative, broad-minded, curious, and seeks new experiences
Emotional stability	Degree to which a person is anxious, depressed, angry, and insecure
Agreeableness	Degree to which a person is courteous, likable, good-natured, and flexible

Sources: Based on descriptions provided by Norman, W. T. (1963). Toward an adequate taxonomy of personality attributes: Replicated factor structure in peer nomination personality ratings, *Journal of Abnormal and Social Psychology, 66*, 547–583; Digman, J. M. (1990). Personality structure: Emergence of the five-factor model, *Annual Review of Psychology, 41*, 417–440; and Barrick, M. R., & Mount, M. (1991). The five big personality dimensions and job performance: A meta-analysis. *Personnel Psychology, 44*(1), 1–76.

Extraversion also has some impact on job performance, especially for jobs that require social interaction, such as sales or management.[35] However, extraversion is not a requirement of leadership or success. For example, out-going Intel CEO, Paul Otellini, is known for being quiet and reserved and has shied away from the media spotlight.[36] Roberta Matuson, an expert on productivity and maximizing employee contributions says: "Sometimes we forget that the most productive people in an organization aren't the ones who make the most noise. In fact, it's often the quiet ones who out-produce everyone else."[37]

Other dimensions of the Big Five, such as openness to experience, can further be helpful in some aspects of work. Leaders who are open to new experiences may be more motivated to learn and explore new ideas and more successful when working in new cultural environments. Amex's CEO, Ken Chenault, believes that: "It's not the strongest or the most intelligent who survive, but those most adaptive to change."[38]

The last two dimensions appear to be less related to organizational performance. Some degree of emotional stability is needed, and individuals who are unstable are obviously not likely to perform well. People with high emotional stability tend to be more positive, have higher job satisfaction, and lower stress. Similarly, agreeableness may be desirable is social relationships, but it is not a factor that is directly related to job performance.

Narcissism

Chances are you have come across people who always need to be the center of attention, are self-important, and seem unable to think about others. They are selfish or self-absorbed, and as result, difficult colleagues. These behaviors are part of the concept of narcissism, which when occurring to an extreme is called the Narcissistic Personality Disorder (NPD).[39] Table 3.4 shows the characteristics of narcissists. The two defining characteristics of narcissists are grandiosity and entitlement (see Self-Assessment 3.3).[40] Narcissists are arrogant and self-absorbed, seek constant attention, are preoccupied with power, unconcerned about others, unable to show empathy, intolerant of criticism, comfortable with exploiting others, and—not surprisingly—have trouble building meaningful relationships.

Although narcissism in the extreme is a psychological disorder, it is also used to describe a range of "normal" behaviors.[41] As a matter of fact, narcissism is related to being confident and having a healthy self-esteem. As you may suspect, many celebrated and successful political and business leaders can be considered to be narcissists. However,

Susan Cain, who wrote the *New York Times* bestseller *QUIET: The Power of Introverts in a World That Can't Stop Talking,* argues that a dominant extrovert culture in business that forces individuals into collaboration can possibly stand in the way of innovation. Cain advocates that there are business situations in which an introverted approach is warranted.

TABLE 3.4 CHARACTERISTICS OF NARCISSISTIC PEOPLE

Narcissistic Characteristics
Arrogance
Exploiting others
Grandiosity
Inability to tolerate criticism
Indifference to others
Lack of empathy
Preoccupation with power
Trouble with relationships

NARCISSISM

For each of the following statements, indicate the degree to which you think each describes you by writing the appropriate number.

1 = Does not sound like me at all   3 = Sounds like me

2 = Does not sound like me   4 = Sounds a lot like me

_____ 1. I see myself as a good leader.

_____ 2. I know that I am good because everyone tells me so.

_____ 3. I can usually talk my way out of anything.

_____ 4. Everybody likes to hear my stories.

_____ 5. I expect a great deal from other people.

_____ 6. I am assertive.

_____ 7. I like to display my body.

_____ 8. I find it easy to manipulate other people to get what I want.

_____ 9. I don't need anyone to help me to get things done.

_____ 10. I insist on getting the respect I deserve.

_____ 11. I like having authority over other people.

_____ 12. I enjoy showing off.

_____ 13. I can read people like a book.

_____ 14. I always know what I am doing.

_____ 15. I will not be satisfied until I get all that I deserve.

_____ 16. People always seem to recognize my authority.

_____ 17. I enjoy being the center of attention.

_____ 18. I can make anybody believe anything.

_____ 19. I seem to be better at most things than other people.

_____ 20. I get upset when people don't notice me or recognize my accomplishments.

_____ 21. I enjoy being in charge and telling people what to do.

_____ 22. I like to be complimented.

_____ 23. I can get my way in most situations.

_____ 24. I think I am a special person.

_____ 25. I deserve more than the average person, because I am better than most people.

_____ 26. I have a natural talent for leadership.

_____ 27. I like to look at myself in the mirror.

(Continued)

(Continued)

_____ 28. I know how to get others to do what I want.

_____ 29. The world would be a better place if I was in charge.

_____ 30. I am going to be a great person.

Scoring Key

Desire for power and leadership (L): add up scores for items: 1, 6, 11, 16, 21, and 26.
Total: _____

Need for admiration and self-admiration (SA): add up scores for items: 2, 7, 12, 17, 22, and 27.
Total: _____

Exploitiveness (EX): add up scores for items: 3, 8, 13, 18, 23, and 28.
Total: _____

Arrogance and a sense of superiority (A): add up scores for items: 4, 9, 14, 19, 24, and 29.
Total: _____

Sense of Entitlement (ET): add up scores for items: 5, 10, 15, 20, 25, and 30.
Total: _____

Add up the total for the five subscales: _____ (30 lowest to 120 highest possible score).

Interpreting Your Score

The five subscales are the key factors in narcissism. The highest possible total in each subscale is 24, with a highest possible total score of 120. The higher your scores, the more narcissistic characteristics you have. Some degree of narcissism is associated with healthy self-esteem and effective leadership.

Sources: Based on Emmons, R. A. (1987). Narcissism: Theory and measurement. *Journal of Personality and Social Psychology,*
52, 11–17; Raskin & Hall (1979); Rosenthal, S. A., & Pittinsky, T. L. (2006). Narcissistic leadership. *The Leadership Quarterly, 17:*
617–633.

Extraverts Live
Happier Lives

Does Presidential
Personality
Matter?

destructive narcissistic leaders self-promote, deceive and manipulate others, respond poorly to criticism and feedback, and blame others for their failures.[42] Positive narcissistic leaders may have an exaggerated sense of self and entitlement, but they use their self-confidence, power, and influence to achieve organizational goals. They are often charming and initially well liked.

Proactive Personality

Do you know someone who can identify opportunities, take initiatives, and persevere even when blocked by obstacles? No matter what happens, that person seems to stay positive and keep going. Chances are that the person has a *proactive personality*. Proactives believe that they control events in their lives and attribute things that happen to them, particularly positive events, to their own efforts or abilities.[43] Research indicates that proactives have more job satisfaction and a more positive outlook about their career and life. Because of these characteristics, proactive people are more likely to create change and be more entrepreneurial,[44] characteristics that are associated with creative leadership. Shelly Provost, a partner at the venture incubator Lamp Post Group describes fearless entrepreneurs as people who speak up, inject energy and enthusiasm into their activities, and are positive, focused, and hard working. "The grittiest people don't just work longer and harder, although that is part of the equation. They keep a laser focus on their goal and say, 'no thanks,' to anything that gets in their way."[45]

Each of the preceding individual characteristics and traits plays a role in how people interact with others or make decisions. Any one trait alone, or even a combination, cannot explain or predict effectiveness in organizations. These characteristics can be useful tools for self-awareness and understanding and can be used as guides for leadership development.

Values

The Importance of Values

Personal values lie at the core of a person's behavior and play a significant role in unifying one's personality. *Personality* refers to a person's character and temperament, whereas values are principles that a person believes. Both guide behavior. For example, someone who holds the value that hard work is important will show up at work early, work late, and do his or her best on a daily basis. Like personality, values are shaped early in life and are resistant to change. They are also heavily influenced by culture.

There are two types of values. **Instrumental values** prescribe desirable conduct or methods for attaining an end. **Terminal values** are desired states or end goals. Honesty, kindness, and hard work are examples of instrumental values; happiness, health, and prosperity are terminal values.

We differ in our level of value maturity, so different instrumental values are held by individuals at different stages of development. Kohlberg's model of moral development, presented in Figure 3.5, focuses on the kind of reasoning used to reach a decision with value or moral connotations.[46] At the *preconventional level,* moral reasoning and instrumental values are based on personal needs or wants and on the consequences of these acts. For example, cheating on an exam is considered okay at this stage because it achieves the personal need of passing the exam and it does not hurt the person whose paper one copied. At the *conventional level* of moral development, people behave morally by conforming to standards as determined by society, and respect from others is valued. Cheating on an exam is wrong because there are rules against it, and respect for one's ability will be lost from the professor and peers. Most adults continue to operate at this level of moral development. The third and final stage is the *postconventional*. In this stage, right and wrong are judged on the basis of the internalized principles of the individual. Thus, cheating on the exam continues to be wrong, but not because

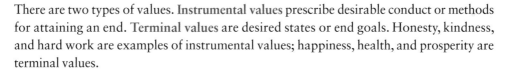

We all know that we have to be careful with what we say and do when we work with people from different cultures, but who would have thought that even apologizing can be a complex act that requires cultural knowledge? Just because the concept of an apology is universal, it does not mean that its form and content are also universal.[47]

An apology can mean anything from expressing regret to admitting guilt, or even asking for forgiveness, and different cultures use apologies differently. Language can play a role since some languages have more complex and extensive vocabulary related to apologies than others.[48] Cultural values of humility and saving face also impact how we apologize. Many Asians routinely apologize as a way of showing humility and softening a hard message that they may be delivering.

So when Toyota executives Akio Toyoda and Yoshimi Inaba apologized for their company's accelerator malfunctions, most Americans were left wanting.[49] They used strong words such as shame, humility, modesty, and regret and still were criticized for not showing enough remorse and for not taking appropriate action.[50] Similarly, when the commander of a U.S.

submarine and the U.S. government did not quickly apologize for their part in the sinking of a Japanese high-school fishing boat off the coast of Hawaii, most Japanese were offended. In both cases, as in many other international incidents, people say the words that convey an apology—they do say "I'm sorry." However, how these words are interpreted can create a storm of their own.

In the United States, an apology often means an admission of guilt. So business executives and political leaders are careful and often reluctant to apologize. However, in Japan, as well as in China, an apology does not mean culpability; but rather, it is an expression of sorrow and a willingness to fix a long-term relationship.[51] This difference means that while the Japanese will apologize profusely and much more easily, Americans will not since it often implies personal responsibility.

1. How much of the managers' behaviors are determined by their personal characteristics rather than their culture?

2. To what extent do individual factors affect how we apologize?

---

of rules and regulations or respect, but because one has developed this principled judgment. According to Kohlberg, few individuals reach this level of moral maturity. You will have the opportunity later to relate the model to a case in this chapter.

You'll Be Different

What we value has a direct bearing on the decisions we make, whether we are at work or at home. Values are viewed as the core of the social contract between company and employee. We are usually attracted to organizations that match our values and more likely to leave those that do not.[52] Your values can therefore impact your career choices. For example, a person who is financially oriented might be better suited for a sales position than for a position as a caseworker in a social service agency. The opposite would be true for a person with a human orientation, who likely would find the caseworker's assignment to be highly motivating and would not like the sales position. Reddin's (1978) Personal Values Inventory describes six different value orientations presented in Table 3.5 (see also Self-Assessment 3.4).

FIGURE 3.5 KOHLBERG'S MODEL OF MORAL DEVELOPMENT

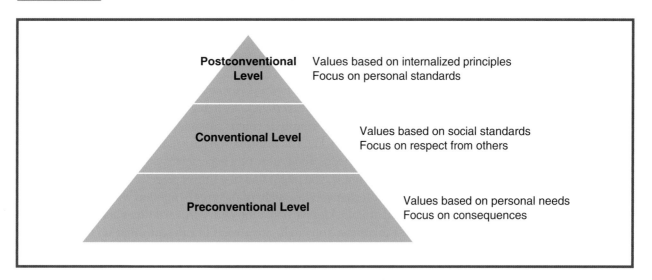

Postconventional Level — Values based on internalized principles. Focus on personal standards

Conventional Level — Values based on social standards. Focus on respect from others

Preconventional Level — Values based on personal needs. Focus on consequences

TABLE 3.5 REDDIN'S PERSONAL VALUES INVENTORY

Value Orientation	Description
Theoretical	The person is interested in ordering and systematizing knowledge, likes to reason and think, and is rational and analytical
Power oriented	The person is interested in the use, implications, and manifestations of power
Achievement oriented	The person is practical, efficient, and concerned with obtaining results
Human oriented	The person views people and relationships in a positive manner, a humanitarian
Industry oriented	The person likes to work and sees work as an end in itself
Financial oriented	The person is interested in the power of money and in rewards for effort and personal gain

Knowing your value orientation and generally what things you value allows you to develop self-awareness that can help you set priorities and make career choices that are most appropriate for you. Additionally, as you will learn throughout the book, leaders must be clear about their own values and communicate them to followers in order to engage and motivate them.

Developing Self-Awareness

An essential aspect of management and leadership development is self-awareness. There are several things you can do to develop your self-awareness (see Figure 3.6). First, you have to be a *reflective practitioner* and engage in reflection-in-action in order to allow practice to provide the laboratory where learning can take place.[53] Through reflection, you can develop your personal narrative about who you are, what you value, what you stand for, and what your personal mission is. A self-narrative speaks to your identity. Telling your story allows you to interpret the events in your life, invent and reinvent yourself in light of those events, and create and reinforce your identity.[54]

In addition to self-narrative and employing instruments such as those included in this chapter, you can enhance your self-awareness by being *attentive to feedback* that you receive from others, either informally through personal conversations or formally through performance evaluations. The information gained through these interactions can provide you with knowledge about how others perceive you, offering opportunities for improvement. For example, you might find that others perceive you as concentrating so strongly on the details that you lose sight of the overall mission with which you have been charged; or that your lack of participation in the organization's activities is viewed as a lack of interest in others. You might not always like the information that you learn through feedback and self-discovery, but that information can be quite valuable. The key is to use the newly acquired information to enhance your self-awareness, and your personal growth and competence.

Self-disclosure requires that we reveal ourselves to others through verbal or nonverbal means. We disclose our beliefs, values, and desires not only through conversation but also through artifacts and nonverbal communication. For example, the pictures that we have in our offices speak of our families, preferred landscapes, places we have traveled,

Career Stages and Anchors

FIGURE 3.6 DEVELOPING SELF-AWARENESS

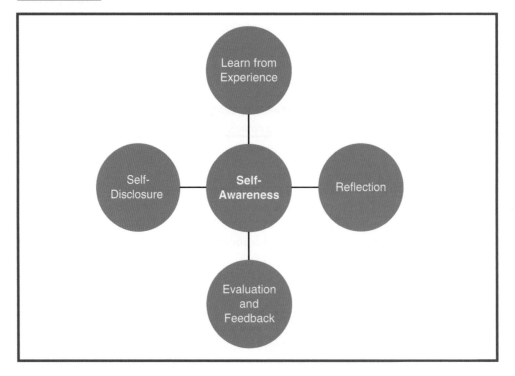

and so on. We become human by sharing our interests and desires with others. Self-disclosure also affects the way in which others see us. For example, studies have shown that people are more likely to trust leaders who are self-disclosing.[55]

To practice self-disclosure, spend an evening with a relative or close friend discussing the results of your personal assessment instruments and their implications. Your relative or friend might want to complete the instruments in this chapter as well. Use questions such as the following: Who am I? What are my values? What are my strengths? What are my weaknesses? What will be necessary for me to be happy in a career or in my personal life? What changes do I need to make in my life? What legacy do I want to leave?

Managers desperately need to be able to stop and think, to step back and reflect thoughtfully on their experiences. Some believe that events, or "happenings," become experience only after they have been reflected upon thoughtfully. Accordingly, most of us undergo events or happenings that are barely processed. These happenings become experiences once we process or digest them by reflecting on them and relating to other aspects of our lives.[56] This means going beyond introspection. It means looking in so that you can better see out in order to perceive a familiar thing in a different way—perhaps a product as a service or a customer as a partner.

Whatever its source, self-knowledge is essential to your productive personal and interpersonal functioning, especially in understanding and empathizing with others. Based on your experiences, feedback from others, information from the inventories, and your personal vision, are there skills and competencies that you would like to enhance? Did you gain knowledge that you will draw on in making important career decisions? What changes in your life do you want to make as a result of your increased knowledge?

Receiving feedback is one way you can further develop your self-awareness. Understanding how others perceive you can help you better understand your strengths and areas for improvement.

▶ Summary and Applications for Managers

Although strategies for learning about yourself and enhancing self-knowledge remain somewhat less fully developed than strategies for building cognitive knowledge and behavioral skills, there are several suggestions that you might consider.

1. *Focus on learning from your experience.* To learn from your experience, you must engage in self-reflection and self-critique. Your past experiences must be translated into an action agenda for personal development. Annual evaluations at work may be a good place to begin the journey, but other means also are available. These include asking or surveying others about your work performance as well as the attitudes and values you express.

2. *Keep a journal.* A journal allows you the opportunity to engage in self-reflection and self-critique over a sustained period of time. Writing in a journal also gives structure to your examination of events.

3. *Talk regularly with people you trust.* In addition to self-reflection and self-critique, the insights and support of trusted friends can be a great boost to developing your confidence and self-esteem.

4. *Find mentors.* In addition to friends, look for people you admire in your company or your professional network and ask them to mentor you. It is helpful to select more than one mentor and to rely on them for advice and support in areas in which each excels.

5. *Watch and read how others handle change.* Learning from the experiences of respected managers and leaders also is helpful. In the rapidly changing world in which we live, it is important to be able to handle change. Others who have been successful before us provide important lessons toward this end.

6. *Strive for balance and insight.* Although the pressure to perform might seem overwhelming, effective performance can be undermined by stress, which can be harmful to your health. Take time to relax and to participate in activities that are not work related. Relaxation will provide for renewed energy with which to improve productivity and creativity.

7. *Set an example.* As a manager, you should not only be concerned with developing your own maturity and self-confidence; you should also encourage and energize others to develop theirs. Such an understanding of yourself not only helps you as an employee but also can help the organization.

8. *Carefully examine the explanations that you give.* You might refuse an assignment by saying, "I am too busy to take on this assignment," when, in fact, the assignment simply might not be of interest to you. Although we all have aspects of our jobs that are less enjoyable, knowing our values and preferences can help us to make prudent job choices.

9. *Look for several causes.* When attempting to interpret behavior, look for various causes that might have triggered the behavior. For example, if someone takes too long to complete an assignment, do not be too quick to determine that the person was uninterested in completing the assignment in a timely manner. Perhaps the delay was due to faulty equipment, pressures from peers to complete other assignments, or other external forces.

10. *Account for individual differences.* Try to account for individual differences and do not overgeneralize or project your own preferences onto others. For example, you might like to be publicly recognized for your achievements, but a highly introverted employee might be quite embarrassed by such public recognition.

11. *Use past behavior as an indicator, but not necessarily a predictor, of future behavior.* How someone behaved in the past might indicate how he or she will behave in the future, but you should not ignore the possibility of change. For example, if someone has not been timely in producing necessary work, then you might assume that he or she will continue to delay the process. But the person might decide that it is in the best interest of everyone concerned to turn in the next assignment on time.

12. *Recognize personality differences.* Consider personality differences when selecting assignments. For example, proactive people will be much more internally motivated than others. If you are one of these individuals, then you might prefer to work in autonomous situations. On the other hand, if you are an externally motivated individual, then you might function best in team assignments.

13. *Celebrate diversity and the contributions diversity brings to the organization.* We are working in an environment with increasing differences in age, race, gender, nationality, political views, and religion. Rather than fearing or judging differences, evaluate how those differences may add to the organization.

▶ Key Terms

Abilities   75

Cognitive
knowledge   77

Conceptual skills   78

Emotional challenge   76

Emotional
dissonance   82

Emotional
intelligence   80

Emotional labor   82

Emotions   82

Feelings   82

Instrumental
values   89

Interactionist view   74

Interpersonal skills   78

Personality   76

Self-awareness   81

Self-management   81

Skills   75

Social skills   81

Technical skills   78

Terminal values   89

Values   76

▶ Exercise 3.1   Increasing Self-Knowledge

The focus of the exercise is to increase self-knowledge by using self-reported instruments and feedback from others.

A self-narrative is a narrative that makes a point about the narrator and increases self-knowledge. You will increase your self-knowledge by answering the following questions with the support of the methods and instruments in this chapter.

Where have I been? The timeline described earlier in the chapter will help in answering this question. Develop a 5- to 10-page autobiographical sketch that will assist you in improving your sense of self by reflecting on the past and how it will influence the future.

Where am I going? Develop interview guides and interview several individuals in positions to which you might aspire. Following are some examples of questions to include:

- How would you describe your typical day at work?

- What are the most critical skills you draw on during a typical workday?

- What qualities do you see as necessary for your line of work?

- If you had to find someone to replace you, on what key abilities would you focus?

Do I have what it takes in terms of ability, motivation, and personal traits to get there? This question may be answered through inventories or evaluations or through questioning others who are familiar with your abilities.

Do not be afraid to engage in self-disclosure. Several studies have shown that low self-disclosers are less healthy and more self-alienated than high self-disclosers.

Write out an action plan for implementation to help you accomplish your vision.

Work with close friends and colleagues to determine what your personal lifetime vision might look like. Try to focus on what you believe an ideal future would look like, or consider looking back on your life and career from an advanced age. What are the things that you would like to have done? Write your vision statement:

Write down a set of values that are important to you. Ask family members and friends to encourage you to live according to your values.

Describe key areas of your life that are important to you, and write down one or two goals in each major area.

Select one or two goals and imagine the goal(s) being achieved to your full satisfaction. How does this goal, or how do these goals, relate to your vision? Experience the achievement of your vision in every way possible.

Develop a detailed action plan to achieve this vision, and make commitments for particular actions necessary to bring your vision to fruition.

▶ Exercise 3.2   Valuing Diversity

In managing a diverse workforce, it is important that we understand our own feelings and the messages that we convey about our value of diversity. Reflect on how you and the organization that you work for react in terms of accepting differences and otherness.[57]

1. Do others see you acting comfortable around colleagues with nontraditional demographics (examples include others of a different age, education, ethnicity, gender, race)?

2. Do colleagues of nontraditional demographics provide evidence that they feel comfortable around you?

3. Do these same employees report that their differences are respected?

4. Do you actively solicit the opinions, feelings, and suggestions of all colleagues, regardless of demographics?

5. Do you receive a relatively equal amount of opinions, feelings, and suggestions from all employees?

6. Does the organization that you work for hire and promote in such a way that employee diversity reflects the diversity of society?

7. Do the organization's social activities reflect diversity?

8. Do the organization's fringe benefits reflect diversity?

9. Are there consequences for colleagues who engage in demeaning or prejudicial behavior toward others?

10. Does your organization maintain a committee charged with improving the working climate for all employees?

▶ Self-Assessment 3.4

REDDIN'S PERSONAL VALUES INVENTORY

Instructions for Answering

The inventory contains instructions for answering the statements. (Remember that there are no right or wrong values here.) Once you have completed the statements, score your answers using the form at the end of the survey. Be sure to add your subtotals to compute your total factor score. When you add up all of your factors, your score should equal 84. The highest scored factor is your preference. For example, if Factor F is your highest total factor score, then you are interested in the power of money and in reward for effort and personal gain. On the other hand, if Factor D is your highest factor score, then you place a higher value on people and relationships. Consider your scores and, if possible, discuss them with someone else.

Read the first set of three statements (A, B, C) and decide to what extent you agree with each. Assign exactly three points among the three statements. The more points you give a statement, the more you agree with it.

EXAMPLE 1: Suppose that you agree with Statement A but not at all with any of the others; then, you would distribute your points in this way:

STATEMENT A

STATEMENT B

STATEMENT C

A3	B0	C0			

EXAMPLE 2: Suppose that in another group of statements, you agree somewhat with Statement B, disagree with Statement C, and do not totally disagree with Statement A; then, you would distribute the three points this way:

STATEMENT A

STATEMENT B

STATEMENT C

A1	B2	C0			

Survey

1. A. Examples and events of history press down on the mind the weight of truth.

   B. As wealth is power, so all power will draw wealth to itself.

   C. Success is always achievement.

A	B	C			

2. A. By what means can the man please who has no power to confer benefits?

   B. A manager's only job is to be effective.

   C. What will money not do?

	A	B			C

3. A. The worst of faces is still human.

   B. Never put off to tomorrow what you can do today.

   C. Money answers all things.

			A	B	C

(Continued)

(Continued)

4. A. Everything includes itself in power.

   B. Life teaches us to be less severe with ourselves and others.

   C. It is pretty to see what money will do.

	A		B		C

5. A. Truth is always strange—stranger than fiction.

   B. It is not enough to do good; one must do it well.

   C. Work keeps at bay three great evils: boredom, vice, and need.

A		B		C	

6. A. The smallest atom of truth represents some man's bitter toil and agony.

   B. We never do anything well till we cease to think about the manner of doing it.

   C. All work is noble; work alone is noble.

A		B		C	

7. A. The father aims at power, the son at independence.

   B. The only way to have a friend is to be one.

   C. Money is indeed the most important thing in the world.

	A		B		C

8. A. All truths begin as blasphemies.

   B. The ornament of a house is the friend who frequents it.

   C. There are few sorrows in which good income is of no avail.

A			B		C

9. A. Disinterested intellectual curiosity is the lifeblood of real civilization.

   B. Labor conquers everything.

   C. Money is like a sixth sense—and you cannot make use of the other five without it.

A				B	C

10. A. God gives to some men despotic power over other men.

    B. He who attempts to do all will waste his life doing little.

    C. Instead of loving your enemies, treat your friends a little better.

	A	B	C		

11. A. A man of words and not of deeds is like a garden full of weeds.

    B. Man's happiness is to do a man's true work.

    C. If you mean to profit, you are wise.

		A		B	C

12. A. The only means of strengthening one's intellect is to make up one's mind about nothing.

    B. To know the pains of power, we must go to those who have it.

    C. If you have one true friend, you have more than your share.

A	B		C		

13. A. The prize of the general is not a bigger tent but command.

    B. The reasonable man adapts himself to the world; the unreasonable man tries to adapt the world to himself.

    C. No man is born into the world whose work is not born with him.

	A	B		C	

14. A. The highest intellects, like the tops of mountains, are the first to catch and reflect the dawn.

    B. A man should keep his friendship in constant repair.

    C. Work brings its own relief; he who is most idle has most of the grief.

A			B	C	

15. A. Man is a social animal.

    B. Actions speak louder than words.

    C. Wherever I found a living creature, there I found the will to power.

		A	B	C	

(Continued)

(Continued)

16. A. There are many wonderful things in nature, but the most wonderful of all is man.

     B. The shortest answer is doing.

     C. Irrationally held truths may be more harmful than reasoned errors.

		A	B		C

17. A. Every man's work is always a portrait of himself.

     B. To know the pleasure of power, we must go to those who are seeking it.

     C. To think is to live.

	A			B	C

18. A. Go to your work and be strong.

     B. The great end in life is not knowledge but action.

     C. Guns will make us powerful; butter will only make us fat.

	A		B	C	

19. A. The mind of a man is cheered and refreshed by profiting in small things.

     B. All work is as seed sown; it grows and spreads, and it sows itself anew.

     C. Life is not long, and too much of it must not pass in idle deliberation over how it shall be spent.

A	B		C		

20. A. There is no substitute for hard work.

     B. The highest duty is to respect authority.

     C. Knowledge is capable of being its own end.

A	B		C		

21. A. Ill blows the wind that profits nobody.

     B. Genius is 1 percent inspiration and 99 percent perspiration.

     C. Logical consequences are the scarecrows of fools and the beacons of wise men.

A	B				C

22. A. Time is money.

   B. The true science and study of mankind is man.

   C. Bustle is not industry.

A		B	C		

23. A. In all labor, there is profit.

   B. Human existence always is irrational and often painful, but in the last analysis it remains interesting.

   C. He who has the longest sword is the leader.

A		B		C	

24. A. Money speaks in a language that all nations understand.

   B. To cultivate kindness is a valuable part of life.

   C. A good catchword can obscure analysis for 50 years.

A		B			C

25. A. They say that knowledge is power, but they meant money.

   B. Every man is the architect of his own fortune.

   C. Make a model before building.

A			B		C

26. A. It is a bad bargain where nobody gains.

   B. In the country of the blind, the one-eyed man is king.

   C. It requires a very unusual mind to undertake the analysis of the obvious.

A				B	C

27. A. What we have to learn to do, we learn by doing.

   B. It is more blessed to give than to receive.

   C. Whatever is worth doing at all is worth doing well.

	A	B	C		

(Continued)

(Continued)

28. A. Doubt can be ended by work alone.

   B. To err is human, to forgive is divine.

   C. Power is a grand objective.

	A	B		C	

Values Inventory: Scoring

A_1 = 1A + 5A + 6A

= ___ + ___ + ___   = ___ = A_1

B_1 = 1B + 2A + 4A + 7A

= ___ + ___ + ___ + ___   = ___ = B_1

C_1 = 1C + 2B + 5B + 6B

= ___ + ___ + ___ + ___   = ___ = C_1

D_1 = 3A + 4B + 7B

= ___ + ___ + ___   = ___ = D_1

E_1 = 3B + 5C + 6C

= ___ + ___ + ___   = ___ = E_1

F_1 = 2C + 3C + 4C + 7C

= ___ + ___ + ___ + ___   = ___ = F_1

A_2 = 24C + 25C + 26C

= ___ + ___ + ___   = ___ = A_2

B_2 = 23C + 26B + 28C

= ___ + ___ + ___   = ___ = B_2

C_2 = 22C + 25B + 27C

= ___ + ___ + ___   = ___ = C_2

D_2 = 22B + 23B + 24B + 27B + 28B

= ___ + ___ + ___ + ___ + ___ = ___ = D_2

E_2 = 27A + 28A

= ___ + ___   = ___ = E_2

F_2 = 22A + 23A + 24A + 25A + 26A

= ___ + ___ + ___ + ___ + ___ = ___ = F_2

A_3 = 8A + 9A + 12A + 14A

= ___ + ___ + ___ + ___   = ___ = A_3

B_3 = 10A + 12B + 13A

= ___ + ___ + ___   = ___ = B_3

C_3 = 10B + 11A + 13B

= ___ + ___ + ___   = ___ = C_3

D_3 = 8B + 10C + 12C + 14B

= ___ + ___ + ___ + ___   = ___ = D_3

E_3 = 9B + 11B + 13C + 14C

= ___ + ___ + ___ + ___   = ___ = E_3

F_3 = 8C + 9C + 11C

= ___ + ___ + ___   = ___ = F_3

A_4 = 16C + 17C + 20C + 21C

= ___ + ___ + ___ + ___   = ___ = A_4

B_4 = 15C + 17B + 18C + 20B

= ___ + ___ + ___ + ___   = ___ = B_4

C_4 = 15B + 16B + 18B + 19C

= ___ + ___ + ___ + ___   = ___ = C_4

D_4 = 15A + 16A

= ___ + ___   = ___ = D_4

E_4 = 17A + 18A + 19B + 20A + 21B

= ___ + ___ + ___ + ___ + ___   = ___ = E_4

F_4 = 19A + 21A

= ___ + ___   = ___ = F_4

Note: The scoring sheet was developed by Donald Coons.

Scoring Interpretation

Add up your subtotals for all of the factors, and your score should equal 84. The highest single factor is your preferred value:

Factor A   *Theoretical:* Interested in ordering and systemizing knowledge, likes to reason and think, and is rational and analytical

Factor B   *Power oriented:* Interested in the use, implications, and manifestations of power

Factor C   *Achievement oriented:* Practical, efficient, and concerned with obtaining results

Factor D   *Human oriented:* Views people and relationships in a positive manner; a humanitarian

Factor E   *Industry oriented:* Likes to work and sees work as an end in itself

Factor F   *Financial oriented:* Interested in the power of money and in rewards for effort and personal gain

Source: From Reddin, W. J. (1978). *Values inventory.* La Jolla, CA: Learning Resources.

Case 3.1 Privatizing the Cafeteria

Ramon Smith is city manager of a midsize town in Louisiana. The city that he is managing has run its own cafeteria for many years. The staff has been with the city for 20 to 30 years and is in their 40s and 50s. The city's evaluation unit, at Ramon's request, has conducted a study showing that great saving would be available to the city by privatizing the cafeteria services. Ramon knows the staff well, and their level of skill would make it very difficult for them to attain jobs in the same industry with the pay and benefits that the city currently pays them.

Employing Kohlberg's model of moral development, answer the following questions:

1. What decisions would a city manager at the preconventional level be expected to make?

2. What reaction would you expect of employees at the preconventional level?

3. What decisions would a city manager at the conventional level be expected to make?

4. What reaction would you expect of employees at the conventional level?

5. What decisions would a city manager at the postconventional level be expected to make?

6. What reaction would you expect of employees at the postconventional level?

7. What reaction will you make as the city manager?

8. How will you explain your decision to the city council?

Case 3.2 Laura's Employment Dilemma

Laura Gomez just completed her MBA program at the University of Missouri. She entered the program as a midcareer student after spending 12 years as a clerk in a high-fashion design studio. During those 12 years, she worked in a financial office, where she found the work to be tedious and routine, a far cry from the exciting life she expected of the design studio. She wanted a change and thought that the best way of going into the job market was to have an MBA in hand. During her academic program, she concentrated on marketing. At home, she is a single parent with two children, 8 and 10 years of age. She feels a great deal of responsibility for her children and wants to be available to participate in their lives on a daily basis.

Laura has been interviewing, and with her experience and especially her education she has had several job offers. The first came from a management consulting firm in the Midwest. The management consulting firm is interested in more work in the retail sector, and Laura's experience in the design studio was viewed as highly valuable. The salary is higher than she had been expecting to receive as an entry-level MBA graduate. She would be expected to travel the Midwest approximately 80 percent of the time.

The second job offer came from a nonprofit organization in St. Louis, Missouri. This nonprofit has been in existence for about 5 years and now is in the position of hiring someone to handle all aspects of its finances, including fund-raising. Laura does not have experience in fund-raising but has been recommended to the organization as a quick learner. The salary is lower than what she was making before she returned to school 2 years ago. There are expectations that, with successful fund-raising, her salary would increase. The office location is 3 miles from her current residence. The job would require very little traveling.

The third job offer came from the federal government in Washington, D.C. In this position, Laura would be fully trained to work in evaluation for the Department of Health and Human Services. This is not an area in which she has worked before, but she is known to pay a great deal of attention to detail, to have good interpersonal skills, and to be a fast learner. The salary is higher than what she was making prior to entering the MBA program but not as high as that offered by the consulting firm in the Midwest.

You are Laura Gomez. Given what you know about yourself from information in this chapter, respond to the following questions:

1. Which position would you take? Why?

2. How does this fit with your preferences and values?

3. Is your choice different from that which you would recommend to Laura? If yes, then why?

---

⑤SAGE edge™

Sharpen your skills with SAGE edge at edge.sagepub.com/nahavandi

SAGE edge for students provides a personalized approach to help you accomplish your coursework goals in an easy-to-use learning environment.

▶ Endnotes

1. Snider, M. (2012). DreamWorks Animation CEO Katzenberg offers advice. *USA Today*, October 22. Retrieved from http://www .usatoday.com/story/tech/2012/10/22/ ceo-forum-dreamworks-jeffrey-katzenberg/1646191/ on November 13, 2012.

2. Borden, M. (2010, December/January). The redemption of an ogre. *Fast Company*, p. 106.

3. The world is us—Jeffrey Katzenberg zeitgeist Americas [Video]. (2012). *YouTube,* October 16. Retrieved from line at http://www.youtube .com/watch?v=kqlbz455_vk on November 13, 2012.

4. Ten minutes that mattered. (2010). *Forbes.com,* February 5. Retrieved from http://www.forbes .com/2010/02/04/disney-dreamworks-shrek-intelligent-technology-katzenberg.html on November 13, 2012.

5. Bryant, A. (2009). The benefit of a boot out the door. *New York Times—Corner Office*, November 7. Retrieved from http://www .nytimes.com/2009/11/08/business/08corner .html?_r=1 on March 2, 2010.

6. Bryant, 2009.

7. Amidi, A. (2012). Jeffrey Katzenberg says honoring employees is good business strategy. *Cartoon Brew*, May 30. Retrieved from http:// www.cartoonbrew.com/ideas-commentary/ jeffrey-katzenberg-says-honoring-employees-is-good-business-strategy-60131.html on November 14, 2012.

8. Johnson, W., Turkheimer, E., Gottesman, I. I., & Bouchard, T. J., Jr. (2009). Beyond heritability: Twin studies in behavior research. *Current Directions in Psychological Science, 18*(4), 217–220.

9. Seligman, M. E. P. (2011). *Flourish*. New York, NY: Free Press.

10. Seligman, 2011.

11. Mischel, W. (1973). Towards a cognitive social learning reconceptualization of personality. *Psychological Review, 80,* 252–283; Weiss, H. M., & Adler, S. (1984). Personality in organizational research. In B. Staw & L. Cummings (Eds.), *Research in organizational behavior* (Vol. 6, pp. 1–50). Greenwich, CT: JAI Press; Zhang, A., Ilies, R., & Arvey, R. D. (2009). Beyond genetic explanations for leadership: The moderating role of the social environment. *Organizational Behavior and Human Decision Processes, 110,* 118–128.

12. Holmer, L. L. (1994). Developing emotional capacity and organizational health. In R. H. Kilmann & I. Kilmann (Eds.), *Managing ego energy: The transformation of personal meaning into organizational success*. San Francisco, CA: Jossey-Bass.

13. Tjan, A. (2012). How leaders become self-aware. *Harvard Business Review—Blog Network*, July 19. Retrieved from http://blogs.hbr.org/tjan/2012/07/how-leaders-become-self-aware.html on November 13, 2012.

14. Denhardt, R. B., & Aristigueta, M. P. (1996). Developing intrapersonal skills. In J. L. Perry (Ed.), *Handbook of public administration*. San Francisco, CA: Jossey-Bass.

15. Hirst, G., Mann, L., Bain, P., Pirola-Merlo, A., & Richter, A. (2004). Learning to lead: The development and testing of a model of leadership learning. *The Leadership Quarterly, 15*, 311–327.

16. Armstrong, M. (2004). *How to be an even better manager: A complete A–Z of proven techniques & essential skills*. United Kingdom: Kogan Page.

17. Sternberg, R. J. (2007). A systems model of leadership. *American Psychologist, 62*, 34–42.

18. Rubin, R. S., Bartels, L. K., & Bommer, W. H. (2002). Are leaders smarter or do they just seem that way? Exploring perceived intellectual competence and leadership emergence. *Social Behavior and Personality, 30*, 105–118; and Gladwell, M. (2008). *Outliers: The story of success*. New York, NY: Little, Brown.

19. Carvell, T. (1998). By the way, your staff hates you. *Fortune, 138*(6), 200–212.

20. Kelly, K., & Marr, M. (2005, September 26). Boss-zilla. *Wall Street Journal*, p. A5, Europe edition.

21. Gawker. (2007). *New York's worst bosses*. Retrieved from http://gawker.com/243908/new-yorks-worst-bosses-scott-rudin on March 1, 2010.

22. Carvell, 1998, p. 201.

23. Goleman, D. (1995). *Emotional intelligence*. New York, NY: Bantam.

24. Gardner, L., & Stough, C. (2002). Examining the relationship between leadership and emotional intelligence in senior level managers. *Leadership & Organization Development Journal, 23*(1/2), 68–78.

25. Schwartz, N. D. (2001, January 22). What's in the cards for Amex? *Fortune*, pp. 58–70.

26. Colvin, G. (2009). Crisis chief: Amex's Chenault. *Fortune*, October 15. Retrieved from http://money.cnn.com/2009/10/14/news/companies/american_express_chenault.fortune/index.htm on March 1, 2010.

27. AmEx's Ken Chenault talks about leadership, integrity and the credit card business. (2005). *Knowledge@Wharton*, April 20. Retrieved from http://knowledge.wharton.upenn.edu/article.cfm?articleid=1179 on July 16, 2007.

28. Ashforth, B. E., & Humphrey, R. H. (1993). Emotional labor in service roles: The influence of identity. *Academy of Management Review, 18*, 88–115; and Hochschild, A. (1983). *The managed heart*. Berkeley: University of California Press.

29. Ekman, P., Friesen, W. F., & O'Sullivan, M. (1997). Smiles when lying. In P. Ekman & E. L. Rosenberg (Eds.), *What the face reveals: Basic and applied studies of spontaneous expression using the facial action coding system (FACS)* (pp. 201–216). London: Oxford University Press.

30. Lazarus, R. S., & Lazarus, B. N. (1994). *Passion and reason: Making sense of our emotions*. Oxford, UK, and New York, NY: Oxford University Press.

31. Jung, C. (1971). *Psychological types*. Princeton, NJ: Princeton University Press.

32. Tosi, H. L., Mero, N. P., & Rizzo, J. R. (2000). *Managing organizational behavior* (4th ed.). Malden, MA: Blackwell Business.

33. Tosi, Mero, & Rizzo, 2000, p. 50.

34. Barrick, M. R., & Mount, M. (1991). The five big personality dimensions and job performance: A meta-analysis. *Personnel Psychology, 44*(1), 1–76.

35. Poropat, A. E. (2009). A meta-analysis of the five-factor model of personality and academic performance. *Psychological Bulletin, 135*(2), 322–338; Seibert, S. E., & Kraimer, M. L. (2001). The five-factor model of personality and career success. *Journal of Vocational Behavior, 58*(1), 1–21; Caligiuri, P. M. (2000). The big five personality characteristics as predictors of expatriate's desire to terminate the assignments and supervisor-rated performance. *Personnel Psychology, 53*(1), 67–88.

36. Anderson, C., Spataro, S. E., & Flynn, F. J. (2008). Personality and organizational culture as a determinant of influence. *Journal of Applied Psychology, 93*(3), 702–710.

37. Matuson, R. (2012). The link between quietness and productivity. *Fast Company,* August 7. Retrieved from http://www.fastcompany.com/3000226/link-between-quietness-and-productivity on December 11, 2012.

38. Chester, A. (2005). Kenneth Chenault, AMEX CEO, speaks on leadership. *Wharton Journal,* March 28. Retrieved from http://media.www.whartonjournal.com/media/storage/paper201/news/2005/03/28/News/Kenneth.Chenault.Amex.Ceo.Speaks.On.Leadership-904135.shtml on July 14, 2007.

39. American Psychiatric Association. (2000). *Diagnostic and statistical manual of mental disorders-IV-Tr* (4th ed., text revision). Washington, DC: Author.

40. Brown, R., Budzek, K., & Tamborski, M. (2009). On the meaning and measure of narcissism. *Personality and Social Psychology Bulletin, 35*(7), 951–964.

41. Emmons, R. A. (1987). Narcissism: Theory and measurement. *Journal of Personality and Social Psychology, 52,* 11–17; Morf, C. C., & Rhodewalt, F. (2001). Unraveling the paradoxes of narcissism: A dynamic self-regulatory processing model. *Personality Inquiry, 12,* 177–196; and Raskin, R., & Hall, C. S. (1979). A narcissistic personality inventory. *Psychological Reports, 45,* 590.

42. Delbecq, A. (2001). "Evil" manifested in destructive individual behavior: A senior leadership challenge. *Journal of Management Inquiry, 10,* 221–226; and Rosenthal, S. A., & Pittinsky, T. L. (2006). Narcissistic leadership. *Leadership Quarterly, 17,* 617–633.

43. Crant, J. M. (2000). Proactive behavior in organizations. *Journal of Management, 26*(3), 436; and Seibert, S. E., & Kraimer, M. L. (2001). The five-factor model of personality and career success. *Journal of Vocational Behavior, 58*(1), 1–21; Li, N., Liang, J., & Crant, J. M. (2010, March). The role of proactive personality in job satisfaction and organizational citizenship behavior: A relational perspective. *Journal of Applied Psychology, 95*(2), 395–404.

44. Crant, 2000; Becherer, R. C., & Maurer, J. G. (1999). Proactive personality disposition and entrepreneurial behavior among small company presidents. *Journal of Small Business Management, 37*(1), 28–36.

45. Haden, J. (2012). 8 qualities of fearless entrepreneurs. *Inc.,* October 24. Retrieved from line at http://www.inc.com/jeff-haden/8-qualities-of-fearless-entrepreneurs.html?nav=next on December 11, 2012.

46. Kohlberg, L. (1971). From is to ought. In T. Mishel (Ed.), *Cognitive development and epistemology* (pp. 151–235). New York, NY: Academic Press.

47. See Wagatsuma, H., & Rosett, A. (1986). The implications of an apology: Law and culture in Japan and the United States. *Law and Society Review, 20*(4), 461-498; and Sidebotham, B. (2011). *A lesson on apology for soldiers and diplomats.* January 13. Retrieved from http://www.oprev.org/2011/01/apologizing-cross-culturally-is-most-challenging-feat/ on December 11, 2012.

48. See Zhang, H. (2001). Culture and apology: The Hainan Island incident. *World Englishes, 20*(30), 383–391; and Avruch, K., & Zheng, W. (2005). Culture, apology and international

negotiation: The case of the Sino-U.S. "spy plane" crisis. *International Negotiation, 10*(2), 337–354.

49. Maddux, W. W., Kim, P. H., Okumura, T., & Brett, J. M. (2012). Why "I'm sorry" doesn't always translate. *Harvard Business Review,* June. Retrieved from http://hbr.org/2012/06/why-im-sorry-doesnt-always-translate/ar/1 on December 11, 2012.

50. Maynard, M. (2010). An apology from Toyota's leader. *The New York Times,* February 24. Retrieved from http://www.nytimes.com/2010/02/25/business/global/25toyota.html on December 12, 2010

51. Maddux et al., 2012.

52. Schon, D. A. (1983). *The reflective practitioner: How professionals think in action.* New York, NY: Basic Books.

53. Ibarra, H., & Barbulescu, R. (2010). Identity as narrative: Prevalence, effectiveness, and consequences of narrative identity work in macro work role transitions. *Academy of Management Review, 35*(1), 135–154.

54. Kouzes, J. M., & Posner, B. Z. (1995). *The leadership challenge: How to get extraordinary things done in organizations.* San Francisco, CA: Jossey-Bass.

55. Gosling J., & Mintzberg, H. (2003, November). The five minds of a manager. *Harvard Business Review,* pp. 54–63.

56. Alinsky, S. (2010). *Rules for radicals.* New York, NY: Random House.

57. Adapted from Deep, S., & Sussman, L. (2000). *Act on it! Solving 101 of the toughest management challenges.* Cambridge, MA: Perseus, p. 33.

4

Perception and Attribution

LEARNING OUTCOMES

After reading this chapter, you will be able to:

1. Discuss the perception processes

2. Explain how culture affects perception

3. Present a three-stage model for understanding social perception

4. Highlight the factors that affect each stage of the perception process

5. Discuss the biases that affect perception and the difficulties of overcoming them

6. Present ways to manage perceptual biases

A Texas Woman CEO in the United Kingdom ▶

When Marjorie Scardino cracked the ultimate glass ceiling at Pearson PLC in 1977, she challenged well-established perceptions on both sides of the Atlantic. Scardino was the first woman to become CEO of a U.K. top 100 company, a conglomerate that owns the Financial Times newspaper, Penguin Books, Madam Tussaud's wax museums, several educational institutions in various countries, and half of The Economist. Pearson had over 17,000 employees at the time. Scardino's credentials were clearly not the usual credentials for the top executive of a British conglomerate. She is an Arizona-born Texan, a former rodeo-barrel racer, a lawyer, and a former journalist, and someone at the time with little experience running a major multibillion dollar global conglomerate.

But it worked. When Scardino took over, Pearson's returns on equity lagged far behind those of its competitors. Before she stepped down in 2012 after a 15-year tenure, Scardino's achievements included doubling the number of Pearson's employees, tripling its profits, seeing an increase in share prices of more than 80%, and transforming a sleepy company into a global powerhouse.[1]

How did this unlikely "outsider" rise to the top of a very conservative corporation based on another continent and become one of the most respected CEOs in the United Kingdom? After law school, Scardino joined the Associated Press in West Virginia. She then teamed up with her husband to start a Pulitzer–winning newspaper in Georgia. When the newspaper failed, the couple came to New York, where Scardino became CEO of the Economist's North American operations and later the CEO of the magazine's global operations, where she boosted earnings by 130 percent in just four years.[2]

Scardino admits to being aware of the skepticism she faced at Pearson: "I had analysts in on the first day and I could feel them thinking, 'Who is this person?' and I started wondering, 'Who is this person?'"[3]

There are things known and there are things unknown, and in between are the doors of perception.

—Aldous Huxley

> *What you see and what you hear depends a great deal on where you are standing. It also depends on what sort of person you are.*
>
> —*C. S. Lewis*
>
> *The more I see, the less I know for sure.*
>
> —*John Lennon*

But she moved quickly to establish herself and push the company forward. During her first week, she sent an e-mail of self-introduction to all 17,000 employees. "I do my best in an atmosphere of energy, some urgency, and a good amount of humor," she wrote. "I do not want to be associated with an organization that's not decent and fair."[4] After just seven months on the job, she announced her intention to double Pearson's market capitalization and sent the company's stock soaring. She promised: "There will be more changes. But for now our aim is to get every business to perform better."[5]

Scardino often wore a baseball cap at meetings and sprinkled colorful American slang throughout her communications. She clearly was not shy about getting attention. Pearson's chairperson called her "an enthusiast and enthuse."[6] Her egalitarian attitude, in contrast to traditional British reserve, made her decidedly approachable. Her style was described as a mixture of Boston blue stock, Southern good ol' girl, and dock-worker,[7] with a self-deprecating style.[8] Scardino, the feisty executive who says she learned from her failures—"I learnt that you can fail and you don't die"—is not ready to retire at 66: "I don't even use that word because, first of all, that's what old people do, and secondly, that's what you do after dinner."[9]

Marjorie Scardino's career and challenges illustrate the role of perceptions in organizations. She has had to cope with cultural and gender stereotypes and to manage people's perceptions in order to operate effectively in her role as leader of a major corporation. A key to her success has been understanding herself, others, and the world around her. As all leaders do, Scardino had to observe people and situations, gather information, interpret that information, and make decisions based on facts and on many subjective interpretations. To be effective, she had to manage how others viewed her. That's something all leaders and managers have to do.

Stereotyping
Muslims

We are constantly bombarded with so many cues from our environment that we cannot pay attention to them all. It may be pleasantly cool in the room where you are now sitting. You may have some music in the background and hear the hum of the air conditioner. The chair you are sitting on may be comfortable but your reading light insufficient. You will likely pay attention to some of these cues and ignore others. The world is not so much an objective reality, but is rather what we perceive it to be. This is especially true in social situations. A large majority of a leader's job involves sifting through information and deciding what is relevant and what is not, then acting based on those choices. People working with Scardino were undoubtedly distracted by her accent and even by the fact that she was a woman in what had always been a man's position. They had to decide whether those factors were important or not. They had to decide what was perception and what was reality. This chapter will explore the way we perceive other people, our organizations, and the world beyond.

WHAT STEREOTYPES DO YOU HOLD?

All of us have stereotypes of various groups. The stereotypes we hold depend on our culture, where we grew up, and many other influences from our family, friends, and personal experiences. The following self-assessment is designed to help you explore the stereotypes you hold, their sources, and their consequences.

1. Identify Your Stereotypes

Using the following table, identify several stereotypes that you hold about different groups; for each one, write down what you believe to be its source and any possible personal experience you have had that you think directly supports the stereotype. You should target stereotypes that you would like to change. One example is provided. Remember that this is a self-assessment, not to be shared with the class or your instructor; there are no right or wrong answers. The more honest you are, the more you will benefit from the exercise.

Stereotype	Source	Personal Experience
Example: • Asians are team members, not leaders.	• My grandfather always said that • I've learned about Asian cultures being community oriented • The business press always says they work well in groups	• My Chinese team member last semester was very quiet • Asian students rarely talk in class or try to take over team meetings • My friend's roommate is Asian and very quiet
• • •	• • • • •	• • • • •

How easy was it for you to remember your stereotypes? How easy is it to remember their source? How about the personal experiences?

2. Looking for Disconfirmation

For each of the stereotypes you listed in step 1, consider events or evidence that you have directly or indirectly experienced that contradict your stereotype. You may have to work hard at this step, as you are not likely to remember contradictory examples easily. Again an example is provided.

(Continued)

(Continued)	
Stereotype	**Disconfirmation**
Example	
• Asians are team members, not leaders	• The Chinese are leading the world in many areas of business • Asians are leaders and entrepreneurs in the high tech industry • The Japanese are courageous military leaders • Japan is one of the leading economies in the world • •

How easy was it to come up with disconfirming examples? Why is it so hard to remember disconfirming evidence and information? What can you do to start changing the stereotypes you hold?

Perception

Perception: the mental process we use to pay attention selectively to some stimuli and cues and not to others

Social perception: the process of gathering, selecting, and interpreting information about how we view ourselves and others

Closure: the process of filling in missing information to understand a stimulus

What Do You Think?

▶ Some people argue that giving many people in the organization impressive sounding titles helps them gain "presence" in their interactions with others and thus improves the work. Others say that only applies to certain industries. Others say it makes no difference anywhere. What do you think?

What Is Perception?

Perception is the mental process that we use to understand our environment, while **social perception** is the process of gathering, selecting, and interpreting information about how we view ourselves and others. Whereas perceiving the physical environment is relatively objective and testable, information about people is often subjective and open to interpretation. This makes social perception a subjective rather than objective process.[10] When we interact with others, there are many cues and signals that beg for our attention. We consider the way people dress; their facial and other physical characteristics; their tone of voice and accent; nonverbal behaviors; their eye contact with others; how often they smile; and the message they communicate. We cannot pay attention to everything at once, so we pick and choose what is important. A key part of a manager's job is to assess social situations, to pick and choose what is important and what is not, to evaluate people, and to act on that evaluation. The perception process is an essential part of managing people.

Perception Process

Because the perception process requires us to select, interpret, and use stimuli and cues, the process is subject to considerable error, a serious drawback. Take a few minutes to examine the images in Figure 4.1 and Figure 4.2. The drawings in the first figure are classical tests of physical perception. Did you make the same errors as most people? Even though we can measure the images objectively, and we know we are making errors in our perception, we are still not able to perceive the images accurately. In Figure 4.2, the corporate logos have hidden cues; but once you see them, you won't miss them again. What we see is subject to perception and therefore to error.

Another example that highlights the power of perception is shown in Figure 4.3. The figure demonstrates **closure**, which refers to how we fill in missing information to understand a stimulus. We know that the figures are a rectangle and a

FIGURE 4.1 COMMON PERCEPTION ILLUSIONS

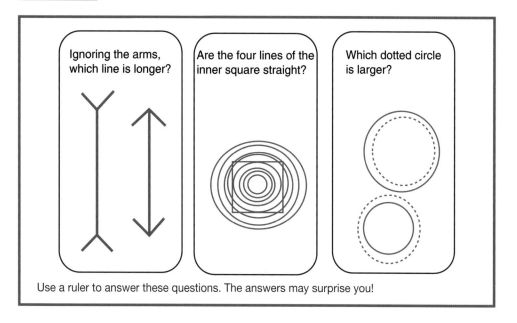

Ignoring the arms, which line is longer?

Are the four lines of the inner square straight?

Which dotted circle is larger?

Use a ruler to answer these questions. The answers may surprise you!

FIGURE 4.2 PERCEPTION AT WORK: WHAT DO YOU SEE IN THESE FAMOUS CORPORATE LOGOS?

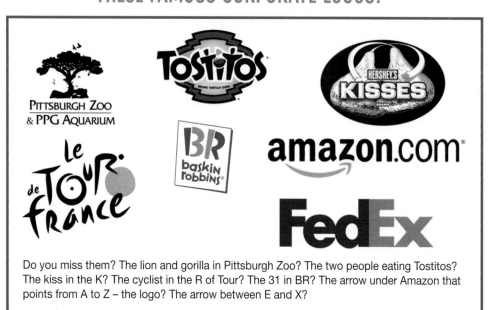

Do you miss them? The lion and gorilla in Pittsburgh Zoo? The two people eating Tostitos? The kiss in the K? The cyclist in the R of Tour? The 31 in BR? The arrow under Amazon that points from A to Z – the logo? The arrow between E and X?

triangle, although the lines are not complete. We complete them. Closure is a crucial part of the perception process. When we do not have all the facts—which is most of the time— we rely on assumptions to fill in missing information. Closure allows us to finish an unfinished picture or to interpret an unclear situation by completing it based on our previous experiences. Figures 4.1, 4.2, and 4.3 illustrate physical perception. However, similar processes affect social perception. We simply do not see everything and we fill in information as needed.

FIGURE 4.3 CLOSURE

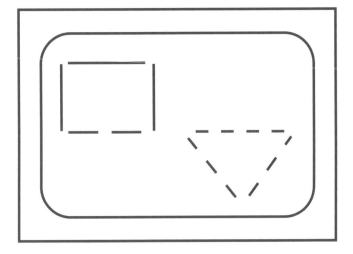

Consider how closure can affect a manager's evaluation of an employee. A manager who supervises 25 people has limited contact with each employee. Over the past six months, however, one customer has complained about a particular employee and the manager has personally observed a loud argument between the same employee and a supervisor from another department. When compared to everything else the employee may have done, these two samples of behavior are limited, but they are the most direct information the manager has and are the ones that stand out. Based on these two samples, and having little time to gather more information, the manager may use closure to fill in the picture and decide that the employee has a short fuse and the potential of being a troublemaker.

Culture and Perception

Culture includes the behavior, norms, values, and assumptions associated with a certain group. Culture, then, affects how we view the world and interpret events. All work-related behaviors—from your method of greeting others, to your style of work, the way you dress, how you resolve conflict, and how you provide feedback to your employees—are affected by culture.[11] Behaviors have meaning only within a certain cultural context. Once outside a familiar cultural context, people interpret what you say and do in different and unexpected ways.

For example, an Australian or American employee interprets a manager's admission that he does not know the answer to a question as an indication that the manager hasn't come across the situation before. He simply doesn't know the answer. In contrast, a French or Brazilian employee is more likely to interpret the manager's admitted lack of knowledge as incompetence. The interpretations differ because France and Brazil have cultures in which there is a higher power differential between managers and employees than in Australia or the United States. In high-power distance cultures, people with power are treated with high deference and expected to have corresponding knowledge. Simple behaviors that are perceived and interpreted one way in one culture are interpreted differently in another culture.[12] We see and interpret situations from our own cultural perspectives, and, not surprisingly, misperceptions are at the core of many cross-cultural communication problems. If managers or employees lack information or are unfamiliar with cross-cultural situations, they are likely to provide closure by relying on information and assumptions based on their own culture. And they may completely miss what is really happening.

Consider the example of a native of America, Ms. Thompson, who starts working for a large firm in Spain. Her boss, Mr. Rodriguez, meets with her on the first day. After lengthy greetings, Mr. Rodriguez inquires about Ms. Thompson's family, her father's and her grandfather's professions, her mother's family, and her siblings. He spends a considerable amount of time making what appears to Ms. Thompson to be irrelevant and inappropriate small

What Would You Do?

▶ You are interested in working for a company that does extensive business in Central and South American countries. You know that being fluent in Spanish will give you an edge. You are currently taking a Spanish course that will improve your basic conversational knowledge of the language. Since you expect to be somewhat fluent by the time you actually get the job, you are wondering if you should write in your résumé that you are fluent in Spanish.

Sorry
Doesn't
Translate

talk about her family and personal background, travels, personal interests, and her impressions of Spain. Ms. Thompson, who is experienced at interviewing and avoiding personal questions, carefully sidesteps all these inappropriate questions. The meeting lasts one hour without her having been told much about her assignments or Mr. Rodriguez's expectations. She is baffled. Mr. Rodriguez for his part is irritated and concerned that Ms. Thompson does not talk about her family and is evasive about her background. How does she expect to connect with people if they know nothing about her and her family? He cannot trust someone without knowing her personal background. Both individuals in this case perceive and interpret the situation from their own cultural perspective. Social and family ties are the key to the fabric of Spanish society[13] and therefore important to Mr. Rodriguez. Ms. Thompson, on the other hand, is used to the U.S. workplace where personal issues are not relevant and considered inappropriate. Mr. Rodriguez is simply trying to establish that his new employee has the essential and necessary family background to be trustworthy; Ms. Thompson, based on her cultural background, is appropriately avoiding these personal issues. From our outside view, it is obvious that the cultural misperceptions here are based on different cultural values and assumptions.

What Do You Think?

▶ You are a manager conducting the first 6-month performance review of an engineer in your department. He is from New Delhi, India, and where he studied in a well-regarded program. He married a U.S. student who was studying abroad in India and has been in the United States for less than one year. You have not had much time to interact with him and have heard neither positive nor negative things about him. While you are asking him a series of questions, he keeps looking down and seems to avoid making eye contact with you. This is making you uncomfortable. What do you think?

The Three Stages of Perception

Social perception is a multistage process, as presented in Figure 4.4. In the following sections, we examine each of the three stages and consider the factors that affect each.

FIGURE 4.4 THE THREE-STAGE PERCEPTUAL PROCESS

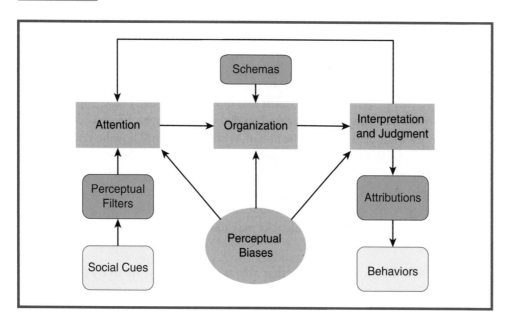

Our perception of others often depends on superficial things such as physical characteristics. Even how someone dresses can heavily impact how we view or judge others. Does your perception of the man on the right differ from your perception of the man on the left? How so?

Attention Stage

The first stage of social perception involves paying attention to signals from the environment. The **attention stage of perception** involves selection of stimuli, cues, and signals to which we will pay attention. What do we notice? What grabs our attention? For example, as your professor stops to read his notes for a moment in class, you suddenly pay attention to the keys he is jiggling in his pocket. That noise may then lead you to pay attention to his particularly ill-fitting baggy pants. Or, in a work situation, your new boss's Southern accent may be terribly distracting. Or an older manager may first notice her new employee's barely hidden tattoos and multiple piercings. In all these cases, something out of the ordinary grabs the attention of people and may distract them from their task.

In the attention stage of perception, we consciously or unconsciously select what we will pay attention to. The process of letting some information in while keeping out the rest is called the **perceptual filter**. At the core of the perceptual filter is **selective attention**—that is, we pay attention to some, but not all, physical and social cues. Many factors determine what makes it through our perceptual filter during the attention stage. Culture is one factor; another is salience.[14] **Salient cues** are those that in some way stand out. We use salient elements and cues more heavily than others in our perceptual process. In the examples above, the jingling keys and baggy pants, the Southern accent, and the tattoos and piercings all became salient.

Attention stage of perception: the selection of stimuli, cues, and signals to which we will pay attention

Perceptual filter: the process of letting some information in while keeping out the rest

Selective attention: the process of paying attention to some, but not all, physical and social cues

Salient cues: those cues that are somehow so striking that they stand out

What determines the salience of one cue as opposed to others? All else being equal, we pay attention to cues that are novel, unusual, brighter, more dynamic, or noisier than others. Factors that are visible and obvious are also likely to be more salient. For example, race, particularly skin color, can be a key factor in salience for some but not for others.[15] Similarly, a tattoo and piercings that may appear mundane to a 21-year-old may be unusual and therefore salient for the older manager. A new employee is novel by definition, particularly in a department that does not hire many new employees. The other employees' attention will be focused on that new employee. For a while, everyone will remember what he wore, how he talked, what he said, and how he reacted. Similarly, women and minorities still stand out in some situations and therefore receive more attention than others. When a person is the salient element in the environment, he gets caught in everybody's perceptual filter and therefore gets attention. Similar behaviors from other employees are likely to go unnoticed, but everyone sees the new person. In such a case, the smallest slipup or mistake may damage the new person's future in the organization.

Intensity of stimuli is another factor that affects salience. You are likely to pay attention to a loud voice, a brightly colored shirt, or someone's strong perfume. For example, those who wear brightly colored clothes are more likely to be remembered after a meeting—though not always positively.[16] Cultural differences may also make events stand out in our minds. For instance, standing close to others during conversation is considered normal in Middle Eastern and Mediterranean cultures. These behaviors go unnoticed in those regions. However, the same behavior is, for the most part, unusual in the United States where people feel uneasy if a coworker stands too close while talking to them or touches their arm or shoulder during a conversation. That coworker's behavior is salient, which means it is something that you are likely to pay attention to and remember.

In all these examples, we remember people and make decisions about them because they stand out. Their salience gets them trapped in our perceptual filter. This does not mean that you should necessarily work at making yourself salient so others can remember you better. People may remember you better, but they may also evaluate you in more extreme ways.[17] Once information grabs our attention, we need to organize the cues and information in meaningful sets that we can use later.

Organization Stage

The second stage of the perception process is **organization**. During this stage we organize the information that our filters have allowed through. We group information into meaningful, orderly, and useful sets. We assign new information to categories that already exist and are familiar to us; we create relationships among the various parts; create new sets; and put things into bundles that we can remember.

Schemas

The major process at work in this stage is the use of schemas.[18] **Schemas** are mental or cognitive models or patterns that people apply to understand and explain certain situations and events. They are frameworks that allow us to fill in information in social settings. For instance, people use schemas in the closure process to help complete incomplete pictures. Although we may be aware of some of the schemas we hold, they usually operate at a subconscious level.

Schemas at Work

Here's an illustration of the schema process. We all have schemas about what happens on the first day of a new job. You'll meet with your new boss and coworkers, get a tour of the department or building, be introduced to others, and be given information about the job and assignments. You expect a light work day with a lot of information overload. The schema about "the first day at a new job" tells you what is "normal" and what is not. Based on this schema, you can determine whether anything unusual takes place. Not meeting with your boss (who sat in her office all day and never acknowledged you) or being given a stack of work without any introduction would suggest something negative because it violates the expectations set by your first-day schema.

Schemas are useful in that they allow us to process information quickly. They help us remember details and complete gaps in what we perceive. Using schemas makes us very efficient information organizers, and, for that reason, they allow us to remember people and events better. On the negative side, schemas can lead to error: We use closure too quickly to fill in information we do not have and come to a hasty conclusion. (The advantages and disadvantages of schemas are summarized in Table 4.1.) Think back to the

Holding a Gun

Organization stage of perception: the organization of information that the perceptual filter has allowed through during the attention stage

Schemas: mental patterns that people apply to understand and explain certain situations and events

GLOBAL SOCIETY   HEINEKEN'S PR CHALLENGE

How does a Dutch beer maker find itself entangled in a dog fighting event in Mongolia? The wonders of instant viral communication!

Heineken is a century and half-old Dutch beer company with 70,000 employees in 71 countries and over 250 international, regional, local, and specialty beers, including Amstel Light and Dos Equis, and other beverages that cater to a global market. It calls itself the world's most international brewer and carefully manages its image by selecting events and partners to showcase its brands. It most recently sponsored the latest Bond movie, Skyfall, and actively participated in a global campaign to reduce the harmful effects of alcohol. The company emphasizes respect for individuals, the cultures and the communities where it operates, and relies on a clear code of ethics.[19] In spite of the careful image and culture building, Heineken was surprised when a picture of an organized dog fighting event in a night club in Mongolia showed up on the Internet with Heineken banners in the background in April of 2012.

The picture quickly went viral and animal rights activists and many others all over the world called for a boycott of Heineken. Social media was buzzing with denunciations and cries of outrage. One Facebook user stated: "I'm not having anything to do with your product or events you sponsor—anywhere—until you sort this out. Disgraceful!"[20] It took Heineken some time to confirm the veracity, and even the location of the picture, which was taken almost a year prior, and then find the venue to investigate why its banners where so clearly visible next to a dog fighting ring. It was finally clarified that the company had sponsored an event, unrelated to dog fighting, in the same nightclub the evening before, and that the banner had not been removed.

The response from Hieneken was strong: "We fully understand the level of negative feeling amongst consumers based on what they have seen. We encourage our consumers to continue to use social media channels to alert us to any situation where they feel our brands are being misrepresented, so that we can take the appropriate actions."[21] The company further moved to cut all relationships with the venue where the fight had occurred and reiterated that: "As a company and a brand owner, we do not and would never knowingly support any event, outlet or individual involved in this type of activity. It is against our company and brand rules and—more important—against our company values."[22]

The controversy was a reminder of the challenges that today's companies face from events all over the world over which they have limited control. A carefully developed and managed image and reputation can quickly go up in smoke due to a viral campaign. Constant vigilance and preparation to expect the unexpected are part and parcel of managing in a global world. Heineken's success in dealing with this crisis was due to its quick response and to putting a strong, very human face on its apology, a response that addressed the concerns of its large, global customer base.

1. How does culture impact perceptions?

2. What can managers do to avoid misperceptions based on culture?

first-day-on-the-job example. You may interpret the boss's failure to greet you and your getting work without explanation as negative and as an indication of a cold workplace. But your boss and coworkers may have been dealing with a major crisis that day and simply did not have time to chat with you.

TABLE 4.1 SCHEMAS IN THE BALANCE

Disadvantages of Schemas	Advantages of Schemas
May lead to over-interpretation	Efficient way to organize information
Ignores information that does not fit	Provides information
Hard to change	Helps us remember

Another disadvantage of schemas is that they resist change. This resistance is due in part to our lack of awareness of the schemas we hold—we cannot change something we do not know exists. Another problem is that even when we are aware of schemas, we are not willing to give them up easily. If you have several years of good work experience, you have already formed schemas of appropriate boss-employee relationships, the way coworkers are supposed to behave, and the way leaders are supposed to behave. You have developed those schemas over a long period of time and you consider them effective. But that might also mean that you find it difficult to accept anything that is different from what you are used to. Facing situations that do not fit our schemas often requires us to spend extra energy and creates some stress, until we can interpret the information that does not fit correctly.

Schemas and Culture

Our schemas for various situations and events are greatly influenced by our cultural background.[23] In the northeastern part of the United States, interaction among people tends to be more formal and businesslike. In southern states, social hospitality and politeness are the norm. A Southerner working in New York City may find her coworkers cold and rushed; a New Yorker in Arkansas may feel that people are not moving fast enough and spending too much time on useless greetings and niceties. Crossing international borders leads to further challenges, as you may remember from the example of Ms. Thompson in Spain.

In many parts of the world, formal interaction, respect for authority, and the presence of clear status symbols characterizes the boss-employee schema. An employee in India calls her boss by his last name and shows him many signs of respect and deference. Because typical U.S. schemas are based on more informal work relationships, the U.S. employee working in India who does not defer to the boss and uses first names is likely to appear rude. His behavior does not fit in the Indian schema of proper boss-employee relationships. Similarly, the U.S. schema about smiling differs from those of others culture. In the United States, smiling is a sign of friendship and indicates a person's degree of niceness and happiness. In many Asian cultures, smiling, especially for men, can indicate a lack of seriousness or respect. The Korean proverb "The man who smiles a lot is not a real man" spotlights how the Korean smiling schema contrasts with beliefs in some Western cultures.

Different organizations with different corporate cultures also create different schemas regarding what is and is not expected and acceptable. For example, joking, being goofy and playful and very informal is part of the culture of Southwest Airlines. Those flying regularly with Southwest are used to the flight attendants singing safety instructions, cracking jokes, and playing tricks on passengers, all behaviors that are a reflection of the values of the company. Having fun, enjoying yourself, and not taking yourself too seriously are part of the stated culture.[24] Part of a job interview at Southwest is to ask candidates to tell jokes—not a likely event in most other airlines in the world.

Shaping Work
Perceptions

Southwest Airlines Advertising Specialist Lindsey Bailey poses inside the engine at a launch party at Southwest Airlines headquarters at Love Field in Dallas. Southwest Airlines is known for its fun and friendly culture.

When interacting with others, we need to be aware that our schemas are likely to affect our perception. Some information fits into existing schemas and is quickly organized and stored away. Other information may not fit an existing schema. This may lead to the creation of a new schema, or may cause what does not fit to be forgotten because it contradicts what we already know and we may have no ready-made category to help us store it. For example, many women have experienced making statements and suggestions in meetings and their male colleagues either not remembering those suggestions or attributing them to male colleagues.[25] The traditional schema of women being less competent, able to deal only with people, and maybe not fully belonging in the workplace, is still operating for many people and prevents them from remembering when women make contributions. Even Marjorie Scardino faced such stereotypes when her successes were attributed to male executives who reported to her!

Interpretation and judgment stage: the clarification and translation of organized information to allow for the attribution of meaning

Interpretation and Judgment Stage

In the third part of social perception, the **interpretation and judgment stage**, we clarify and translate information we have organized so we can decide on its meaning (see Figure 4.5). Through interpretation, we make a judgment or form an opinion about the event or the person and we decide the cause of the behavior. This process is critical in organizations where a manager's job involves evaluating employees, customers, suppliers, and various business partners. For instance, you observe that your new employee is polite and friendly to the people she meets and spends time getting to know them. You wonder whether she is simply behaving as most people would when they start a new job or whether she is a particularly nice and outgoing person. To decide, you need to assign a cause to her behavior, a process we discuss next.

FIGURE 4.5 ## THE INTERPRETATION AND JUDGMENT STAGE: ATTRIBUTIONS

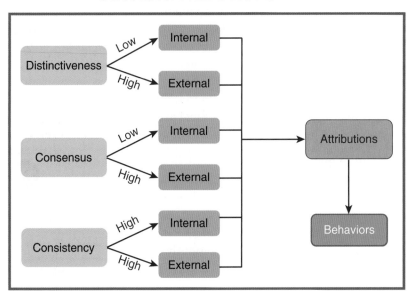

The Attribution Process

The process of inferring and assigning a cause to a behavior is called the **attribution process**.[26] One of the first steps in the attribution process involves deciding whether the cause of a behavior is internal or external (see Figure 4.5). If you make an **internal attribution**, you attribute the cause of behavior to factors within the control of or "inside" the person. These are factors that are permanent and stable (such as personality, values, or natural ability) or less permanent (such as effort or motivation). Because internal attributions refer to the person, they are also called personal attributions. For example, you would say: "Mary is late for work because she is lazy," or "Sergio did well on the exam because he worked hard." We make **external attributions** when we think that factors "outside" the person are the cause of behavior. These are factors such as the physical setting, task difficulty, the organizational culture, the presence and behavior of other people, or luck. Because external attributions refer to the situation as the cause of behavior, they are also called situational attributions. An example would be: "Mary is late for work because she has to drop her child off at day care," or "Sergio did well on the exam because it was easy."

Attributions are a central factor in any social perception process. In managerial situations, most decisions regarding people require managers to make attributions about the cause of behavior (see Figure 4.5). For example, when interviewing a potential employee, managers need to decide whether the person has real talent and potential—an internal attribution, or whether he is simply well prepared for the interview—an external attribution. The same attribution process operates in performance reviews. While some performance data may be objective, it is still subject to some interpretation. Is the high performer bright and hardworking (internal attributions) or just lucky to have landed a big client through pure coincidence (an external attribution)? What about the employee who had a bad year? Was it for lack of effort or ability, or because of a tough territory or uncooperative coworkers?

Deciding the cause of behavior—making attributions—is essential in the manager's decision about what to do about an employee's good or bad performance. A manager might not rank a performer who had top results in an easy territory as high as a person whose performance results were slightly lower but worked very hard and had a tougher assignment. The poor performer who did not try will be rated more harshly than the equally poor performer who tried hard but lacked the necessary training to do the job well. All personnel decisions regarding raises, training, promotions, discipline, and so forth similarly require managers to make attributions.

As demonstrated by the examples, effort and ability are used in internal attributions, while task difficulty and luck are the major factors used in external attributions.[27] Managers, just like all of us, are likely to overuse internal attributions and underutilize external ones.[28] For example, managers evaluating employees are more likely to assume that lack of ability or effort and motivation are the cause of poor performance. They are much less likely to attribute poor performance to situational factors, such as lack of training, poor support from other employees, poor equipment, or even their own poor leadership.

Information We Use to Make Attributions

When making either internal or external attributions, we use three types of information: distinctiveness, consensus, and consistency[29] (see Figure 4.5).

Causal Attribution Theory

Attribution Theory

Attribution process: the process of assigning or attributing a cause to a behavior or event

Internal or personal attribution: the process of assigning a cause to a behavior that is related to internal factors within a person

External or situational attribution: the process of assigning a cause to a behavior that is related to factors external to the person

- First, we consider whether the behavior we are evaluating is unique or *distinctive* to a particular task or situation. Does the person behave like this in all situations? If yes, then we are likely to attribute the cause of the behavior to the person. If not, then we may consider situational causes. To show how this factor applies in an organizational setting, a manager evaluating his employees would look at the distinctiveness of the employees' performance histories. Do they perform as well at all tasks or is the good performance unique and specific to computer-related tasks? If the performance is specific to one or a few tasks and therefore distinctive to a situation, an external attribution is more likely.

- The second factor in making attributions is *consensus*. Does everybody act the same way or is the person acting in a particularly unusual way? Did everyone in the poor performer's team have trouble with a new process or is the employee in question the only one? If others behave similarly, meaning that there is consensus, we are likely to make an external attribution.

- The last factor is *consistency*, whether there is a consistent pattern of behavior. Depending on what is consistent, we may make either internal or external attributions. If there is no consistency, we have trouble making any kind of judgment; high consistency is needed in order to make an attribution. A manager would have trouble making an attribution about an employee whose performance is highly inconsistent from one month to the next and from task to task.

Attributions we make about others' behavior determine our own actions. If a manager attributes poor performance to lack of training rather than lack of effort, she is likely to be less critical and offer a constructive course of action. Although the process of making attributions about others is somewhat similar to that of making attributions about our own behaviors and actions, there are several key differences.

Making Attributions About Our Own Behavior

Attributions and Actions

Although we have access to more information about ourselves than we do about others, researchers have found that we tend to follow the same patterns to decide the cause of our own behaviors as we do to decide why others behave as they do.[30] We consider our actions and behaviors and deduce our intentions and attitudes from them. This concept, known as **self-perception theory**, refers to people's tendency to look for internal and external factors when asked to explain the cause of their own actions.[31] Self-perception suggests that we do not always behave intentionally or consciously know the cause of our own behavior. Instead, we do something, and then we try to figure out why we did it.

Self-perception theory: a theory suggesting that people make attributions about themselves by looking at their behavior

The self-perception theory of attribution leads to some interesting results. Consider how we explain our action when we're rewarded for what we did. For example, how would a professional basketball player who gets a large bonus for playing well explain his performance? Would he say he really loves the game or attribute his performance to the high bonus? How would the employee who often volunteers to help other coworkers without getting any tangible reward explain her behavior? Interestingly, when we receive high tangible external rewards for our actions, such as money or public recognition, we are more likely to see the external reward as the cause of our behavior. Conversely, when there are no clear external rewards, we tend to attribute our behavior to internal causes. The top designer is more likely to tell you that she worked hard because of the bonus rather than the love of her job. The helpful employee who gets no obvious reward will tell you that he really enjoys helping others. The tendency to make external attributions about our own behavior when an external reward is given is called overjustification.[32]

Overjustification has many implications for managers. It suggests that giving people substantial external rewards for doing tasks they enjoy may reduce their internal motivation to do the task. If the reward is large and important enough, people are likely to make an external attribution—that is, they see the reward rather than their internal motivation as the cause of their actions. As a result, their internal motivation to perform may be reduced and they may be less likely to perform as well, unless they keep receiving the high rewards. This process may provide one explanation for the low performance of some star athletes, who seem to put forth little effort, in spite of high salaries. The implications of overjustification are that, whenever possible, managers should emphasize internal factors and make them salient to maintain employees' internal interests and motivation. High public recognition and reward can provide short-term results, but they may backfire in the long run.

Because we act on the basis of our attributions about others and ourselves, it is essential that our attributions be as objective as possible. Misjudging an employee may have serious legal, ethical, and performance-related consequences. It is important that managers hire, promote, demote, reward, and fire the right people for the right reasons.

Perceptual Biases

As you saw in Figures 4.1 and 4.2, our perception can be inaccurate and incomplete. We pay attention to some but not all information, we use closure and schemas to be quick and to organize information, and we make interpretations and judgments that are subject to biases and errors. These errors are, to a large extent, a normal and inevitable part of the physical and social perceptual processes. However, we can manage specific perceptual errors. In the following section, we identify several common perceptual biases, the difficulty in overcoming them, and ways to manage them.

Our perceptual abilities allow us to process a vast amount of information quickly and efficiently. However, this efficiency often leads to ineffective decisions because we do not process the information thoroughly or correctly. Instead we often take cognitive shortcuts, such as ignoring information that does not fit our expectations or making assumptions based on perceptions rather than objective facts. The shortcuts we use to be efficient and that can create distortions are called **perceptual biases** (see Table 4.2 for a summary). These, in turn, lead to mistakes in judgment. When these biases operate, we stop gathering information and instead rely on our assumptions to fill in the missing information.

What Would You Do?

▶ Anita has been at her job for three years. She has not been the highest performer, but she has received consistently good evaluations. She is part of a 30-person department with just one supervisor. Anita has applied for a promotion. While reviewing her file, her manager notices occasional mentions of less-than-average performance in a few tasks. One is related to dealing with customers; another is related to some budget issues; a third has to do with a poorly done report. The manager is wondering what is going on. Should she consider Anita for a promotion? What would you do?

Fuzzy Attribution Styles

How Perceptions Shape Our Lives

Overjustification: the tendency to make external attributions about our own behavior when an external reward is given

Perceptual biases: distortions in perception, often caused by cognitive shortcuts, and that lead to mistakes

TABLE 4.2 PERCEPTUAL BIASES

Biases	Description
Fundamental attribution error	The tendency to underestimate situational factors and overestimate personal factors when making attributions about others' actions
Actor-observer difference	The tendency to rely more on external attributions when explaining our own actions
Stereotypes	A generalization about an individual based on the group to which the person belongs
Halo or horn effect	Use of a one characteristic to create a positive or negative impression that dominates other information
Similar-to-me effect	Developing a liking for a person that we perceive is similar to us and disliking those who are different
Primacy and recency	A tendency to overemphasize either early information—in the case of primacy, or most recent information—in the case of recency
Self-serving bias	The tendency to accept credit for success and reject blame for failure

Fundamental Attribution Error

Fundamental
Attribution Error

We mentioned earlier our tendency to underestimate situational factors and overestimate personal factors when making attributions about others' actions. This tendency is called the **fundamental attribution error**.[33] For example, if your boss is unresponsive, you are more likely to blame the behavior on his lack of interpersonal skills or on his being distant and cold than on the pressures he is facing or how overloaded he is. Similarly, you are more likely to attribute the uncooperative behavior of a fellow manager to her personality rather than to a lack of time. These attributions lead us not to give people the benefit of the doubt.

The fundamental attribution error can have serious consequences. Because of this bias, we often make an incorrect internal attribution about people who are victims, blaming them for what happens to them. For example, in the much publicized case of the Floridian teenager, Trayvon Martin, who was shot by a self-appointed neighborhood watchman, the fact that Trayvon was wearing a hoodie became the focus, overshadowing many of the critical issues in the case.[34] In perceiving others, we tend to focus on internal factors.

Fundamental attribution error: the tendency to underestimate situational factors and overestimate personal factors when making attributions about others' actions

Actor-observer difference: the tendency to rely more on external attributions when explaining our own actions

But the fundamental attribution error works in reverse when we are looking for causes of our own behavior. When we explain our own actions, we rely more on external attributions. This process is called the **actor-observer difference**.[35] While we tend to make internal attributions about the behavior of others and often fall prey to the fundamental attribution error, we tend to make external attributions about our own behavior. The reason for this difference is that access to different types of information leads to different perspectives. In contrast to what others perceive, we have information about our own history and how we behave in different situations. As a result, we have views of the distinctiveness and consistency of our own behavior that are likely to differ from observers' views. Because of the different perspectives, environmental factors are more salient to the actor than to the observer, so an actor is more likely to make external attributions.

Consider the case of a relatively new employee who has just had a run-in with a client. The employee knows from his prior encounters with other clients in previous jobs that this particular client is unusually rude, difficult, and overly demanding. The employee has been in sales for many years and has rarely run into this type of trouble. He also knows that his father's recent illness has created a lot of stress for him and contributed to his uncharacteristic lack of patience. The employee knows that his behavior is distinctive to this situation. From his point of view, the client's rudeness is the focus. These factors all lead the employee to decide that the cause of the problem is the client, an external attribution, not himself.

The situation looks different to his boss. She does not yet have extensive information about her new employee's style or performance. Because the client has complained about the employee's lack of responsiveness, her attention will be focused on the complaint and the employee. Another factor that could affect her perception is that clients rarely call to complain. The manager who observes the situation makes an internal attribution about the cause of the employee's behavior. She may decide that he is inexperienced and needs training or that he is impatient and not well suited for this type of job (both internal attributions.)

The example illustrates how the actor-observer difference and the fundamental attribution error can lead to poor judgment, disagreement, and misunderstanding. Awareness of the bias, however, can help managers avoid these pitfalls. Managers can also take extra steps to overcome the bias. In our case, for instance, the employee and the manager could resolve their differences with an exchange of information, more objective data collection, good listening, and more experience working together.

Perception and stereotypes played a key role in the Trayvon Martin case. Something as simple as a hoodie, which Martin was wearing the night he was shot, can impact how we view others.

What Would You Do?

▶ You have a brilliant jerk in your office, smart, insightful, but overly self-centered and, to be honest, supremely annoying. What would you do?

Stereotypes

A **stereotype** is a generalization about an individual based on the group to which the person belongs. Such groups may include race, gender, sexual orientation, functional area, and so forth. Stereotypes are so powerful that they can prevent us from recognizing individual differences and performance. For example, research shows that the majority of the U.S. population still has negative views of African Americans and Hispanics.[36] Other recent research suggests that the color of a political candidate's skin continues to affect voters' decisions.[37] Similarly, women managers continue to be viewed as primarily able to deal with people well,[38] while other studies indicate that people generally fail to give female managers credit for their accomplishments.[39]

Why do stereotypes operate? The main reason is that they allow us to become fast and efficient information processors. Based on our stereotypes, we can quickly select information we will pay attention to in making a judgment about the person. We therefore

Shrewd GA
Business Woman

Stereotype: a generalization about an individual based on the group to which the person belongs

do not have to continue gathering information and can concentrate on the many other stimuli that beg for our attention. But although stereotypes help us process information quickly, they compromise effectiveness and accuracy. Once formed, stereotypes are resistant to change.

How do stereotypes operate? If a stereotype is activated in the attention stage, we use it as the basis of our perception and stop gathering information. Because we stop paying attention, we fail to notice information that may contradict the stereotype. Stereotypes also influence the way we interpret and judge a person. For instance, a commonly held stereotype of the Asians is that they are good followers and team members, but not good leaders. If you rely on this stereotype, you are likely to stop collecting information about the leadership behaviors that your Asian employee is demonstrating. Instead, you may start searching for information that confirms her excellent team behaviors. Think back on the exercise at the beginning of this chapter. Your stereotypes are likely to make it easy to remember information and examples that confirm them, but it may be harder for you to remember disconfirmatory evidence. How can you change if you simply do not have the right data?

Consider the challenges that Marjorie Scardino of Pearson faced. She used to be a rodeo-barrel racer, then moved to newspaper publishing to the *Economist* to CEO of a global conglomerate. Since her first day, the British newspapers questioned her credentials and her fitness for the job. Some questioned how a mother of three had time to run a major British company. Others poked fun at her spouse, calling him the "househusband." People even attributed several of her successful decisions to male executives in the company rather than to Scardino's creativity and strategic skills. Scardino fought back against the stereotypes with disarming humor and excellent people-management skills.[40]

Halo-Horns and Similarity Effects

The halo-horn effect is another bias that usually affects perception during the attention and organization stages.[41] The **halo effect** occurs when a general impression or evaluation of one characteristic of a person or situation creates either a halo, a positive impression, or horns, a negative impression, that becomes the central factor around which all other information is selected, organized, and interpreted. For example, a study in the United Kingdom indicates that a person's first name can have a significant impact on how the person is perceived. Another example is when someone is introduced as an "Apple" or "Google" employee. Because of the reputation of these companies, we are likely to quickly form an impression of the person.

A powerful factor that can create a halo or horns is the "similar-to-me" effect.[42] The **similar-to-me** effect occurs when we develop a liking for a person that we perceive is similar to us and dislike those who are different. A lack of similarity can be very serious in a cross-cultural situation when the other person is bound to be different, and as a result, potentially disliked.

Halos and horns are triggered automatically as we interact with people. As with other biases, they are not easy to avoid. Being aware of how halos or horns operate and understanding their effect on our perception is one of the best defenses. If we allow them to operate, we will fail to see individual differences in people with whom we work, thereby clouding our judgments about others' behavior.

Halo Effect

Halo effect: a bias that occurs when a general impression or evaluation of one characteristic of a person or situation creates a positive impression that becomes the central factor around which all other information is selected, organized, and interpreted

Similar-to-me: developing a liking for a person that we perceive is similar to us and disliking those who are different

Primacy and Recency

Do you believe that first impressions are important? If you do, you are correct. The importance of early impressions is called the **primacy effect**. It refers to a tendency to overemphasize early information. People tend to remember early information and it tends to color their later perceptions. The early information provides an organizing structure that influences other perception stages. In some cases, the first impression becomes a halo or horns that affects later information gathering and interpretation of a person's behavior. Shawn Graham, partner in a marketing brand strategy company, believes that the first impression you make on your new boss is essential: "I've got to be on my best behavior **because the way I present myself early (both good and bad) could typecast me for months to come.**"[43]

The primacy effect suggests that the new employee who makes a bad mistake will have difficulty overcoming it. As a matter of fact, research indicates that most of us form a strong and long-lasting impression in the first few minutes we meet someone. The flip side of the primacy effect is the **recency effect**, whereby we pay attention to the most recent information at the expense of earlier data. The recency effect takes place most often when there is a time lag between the early and later information. For instance, consider a manager who has not had much contact with an employee during recent months. The manager is likely to base her performance review on the employee's activities on the latest project, without giving enough weight to earlier examples of work and performance. Similar to halos and horns, primacy and recency bias our perception mostly at the attention and organization stages. They provide organizing structures that influence the other information that is gathered and how it is organized.

Self-Serving Bias

Although actors are quick to make external attributions about their own shortcomings, they are also quick to accept credit—an internal attribution—when they succeed. The tendency to accept credit for our success and reject blame for failures is called the **self-serving bias**.[44] On the one hand, when we do poorly on a test, mess up a presentation, lose a client, or fail to achieve our goals, we blame situational factors rather than make internal attribution about our own lack of effort or ability. We blame the unfair professor, the inattentive audience, the demanding client, or unreasonable company goals. On the other hand, we tend to believe we are successful because we are smart and work hard. Few of us give credit readily or completely to our boss's coaching and motivational skills or to simply having been lucky when we perform well. Case studies of cheating in schools show that cheaters even consider their cheating to be act of selflessness and generosity. One student caught giving another an inflated score said: "**A kid who has a horrible grade-point average, who, no matter how much he studies is going to totally bomb this test, by giving him an amazing score, I totally give him . . . a new lease on life.**"[45]

You can see many examples of the self-serving bias operating in the business press. Have you noticed how often business executives take credit for the success of their firms, but blame the economy, the competitors, government regulations, the global market, or other external factors for poor performance and failure? We all have a tendency to glorify ourselves and give positive consideration to things that directly affect us.[46] The recent case of Lance Armstrong, the now infamous Tour de France cyclist, provides yet another example.

Primacy effect:
a tendency to overemphasize early information

Recency effect:
a tendency to overemphasize the most recent information rather than earlier data

Self-serving bias:
the tendency to accept credit for our success and reject blame for failures

With accusations of doping and Armstrong being stripped of his seven titles, neither Armstrong himself, nor any of the officials of the International Cycling Union, accepted any responsibility for what has been described as a successful and professional doping program; they simply blamed one another.[47]

The combination of all the biases makes for interesting interaction between managers and their employees. Stereotypes, halos-horns, and primacy-recency may bias the information managers gather. Additionally, managers are likely to blame poor performance on their employees' lack of skills and effort whereas the employees blame it on their managers' poor leadership skills. On the other hand, both will tend to believe that their own ability and hard work led to success and they forget to give the other side much credit. Given the amount of information we have to process, being efficient is necessary and desirable. Perceptual biases allow us to be efficient and quick in our social perception, but they can also cause errors.

Difficulty in Overcoming Biases

Now that we are aware of the potential biases in perception, why can't we simply avoid them? Three factors make this task harder than it looks. First, we have a *need for consistency* that pushes us to look for information that supports our assumptions and beliefs.[48] As a result, we either avoid looking for or we ignore information that disproves our perceptual biases. These avoidance techniques give us a greater sense of control over events. For instance, managers who have already decided to open an international branch office may look only for positive information that confirms their decision and ignore any contradictory input.

Second, *channeling* reinforces our biases.[49] **Channeling** is the process of limiting our interaction with another so that we avoid receiving information that contradicts our judgment. Channeling is also called **confirmatory hypothesis testing** because we set up the situation to confirm our hypotheses about others. Research suggests that managers evaluating various opportunities use confirmatory strategies and as a result make poor decisions.[50] For example, if you dislike someone, you may not interact with or may be aloof toward her. Because of your actions, the other person is likely to respond in cold and unfriendly ways, thereby providing you with further evidence of the correctness of your perception. In another instance, a manager's perception that a Japanese subordinate lacks creativity may lead her to assign him to routine tasks. The employee then does not have the chance to demonstrate his creativity. The manager has channeled the employee's behavior to confirm her perceptions.

Sheryl Sanberg, Facebook COO, believes that women are held back by others' stereotypes and by how they perceive their own roles in organizations and in their family. In your own words, explain how this is an example of channeling.

Channeling or confirmatory hypothesis testing: the process by which we limit people's interactions with us so their behavior supports our expectations

Channeling can have a profound effect on organizational behavior. For example, research indicates that women are generally perceived by both male and female managers to be less competent, less capable of leading, and more likely to quit because of family pressures. In accordance with such stereotypes, many managers behave in ways that will confirm them. They provide women with fewer training opportunities, limited exposure to diverse experiences, and more routine, less challenging assignments. Why should they waste resources on low-potential employees who are likely to leave? In many professions, women are still bypassed for key promotions because the position requires that they supervise men or that they travel extensively.

What Would You Do?

▶ Are there reasons to think men are more effective leaders or managers; are there reasons to think that women are more effective leaders or managers?[51]

The third reason it is difficult to overcome our biases is one of the most powerful. The **Pygmalion effect** or **self-fulfilling prophecy** refers to the way in which the strength of one's expectations and perceptions cause those expectations to become reality.[52] Pygmalion was a mythological Greek sculptor who fell madly in love with the beautiful female statue he had carved and named Galatea. The strength of his love and his prayers to the goddess Aphrodite brought his creation to life. The myth of Pygmalion is used to describe the process by which our beliefs and expectations come to be reflected by others to the point that they behave as we originally expected.

Research into the Pygmalion effect showed that when teachers were given bogus information about their pupils' reading ability and even their IQ scores, the children's performance began to actually mirror those expectations.[53] Other research relating the concept to management has shown similar results. For example, successful CEOs use more positive language and believe that they will succeed whereas less effective ones focus on negative factors.[54] Through a variety of verbal and nonverbal messages and behaviors, managers consciously and unconsciously communicated their expectations to their employees and even to outsiders. The employees who are perceived to have potential, who have a positive halo, or who are similar to the manager based on work and non-work-related factors are treated differently from those who are not on the "A" list. Those who are expected to succeed are assigned more challenging tasks, benefit from clearer communication and more frequent and more positive feedback, and are coached more actively. Those who are not expected to succeed typically do not receive any of these benefits. Both groups are rewarded further for confirming the original stereotype and any actions and behaviors that do not fit expectations are ignored, forgotten, or explained away. Eventually, employees in both groups confirm the managers' expectations, further reinforcing the managers' belief that their perceptions are reality.

Perceptual biases in organizational settings have serious repercussions. The organization may not treat individuals fairly and may be held legally accountable as a consequence. Additionally, the organization may be deprived of potentially high performers and saddled with poor performers. For example, if several top managers' negative stereotypes of older workers result in those workers being passed over for promotion or being fired, the organization may never be able to take advantage of marketing to and developing products for aging baby boomers and senior citizens, a growing segment of the market. Similarly, organizations that channel women's behavior because of gender stereotypes ensure that the stereotypes become reality. The serious legal implications aside, the potentially missed opportunities are costly and the organization is the ultimate loser.

Nixon's Perceptions

Pygmalion effect or self-fulfilling prophecy: the process by which one's expectations and perceptions becoming reality because of the strength of the original expectation

The social perception process is by nature subjective, so it is bound to have some biases and errors. Although biases cannot be avoided entirely, awareness of the potential pitfalls of the social perception process can help managers minimize errors and help turn potential problems into advantages. In addition, managers and employees must learn to actively manage the perceptual process.

Managing Biases

Individuals and organizations can take four key steps to reduce the negative effects of perceptual biases and to improve decision making (see Figure 4.6).

FIGURE 4.6 MANAGING BIASES

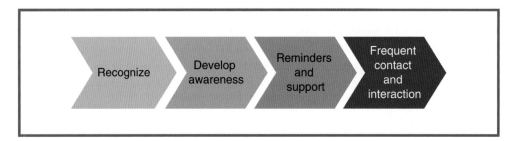

1. *Recognize the biases.* In this first step, you can learn to recognize biases through informal and formal training. For instance, this chapter should help you identify situations in which your decisions might be affected by perceptual biases. But you can also help others recognize their biases. Cross-cultural and diversity training is a specialized type of training that can help manage cultural stereotypes and attributional biases. Such training can encourage participants to identify stereotypes they hold, recognize when those stereotypes may be influencing them, and work on developing alternative views.

2. *Develop awareness of the areas and situations in which biases are most likely to operate.* Training helps to develop this awareness, but training and awareness alone are usually insufficient. You may be quite sensitive to perceptual biases immediately after reading this chapter but may find that in a few weeks or months you've forgotten about them.

3. *Offer constant reminders and support.* Leaders and managers in organizations need to offer reminders and support to others to prevent them from reverting to old biases. Repeatedly and consistently, leaders need to discourage negative biases and reinforce the positive aspect of any stereotyped groups.

4. *Provide opportunities for frequent contact and interaction.* Given that the biases prevent us from gathering information, any opportunity to interact with others enhances the chance that people will come across more objective information. Increased contact can help reduce stereotypes, the negative impact of the primacy effect, or attributional errors that often take place. You should look for chances to engage with different types of people.

CREATIVITY AND CHANGE

SPEAKING OF LEADERSHIP . . . MASCULINE OR FEMININE?

Many years ago, Jan Perkins and I wrote an article that asked whether the rising tide of women in positions of management and leadership would change those fields, or whether those same women would be changed by their experience and the traditional leadership model would prevail. That same question has been raised again in a variety of books and articles over the last couple of years, many probably stimulated by Sheryl Sandberg's highly publicized book *Lean In.*

One article reported on a worldwide survey that asked respondents what they thought were the most important skills and characteristics of leaders, then asked which of those characteristics were associated with a feminine perspective and which were associated with a masculine perspective. The first finding was that people who demonstrate collaboration, flexibility, selflessness, and are ready to share credit were likely to be the most successful leaders—and that these were all considered feminine qualities. Some masculine qualities, like resilience and decisiveness, were on the list of positives but further down, whereas others like ego and pride were all the way at the bottom of the list.

A similar article offered the seven most important characteristics of today's leader:

1. Empathy: Being sensitive to the thoughts and feelings of others

2. Vulnerability: Owning up to one's limitations and asking for help

3. Humility: Seeking to serve others and to share credit

4. Inclusiveness: Soliciting and listening to many voices

5. Generosity: Being liberal with time, contacts, advice, support

6. Balance: Giving life, as well as work, its due

7. Patience: Taking a long-term view

While we can question whether these surveys convey an accurate picture of leadership today, certainly most folks would acknowledge that effective leadership is increasingly becoming "feminized." This doesn't necessarily mean that women are better leaders than men, rather it means that people showing more traditionally feminine traits—and these could be men as well as women—are likely to be more successful in their leadership roles. It doesn't appear to be a matter of gender but one of style.

In an earlier post, I wrote that leadership styles need to change with the times, with cultural history. "To be a better leader, you have to relate to the particular time and culture in which you live. That time and that culture are constantly changing. And your leadership must change as well. In fact, the best leaders are those who can match their personal growth and development with the changing world around them."

Most men who occupy top positions in business, governments, and nonprofits—and they are still mostly men—entered their first jobs in an era dominated by top-down hierarchical practices and the tough, masculine traits associated with them. But time and culture march on. Today neither men nor women employees are likely to respond well to that traditional masculine model. They don't want to be bossed around, regulated in their behavior, or told what to do. Wise leaders, both men and women, will see the evolving set of expectations and adopt many of the more feminine characteristics listed above.

In this, women probably have a little head start, but we all know women managers who adopted the most heavy-handed masculine traits as they rose up the corporate ladder. If they can adapt in one way, men can surely adapt in the other.

When Jan and I wrote our article over thirty years ago and asked whether women would change the workplace or be changed by it, we expected to know the answer by now. But we don't. Cultural change takes a long time. And, of course, there are other variables at play. The environment of business and government is changing in ways that support new styles of leadership that, for example, require more flexibility and less ego.

Both men and women leaders will have to be attentive to those changes and the changes in leadership they will demand. At this point, however, we can say that, whether it's the influence of more women in the workplace or whether it's the influence of changes in the environment, a more feminine model of leadership seems to be emerging. Leaders of all types should take notice.

Source: Adapted from Robert B. Denhardt, Speaking of leadership . . . masculine or feminine? Leadership@USC Blog, accessed at http://leadershipusc.blogspot.com/.

► Summary and Applications for Managers

Perception is a mental process that involves paying attention selectively to some stimuli and cues. Social perception plays a key role in our everyday life and in our activities at work, but it is inherently flawed and subject to many biases. These biases are often accentuated when we move across cultural boundaries. The same behavior may be perceived differently in different cultures and therefore have very different meanings. Effective managers use information about the social perception process to become aware of their biases and how others may perceive them.

1. *Remember that the perceptual process is inherently flawed and subject to bias.* People see the world differently and how we each view the world shapes how we make judgments and how we behave. Be aware of the various instances where biases and perceptual errors may affect how you view and interpret things.

2. Because culture provides complexity and often an unknown situation, *cross-cultural interactions are particularly subject to perceptual errors.* We are more likely to use closure and fall prey to perceptual biases when we are unfamiliar with a situation. Therefore, being in a new cultural environment or interacting with someone from a different culture is a situation that is especially likely to be subject to biases and errors. When you are facing a cross-cultural encounter, whether it is while traveling abroad, working with a foreign national, or even when working with someone from another cultural group within your own country, take a minute to stop and slow down your attributional processes. You are more likely to jump to inaccurate judgments in those situations, so stop and ask yourself where your reaction is coming from.

3. *Spend some time to become aware of your stereotypes.* Everyone has stereotypes about one group or another. It is part of being human. While stereotypes are often wrong, they are also a natural part of how we perceive the world. Having stereotypes about various groups may be a personal matter, but acting based on those stereotypes as a manager is an entirely different thing. You should examine your personal stereotypes and decide whether you would like to change them, but you should not act based on them when you are managing others.

4. *Increased interaction helps provide more information.* The more time we spend with our coworkers and employees, the more we get to know them and the less likely we are to base our judgments and attributions on biases or errors. While it is not always practical to get to know every one of your employees well, especially if you have a large group of people reporting to you, you should make an effort to interact with them and keep track of their performance.

5. *Don't rely on your memory; we don't remember things as well as we think we do.* In order to prevent various biases and errors from affecting your judgment and causing mistakes, keep notes on events and important issues. You are less likely to simply "fill in" the missing parts based on your own biases, or to use the most easily available piece of information instead of the most relevant one, to make a decision.

6. *Be aware of the power of the fundamental attribution error.* We are much more likely to make personal attributions about the cause of others' behaviors. We tend to think, often inaccurately, that people behave the way they do because of who they are, rather than because of external factors. Stop and think before you assume that your employees are performing poorly because of their own traits or abilities. Make an effort to fully consider the power of the situation in shaping people's behavior.

7. *The self-fulfilling prophecy and other errors make it very hard for us to disconfirm our expectations.* Be aware of how much power, subtle and not so subtle, expectations have on people's behavior. You shape what others do, and they shape what you do, to a much greater extent than you think. Stop and evaluate your own behavior and how it influences what others do, before you judge and evaluate them.

8. *Perceptual biases and errors are very important in managerial decision making and in many other managerial situations.* While our biases may lead us to misjudge people and miss out on great opportunities in our personal lives, in organizations,

our errors can have serious ethical and legal consequences. Managers have the responsibility of being as objective as possible. An inaccurate judgment about an employee may lead to serious consequences for the employee, for you, and for your organization. Use the information about the perceptual process wisely to become more effective.

9. *Carefully manage the image you present in the workplace.* Managing impressions and careful self-presentation are neither unethical nor shady. The key is to focus on providing accurate information and actively managing when and how you present that information. Knowledge of perceptual issues can help you in that process.

▶ Key Terms

Actor-observer difference   126

Attention stage of perception   118

Attribution process   123

Channeling or confirmatory hypothesis testing   130

Closure   114

External or situational attribution   123

Fundamental attribution error   126

Organization stage of perception   119

Overjustification   125

Halo effect   128

Internal or personal attribution   123

Interpretation and judgment stage   122

Perception   114

Perceptual biases   125

Perceptual filter   118

Primacy effect   129

Pygmalion effect or self-fulfilling prophecy   131

Recency effect   129

Salient cues   118

Schemas   119

Selective attention   118

Self-perception theory   124

Self-serving bias   129

Similar-to-me   128

Social perception   114

Stereotype   127

▶ Exercise 4.1   Dealing With Stereotypes and Ethical Issues

You are aware that a manager in your department holds strong negative stereotypes about African Americans. The manager makes numerous jokes and other derogatory comments in private conversations. Although you cannot point to specific instances where his bias has affected his business decisions, you are uncomfortable with his behavior and worried about its implications for your organization. Do you consider his behavior unethical or politically incorrect? Would that make a difference in what you would do?

▶ Exercise 4.2   Perceptual Process at Work

1. Individual Work

Read the following short case carefully and as often as you think is necessary for full understanding. You will not be able to refer to it until the end of the exercise as instructed by your instructor.

A well-liked college instructor had just completed making up the final exam and had turned off the lights in the office. Just then, a tall, dark, and broad figure appeared and

demanded the exam. The professor opened the drawer. Everything in the drawer was picked up and the individual ran down the corridor. The dean was notified immediately.

Answer the following questions about the case you have just read without referring back to the case. Circle *T* if the statement is true or correct, *F* if it is false, and *?* if you are not sure or cannot tell.

1.	The thief was tall, dark, and broad.	T	F	?
2.	The professor turned off the light.	T	F	?
3.	A tall figure demanded the examination.	T	F	?
4.	The examination was picked up by someone.	T	F	?
5.	The examination was picked up by the instructor.	T	F	?
6.	A tall dark figure appeared after the professor turned off the light.	T	F	?
7.	The man who opened the drawer was the professor.	T	F	?
8.	The professor ran down the corridor.	T	F	?
9.	The drawer was never actually opened.	T	F	?
10.	Three people are referred to in this case.	T	F	?

2. Group Work

- Without turning back to the case or changing any of your answers, compare your answers with those of your group members. Discuss any discrepancies. The goal is not to come to an agreement and a common group answer, but to explore areas of differences and their causes.

- Now that you have discussed the case in your group, how many questions do you think you answered correctly?

3. Scoring and Discussion

Your instructor will provide you with the scoring key for the questions. What explains your score? What processes are operating? What are the implications?

▶ Case 4.1 A Smile Is Just a Smile, or Is It?

After obtaining a business and engineering degree in South Korea, Hun Lee Kim spent six months in a management training program at a prestigious U.S. university. He had three years of work experience in Korea and Singapore and he was hoping to get a one- or two-year internship in a large U.S. high-tech firm before he returned home. He was most interested in the experience, and salary and benefits were not of consequence to him. All his efforts for the past three months had failed and Hun Lee was very discouraged.

Hun Lee had prepared a detailed résumé and attached a picture of himself in which he was careful to project a serious expression that would show potential employers his respect for them and the importance he attributed to finding a job. Out of the fifty letters and resumes he sent out, he received only two in-person interviews and one phone interview. Even with the poor economy, all his other classmates, several of whom were foreign nationals like him, had eight to ten interviews within the first few weeks, and most had had attractive offers.

For both his interviews, Hun Lee gathered considerable information about the company and was extremely well prepared. During the interview, he was careful to show respect, not to interrupt the managers who were talking to him, and to answer their questions very clearly. In both cases, Hun Lee found the interviews silly and childish. He thought that they joked around too much and did not appear to be taking the interviews seriously. However, he made sure that he demonstrated his commitment and avoided conveying a frivolous attitude.

Jerri Hirsch, the internship director, was puzzled by Hun Lee's lack of success. He was one their best students and had much to offer as an intern. She decided to call the HR directors of the companies that interviewed him to find out what was going on. The first one said, "The guy was really unfriendly. He looks good on paper, but is he just too uptight. We have a lot of young employees here and we are open and friendly. He just didn't fit well." The response from the second one was kinder. "Hun Lee did not appear to have much initiative. This is just an internship, but we always look for people who have the potential to contribute long-term. He knew the facts, but not much more." The phone interviewer was kinder; she stated: "Maybe he was nervous on the phone. I'm sure he is nice, but he was so serious."

1. What are the causes of Hun Lee's lack of success?

2. What role do cultural stereotypes play?

3. What attributional processes may be operating?

4. If you were Jerri Hirsch, how would you explain the situation to Hun Lee, and what advice would you give him?

⑤SAGE edge™

Sharpen your skills with SAGE edge at edge.sagepub.com/nahavandi

SAGE edge for students provides a personalized approach to help you accomplish your coursework goals in an easy-to-use learning environment.

▶ Endnotes

1. Schweizer, K. (2012). Pearson CEO Scardino will step down as Fallon takes over. *Bloomberg*, October 3. Retrieved from http://www .bloomberg.com/news/2012-10-03/pearson- names-fallon-as-new-ceo-from-january-to- replace-scardino.html on October 18, 2012.

2. Angelo, B. (1977). Marjorie Scardino yanks their chain. *Columbia Journalism Review, 36*(1), 44.

3. Rushton, K. (2012). Marjorie Scardino: The softly-spoken American who rose to the top of Pearson. *The Telegraph, October 6. Retrieved from http://www.telegraph.co.uk/finance/ newsbysector/mediatechnologyandtelecoms/ media/9591486/Marjorie-Scardino-the-softly- spoken-American-who-rose-to-the-top-of- Pearson.html on October 18, 2012.

4. Angelo, 1977.

5. Colby, L. (1998). Yankee expansionist builds British Empire. *Fortune, 137*(5), 102–104.

6. Colby, 1998.

7. Colby, 1998.

8. Rushton, 2012.

9. Rushton, 2012.

10. Fiske, S. T., & Taylor, S. E. (1991). *Social cognition*. Reading, MA: Addison-Wesley; and Schiffman, H. R. (1990). *Sensation and perception: An integrated approach*. New York, NY: Wiley.

11. Hofstede, G. 2001. *Culture's consequences: Comparing values, behaviors, institutions, and organizations across organizations*. Thousand Oaks, CA: Sage; also, House, R. J., Hanges, P. J., Javidan, M., Dorfman, P. W., & Gupta, V. (2004). *Culture, leadership, and organizations: The GLOBE study of 62 countries*. Thousand Oaks, CA: Sage.

12. Trompenaars, A., & Woolliams, P. (2003). *Business across cultures*. Chichester, UK: Capstone.

13. Rodriguez, C. (2008). *International management: A cultural approach* (3rd ed.). Thousand Oaks, CA: Sage.

14. Fiske & Taylor, 1991.

15. Hutchings, V. L., & Valentino, N. A. (2004). The centrality of race in American politics. *Annual Review of Political Science, 7,* 383–408.

16. Fiske & Taylor, 1991.

17. Taylor, S. (1981). A categorization approach to stereotyping. In D. L. Hamilton (Ed.), *Cognitive processes in stereotyping and intergroup behavior* (pp. 83–114). Hillsdale, NJ: Erlbaum.

18. Fiske, S. T., & Neuberg, S. L. (1990). A continuum of impression formation from category-based to individuating processes: Influences of information and motivation on attention and interpretation. In M. P. Zanna (Ed.), *Advances in experimental social psychology* (Vol. 23, pp. 1–74). New York, NY: Academic Press.

19. Values and principles. (2012). *Heineken International*. Retrieved from http://www.heinekeninternational.com/valuesandprinciples.aspx on October 27, 2012.

20. Allen, K. J. (2012). *3 PR lessons from Heineken's bizarre dog-fighting crisis*. Retrieved from http://www.ragan.com/Main/Articles/3_PR_lessons_from_Heinekens_bizarre_dogfighting_cr_44761.aspx on October 28, 2012.

21. Robinson, M. (2012, April). Did Heineken sponsor brutal dog fighting in Asia? *Daily Mail*, April 2012. Retrieved from http://www.dailymail.co.uk/news/article-2131506/Heineken-launches-probe-new-photo-shows-beer-giant-sponsored-brutal-dog-fighting-Asia.html on October 27, 2012.

22 Eims, P. (2012, April 19). Heineken addresses allegations that they promote dog-fighting. *Examiner.com*, April 19. Retrieved from http://www.examiner.com/article/heineken-addresses-allegations-that-they-promote-dog-fighting on October 27, 2012.

23. Adair, W. L., Taylor, M. S., & Tinsley, C. H. (2009). Starting out on the right foot: Negotiation schemas when cultures collide. *Negotiation and Conflict Management Research, 2*(2), 138–163.

24. Our culture. (2012). *Southwest Airlines*. Retrieved from http://www.southwest.com/html/about-southwest/careers/culture.html on October 27, 2012.

25. Lynnes, K. S., & Heilman, M. E. (2006). When fit is fundamental: Performance evaluations and promotions of upper-level female and male managers. *Journal of Applied Psychology, 91*(4), 777–785.

26. Kelley, H. H. (1973, February). The process of causal attribution. *American Psychologist,* 107–128.

27. Weiner, B. (1985, October). An attribution theory of achievement motivation and emotion. *Psychological Review*, pp. 548–573.

28. Ross, L. (1977). The intuitive psychologist and his shortcomings: Distortions in the attribution process. In L. Berkowitz (Ed.), *Advances in experimental social psychology* (Vol. 10, pp. 174–221). New York, NY: Academic Press.

29. Kelley, 1973.

30. Nisbett, R. E., & Wilson, T. D. (1977). Telling more than we can know: Verbal reports on mental processes. *Psychological Review, 84,* 231–259.

31. Bem, S. (1972). Self-perception theory. In L. Berkowitz (Ed.), *Advances in experimental social psychology* (Vol. 6, pp. 1–62). New York, NY: Academic Press; and Riding, R. J., & Rayner, S. G. (2001). *Self-perception: International perspectives on individual differences*. Westport, CT: Ablex.

32. Tang, S. H., & Hall, V. C. (1995). The overjustification effect: A meta-analysis. *Applied Cognitive Psychology, 9*(5), 365–404.

33. Ross, 1977; also Stadler, D. R. (2009). Competing roles for the subfactors of need for closure in committing the fundamental attribution error. *Personality and Individual Differences, 47*(7), 701–705.

34. Fung, K. (2012). Geraldo Rivera: Trayvon Martin's "hoodie is as much responsible for [his] death as George Zimmerman" [Video]. *The Huffington Post*. Retrieved from http://www.huffingtonpost.com/2012/03/23/geraldo-rivera-trayvon-martin-hoodie_n_1375080.html

35. Jones, E. E., & Nisbett, R. E. (1972). The actor and the observer: Divergent perception of the causes of behavior. In E. E. Jones, Kanouse, D. E., Kelley, H. H., Nisbett, R. E., Valins, S., & Weiner, B. (Eds.), *Attribution: Perceiving the causes of behavior*

(pp. 79–94). Morristown, NJ: General Learning Press; and Epley, E. N., & Dunning, D. (2000). Feeling "holier than thou": Are self-serving assessments produced by errors in self- or social prediction? *Journal of Personality and Social Psychology, 79*(6), 861–875.

36. Junius, D. (2012). AP poll: U.S. majority have prejudice against Blacks. *USA Today,* October 27. Retrieved from http://www.lohud.com/usatoday/article/1662067?odyssey=mod%7Cnewswell%7Ctext%7CNews%7Cs on October 27, 2012.

37. Weaver, V. (2005). *Race, skin color, and candidate preference.* Paper presented at the 2005 annual meeting of the Midwest Political Science Association.

38. Ryan, M. K., Haslam, S. A., Herby, M. D., & Bongiorna, R. (2011). Think crisis—think female: The glass cliff and contextual variation in the think manager—think male stereotype. *Journal of Applied Psychology, 96*(3), 470–484.

39. Heilman, M. E., & Haynes, M. C. (2005). No credit where credit is due: Attributional rationalization of women's success in male-female teams. *Journal of Applied Psychology, 90*(5), 905–916.

40. Colby, 1998.

41. Bechger, T. M. (2010). Detecting halo effects in performance-based examinations. *Psychological Measurement, 34*(8), 607–619.

42. Pulakoz, E. D., & Wexley, K. N.(1983). Relationship among perceptual similarity, sex, performance, and rating in manager-subordinate dyads. *Academy of Management Journal, 26,* 129–139.

43. Graham, S. (2008). Careers: There's a new sheriff in town. *Fast Company*, January 2. Retrieved from http://www.fastcompany.com/661452/careers-theres-new-sheriff-town on October 15, 2012.

44. Miller, D. J., & Ross, M. (1975). Self-serving bias in attribution of causality: Fact or fiction. *Psychological Bulletin, 82,* 213–225; and Shepperd, J., Malone, W., & Sweeny, K. (2008). Exploring the causes of the self-serving bias. *Social and Personality Psychology Compass, 2*(2), 895–908.

45. Kolker, R. (2012). Cheating upwards. *New York Magazine*, September 16. Retrieved from http://nymag.com/news/features/cheating-2012-9/ on October 25, 2012.

46. Hausdorf, P. A., Risavy, S. D., & Stanley, D. J. (2011). Interpreting organizational survey results: A critical application of the self-serving bias. *Organizational Management Journal, 8*(2), 71–85.

47. Scott-Elliot, R. (2012). Cycling: UCI rejects any blame for "greatest crisis" over Lance Armstrong. *The Independent,* October 23. Retrieved from http://www.independent.co.uk/sport/general/others/cycling-uci-rejects-any-blame-for-greatest-crisis-over-lance-armstrong-8221930.html on October 25, 2012.

48. Festinger, L. (1957). *A theory of cognitive dissonance.* Evanston, IL: Row Peterson; and Strack, F., & Gawronski, B. (2012). *Cognitive consistency: A fundamental principles in social cognition.* New York, NY: Guilford Press.

49. Snyder, M., & Swann, W. (1978). Hypothesis-testing processes in social interaction. *Journal of Personality and Social Psychology, 36,* 1202–1212; and Swann, W. B., Jr., & Giuliano, T. (1987). Confirmatory search strategies in social interaction: How, when, why and with what consequences. *Journal of Social and Clinical Psychology, 5,* 511–524.

50. Shepherd, D. A., Haynie, J. J., & McMullen, J. S. (2012). Confirmatory search as a useful heuristic? Testing the veracity of entrepreneurial conjectures. *Journal of Business Venturing, 27*(6) 637–651.

51. See Casse, P., & Turnbull, S. (2011, January). For female leadership: Who is the winner. *Business Leadership Review, 8*(1), 1–7. Retrieved from http://www.mbaworld.com/blr-archive/issues-81/6/index.pdf

52. Rosenthal, R., & Jacobson, L. (1968). *Pygmalion in the classroom: Teacher expectation and pupils' intellectual development.* New York, NY: Holt, Rinehart & Winston.

53. Spiegel, A. (2012). Teachers' expectations can influence how students perform. *National Public Radio,* October 16. Retrieved from http://www.npr.org/blogs/health/2012/09/18/161159263/teachers-expectations-can-influence-how-students-perform?sc=emaf on October 17, 2012.

54. Goodwill, D. (2008, April). Self-fulfilling prophecies. *Canadian Transportation Logistics, 111,* 46.

5 Motivation and Engagement

A Case Study: Happiness at Work ▶

For years, scholars and businesspeople have known that employee engagement was positively correlated with the organization's productivity; indeed, research shows that engaged groups of employees are more than 25% more productive. Engagement means that people want to come to work, they feel emotionally connected with others at the workplace, and they find their work both challenging and meaningful. But is that all there is?

Some executives today are saying "no," and, taking a page from Zappo's playbook, are trying to extend beyond engagement to something called happiness. (It's an old term, but you may have heard of it.) For example, Russ Lidstone, CEO of Havas Worldwide, an advertising firm, is trying to build a more resilient and more creative workforce through efforts to enhance his employees' happiness.

The idea is related to the positive psychology approach (see Chapter 1), an approach that suggests that instead of trying to fix problems (which only continue to pop up), managers and leaders should focus on the positive aspects of what's happening in their organizations and build on their strengths.

Lidstone comments, "Ours is a young culture with high levels of engagement—one of our agency's strengths, and I was interested to see how we could magnify this across every member of the staff." The idea is that more liberated and confident people—happy people?—are freed to think and act more creatively, which, in this case, means more productively.

How do you make workers happier? By giving them a basic course in happiness, one that all of Lidstone's employees will take. The course presumably will improve the quality of jokes and pranks in the office, but, more seriously (or happily), build the employees' capacity for emotional intelligence, something that should positively impact their work life and their personal life for a long time to come.[1]

You can buy people with your wallet or stimulate them with your academic prowess, but neither lasts long. What you need is their hearts. . . . They need to believe in what they are doing.

—Andrew Liveris, CEO, Dow Chemical

> *Any company trying to compete . . . must figure out a way to engage the mind of every employee.*
>
> —Jack Welch, former CEO of General Electric

The key to organizational success is to develop employees who are motivated to consistently, creatively, and energetically work toward the attainment of organizational goals. As we all know, in any group of employees—like those in the case study above—some will be more motivated than others. And those who are most highly motivated will likely be those who are most productive. Motivation also is critical to our own personal success. The more motivated we feel to do our best, to accept new challenges, and to help others accomplish their goals, the more satisfied and successful we will be in our work. But motivation is complex: some are motivated by money, some are motivated by prestige and position, and others are hardly motivated at all.

What's My Motivation?

How do you motivate an individual or a group to be more productive? Will motivating factors change from place to place or situation to situation? Are there specific motivating factors that the manager needs to know? Or are people simply motivated by good management, whatever that might be? Understanding motivation is also important to your own personal achievement and commitment to organizational success. What motivates you to behave as you do at work? This chapter focuses on these questions and challenges.

SELF-ASSESSMENT 5.1

WHAT MOTIVATES YOU?

There are several reasons for beginning our discussion of motivation with ourselves. First, to enhance your own experience at work, it is important to understand what motivates you. Second, if you are highly motivated, then that can influence others in a constructive way. Conversely, if you do not appear highly motivated, then others are likely to reflect the same level of motivation. Third, understanding what motivates us can help us to make good choices about motivating others. We can seek out circumstances that offer the greatest value to us and to others.

The following are self-assessments that can begin to help you think about motivation. Remember as you work through these exercises that motivation is multifaceted; it is influenced by your work situations, your life stage, your personality, and many other factors. As a result, you will find that your motivations change over time and from situation to situation.

What Motivates You Now?

Read through the following statements. Then select those eight items that are most important in terms of motivating you in your present (or most recent) work environment.

1. A positive working relationship with my boss

2. Good pay

3. Lots of freedom on the job

4. Praise for a job well done

5. Interesting and challenging work

6. People with whom I enjoy working

7. Knowing that there will be consequences for poor performance

8. A clearly written job description

9. Chance for promotion

10. A nice office

11. Personal respect

12. A generous retirement program

13. Performance evaluations

14. Doing important work

15. Time off from work

16. Serving the public and making the community a better place to live

17. Regular hours

18. Knowing "inside" information about what is going on at work

19. Opportunity for learning and growth

Keep your answers. When we discuss need theories later in the chapter, we will come back to score this instrument.

What Will Motivate You in the Future?

You have been invited to interview for your dream job. At the time the interview was scheduled, you were asked to be ready to discuss what factors would be most important in motivating you in this position. What will you say? Compare what would motivate you in your dream job with what motivates you in your current job. Are there differences? Why?

Source: Statements are from Herzberg, F. (2003, January). One more time: How do you motivate employees? *Harvard Business Review*, pp. 2–12.

Approaches to Motivation

As we saw in Chapter 1, the study of motivation was not a central part of early management theorizing in the United States. But during the decades following the Hawthorne experiments (published during the 1930s), a number of different writers offered alternative views of motivation. While these models are not mutually exclusive, we can categorize them by which part of motivation they emphasize—human needs, the goals people seek to attain, the factors people consider in choosing behavior, the effect of cognition on motivation, the characteristics of people that may influence the motivational process, and the influence of rewards. These perspectives are considered in the sections that follow. But first, let's discuss why motivation is important.

Why Does Motivation Matter?

Motivation is a state of mind, desire, energy, or interest that translates into action. You are motivated when you are interested in doing something. Motivation has a strong behavioral component and it is important for managers because it is one of the elements that affects performance. Performance in any setting is a function of three things (see Figure 5.1). First, the person must be motivated or willing to perform. For example, you may be motivated to play basketball. Second, the person must have the ability to perform. For example, while many of us may be motivated to play professional basketball, few have the ability and talent to do so. Finally, given both motivation and ability, the person must be given the opportunity to perform. In the basketball example, the motivated and talented athlete must get a try-out with a team, and if selected, get time to play to be able to perform. While managers cannot control the ability element of performance, they can provide opportunity and they can affect their employees' motivation through a variety of means.

It is important to differentiate between job satisfaction and motivation. Job satisfaction is an attitude or feeling about one's job. It includes satisfaction with pay, coworkers, supervision, promotion, and the organization. Motivation has deeper roots. It includes not only attitudes about the job, but also factors such as individual needs. **Needs** are based on personality and values and are related to things that are lacking and are desired. As you will see in the next section, needs relate to work motivation. In addition to needs, motivation has a strong behavioral aspect—the drive to act—that is not necessarily present in job satisfaction. In spite of the differences, motivation and job satisfaction are closely linked. Being motivated to do a job well is difficult when you are dissatisfied. Similarly, a highly satisfying job is likely to motivate. You can also be satisfied with the job, but not motivated to work hard because of dissatisfaction with the pay, your manager, or other factors.

Finally, motivation has three general components that are addressed by the various theories that you will learn about in this chapter.

Motivation

FIGURE 5.1 ELEMENTS OF PERFORMANCE

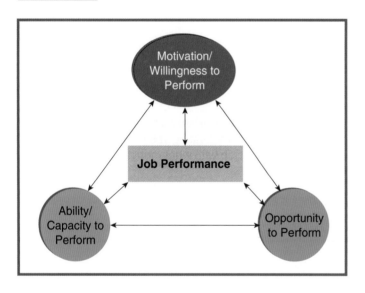

- First, motivation is related to *individual differences* that we discussed in chapter 2. For example, proactive people may have more motivation and show more initiative than those who are not proactive. Values are another individual difference that may affect motivation. For example, people who value hard work are more likely to be motivated to actually work hard.

- Second, the *actual job* that people do affects their motivation. As you will see, many motivation theories consider the job one of the most important factors in motivation. If the job is interesting and challenging and provides a sense of achievement, employees are more likely to be engaged and motivated to perform it. A boring, repetitive, and tedious job is less likely to motivate most people.

Motivation: a state of mind, desire, energy, or interest that translates into action

Needs: based on personality and values and related to things that are lacking and are desired

- Third, *the organization* plays a role in motivation. To motivate employees to do their job, the organization must provide the right climate and opportunities. Factors such as the organizational culture, the mission, the management style, the structure and goals and strategies all provide the setting in which employees work. They therefore can affect motivation.

Need Theories

Among the most influential and intuitively appealing approaches to understanding motivation are the theories that describe behavior as being directed toward the satisfaction of human needs. The theoretical foundation for many of these approaches is found in the work of Abraham Maslow. Maslow, a clinical psychologist, published in 1943 *A Theory of Human Motivation,* which remains one of the best-known and most widely cited works on motivation. In simple terms, Maslow argued that people are motivated to behave in ways that will satisfy their needs. Maslow conceptualized human needs in an ascending hierarchy from lowest level (most basic) needs to highest level needs. In this model, different levels of human needs are aroused in a specific sequence, and as each basic or lower-level need is substantially satisfied, the person is motivated to seek to satisfy the next higher level of need. This **hierarchy of needs** is depicted as a pyramid in Figure 5.2.

FIGURE 5.2 MASLOW'S HIERARCHY OF NEEDS

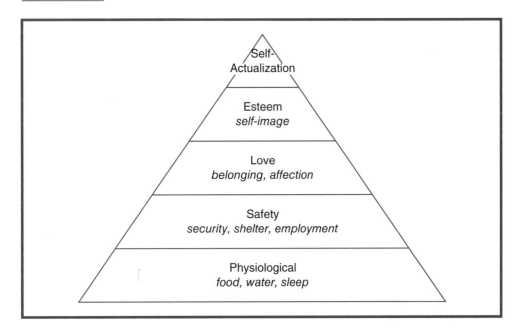

Maslow's Hierarchy of Needs

A basic assumption of this model is that as we satisfy one type of need, other needs then occupy our attention. Once we satisfy our need for food, air, water, and shelter, then we can move on to safety needs, love needs, and so on. Although Maslow argued that most people tend to experience these needs in the order that he described, for some people, the so-called higher-level needs will dominate lower-level needs. Some people will be so enthralled by a book or a movie that they will forget they are really hungry. It also is important to emphasize that Maslow did not suggest that each level of need has to be fully satisfied before you move on. "Most members of our society who are normal are partially satisfied in all their basic needs and partially unsatisfied in all their basic needs at the same time."[2]

Hierarchy of needs: Maslow's theory that different levels of human needs are aroused in a specific sequence, and as each lower-level need is substantially satisfied, the person is motivated to seek to satisfy the next higher level of need

The founder of Circuit City, Sam Wurtzel, built his highly successful company based on a Theory Y view of people. Although it was the nation's largest retailer of electronics in 2000, by the time the company declared bankruptcy in 2009, Theory X had become the norm.

Motivating
Employees

What Would You Do?

▶ According to another manager at your level, one of your employees yelled at one of his employees about being left off a meeting invitation. You didn't see or hear the incident yourself, but this is consistent with other comments you've heard about this employee. What would you do?

Maslow's work served as the point of departure for Douglas McGregor, another highly influential management thinker. As we saw earlier, McGregor used Maslow's hierarchy of needs to capture the dramatic shift in management thinking that was occurring based on changing conceptions of human motivation and the needs of people at work. In an article titled "The Human Side of Enterprise," McGregor[3] contrasted the conventional view of "management's task in harnessing human energy" (which he called Theory X) with a "new theory of management" (which he called Theory Y). Theory X is based on conventional assumptions about worker motivation such as those represented in the works of Taylor. Conversely, Theory Y is based on the recognition that people need opportunities at work to satisfy not only lower-level needs for wages and decent working conditions but also higher-level social and ego needs.

McGregor argued that the responsibilities of managers change as the managers change their beliefs about workers. Theory Y assumptions require management to accept responsibility for arranging "organizational conditions and methods of operation so that people can achieve their own goals best by directing their own efforts toward organizational objectives."[4] McGregor suggested strategies such as delegation, job enlargement, and participative management as consistent with Theory Y assumptions. The implication is that if workers are not motivated, then it is because of poor management practices that do not allow people's natural positive attitudes toward work to emerge.

In 1960, Sam Wurtzel, founder of Circuit City, read Douglas McGregor's book *The Human Side of Enterprise*, and immediately traveled to Boston to meet McGregor. He was told several times that the professor was unavailable, but finally his persistence paid off and he was granted an appointment. Wurtzel was particularly struck by McGregor's clear presentation of an approach to management that Wurtzel had long held himself—that success comes by working with people and treating them with respect. Between that time and the year 2000, Circuit City became the largest retailer of consumer electronics in the country. According to Sam's son, Alan, after that, the company experienced more of a Theory X management, which, combined with other environmental conditions and mistakes, led to the company's demise.[5]

Frederick Herzberg,[6] who also studied motivation in work settings, took a different approach, what was called a two-factor approach. He suggested that the factors that produce job satisfaction or motivation are different from the factors that lead to dissatisfaction. The satisfaction of lower-level needs, which he called hygiene or extrinsic factors, does not lead to motivation; it only leads to the absence of dissatisfaction. In other words, factors such as pay or working conditions, supervision, interpersonal relations, status, and security can cause dissatisfaction, but satisfying these needs will not lead to motivation.

Motivating or intrinsic factors, on the other hand, are those associated with the nature of the work itself—achievement, recognition, challenging work, responsibility, and growth.

Now we can return to the self-assessment exercise presented earlier in the chapter. Compare your questionnaire answers to Herzberg's categories as shown here:

Hygiene or Extrinsic Factors	Motivating or Intrinsic Factors
Items 1, 2, 6, 7, 8, 9, 10, 12, 13, 14, 15, 17, and 18	Items 3, 4, 5, 11, 16, and 19

What do your answers tell you about what motivates you? What do your answers tell you about your levels of satisfaction, dissatisfaction, and motivation in your present work environment? Remember that, according to need theories of motivation, we are most preoccupied with unmet needs. What do you need to be motivated? Although there are important differences among these approaches, Maslow, MacGregor, and Herzberg all emphasized the innate needs that people have in common. David McClelland,[7] on the other hand, suggested that some important needs differ from individual to individual: (1) the need for achievement, (2) the need for power, and (3) the need for affiliation. McClelland suggested that people have different dispositions that he defined as a "current concern about a goal state that drives, orients, and selects behavior."[8] According to this model, the need for achievement drives some of us, whereas the need for affiliation might be more important for others. As a result, the same set of incentives or circumstances in a particular work environment may cause different people to react in different ways. McClelland found that those with high achievement needs perform better when they work on moderately difficult tasks, want feedback on how well they are doing, and take personal responsibility for their performance. Because they seek challenges, they try new and more efficient ways of doing things.

McClelland also found that individuals with high power needs, on the other hand, are more sensitive to power-related stimuli, recall "peak" experiences in terms that involve power, strive to be assertive, are risk takers, and gravitate to careers in which they can exercise power and influence. Such individuals tend to be motivated by the symbols of power or the acquisition of "prestige possessions." Still others, according to McClelland, seem to be motivated primarily by the desire to affiliate or be with other people. People with a strong affiliation motive will do better on tasks if the incentives are social in nature. They want to please others, they learn social relationships more quickly, "read" people well, and tend to engage in more dialogue with others. They prefer having friends rather than experts as work partners, and they avoid conflict whenever possible.

Need to Know

Expectancy Theory

Instead of focusing on individual needs, whether innate or learned, **expectancy theory** suggests that people will be motivated when they expect that their efforts will result in desirable outcomes. This model assumes that motivation is a cognitive or mental process. Because it is a cognitive model, the individual's perception of events is equally important, and in some cases, more important than the objective or actual state of affairs. The focus on perception is crucial for managers because what an employee believes, although it may be inaccurate or biased, will affect his behavior. Therefore, to motivate employees, managers must consider how employees perceive the situation.

Expectancy theory: a motivation theory that holds that people will be motivated when they expect that their efforts will result in desirable outcomes

MOTIVATION AT SEMCO

Semco is a diverse Brazilian company that is a market leader in industrial equipment and solutions for document management. The company may be better known for its innovative and unorthodox management techniques and its radical form of workplace democracy. Workers set their own work targets and wages and select their managers.[9] Meetings are voluntary says Ricardo Semler, the CEO: "All our meetings are on a voluntary basis. Because if it's getting boring, go. . . . If no one's left, do we really need to do this?"[10]

Semler was one of the early proponents of open-book management, a method based on sharing financial information with employees and training them to interpret and use it to set and achieve performance goals. He

CEO of Semco, Richard Semler, gives employees both freedom and responsibility.

also believes in sharing information and power. He proposes that people who make far-reaching and complex decisions in their own lives every day are fully capable of managing themselves at work. He believes, "Freedom is the prime driver of performance,"[11] however, according to Semler democracy is badly lacking in organizations. At Semco, employees not only pick the color of their uniforms and their work hours, but also vote on adopting new products and undertaking new ventures.

Work-life balance is also key to Semco's radical management style. The company has set up hammocks in offices to allow employees to relax so that they can be more creative. Employees can take sabbaticals and "Retire-A-Little" time, where they can take time off to do what they would do when they retire.

However, these perks and freedoms come with both responsibility and high performance expectations. The company has grown 900 percent under Semler's leadership, is either number one or number two in all the markets in which it competes, and has grown 27.5 percent a year for 14 years.[12]

Employees who cannot work in the culture or who do not perform do not survive. Semler suggests that his management philosophy is not easy to implement everywhere because of two lacking elements: "One, the people in charge wanting to give up control. This tends to eliminate some 80 percent of businesspeople. Two, a profound belief that humankind will work toward its best version, given freedom; that would eliminate the other 20 percent."[13] Both these elements make empowerment and engagement possible at Semco.

1. What are the unique elements of Semco's management?

2. To what extent does culture play a role?

Expectancy theory holds that before people exert effort, they engage in a rational calculation of expected performance and rewards and an assessment of how much those outcomes matter to them (see Figure 5.3). In order to be motivated to act or perform their job, employees must perceive that their *efforts* (E) are likely to lead to good *performance* (P). In other words, effort has to be *instrumental* to good performance. Second, people must *expect* that their performance is clearly linked to certain *outcomes* (O).

FIGURE 5.3 EXPECTANCY THEORY

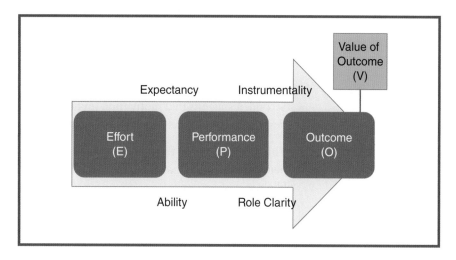

And finally they have to *value* (V) the outcome they obtain when they perform. If all these paths and linkages are clear, the person will be motivated.[14] Two other factors that can affect motivation are ability and role clarity.[15] A person might be highly motivated, but if she does not have the ability to perform the job or task and a clear understanding of how to direct her efforts in a manner that is appropriate to her organizational role, then the task might not be accomplished.

Expectancy Theory of Motivation

Consider the example of highly paid professional athletes. Fans often are bewildered when some basketball or football players earn several millions dollars a year but do not put in much effort or perform to their potential. In spite of the high salaries (valued outcomes), they may not perceive that their performance is linked to those outcomes (weak P-O). Instead, the negotiation skills of agents, the player's free agency status, and bidding for the player by other teams strongly determine the salary. Similarly, because of the presence of many talented athletes on any given team and intense competition, working hard and playing well alone do not guarantee performance and recognition (weak E-P). As a result, the athletes' efforts do not always lead to performance or to their getting the desired outcomes. When applying the expectancy model, one can understand why such highly paid athletes may not be motivated to play hard, in spite of astronomical salaries.

Expectancy theory argues that motivation is about more than salaries, even very high salaries. A star athlete in the NBA may be paid a high salary (valued outcome) but may not view his performance on the court as linked to those outcomes (weak performance outcome).

Smart Goal

Self-Efficacy,
Motivation, and
Goal Revision

Similarly in organizations, if people believe in their ability to get the job done but do not believe that the reward will be forthcoming or do not want the reward, then they will be less likely to put forth much effort.[16]

Expectancy theory goes beyond need-based theories of motivation in several respects:

- First, it introduces a cognitive aspect to motivation—that people at work think about the expected payoffs for their efforts.

- Second, it suggests that motivation involves not just the individual but also opportunities, rewards, and incentives in the work environment.

- Third, it reminds us that different people have different skills and abilities and that people will tend to exert more effort in those areas where they believe they are more likely to perform well.

Expectancy theory suggests that motivations can be enhanced in three ways. First, as a manager, you can offer rewards or outcomes that are of value to a particular worker or group of workers. Second, you can work to change the expectancy of existing outcomes so that the link between hard work and rewards is strengthened. For example, you can reduce political in-fighting that may prevent someone's performance resulting in the desired outcomes. Third, you can attempt to change the valence of existing outcomes. The first two ways, which involve changing the situation or organizational circumstances, probably are more amenable to influence than the third way, which would require manipulating how much people value a particular outcome.[17]

Goal Theories

As we discovered in Chapter 1, much of the theoretical base of the field of organizational behavior assumes that behavior is purposeful or goal directed.[18] Therefore, having goals is key to motivation. Having or setting goals, in and of itself, can motivate behavior. As early as the 1960s a series of experiments showed that individuals who were assigned difficult goals performed better than those who were assigned easy or moderately easy goals.[19] Later studies further showed that specific and challenging goals can increase performance because they direct the individuals to what they need to do.[20] In turn, individuals who accomplish the goals get a sense of achievement that further motivates them toward performance. Generally, difficult and specific goals work better than goals that are not challenging and are vague.[21] In other words, you should state a specific goal rather than simply urge workers to do their best. The acronym SMART is often used to remind people that in order to motivate them, the good goals must be specific, measurable, achievable, reasonable, and have a timetable (see Table 5.1).

Goal setting and expectancy theories are compatible approaches to increasing motivation, because goal setting enhances feelings of self-efficacy.[22] **Self-efficacy** is defined as people's judgments of their capabilities; in other words, it is our assessment of what we can do with the skills we possess.[23] Positive self-efficacy translates into a belief that we can do something—a belief that can become a self-fulfilling prophecy. Put in the language of expectancy theories, as workers' "expectancy," or judgment that their efforts likely will pay off, is increased, they will be more likely to choose to exert more effort toward goal attainment.

Self-efficacy: people's judgments of their capabilities; in other words, it is our assessment of what we can do with the skills we possess

TABLE 5.1 SMART GOALS

Smart Goals
Specific
Measurable
Achievable
Reasonable
Timetable

Equity Theory

Equity theory presents another cognitive model of motivation based on the notion of social exchange. It suggests that people make choices based on their assessments of particular situations before exerting effort to achieve organizational goals. Equity theory suggests that people evaluate what they bring into a situation and what they get out of it based on what they perceive to be fair or advantageous compared with what others receive or the effort required.[24] We generally expect the world to be balanced and fair, something called the *equity norm*. We therefore expect that those who contribute more to an organization should receive more rewards.[25]

Motivation, according to this model, is a consequence of perceived inequity. People can either feel guilty because they think they are paid too much (overpayment inequity) or be angry because they believe they are paid too little (underpayment inequity). Figure 5.4 represents three typical situations that lead to inequity. In each case, people who feel that there is no equity will be motivated to balance out the outcomes. Individuals will be motivated to reduce this tension by either changing what they do or changing what they think. Equity theory suggests six ways of reducing tension and achieving a sense of equity presented in Table 5.2.

FIGURE 5.4 STATES OF INEQUITY

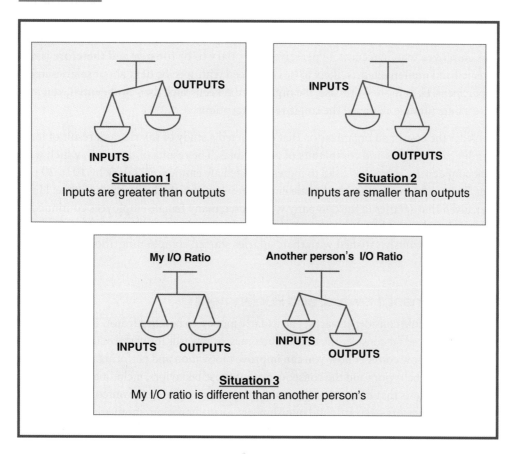

TABLE 5.2 POTENTIAL REACTIONS TO INEQUITY

Reaction	Example
1. Increase outputs	Employee asks for a raise or promotion
2. Decrease inputs	Employee works fewer hours or holds back ideas from the organization
3. Decrease outputs	Employee refuses a raise or promotion
4. Increase inputs	Employee works harder or goes to college to get a degree
5. Pick a different comparison person	Employee finds someone who, in his opinion, is more similar to him
6. Increase the comparison person's inputs	Employee sabotages or refuses to cooperate with the comparison person, which make the person's job harder and therefore increases that person's inputs
7. Decrease the other person's output	Employee complaints about the comparison person's output prevents the person from receiving a raise or promotion
8. Quit or transfer	Employee leaves to avoid feelings of inequity

Source: Based on Adams, J. S. (1965). Inequity in social exchange. In L. Berkowitz (Ed.), *Advances in experimental psychology*. New York: Academic Press.

How can you use equity theory to increase employee motivation? You must recognize than an employee's *perception* of inequity is often more important than objective reality. You shouldn't dismiss an employee's views as unfounded but should instead address the employee's perceptions and provide hard facts and data to change inaccurate perceptions. The employee who inaccurately perceives her salary to be too low and therefore is dissatisfied and unmotivated, is likely to be convinced with specific data about salaries in her department. If, as is often the case, the organization keeps such data confidential, you may have a difficult time changing the employee's perceptions.

Consider the case of an organization that conducted a study of salaries as a result of long-standing accusations and complaints of gender bias. The results of the study, which were kept confidential, were then used to increase all female employees' salary by 10 to 20 percent. You might expect that the female employees were satisfied with the outcome. However, given that salaries in the company were secret, many female employees continued to suspect that the problem was worse than originally thought. In addition, male employees who were previously satisfied with their salaries started complaining about inequitable treatment.

Reinforcement, Reward, and Punishment

Many of us would consider rewards, particularly money, to be a motivator. The theories we have presented so far consider the role of outcomes, or rewards for performance in a variety of ways. Let's now consider how you can improve motivation and performance by focusing on employee's behaviors and the consequences of those behaviors, including rewards. This approach suggests that behavior is learned and that manipulating the outcomes that result from those behaviors—rewards and punishments—can change our motivations and behavior. At the heart of this approach is the idea that people repeat behaviors that bring them satisfaction and pleasure, and stop those that bring them dissatisfaction or pain. This is known as the **law of effect**.[26] B. F. Skinner is perhaps the person most closely identified with this idea. His work focused on what he called operant behavior, or behavior that is controlled by the individual. Based on Skinner's work and the law of effect, **reinforcement theory** recommends providing an organizational environment and response patterns that reward and encourage desirable behaviors while discouraging or punishing undesirable ones.[27] Reinforcement theory is therefore based on the idea that external factors can determine a person's behavior. Accordingly, a manager's reaction to an employee's poor performance will determine whether the employee will continue to perform poorly or decide to work harder.

To control behaviors through consequences, managers must use positive reinforcement, negative reinforcement, and punishment, as summarized in Table 5.3. A **reinforcement** is an outcome or event that increases the likelihood that a behavior will occur again. It is easy to confuse reinforcers with rewards. **Organizational rewards** are positive outcomes that organizations provide to individuals. Examples include promotions, raises, bonuses, public recognition such as employee-of-the-month, and letters of commendation. Whether an organizational reward encourages the desired behavior depends on the needs of the individual. Therefore, not all organizational rewards act as reinforcers for all individuals. Additionally, not all reinforcers are positive and pleasant.

TABLE 5.3 CONSEQUENCES OF BEHAVIOR

Type	Nature	Goal	Timing
Positive Reinforcer	Pleasant event or outcome	Increase a certain behavior	After behavior takes place
Negative Reinforcer	Unpleasant event or outcome	Increase a certain behavior	Before behavior takes place
Punishment	Unpleasant event or outcome	Decrease a certain behavior	After behavior takes place

A **positive reinforcer** is a pleasant outcome that follows a desired behavior and is aimed at encouraging the behavior. A manager who publicly recognizes her best sales person at the end of each month is trying to create positive reinforcement. Like a positive reinforcer, a **negative reinforcer** is aimed at encouraging a certain behavior. However, it is unpleasant and comes before the behavior occurs. The supervisor who threatens a regularly tardy employee with a reprimand or a reduction in pay is using negative reinforcement. The goal is to encourage the employee to be on time. The threat, a negative event, takes place before the behavior occurs and stops when the employee comes in on time.

Those of us who nag our friends, spouses, roommates, and children to get them to do what we want are using negative reinforcement. The appreciation we express, the hugs and kisses, and other positive events we deliver after they do what we asked, are positive reinforcements. Although one reinforcer is positive and the other one negative, they are both called reinforcers because they aim at increasing a desired behavior. The focus on increasing the rate of a behavior distinguishes reinforcement, especially negative reinforcement, from punishment.

The third option for a manager to manage behavior through consequences is to use punishment. **Punishment** is a negative event that occurs after an undesirable behavior and is aimed

Law of effect: people repeat behaviors that bring them satisfaction and pleasure, and stop those that bring them dissatisfaction or pain

Reinforcement theory: recommends providing an organizational environment and response patterns that reward and encourage desirable behaviors while discouraging or punishing undesirable ones

Reinforcement: an outcome or event that increases the likelihood that a behavior will occur again

Organizational rewards: positive outcomes that organizations provide to individuals

Positive reinforcer: a pleasant outcome that follows a desired behavior and is aimed at encouraging the behavior

Negative reinforcer: an unpleasant outcome aimed at encouraging a certain behavior

Punishment: a negative event that occurs after an undesirable behavior and is aimed at stopping that behavior

at stopping that behavior. The typical punishments in organizations are oral and written reprimands, docking of pay, demotion, and firing. All these negative actions are aimed at getting employees to stop doing something they are not supposed to do. The consistently tardy employee who does not respond to the threats (negative reinforcement) may receive a formal reprimand and have his paycheck docked; eventually he may even be fired (punishment).

Managers can use a combination of positive and negative reinforcers and punishment to manage employee performance. In order to use these principles well, you must recognize several rules, which are summarized in Table 5.4. First, whether you use reinforcement or punishment, the key is to focus on *work-related behaviors*. The goals should not be to change an employee's personality or non-work-related behaviors. Second, it is important that managers provide a *quick response* to either positive or negative behaviors. If an employee is late or makes too many personal phone calls, his manager should discuss the problems as soon as they occur rather than wait weeks or even months for a regularly scheduled evaluation. Third, managers must be *consistent* with different employees and across situations to encourage desired behaviors. Fourth, the *reinforcers must be meaningful* and valued by the employee to have the desired impact. Compare the organization that provides movie tickers or a complimentary dinner to employees who share ideas that save the organization millions of dollars to one that offers an employee a percentage of profits for a new product that is developed as result of his or her idea and work. Which one is meaningful enough to motivate other employees to contribute their best ideas?

TABLE 5.4 RULES FOR USING REINFORCEMENT AND PUNISHMENT

Rule	Description
Focus on specific, job-related behaviors	Identify specific behaviors rather than general attitudes
Respond quickly	Provide reinforcement and punishment as soon as possible to make the connection between the behavior and its consequence clear
Be consistent (the "hot stove" rule)	The same behavior, good or bad, should lead to the same consequences every time and for every employee (the hot stove burns every one, every time!)
The larger the positive reinforcer the better	Provide as large a positive reinforcer as possible
Use punishment sparingly	Although sometimes necessary, it can have negative consequences; therefore, it should be used sparingly and as a last resort
Give praise in public; punish in private	With the exception of some cultures, public praise is more effective than private praise; punishment should always be delivered in private
Provide alternative behaviors after punishing	Because punishment is aimed at stopping undesirable behaviors, follow up with examples of alternative positive behaviors

The last three rules address the use of punishment in organizations. Punishment requires careful application because it has many negative consequences. Managers should use it *sparingly* and as a last resort. Relying on punishment as the primary method of managing employee behavior can lead to fear, resentment, lack of productivity, and potentially damaging behaviors. Another very important point is that employees should be *punished in private*. Public reprimands humiliate the employees and increase the negative effects of punishment. In one organization, a manager believed in openly and publicly berating the telemarketing agents who worked for him. He stated that that they worked harder when they were scared and knew he would get them when they made mistakes. Interestingly, he was perplexed that his business had 100 percent yearly turnover, unaware of the negative and intolerable climate that he was creating. Finally, if punishment is used, managers should clearly indicate *what behaviors they consider desirable*.

Financial rewards and incentives have been considered as primary motivators for a very long time. Depending solely on financial incentives, however, may be an overly simplistic and even ineffective approach to motivation. Financial incentives can motivate employees, but their effect is limited and they work only when other organizational conditions are favorable.[28] In order to motivate workers in a way that will improve performance and the quality of work, managers must consider other motivational factors such as attention to job design and work schedules, fostering participation, and setting goals that are challenging and creative.

In analyzing the results of a number of existing experimental studies on the effects of pay-for-performance, Weibel, Rost, and Osterloh found that there may be benefits, but also hidden costs in the use of pay-for-performance or merit-pay approaches. Interestingly, they found that "pay for performance has a strong, positive effect on performance in the case of noninteresting tasks. Pay for performance, however, tends to have a negative effect on performance in the case of interesting tasks."[29] In other words, the more intrinsically satisfying the work is, the more there is to lose.

What Do You Think?

▶ Some have argued that using reinforcement theory in management amounts to manipulation of employees. Some would say that it is no more manipulative than other approaches to motivation. Others would say that is simply what managers have to do. What do you think?

Meaningfulness, Commitment, and Engagement

Current Debates and Perspectives

Motivation and Life Stages

Interest in adult life stages has been strong in studies of human behavior and motivation during recent decades. Based on adult life-stage theories, certain issues can be expected to present themselves for resolution during the different life stages of employees. For example, the major issues facing employees during early adulthood are the establishment of careers and finding personal intimacy. During middle life, employees encounter opportunities for growth and change, and they experience a shift from concentration on external concerns to concentration on internal or self-oriented concerns. During later life, employees search for meaning and integrity.

Life stages also influence an individual's motives and cognitive and intellectual capabilities. In the early stages of their careers, young adults have fluid intellectual abilities, which are most

Our motivations, goals, and attitudes toward work may differ based on the era in which we grew up.

associated with working memory, abstract reasoning, attention, and processing of novel information.[30] In middle age, they tend to suffer the loss of these abilities. Instead, middle-aged workers gain occupational and avocational (hobbies, music, art, culture) knowledge, which may be very useful for the organization. Not only do skills change, but motives change as well. While in an early career it is important for the individual to look for future opportunities, to require novel information and promotion, middle-aged workers have preferences for job security, salary, and opportunities to use their skills.[31]

Generational Differences at Work

Awareness of generational differences, a topic we discussed in Chapter 2, can be helpful in understanding needs and expectations of employees. We should not assume, for example, that a 21-year-old employee necessarily wants the same things or has the same values older workers had when they were 21-years-old. In today's organizations, there may be at least three generational groups: baby boomers, Generation Xers, and millennials. While there are great individual differences, researchers have found that growing up in different eras has resulted in generational shifts in values and needs that are relevant to the workplace and to how you motivate employees. Baby boomers, for example, grew up in the post–World War II era, with general prosperity. They experienced marked social and technological changes ranging from the development of television in the 1950s to Vietnam and the civil rights movement in the 1960s. They represent the largest generational group in the workplace and have been found to be more competitive and dedicated, as well as self-absorbed, than other age cohorts. They tend to embrace change and personal growth and to question rules. Baby boomers also may be more likely than other generations to be motivated by praise, money, and position and to be loyal to their organization.[32]

What Would You Do?

▶ A sixth grader is asked, "What happens when someone is making noise in the classroom while you are trying to study?" The answer is, "The teacher makes them be quiet." "And if the teacher is out of the room?" "Then we have to do it ourselves." Can you think of parallels in the business world? What would you do?

Generation X adults, on the other hand, matured in a very different world than baby boomers. Many grew up in families when both parents worked or in single-parent households. They saw the beginning of the AIDS epidemic and the end of the Cold War, as well as numerous government and business scandals. As a group, they tend to value independence and creativity, be somewhat cynical, distrust large corporations, and want fulfilling work.[33] Motivation for this generation may revolve around allowing greater independence and involvement.[34]

Millennials (or Generation Y) are generally highly educated, well traveled, and technologically sophisticated. This is a generation that "*works to live* rather than *lives to work*."[35] This generation has been found to place more emphasis on the meaning of their work and the feeling that they are making a difference. While other generations may be willing to pay their dues before finding meaning in their work, millennials tend to seek meaning and fulfillment as the most important aspect of their jobs from the beginning.[36] They want to know *why* before *what*. They want to know why something is worth doing before doing it, not out of defiance, but out of the value placed on making a meaningful contribution. In a sense, they can be said to arrive at the workplace at the top levels of Maslow's hierarchy of needs, between the belongingness and esteem levels.[37]

What Work Means

"Anti-Motivation" Theories

Some people now argue that when we ask how to motivate employees, we actually are asking the wrong question. Motivation is not something that managers do for their employees. It is something inside the person. When managers try to implement motivation theories, they are manipulating their employees.[38] Trying to motivate employees is paternalistic, narrow, and relies too much on external rewards that do not work in the long term.

Instead, managers should think in terms of voluntary engagement with work activities rather than in terms of carrot-and-stick motivational approaches. Two essential elements of engagement theory are learning and involvement. The idea is that if people are allowed a degree of self-determination, they will become voluntarily engaged in work that is interesting and enjoyable to them. People will choose work that they are good at, and once they are engaged, people will challenge themselves and be persistent. The acquisition of more and better knowledge is a primary goal. The result is self-determination and continuous engagement with work activities rather than episodic motivation. Although this might seem to be a rather radical approach, it challenges us to think about the nature of work and our assumptions about workers and ourselves. Next we consider research that supports the importance of engagement.

What Retirement?

Trust and Engagement

As you are probably aware, trust in all major institutions, including business, labor, and government, has decreased substantially over the last decades. That decrease has been especially marked in the last several years with respect to business. Of course, that's understandable given the difficult economic conditions, the uncertainty of employment, and the requirement to do more with less. But it presents a major problem for managers and leaders in business and elsewhere. Gallup studies show extremely low rates of employee engagement in Europe and the United States: 7% in France, 12% in Germany, 17% in the United Kingdom, and 28% in the United States.

Building Trust
Partnerships

Does that make a difference? Actually, it does. As we saw in Chapter 1, there is a correlation between trust and employee engagement, on the one hand, and profit and productivity, on the other. For example, we noted that work units scoring in the top half on Gallup's employee engagement inventory essentially doubled their odds of success compared to those with scores in the bottom half. Moreover, employee engagement clearly had an impact in terms of productivity, quality, and customer service.[39]

Obviously, the recommendation for managers and leaders under these circumstances is that building trust and employee engagement should be very high on their agendas. It turns out that there is a long tradition in management that recommends higher levels of employee participation in organizational decision making. For many years, researchers have argued that an overall management philosophy that emphasizes a participative approach is positively related to employee motivation and performance[40] and have advocated participative or high involvement approaches to management.[41] Management researchers and practitioners are finding that participation influences motivation because it increases the amount of information that people have on the expected outcomes of performance. It helps to ensure that rewards have high significance for workers, and it helps people to see the relationship between performance and outcomes.

Employee engagement: the rational and emotional attachment and commitment employees have to their work and their organizations or the involvement, satisfaction, and enthusiasm employees have for their work

More recent studies have confirmed these early recommendations, though they increasingly use the term **employee engagement**—the rational and emotional attachment and commitment employees have to their work and their organizations or the involvement, satisfaction, and enthusiasm employees have for their work[42] (see also Figure 5.5). In Chapter 1, we reported on a 2005 study that found that supervisors play an

GENERAL STANLEY MCCHRYSTAL

In 2009, four-star General Stanley McChrystal became commander of all U.S. and international forces in Afghanistan. During his command, McChrystal guided a major escalation of American troops and other resources in Afghanistan. He also developed a somewhat controversial approach to counterinsurgency, emphasizing the importance of protecting citizens over engaging insurgents and restricting airstrikes to reduce civilian casualties. Our interest here is in his leadership style and his emphasis on trust and relationships.

To former general McChrystal, building consensus or a shared purpose is more important than giving orders. This requires investments in communications, trust, and relationships.

McChrystal's approach to leadership was quite different from the traditional military leadership. "We grew up in the military with this [classic hierarchy]: one person at the top, with two to seven subordinates below that, and two to seven below that, and so on." However, fighting Al Qaeda proved to require a different sort of military. "We had to change our structure, to become a network. We were required to react quickly. Instead of decisions being made by the people who were more senior—the assumption that senior meant wiser—we found that the wisest decisions were usually made by those closest

to the problem."[43] So McChrystal instituted more of a shared leadership approach to command, with all officers being encouraged to become more active in decision making at their level.

At the same time, McChrystal and other leaders wanted to make sure that everyone was moving in the same direction. Particularly in the chaos of war, it is easy to see how lower-level commanders might drift away from the direction sought by the upper level commander. In order to counter this tendency while at the same time supporting those throughout the organization, McChrystal tried to instill a "shared consciousness" so that everyone in the organization would know "the commander's intent." Once that was clear, people in the field were free to make decisions on their own. "My command team and I guided our values, strategy, and priorities. The leader's lower in the organization made tactical and operational decisions in line with those principles."[44]

Pursuing this approach meant that McChrystal would need to emphasize communications from top to bottom and throughout his organization. He was known for spending discretionary funds not on guns but on communications equipment and information technology. He insisted that communications flow in all directions from top to bottom and throughout the assembled forces. Of course, that required the latest communications technology so that networks within his command could communicate with other networks as well as with the upper level commanders. You can imagine how difficult this was in Afghanistan, with many roadblocks to effective communication, some having to do with weather and terrain, some having to do with distance, and some having to do with enemy interference. And, of course, McChrystal was dealing with troops from 20 different countries and 20 different command posts around the world; that meant that you could never have a face-to-face meeting with everyone in the room. So McChrystal came to rely on e-mail, chat, video teleconferencing, and many other technologies not only for communication, but for leadership.

Now McChrystal is teaching leadership. In a recent class, he opened by commenting, "The point of today is to understand trust and relationships, which underpin the difference between success and failure."[45] In McChrystal's view, communications is all-important but trust and relationships hold everything together. This is especially true when you are dealing with such a diverse set of troops in terms of nationality, gender, generation, and background. In this kind of situation you're not giving orders but you're building consensus or shared purpose. And that requires communications, trust, and building sound relationships.

1. In what ways do you think McChrystal was successful?

2. In what ways do you think he was unsuccessful?

3. What lessons about motivation and leadership does his experience provide?

important role in employee engagement and trust, factors that in turn impact key business outcomes, such as productivity, profitability, retention, and customer service. But a more recent study examined what managers actually *did* that led to these results. Specifically, they looked at whether managers used a strengths-based approach, whether they maintained a positive attitude when difficulties arose, and whether they provided frequent recognition and encouragement. There is great value in using a strengths-based approach. Many leaders and managers are focused on fixing the problems or weaknesses they find in their organizations, as opposed to building on the strengths that exist in the organization. On the other hand,

Trust Building on CNN

FIGURE 5.5 ENGAGEMENT IN ORGANIZATIONS

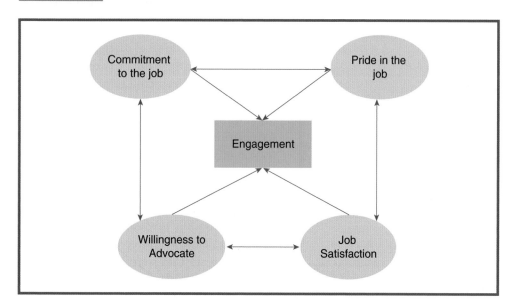

Source: Adapted from Haid, M., & Sims, J. (2009). *Employee engagement* (pp. 1–24). Philadelphia, PA: Right Management. Retrieved from http://www.right.com/thought-leadership/research/employee-engagement---maximizing-organizational-performance.pdf

Trust

Managers who take a strengths-based approach help employees identify strengths and align their talents with their work. These managers don't ignore employee weaknesses, but fixing them isn't their primary focus. Instead, positive managers focus more on what the employee is good at and how his or her strengths can be leveraged to the benefit of the employee, team, and organization.[46]

We should also note that other management behaviors, such as maintaining a positive attitude and providing recognition and encouragement, extend the strengths-based approach. The study concluded that managers who maintain the strength oriented approach ranked in the upper quartile of managers in terms of performance and productivity. Gary Tranter, senior vice president and CIO of Hanover, the company that was studied, commented, "The results helped to validate my beliefs and hypothesis that managers who maintain a positive perspective, who ensure that timely and meaningful recognition of people occurs, and who have a keen awareness of employees' strengths [help create] a more engaged workforce. What surprised me about the outcomes was that the correlations were much stronger than I had anticipated."[47] Another study, conducted by the consulting firm Right Management, involved more than 28,800 employees in 15 countries. That study concluded that engagement levels affected an organization's culture, its strategy execution, leadership ability, and structure and processes. More specifically, the study confirmed that engagement leads to higher financial performance, higher customer satisfaction, and higher employee retention. Employees who indicated that their companies were among the top performers in their field were twice as engaged as those who saw their companies as underperforming. "Fifty-three of those who saw their organizations as top performers were highly engaged, while only 8% of those who reported their organizations as underperforming were engaged."[48] But combining this work with a study conducted by the Institute for Employment Studies in the United Kingdom led to the conclusion that engagement is actually a two-step process (see Figure 5.6).

Engagement
Bottom Line

One element is the level of engagement that people have for their job or career or profession. For example, a college professor might be deeply involved in his or her professional organization, say, the American Psychological Association, and highly committed to the profession of psychology, but care little about the specific university where he or she works. The situation could also be reversed and a person might show high engagement with a specific organization but low engagement with the profession. The obvious conclusion is that the highest and most impactful employee engagement combines job or professional engagement with organizational engagement. And that in turn affects performance, profitability, productivity, and retention.

FIGURE 5.6 **IMPACT OF ENGAGEMENT**

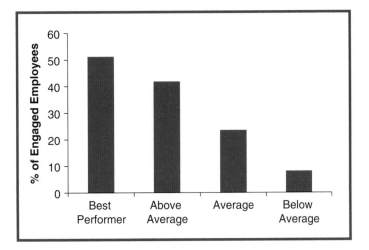

Source: Adapted from Haid, M., & Sims, J. (2009). *Employee engagement* (pp. 1–24). Philadelphia, PA: Right Management. Retrieved from http://www.right.com/thought-leadership/research/employee-engagement---maximizing-organizational-performance.pdf

What are the things that you as a manager can do to increase trust and engagement? (1) Obviously, the first and most important thing to do is to increase the involvement of people in decisions that affect them. Even if employees don't make the final decision, they are more likely to endorse the decision and help in its implementation if they have been a part of the process. People usually like decisions that they themselves have made or at least have contributed to. But employee involvement must be authentic. It can't be just a matter of making people feel they are involved when they really aren't or when they really don't have any impact on the decision. (2) Another way to increase trust and engagement is for you to exhibit a high degree of caring and compassion. One finding in the Gallup studies was that engagement is connected to a high degree of emotional caring on the part of the immediate boss. When caring or compassion was present, employees were more likely to take risks and to stretch themselves to achieve more. Though the top level leaders can't engage personally with every employee, they can certainly encourage a culture of caring and compassion throughout the organization. (3) Leaders and managers should also try to be as transparent as possible in the decision-making process. People are more likely to be engaged if they understand how decisions are made, even if those decisions don't go in their direction. One study, for example, showed that people who understood how their performance bonus was decided upon were more satisfied than those who received more money but didn't understand the process.[49] (4) Managers and leaders should always be attentive to relationships.

New managers particularly will be aided by giving top priority to building relationships. When Laura Ching, founder and chief merchandising officer of TinyPrints.com, was asked what she looks for in new employees, she replied, "First, do they have the right skills? But on a more personal level, we want someone who's genuine and memorable and enjoys connecting and relationships."[50]

When Your Boss
Is Too Nice

Gary Burnison, CEO of Korn/Ferry, the world's largest executive recruiting firm, builds on this theme based on his experience as a business leader. He argues that leadership starts with the leader, but it is never about the leader. The leader, he argues, must be hands-on, but the primary objective is "to empower others to make decisions and take actions that are aligned with the organization's vision, purpose, and strategy."[51] The leader's role is to build leadership and collaboration throughout the organization. In doing so, the leader must be especially attentive to what is being said and also what is left unsaid (the latter often being the more important). The leader must also remain humble and reinforce the importance of the role employees play in the organization. The leader can express a vision and encourage people to move toward that vision, but the real work of the organization requires the collaboration of people at all levels of the organization and with stakeholders outside. "As a leader, you rise above 'me' to embrace 'we.'"[52]

Creativity and Engagement

In this book we are especially concerned with creative change in a global society. For that reason, we should spend some time thinking about how changing leadership and changing environmental conditions are likely to affect the motivation of our employees. Traditional approaches to motivation have largely assumed a one-on-one relationship between the manager and the employee, with the manager trying to do those things that will increase the motivation of the employee to contribute to the organization. And that one-on-one relationship, typically a relationship between a front-line manager and the employee, remains important. But as society becomes both more global and more complex, more is needed. If your employees are scattered all over the world, the job of inspiring employees to contribute to and engage with the organization is something that can't be left to the front-line managers, but is something the leaders of the organization must attend to. By establishing a particular culture in the organization, those at the top can affect the way in which employees regard the organization and choose to engage. One way to sort this out is to think of motivation as a responsibility of the front-line manager, and engagement as a responsibility of top leadership.

The front-line manager has the opportunity to have discussions regularly with her employees. What happens in those discussions can determine the extent and the nature of an individual's contribution. In this interaction, the most contemporary advice seems to be that the manager needs to understand the uniqueness of the individual and especially the talents that each individual brings to the job, and then to shape the work so that it is most meaningful to the employee. One writer has put it this way:

> Great managers know that the most effective way to invest their time is to identify exactly how each employee is different and then to figure out how best to incorporate those enduring idiosyncrasies into the overall plan. To excel at managing others, you must bring that insight to your actions and interactions. Always remember that great managing is about release, not transformation. It's about constantly tweaking your environment so that the unique contribution, the unique needs, and the unique style of each employee can be given free rein. [53]

At the same time that the front-line manager is trying to increase motivation, top leadership needs to set a tone or establish a culture that emphasizes employee engagement. We have already seen evidence that changes in organizational engagement can lead to increases in productivity, so this is important work. So where do we begin? One major study of federal employees offered several elements that constitute employee engagement. These are: (1) Pride in one's work or workplace, (2) Satisfaction with leadership, (3) Opportunity to perform well at work, (4) Satisfaction with recognition received, (5) Prospect for future personal growth, and (6) Positive work environment/teamwork.[54] These factors in turn can become drivers of productivity and profit. What's important to note here is that these factors all can be influenced by the top leaders' encouragement of an open and engaged workforce. Top leadership can establish organization-wide policies and structures that affect these matters, but leadership can also inspire people to connect emotionally with the organization and in turn increase their contributions to the organization.

Let's unpack this issue a little further. While we will elaborate the notion of creative leadership later, we can say again that leadership in the future is likely to be quite different from leadership today. As we have already seen, many are talking about shared leadership and group-centric leadership, both of which suggest the decline of the concept of a leader as an individual and the ascendancy of the concept of the group as leader.

Create a Friendly Environment

They also suggest the withering away of hierarchy and top-down leadership. And, as a result, they build a more creative and innovative organization, as well as one that can react quickly to rapid changes in the environment. Another important element of creative leadership, however, is that it comes from inside; that is, your personal growth and development is a prerequisite to your maturity as a leader. Business school dean Doug Guthrie writes, "For me, creative leadership is not about the position you hold inside the organization, it is about how you live in that position. It is your state of mind and how you approach your work and the values you bring to that work that makes you a leader."[55] And, if we assume that leadership should be extended throughout the organization, then we should be concerned about the "inner life" of those throughout the organization.

What Do You Think?

▶ A progressive and highly successful leader of a clothing design and manufacturing firm believed that process innovation—for example, new ways to engage employees—was much more important than product innovation, so he talked process innovation at every meeting, indeed in every opportunity he had. Is process innovation more important than product innovation? What do you think?

Leadership and Temperament

This perspective shines new light on the issue of motivation and engagement, suggesting that we give greater attention to the emotions, the psychological attachments, and the developmental state of those throughout the organization. Recent research has developed several points that are significant in this regard. A study based on over 12,000 daily diary entries by leaders and managers in a variety of firms analyzed the psychological state of mind of people who were experiencing good days in terms of their creativity and productivity, as opposed to those who were having bad days. What the researchers found was that people perform better when they are experiencing positive emotions, more passion for their work, and positive perceptions of those around them, from coworkers to top leadership. But the single most important driver of high performance turned out to be the individual's making progress on meaningful work. Incidentally, the study also found that leaders and managers played an important role in appropriately acknowledging both progress and the meaningfulness of the work. When managers praised work that employees thought was minimal, suspicion, cynicism, and even anger resulted. When managers failed to praise work that employees thought was highly creative and positive, or even criticized employees over trivial matters, the results were even more negative. As you might expect, when managers praised work that employees felt was their best, there were positive effects in the inner life of both managers and employees.[56]

This raises an important theme that we will see repeated in our various discussions of creative leadership, the idea that the inner world of the leader dramatically affects what happens in the outer world. So for the leader, the manager, or the employee, we might ask what the organization is doing to encourage self-examination, self-reflection, and personal growth. Brené Brown, author of *Daring Greatly*, writes that "what we know matters, but who we are matters more. Being rather than knowing requires showing up and letting ourselves be seen. It requires us to dare greatly, to be vulnerable. The first step of that journey is understanding where we are, what we're up against, and where we need to go."[57] Understanding where we are, what we are up against, and where we need to go obviously sets us on a path to personal development. And, in organizational terms, the same steps lead to a more committed and engaged leader, manager, or employee.

▶ Summary and Applications for Managers

The preceding sections presented an almost dizzying array of perspectives on motivation and behavior. The reader might be left wondering what might be the best way of understanding behavior. Is it need satisfaction? Based on learning and reinforcement? Shaped by our values and personality? Influenced by rewards? Affected by different management approaches? Intrinsic in the nature of the job? Based on a rational calculation of effort, performance, and expected outcomes? Influenced by our life stages? Based on our assessments of fairness?

The short answer to all of these questions is *yes*. As we mentioned at the beginning of the chapter, motivation is complex, and the models developed to explain it represent a complicated foundation on which to base our attempts to influence our own motivation as well as that of others. But as we also suggested, the various models presented here are not necessarily mutually exclusive. Particularly when we think about the actions that are suggested in looking across the varied perspectives, several commonalities emerge. Although motivation is complicated, in general it may be useful to think about the following.

1. *Be self-reflective and proactive about your own motivation.* It is difficult, if not impossible, to motivate your employees if you lack motivation yourself. Carefully consider the factors that motivate you and keep you motivated. Are you motivated by challenging goals? Promotion? Achievement? Whatever your answer, do what you can to create situations for yourself that keep you excited and motivated about your work. Your attitudes and behavior can be an important and positive contributing factor in the overall motivational climate.

2. *Be aware that what motivates you is not necessarily what will motivate others.* Talk with your employees and listen carefully to what they say about the motivational factors that are important to them. Help them to clarify their goals, desires, and needs. There is no "one size fits all" approach to motivating people. Be cognizant of the differences among people in terms of what they need from you and the organization to motivate them. People differ in terms of needs, personality, attitudes, and values.

3. *Have realistic expectations about the extent to which you can influence the motivation of others.* Certainly, there were many things suggested in this chapter that have been shown to positively influence motivation. But it also is important to remember that motivation is internal to the individual. As a manager, you cannot motivate everyone. There might be people who, despite your best efforts, simply are not motivated to work toward organizational goals. In those cases, it might just be a poor fit between the organization and the individuals.

4. *Participate in setting clear and challenging goals.* Goal setting is important from several perspectives. Particularly if established in a participative process, goal setting clarifies shared objectives, provides an opportunity for communication, enhances self-efficacy and commitment, and provides the basis for tracking performance. Once goals are established, you should provide information so that people can track their progress and know when and how well they have reached the goals. This information can be motivating in and of itself for some people. Feedback is particularly important to people with a high achievement need, but in general, people who participate in the formation of goals and become committed to them want information so that they can assess their progress in achieving the goals.

5. *Think about the salience of various rewards.* Because different people are motivated by different things, different rewards will have more or less value to them. Do not assume that the rewards that would be meaningful for one person will be the same for everyone else. Ask people about their plans, personal goals, and aspirations. Talk to them about what makes their work rewarding for them. Ask them what they want from you so that they will do their best. Listen to what they tell you about what makes them enthusiastic, discouraged, or energized. Then do what you can to provide rewards that are valuable to them. Also make clear the connections between performance and rewards. Let people know what they will need to accomplish to earn the rewards they desire.

6. *Be honest with people about what rewards are possible and what rewards are not.* If you promise more than you actually can deliver, then you might end up doing more damage than good. It is critical to be clear about what you can and

cannot do in terms of monetary rewards, promotions, changes to assignments, and other matters over which you might not have complete control. If there is something that is important to a particular employee, then explain clearly what you can and cannot do in that regard. For those things that you cannot control, try to work creatively with the employee.

7. *Although people might be different in terms of personality, wants, goals, and needs, realize that they also want to be treated fairly.* Employees do not work in a vacuum. They make comparisons. When employees think that there is an inequity, they might well act to correct it. Rewards, consequences, and outcomes need not be the same for everyone, but they should be perceived by employees as fair and equitable relative to how their inputs compare with the inputs of others.

8. *Remember that motivation is not just about the characteristics of people;* it also is about the work that you ask them to do and the organization they work in. To maintain motivation, the work itself needs to be satisfying and meaningful. Jobs that are repetitive, lack variety, allow little autonomy, or have little effect on others are inherently unsatisfying, not to mention boring. It makes sense, then, to work with employees to make their work as interesting and satisfying as possible. But we should mention a cautionary note: Make sure that people want to enrich their jobs. Ask them what they would like to see changed.

9. *Think about the life stages of the people you work with* as a means of understanding the challenges they face and offering appropriate support. But as critics note, life-stage theories cannot be applied unthinkingly or used as the only means of understanding what motivates behavior. It is important to recognize the roles of other factors such as lifestyle, gender, cultural differences, and changes in family structure, as well as the influence of factors related to the organizational context, such as perceptions of climate and the positions and levels of employees.

10. *Keep in mind the importance of trust and engagement.* You may not have unlimited power or control, even if you are in a higher level position, but you can always think about ways to build trust in your team and ways to engage people who work with you or for you. Focus on making work meaningful and encouraging participation and contribution.

▶ Key Terms

Employee engagement   157

Expectancy theory   147

Hierarchy of needs   145

Law of effect   153

Motivation   144

Needs   144

Negative reinforcer   153

Organizational rewards   153

Positive reinforcer   153

Punishment   153

Reinforcement   153

Reinforcement theory   153

Self-efficacy   150

▶ Exercise 5.1 Staying Motivated

For this exercise, focus on some aspect of your job where you do not feel motivated. Then go over the following steps.

1. Identify the barriers to motivation. Is the work challenging? Do you feel competent to perform the work? Are you getting needed feedback? Do you understand the expectations? Do you have the time and resources needed to perform well? What other problems, obstacles, and unmet needs do you confront?

2. Formulate a plan, including action steps, for overcoming the barriers to motivation. Discuss the plan with affected parties and get commitments from them (if appropriate).

3. Implement the action steps. After a reasonable time period, assess the results. Has your motivation increased? Has your interest, satisfaction, or performance improved? What else might you do to stay motivated?

► Exercise 5.2   Being an Energizer

Earlier we talked about how positive energy is a very important source for motivation. Over the next week, observe people in your organization who act as "energizers" and "de-energizers." How do you respond to these people? Then carefully observe how often you are an energizer or a de-energizer at work and how people react to you. Over time, consciously and authentically adopt a more positive attitude and engage in energizing behaviors such as seeing opportunities for positive action, taking into account others' opinions and ideas, and openly showing appreciation for others' efforts. As you continue to practice this behavior, can you observe any changes in the behavior and attitude of the people around you? How do those changes, if any, influence you?

► Case Study 5.1   SOS in DHS: A Problem of Motivation

About 18 months ago, Jess Johnson was appointed to direct a newly created unit in the state's Department of Human Services (DHS). Shortly thereafter, she interviewed and hired six new employees to staff the unit. The name of the unit is Service Outreach for Seniors (SOS). Its purpose is to coordinate services for the vulnerable elderly. This is Jess's first supervisory position.

Susan Jones and Bob Martin were two of the new employees Jess hired. Initially, both were very productive, enthusiastic, and industrious. Bob had taken the initiative to work closely with several prominent private service providers to ensure their cooperation and involvement in the new program. Susan had done a terrific job of producing publications and other materials describing the goals of the unit and explaining SOS services to the elderly. But since this initial spurt of activity and enthusiasm, both Susan and Bob have become less-than-ideal employees in Jess's estimation.

Within 6 months of his hiring, Bob developed what Jess considers to be poor work habits (e.g., very long lunches and coffee breaks, tardiness, absenteeism). Bob demonstrates little interest in or enthusiasm for his work. Although he generally accomplishes, at least in a minimal manner, those tasks that are directly assigned to him, he rarely volunteers ideas or takes the initiative. From Jess's perspective, employees who take initiative and demonstrate creativity are critical in helping the unit to establish itself politically and to create a service where none had existed before.

Susan, on the other hand, has become quite "creative" in the sense that she has ceased to check with Jess (or anyone) on important policy matters before speaking to external groups and individuals. On several occasions, she has promised things to representatives of organizations and to elected officials that the SOS program simply could not deliver. On other occasions, she has misrepresented her role as a staff member, instead leaving the impression that she was directing the unit. This has embarrassed Jess and her supervisors more than once. Despite Susan's apparent desire to be "in the limelight" in the political and community arena, she has developed an open disdain for the regular workload in her area. She routinely misses deadlines and fails to complete important paperwork.

Jess has met with Bob and Susan separately to discuss her dissatisfaction with their performance. Being a matter-of-fact person, Jess simply told them that their work was not up to par and that she expected them to improve. For a week or so, things seemed to get better. But the same problems quickly resurfaced.

The other four employees Jess hired are doing well. They have what she considers good work habits: They usually are on time and are willing to work hard to help the new unit succeed. They seem to be eager to do well. She can count on them to complete assigned tasks and meet deadlines. Each of them, in his or her own way, also has demonstrated a willingness to go "above and beyond" and to make positive suggestions for improving the operations and services of the unit.

But the problems with Susan and Bob are beginning to drag down the morale of the other employees and certainly are causing Jess's attitude toward work to suffer. Jess has not talked to either of them about these problems for several weeks because she has not been able to figure out what to do or say. But at different times this morning, both Susan and Bob came to Jess's office asking her to recommend them for promotion to a position that opened up recently in the Child Welfare unit similar to SOS. Jess does not know how to handle these requests. More troubling, she does not know how to address the longer term problems of motivating all of her employees to do well.

1. Define the problem(s) in this case, using as many theories of motivation from this chapter as you think might apply.

2. Discuss the practical implications for each of the models you use. In other words, what do these models suggest the supervisor should *do or say* as a consequence of defining the problem from that perspective?

3. What are some of the perspectives on organizational behavior that could explain the apparently high levels of motivation among the four employees? What models might explain Jess's motivation?

4. Which of the theories or models do you think fit best with which employees and why?

5. What conclusions can you draw, or what observations can you make, about motivation theory and research?

⑤SAGE edge™

Sharpen your skills with SAGE edge at edge.sagepub.com/nahavandi

SAGE edge for students provides a personalized approach to help you accomplish your coursework goals in an easy-to-use learning environment.

▶ Endnotes

1. Carter, M. (2013). Happiness means creativity: One company's bet on positive psychology. *Fast Company*, July 1. Retrieved from http://www.fastcocreate.com/1683288/happiness-means-creativity-one-companys-bet-on-positive-psychology on September 10, 2013.

2. Maslow, A. (1943). A theory of human motivation. *Psychological Review, 50*, 388.

3. McGregor, D. (1957, November). The human side of the enterprise. *Management Review*, 22–28, 88–92.

4. McGregor, 1957, pp. 88–89.

5. Wurtzel, A. (2012, October 23). *What Circuit City learned about valuing employees*. Retrieved from http://blogs.hbr.org/cs/2012/10/what_circuit_city_learned_abou.html on December 12, 2012.

6. Herzberg, F. (2003, January). One more time: How do you motivate employees? *Harvard Business Review*, reprint, 2–12.

7. McClelland, D. (1985). *Human motivation*. Glenview, IL: Scott, Foresman.

8. McClelland, 1985, p. 183.

9. Interview with Ricardo Semler [video]. (2007). Retrieved from http://www.youtube.com/watch?v=gJkOPxJCN1w on December 12, 2012.

10. Linderman, M. (2007). *Signal vs. Noise: Inspiring Ricardo Semler lecture at MIT*. Retrieved from http://37signals.com/svn/posts/649-inspiring-ricardo-semler-lecture-at-mit on December 12, 2012.

11. Shinn, S. (2004, January/February). The Maverick CEO. *BizEd*, 18.

12. Fisher, L. M. (2005). Ricardo Semler won't take control. *Strategy and Business*, Winter. Retrieved from http://www.strategy-business.com/media/file/sb41_05408.pdf on December 12, 2012.

13. Fisher, 2005.

14. Vroom, V. (1964). *Work and motivation*. New York, NY: Wiley.

15. Porter, L., & Lawler, E. (1968). *Managerial attitudes and performance*. Homewood, IL: Irwin.

16. Burton, F. G., Chen, Y. N., Grover, V., & Stewart, K. (1992–1993). An application of expectancy theory for assessing user motivation to utilize an expert system. *Journal of Management Information Systems, 9*(3), 183–198; Mastrofski, S. D., Ritti, R. R., & Snipes, J. (1994). Expectancy theory and police productivity in DUI enforcement. *Law and Society Review, 28*, 113–148; and Smith, C. G., Hindman, H. D., & Havlovic, S. J. (1997). A discriminant analysis of employee choice in a multi-union representation election. *Canadian Journal of Administrative Sciences, 14*(3), 235–245.

17. Hackman, J. R., & Porter, L. (1968). Expectancy theory predictions of work effectiveness. *Organizational Behavior and Human Performance, 3*, 417–426.

18. Locke, E. (1978, July). The ubiquity of the technique of goal setting in theories of and approaches to employee motivation. *Academy of Management Review*, 594–601; see p. 594.

19. Locke, E. (1968). Toward a theory of task motivation and incentives. *Organizational Behavior and Human Performance, 3*, 157–189.

20. Latham, G., & Baldes, J. J. (1975). The "practical significance" of Locke's theory of goal setting. *Journal of Applied Psychology, 60*(1), 122–124.

21. Tubbs, M. (1986). Goal setting: A meta-analytic examination of the empirical evidence. *Journal of Applied Psychology, 71*(3), 474–483.

22. Eden, D. (1988). Pygmalion, goal setting, and expectancy: Compatible ways to boost productivity. *Academy of Management Review, 13*(4), 639–652.

23. Bandura, A. (1986). *Social foundations of thought and action: A social cognitive view*. Englewood Cliffs, NJ: Prentice Hall.

24. Adams, J. S. (1965). Inequity in social exchange. In L. Berkowitz (Ed.), *Advances in experimental psychology*. New York, NY: Academic Press.

25. Goodman, P. S. (1977). Social comparison processes in organizations. In B. M. Staw & G. E. Salancik (Eds.), *New directions in organizational behavior*. Chicago, IL: St. Clair.

26. Thorndike, E. L. (1913). *Educational psychology: The psychology of learning*. New York, NY: Columbia University Press.

27. Skinner, B. F. (1971). *Beyond freedom and dignity*. New York, NY: Knopf.

28. Durant, F. R. (Ed.), Kramer, R. (Assoc. ed.), Perry, J., Mesch, D., & Paarlberg, L. (2006). Motivating employees in a new governance era: The performance paradigm revisited. *Public Administration Review, 66*(4), 505–514.

29. Weibel, A., Rost, K., & Osterloh, M. (2009). Pay for performance in the public sector. *Journal of Public Administration and Theory, 20*, 387–412; see p. 404.

30. Kanfer, R., & Ackerman, L. P. (2004). Aging, adult development, and working motivation. *Academy of Management Review, 29*(3), 442.

31. Kanfer & Ackerman, 2004, p. 446.

32. Gibson, J., Greenwood, R., & Murphy, E. (2009). Generational differences in the workplace: Personal values, behaviors, and popular beliefs. *Journal of Diversity Management, 4*(3), 1–8.

33. Gibson, Greenwood, & Murphy, 2009.

34. Crampton, S., & Hodge, J. (2007). Generations in the workplace. *The Business Review, 9*(1), 16–22; and Gibson, Greenwood, & Murphy, 2009.

35. Crampton & Hodge, 2007, p. 16.

36. Lancaster, L. C., & Stillman, D. (2010). *The M-factor: How the millennial generation is rocking the workplace*. New York, NY: Harper Business.

37. Espinoza, C., Ukleja, M., & Rusch, C. (2010). *Managing the millennials: Discover the core competencies for managing today's workforce.* Hoboken, NJ: Wiley.

38. Marcum, J. (1999, Autumn). Out with motivation, in with engagement. *National Productivity Review,* 43–46.

39. Asplund, J., & Blacksmith, N. (2013). The secret of higher performance. *Gallup Business Journal,* May 3, 2011. Retrieved from http://businessjournal.gallup.com/content/147383/Secret-Higher-Performance.aspx#1 on September 12, 2013.

40. Likert, R. (1967). *The human organization.* New York, NY: McGraw-Hill.

41. Lawler, E. E. (1990). *High involvement management.* San Francisco, CA: Jossey-Bass.

42. Wefald, A. J., & Downey, R. G. (2009). Job engagement in organizations: Fad, fashion, or folderol? *Journal of Organizational Behavior, 30*(1), 141. Retrieved from http://login.ezproxy1.lib.asu.edu/login?url=http://search.proquest.com/docview/224878200?accountid=4485 on September 12, 2013.

43. Safian, R. (2012). The secrets of generation flux. *Fast Company,* October 15. Retrieved from http://www.fastcompany.com/3001734/secrets-generation-flux on September 12, 2013; see p. 102.

44. Safian, 2012, p. 102.

45. Foxhall, E. (2011). Professor McChrystal. *Yale Daily News,* January 18. Retrieved from http://www.yaledailynews.com/news/2011/jan/18/professor-mcchrystal/ on September 1, 2013.

46. Robison, J. (2012). The business benefits of positive leadership. *Gallup Business Journal,* May 10, 2007. Retrieved from http://businessjournal.gallup.com/content/27496/Business-Benefits-Positive-Leadership.aspx on September 15, 2013.

47. Kastelle, T. (2012). Why you need to be vulnerable to innovate. *Innovation Excellence,* November 5. Retrieved from http://www.innovationexcellence.com/blog/2012/11/05/why-you-need-to-be-vulnerable-to-innovate on September 10, 2013.

48. Haid, M., & Sims, J. (2009). *Employee engagement* (pp. 1–24). Philadelphia, PA: Right Management. Retrieved from http://www.right.com/thought-leadership/research/employee-engagement—maximizing-organizational-performance.pdf; see p. 8.

49. Atkins, A. (2012). How leaders build trust. *Fast Company,* August. Retrieved from: http://www.fastcompany.com/3000204/how-leaders-build-trust?utm_source on September 10, 2013.

50. Bryant, A. (2011). On Mondays, look forward to coming in. *New York Times,* February 19. Retrieved from http://www.nytimes.com/2011/02/20/business/20corner.html?pagewanted=1&_r=0 on September 10, 2013.

51. Burnison, G. (2012). The softer side of management. *Fast Company*, March 13. Retrieved from http://www.fastcompany.com/1823211/learning-softer-side-leadership on September 10, 2013; see p. 1.

52. Burnison, 2012, p. 1.

53. Buckingham, M. (2005). What great managers do. *Harvard Business Review,* March, 1–7. Retrieved from http://hbr.org/2005/03/what-great-managers-do/ar/1 on September 10, 2013.

54. Nierle, D., Ford, J., & Tsugawa, J. (2012). *The power of federal employee engagement.* Retrieved from MSPB: http://annex.ipacweb.org/library/conf/10/nierle.pdf on December 10, 2012.

55. Guthrie, D. (2012). Creative leadership: Democracy. *Forbes.* July 12, p. 1. Retrieved from http://www.forbes.com/sites/dougguthrie/2012/07/12/creative-leadership-democracy/ on September 10, 2013.

56. Amabile, T. M., & Kramer, S. K. (2007, May). Inner work life: Understanding the subtext of business performance. *Harvard Business Review, 85*(5).

57. Quoted in Kastelle, 2012.

6 Managing Stress

LEARNING OUTCOMES

After studying the material in this chapter, you should be able to:

1. Recognize the symptoms of stress you may be experiencing

2. Understand the personal and organizational consequences and cost of stress

3. Explain individual and organizational sources of stress

4. Use personal and organizational strategies for managing and coping with stress

5. Recommend strategies for managing stress in the workplace

Marissa Mayer of Yahoo ▶

In July 2012, Marissa Mayer became CEO of Yahoo!, the Internet provider. Mayer, certainly one of the most powerful women in the tech industries, came to Yahoo! after thirteen years with Google (she was one of its earliest employees). In accepting the position, she acknowledged the company's difficulties, but also pointed out the significance of the Yahoo! brand. She also announced that she was pregnant. On all the scales of stress, Mayer should be a psychic wreck, but she seems to thrive on the difficulties she faces.

She commented, "I have a theory that burnout is about resentment. And you beat it by knowing what it is you're giving up that makes you resentful. I tell people: Find your rhythm. Your rhythm is what matters to you so much that when you miss it you're resentful of your work. . . . So find your rhythm, understand what makes you resentful, and protect it. You can't have everything you want, but you can have the things that really matter to you. And thinking that way empowers you to work really hard for a really long period of time."

Stress: an individual physiological, behavioral, and psychological response to perceived challenges and threats in the environment

Stressors: environmental threats perceived by an individual

Stress is an inevitable part of life. All of us recognize the feeling of being overwhelmed and tired from too much work, lack of balance, or pressure from various factors. All these stressors are compounded by the realities of everyday life during the 21st century. Traffic, noise, family issues, health problems, time pressures, and all of the other everyday stresses and strains of living can take their toll. Two-income families, changing role expectations, the divorce rate, and changing demographics all challenge our sense of family, not to mention our free time. We are bombarded with information and new technology demanding that we change our ways of communicating and even our ways of thinking.

But before throwing up your hands in despair, you should recognize that stress is a part of being human; and it is not always a bad thing. **Stress** can be defined as an individual physiological, behavioral, and psychological response to perceived challenges and threats in our environment. These environmental threats are called **stressors**. You can experience stress anytime you are put in the position of having to adapt or change; indeed, it is difficult to imagine a meaningful

Much of the stress that people feel doesn't come from having too much to do. It comes from not finishing what they started.

—David Allen, writer on productivity and time management

> *One of the symptoms of an approaching nervous breakdown is the belief that one's work is terribly important.*
>
> — Bertrand Russell

> *Stress: The confusion created when one's mind overrides the body's basic desire to choke the living daylights out of some jerk who desperately deserves it.*
>
> — Anonymous

existence that does not include some level of stress. Completely eliminating stress is not only bad for you, but impossible; life requires that we adapt to changes that occur and respond to demands that are encountered. To put it bluntly, to have no stress, we probably would have to be dead.

In fact, the stress response can contribute to our sense of well-being, motivation, and performance. Stress does not kill people; rather, it is the capacity of people to adapt to the demands of life that enables them to live.[1] It is stress that is too intense, too frequent, or poorly managed that can be personally and organizationally destructive.[2] The key, of course, is to manage stress both in our personal lives and in the organizations where we work so that it is a mostly constructive force rather than a mostly destructive one. Although we concentrate on organizational stress, it is important to recognize from the outset that we cannot completely isolate work-related stressors from stresses arising from factors outside of the organization. The reality is that we experience stress as individuals who must respond to demands that arise in both our private and professional lives. Fortunately, if we can understand stress, recognize its effect on us and those around us, and learn ways of coping with it, there will then be both personal and organizational benefits.

Defining Stress

What Is Stress?

Are you stressed? That might seem like a ridiculous question, particularly because many of you are in school at the same time as you are working and handling family and other responsibilities. Of course you are stressed, you might say. The truth, again, is that all of us experience stress at some level. We all face challenges and threats. The word *stress* is an everyday part of our vocabulary. If you talk about being "stressed out" at work, you are likely to elicit knowing nods and personal stories of feeling overworked, overpressured, and overwhelmed. Some might claim to be immune to it, and others might claim to be almost paralyzed by it, but seemingly everyone knows what it is.

Stress

How do we know when we are exhibiting the symptoms of stress that is too frequent or too intense? In answering that question it is helpful to begin by examining in more detail what exactly happens to us when we become overly stressed. By doing so, it becomes clear that stress is not just "all in our minds," as some people seem to suggest. Remember from the definition at the beginning of the chapter that stress is physical, psychological, and behavioral.[3] It involves first how your body responds. The word *stress* is derived from the Latin word *strictus*, which means tight or narrow. Subjectively, stress sometimes can feel like being internally constricted. But the actual physiological changes associated with stress are much more complex.

General adaptation syndrome (GAS): the three stages that individuals go through when they respond to stressors and try to adapt to them

The General Adaptation Syndrome

The **general adaptation syndrome (GAS)** describes the three stages that individual go through when they respond to stressor and try to adapt to them.[4] When a person is stressed, the brain sets off a type of emergency signal to the nervous and endocrine (hormonal) systems. This often is called the fight-or-flight response, which is the starting point for stress (see Figure 6.1). Our bodies are programmed to either fight the threat or run away from it to survive.

SYMPTOMS OF STRESS

Now that you know that stress is a physical, psychological, and behavioral response, consider how often you feel or experience these symptoms.

	Never	Occasionally	Often	Nearly Always
Dry mouth	0	1	2	3
Irregular or fast heartbeat	0	1	2	3
Aches in back, neck, or other muscles	0	1	2	3
Watery eyes	0	1	2	3
Excessive perspiration or feeling too warm	0	1	2	3
Headache	0	1	2	3
Upset stomach or other digestive problems	0	1	2	3
Loss of appetite	0	1	2	3
Shortness of breath	0	1	2	3
Changes in sleep pattern	0	1	2	3
Fatigue and exhaustion	0	1	2	3
Cold or sweaty hands	0	1	2	3
Lump in throat	0	1	2	3
Anxious or nervous	0	1	2	3
Irritable and frustrated	0	1	2	3
Accident prone	0	1	2	3
Increased drug or alcohol use	0	1	2	3
Emotional outbursts	0	1	2	3
Unable to make decisions	0	1	2	3
Poor concentration and short attention span	0	1	2	3
Hypersensitivity to criticism	0	1	2	3

It is not your total score that is important, but the number of items on which you score 2 or 3. If you are experiencing more than 4 or 5 items with scores of 2 or 3, it is likely that you are experiencing some of the negative impacts of stress.

FIGURE 6.1 THE GENERAL ADAPTATION SYNDROME

Understanding
Stress

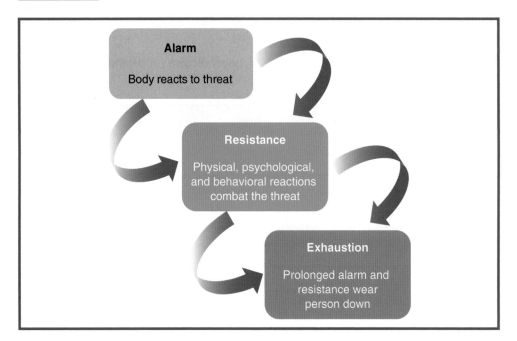

1. **Alarm** is the first physical reaction that occurs when a person feels threatened because she perceives and recognizes stressors. The body reacts to the threat instinctively. Heart rate and blood pressure go up, muscles tense, and perspiration increases as the body readies itself for an emergency. Blood rushes to the heart, muscles, and brain while it rushes away from the intestines, skin, and other organs. The breathing rate increases, and bronchial tubes dilate to facilitate an increased flow of oxygen. The pupils of the eyes enlarge to enhance vision. Your body produces adrenaline. People who are roller-coaster fans readily recognize these reactions when they realize the drop is about to happen. If the stressors continue to be present, the second stage of GAS starts.

2. **Resistance** occurs when the person fights the threat. After the alarm stage described previously, there is a countershock phase in which the body's physical and psychological defenses are mobilized. Initially, the person might feel energized to find ways of dealing with the situation. Under ideal circumstances, the individual successfully adapts to the demand and the body returns to normal functioning. But if the stressors persist or the individual is unable to cope, fatigue sets in. The individual's resistance eventually wears down and he moves to the final stage of the GAS.

3. **Exhaustion** results from long-term exposure to stressors. Continuous and unsuccessful resistance to stressors wears down the individual. All of us have limits in terms of the degree of alarm and resistance we can handle before our physical and mental defenses collapse.

Continued and prolonged exposure to stressors puts people in a continual GAS cycle where they experience alarm and resistance. Even when the stressors are managed successfully, people eventually lose their ability to cope and become exhausted and unable to function. This is the state that most of us describe as being stressed out. In addition to a sense of being overwhelmed, stress has serious physical consequences, particularly when stress becomes chronic and exhaustion sets in. For example, when under stress, our bodies produce corticoids that regulate metabolism

Alarm: the first GAS stage; includes the initial physical reaction to stressors

Resistance: the second GAS stage; occurs when one fights the threat

Exhaustion: the third GAS stage; results from long-term exposure to stressors

and release fatty acids into the bloodstream. Over time, these fatty acids can accumulate in the arteries and ultimately compromise the body's ability to deal with injury and infections. Other hormones are released that increase anxiety, feelings of fatigue, and other mental and psychological responses to stress. As our bodies are bombarded with stress-related chemicals over time, all types of health problems can emerge, ranging from migraines to muscle tension, heartburn to rashes, and coughing to tremors.

You might be asking yourself why all of this physiological mayhem results from a late report, an unexpected presentation, or a bad traffic jam. The reason is that stress is a *nonspecific* bodily response to anything that places a demand on us.[5] In other words, in terms of physical reaction, our bodies do not distinguish between a crisis at work and a car accident, between being physically assaulted and being verbally attacked, or between running from a wild animal and trying to meet an impossible deadline. Even more surprising to some, stress can occur with both happy and sad events. As indicated in Self-Assessment 6.2, change good or bad, both marriage and divorce, as well as both getting promoted and getting fired, can be stressful. From a physical, biochemical, and medical standpoint, it is all the same.

There is, however, some evidence that men and women may behave differently in reaction to these changes. For example, research shows that the fight-or-flight response described previously is the dominant behavioral response among males, but that females are more likely to engage in what they called "tend and befriend" behaviors in response to stress.[6] Nurturing and befriending behaviors among females have been beneficial under conditions of stress, and through the process of evolution and natural selection, those responses have been reinforced. So, humans appear to have a broader repertoire of responses to stress, including affiliative, protective, and caretaking behaviors.

The Consequences and Costs of Stress

The consequences and costs of stress to individuals, to organizations, and to society at large are nothing short of enormous. "Job stress alone is estimated to cost U.S. businesses at least $300 billion each year in absenteeism, diminished productivity, employee turnover and direct medical, legal and insurance fees."[7] If stress leads to depression, the costs go even higher. The U.S. Centers for Disease Control and Prevention estimate that 18.8 million American adults, or about 9.5 percent of adults, will suffer from a depressive illness in a given year. "In a three month period, patients with depression miss an average of 4.8 workdays and experience 11.5 days of reduced productivity. It is estimated that depression causes 200 million lost workdays each year at a cost to employers of $17 billion to $44 billion."[8] In a 2012 study of the IT industry 7% of respondents said they were stressed, 67% considered switching careers, 85% said their job interfered with their personal life, and 42% admitted losing sleep because of work.[9]

Too much stress can lead to a variety of health problems.

What Do You Think?

▶ Many people have tricks to turn stress into a positive force. For example, someone experiencing stage fright might "get mad" at the stage fright for getting in the way of an excellent performance and beat it into submission. There may be other ways of handing the same stress. What do you think?

Avoid Burnout

SOURCES OF STRESS

Although in this chapter we primarily concentrate on the sources of stress that are work and job related, as you read, it is important to remember that all types of life events and changes can lead to stress. Furthermore, it is not only big changes and life events that cause stress. In addition to events such as major job moves, shifts in responsibilities, and organizational changes, the day-to-day realities of work can make you feel stressed. How often do you experience the following at work?

	Never	Occasionally	Often	Nearly Always
Too much work	0	1	2	3
Conflicts with coworkers	0	1	2	3
Too much e-mail	0	1	2	3
Irate customers	0	1	2	3
Unreasonable demands	0	1	2	3
Travel or commuting problems	0	1	2	3
Telephone interruptions	0	1	2	3
Trouble with supervisor	0	1	2	3
Problems with employees	0	1	2	3
Unpleasant working conditions	0	1	2	3
Job interfering with family life	0	1	2	3
Not enough to do	0	1	2	3
Tasks are boring	0	1	2	3
Lack of resources to do job	0	1	2	3
Unproductive meetings	0	1	2	3
Goals not reachable	0	1	2	3
Too many objectives at once	0	1	2	3
Unclear guidance	0	1	2	3
Family life interfering with work	0	1	2	3
Deadlines	0	1	2	3
Difficult work	0	1	2	3
Lack of advancement	0	1	2	3
Not enough training	0	1	2	3
Lack of input on decisions	0	1	2	3
Too little autonomy	0	1	2	3
Too many hours	0	1	2	3
Unsatisfying work	0	1	2	3

Stress can lead to behavior that interferes with our relationships with others. We might become irritable, less patient, angry, or withdrawn. We might lash out at others or react out of proportion to the situation. We are less able to deal with situations calmly, effectively, and appropriately. Obviously, this can affect the nature of our relationships with our supervisors, our employees, citizens, and our peers, families, and friends. Ask yourself, would you rather work with someone who is constantly stressed and "on edge" or with someone who manages his or her stress successfully? In other words, being an effective manager or leader requires us to manage our own stress, not only for our own benefit but also for the benefit of the people working with us and the citizens we serve.

Stress also can make us accident-prone and cause work-related accidents.[10] Stress can make us hurry through tasks, making us more apt to make mistakes. Stress can decrease our reaction time and attention and also can distort cognitive processes. The U.S. Bureau of Labor Statistics estimates that there were over 1 million workplace accidents in 2011, with an average 8 days of work lost per incident.[11]

In extreme cases, stress also can lead to workplace violence. In 2011, 17 percent of fatal work injuries in the United States were related to workplace violence.[12] An average of 20 workers a week were killed and 18,000 were assaulted. From 2006 to 2010, over 500 people were killed in

Candlelight vigil held on November 2012 in Fresno, California, after Lawrence Jones opened fire on four co-workers, killing two and wounding two others. In extreme cases, stress can result in workplace violence.

work-related homicides with shootings accounting for 70% of those deaths in 2010.[13] While not all these deaths are related to stress—many are caused by criminals—stress plays a part in many. An FBI report acknowledges that angry and disturbed and aggrieved employees pose a serious threat to others in the workplace.[14] Whereas these behavioral consequences of stress have serious implications for our health, there also are other medical issues associated with stress. Stress compromises our immune systems, making us generally more vulnerable to illness and disease. It disrupts our sleep patterns, leading to impaired concentration, memory, and alertness.[15] Heart attacks, strokes, cancer, ulcers, hypertension, headaches, back troubles, and arthritis all have been linked to or found to be worsened by stress.

Job dissatisfaction is linked to stress as well.[16] **Job burnout**, characterized by exhaustion, sense of powerlessness, cynicism, and disengagement, often is related to stress.[17] "The business climate has become so fiery and competitive that leaders are focused on competition and getting the most out of their people. Everyone's working to their max."[18] In short, stress imposes significant costs, lowers productivity, compromises effectiveness, and decreases the quality and safety of work life.

Stress: Good, Bad, and Ugly

Why do we not avoid stress at all costs? There are two answers to this question. The first is relatively simple: We cannot avoid stress while still living normal lives. But, second, despite all of its negative consequences and costs, some stress can be very beneficial. It can increase our energy, motivation, and drive. Appropriate levels of stress help us to focus our attention, make our awareness more acute, and promote sound decision making. Seyle[19] expressed this distinction between the positive and negative aspects of stress as the difference between *eustress* (*eu* is the Greek root for "good") and distress. Eustress is healthy stress that is experienced positively with constructive outcomes. Rather than feeling overwhelmed, people feel challenged and motivated.

The link between stress and performance is presented in Figure 6.2. When stress levels are too low, performance will suffer. Too little stress leads to apathy, boredom, and impaired attention. As stress (arousal) increases, performance improves. People might feel challenged and exhilarated. Their attention becomes more focused, and their senses become more acute. Decision-making capacity and judgment are enhanced. But as stress continues to increase, performance declines. People might withdraw, become overwhelmed, and experience the negative physical and mental symptoms of stress.

FIGURE 6.2 IDEAL LEVEL OF STRESS

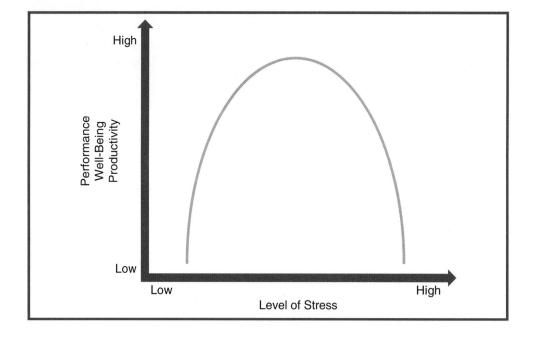

Job burnout: characterized by exhaustion, sense of powerlessness, cynicism, and disengagement

What makes the situation even more complicated is the fact that individuals may respond to the same set of circumstances differently. Stress is subjective, and people respond to it in various ways. One person might see a situation as highly motivating and energizing, whereas another might become quite distressed. It is important to remember, then, that what causes stress for others might not be what causes you to feel stress. Conversely, something that you find to be very stressful might be seen as an invigorating challenge by others, or they might not notice it at all. But what is an appropriate or moderate level of stress? Is it daily deadlines and a boss who is always pushing you to learn new things? Or is it weekly deadlines with a boss who leaves you alone? Do you work best when you are pushed and face competition and challenge or do you like to work at your own pace?

The fact that stress is different for different people has important implications for managers and organizations. If you seek challenge and can handle high pressure, you may assume that your employees are the same and push them to levels that you may personally prefer. Not all those who report to you will feel the same way. Some can handle even more stressors; others may be overwhelmed. Similarly, some organizational cultures are more high pressure than others. The key to effective management is to take individual differences into consideration. A good manager gets to know her employees and understands what motivates and challenges each of them without stressing them out. Additionally, through the interviewing and hiring process, organizations can select individuals who best fit the job.

Sources of Stress

As explained previously, stress occurs in response to some demand or need to adapt. There are a number of situations or conditions at work that can evoke a stress response. Job stress occurs when job-related factors interact with the worker's individual characteristics in a way that either enhances or disrupts the worker's psychological or physiological functioning.[20] There are a variety of job-related factors that may play a role; however, individual personal factors also impact stress level and therefore an employee's performance. The sources of stress are presented in Figure 6.3. When reading about these potential stressors, keep in mind that they are just that—potential. Not all people will respond to these factors in the same way, and the existence of a stress response does not necessarily mean that it is altogether negative. Many managers have found ways of coping successfully and creatively with the challenges they face, to their own and their organizations' advantage. Some of those coping strategies are discussed in a later section of this chapter. But for now, it is useful to explore some of the factors at work that may trigger the stress response in the first place.

Stress at the Workplace

Individual Factors

Individual sources of stress stem from our personalities or events in our personal lives. The primary source of stress is life changes (see Self-Assessment 6.2 and Self-Assessment 6.3). We all know that negative changes, such as loss of a loved one, lead to stress. But even positive changes—such as getting married or moving to a new house—carry the potential of stress. Classic research by Holmes and Rahe showed that people who experience more changes, both good and bad, experience more symptoms of stress and are more likely to have health problems.[21]

A factor that moderates the effect of life changes and affects stress is personality. For example, individuals with internal locus of control tend to experience less stress.[22] Similarly, **Type A individuals**—those who are hard driving and have a high need for

Type A individuals: those who are hard driving and have a high need for control

FIGURE 6.3 SOURCES OF STRESS

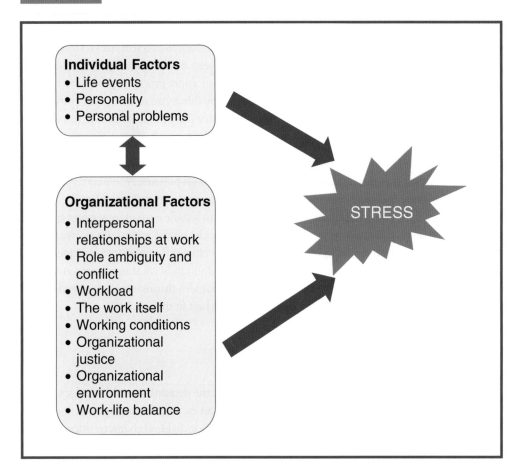

Job Stress

control, are more prone to experience stress.[23] On the other hand, individuals who have a **proactive personality** are action oriented, tend to identify opportunities and take advantage of them, and generally persevere in the face of obstacles and change.[24] They also are less likely to experience stress and burnout.[25]

Various other personal factors such as financial pressures, family troubles, abusive relationships, addiction, and so forth, can be both a source and a consequence of stress. While these factors are related to the individual and not within the purview of managers, they impact people's behavior at work. An employee who is involved in an abusive relationship or whose spouse has lost his job will bring those issues to work. Organizations are recognizing the role of personal stress factors and providing assistance to their employees to resolve such problems. **Employee Assistance Programs (EAP)** cover areas such as counseling, drug and alcohol abuse, abusive relationships, housing, and grief counseling. For example, the Department of Homeland Security provides its employees with help in managing things such as divorce, having a new baby, aging parents, managing difficult people, as well as traditional job stress and burnout.[26]

Organizational Factors

In addition to personal factors, many factors in organizations have the potential to create stress for employees. We review these next.

STRESS INVENTORY

The list below was developed by researchers Holmes and Rahe (1967).[27] They discovered that change, whether positive or negative, is a major source of stress. The more changes a person experiences in any given year, the more the person is likely to have health problems. How many of these changes have you faced in the previous year?

Rank	Life Event	Mean Value
1	Death of a spouse	100
2	Divorce	73
3	Marital separation	65
4	Jail term	63
5	Death of a close family member	63
6	Personal injury or illness	53
7	Marriage	50
8	Fired from job	47
9	Marital reconciliation	45
10	Retirement	45
11	Change in health of family member	44
12	Pregnancy	40
13	Sex difficulties	39
14	Gain of a new family member	39
15	Business readjustment	39
16	Change in financial state	38
17	Death of a close friend	37
18	Change to a different line of work	36
19	Change in number of arguments with spouse	35
20	Mortgage more than $50,000	31
21	Foreclosure of mortgage or loan	30
22	Change in responsibilities at work	29
23	Son or daughter leaving home	29
24	Trouble with in-laws	29
25	Outstanding personal achievement	28
26	Spouse beginning or stopping work	26

(Continued)

	(Continued)	
Rank	**Life Event**	**Mean Value**
27	Beginning or ending school	26
28	Change in living conditions	25
29	Revision in personal habits	24
30	Trouble with boss	23
31	Change in work hours or conditions	20
32	Change in residence	20
33	Change in schools	20
34	Change in recreation	19
35	Change in church activities	19
36	Change in social activities	18
37	Loan less than $50,000	17
38	Change in sleeping habits	16
39	Change in the number of family get-togethers	15
40	Change in eating habits	15
41	Vacation	13
42	Religious holiday (e.g., Christmas, Hanukkah)	12
43	Minor violations of the law	11

Scoring: Next to each item is its ranking. Life Change Units (LCUs) are the amount of stress a person experiences during a period of time. LCUs are calculated by adding the value for all the stressors a person has experienced. Those experiencing LCUS of 150 points are typically not heavily affected. Those with LCU scores between 150 and 300 points have a 50 percent chance of developing health problems. A score over 300 increases the likelihood of problems to 70 percent.

Source: List adapted from Holmes, T. H., & Rahe, R. H. (1967). The social readjustment rating scale. *Journal of Psychosomatic Research, 11,* 213–218. © 1967. Used with permission from Elsevier Science.

What Do You Think?

▶ While many organizations provide EAPs for their employees, they are most often part of the benefits that are offered to full-time employees. What are the consequences of not offering such assistance to part-time employees? What about the many temporary employees who work in organizations in increasing numbers?

Interpersonal Relationships

Although working with people can be a great source of satisfaction, work also can become stressful when we encounter interpersonal conflicts. Both the quality of relationships and the availability of support from peers, supervisors, and others in the organization can influence stress levels.[28] If people believe that coworkers, supervisors, or others are treating them inappropriately or rudely, then interpersonal difficulties can arise. These conflicts can manifest in a variety of ways. In any case, it is not uncommon for such conflicts to cause stress for the people involved. Competitiveness may play a role in encouraging such conflict. Workplace bullying can also be a very significant source of stress. One study found that the cost of workplace bullying and harassment can be as high as $180 million annually.[29] Such behavior not only creates stress for those individuals who are directly involved, but can also have repercussions for the work group and the organization as a whole. Particularly if the behavior is tolerated, or the participants are simply separated, it can send a message to both the perpetrator and the work group that bullying is part of the organizational culture.[30] Instead, bullying should be confronted directly and a clear message sent to the perpetrator and others that it will not be tolerated.

Role Ambiguity and Conflict

Organizational roles can be thought of as a set of expectations about what an individual should do. **Role conflict** occurs when compliance with one role makes it impossible to comply with another role or when individual needs conflict with role demands.[31] Role conflict has been found to be associated with tension, anxiety, and poor performance.[32] When faced with role conflict, individuals may withdraw, change their personal values, rationalize, or become aggressive. Many people experience a conflict between their personal and work roles, for example being a parent and being a manager. You may find that your work life can bleed into your home life: "Then I can never relax, because, just like an ax murderer in a horror movie, my work is always lurking."[33] Women particularly feel this type of conflict. One recent survey indicated that over 80% of women felt that taking leaves, reducing work hours, and prioritizing family over work are all factors that are holding back their careers.[34]

Role ambiguity is the lack of clarity about the role one is playing. Not having a clear job description and not knowing the performance expectations are both examples of role ambiguity. Working in teams in which each person's role is not clear and leadership is shared may be a source of ambiguity. Employees who are used to being assigned tasks and told what to do by a manager may experience confusion and stress when they work in self-managed teams (you will learn more about these in Chapter 9).

Workload

Workload, or (more accurately) perceptions of workload pressures, can cause stress for people in the workplace. Workload demands can vary not only with the amount of work but also with the difficulty of the work. Very low work complexity can lead to boredom, and very high work complexity can lead to fatigue, anxiety, and stress.[35] Time stress can be related to work–life balance as well as the characteristics and demands of the job itself, or to organizational practices. For example, although meetings are often an "essential part of organizational life, . . . the more time employees spend in these meetings, the more time stressed they are."[36] Time stress is exacerbated when goals are unclear, making it difficult for employees to determine priorities and to plan for particularly busy times.

Intrinsic Nature of the Work

Some jobs involve tasks that are inherently stressful. Nurses, police officers, and air traffic controllers, for example, have high levels of responsibility for life-and-death consequences coupled with a variety of organizational constraints and environmental factors. As a result, many have significant physical, psychological, and behavioral symptoms of stress. In general, the jobs that are perceived to be most stressful are those in which the workers believe that they have the least amount of control.[37] When workers lack a sense of control, because of either the lack of autonomy or the lack of opportunity to participate

Working conditions, including long hours and frequent travel, can exacerbate stress.

Burnt Out
or Unhappy
Employees

Meaningful Work

Distributive justice: the fairness of the outcome or decision

Procedural justice: the fairness of the process used in making the decision

Interactional justice: the nature of communication and how a person is treated

in decisions that affect them, stress often results. It is not difficult to imagine becoming stressed under conditions where you have important responsibilities but lack the freedom to make choices or the opportunity to influence how the work is done. Secretaries, for example, may exhibit stress symptoms when they have little or no control over their work, particularly if they perceive that they are expected to do everything for everyone with no say in how or when it is to be done.

Working Conditions

Working conditions also can exacerbate stress. Noise, lighting, smells, temperature, physical discomfort, and danger can influence our overall mental state.[38] Long working hours also take their toll on worker stress levels. Some jobs involve travel—either short or long distances—that can involve traffic jams, frustration over incorrect addresses, and delayed flights, buses, or trains. Shift work also has been connected with stress reactions due to the disruption of sleep patterns and personal lives.[39] Furthermore, heat, the degree of danger, and even the design of the rooms in which individuals work can be important variables.[40] Particularly workplace changes occurring simultaneously on multiple dimensions have been linked to employee stress and health problems.[41]

Organizational Environment and Justice

The organizational environment of work also can influence our stress levels. Office politics, lack of participation or involvement in decisions, and poor communication can result in worker stress. Ferris and colleagues,[42] for example, found that although politics may be an inherent part of organizational life, the higher the perceived level of politics, the higher the stress for employees. This may occur when people experience politics as a threat to their positions, their resources, and their sense of organizational security. Unfortunately, stress might make them even less able to cope with organizational politics successfully.[43] Poor communication and low levels of participation can make people feel powerless, frustrated, and stressed. For example, during times of significant organizational change, poor communication might cause increasing levels of uncertainty, fear, and stress. Moreover, ineffective communication can exacerbate stress caused by role ambiguity and conflict.

The perception that we are being treated unfairly in organizations can also be a source of stress. As discussed in Chapter 5 on Motivation, our evaluation of organizational justice influences motivation, but it also is related to stress. If employees feel that they do not receive what they deserve (distributive justice), especially if they think that others in the organization receive more than they do, they may experience anxiety and stress. But if there are clear reasons and procedures that justify the inequity, it will be less likely to provoke anxiety. What is key here is whether the worker knows the procedures (procedural justice) and the manager has openly, fully, and respectfully communicated how the process works (interactional justice). You can't treat everyone exactly the same way, but it is important that the reasons for the differences are clearly and respectfully communicated and understood.

CREATIVITY AND CHANGE

A TOP MANAGEMENT TEAM UNDER STRESS

In the afternoon of October 2002, senior managers in British Columbia's environment ministry found out that shots had been fired and some staff were trapped in a regional office of the Environmental Protection Division. When I was told that my co-director was there, my gut instinct said he was gone. Later I learned the purpose of his trip was a disciplinary meeting with the regional manager. The next hours were marked by shock, fear, disbelief, and uncertainty. It wasn't until late the next morning that we learned that there had been a double-murder suicide involving my co-director, the regional manager, and a staff member and that two other staff had been hiding in fear in the building until the police thought it safe to enter.

When the tragedy occurred the environment ministry was less than a year into transformational change, having been directed to adopt a new business model and reduce the budget by 35% over three years. From the start our leadership team kept a focus on promoting and practicing wellness and positive energy. Each of us had personal resilience rituals including cycling, practicing yoga, and listening to and/or playing music. We used humour to advantage when we were together, even in very stressful times. Early on we held our first off-site team meeting and identified our core personal values—family, integrity, and wellness—and discussed how we would model those values while leading change. The session solidified our already strong relationships and boosted our confidence in our ability to effectively lead our people through chaos and complexity.

Although wellness was a key organizational value, it proved a difficult one to model and sustain. After the tragic loss of our three colleagues, the leadership team again met off-site and rated our resilience using a "heart battery" our management coach had created. The heart ratings ranged from "thrilled" at 90% to "ill health" at 20%. Each of the three original team members rated ourselves between ill health and exhaustion (20%–40%); the new member between tired and comfortable (60%–70%). Afterwards we regularly used the heart battery to discuss resilience. After self-rating we'd then invite the other three members to provide their (often differing) perspectives. Healthy debates would ensue, always involving laughter and ending with agreement on priority areas requiring attention to and practical actions to pursue. We used both 360 reviews and individual and team emotional intelligence profiling to deepen our understanding of our leadership behaviours and patterns.

In addition to our off-site sessions for strategic reflection and renewal, our team started each weekly business meeting with a personal check-in to take the pulse of our resilience levels. Our personal commitments around wellness were incorporated into our annual performance plans and we used a buddy system to hold each other accountable to the commitments set in those plans. Ours was a decentralized organization (11 offices across the province) and the resilience techniques modeled by the leadership team were also conducted by all 15 of our management teams.

Our goal was to create a resilient learning culture, to create effective relationships, and to achieve outstanding results. To support this goal we conducted a pilot training project for all middle managers in the regions. The purpose of the training was to strengthen the capacity and effectiveness of our managers and to have them learn new tools for addressing both people and business challenges. In turn, the managers were charged with sharing their learning with their staff. Near the end of the two-year initiative a tipping point was reached. The managers concluded it was time to rebrand the learning and wellness culture work and simply recognize it as the way we did our business, providing us the adaptive capacity to deal with our fast-moving and reactive work.

About five years into our cultural transformation, our work reflects the importance of wellness and resilience to the organization as a whole. Wellness is an

(Continued)

(Continued)

organizational value: "We will foster a working environment that promotes our health and well-being." One of the six organizational health principles is "We integrate health and wellness into our work." Each principle is further described by identifying associated behaviours. The behaviours that demonstrate this principle are, "We support flexible work hours and arrangements," "We create a work environment that is environmentally friendly and sustainable," and "We emphasize humour, camaraderie and fun at work."

The Environmental Protection Division's motto is "Taking care of our people; taking care of our business." Our experience is that even in extraordinarily turbulent times outstanding business results can be achieved by taking care of your people and paying attention to the resilience of your organization.

1. This is an organization already under the stress of reorganization and budget reductions when a colleague is killed. How much stress can an organization take?

2. The organization then began to emphasize wellness in its change efforts. Do you think helping with the stress individuals feel will lead to improvements in the organization's productivity?

3. And does the productivity issue really matter? Isn't concern for the wellness of individuals in the organization simply the right thing to do?

Source: This case was contributed by Lynn Bailey, former Assistant Deputy Minister of the British Columbia Environmental Protection Division.

Coping With and Managing Stress

Justice at Work

Recognizing and evaluating how stress is influencing both our own performance and that of others is the first step in using stress constructively and avoiding its destructive aspects. As a starting point, we need to be sufficiently self-aware to first recognize the symptoms of stress in ourselves (refer to the Self-Assessment at the beginning of this chapter). You also want to know when you might be getting into the unproductive and destructive ends of the stress curve. From an organizational and personal standpoint, managing stress has a lot in common with what we would consider to be some of the basics of good management practice—establishment of clear goals, development of resources and support, effective communication, and self-awareness. In the following sections, a variety of strategies that might be useful in managing and controlling stress are discussed.

Personal Strategies
Lifestyle Adjustments

Learning to
Navigate Stress

Perhaps one of the most important things we can do for ourselves in managing stress and enhancing our ability to deal with it constructively is to consider our lifestyles. Lifestyle decisions play a significant role in influencing our physical health and well-being as well as our ability to cope successfully with the demands, challenges, and stresses of our work. As explained earlier, stress is a nonspecific bodily or physical response to demands. It only makes sense, then, that one of the most important and effective ways in which we can manage stress is to maintain our physical health. To handle stress well, we need to be healthy enough to cope with the demands and challenges we face and to deal with the physical manifestations of stress when we experience them (see Figure 6.4).

FIGURE 6.4 STRATEGIES FOR MANAGING STRESS

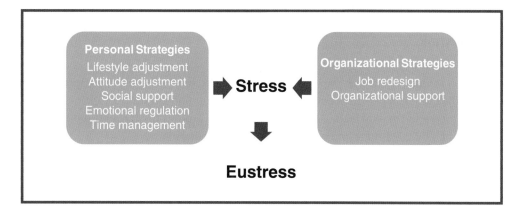

As you know, it is important to eat a balanced diet, get enough sleep, and exercise regularly. As our mothers might have told us, moderation is the key. Following these tried-and-true prescriptions for a healthy life helps to prevent some of the negative manifestations of stress and to cope with stress-related symptoms. Exercise is particularly important, in part because of chemicals that are released in our bodies during the fight-or-flight response that stress can evoke. Exercise provides that outlet and counteracts the negative effects of the chemical changes associated with stress. A regular exercise program, then, is a central component of stress management. It can also be used as a more immediate antidote when we begin to feel stressed. For example, by taking a brisk walk during our lunch hour, we might be able to better handle a tense meeting or the pressures of a deadline.

In considering lifestyle questions, it also is constructive to evaluate and make appropriate changes to maintain a balance between work and outside interests. As noted previously, those whose whole lives revolve around work and work-related issues seem to experience more stress. For this reason, leisure and recreational time not only are important to quality of life but also may contribute to enhanced work performance. Put more bluntly, working 24/7 not only is bad for our physical and mental health as individuals but also is unlikely to be an effective or productive strategy for making professional or organizational contributions. Although there might be times and circumstances that demand extra hours and personal sacrifices, as a long-term approach, such demands are not likely to be good for us or our organizations.

Attitude Adjustment: Positivity and Resilience

In a survey of human resources managers in 400 organizations, 94% of the respondents said that "healthy attitudes" helped people to increase their tolerance for stress. This might seem somewhat ironic given that stress is a bodily response and not "all in your head." Although this is true, it also is the case that our perceptions and attitudes can make a difference in how we respond to potentially stressful situations as well as alter our subjective experiences of stress when it occurs. This is not a matter of simply ordering ourselves or others to "pull yourself together and get back to work." As suggested previously, individuals may respond to the same demands in very different ways. Recent research on positive psychology indicates that having a positive attitude can have a considerable impact on well-being and happiness. Renowned psychologist Martin Seligman, who is often considered to be the father of positive psychology, considers five elements to be essential to

Wheel of Life

Holistic Self

NOKIA'S CULTURE

The Finnish mobile telecom company Nokia, once the dominant cell phone company in the world, is no longer the market leader, dislodged from its top position by the iPhone and other new smart phones. In 2007, Nokia controlled 40 percent of the cell phone market; it now holds around 4 percent, with financial performance to match.[44] With a new CEO, Stephen Elop in 2010, the first non-Finnish CEO, and a new Windows 8-based phone, Nokia is hoping to regain some of its past glory.

In spite of the poor performance, Nokia continues to get high marks from its employees all over the world as one of the best workplaces with high ratings for supporting work-life balance, growth opportunity, and career advancement, among others. One of the company's senior program managers states: "Great people; always look for a better way from all team members."[45] The focus on team work and its importance to the company was also emphasized by its CEO, Stephen Elop, who is Canadian, during their 2013 annual leadership meeting in Istanbul, Turkey. He used an orchestra that played Ravel's Bolero to full effect and said: "My message was that the way we would succeed in the end was if each of us played our role, and each instrument came together to build this beautiful symphony."[46]

Nokia is known for a "fiercely insular culture."[47] While one of the most global companies in the world, its top leadership has been almost exclusively Finnish and some say the company is highly male-dominated with deals made during visits to saunas that have been installed in many company offices worldwide. However, employees are highly loyal and many consider the company to be part of their family, as it is also highly regarded as a symbol of Finland. A former Nokia executive, Tomi Ahonen, attributes the company's success to its radically driven culture that is different from that of U.S. companies that focus on short-term and quick results.[48] The company headquarters in Helsinki is a modern building called NoHo (Nokia House) with offices built around the largest public space in the building, the cafeteria.

While employees are aware of the challenges ahead of them, they are highly confident in their company's ability to succeed. Stefan Pannenbecker, the head of industrial design states: "With my team, the only thing I'm interested in is whether people love this product or not. We could have the best quarter in Nokia's history, and I wouldn't care a bit about it if I didn't feel the products were exciting."[49] Hans Henrik Lund, head of marketing, echoes the sentiment: "I'm motivated by a turnaround. I need that kick to do my best."[50] The company's bureaucratic culture based on avoiding mistakes has been shaken up through the use of teams to encourage creativity.

However, the strength of Nokia is its Finnish cultural roots with an emphasis on integrity, determination, and hard work, believes one of the company's top leaders.[51] Nokia continues a strong emphasis on diversity with 60,000 employees who come from 115 different countries and with close to 41% women. The company documents state: "Above all, it's about being human in everything we do—respecting and caring, even in tough business situations,"[52] principles that are clearly presented in the company code of conduct that is available in 34 languages on its website.[53] It focuses on communication, ethical conduct, fair labor practices, compensation, and benefits, respect for employees, their health and well-being, and a strong message on integrity.

1. What are the factors that help Nokia's managers and employees manage the pressure and stress of competition?

2. What role does culture play in how they manage?

well-being. He uses the term **PERMA** to summarize them.[54] PERMA and positive psychology further rely on the concept that our cognitive appraisal of a situation influences whether or not we will experience it as stressful (Table 6.1).[55]

TABLE 6.1 ESSENTIAL ELEMENTS OF WELL-BEING: PERMA

Element	Description
P: Positive Emotion	Typical view of happiness involves enjoying yourself and experiencing pleasant feelings such as satisfaction, pleasure, hope, etc.
E: Engagement	Being fully engaged and engrossed in a task or situation so that you experience flow and can remain fully concentrated
R: Positive Relationships	Having good and meaningful relationships with other people
M: Meaning	Being involved in something bigger than ourselves such as a charity, a social movement, religion, or community
A: Accomplishment/ Achievement	Achieving goals or mastering new skills

Source: Based on Seligman, M. (2011). *Flourish: A visionary new understanding of happiness.* New York, NY: Free Press.

Remember that depending on how you handle it, stress can be good for you and make you better able to handle future challenges. In fact, developing psychological resilience only occurs through having problems, challenges, and failures. Key to psychological resilience is the idea that individuals do not simply survive or recover, but that they can actually adapt, learn, and change, and as a result, become more resilient over time. First, people can become more resilient by facing the realities of a particular situation or problem.[56] Realistic optimism is better than misguided optimism. Only by honestly and pragmatically assessing what is happening can we develop realistic and constructive responses. Second, having a strong value system that helps us set priorities, and make sense of the challenges we face, enhances resilience. Finally, Coutu suggested that ingenuity fosters resilience by improvising and being creative with the resources that are available to us. At the core, resilient people "turn challenges into opportunities."[57] Accordingly, it makes sense to become more aware of our attitudes toward demands for change and adaptation in the work environment. As we become more attentive, we might discover ways of thinking that could use some reappraisal.

Importance of Resilience

How might we think about problems as challenges or about demands as opportunities? This cognitive reappraisal can be aided by *self-talk*. For example, we might find it helpful to consciously ask ourselves how we might see a potentially stressful situation in a more positive light. Or, we might find it useful to remind ourselves of how we have handled such challenges successfully in the past. Some people might even find it helpful to ask themselves what the worst outcome of a stressful situation would likely be. After thinking through the worst-case scenario of failure (loss of relationship, goal not met, loss of job, bypassed for promotion, etc.), most people conclude that they could indeed survive it. Ironically, doing so might even take away some of the fear and lead them to take constructive action to avoid the worst outcome.

PERMA: Positive emotion; Engagement; positive Relationships; Meaning; Accomplishment

Twitter employees taking a break in the cafeteria. Studies show that social connections can have a positive effect on both job performance and how we handle stress.

Dogs at Work

As with many areas of organizational behavior and leadership, self-knowledge is critical (see Chapter 2). Knowing our strengths and weaknesses, and evaluating our ambitions in light of them, helps to keep us focused on realistic goals. For example, if you are a perfectionist, then you might have a number of unspoken assumptions that cause stress. You might think, either consciously or unconsciously, that you must (1) do all things for all people at all times, (2) avoid failure while trying new things, (3) always make everyone completely happy, and (4) do more than is humanly possible. An acceptance of the fact that none of us can be perfect can go a long way toward avoiding unnecessary levels of stress associated with unrealistic self-expectations. If, on the other hand, you find on reflection that you try to avoid having high expectations for yourself, avoid all risks, or find yourself bored and dissatisfied at work, then you might want to find ways of increasing the demands and stresses of your job. You might try new things, seek out new challenges, set goals, and take some measured risks. Remember that some stress is a normal and beneficial part of life.

Social Support

People are social beings. From a medical standpoint, in fact, social isolation is a major risk factor in human morbidity and mortality. For example, research has shown that our personal relationships are linked to our immune function and our ability to fight disease.[58] Similarly, one of the key mediating factors in determining how well people cope with stress is the amount and quality of social support that they receive. Positive relationships with and support from the people we work with can act as a buffer or mediator to job-related stress. Relationships with our supervisors, our employees, or our coworkers can provide structural, functional, emotional, and tangible support, thereby enabling us to ameliorate the potentially harmful effects of stress in the workplace.[59] Structural social support comes from being embedded in and connected to a network of people whom we know can potentially provide support.

Laughter and positive humor have been shown as highly effective tools to help people handle stress. Laughter in the workplace can result in a significant and long-lasting "increase in several different aspects of self-efficacy, including self-regulation, optimism, positive emotions, and social identification."[60] Interestingly, laughter has become part of the ancient Indian practice of Yoga. Laughing clubs and laughter yoga are common in India where people get together to laugh together for exercise and stress relief.[61] In order to be constructive, humor needs to be positive, rather than a disguised attack or insult. Successful humor accordingly increases positive emotions, lowers stress, and even increases productivity.[62] Furthermore, humor can "create psychological safety and higher levels of group cohesion, allowing members to see the group as a 'safety net' that would enable them to focus on the task at hand, take necessary risks, and experience less psychological and physical stress."[63]

The importance of structural, emotional, and functional social support has implications for both what we can do for ourselves as individuals and what we can do to help others in our organizations. The evidence would suggest that making social connections with others at work can help us to do a better job and cope with stresses as they arise. At the same time, it is important to understand how *our* support—be it emotional, tangible, or functional—can strongly influence other people's capacity to cope with the stresses and strains of organizational life. We all need a little help from our friends.

Emotional Regulation

All of us regulate our emotions to a greater or lesser extent under different kinds of circumstances. Particularly at work, we may choose to conceal or alter the external display of our emotions for our own reasons or because the employer has set up certain rules for behavior. While emotional regulation can cause stress, it can also be important to smoothing the cycles of social interaction. It is not hard to imagine how the lack of emotional regulation, resulting in all people expressing all their emotions at all times, might make social interaction quite difficult.

Happiness at Work

But the effects of emotional regulation are actually quite complex, in part because emotional regulation occurs in a social context. If emotional regulation results in improved social interaction, it is less likely to cause stress.[64] If, for example, in an interaction a person conceals his or her frustration or stress and tries to appear relaxed, and the other person responds pleasantly, this might reduce the level of stress. Performing work that involves "emotional labor" in this context can actually be rewarding to the employee and contribute to job satisfaction.[65]

But not all emotional regulation evokes positive responses. Emotional work that involves "false face" or "surface acting" (what is displayed compared to what is the real emotion) increases strain when "inauthentic displays of emotion evoke adverse responses from receivers."[66] In fact, emotional labor of this type contributes to worker burnout.[67] Despite this, while there are situations in which workers feel stressed because of emotion regulation, managers can still have an important role in reducing it.

Time Management

Time pressures coupled with too much to do are a major source of stress. What can you do to manage your time better and take control of how your time is spent? At its core, effective time management involves establishing and reaffirming priorities, taking stock of how you spend your time, and then organizing your time to better reflect your goals, plans, and commitments. It does not mean that you have to become a slave to the clock or become compulsive about planning and consulting your calendar. Time management for some individuals might include detailed scheduling, but for many others, a less-structured approach might work best.

It is not just a matter of completing all of the tasks presented to us. In fact, at the end of the day, after we have done everything that everyone has asked and that we were expected to do, we still might experience stress if we have not made time to do things that we judge to be the most important. The first step is to determine what your priorities are (see Figure 6.5). You might find it helpful to draw a pie chart and assign to the chart different-sized slices of your time that you think ought to be devoted to your various roles and tasks. (Although this exercise is described here in terms of work tasks and responsibilities, it also can be very useful as a "whole" life exercise.) Alternatively, you could list all of your tasks and responsibilities and use an "ABC" system in which high-priority items are assigned an

A and moderate- or low-priority items are assigned a B or C. Either way, after making your priorities explicit, you evaluate how you actually spend your time. You might well discover that the actual allocation of your time does not always match your priorities and the degree of importance you assign to each of your responsibilities.

FIGURE 6.5 STEPS IN TIME MANAGEMENT

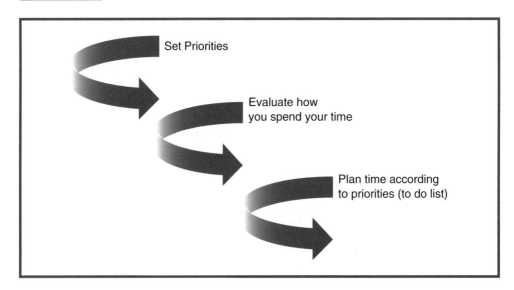

Set Priorities

Evaluate how you spend your time

Plan time according to priorities (to do list)

In planning your time, you should also allocate some part of the day for reflection, rest, creativity, and social contact. The first three of these (reflection, rest, and creativity) might involve setting aside time when you will not be interrupted, whereas the last of these (social contact) might involve forcing yourself out of your office. Although it might not be possible to "do it all" every day, it *is* possible to do the things that are most important. Doing so increases your feelings of accomplishment and control and, as a result, reduces stress while increasing your effectiveness.

Organizational Strategies

Job Redesign

Some stress arises from the nature of the work itself. Modifying and redesigning jobs so that they fit employees' needs can ameliorate some sources of work-related stress. Although this is largely an organizational issue, it also might be possible for us to make some changes to our own jobs—or how we approach them—that will make positive differences. Jobs that have skill variety, task identity, and task significance are intrinsically more motivating. Such jobs increase satisfaction, give a sense of meaning to our work, and reduce stress,[68] particularly if the individual employee needs a more challenging job. As such, we feel as though we are responsible for an identifiable and interrelated set of tasks and that our work produces results.

Although most of us are not free to redesign our jobs, we can often make small changes and adjustments in our work to reduce stress. What are the major stressors in your job? Do

What Would You Do?

▶ Your boss wants a report you prepared significantly revised by eight in the morning. It's now five in the afternoon. Though she says she doesn't want to "Kill you," it's clear the report is needed the next morning. What would you do?

you have too much or too little challenge? Does the job fit what you need and want and how much you want to be challenged? How might you increase your sense of control over the tasks for which you are responsible? If goals are lacking, can you talk with your supervisor about the goals you would like to pursue? Perhaps making a schedule of work in which you set some of the priorities could help.

Preventative Strategies

In addition to what we can do for ourselves and others, there are a number of organizational-level considerations related to stress management. Organizations must be attentive to preventive strategies in recruiting, selecting, and socializing employees.[69] Because stress is, in part, a consequence of the "fit" between people and their organizational environment, recruitment and selection should be seen as an opportunity to ensure better person–organization matches. For example, if people are given accurate and complete information about the nature of the work prior to hiring, then they are more likely to have realistic expectations and higher levels of job satisfaction. Taking time to carefully analyze what the job requirements are and assessing candidates in light of those demands also help to decrease the likelihood of mismatches between people and organizational environments.

Software engineer Amanda Camp uses the climbing wall at Google Inc.'s new campus in Kirkland, Washington, during a break from her work. Exercise can be an excellent way to manage stress and prevent burnout.

Health promotion programs can encourage employees to engage in behaviors promoting a healthy lifestyle, and, as noted earlier, employee assistance programs (EAPs) can provide assistance or refer employees to outside resources when troubles arise. Workers' performance can be positively influenced by promoting their psychological well-being and happiness.[70] Happier workers cope with stress more efficiently than their unhappy counterparts, and as a result they are more productive. Although a person's psychological well-being remains relatively stable over time, managers can have a positive influence. Training programs can help employees cope with stress by emphasizing the importance of happiness and a positive outlook. Happy workers not only are more pleasant companions, but also are more willing to work and are better motivated, and they usually outperform those who feel unhappy and overly stressed.[71] Particularly in times of organizational change, stress management programs and strategies can help enhance employee trust, reduce stress, and increase effectiveness.[72] Specifically, cognitive-behavioral approaches, designed to educate employees about stress as well as enhance their coping skills, have been shown to be the most effective type of organizational intervention. "These interventions encourage individuals to take charge of their negative thoughts, feelings, and resulting behavior by changing their cognition and emotions to more adaptive ones and by identifying and practicing more functional behavior responses."[73]

▶ Summary and Applications for Managers

We can now review how we can use all of the information in this chapter to take action to prevent and/or cope with stress so as to improve personal and organizational effectiveness.

1. *Take charge.* Identify the major stresses in your life and evaluate which you can control or influence and which you cannot. For those things that you cannot change, accept them and use coping skills such as relaxation and exercise to counteract the negative effects of stress. For those things that you can change, think of strategies for eliminating or reducing the stress that they cause. For example, if you are experiencing stress because of a lack of clear objectives for your job, then develop some of your own and propose them to your supervisor. Within your own area of discretion, set personal goals for work accomplishment and then reward yourself when you attain your goals. If you are stressed by the confusion at work, then find ways of getting organized and find mental or physical places of clarity or simplicity. If you are bothered by interruptions, then take charge by setting some time aside each day when you will not be interrupted by phone calls or drop-by visitors. The message: Do not wait for your life and work to become calmer or simpler; change the things you can to make things better.

2. *Take care of yourself.* Keeping yourself healthy makes you more resilient in the face of stress and stress-related health problems. Use relaxation techniques, eat well, exercise, and get enough sleep. Remember that the stress response is physiological. Fight back by being physically rested, well nourished, and healthy.

3. *Reach out to others.* Time with friends at work or outside of work will help you to cope with stress and keep you mentally healthy. Do not forget to laugh and enjoy yourself. It is hard to feel stress and tension when you are laughing and having fun with your family or friends. When the pressure mounts and you find yourself becoming stressed, find a trusted person with whom you can talk. Sometimes the best person to talk with is a friend, sometimes it is a family member, and sometimes the objectivity of a counselor might

be what is needed. Whoever it is, ask for help and support if you need it. Helping others also is a great stress reducer. Remember that you are not the only one who experiences stress. Support others and offer assistance when possible. A little encouragement, a favor, or an offer of assistance can go a long way when someone is feeling overwhelmed. As an added bonus, it can make you feel better about yourself. When you find yourself experiencing the negative signs of excessive stress, such as depression, anger, anxiety, health problems, and excessive drinking, consult a professional. Seek out assistance through your EAP, consult your doctor, or find an appropriate program or counselor on your own. Do not be afraid to get help.

4. *Find a balance.* If work is your whole life, then you and your work probably will suffer. Those who seem to handle stress best are those who have interests outside of work. It is possible and appropriate to be a dedicated, hardworking, extremely effective public servant while still having other interests. Pursue a hobby, nurture your family, or do something new. Find things that relax or distract you. Listen to music, get involved in sports, start a garden, take up photography—do anything that gives you an opportunity to express yourself, relax, enjoy your time, access your creativity, or learn new things.

5. *Be prepared.* It is helpful to try to be well organized so that you can keep up with things. Planning ahead and setting priorities, thinking ahead, and gathering needed information will help to give you a sense of control and avoid being caught unprepared and ill equipped. Whereas many situations are difficult to predict, many can be thought out in advance and allow for some preparation.

6. *Build your competence.* Feeling like you are not doing your job well can be very stressful. Build your competence and confidence by enhancing your skills, abilities, and knowledge. Honestly assess your strengths and weaknesses on the job. Explore training and educational opportunities that can capitalize on your assets and enhance your skills in areas that are weak. Find a mentor

and seek his or her advice and guidance. Learn all that you can about your job, your organization, and your profession.

7. *Get creative*. Find ways of innovating on the job. What can you change to make your work more manageable, more satisfying, and more interesting? What can you reformulate? What can you delegate? How can you better use time? (See Chapter 3.)

8. *Adjust your attitude*. Remember that although stress is not "all in your head," how you perceive situations affects how stressed you become.

Focus on the PERMA elements and pay particular attention to your self-talk. Are you sabotaging yourself with negative messages? Do you tell yourself that you are unable to cope and that you never will be able to solve the problems you confront? Try telling yourself that problems can be seen as challenges and that demands can offer opportunities. Then figure out some strategies for taking advantage of the challenges and opportunities that you encounter. Don't beat yourself up for not being able to do it all and do it perfectly. Remind yourself that being normal and happy is better than being perfect.

▶ Key Terms

Alarm 174

Distributive justice 184

Employee Assistance Programs (EAP) 180

Exhaustion 174

General adaptation syndrome (GAS) 173

Interactional justice 184

Job burnout 178

PERMA 189

Proactive personality 180

Procedural justice 184

Resistance 174

Role ambiguity 183

Role conflict 183

Stress 170

Stressors 170

Type A individuals 179

▶ Exercise 6.1 Coping With Stress

Now let us look at how you cope with stress. For each of the following items, circle the number that indicates how often you respond to conditions of high stress in this manner.

	Never	Occasionally	Often	Nearly Always
1. Skipping meals	0	1	2	3
2. Talking with friends	0	1	2	3
3. Setting priorities	0	1	2	3
4. Sleeping less to work more	0	1	2	3
5. Increasing alcohol consumption	0	1	2	3
6. Getting angry	0	1	2	3
7. Crying	0	1	2	3
8. Eating healthy	0	1	2	3
9. Exercising	0	1	2	3
10. Deep breathing and relaxation	0	1	2	3

(Continued)

(Continued)

	Never	Occasionally	Often	Nearly Always
11. Spending less time with family	0	1	2	3
12. Distancing self from the stress	0	1	2	3
13. Problem solving	0	1	2	3
14. Smoking more	0	1	2	3
15. Withdrawing from others	0	1	2	3
16. Confronting those responsible	0	1	2	3

What are your preferred coping mechanisms? Note that Items 2, 6, 7, 12, and 15 may be considered primarily emotional coping strategies. Items 3, 13, and 16 may be seen as focused on problem solving. Items 1, 3, 4, and 11 may be viewed as attempts to manage and control time. Attempts to cope with the physical symptoms of stress may be manifested in the behaviors described in Items 5, 8, 9, 10, and 14. Although all of these coping mechanisms are normal in the sense that they are things that people do under conditions of stress, some are healthy and effective, whereas others (e.g., skipping meals, smoking, drinking, cutting oneself off from friends, getting insufficient sleep) most certainly are detrimental in the long term. As you study this chapter, try to think about the things that cause you stress, reflect on how you typically respond, and (if appropriate) consider how you might respond more positively and effectively in the future.

▶ Exercise 6.2 Building Resilience

Look back at some of the major challenges and problems that you have faced in your work and personal life. What have these experiences taught you? Identify a specific instance in which you faced a challenge in a manner that left you stronger and better able to handle such problems in the future. Then answer the following questions:

1. How do you think and feel about the challenge now, and how did you at the time you faced it?

2. What did you do in response to the challenge? How did your responses improve your ability to cope or make you stronger, more flexible, or capable?

3. How might you apply these lessons to the challenges you face currently?

▶ Exercise 6.3 Life Balance

1. Draw a circle on a sheet of paper. Then divide the circle into sections representing the importance of each of the following in your life:

   o Work

   o Family and friends

   o Intellectual pursuits

   o Spiritual life

   o Recreation and physical exercise

   o Creative and cultural activities

2. Now draw another circle. Divide this circle into sections representing the relative amount of time and energy you *actually devote* to each. Compare the size of the sections in each circle. How does the relative importance of each compare with the time that you actually spend?

3. If some adjustments are in order, then first consider how you might eliminate some activities or time spent on doing things that are less important or out of balance. Then identify

some specific activities that you can do to enhance your growth and development in neglected areas. For example, if you find yourself neglecting recreation and exercise, and if that is important to you, then you might find that you can schedule a brisk walk at lunch if you batch phone calls (and limit their duration) at work. Or you might find that reading a new and important book that you have been wanting to read, rather than going to the gym for the fifth time this week, will make you feel less pressured. The key is balance. What do you want your "life circle" to look like, and what changes can you make to more closely align the activities in your life with the values, priorities, and ideals it represents?

▶ Exercise 6.4 Having Fun at Work

Public Service Week (PSW) in British Columbia is held every year to recognize and celebrate employees with barbecues, picnics, and a variety of other activities. For PSW week in 2010, the British Columbia Ministry of the Environment made a video of ministry employees at all levels of the organization lip-synching to the *Glee* television show version of Journey's "Don't Stop Believin'." In the video, employees incorporated a variety of educational posters and props to show the ministry's work, goals, and priorities. It was a light-hearted and simple way for the organization to reinforce a commitment to the public service mission and celebrate the hard work and dedication of its employees. The video was planned and taped during lunch hours, and the participants reported the project to be a great morale booster and highly successful in engaging a wide variety of employees in doing something both fun and inspirational.[74]

What might you do in your organization to encourage laughter and fun at work in a way that contributes to stress reduction and increased effectiveness and productivity?

▶ Exercise 6.5 Developing Your Own Stress Management Program

Use the following steps as a guide to design your own personal stress management program:

1. Identify the primary stressors in your life. It may be helpful to keep a stress journal to write down those times and situations that make you feel the most stressed.

2. Identify the thoughts and behaviors you engage in as a response to these stressors. Are these thoughts and behaviors constructive or destructive?

3. What constructive coping skills do you want to develop or enhance? Do you, for example, want to start exercising more, learn meditation, manage your time better, develop a new hobby or activity, spend more time with family or friends? Do you need to get help in developing these skills? If so, what resources can you identify or seek out?

4. What are the barriers to effective stress management in your life and how can you overcome them? What specific action steps can you take in this regard?

▶ Exercise 6.6 Finding Happiness

Being happy helps us handle stress, stay healthy, and improve the quality of our lives and the lives of others—including our coworkers and the people we serve. Accordingly, being happier can help make us better managers. Finding happiness can be thought of as a deep, philosophical life quest similar to finding "the meaning of life." Or, it can be thought of as a simple practice of learning to enjoy everyday things, people, situations, and activities. Think about simple things that you do, or could do, to make yourself and others happy. Make a list, if that makes you happy. In any case, do these things more often.

► Case 6.1 Distress at DES

Your friend Diane works at the Department of Economic Security (DES) as a child protective service worker. You have known Diane personally and professionally for a number of years, and she has asked you to advise her on managing stress. She told you that she admires the way in which you seem to handle stress in your own job at the Department of Motor Vehicles, and she wants advice and counsel for reducing stress where possible and coping with the rest.

Because you are such a good friend, you have decided to set aside an afternoon to talk to Diane. You begin by asking her to simply talk about the sources of stress in her life. She tells you the following:

"First let me say, I love my job. I really think I am making a difference in the lives of children and their families. It's not that it isn't frustrating—it is. Sometimes the system just won't let me do what I think is best. I do care about my work and want to stay in the job, but I guess the stress is getting to me. I can't figure out what the problem is. After all, I've been on the job for three years. But I feel terrible, I can't sleep, I'm anxious, my stomach hurts, and my blood pressure is up. I even have this annoying rash that seems to appear on my neck when things get tense.

"I have a new supervisor. She's part of what is making me crazy. According to my training and what I have been taught here, I am a social worker. I am supposed to help families and kids the best I can. By law, my first priority is preserving families, which means that sometimes I have to make some pretty tough judgments between protecting the kids and keeping the family intact. This new supervisor says we're just supposed to investigate, not do social work. As she puts it, 'we don't have time to babysit or be neighborhood do-gooders.' This, she says, will free us up to increase our workload by a third.

"My husband has been so supportive. But he has gone back to school, you know. That means I have to be at the day care at exactly six o'clock every day of the week. Morgan, our four-year-old, can't seem to shake the ear infections. The doctor has suggested surgery. I don't know when we're supposed to fit that in, but I guess we have to get it done.

"But back to the job. I am in the car half the day, going from case to case. I can't even tell you how often I have incomplete information. Sometimes it's a wrong address, but the bigger problem is that I just don't know what I'm walking into. We don't routinely share information with the police. Sometimes I walk into dangerous situations; sometimes it's just a nuisance call from a crazy neighbor. But I can't predict. Three weeks ago, an angry father threatened me. It normally wouldn't have bothered me so much, but I just have felt vulnerable lately.

"When I get back to my office, I have a mountain of paperwork, and of course the phone rings constantly. I used to try to have lunch sometimes with some of the other workers—talk about cases and let off some steam—but I have felt too pressured to do that in the last several months. I've got to catch up on the paperwork!

"So, I've been doing this job for a while. Why am I feeling so stressed all of a sudden? What's wrong with me? What should I do?"

Respond to the following questions.

1. What will you say to Diane? Are there additional questions you would like to ask?

2. What advice will you give her? What do you think are some of the sources of her stress? How will you work with her to develop strategies for reducing her stress?

3. What are your recommendations for coping with the stress that Diane is experiencing? What will you caution her not to do?

4. What actions have you taken in the past that have helped you to cope successfully with stressful circumstances? Could any of these approaches be useful to Diane?

⑤SAGE edge™

Sharpen your skills with SAGE edge at edge.sagepub.com/nahavandi

SAGE edge for students provides a personalized approach to help you accomplish your coursework goals in an easy-to-use learning environment.

▶ Endnotes

1. Vaillant, G. E. (1977). *Adaptation to life.* Boston, MA: Little, Brown.

2. Quick, J., Quick, J., Nelson, D., & Hurrell, J. (1997). *Preventive stress management in organizations.* Washington, DC: American Psychological Association.

3. Seyle, H. (1974). *Stress without distress.* Philadelphia, PA: J. B. Lippincott.

4. Seyle, 1974; and Smith, J. (1993). *Understanding stress and coping.* New York, NY: Macmillan.

5. Seyle, 1974.

6. Taylor, S., Klein, L., Lewis, B., Gruenewald, T., Gurung, R., & Updegraff, J. (2000). Behavioral responses to stress in females: Tend-and-befriend, not fight-or-flight. *Psychological Review, 107*(3), 411–429.

7. Singer, J. (2011). Heal your workplace. *Collector, 76*(7), 18–20.

8. Schramm, J. (2013). Manage stress, improve the bottom line. *HRMagazine, 58*(2), 80.

9. Stern, G. M. (2012). Employee burnout: Around the corner? Already here? *Fortune CNN,* May 12. Retrieved from http://management.fortune.cnn.com/2012/05/21/employee-burnout-around-the-corner-already-here/ on April 20, 2013.

10. Hilton, M., & Whiteford, H. (2010). Associations between psychological distress, workplace accidents, workplace failures and workplace successes. *International Archives of Occupational and Environmental Health, 83*(8), 923–933.

11. Nonfatal occupational injuries and illnesses requiring days away from work [News release]. (2012). *Bureau of Labor Statistics,* November 8. Retrieved from http://www.bls.gov/news.release/osh2.nr0.htm on September 14, 2013.

12. Feds: Workplace violence caused nearly 17 percent of all fatal U.S. work injuries in 2011. (2012). *Security Info Watch,* November 27. Retrieved from http://www.securityinfowatch.com/news/10834285/feds-workplace-violence-caused-nearly-17-percent-of-all-fatal-us-work-injuries-in-2011 on April 20, 2013.

13. Workplace homicides from shootings. (2013). *Bureau of Labor Statistics,* January. Retrieved from http://www.bls.gov/iif/oshwc/cfoi/osar0016.htm on April 20, 2013.

14. Workplace violence: Issues in response. (2004). *US Department of Justice: FBI.* Retrieved from http://www.fbi.gov/stats-services/publications/workplace-violence on April 20, 2013

15. Quick, Quick, Nelson, & Hurrell, 1997.

16. Crampton, S., Hodge, J., Mishra, J., & Price, S. (1995). Stress and stress management. *SAM Advanced Management Journal, 60*(3), 10–18.

17. Beehr, T. (1995). *Psychological stress in the workplace.* London: Routledge.

18. Stern, 2012.

19. Seyle, H. (1975). Confusion and controversy in the stress field. *Journal of Human Stress, 75*(1), 37–44.

20. West, J., & West, C. (1989). Job stress and public sector occupations: Implications for personnel managers. *Review of Public Personnel Administration, 9*(3), 46–65.

21. Holmes, T. H., & Rahe, R. H. (1967). The Social Readjustment Rating Scale. *Journal of Psychosomatic Research, 11,* 213–218.

22. Nonis, S. A., & Hoyt, D. R. (2004). Coping strategies used by managers in the People's Republic of China: Relationship with personal characteristics and job outcomes. *Journal of Asia-Pacific Business, 5*(3), 45.

23. Watson, W. E. (2006). Type A personality characteristics and the effect on individual and team academic performance. *Journal of Applied Social Psychology, 36,* 1110–1128.

24. See Batemam, T. S., & Crant, J. M. (1993). The proactive component of organizational behavior: A measure and correlates. *Journal of Organizational Behavior, 14*(2), 103–118; and Seibert, S. E., Kraimer, M. L., & Crant, J. M. (2001). What do proactive people do? A longitudinal model lining proactive personality and career success. *Personnel Psychology, 54*(4), 845–874.

25. Alarcon, G., Eschleman, K. J., & Bowling, N. A. (2009). Relationship between personality variables and burnout: A meta-analysis. *Work and Stress: An International Journal of Work, Health & Organisations, 23*(3), 244–263.

26. Employee Assistance Program (EAP) (2013). *Homeland Security.* Retrieved from http://www.dhs.gov/employee-assistance-program-eap on April 21, 2013.

27. Holmes & Rahe, 1967.

28. Riley, A., & Zaccaro, S. (Eds.). (1987). *Occupational stress and organizational effectiveness.* New York, NY: Praeger.

29. Farrell, I. (2002, March 18). Workplace bullying's high cost. *Orlando Business Journal.*

30. Heames, J., & Harvey, M. (2006). Workplace bullying: A cross-level assessment. *Management Decision, 44*(9), 1214–1230.

31. Vasu, M., Stewart, D., & Garson, G. D. (1990). *Organizational behavior and public management* (2nd ed.). New York, NY: Marcel Dekker.

32. Jackson, S., & Schuler, R. (1985). A meta-analysis and conceptual critique of research on role ambiguity and role conflict in work settings. *Organizational Behavior and Human Decision Processes, 36,* 16–78.

33. Beck, M. (2013). Finding work-life balance; how to keep your job and home lives separate and healthy. *Huffington Post,* April 10. Retrieved from http://www.huffingtonpost.com/2013/04/10/work-life-balance-job-home-strategies-for-women_n_3044764.html on April 21, 2013.

34. Everitt, L. (2013). Leaning elsewhere: Are Harvard B-school women opting out? *Fortune CNN,* April 12. Retrieved from http://management.fortune.cnn.com/tag/work-life-balance/ on April 21, 2013.

35. Xie, J. L., & Johns, G. (1995). Job scope and stress: Can scope be too high? *Academy of Management Journal, 38,* 1288–1309.

36. Im, T. (2009). An exploratory study of time stress and its causes among government employees. *Public Administration Review, 69*(1), 104–115; see p. 112.

37. Jex, S. (1998). *Stress and job performance.* Thousand Oaks, CA: Sage.

38. Cooper, C. L., & Smith, M. J. (1985). *Job stress and blue collar work.* New York, NY: Wiley.

39. Cartwright, S., & Cooper, C. (1997). *Managing workplace stress.* Thousand Oaks, CA: Sage; and Riley & Zaccaro, 1987.

40. Riley & Zaccaro, 1987.

41. Dahl, M. (2011). Organizational change and employee stress. *Management Journal, 57*(2), 240–256.

42. Ferris, G., Frink, D., Galang, M., Zhou, J., Kacmar, K. M., & Howard, J. (1996). Perceptions of organizational politics: Prediction, stress-related implications, and outcomes. *Human Relations, 49*(2), 233–266.

43. James, K., & Arroba, T. (1990). Politics and management: The effect of stress on the political sensitivity of managers. *Journal of Managerial Psychology, 5*(3), 22–27.

44. Cheng, R. (2012). Nokia on the edge: Inside an icon's fight for survival. *C/net,* December 18. Retrieved from http://news.cnet.com/8301-1035_3-57559620-94/nokia-on-the-edge-inside-an-icons-fight-for-survival/ on April 24, 2013.

45. Nokia. (2013). *Career bliss*. Retrieved from http://www.careerbliss.com/nokia/reviews/ on April 24, 2013.

46. Hill, A. (2013). Nokia: From "burning platform" to a slimmer management model. *Financial Times*, February 25. Retrieved from http://www.ft.com/intl/cms/s/2/8a68e12e-7d0a-11e2-8bd7-00144feabdc0.html#axzz2RQAHgkec on April 24, 2013.

47. Johnson, B. (2011). Nokia crisis highlights internal struggle. *BBC Technology*, February 10. Retrieved from http://www.bbc.co.uk/news/technology-12414595 on April 24, 2013.

48. Johnson, 2011.

49. Cheng, 2012.

50. Cheng, 2012.

51. Rushton, K. (2012). Nokia needs to be "Finnish to its core" says new chairman Risto Siilasmaa. *The Telegraph*, May 3. Retrieved from http://www.telegraph.co.uk/finance/newsbysector/mediatechnologyandtelecoms/telecoms/9244443/Nokia-needs-to-be-Finnish-to-its-core-says-new-chairman-Risto-Siilasmaa.html on April 24, 2013.

52. Nokia—Our people & culture. (2013). Retrieved from http://www.nokia.com/global/about-nokia/about-us/culture/our-people-and-culture/ on April 24, 2013.

53. Nokia—Green and ethical operations. (2013). Retrieved from http://www.nokia.com/global/about-nokia/people-and-planet/operations/operations/ on April 24, 2013.

54. Seligman, M. (2011). *Flourish: A visionary new understanding of happiness*. New York, NY: Free Press.

55. Lazarus, R. S., DeLongis, A., Folkman, S., & Gruen, R. J. (1985). Stress and adaptational outcomes. *American Psychologist, 49*, 770–779.

56. Coutu, D. (2002). How resilience works. *Harvard Business Review, 80*(5), 46–55.

57. Harland, L., Harrison, W., Jones, J., & Reiter-Palmon, R. (2005). Leadership behaviors and subordinate resilience. *Journal of Leadership & Organizational Behavior, 11*(2), 2–14; see p. 4.

58. Quick, Quick, Nelson, & Hurrell, 1997.

59. Beehr, 1995.

60. Beckman, H., Regier, N., & Young, J. (2007). Effect of workplace laughter groups on personal efficacy beliefs. *The Journal of Primary Prevention, 28*(2), 167–182; see p. 167.

61. To see an example of a laughing club go to http://www.youtube.com/watch?v=-AkDvvePb-A . A description of laughing clubs can be found at http://www.laughteryogaamerica.com/learn/laughterclubs/what-are-laughter-clubs-2-1510.php.

62. Romero, E., & Pescosolido, A. (2008). Humor and group effectiveness. *Human Relations, 6*, 395–418.

63. Romero & Pescosolido, 2008, p. 412.

64. Guy, M., Newman, M., & Mastracci, S. (2007). Recognizing the emotion work of public service. *Public Management, 89*(6), 25–28; and Côté, S. (2005). A social interaction model of the effects of emotion regulation on work strain. *Academy of Management Review, 30*(3), 509–530.

65. Jin, M., & Guy, M. (2009). How emotional labor influences worker pride, job satisfaction, and burnout. *Public Performance and Management Review, 33*(1), 88–105.

66. Côté, 2005, p. 522.

67. Jin & Guy, 2009.

68. Quick et al., 1997, p. 165

69. West & West, 1989.

70. Wright, T. A., & Cropanzano, R. (2004). The role of psychological well-being in job performance: A fresh look at an age-old quest. *Organizational Dynamics, 33*(4), 338–351.

71. Wright & Cropanzano, 2004.

72. Yu, M. (2009). Employees' perception of organizational change. *Public Personnel Management, 38*(1), 17–32.

73. Richardson, K., & Rothstein, H. (2008). Effects of occupation stress management intervention programs. *Journal of Occupational Health Psychology, 13*(1), 60–93; see p. 88.

74. Adapted from Denhardt, J. V., & Denhardt, R. B. (2011). *The new public service: Serving, not steering* (3rd ed.). Armonk, NY: M. E. Sharpe.

7 Fostering Creativity and Innovation

LEARNING OUTCOMES

After reading this chapter, you should be able to:

1. Interpret the steps in the creative process

2. Distinguish between creativity and innovation and understand how they work together

3. Recognize and resolve impediments to creativity and innovation in organizations

4. Employ various tools and approaches to enhancing creativity

5. Explain the role of leadership in enhancing organizational creativity and innovation

Creativity at J.Crew ▶

On the inside cover of a spring 2013 mail catalog, Jenna Lyons, Creative Director of J.Crew wrote "You may remember us from years ago—J.Crew, all about the classics. You'll still find them here, but we've changed a lot since then. These days, you might be surprised by what you find."

In that short statement, Lyons summarizes a much more complex series of developments that have occurred at J.Crew over the last 10 years. Not only has the company tripled its annual revenue, but it has become an almost cult-like brand. Much of the credit for the change goes to Mickey Drexler who became chairman and CEO at J.Crew in 2003. Under Drexler and Lyons (as Creative Director), the J.Crew product design would be no longer dictated by corporate strategy. In fact, this approach would be turned on its head: the focus would be on the creative process and building a unified aesthetic for the brand. Early in his tenure, Drexler appointed Lyons not only Creative Director, but also president of the company. "What it says," Lyons argues, "is that no financial decision weighs heavier than a creative decision. They are equal."[1]

But maintaining the creativity of the product design staff is not an easy job. Managing creative people is difficult, and Lyons recognizes that some designers require a lot of emotion and a lot of stroking. In the world of design, there are no right or wrong answers and, as Lyons notes, when someone creates something and puts it in front of you, that thing came from inside of them, and if you make them feel bad, it's going to be hard to fix, because you've actually crushed them."[2] Lyons's approach is to model the creativity and freedom she wants. (Incidentally, it's hard to find anyone working at J.Crew wearing socks—in fact, look through a catalog and notice that, while J.Crew sells socks, almost nobody is pictured wearing them.) Lyons also gives her designers and her staff implicit permission to take risks. When new designs don't work out, Lyons simply requires that people take responsibility and move on to fix the problem. But when new designs do work out, they

To generate creative ideas we search beyond reason, we venture out into the impossible, the fantastic world of dreams. . . . Yet we know that a truly creative idea is not silly for it must be solid, rational, and logical.

—Dimis Michaelides, global business consultant and author of The Art of Innovation

are widely heralded and become central to the company's identity.

Recently Lyons worked on a bold overhaul of the catalogs, of which 40 million are distributed each year. The redesigned catalog supports the creative image of J.Crew and its new posture as a leading fashion icon. And it gives Jenna Lyons the chance to tell the story of the last 10 years in very simple and direct terms—when in truth the move toward an all-out emphasis on creativity and design excellence required a huge change in the way the company operated. But, as we noted, it's paying off big time.

Managing
Innovation

Creativity and innovation are essential to meeting the challenges of a rapidly changing and global corporate environment. Recall that in the 2010 IBM Global CEO Study, creativity was identified as the single most important attribute of future leaders. Creativity suggests innovation and originality—the ability to see old problems in novel ways and to devise new ways of thinking, analyzing, and doing. How do we tap creativity and make organizations more innovative?

One of the first steps in becoming more innovative is to challenge ourselves to think differently about what creativity means to us and our organizations. According to the conventional wisdom, organizations are focused on achieving efficiency, management control, predictability, and rules. In contrast, creative and innovative organizations are fluid, embrace uncertainty, and thrive on the freedom to think and act outside of normal procedures. Contrary to a management philosophy based on avoiding errors, innovation requires both risk taking and failure. On a personal level, we may initially think of "creative types" as different from us: eccentric, unpredictable, and even a little strange. But increasingly we have come to realize that each of us has a role to play in making our organizations creative, innovative, and responsive.

Creativity and
Innovation

Creativity and innovation are essential to sustained business success. They are what helps organizations keep up with changing markets, enhance customer satisfaction, improve the quality of products and services, take advantage of new technologies, and increase profitability. Further, creativity is not just the responsibility of the traditional research and development department or the stereotypical "creative types." According to Apple CEO Tim Cook, "Everybody in our company is responsible to be innovative, whether they're doing operational work or product work or customer service work."

Creativity: the
generation of new and
useful ideas

Innovation:
the successful
implementation of
creative ideas

The Importance of Creativity and Innovation

Creativity and innovation are not necessarily the same thing, but one isn't very useful without the other. While the terms are often used interchangeably, **creativity** is the generation of new and useful ideas, while **innovation** is the successful implementation of

HOW CREATIVE ARE YOU?

Rate yourself on the following dimensions of creativity:

	Not skilled at all	A little skilled	Somewhat Skilled	Very Skilled
1. Perceiving problems	1	2	3	4
2. Thinking intuitively	1	2	3	4
3. Developing lots of ideas	1	2	3	4
4. Being imaginative	1	2	3	4
5. Visualizing my thoughts	1	2	3	4
6. Creating new combinations of ideas	1	2	3	4
7. Communicating ideas	1	2	3	4
8. Reconceptualizing problems	1	2	3	4
9. Relaxing and allowing my mind to wander	1	2	3	4
10. Discovering new ways of doing things	1	2	3	4
11. Seeing things from multiple perspectives	1	2	3	4

Based on this inventory, think about the following questions:

1. In what ways are you creative?

2. What limits your creativity?

3. What do you do to stimulate and support creativity in others?

those ideas.[3] In order to be successful, organizations need both creativity and the ability to innovate based on that creativity. Creativity, by itself, does not directly improve performance. A company's ability to take action or innovate based on that creativity is the key to success.[4]

Interestingly, the people who are best at producing new ideas may not be the same people who are best at putting those ideas into practice. For the purposes of this chapter, we will treat creativity as the beginning of the process and innovation as the next step. We will begin by exploring creativity, how it works and how to enhance it. We will then explore how to build organizations that are innovative: resilient, adaptive, and responsive to changing markets, technologies, and other environmental factors.

First, however, we should ask some fundamental questions. What are the consequences of creativity for organizations? Why should organizations strive to be innovative? Creativity is directly and positively linked to organizational effectiveness and to improvements in quality and productivity. It increases the quality of solutions to organizational problems, helps to stimulate innovation, revitalizes motivation, and promotes team performance.[5] Creativity helps organizations respond to challenges, demands, and opportunities for change.

In addition to driving innovation, there are other benefits to creativity as well. Employees and potential employees strongly value the chance to use their creativity. For example, in a poll conducted by Louis Harris and Associates of the class of 2001, the top-ranked qualities desired in a job were committed coworkers, creativity, responsibility, and the ability to work independently.[6] Managers who are creative and have opportunities to use their creativity on the job are less likely to want to leave their organizations.[7] Innovation and creativity can also reduce workplace stress. Helping people to become more innovative and creative "not only makes the work environment less stressful but also leads to the introduction of procedures which enhance productivity and quality of work."[8]

In short, creativity allows organizations to be responsive and to develop new and better ways of serving customers and using resources wisely. The opportunity to be creative helps to motivate people, keeps them interested in and committed to their work, and reduces stress. Creativity is not just something for "creative types" or a matter of a "flight of fancy" if people happen to have some extra time. It is a critical component of managing organizational behavior and business success and everyone can play a role, even if it is just to stay out of the way!

End of Creativity?

How Creativity
Works

What Is Creativity?

There is no single, commonly accepted definition of creativity. Creativity has been described as "any form of action that leads to results that are novel, useful, and predictable";[9] as "seeing things that everyone around us sees while making connections that no one else has made";[10] as "a process or change from what is and has been to what might be";[11] and as "the entire process by which ideas are generated, developed, and transformed into value."[12] What is particularly important to note is that creativity is not about doing random things, creativity is measured by how well it solves a problem or accomplishes a goal. Creativity occurs when something actually works, is useful, and accomplishes some purpose. In the arts, the purpose of creativity might be to achieve a particular aesthetic, provoke an emotion, or to make a statement. In business, the purpose can be to make a product more attractive, make a system more responsive, or to make a process more efficient and effective.

Views of Creativity

Definitions and interpretations of creativity differ, in part, because they emphasize different aspects of creativity in different settings. As shown in Table 7.1, these varying perspectives can be grouped according to whether they focus on the personal characteristics or attributes of individuals, the possession of a group of conceptual abilities, the demonstration of particular behaviors, or creativity as an integrated process.[13] Each of these perspectives provides insights and has practical implications for how we view creativity in ourselves and others.

TABLE 7.1 ALTERNATIVE VIEWS OF CREATIVITY

Perspective on Creativity	Main Points	Practical Implications
Creativity as a trait	People have innate characteristics that predispose them to be creative.	Some people have traits that make them naturally creative; such people probably will be creative wherever they are situated.
Creativity as cognitive skills and abilities	Creativity is based on conceptual skills and abilities such as divergent and abstract thinking.	Creativity can be enhanced by learning and improving certain cognitive skills.
Creativity as behavior	Creativity is whatever results in the formation of new ideas or solutions that are useful.	The value of the creativity lies in what useful outcomes are produced.
Creativity as a process	Creativity is a process of generating and testing ideas.	The creative process may or may not yield a new product or process; individuals can play different roles in the process.
Integrated views of creativity	Creativity is a function of the interaction among the person, the environment, and the task.	Some types of tasks and organizational environments can be more or less conducive to creativity.

Characteristics of Creative Individuals

The traditional way to look at creativity is in terms of the traits, attributes, or characteristics that predispose a person to be considered "creative." While this way of thinking about creativity may be somewhat outdated, it still may teach us something useful about what it means to be creative. The trait perspective assumes that personal characteristics are more important than the nature of the organizational environment in which the person works. In other words, it suggests that creative people have particular traits that will probably make them creative wherever they are situated. For example, creativity has been described as synonymous with originality. In fact, people who demonstrate originality have been found to be more intelligent and to have a preference for complexity—traits that also are associated with creativity.[14]

This trait approach to creativity also looks at the personalities of creative people. Figure 7.1 presents the various adjectives and personality traits that have been associated with creative people. Some of the adjectives used that were negatively associated with creativity were *affected*, *commonplace*, *conventional*, *submissive*, and *suspicious*. Those who see creativity as residing in the personal characteristics of the individual would not deny that we all have some creative potential. Rather, it suggests that some of us simply have greater innate creative potential, in the same way as we all can learn to express ourselves artistically, even though only some of us will become artists. But there are limits to this approach. As with trait theories of leadership (which we examine later), trait theories of creativity give us only part of the picture. Creativity involves more than simply the presence of certain traits; it also involves certain skills, motivations, behaviors, and environmental factors.

Creativity and Innovation in the 21st Century

The Creative Personality

FIGURE 7.1 CHARACTERISTICS OF CREATIVE PEOPLE

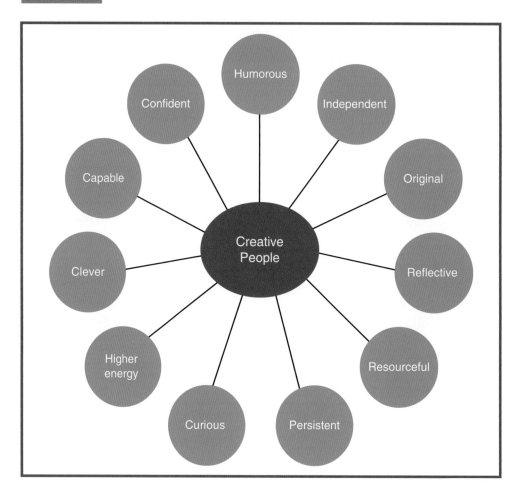

Conceptual Skills and Abilities

Creativity also involves the use of a particular set of conceptual skills and abilities. This perspective differs from trait approaches in that it focuses more on cognition than on personality characteristics. For example, creativity is based on the ability to think on more than one plane or more than one level at a time.[15] "The more adept a person is at rising from lower applied areas to higher intellectual and imaginative planes, the more creative such a fortunate individual is likely to become."[16] Creative people possess cognitive skills in divergent thinking and ideational fluency (the ability to generate alternatives or a stream of ideas), linguistic ability, and a strong ability to find associations between things or ideas.[17]

Although there is a degree of overlap between views of creativity that rely on personal characteristics and those that emphasize conceptual and cognitive skills, there is an important distinction. Skills can be learned, whereas characteristics cannot. While we may have differing innate abilities, we all can learn to be more creative by expanding and enhancing our conceptual and cognitive abilities.

Creativity as Behavior

The behavioral view of creativity focuses on actions and activities that result in the development of something new. From this perspective, creativity is something a person does rather than who and what the person is. What is important is that behavior is judged to be creative based on the extent that it solves a problem or addresses a need. "The ideas must be novel—different from what's been done before—but they can't be simply bizarre; they must be appropriate to the problem or opportunity presented."[18] Again, the emphasis is on the behavior, not on the innate characteristics or cognitions of the individual.

This view of creativity focuses on the outward behavioral manifestations of creativity and places them in context. Importantly, this view of creativity adds the element of usefulness, thereby distinguishing creativity from simply bizarre, erratic, or unusual behavior. Accordingly, creativity not only brings forward new ideas; it is a process that results in actions or behaviors that are functional and useful in a given situation. In that sense, it is not nonconformity for its own sake but rather nonconformity with a purpose.

Creativity as a Process

Creativity also can be seen as a process. In this view, creativity is a highly complex phenomenon involving multiple phases and stages. Creativity is a process of sensing problems, making guesses, formulating hypotheses, and communicating ideas.[19] Creativity involves the engagement of a person in a process where the person "behaviorally, cognitively, and emotionally attempts to produce creative outcomes."[20] The emphasis here is on the process rather than on the outcome, the result. This involves both the generation of ideas and the testing of ideas. This perspective on creativity is useful for thinking about the stages in the creative process and about the roles that different individuals might play in each of these stages.

An Integrated Perspective on Creativity

Perhaps creativity can best be viewed as encompassing all of these views. This view would require that we think of creativity in a way that takes into account expertise in a particular domain, creative thinking ability, and the intrinsic motivation of the individual in a particular work or social environment.[21] It takes creative and innovative individuals and groups, supported by a conducive organizational culture and environment to achieve creative outcomes.[22] Taken together, then, creativity can be viewed as the development of a valuable and useful new product, service, process, or procedure by people working together in a complex social system.

This integrated perspective is illustrated in Figure 7.2, which indicates the mutual influence of personal factors, environmental characteristics, and the nature of the task. This perspective emphasizes the intrinsic motivation of an individual in a particular context, shifting the focus from what levels and types of creativity people are capable of to what they are willing to do. That is, people are most likely to be creative when they love what they do and do what they love.[23] Intrinsic motivation is included as part of an integrated perspective because it involves not only the personal interests and personalities of individuals but also how interesting the problems or tasks are.

Creative People
Must Be Stopped

This integrated approach is a useful one for leaders and managers in today's increasingly complex and global environment. It recognizes that we all are potentially creative, although some of us might be more naturally suited to some parts of the creative

FIGURE 7.2 **INTEGRATED VIEW OF CREATIVITY**

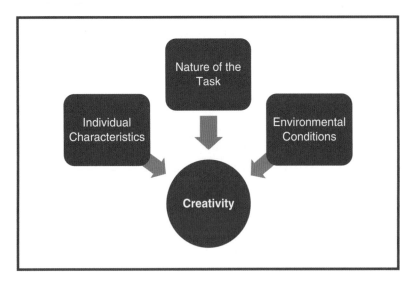

process than others. It suggests that we can learn skills that will enhance our own creativity and that we can support creativity in others. It recognizes that creativity takes place in context and that creativity must be useful and appropriate to the setting or problem at hand. It leads us to think about ways in which the organizational environment may enhance or impede the development of creative ideas and solutions to problems. Finally, it suggests that creativity is an important component of a larger process of change and innovation (a subject that is dealt with in more depth in Chapter 15). Finally, because we all have the capacity to be creative, in a sense, we are all "the creative type."[24]

The Creative Process

Creativity is more than a flash of insight. Instead, creativity can be thought of as a process with five identifiable steps or stages: (1) preparation, (2) concentration, (3) incubation, (4) illumination, and (5) verification.[25] These stages are illustrated in Figure 7.3.

FIGURE 7.3 **STEPS IN THE CREATIVE PROCESS**

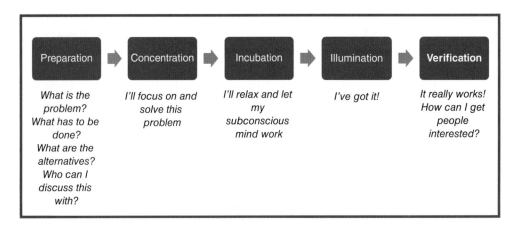

1. *Preparation* is the first step in the creative process. In the preparation stage, all parts of the problem are thoroughly investigated. This includes consciously gathering and examining information, defining the problem, and generating alternative ideas for addressing the problem. Of particular importance is figuring out what the right questions are. "Questions are places in your mind where answers fit" (Christensen, http://www.inc.com/magazine/201210/jason-fried/a-conversation-with-innovation-guru-clayton-christensen.html). In the preparation stage, a person not only searches

for facts but also searches for ideas and alternative perspectives. Preparation is a conscious mental activity. Therefore, most efforts at enhancing creativity are focused on this stage of the creative process.

2. In the *concentration* stage, the energy and resources of the person (or of the organization) are focused on solving the problem. The individual, in essence, concentrates his or her efforts on the problem or situation. There is a choice to engage with the process and a commitment to find a solution. This stage is not so much a matter of mental activity as it is a matter of choice.

3. The *incubation* stage is a largely unconscious phase of the creative process. It is, in essence, the "black box" of creativity. There is an internalization and subconscious ordering and reordering of information gathered in the preparation stage. The person cannot force this process; the best that the individual can do is attempt to relax and allow the subconscious to work and ideas to surface. This may involve the combination of previously unrelated thoughts and a subconscious struggle between what is and what might be. Conscious thought and effort probably interfere, rather than help, in this stage. In fact, research has demonstrated that psychological distance leads to clearer and more integrated thought and judgment.[26]

4. *Illumination* is the "Eureka!" of the creative process. This is the moment of insight or discovery when the answer simply seems to arrive in the person's conscious mind from his or her subconscious mind. It has been called an epiphany, a revelation, or a brainstorm—a sudden realization of something new or novel. But when viewed as part of the creative process, such insights actually occur after the individual has gathered information and gone through a period of subconscious mental activity during which the brain has "worked on" the problem.

5. The final stage of the creative process is *verification*. This involves testing and verifying the idea or insight as viable. In other words, the creative solution is evaluated against some standard of appropriateness or acceptability, and the creator seeks corroboration and acceptance of the idea.

In addition to these identifiable stages, Foster[27] provided a useful summary of the characteristics of the creative process, including the following:

- Long rather than short in duration

- Ambiguous rather than certain and concrete

- Information rich rather than based on "existing" information

- Involving multiple mental models rather than a particular point of view

- Oriented to defining problems rather than finding short-term fixes

- A continuing process rather than a one-time event

The creative process may unfold in a much less linear, orderly fashion than we might expect or prefer.

In the preparation phase of creativity, the individual is focused on gathering information, defining the problem, and generating alternative ideas.

Based on what has been called "chaordic systems thinking" (CST), we can see the creative process as marked by the coexistence of both chaos and order.[28] Put simply, the process may look chaotic because it so dynamic and complex, but there are actual patterns and order in the process that can be recognized. Rather than being fearful of or distrusting the chaos and uncertainty, this perspective suggests that we recognize that creativity and new ways of thinking are often found at the edge of chaos.[29] Efforts to force order and control into a process that is, by its nature, a bit messy can be counterproductive.

It is useful to remember the following:

- Recognition of the steps in and characteristics of the creative process is important from several perspectives. First, creativity does not just "happen." It is a process that can be observed, nurtured, and supported over time. It is a process that requires an investment in time, a search for information, a commitment to openness, and a tolerance for uncertainty and ambiguity.

- Second, we do not all have to be highly skilled at all stages of the creative process; some of us might be better at generating ideas, others might be skilled at synthesizing concepts, some might be good information gatherers, and still others might be excellent "validators" of others' insights. Thus, we can play different roles in the creative process—an idea that is elaborated in the sections that follow.

- Third, not all of the stages of the creative process are amenable to conscious mental effort. As a result, most techniques and training to improve creativity focus on the preparation stage when conscious mental activity is dominant. Such techniques and training activities, which have been shown to be highly effective, are described in later sections of this chapter.

- Finally, being creative requires not only tolerating uncertainty and unpredictability, but embracing the idea that creativity can be to some extent **chaordic**—chaotic and orderly at the same time.

Chaordic: chaotic and
orderly at the same time

According to Apple CEO Tim Cook, "Everybody in our company is responsible to be innovative, whether they're doing operational work or product work or customer service work."

Roles in the Creative Process

All phases of creativity ultimately stem from the work and insights of individuals. But there are different types of individuals. Similarly, different individuals are more or less adept at playing varying roles in the creativity and innovation process. While he uses the term "innovation" differently than we have here, Kirton's Adaptation/Innovation Inventory[30] helps us to understand where different individuals might fall on the creativity spectrum. Kirton described *adaptors* as the type of people who try to find better ways of doing their work. These are the people who make improvements in existing practices, devise ways of cutting costs, and develop approaches to modify programs so as to better meet the needs of customers. Goldsmith[31] found that adaptors prefer short-term efficiency, seek consensus, and value conformity to rules and group norms. *Innovators*, on the other hand, are the dreamers and big thinkers. They have an ability to take two previously unrelated ideas of things and combine them in a new way. Innovators seek change-oriented solutions, look for new paradigms, are less tolerant of rules, and prefer big changes over small ones. In simple terms, adaptors do things better and innovators do things differently.

Obviously, organizations need multiple types of creativity and people who fall on both ends of Kirton's adaptor/innovator scale.[32] The key is to find a balance. Too much innovation can result in organizations being in constant flux, thereby failing to secure and perfect improvements before changing to something else. The goal may be creativity, but too much innovation can lead to chaos. On the other hand, if creative efforts are limited to making only small improvements and changes to the status quo (as preferred by adaptors), then organizations might stagnate. Sometimes incremental improvements simply are not enough; in all organizations, there are times when quantum change is needed. According to Kirton, when innovators and adaptors collaborate, adaptors provide stability, order, and continuity; are sensitive to people; help to maintain cooperation; and provide a safe foundation for the innovators' riskier ideas. Innovators, on the other hand, bring to such collaborations the task orientation and dynamics needed to bring about change.

Social and Structural Factors

Creativity is related to the social connections within and outside the organization. "Communication with others in the domain should enhance one's understanding of the area and facilitate the generation of approaches that are feasible and appropriate, but also unique."[33] When individuals connect with other people, they exchange information and ideas, increasing the likelihood that new approaches and solutions will be created.

Boost U.S. Economy

The degree of creativity these social connections foster will depend on the "strength and the position" of the relationship. Under some circumstances, weak ties can actually facilitate creativity more than strong ties. When the relationship is strong, the "parties truly like each other and are concerned about one another, see each other relatively frequently, and have similar perspectives and outlooks on the importance of their relationship."[34] Since the parties involved in a close relationship often share very similar points of view, they may be less likely to challenge ideas. Weak ties, on the other hand, may give individuals more information and "the exposure to different approaches and perspectives."[35]

There is a limit, however, to how many of these social connections a person can effectively and productively handle. When an individual has too many weak ties, he or she may spend too much time exchanging and processing information. This can result in higher levels of stress and conflict rather than in higher levels of creativity. Weak relationships may foster creativity up to a point, beyond which the number of ties may even constrain creativity at work. The people who have the greatest potential for creativity are those who occupy what the authors call "peripheral network positions." People in these positions have enough connections within the organizations to stay informed and gain organizational knowledge, but their outside connections give them the opportunity to hear something new.

Impediments to Creativity

There are a number of common impediments or barriers to creativity.[36] Removing these barriers can be the first step in fostering creativity in ourselves and others. Figure 7.4 summarizes the impediments to creativity.

Conform and Inspire Creativity

FIGURE 7.4 IMPEDIMENTS TO CREATIVITY

Impediments to Creativity				
Incorrect problem definition	Judging too quickly	Stopping at first idea	Lack of support	Hostility to sharing knowledge

Defining the Problem Incorrectly

If the problem is defined incorrectly, incompletely, or inappropriately, then creative approaches to solving it will be misplaced. One of the ways in which this can occur is when individuals engage in what is called **vertical thinking**.[37] Vertical thinking occurs when a problem is defined in a single way and there are no deviations or alternative definitions considered until the solution is reached. For example, an organizational problem might be defined as one of excessive costs in a particular service unit. If there are no challenges to this definition of the problem, then people will logically pursue cost-cutting efforts such as reducing hours of service, laying off staff, decreasing the variety of services, and postponing purchases of equipment and supplies. But such approaches might make the problem worse if it is later discovered that the real problem was failure to understand and respond to changes to increasing customer needs.

Judging Ideas Too Quickly

People often reject ideas that are inconsistent with their current thinking. We all have heard people defend current practices by saying, for example, "We've always done it that way." Although constancy and consistency might be a human need and a virtue in certain circumstances, blind adherence to the status quo in organizations is not. As Allison argued in his analysis of the Cuban missile crisis,[38] sometimes organizations (and the people in them) try to fit problems into particular organizational routines, whether or not the situation really calls for a novel response.

> **Vertical thinking:** when a problem is defined in a single way until the solution is reached

Stopping at the First Acceptable Idea

Because people often are under pressure to come up with solutions to problems, sometimes the response is to accept the first good idea that comes along. Time pressures, different problems competing for our attention, or simply lack of recognition that other ideas might be better can lead us to choose alternatives too quickly. Obviously, this can result in forgoing what might have been a later—but better—idea.

What Would You Do?

▶ You have just become the creative director of a major fashion magazine, meaning you supervise artists, designers, writers, and other creative types. You are thinking that your previous management style, which was pretty directive, won't work here. What would you do?

Lack of Support

Creative ideas can wither on the vine. If someone comes up with an interesting and original idea but no one listens or considers it, then the idea probably will not go anywhere. We might learn over time that curiosity and questioning are not welcome in our work environment. Sometimes we are not creative because it takes a great deal of mental energy, and the demands of our daily jobs simply consume all of our reserves. Moreover, thinking does not *look* like working.

We might be concerned with appearing busy and engaged with our work and, as a result, become mentally and creatively lazy. The truth is that it often is easier and less demanding to keep doing things in the way we always have.

Hostility to Sharing Knowledge

In some organizations, there is not only a lack of support, but also an outright hostility to creativity and the sharing of ideas. This may take the form of supervisors insisting the workers do not deviate from standard procedures, to not "waste time" by talking among themselves, or routinely tell employees that "we don't have time to experiment" or "we tried that once and it didn't work." In such cases, "it is unrealistic to expect or assume that individuals are basically willing to share knowledge even when incentives are introduced."[39] For example, if there is an organizational norm that employees should not know more than their managers, it is unreasonable to expect any initiative from the lower levels. If managers believe that they are solely responsible for innovation, "competition" from someone who is at a lower level in the organizational hierarchy may be unwelcome. Creativity is also thwarted in organizations where mistakes are taboo. When mistakes are punished, employees will avoid risk and are often scared to admit when they make a mistake. There is also what is called the "NIH syndrome" (Not-Invented-Here Syndrome) where ideas from outside the organization are considered less valuable than ideas that come from the inside. This obviously limits a potentially important source of information and inspiration for creativity.[40]

The truth is that it is relatively easy to kill creativity. First, there are structural, psychological, and behavioral barriers to creativity found in all formal organizations. Traditional organizations, after all, are designed for predictability and control, not creativity. Second, however, you can make it worse by simply dragging your feet, failing to act on other's ideas, postponing action, calling for endless analysis, over-estimating costs and risks, and sticking to the way it has always been done before. Achieving creativity and innovation, on the other hand, requires conscious, strategic, and determined effort. Fortunately, based on the experience of innovative and creative companies, we have learned a great deal about how to be successful in doing so.

Fostering Creativity in Organizations

Successful companies recognize that if people choose to exercise their creative abilities, then they have to be motivated to do so, and that this motivation comes from within the person and through collaboration, not from incentive programs or competitions. Extrinsic motivations (those coming from outside a person), like money, are much less effective: "Money doesn't necessarily stop people from being creative, but in many situations, it doesn't help."[41] Instead, not interfering, and trying to build on people's natural interests and passions, most effectively fosters creativity.[42]

Organizational Cultures Influence

The motivation to be creative resides largely within individuals, but their social environment also influences creativity. A positive climate can create an atmosphere in which creativity and innovation flourish, whereas a negative one can squash such efforts. In other words, it is important to both unleash the creative talents of people as well as create an environment which does not inhibit, punish, or discourage creative thinking. Organizations also need the capacity to adapt and use innovations developed elsewhere.[43] Innovation requires resources and time, and organizations do not possess limitless amounts of either. It makes good sense to both encourage internal innovations and take advantage of ideas that come from outside.

IMPLEMENTING INNOVATIVE IDEAS: SOL AND ROBERT PRICE

Sol Price created the concept of low-cost, broad service retailing, starting with FedMart and Price Club and evolving into Costco. In this he was an industry leader and fostered innovations that influenced many others. For example, Sam Walton, who started Walmart admitted he had "borrowed" many of Price's innovations. But Price was not only a business innovator; he was also interested in addressing significant social problems. Through his charitable foundations, for example, he spearheaded the development of City Heights, an economically distressed area of San Diego, leading to new school programs in the area and the building of a new library and police station. In his forward to Sol's son Robert's book about his father, Jim Sinegal, a friend of the Prices' and cofounder of Costco Wholesale, wrote that Sol's "lessons and philosophy—that business is about more than making money and that the company also has an obligation to serve society—are still valuable reminders for many of us in business today. The fact that he instilled these concepts in so many who were around him is, in my mind, his greatest legacy."

Those that followed Sol Price's career recognize that he was much better at conceiving of new businesses as opposed to operating those businesses. For that, his son Robert entered the scene, recognizing the importance of disciplined operations. Robert assumed his larger role in the company at the time the transition was made from FedMart to Price Club, and became chief executive officer and chairman of the board. Under his leadership,

Price Club combined merchandising features with a new warehouse format and differed from its competitors because of the number of items offered for sale.

Throughout their careers, Sol Price and his son Robert Price devoted a great deal of thought, energy, and commitment to causes in which they believed. Sol believed that philanthropy was an obligation of those who had been able to accumulate wealth, that they were obligated to share their good fortune by "giving back." Sol often said that "progressive taxes, public policies that promote fairness, and philanthropy directed to support vital not-for-profit organizations in the community are all part of recognizing the fact that financial success is a shared activity."[44] The more pragmatic reason for philanthropy and a progressive tax system was to avoid a "have and have not" society.[45]

In his book about his father, Robert writes, "Whatever I've learned about business I learned from my father—everything—from how to read a financial statement to management to good judgment and fair dealings. He also taught me to be humble, to appreciate the unpredictability of life, to care for people, to remain hopeful, and always to be there for people who are in need."[46]

In my interview with Robert Price, he commented on what he and his father have in common: "intellectual curiosity, a strong value system, a desire to do good whether in business for philanthropy, dissatisfaction with the conventional, mental restlessness, optimism, a concern for the underdog. I am somewhat risk-averse; a cautious temperament more like my mother, a good leader but nowhere as self-confident and capable of inspiring confidence as my father."

1. What did your parents teach you about taking risks? About being creative? About intellectual curiosity?

2. How have you experienced the difference between creativity and implementation of creative ideas?

3. Sol Price was a creative leader with a great personal impact. Do you think that one individual can carry the creative load of a company today?

Source: Price, R. E. (2012). *Sol Price: Retail revolutionary and social innovator.* San Diego, CA: San Diego History Center. Supplemented by an interview with Robert Price by Robert Denhardt in the spring of 2013.

Today's Costco stores still rely on retailing principles developed by Sol Price.

Creativity and innovation are also enhanced by diversity in the work environment. Multicultural experiences not only benefit individual creativity, organizational diversity also enhances creativity.[47] The link between diversity and creativity has been shown to be even stronger when organizations have high levels of involvement and engagement across cultural, racial and ethnic groups. When people of different backgrounds and experiences come together to collectively explore new and creative ideas, both the individual and the organization benefit.

What else can managers do to create a climate that encourages creativity? Two factors seem particularly important: (1) challenging work and (2) supportive supervision.

In 2013, Forbes gave Citibank and Merck top rankings among companies in the S&P 100 as the best for women, minorities, and people with diverse sexual orientation.

Challenging Work

As suggested previously, intrinsic task motivation is an important component of creativity. Intrinsic task motivation is driven by "deep interest and involvement in the work, by curiosity, enjoyment, or a personal sense of challenge."[48] Intrinsic motivation is the motivation to work on something you want to—because it is exciting, satisfying, involving, challenging, and personally interesting. A key factor in this regard is choice. Research has shown that if a person chooses to do something just because he or she wants to, then that person will approach the task more creatively than if given external incentives or rewards.[49] Obviously, then, intrinsic motivation is heavily influenced by an individual's preferences, values, interests, and attributes. But it also has to do with the nature of the task. Even the most curious, committed, and creative individual might not exhibit these talents if placed in a repetitive, rigid, and uninteresting job. Moreover, the individual probably will be miserable. With a high level of intrinsic motivation, on the other hand, the individual will be more likely to fully engage his or her expertise and creative thinking abilities. Intrinsic motivation can be so powerful that it even can make up for deficiencies in expertise, knowledge, and creative thinking skills because it drives people to look to other domains or to exert the effort to acquire those skills.[50]

Job design is critical in this respect. Challenging jobs with complex tasks, high levels of autonomy, skill variety, significance, and feedback are associated with higher levels of motivation and creativity than are jobs that are simple and routine.[51] When jobs are designed to be interesting and challenging, people are more likely to be excited about and willing to invest themselves in their work in the absence of external controls and constraints.[52] It also has been found that intrinsic interest and creativity can be enhanced by designing jobs in a way that gives people choices about how to perform their job tasks.[53] Intrinsically creative jobs, then, are jobs in which there is a measure of worker control and freedom in deciding what work to do and how to do it.

What Do You Think?

▶ A friend argues that Microsoft is not an innovative company, because it takes creative ideas from elsewhere and them implements them. What do you think?

Supportive Supervision

How you interact with your employees can have a significant effect on their creativity at work. Supervision that is supportive of employees fosters their creative achievement, whereas supervision that is controlling usually diminishes it.[54] Research has shown that supervisors who encourage risk-taking and novel ideas help unleash creative potential.[55] Supervisors can be supportive by demonstrating concern for employees' feelings, encouraging employees to voice their concerns and needs, providing positive and information-rich feedback, and facilitating worker skill development.[56] Doing so can bolster workers' feelings of self-determination and control, which in turn can positively influence intrinsic motivation and creativity. Because offering people more choices in what they do enhances intrinsic motivation, participative decision making also is important in creating an organizational climate supportive of creativity. Workers who believe they have meaningful input into organizational decision making are more creative than those who do not.[57]

Conversely, supervision that is controlling and limiting, sometimes called **micromanaging**—where employees are closely monitored, allowed few choices, denied opportunities to participate in decisions, and pressured to think, act, or behave in particular ways—can easily thwart creativity. Supervision that is overly controlling undermines intrinsic motivation and shifts workers' attention away from the job itself and toward external concerns.[58]

Organizational and Work Group Culture

Creativity as a System

Organizations that are successful at developing innovative and creative approaches to business have organizational cultures in which there are fair and constructive evaluation of ideas, reward and recognition for creativity, mechanisms for developing new ideas, and a shared vision.[59] An organization with a climate or culture that supports and enhances creativity might express these values in a number of ways. In addition to supervisory attitudes and practices discussed in the preceding subsection, organizations can cultivate these values, for example, by talking about the values of creativity, developing a shared sense of organizational vision, providing time and opportunities to develop new ideas, offering special recognition and rewards for creative solutions to problems, providing creativity training and education, and other activities and actions that reflect an attitude or mind-set that is receptive to creative efforts. The climate of an individual's work group also can have a positive effect. When group leadership is democratic and collaborative, the structure is flexible, and the group is composed of people with diverse backgrounds, creativity is enhanced.[60]

As noted in Chapter 12, leaders play a particularly important role in shaping organizational culture. Transformational leadership, in particular, has been shown to be an important factor in organizational innovation. This suggests that leaders who want to foster creativity should build positive relationships with employees based on their needs, aspirations, and skills, focus on a shared vision, as well as inspire, encourage and stimulate employees to think in new ways.[61]

Micromanaging: when employees are closely monitored, allowed few choices, denied opportunities to participate in decisions, and pressured to act in particular ways

Cultural artifacts are also important in communicating and reinforcing a culture of innovation. Symbols and cultural artifacts "shape the attitudes and behavior of new as well as veteran employees."[62] In order to create a culture of innovation, organizations often have to modify or even create new myths and stories, language, and metaphors. Telling success

ALESSI EMBRACES FAILURE

"Alessi is an example of an Italian design factory, meaning a small or medium-size company that specializes in one area, such as furniture, lighting, or, for Alessi, accessories. In my opinion, there is a kind of historical DNA in Italy, dating at least from the Italian Renaissance, when workshops that had these very specialized, niche production factories originated," is how Alberto Alessi describes his family-owned company.

In 1921, Giovanni Alessi, a skilled lathe turner, established his company in a village on the foothills of the Alps in Novara, Italy. Because of his skills and creativity, it was not long before the household objects the company manufactured from fine metals, such as nickel-coated brass flask holders and cheese trays, became collectibles all over the world. His son Carlo trained as an industrial designer and moved the company to the forefront of design, not only by putting his own skills to work, but also by hiring famous freelance designers who contributed to Alessi's reputation for unusual yet practical objects.[63]

Alessi's design objects are part of permanent museum collections more that any other design company. By relying on hundreds of cutting-edge designers such as Philip Starck and Michael Graves, from all over the world, the company has maintained it leading position. The current head of the company, Alberto Alessi, believes that one secret to working with a group designers with big egos who contract with the company is keeping them separate.[64] As the person who has final say on what the company will market, he relies on his own intuition for inspiration: "I have a good nose to smell the true spirit of our times. Intuition comes from inside, not by watching what somebody has done or established trends. I prefer to stay home and listen to people."[65]

Alessi is not a mass-production company. It's a research lab for the applied arts where failure is celebrated. To Alberto Alessi, failure is the source of success. He values it so much that he prominently displays his company's biggest flops in a museum and has published a book about the prototypes that never made it to market.[66] He says: "We work as close as we can to the borderline and accept the risk of failing into the other area."[67] These failures remind Alessi that they have to stretch their limits. While Alessi is a savvy marketer and uses a special formula to decide what to market, the company considers itself to be an artistic endeavor. Alberto Alessi likens what his company and its designers do to Picasso's creative process: "Picasso shows us a completely different approach: starting from yourself, as a creator, and using your sensibility and your intuition in order to touch other people's hearts or sensibility or intuition. And by the way, he also built an interesting business."[68]

1. What is the key to Alessi's success?

2. How do management practices and organizational culture encourage creativity?

stories about innovation can reinforce those cultural values and make the employees feel free to express their ideas. Value systems and behavioral norms are also powerful tools that can enhance innovation. If innovation is recognized and rewarded over time, employees can become more aware that the organization values such behavior. Physical artifacts and surroundings can be important in fostering creativity as well. The shape and the size of the office, the building itself, the amenities around the building—sport courts, parks, and so forth—not only encourage creativity but also can increase overall productivity of the organization.[69]

The "Tell Your Stories Here" sitting area is one of the features that Sara Morishige Williams had installed in the new Twitter offices seen in San Francisco. Why do you think symbols and physical artifacts have an impact on organizational creativity?

What Would You Do?

▶ Your employees have suggested that they be given one full afternoon each week to visit art galleries, listen to concerts, read the latest novels, and otherwise stimulate their creativity. What would you do?

Workload Pressures and Resources

The effect of workload pressure on creativity is difficult to gauge. On the one hand, excessive workload demands can undermine creative efforts. On the other hand, some degree of pressure or urgency can have a positive influence, particularly when it arises out of the nature of the problem itself.[70] Similarly, some time pressure can enhance creativity, but too much can stifle it.[71] Part of the issue seems to be whether the time and workload pressure is externally imposed as a form of control (in which case it would tend to hamper creativity) or the urgency and challenge come from the person's perception of the problem or the work itself (in which case creativity can be enhanced).

The resources allocated to a project also can affect creativity. The obvious effect of extreme resource restriction is to limit what people can accomplish. In addition, however, if a business does not commit adequate resources to a particular project or task relative to others, it can also have a symbolic and psychological effect in that it may lead to the belief that the work is not valued or considered important by the organization.[72] Of course, money is not the only resource that can be invested in creative efforts. Another way in which organizations can emphasize creativity is to provide the time needed to think about problems and to develop innovative solutions.[73]

Positive Emotions

Emotions also play an important role in creativity. Put simply, positive emotions (such as happiness), foster creativity and creativity fosters positive emotions. "Creative activity appears to be an affectively charged event, one in which complex cognitive processes are shaped by, co-occur with, and shape emotional experience."[74] Positive emotions can help loosen inhibitions, increase visual and spatial attention and enhance the ability to use language. Fortunately, positive affect and creativity can be mutually reinforcing. When people have opportunities to exercise creative problem solving, and have success in doing so, they can experience positive emotions, which can lead to more creativity.

There are a number of ways to enhance positive emotions at work including using humor, eliminating extreme workload pressures, making sure groups have some members with positive affect, meditation, and even providing background music.[75] Leadership style and emotional intelligence, as described in Chapter 12, also play an important role in fostering positive emotions and creativity. Leaders who demonstrate emotional intelligence are also more likely to foster creativity in their organizations.[76] Individuals with higher levels of emotional intelligence are also more likely to be creative themselves.[77]

Fostering Creativity: Techniques and Tools

Creativity is not something that you are necessarily born with, it takes practice. The environment for this practice matters. Job design, supervision, organizational climate, and the allocation of adequate time and resources can have a potent and synergistic effect on individual and organizational creativity. When people have interesting and challenging jobs, when they are supervised in an open and supportive manner, and when they work in an environment that encourages and rewards creativity, they are more likely to respond with creativity and enthusiasm.[78]

But it should be remembered that motivation—including the motivation to be creative—resides within the individual. Although it can be influenced, it cannot be directly controlled. In other words, despite environmental conditions designed to promote creativity, different individuals will respond in varying ways. Furthermore, we can unintentionally and unwittingly contribute to inhibiting our own creativity by blaming others or by blaming the organization for producing conditions that discourage creativity.[79] In this case, our own defense mechanisms might lead us to blame the organization for our lack of creativity, to avoid change, and to deny the importance and intrinsic value of public service work. It is important to remember that just as all of us are products of our work environments, we also contribute to shaping those environments. As we work to foster creativity in others, we also need to be self-reflective and take responsibility for the levels of enthusiasm, creativity, and energy that we invest in our work.

Creative skills can be enhanced by learning and practicing. Businesses often use creativity training to build and foster creativity approaches and skills. The following subsections offer a sampling of some of the tools used in organizations to enhance creativity.

The Idea Box or Matrix Analysis

In matrix analysis, a two-dimensional "idea box" is used to explore new ideas or alternatives.[80] There are four steps to generating an idea box:

1. specifying your purpose or what you are trying to accomplish,

2. identifying the parameters of the problem,

3. listing variations, and

4. trying different combinations.

Consider a situation in which your purpose is to more closely connect and "customize" your chain of coffee shops to the neighborhoods where they are located, but you are not sure how to do it and resource limitations are such that you will be limited in the number of approaches you can use. You could begin by asking yourself what the parameters of the problem might be. For example, perhaps you could consider methods of input, timing or frequency, subjects, and target groups as your parameters. For each of those parameters, you would develop options. Methods of input might include social media, neighborhood open houses, mailed questionnaires, or suggestion boxes. For target groups, you might think about seniors, teenagers, neighborhood groups, and businesspeople. Table 7.2 provides an example.

Using the idea box, you then would randomly combine one item from each column (e.g., an open house held semiannually on facilities for seniors, a questionnaire mailed quarterly

TABLE 7.2 EXAMPLE OF AN IDEA BOX

	Input	Timing	Subject	Target Group
1.	Social Media	Once	Events	Seniors
2.	Open Houses	Quarterly	Facilities	Teenagers
3.	Questionnaire	Semiannually	Access and hours	Neighborhood Groups
4.	Suggestion Boxes	Ongoing	Community involvement	Businesspeople

to businesspeople). The matrix, or idea box, provides a structure to combine and recombine ideas to develop new alternatives. The 4 × 4 box depicted yields 1,024 different combinations—a far greater number than you are likely to generate without the aid of such a structure. Of course, it is not necessary to consider all of these combinations. The purpose of the idea box is simply to get you to start thinking about multiple options.

Synectics

Synectics

The word **synectics** means joining together different and apparently unconnected or irrelevant elements. In synectics, problems are defined by "making the strange familiar," and ideas are sought by "making the familiar strange."[81] In the former case, the aim is to understand or define the problem using terms that are familiar to you. In the latter case, the purpose is to make the familiar strange by purposely distorting, inverting, or transposing the problem to something unfamiliar. This can "transpose both our usual ways of perceiving and our usual expectations about how we or the world will behave."[82] Synectics uses four types of metaphors in this process: (1) the personal analogy, (2) the direct analogy, (3) the symbolic analogy, and (4) the fantasy analogy.

In using a *personal analogy,* you actually imagine yourself as the object or problem. For example, if the purpose is to reduce the incidence of shoplifting, then you might want to imagine yourself as a shoplifter. Or if the purpose is to reduce air pollution, then you might want to imagine yourself as the air. This might sound far-fetched, but such an exercise probably will increase the number of ways that you think about the problem. Even Einstein used visual and muscular analogies in understanding mathematical constructs. The *direct analogy* is similar to the problem or issue in terms of facts, knowledge, or technology. For example, in organizational theory, we often talk about organizations functioning as organic systems, using a biological metaphor where there are inputs, a conversion process, outputs, and a feedback loop. The *symbolic analogy* uses an image or symbol to represent the problem. For example, developing a work team might be thought of as analogous to creating a collage with a common theme, or your role as a supervisor might be thought of as analogous to the role of a conductor, a coach, a gardener, a teacher, or a tugboat. Finally, in a *fantasy analogy,* you might ask yourself, "What is my wildest fantasy about how to make this work?" The purpose is to imagine the best of all possible worlds or outcomes. This frees you to think about problems without becoming prematurely limited by present constraints and limitations.

Playing with analogies as a means to making the familiar strange and the strange familiar can lead us to think about problems and solutions in new ways. By thinking about the

What Do You Think?

▶ Many organizations struggle to balance creativity and innovation with more structured ways to keep the basic functions of the organization running smoothly. Many wonder if these can be reconciled. What do you think?

Synectics: joining together different and apparently unconnected or irrelevant elements

problem in the form of an analogy, new insights about the nature of the problem and possible solutions can emerge. For example, imagine that the problem is a work group with low levels of creativity and innovation. You might ask yourself what this problem reminds you of or how it makes you feel:

Is it like working underwater? If so, then how can you create bubbles that will allow ideas to float to the surface? Ensure that people have flippers and oxygen tanks? Build islands of dry land? Drain the pool?

Is it like trying to open a rusted lid on a jar? If so, then how can you loosen the lid? Remove the rust? Prevent rust? Break the jar?

Does it look like a bleak winter landscape? How can you add color? Change the season? Get yourself out of hibernation?

Mindmapping

Mindmapping is a technique designed to help us think visually and spatially about issues and problems. Mindmapping uses pictures and images to define a vision, a problem, or a situation. It can be a simple representation intended to be used as a memory trigger or as a detailed representation of a situation, process, or "territory." A mindmap should begin with a central image in the middle of the page. Then colors, pictures, and symbols should be used to map the situation, using only one key word per image. All lines branch from the central image. Mindmapping can be done individually or in a group. One possibility is to draw individual maps and then pair people off to explain their maps to each other and create a shared map. The map can be a depiction of a process, a goal, an interaction, or the multiple facets of a complex problem. The following questions can help to get the process going:[83]

Unleash Your
Creativity

- How can we visually describe our goals?

- What metaphors might describe how we work together?

- How would we like to see ourselves?

- What is the environment we are trying to create?

- What are some of the possible scenes from our future?

Mindmapping can be a highly useful tool for organizing information, generating and communicating ideas, and creating a framework for solving problems. There are a number of variations, such as a tree and a fish bone map. Using a tree, some dominant idea or problem is linked to a set of its components or branches. In fish boning (a technique popular in Japan), problems are diagrammed in terms of cause and effect. The head of the fish is the problem, and the fish bones are labeled as the various causes of the problem. Whatever type of picture or representation is used, a map does not need to stand alone. It can be used as a supplement to other forms of idea generation, communication, and presentation. Several web-based or standalone programs are available to help with mind mapping. For example, see Visual Root (http://www.visualroot.com/roots.php) or Free Mind (http://freemind.sourceforge.net/wiki/index.php/Main_Page).

Design Thinking

Design thinking is an approach to using creativity to solve problems that incorporates graphic and industrial designers' original methods to "engage people, communicate information,

Mindmapping: a specific technique to aid visually and spatially thinking about issues and problems

Design thinking: an approach to creativity that incorporates graphic and industrial design methods which involves brainstorming and rapid prototyping to test ideas

generate ideas, or inquire into a design problem."[84] This process, based on the process used in the physical design of objects (e.g., chairs, computers, and bicycles), is being applied to organizational problems as well. It offers a way to approach issues and problems that is directed at "inventing" ways of doing things that make sense to the humans who use them in a particular context. Some see design thinking as a complement to scientific thinking. In scientific thinking, the scientist analyzes facts to find patterns and insights. In design thinking, the designer "invents new patterns and concepts to address facts and possibilities."[85] Others see design thinking as a combination of analytical and intuitive thinking.[86] Miller suggested that even organizations deeply ingrained in traditional analysis can develop and use innovative and intuitive skills by focusing less on what has been reliable in the past, and focus more on what will be valid in the future.[87] The goal is to create "useful, usable, and desirable" outcomes for the people who will use or benefit from the design.[88] Accordingly, the process actively engages the people who will ultimately use the design at all stages of the design process.[89]

Framing questions in a positive light, using "how might we" instead of "can we," can be an effective strategy for generating new ideas.

Design Thinking:
Empathy and
Collaboration

Innovation
Through Design
Thinking

The process can be taught to nondesigners using relatively simple, hands-on workshops. For example, a team from the School of Design at Carnegie Mellon University worked with the United States Postal Service as part of a project to transform its cumbersome and difficult to use *Domestic Mail Manual* into a highly usable and useful guide. The process of design thinking was introduced to the Postal Service using an exercise in organizing objects. In one of the first meetings, each of three teams were given a pile of random "stuff" and told they had 15 minutes to organize it. The three teams used very different approaches—one team created a sculpture, one sorted according to the potential use of the objects, and another categorized the objects by the material they were made from. The various approaches were used as the basis for a dialogue about the human experience of organizing and design. Over the course of the project, research was conducted on each of four customer groups—(1) household mailers, (2) small business mailers, (3) large and online businesses, and (4) specialty or "exceptional" mailers—to create focused, easy-to-use guides for each group.[90]

Design companies, like Continuum and IDEO, use two methods that are highly adaptable to most business environments. The first is that ideas are generated using the "how might we?" approach. This wording is surprisingly effective in generating ideas because positive framing helps avoid the "we can't do that because" response. Instead, it asks us to think through possibilities in relation to our objectives rather than barriers to implementation. They also use a method called "rapid prototyping." In rapid prototyping, ideas are tested using simple, quick, and inexpensive mock-ups of new products, services, or processes. The goal is to find and correct design flaws early in the process, long before there is any commitment to a particular approach. These mockups may take the form of a skit; a physical model built from string, duct tape, and clothespins; or a picture board.

Enhancing Your Personal Creativity

In our efforts to create a positive climate for others to be creative, it also is important to think about how to support our own creativity. Fortunately, there are a number of ways for individuals to improve their own creative process. Many are analogous to the types of things that help to foster creativity in others, but it also is worthwhile to think about them as things that we can do for ourselves.

Personal Creativity

- *Be aware.* To be creative, it often is necessary to have an understanding of the current situation. What are the facts? What information is available? By immersing ourselves in a particular subject, we ground our creativity in reality. After all, as noted earlier, creativity is the development of novel and useful ideas. How can we know what is novel or useful if we do not know how things work at present?

- *Be persistent in your vision and values.* Applying consistent energy in a particular direction increases the probability of realizing your goals. A vision, or purpose or goal, guides our efforts and motivates us to be persistent. Creativity is, at its core, a personal enterprise in that it brings forth something that you, as an individual, value. Maintaining a vision requires self-reflection, the creation of a clear idea or picture of what you want to accomplish, and a conscious investment of energy.

- *Consider all of your alternatives.* Dream up as many ideas as you can. Do not rush to find a solution. Avoid mental idea killers such as when we say to ourselves, "Oh, that will never work," "That's dumb," or "We already tried that and it didn't work." Keep your evaluation of alternatives separate from your development of ideas and alternatives.

- *Entertain your intuition.* Allow your intuition to give the answers that you are seeking. Relax and allow your mind to work. Creativity involves hard work, but the importance of the intuitive part of the creative process cannot be overlooked. Your intuitive self compiles information and creates new images and symbols that can lead to new inspirations.

- *Assess your alternatives.* In evaluating your alternatives, two factors are critical. First, be open to the best solution. Let go of your ego, hidden agendas, desire for a convenient solution, and even self-interest in considering what the best solution might be. Second, use not only your analytical abilities but also your intuition (or "gut feelings") in evaluating alternatives. Are you excited about the idea? Does it feel right?

Can You Teach Creativity?

- *Be realistic in your actions.* If your creation is to be realized, then it usually requires you to take action. Even the greatest idea will be unlikely to go anywhere unless someone sells it, works out the details, and implements it. Even Einstein had to defend his data and ideas. New ideas have to be supported within formation and then effectively communicated to others.

- *Evaluate your results.* Many of us want external praise and rewards for our creative efforts. It also is important to set up constructive feedback for yourself. For most of us, the creative process needs a point of completion when we acknowledge what we have accomplished and the results we have achieved. Even if things do not turn out as we hoped they might, self-reflection allows us to evaluate the parts of the process that did and did not work well.[91]

▶ Summary and Applications for Managers

Everyone has creative potential. Creativity is more than simply novelty; it involves the development of new, useful, imaginative, and appropriate approaches to meeting challenges and solving problems. Because creativity is one of the greatest and most important personal and organizational resources, it should be nurtured, supported, and encouraged. There are a number of practical steps that can be taken to bolster your own creativity as well as to encourage the creativity of others in organizations. These methods are highlighted in what follows.

1. *Debunk the myths of creativity.* All people have creative potential; it is not limited to the artistic, eccentric, or unusual among us. Moreover, different people can contribute to the creative process in different ways, all of which are important and constructive for organizations and the people who work in them. Creativity involves the development of novel and *useful* or *appropriate* ideas. To be creative in organizations, we need not embrace or implement the bizarre or unusual. Rather, creativity is about using imagination to make things work better.

2. *Change your vocabulary.* Nothing squashes creativity faster than a negative response. Killer phrases such as "Yes, but . . . ," "We already tried that and it didn't work," and "We can't do that" can be substituted with phrases such as "Yes, and . . . ," or "How might we . . . ?" Remember that it is important not only to use these creativity-building phrases with others but also to use them in our "self-talk." Do not fall into the trap of being overly critical of your own ideas.

3. *Use participatory management approaches.* Using these approaches can increase intrinsic motivation and allow you to actively encourage creative thinking as part of the decision-making process. Creative collaboration is enhanced when everyone understands that a democratic process for generating ideas can lead to something unexpected and valuable. Overcontrolling supervisory approaches have been shown to hamper creativity. Open participatory approaches can encourage creativity and a willingness to try new things.

4. *Make time and information available for creative efforts.* Information fuels creativity by triggering the imagination and providing the foundations of innovation. Make sure that people have the information they need to think creatively, but also realistically, about finding new and better ways of doing their jobs and meeting organizational challenges. Individuals and groups also need time to be creative. Time pressures are undeniable and often unavoidable. But unless it is absolutely necessary, demanding that a task be done or a problem be solved immediately might cost time and money in the long run if it hampers the development of more creative and effective approaches.

5. *Analyze your organizational climate.* Ask yourself the following questions. Does your organizational climate encourage or hinder creativity? Are interactions between people characterized by trust and respect? Are new ideas welcomed and encouraged? Do people feel safe in asking questions and making suggestions? Is supervision characterized by control and micromanagement or by guidance, support, and openness? Within a framework of a shared vision and organizational goals, are people encouraged to do what they love and to love what they do?

6. *Relax and let your mind work.* There is a point in the creative process when you just need to allow the mind to work, letting your subconscious make new connections and recombinations of ideas. This means that taking a short walk, doodling, or simply taking a "breather" or mental break can be important in allowing creative ideas to emerge in your mind. Laughter also can be a good way of breaking down barriers and relaxing your mind.

7. *Use techniques and tools to foster creativity.* Use techniques and tools to foster your own creativity as well as that of others. A sampling of techniques discussed earlier in this chapter included idea boxes, mindmapping, synectics, and design

thinking. These and other tools can help you and others to stimulate your creativity. A variety of training programs also are available to build creative thinking skills.

8. *Identify problems that need creative solutions.* Identify problems that need creative solutions, and challenge yourself and others to find answers. Creativity requires a willingness to look at what is and consider what might be. This willingness can be encouraged by explicitly identifying issues and problems and by asking people to contribute creative energy to addressing them.

9. *Make work interesting and do not oversupervise.* Ask yourself what you can do to make your work and your employees' work more complex, challenging, and interesting. Creativity is enhanced when people have choices in their work and when they feel challenged to do complex and important tasks. Allowing workers to have some flexibility and discretion in how they will accomplish work tasks creates situations that invite innovation, experimentation, and creative approaches. Avoid unnecessarily controlling or overspecifying *how* someone must accomplish a particular objective.

10. *Challenge yourself and others to be creative.* Managing a successful business demands creativity. A rapidly changing, increasing global and complex business environment requires us to solve problems and meet challenges that are messy, difficult, and complicated. In the middle of everyday demands, deadlines, and routines, it is important to sometimes remind yourself and others that innovation and creativity is the lifeblood of survival.

▶ Key Terms

Chaordic 212	Design thinking 223	Micromanaging 218	Synectics 222
Creativity 204	Innovation 204	Mindmapping 223	Vertical thinking 214

▶ Exercise 7.1 Understanding Your Creative Style

Go back and review your answers to the questions in the Self-Assessment near the beginning of the chapter. Do you have any new ideas about what you might do to enhance or develop your creativity? How might you help others to be more creative?

▶ Exercise 7.2 Mindmapping Exercise

Think about a goal that you have for your career or education. Spend a few minutes visualizing the goal. Then create a mindmap that represents how you see the process for achieving that goal. Be attentive to choosing a central image that you think best captures your goal. What has to occur for you to reach that goal? Who and what is involved? What is the nature of the goal? What are the consequences of achieving it? What are the barriers and obstacles? How do you view the future? What factors will influence your efforts? Include pictures, images, and symbols for as many facets of the process and the goal as you think are important.

Sometime after completing your mindmap, go back and look at it again. What can you see that might help you to think differently about your approach to the goal? What does the map tell you about the key factors involved? What are the barriers to reaching the goal? What are the things that might contribute to its attainment? What do you want to change? Does the map satisfy you as a depiction of how to reach the goal? What would you like to add? What would you like to erase? What can you learn from the process?

▶ Exercise 7.3: Using Analogies

Think about your present role in an organization. It can be work, school, family, or any other organization or group with which you are involved. Identify a problem that you encounter in this role that you would like to resolve. Using the following as a guide, take a piece of paper and write down some ideas and create some doodles using four types of analogies:

1. *Personal analogy.* If you were this problem, what would you look like? How would you feel?

2. *Direct analogy.* What is the problem like? What metaphors could you use to describe it?

3. *Symbolic analogy.* What symbol or image best captures what this problem looks like? Feels like? Sounds like?

4. *Fantasy analogy.* What is your wildest fantasy about how to solve this problem? How would solving the problem change the future? What is the best possible outcome?

Now go back and think about your analogies and their implications. If the problem you are trying to resolve actually *was* one of these analogies, then what would you do? For example, if you compared the problem with your present organizational role to a flower that was not blooming, then how could you actually make a flower bloom? Fertilizer? Water? Sunshine? What ideas does that give you for addressing the problem?

▶ Exercise 7.4 Adapting Innovations

One of the best ways to fuel your creativity is to seek out ideas from other individuals and organizations. Read through several journals or magazines to see what innovations other companies are coming up with. Then answer the following questions:

1. What particularly intrigues you about this innovation? Why do you think it is needed and might or might not work in your organization?

2. In what ways might the innovation be adapted to your particular organization's characteristics or needs? How can you build from or depart from what is already being done in another company?

3. Where and how would you begin to work toward getting such an innovation implemented? What factors do you think will support its adoption? What might be the significant barriers?

▶ Case 7.1 A Creativity Challenge

You have just received a promotion to become the manager of the communications office for your company. You are thrilled about your new job and anxiously await the opportunity to work with your staff of seven people both to improve how your company responds to requests for information and to create new avenues for communication between the company and its customers.

At the conclusion of your first staff meeting, you ask your staff to help you begin identifying what they think are some of the problem areas and opportunities that the unit can and should address. The silence that follows is very unsettling to you. Nonetheless, you wait for someone to speak. Finally, the most senior staff member says, "There is never any money around here to try anything new." Another comments, "What's the point? Our unit isn't a priority. Everything we've tried has been shot down." Another adds, "People don't respond to our efforts to communicate with them. They just don't seem to care about what we are doing." After a few more similar comments, you conclude the meeting by expressing appreciation for their comments and your hope and vision that things will change for the better. Still, you feel rather discouraged.

Later, in private meetings, you talk with your staff about your desire to approach problems creatively and to come up with some new and innovative approaches to achieving the unit's mission. In the course of these discussions, you learn that the prior manager not only did not solicit ideas but also routinely shot them down if they were raised. His

favorite response to suggested innovations was, "We tried that once and it didn't work." Staff confided that they had learned a long time ago that they just needed to keep their heads down and do their jobs. One commented, "Besides, it's enough to just keep up with all the requests we get. We don't have staff to do anything else!"

1. What are some of the characteristics of the past management practices and organizational climate that are thwarting creativity?

2. What are some measures that you can take to begin to foster creativity in the individuals you work with and in your unit as a whole?

3. What tools might be helpful?

$SAGE edge™

Sharpen your skills with SAGE edge at edge.sagepub.com/nahavandi

SAGE edge for students provides a personalized approach to help you accomplish your coursework goals in an easy-to-use learning environment.

▶ Endnotes

1. Sacks, D. (2013, April 15). How Jenna Lyons transformed J.Crew into a cult brand. *Fast Company*. Retrieved from http://www.fastcompany.com/3007843/creative-conversations/how-jenna-lyons-transformed-jcrew-cult-brand on October 24, 2013.

2. Ibid.

3. Amabile, T. M. (1996). *Creativity and innovation in organizations*. Boston, MA: Harvard Business School.

4. Weinzimmer, L. G., Michel, E. J., & Franczak, J. L. (2011). Creativity and firm-level performance: The mediating effects of action orientation. *Journal of Managerial Issues, 23*(1), 62–87.

5. Raudsepp, E. (1987). Establishing a creative climate. *Training and Development Journal, 45*(1), 50–53.

6. Committed co-workers, creativity rank high. (1998, March 16). *Industry Week*, 14–16.

7. Koberg, C., & Chusmir, L. (1987). Organizational culture relationships with creativity and other job-related variables. *Journal of Business Research, 15*(5), 397–409.

8. Bunce, D., & West, M. (1996). Stress management and innovation interventions at work. *Human Relations, 49*(2), 209–231; see p. 210.

9. Boone, L., & Hollingsworth, A. T. (1990). Creative thinking in business organizations. *Review of Business, 12*(2), 3–12.

10. Wycoff, J. (1995). *Transformation thinking.* New York, NY: Berkley Books.

11. Singh, P. (1985, Spring). Creativity and organizational development. *Abhigyan,* 108–119.

12. Kao, J. (1996). *Jamming.* New York, NY: HarperCollins, p. xvii.

13. Gundry, L., Kickul, J., & Prather, C. (1994). Building the creative organization. *Organizational Dynamics, 22*(4), 22–37.

14. Foundation for Research on Human Behavior. (1958). *Creativity and conformity.* Ann Arbor, MI: Edwards Brothers; and Gundry, Kickul, & Prather, 1994.

15. Koestler, A. (1964). *The act of creation.* New York, NY: Macmillan.

16. Dimock, M. (1986). Creativity. *Public Administration Review, 46*(1), 3–7.

17. Barron, F. B., & Harrington, D. M. (1981). Creativity, intelligence, and personality. *Annual Review of Psychology, 32,* 439–476.

18. Amabile, T. (1997). Motivating creativity in organizations: On doing what you love and loving what you do. *California Management Review, 40*(1), 39–58; see p. 40.

19. Torrance, E. P. (1988). The nature of creativity as manifest in its testing. In R. J. Sternberg (Ed.), *The nature of creativity: Contemporary psychological views.* Cambridge, UK: Cambridge University Press.

20. Torrance, 1988, p. 290.

21. Amabile, 1997.

22. Woodman, R., Sawyer, J., & Griffin, R. (1993). Toward a theory of organizational creativity. *Academy of Management Review, 18*(2), 293–321.

23. Amabile, 1997; and Drazin, R., Glynn, M. A., & Kazanjian, R. (1999). Multilevel theorizing about creativity in organizations: A sensemaking perspective. *Academy of Management Review, 24*(2), 286–307.

24. Rawlinson, J. G. (1981). *Creative thinking and brainstorming.* New York, NY: Wiley; and West, M. (1997). *Developing creativity in organizations.* Leicester, UK: British Psychological Society Books.

25. Boone & Hollingsworth, 1990.

26. Dijksterhuis, A. (2004). Think different: The merits of unconscious thought in preference development and decision making. *Journal of Personality and Social Psychology, 87,* 586–598.

27. Foster, R. (1995). Do creativity workshops work? *McKinsey Quarterly, 3,* 186–187.

28. Hock, D., & VISA International. (1999). Birth of the chaordic age. San Francisco, CA: Berrett-Koehler; and van Eijnatten, F. (2004). Chaordic systems thinking. *The Learning Organization, 11*(6), 430–449.

29. Overman, E. S. (1996). The new sciences of administration: Chaos and quantum theory. *Public Administration Review, 56*(5), 487–491.

30. Kirton, M. (1976). Adaptors and innovators: A description and measure. *Journal of Applied Psychology, 61,* 622–629.

31. Goldsmith, R. (1989). Creative style and personality theory. In M. J. Kirton (Ed.), *Adaptors and innovators.* London: Routledge.

32. Kirton, 1976.

33. Perry-Smith, J. E., & Shalley, C. E. (2003). The social side of creativity: A static and dynamic social network perspective. *Academy of Management Review, 28*(1), 91–96; see p. 91.

34. Perry-Smith & Shalley, 2003, p. 92.

35. Perry-Smith & Shalley, 2003, p. 94.

36. Gundry, Kickul, & Prather, 1994.

37. de Bono, E. (1992). *Serious creativity: Using the power of lateral thinking to create new ideas.* New York, NY: HarperCollins.

38. Allison, G. (1971). *The essence of decision: Explaining the Cuban missile crisis.* Boston, MA: Little, Brown.

39. Michailova, S., & Husted, K. (2003, Spring). Knowledge-sharing hostility in Russian firms. *California Management Review, 45*(3), 59–77; see p. 60.

40. Michailova & Husted, 2003.

41. Amabile, T. (1999). How to kill creativity. In *Harvard Business Review on breakthrough thinking*. Boston, MA: Harvard Business School Press, p. 6.

42. Amabile, 1999.

43. Chesbrough, H. (2003). The logic of open innovation: Managing intellectual property. *California Management Review, 45*(3), 33–58.

44. Price, R. E. (2012). *Sol Price: Retail revolutionary and social innovator.* San Diego, CA: San Diego History Center. Supplemented by an interview with Robert Price by Robert Denhardt in the spring of 2013, p. 174.

45. Price, 2012, p. 175.

46. Price, 2012, p. 210.

47. Tadmor, C., Satterstrom, P., Jang, S., & Polzer, J. (2012). Beyond individual creativity. *Journal of Cross Cultural Psychology, 43(3),* 384–392.

48. Amabile, 1997, p. 44.

49. Amabile, 1997; and Kruglanski, A. W., Friedman, I., & Zeevi, G. (1971). The effects of incentive on some qualitative aspects of task performance. *Journal of Personality, 39,* 606–617.

50. Dweck, C. (1986). Motivational processes affecting learning. *American Psychologist, 41,* 1040–1048; and Harter, S. (1978). Effectance motivation reconsidered: Toward a developmental model. *Human Development, 21,* 34–64.

51. Deci, E., Connell, J., & Ryan, R. (1989). Self-determination in a work organization. *Journal of Applied Psychology, 74,* 580–590; Hackman, J. R., & Oldham, G. (1980). *Work redesign.* Reading, MA: Addison-Wesley; and Amabile, 1997.

52. Oldham, G., & Cummings, A. (1996). Employee creativity: Personal and contextual factors at work. *Academy of Management Journal, 39*(3), 607–634.

53. Woodman et al., 1993.

54. Cummings, A., & Oldham, G. (1997). Enhancing creativity: Managing work contexts for the high-potential employee. *California Management Review, 40*(1), 22–38.

55. DiLiello, T. C., Houghton, J. D., & Dawley, D. (2011). Narrowing the creativity gap: The moderating effects of perceived support for creativity. *Journal of Psychology, 145*(3), 151–172.

56. Deci, E. L., & Ryan, R. M. (1987). The support of autonomy and the control of behavior. *Journal of Personality and Social Psychology, 53,* 1024–1037.

57. Plunkett, D. (1990). The creative organization: An empirical investigation of the importance of participation in decision-making. *Journal of Creative Behavior, 24*(2), 140–148.

58. Deci & Ryan, 1987.

59. Amabile, 1997.

60. King, N., & Anderson, N. R. (1990). Innovation in work groups. In M. West & J. L. Farr (Eds.), *Innovation and creativity at work.* Chichester, UK: Wiley; also Yang, Y., & Konrad, A. (2011). Diversity and organizational innovation. *Journal of Organizational Behavior, 32,* 1062–1083.

61. Gumusluoglu, L., & Ilsev, A. (2009). Transformational leadership and organizational innovation. *Journal of Product Innovation and Management, 26,* 264–277.

62. Higgins, J. M., & McCallister, C. (2002). Want innovation? Then use artifacts that support it. *Organizational Dynamics, 31*(1), p. 77.

63. Alessi company history. (2013). Retrieved from http://www.alessi.com/en/company/history on May 2, 2013.

64. Tischler, L. (2009). Object lessons: Alberto Alessi. *Fast Company*, September 10. Retrieved from http://www.fastcompany.com/

design/2009/featured-story-alberto-alessi on May 2, 2013.

65. Tischler, 2009.

66. Kirschenbaum, J. (2001, October). Failure is glorious. *Fast Company*, pp. 35–38.

67. Kirschenbaum, 2001, p. 36.

68. Capozzi, M. M., & Simpson, J. (2009). Cultivating innovation: An interview with the CEO of a leading Italian design firm. *McKinsey & Company, Insights and Publications*, February. Retrieved from http://www.mckinsey.com/insights/innovation/cultivating_innovation_an_interview_with_the_ceo_of_a_leading_italian_design_firm on May 2, 2013.

69. Higgins, & McCallister, 2002.

70. Amabile, T. (1988). A model of creativity and innovation in organizations. In B. M. Staw & L. L. Cummings (Eds.), *Research in organizational behavior*. Greenwich, CT: JAI Press.

71. Andrews, F. M., & Farris, G. F. (1967). Supervisory practices and innovation in scientific teams. *Personnel Psychology, 20*, 497–515.

72. Damanpour, F. (1991). Organizational innovation: A meta-analysis of effect of determinants and moderators. *Academy of Management Journal, 34*, 555–590.

73. Redmond, M., Mumford, M., & Teach, R. (1993). Putting creativity to work: Effects of leader behavior on subordinate creativity. *Organizational Behavior and Human Decision Processes, 55*, 120–151.

74. Amabile, T. M., Barsade, S. G., Mueller, S. J., & Staw, B. M. (2005, September). Affect and creativity at work. *Administrative Science Quarterly, 50*(3), 367–403.

75. Davis, M. (2009, January). Understanding the relationship between mood and creativity: A meta-analysis. *Organizational Behavior and Human Decision Processes, 108*(1), pp. 25–38.

76. Castro, F., Gomes, J., & de Sousa, F. C. (2012). Do leaders make a difference? The effect of a leader's emotional intelligence on followers' creativity. *Creativity and Innovation Management, 21*, 171–182.

77. Lassk, F., & Shepherd, C. (2013). Exploring the relationship between emotional intelligence and salesperson creativity. *Journal of Personal Selling and Sales Management, 33*(1), 25–38.

78. Amabile, T. (1987). The motivation to be creative. In S. G. Isaksen (Ed.), *Frontiers in creativity: Beyond the basics*. Buffalo, NY: Bearly Limited; Gundry et al., 1994; and Oldham & Cummings, 1996.

79. Wesenberg, P. (1994). Bridging the individual-social divide: A new perspective for understanding and stimulating creativity in organizations. *Journal of Creative Behavior, 28*(3), 177–192.

80. Miller, W. (1987). *The creative edge: Fostering innovation where you work*. Reading, MA: Addison-Wesley.

81. Gordon, W. (1961). *Synectics*. New York, NY: Harper, p. 33.

82. Gordon, 1961, p. 36.

83. Wycoff, 1995.

84. Junginger, S. (2006). *Human-centered interaction design: A study in collective creativity*. Paper presented at the Academy of Management pre-conference session on Critical Management Studies, August 2006.

85. Owen, C. (2006). Design thinking: What it is, why it is different, where it has new value. *The Business Process Management Institute* (BPMInstitute.org); p. 17.

86. Martin, R. (2009). *The design of business*. Boston, MA: Harvard Business School Press.

87. Miller, 1987.

88. Junginger, 2006, p. 4.

89. Junginger, 2006, p. 3.

90. Junginger, 2006, p. 8.

91. Miller, 1987.

GROUP AND TEAM PROCESSES ◄

PART 3

8 Decision Making

LEARNING OUTCOMES

After reading this chapter, you should be able to:

1. Demonstrate an understanding of the dynamics of the decision process

2. Apply models of decision making

3. Understand the dynamics of involving different parties in decision making

4. Apply techniques that can aid in decision making

5. Analyze information and data to arrive at alternative solutions

6. Evaluate the alternative solutions

7. Make informed decisions

Breaking All the Rules: Steve Jobs ▶

The outstanding design and amazing success of Apple are no chance occurrence. Careful and almost maniacal attention to detail, razor focus on specific goals, and a top-down, quasi-tyrannical decision-making style from founder Steve Jobs were all part of the formula as were his vision, innovative genius, and charisma.[1] In his now famous 2005 Stanford Commencement speech, Jobs encouraged graduates to take action and risks: "Remembering that I'll be dead soon is the most important tool I've ever encountered to help me make the big choices in life. . . . Remembering that you are going to die is the best way I know to avoid the trap of thinking you have something to lose. You are already naked. There is no reason not to follow your heart."[2]

During his career, Jobs made plenty of mistakes, many of them very public, but he also practiced the fundamentals of good decision making: clear goals, quality, focus, learning from mistakes, and passion for what you do. When in 2008, Apple's MobileMe was not meeting with success, Jobs berated the employees: "You've tarnished Apple's reputation, you should hate each other for having let each other down."[3] Jobs's focus and his vision are on the mind of every employee and every manager at all times. Because Jobs was aware of his crucial role in the company's success, he prepared Apple for his passing by institutionalizing the attention to detail, the secrecy, the constant feedback, and the sense of responsibility that he believed ensured success.[4]

While most businesses use the bottom line and profit and loss as criteria for decision making, Jobs considered them distractions. Instead, everyone at the top focuses on ideas and moves as a unified team, focusing on a few things, and moving to make changes sometimes days before a product is launched. Jobs's top-down and highly directive approach further relied on extensive feedback about everything. This constant feedback is used to continually and quickly correct course. A secret group of about 100 Apple

Whenever you see a successful business, someone once made a courageous decision.

—*Peter Drucker*

people, from all ranks, was the sounding board for Jobs. Describing the members he said: "That doesn't mean they're all vice presidents. Some of them are just key individual contributors. So when a good idea comes . . . part of my job is to move it around [and] . . . get ideas moving among that group of 100 people."[5]

Managers face numerous responsibilities and choices. Some of their decisions have limited impact, primarily within their organizations. But other decisions may affect the lives of thousands of people (or more), and they are decisions that just seem to cascade on one another. Imagine the situation faced by transportation officials in the Northeast Corridor when they discovered that a major section of Interstate 95 (I-95) between Philadelphia, Pennsylvania, and Wilmington, Delaware, had been undermined and that repairs would require completely shutting down a 10-mile section of the highway for several months. The decision to do so was itself a major move, affecting not only the incredibly high volume of traffic between New York and Washington, D.C., but also those who commute from Wilmington to Philadelphia to work every day. And, think of the decisions that flow from that. How do they reroute traffic? In so doing, what impact will the action have on businesses and residential neighborhoods adjacent to the detour? How can they minimize the difficulty? Can anyone encourage alternative modes of transportation, perhaps working with Amtrak to add additional commuter trains? What do they do with the cars that people would now want to park at the train station? And think of the issue from the standpoint of businesses affected by the closure. How can they make sure their employees will be able to get to work? How can they solve the inevitable transportation and logistics problems?

Of course, not all decisions are, or should be, treated alike. Some require quick action, whereas others allow more time to decide. Imagine the difference in the I-95 example if, instead of being able to plan for several months for the shutdown, transportation officials were awakened in the middle of the night to learn that the highway was closed by a sudden gas explosion and needed to be shut down immediately and for the next several months. Of course, as we saw earlier, adding time pressures to already difficult situations makes them even more difficult. And as we know, in an increasingly complex world with high-speed information systems, decision makers must respond to events of enormous complexity within minutes or even seconds. Whatever the size and shape of the required decision, it is naive to think that time is always available to undertake a rational and calculated process. By the same token, it also is a mistake to think of decision making as simply a random process.[6]

Making Better Decisions

Defining Decision Making

Let's begin by defining **organizational decision making** as taking place when a person in authority identifies an important issue and carries out a process to make a choice that produces outcomes with consequences.[7] Earlier research found the process to unfold in a sequence of actions that includes intelligence gathering, direction setting, the generation of alternatives, selection of a solution, and solution implementation.[8]

Organizational decision making: when a person in authority identifies an important issue and carries out a process to make a choice that produces outcomes with consequences

A DECISION DIAGNOSTIC

Consider the last three meaningful decisions you have been involved in making and ask yourself the following questions:

- Did a decision need to be made?

- Were the decisions made the right choices?

- Were they made on a timely basis?

- Were the right people involved in the decision-making process?

- Was it clear to you: (1) who would make the recommendation, (2) who would be asked to provide input, (3) who had the final say, and (4) who would be responsible for implementation?

- Were the roles, process, and timeline adhered to by all parties involved?

- Were the decisions based on appropriate facts?

- When there was controversy, was it clear who had the final say?

- Were the right people brought in, and if not, who was left out and why?

- Did the organization's culture and incentives encourage those involved to make the right decision? Explain.

Source: Adapted from Rogers, P., & Blenko, M. (2006). Who has the D? How clear decision roles enhance organizational performance. *Harvard Business Review, 84*(1), 52–61.

There are several ways of thinking about the different types of **decisions** that leaders and managers must make. Some researchers have divided decisions into two types: (1) **programmed decisions** (which are repetitive and routine and for which a procedure or decision rule has been established or may be easily specified; for example, pricing policy or delegation of authority procedures) and (2) **nonprogrammed decisions** (which occur infrequently and are poorly structured). For nonprogrammed decisions, there is no apparent decision rule, and managers are required to engage in difficult problem solving.[9]

Risk may be viewed as an inescapable part of every decision.[10] For most of the decisions that people make, the risks are small. But on a larger scale, the positive and negative implications can be enormous. At a minimum, decisions entail opportunity costs for paths not taken.

Levels of Decision Making

Interestingly, decisions differ at different levels of the organization, leading to another way of characterizing decisions. Decisions that take place at the top of the organization typically are labeled strategic or **high-risk decisions**. These may involve gathering intelligence, setting directions, uncovering alternatives, assessing these alternatives to choose a plan of action, or implementing the plan.[11] For example, a strategic decision may be needed as the company ponders entering a new market. High levels of uncertainty and even the

Decisions: choices made from two or more alternatives

Programmed decisions: decisions that are repetitive and routine and for which a procedure or decision rule has been established or may be easily specified

Nonprogrammed decisions: decisions for which there is no apparent decision rule, and managers are required to engage in difficult problem solving

High-risk decisions: decisions that take place at the top of the organization and are often strategic

possibility of conflict often characterize these decisions, and external events often shape choices (see Figure 8.1).

On the other hand, **low-risk decisions** involve less uncertainty and occasionally permit a degree of delegation. For example, imagine that a change in an organization's benefits package seems advantageous. Such a change might come about by asking the human resources department to research available benefits and provide a recommendation to be approved by top management. Or there might even be more delegation. The human resources department might gather information from representatives of various stakeholder groups (including employees) invited to serve on a "benefits committee." The final recommendation might even be left to the consensus reached by the committee. Figure 8.1 shows the types of decisions that we might expect to be made at different levels of the organization. From this figure, we may conclude that the more uncertain the conditions surrounding the required decision, the higher up in the organization the decision making is likely to take place. Or, to put it differently, nonprogrammed decisions are more likely to be found at the higher levels of the organization, and programmed decisions are more likely to be found at the lower levels.

FIGURE 8.1 DECISIONS AT VARIOUS ORGANIZATIONAL LEVELS

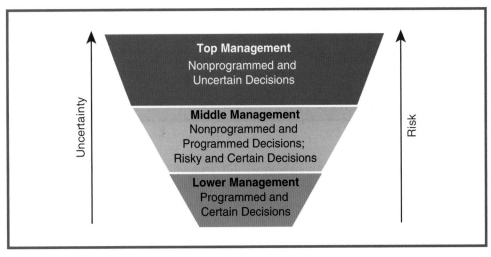

Source: Based on Barney, J. B., & Griffin, R. W. (1992). *The Management of Organizations*. Boston: Houghton Mifflin.

Decision Making and Problem Solving

Decision making is a mechanism for making choices at each step of the problem-solving process. **Problem** solving is a set of activities designed to analyze a situation systematically and generate, implement, and evaluate solutions. Decision making is part of problem solving, and decision making occurs at every step of the problem-solving process.

Effective decision makers know that very few problems or events are unique. Most are manifestations of underlying problems. Therefore, before attempting a quick fix on Problems A, B, C, and D, they will try to find the basic problem, E. Once E is solved, A, B, C, D, and any future problems stemming from E are eliminated. Thus, effective decision makers make few decisions. Indeed, managers often make more decisions than they need to make.

Low-risk decisions: decisions that involve little uncertainty

Problem: a discrepancy between what is actually occurring and the ideal or desired

Because the underlying causes of problems are not always obvious, problems are treated as unique. This results in managers treating symptoms rather than identifying and treating the root causes.[12] It is important to remember that all problems require decisions, but not all decisions will require problem solving.

"If I were given one hour to save the planet, I would spend 59 minutes defining the problem and one minute resolving it," Albert Einstein said. Those were wise words, but from observation, most organizations don't heed them when tackling innovation projects. Indeed, when developing new products, processes, or even businesses, most companies aren't sufficiently rigorous in defining the problems they're attempting to solve and articulating why those issues are important.

Business executive Chester Barnard is credited with importing the term *decision making* into the business world. Barnard's introduction of decision making changed how managers thought about what they did and spurred "a new crispness of action and a desire for conclusiveness."[13]

Bottlenecks in Decision Making

However, even organizations known for their decisiveness may experience ambiguity over who is accountable for the decision and as a result, the decision-making process can stall. Figure 8.2 presents the typical bottleneck in organizational decision making.[14]

Decision Making
Takes a Toll

FIGURE 8.2 BOTTLENECKS IN ORGANIZATIONAL DECISION MAKING

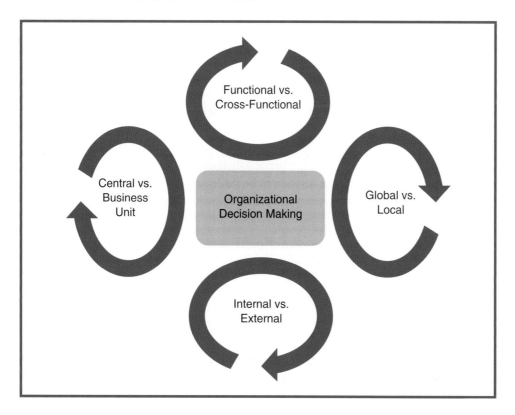

BP came under heavy criticism for its decisions leading up to the Deepwater Horizon oil spill of 2010 that killed eleven people aboard the rig. Among other things, BP was criticized for selecting a well design that was less costly but prone to more risks.

For the manager, the central, functional, and internal bottlenecks are particularly relevant. In the case of the central versus business unit, think of where a policy decision lies: Should the decision to leave a package be made at headquarters, or by the sales people who know the customers? For the functional versus cross-function, consider who is responsible for identifying health care needs for the elderly: Are the needs the responsibility of the heart surgeon alone, or are there partners that should be brought to the decision making to provide for the comprehensive health and well-being of the patient? And finally, networks, collaborations, and contracting exemplify the accountability issues for decision making. For example, internal versus external accountability is questioned when garbage is not picked up in a neighborhood: Who will the residents call to report the problem—the city or the private company that has been contracted for pickup?

We might also consider the concept of "decision debacles," decisions that go so wrong that they are reported by the media. In fact, one scholar found that half of all decisions fail.[15] Executives facing new situations often employ the same strategies and tactics that proved successful in the past without questioning whether those strategies are appropriate for the new circumstances. This has been called the "experience blind spot." While this danger can be particularly perilous for executives who move into a new role or company, this blind spot can also affect tenured executives who face unexpected crises, as experienced with Tony Hayward following the BP (British Petroleum) oil spill.[16]

Why Decisions Fail

Not all failed decisions lead to media attention, but three common elements are found in debacles and failed decisions: (1) faulty decision practices, (2) premature commitments, and (3) misallocation of resources (such as time and money spent on analyses to justify the wrong problem). We have also discovered that the context has less influence on the selection of decision-making practices than previously thought. In other words, best practices can be followed regardless of the decision to be made and the circumstances surrounding it. The prospects of success also improve when managers work to uncover hidden concerns, take steps to manage the social and political forces, identify results, encourage innovation, and estimate risk.[17]

The Critical Decision

Ethical Decision Making

Cognitive biases in decision making and the incentive systems they create can negatively skew behavior. In order to make ethical decisions, one must understand what is influencing the behavior. The five factors that influence ethical decision making[18] are presented in Table 8.1.

TABLE 8.1 FACTORS IN ETHICAL DECISION MAKING

Factor	Description
Goals	Goals that are ill conceived may lead to unethical behavior.
Motivated blindness	This occurs when people may perceive that it is in their best interest to remain ignorant. We need to be mindful of the conflicts of interest not readily visible and work to remove them from the organization, including existing incentive systems.
Indirect blindness	This occurs in organizations, but this time the manager delegates the unethical behavior to others, not necessarily consciously. As managers, we must take responsibility for an assignment's ethical implications and be alert to the indirect blindness that may obscure unethical behavior.
Incremental violations	We are likely to accept increasingly major infractions as long as each violation is only incrementally more serious than the preceding one.
Reward systems	Organizations tend to reward unethical decisions that have good outcomes, thereby encouraging unethical decision making.

In order for us to act on our values, we need skills with which to approach our decisions. When faced with many activities and counter-pressures, the manager needs to be able to think through the problems at hand. This requires not only the use of decision tools, but also the use of what Newell referred to as *moral imagination*.[19] Moral imagination requires that we ask the right questions to act ethically.

Komen Cancel's Charity

Generating Alternatives

Think of a situation that you currently are experiencing at work, at home, or at school. Or just use the following example. You have been offered a data-entry job in a local bank. The job pays well; in fact, it might pay better than the marketing job you have been planning on for the past 3 years. You have been working hard to complete your degree so as to pursue a career in marketing. Going to work at the bank would mean at least postponing graduation.

Why is a choice necessary? Needing to choose implies that a gap exists between what is happening and what you would like to see occur. What alternatives exist in the situation that you are experiencing? The variations to the decision gap might look something like this:

Something is wrong and needs to be corrected.

Something is threatening and needs to be prevented.

Something is inviting and needs to be accepted.

Something is missing and needs to be provided.

Wise Decision Making

Were you able to come up with an action that would close the gap? For example, were you able to justify taking or not taking the job? Through this process, we can say that the decision-making process begins with the perception of a gap and ends with the action that will close or narrow the gap.[20]

CREATIVITY AND CHANGE CIRQUE DU SOLEIL

The Circus of the Sun, better known as Cirque du Soleil, has had a remarkable history of growth and impact since its founding. In its first year, 1984, 73 people worked for Cirque. Today, Cirque has about 5,000 employees worldwide, including more than 1,300 artists. At the Montreal Headquarters alone, there are close to 2,000 employees. More than 100 million people have attended a Cirque du Soleil show since that first year and about fifteen million will see a Cirque show this year.

However, early in 2013, a grim-faced Cirque founder Guy Laliberté, and Daniel Lamarre, the company's president, announced to staff that they had found it necessary to eliminate 400 jobs in the company. This cut was on top of another fifty jobs that were lost the year before. The two principals told the group that the cuts were necessary because of dramatically rising production costs, the strong Canadian dollar, and the worldwide economic downturn. As a result, despite strong ticket sales, the company simply wasn't making any money.

In its glory days, Cirque thrilled audiences with a new concept of the circus, one based on contemporary music, colorful acrobatics, bright and inventive costumes, and a narrative framework. Throughout this period, company spokespersons maintained that the creativity energy of the company led all other decisions, including those that might be considered more "business" functions. Consequently, the company seemed to ignore rising expenses and the cost of mounting as many as nineteen shows worldwide, even as four critical shows had to be terminated. Observers contended the company was "over-extended."

However, Cirque continued to pursue its creative mission of "invoking the imagination, provoking the senses, and evoking the emotions of people around the world." Again, it appeared that artistic decisions were leading even if they involved major business risks. Along the way, then, the company lost track of its competitive position and was shocked to find it was in financial trouble.

Today Cirque faces a difficult decision concerning the future of its operations. Does it return to its traditional strategy of permitting the creative side to lead the company—or does it admit that times are different and that it must pay more careful attention to financial matters, cost containment, and marketing? This is the kind of decision that can make or break a company—even a circus.

1. The last paragraph states the decision that Cirque faces. What further information would you want before deciding?

2. Who should be part of that decision?

3. What would you decide?

Source: Company report, 2010. Retrieved from http://www.cirquedusoleil.com/en/~/media/about/global-citizenship/pdf/Review/Review2005.pdf; *Nelson Wyatt, "Cirque du Soleil Announces 400 Lyoffs," Toronto Star,* January 16, 2013. Retrieved from http://www.thestar.com/entertainment/stage/2013/01/16/cirque_du_soleil_announces_400_layoffs.print.html

Implementing Good Decisions

An effective manager has to identify which problems are within the scope of managerial decision making and then make an effective and responsible decision. A good decision in terms of effectiveness is one that is high in quality, is timely, and is both understandable and acceptable to those whose support is needed for implementation.[21] Time must be spent early in the decision-making process to uncover hidden or ethical concerns.[22] Ethical dilemmas may go undetected while decisions are made and surface later. This can be avoided if the decision maker takes steps to allow the exploration of ethical questions about a decision to be voiced as the decision-making effort unfolds.[23]

The defining characteristic of a high-performing organization is its ability to make good decisions in a timely manner. Table 8.2 presents key principles for successful decision making.

TABLE 8.2 PRINCIPLES OF SUCCESSFUL DECISION MAKING

Principle	Description
Clear priorities	Some decisions matter more than others. Being able to distinguish what truly matters in your organization will be crucial to its success.
Focus on action	The goal should be to move toward an action, not only to reach consensus. Using the term buy-in will likely be more productive than consensus.
Clarity	Ambiguity is the enemy of decisions, as clear accountability is desirable. The RAPID technique discussed later in this chapter can help reduce ambiguity.
Timeliness	Timeliness is crucial for effective decision making, and adaptability is paramount during times of rapid change. Creating an environment where groups are able to meet with short notice is important in most organizations and critical during times of crisis.
The right decision making	The person with the right information and expertise rather than the organization chart or a title should determine who makes the decision.
Measure and reward	Measures and incentives, information flow, and culture reinforce decision-making roles.
Participation	The people who will need to live with the new decisions should be involved in the decision making.

Source: Based on Rogers, P., & Blenko, M. (2006). Who has the D? How clear decision roles enhance organizational performance. *Harvard Business Review, 84*(1), 52–61.

As a manager, you must be aware of two initial steps in the decision-making process. First, you must identify the problem and its elements. In the problem-identification phase, you might ask questions such as the following. Is the problem easy to deal with? Might the problem resolve itself? Is this your decision to make? Is this a solvable problem within the context of the organization? In this process, you probably will want to keep in mind some appropriate models of decision making. Second, you will need to manage the involvement of others in the decision-making process, taking into account trade-offs between quality and speed. If quality is most important and you seek a decision that is accurate, creative, and likely to be accepted by others, then you probably will want to engage various individuals and groups in the decision-making process. In this way, you can have more people contributing ideas, you can divide up complex tasks, you can conduct a more thorough search for alternatives, and you probably can generate more alternatives and stimulate greater interest. But if efficiency is paramount and defined in terms of how quickly the decision is made, then you probably will have to resort to making the decision on your own. In the following subsections, we examine three aspects of the decision process: (1) models of decision making, (2) who should be involved, and (3) what techniques are available.

What Would You Do?

▶ Your employees seem incapable of making a decision and keep bringing even the most trivial decisions to you. You consider this a waste of your time. Why do you think they are unable to make decisions? What would you do?

Models of Decision Making

Graham Allison developed three models for decision making after analyzing the Cuban missile crisis.

In 1971, Graham Allison published *The Essence of Decision,* in which he analyzed the Cuban missile crisis that President Kennedy faced during the early 1960s. Although Allison's specific example is quite dated, the categories he developed to understand the decision process in this case remain extremely helpful and can be applied to other situations. Essentially, Allison suggested that there are three perspectives that one might use to analyze a major decision: (1) the rational model, (2) the organizational process model, and (3) the governmental politics model which we will refer to as the collaborative model. (These sometimes are identified as Model I, Model II, and Model III, respectively.) Allison's basic argument was that, depending on which model or perspective you employ to understand the decision process, you see different things.

Decision-Making Process

As an illustration, Allison described someone watching a chess match. Initially, most observers would assume that the chess players move the pieces in a strategic fashion toward the goal of winning the match. This way of understanding the situation—focusing on the goal as well as strategies and tactics to reach that goal—is consistent with the rational model. But someone else might look at the same match and conclude that the players were not single individuals and that, instead, the game was being carried out by a loose alliance of semi-independent "organizations," each moving its pieces (e.g., rooks, bishops, pawns) according to some standard operating procedures. This view would be consistent with the assumptions of the organizational process model. Finally, still another observer might watch the chess match and assume that the game was the result of a number of distinct players, with separate objectives but with shared power over the individual pieces, operating through a process of collegial bargaining.[24] This view would be consistent with what we refer to as the collaborative model. In any case, Allison described the three models as conceptual lenses that magnify, highlight, and reveal but that also distort or blur our vision. He called for greater awareness of our choices among the three approaches.

In the following subsections, we organize our discussion around these three perspectives of decision making (the rational model, the organizational process model, and the collaborative model). In each case, we examine the basic premises of Allison's approach as well as some of the prior thinking that led to Allison's formulation. Then we note some more recent interpretations of decision making that at least loosely correspond to Allison's three models.

The Rational Model

Decision Making in Organizations

We begin with a general and familiar description of how decision making takes place, whether in organizations or by individuals. Within the organizational context, decision making is the process by which "courses of action are chosen (from among alternatives) in pursuit of organizational goals."[25] From an individual perspective, decision making can be expressed as a course of action chosen from among alternatives in pursuit of personal goals. Basically, when we think of decision making, we tend to think of a process involving the following five phases[26] (see also Figure 8.3):

1. *Pre-analysis phase.* Situations are defined.

2. *Analytic phase.* Situations that affect goals are perceived, and information about them is gathered.

3. *Design phase.* Options are crystallized to deal with the situation.

4. *Choice phase.* Alternatives are evaluated, and the optimal choice is selected.

5. *Implementation phase.* The alternative that is chosen to meet the specific situation is implemented.

In the **rational model**, these phases for decision making are performed deliberately and consciously, relying on the rationality of the decision maker's thoughts and behaviors. Allison[27] proposed the rational model as the classical and dominant orientation to decision making. This model assumes "human purposeness both in individual behavior and in the broader scope issues" such as those found in organizations. Moreover, it assumes that individuals and groups behave rationally in decision making and when they take other actions. And to behave rationally generally is understood to mean that people try to maximize the value they receive in any situation. That is, they make value-maximizing choices.

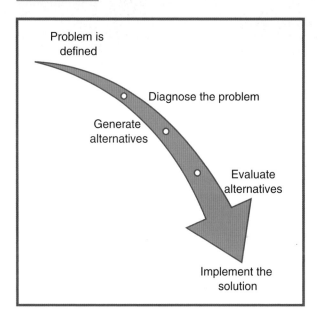

FIGURE 8.3 BASIC RATIONAL MODEL

Problem is defined

Diagnose the problem

Generate alternatives

Evaluate alternatives

Implement the solution

There actually are several variations on the theme of rationality. The classic "economic man" argument suggests that people consider all available alternatives and then make choices that maximize the values they receive. For example, if you are buying a car, then you get complete information on all cars that meet certain minimum criteria and then make the choice that provides the best value—the best combination of price, features, and quality that you desire. But Herbert Simon,[28] in his classic *Administrative Behavior*, argued that real people cannot quite handle all of the information that is available and that they do not have the decision-making prowess required to fit the assumptions of economic man.

Instead, Simon suggested that, as humans, we have cognitive limits. Because we cannot deal with all of the possible aspects of a problem or process all of the information that might be available, we do the next best thing; we choose to tackle meaningful subsets thereof and make decisions that might not maximize value but are at least satisfactory or we "satisfice." In the example of buying a car, instead of searching out all of the information available and making a purely rational decision, you are more likely to look at different cars until you find one that meets your minimum criteria. Then you buy that car. However, note that you still are seeking a rational decision; you just are limited in your capacity to achieve such a decision in all cases. Allison also equated the "rational man" with the classical economic man. In either case, our goal is to make value-maximizing choices to the extent that we can. Also included in the rational model are the assumptions that decisions are orderly (not disorderly), intentional (not unintentional), purposeful (not random), deliberate (not chaotic), consistent (not inconsistent), responsible (not irresponsible), accountable (not unaccountable), explainable (not unexplainable), and rational (not irrational). It is important to note

Strategic Models

Rational model: phases for decision making are performed deliberately and consciously, relying on the rationality of the decision maker's thoughts and behaviors

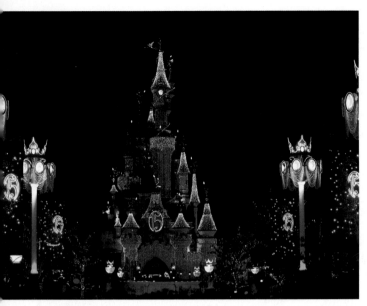

Euro Disney provides a good example of how important it is to take culture into consideration in decision making.

Nathan Steele
Studies

that in a competitive world sometimes irrational decisions put us in a competitive advantage in that the competitors cannot anticipate the decision, for example in the case of pricing discounts. The result is a decision model characterized by rational calculation of the costs and benefits of various alternatives.

Regardless of whether the assumptions of the rational model actually are carried out in practice, the model is attractive as a way of thinking about problems. Indeed, because it is so useful for explaining and predicting behavior, it is the model most familiar to us. Allison and Zelikow[29] illustrated the pervasiveness of the model by asking individuals to react to another nation's unexpected behavior. They specified three occasions: (1) the expansion into Eastern Europe by Hitler, (2) the transfer of missiles into Cuba by the Soviet Union, and (3) the invasion of Kuwait by Iraq. The overwhelming response of those questioned was to make sense of what happened, to develop reasons and motivations, to explore the intentions of various actors, and to assume a careful and deliberate calculation of the consequences of various outcomes. In other words, they tried to fit these aggressive and risky situations into the rational model and assumed that the government action was primarily the result of a single actor behaving under the assumptions of rational behavior. So, even when other models might be more appropriate for explanation and prediction, we tend to rely on the rational model to make sense out of decisions. A recent study of almost 400 nonroutine organizational decisions found that "a rational, goal-directed approach was the most effective way to search" for solutions to problems.[30] Setting goals clears ambiguity and increases the decision makers' chance of success.

The modern rational choice model introduces the element of self-interest, which seeks to explain the inconsistencies between the rational goal of the organization and the individual interests of the actor.[31] The notion of self-interest acknowledges that rationality is just one of the many potential influences on the decision-making process.

Examples of other decision debacles include the British Millennium Dome and Euro Disney. The Dome, which opened on January 1, 2000, was hyped as a futuristic, flashy, and high-tech project to usher in the new millennium. Within weeks of opening, the project became a national embarrassment with high admission fees and lower than forecast attendance. Politicians argued over who was to blame. The government put 785 million pounds into the project and 175 million more to keep it afloat. Now, bidders plan to bulldoze the building and use its picturesque location on the River Thames to build something else.

Euro Disney is another example of decision failure resulting from the building of the Disney park in France without, among other things, taking culture into consideration. An American park in the United States made "Americana" accessible to Europeans; yet in Europe it was less appealing. Disney applied its old formulas, replete with historical and cultural assumptions. It limited its downside cost risk but did not consider how to adapt to European culture to ensure revenues would cover the cost. Warning signs were ignored, although expressed at the press conference. Estimates of park and hotel use were overoptimistic, which suppressed the true risk of the project.[32]

How do decision debacles happen? Are they preventable? Can the risks and the magnitude of the losses be foreseen? Can a debacle be headed off with a midcourse correction? What lessons might we learn from experiences?

There is a growing wave of criticism of the rational model. One part of this criticism is the recognition that values and feelings also play an important role in decision making.[33] In addition, habits, moral feelings, and values that have nothing to do with rationality may guide our behavior.[34] One study examined the influence of emotions on the decision making of traders in four City of London investment banks, a setting where work has been predominantly characterized as dominated by rational analysis. The conclusion was that emotions and their regulation play a central role in traders' decision making.[35] Finally, others criticized the rational approach for its disregard of a holistic picture of human nature, which for us would include culture.[36] Assuming consistency, intentionality, purposefulness, and rationality on the part of individuals invariably leads to misunderstandings and possibly false assumptions. Relying on other models as alternative conceptual lenses avoids this trap and can offer different insights by highlighting different aspects of the decision process.

Critics of the rational model argue that values and feelings play an important role in decision making. Day traders, for example, rely on industry strategies but also make decisions based on emotion—not all decisions are rational.

Future of Decision Making

The Organizational Process Model

An alternative to the rational model sees the organization as composed of many loosely allied units, each with its own set of leaders. One individual leader rarely can control the behavior of so many different units. To accomplish the necessary complex tasks, the behavior of a large number of individuals must be coordinated.[37] According to Allison and Zelikow, Model I (the rational model) "examines the logic of consequences," whereas Model II (the **organizational process model**) "explains the logic of the action."[38] The latter model includes the possibility of multiple agents in the decision-making process. But under this model, decision makers are constrained by standard operating procedures that tend to make decision outcomes somewhat predictable.

We can think of an organization as the pattern of communication and relationships in a group that provides each member with information and assumptions, goals, and attitudes that enter into his or her decisions. These patterns mean that individual members develop standard ways of reacting to situations they confront. "A sales manager reacts like a sales manager because he occupies a particular organizational position, receives particular kinds of communications, is responsible for particular sub-goals, and experiences particular kinds of pressure."[39] More generally, an organization's influence on decision making is exercised by (1) dividing tasks among its members, (2) establishing standard practices,

Organizational process model: relies on incrementalism for decision making

(3) transmitting objectives throughout the organization, (4) providing channels of communication that run in all directions, and (5) training and indoctrinating its members with the knowledge, skills, and values of the organization.[40] The five characteristics of the organizational behavior model are presented in Table 8.3.

TABLE 8.3 CHARACTERISTICS OF ORGANIZATIONS UNDER THE ORGANIZATIONAL BEHAVIOR MODEL

- Individuals must be organized in a structured way to achieve an objective.
- Organizations create capabilities for performing tasks that otherwise would be impossible.
- Existing organizations and programs constrain behavior.
- An organizational culture emerges that shapes the behavior of individuals within organizations.
- Organizations form a sort of technology in which groups of individuals work together in developing procedures to complete designated tasks.

Source: Based on Allison, G., & Zelikow, P. (1999). *Essence of decision: Explaining the Cuban Missile Crisis* (2nd ed.). New York, NY: Longman.

Incrementalism, an alternative to the rational model, is the key to the organizational process model. Charles Lindblom rejected the notion that most decisions are made by rational processes. Instead, he found that decisions are dependent on small incremental choices made in response to short-term conditions. His theory suggests that decision making is "controlled infinitely more by events and circumstances than by the will of those in policy-making positions."[41] According to Lindblom, the bargaining process characteristic of government produces incremental "muddling through" that is quite different from the comprehensive choices of a centralized authority acting according to the dictates of rationality. Inevitably, the analysis of alternatives for action and the choice of values and goals that inform the decision become so intertwined that they are indistinguishable.

Criticisms of the organizational process model include the fact that decision makers are prevented from forecasting the future and acting on the basis of a predetermined vision. Decision makers are forced to make incremental changes based on standard operating procedures. Critics also point out that organizations create their own institutionalized rationality.[42] A study of hospitals and their use of cesarean sections illustrates this point. In an empirical study, Goodrich and Salancik found that the rates of cesarean sections for childbirth in hospitals were not related to best medical practice but rather were based on organizational standards of procedure.[43] This case provides a vivid illustration of the concerns presented by using standard operating procedures instead of what is in the best interest of the mother's health.

A related model emphasizes the legal aspects of decision making. In its most simple and direct form, law is concerned with the conduct of individuals in the context of the social, political, and economic order.[44] The legal model consists of the sum total of principles and procedures that a society has adopted and relies on to function properly. In using this model for decision making, the law is used as a guiding principle, requiring reasoned

Incrementalism: decisions are dependent on small incremental choices made in response to short-term conditions

decisions and fundamental fairness. Legal models are viewed as administrative tools in that "they aid in decision making, enhance efficiency, reduce arbitrariness, improve morale, and provide defenses when agencies' actions are challenged."[45] The legal model in the United States looks to the U.S. Constitution, laws, courts, and contractual obligations for specificity on procedures, requirements, and responsibilities.

The Collaborative Model

The collaborative decision-making model acknowledges that decisions in organizations are made through a collaborative process that, in reality, bears little resemblance to a single executive making a rational choice. Under the collaborative model, decisions are group efforts that involve bargaining among players with different and competing interests. The collaborative model is most readily understood by defining what it is not. First, it is not a model with a single unitary decision maker; rather, it involves a number of managers with their own agendas, priorities, and timetables. Second, this model does not focus on single strategic issues at stake in a decision but rather recognizes complex multilevel issues being considered by the group with multiple interests and agendas and operating in different social spheres simultaneously. Third, this model does not describe a single rational choice; instead, it offers the negotiations and compromises required in collaborating. Bargaining actually is a collection of decisions that often is assembled more haphazardly than logically. Most issues—for example, the Asian economic meltdown, the proliferation of nuclear weapons, or trade with China—emerge piecemeal over time, one lump in one context, a second in another.[46] Hundreds of issues compete for managers' attention every day. Each manager is forced to fix on the relevant issues for that day, deal with each on its own terms, and rush on to the next.

The major contribution of the collaborative model is that it places the actor within a context. Each person is influenced by his or her position, perceptions, practices, and priorities. How problems are defined and how agendas are set are critical considerations in explaining decisions and their results. Issues originate from a variety of sources, ranging from pragmatic considerations to strategic goals and values.

In addition, avoiding what Snyder[47] refers to as "the hubris trap," executives listen to the opinions of others. Carefully considering the input of others, be it agreement or dissent, is critical to making a fully informed decision. It may not change the path an executive takes in the end, but it offers a beneficial speed bump that ensures that several options are considered. For example, a potential increase in tuition at a private university involves various actors. How the potential increase is received will vary among the many actors affected by it—the parents or students paying tuition, employers covering employees' educational expenses, and the faculty and administration of the university. What would be the reaction of these actors? Can you think of additional actors on both the decision-making and receiving ends of the decision process?

Other Decision Making Models

Another popular approach to decision making bearing some resemblance to the collaborative model is what has been called the "**garbage can model**." Cohen, March, and Olsen,[48] whose original work focused on universities as a form of "organized anarchy," developed the garbage can model. "These organizations could then be viewed as having a collection of choice opportunities, solutions looking for problems, and participants looking for work."[49] **Choice opportunities** are occasions when organizations are expected to produce decisions. For example, in the university setting, the administration may ask a university program to decide whether it

Garbage Can Model

Collaborative decision-making model: decisions in organizations are made through a collaborative process that bears little resemblance to a single executive making a rational choice

Garbage can model: decision processes are affected by the timing of problems, solutions, participants, and choice opportunities, all of which are assumed to be independent

Choice opportunities: occasions when organizations are expected to produce decisions

ASIA'S SCOTTISH COMPANY

Fans of James Clavell's novel *Taipan* may recognize aspects of the popular novel in one of Asia's largest multi-national enterprises, Jardine Matheson. The company was founded by two Scotsmen, William Jardine and James Matheson, in Hong Kong in 1832. The opium and cotton trades were the backbone of the company then; now the conglomerate has many different companies including supermarkets, construction and engineering, insurance, property investment, and hotels with 240,000 employees, and an impressive rate of growth and success.[50]

While still controlled by the descendants of the founders, and with a non-Chinese CEO, Henry Keswick, who is married to the Jardine side of the family, Jardine Matheson has developed a distinct culture that is a blend of its European roots with an unmistakable Asian influence based on the traditional Chinese business house or Hong structure. The company has a long and well-respected history in the region with many long-established relationships that are key to business success anywhere, but even more essential in Asia. It also has a strong social presence and expects its leaders to be involved in the life of the communities in which they operate primarily as a way of having access to information. Additionally, because it has always operated in an uncertain environment, the company has a strong focus on collaboration inside and outside the company.[51] Its philanthropic arm, Mindset, focuses on educating people about mental health issues with 42 of the company's executives serving as ambassadors for the program.[52]

In order to develop its leaders in a global market with highly diversified companies, Jardine Matheson exposes its managers to management practices both inside and outside of the company and provides them with one of 200 well-trained performance coaches.[53] They also put particular emphasis on learning about international best practice in order to prepare their managers for the complex environment they face through tightly structured training programs.[54]

1. How does Jardine Matheson prepare for uncertainty?

2. What tools do managers need to make decisions in such a global environment?

would like to implement a doctoral program in the School of Management. *Participants* are characterized in terms of the energy they have available for problem solving. The school director would determine which faculty members would be available to work on the issue and are interested in doing so. The faculty members would be asked to participate in the decision-making process. *Problems* are characterized by how much energy will be required to make a choice. After selecting the faculty members, a committee chair would be assigned. The committee would decide on the issues that must be addressed, such as the curriculum, additional faculty, recruiting of students, and the energy required to supervise doctoral students. *Solutions* recognize the potential energy that is necessary to solve a problem. The committee would then make a decision, given to the department head, on whether or not to consider adding a doctoral program based on the resources that are available.

Under this model, decision processes are affected by the timing of problems, solutions, participants, and choice opportunities, all of which are assumed to be independent. The choice opportunity is viewed as the garbage can in which the participants dump problems, solutions, and energy. Once the garbage can is full, or once all of the alternatives associated with it have been exhausted, it is removed from the decision-making process. The scenarios[55] that would lead to using a full garbage can model are presented in Figure 8.4.

Research revealed that "decision making by flight is a regular feature of the usual decision processes of white-collar workers in Japanese firms."[56] Takahashi found that an increase in workload increases the use of flight when an organization has a high degree of anarchy. He was not surprised by his findings and did not find the high flight ratio to mean failure in an organization with competent organizational workers. "In fact, it is directly [the] responsible managers for efficiency who have the high flight ratio in comparison with the others in Japanese firms."[57] This is attributed to bounded rationality, where the heavy workload makes it difficult for the organization to operate smoothly and satisfactorily.[58]

In addition, critics have noted that because, in this model, managers make decisions in small increments that make sense to them, they may simply generate actions that will make them look good[59] or protect them from looking bad. In fact, an analysis of decision making during the Cuban missile crisis led to the conclusion that decisions were made to avoid failure rather than to achieve success.[60] Finally, Mintzberg and colleagues[61] studied how people actually choose from among alternatives by developing a content analysis of 25 strategic decisions. They found that judgmental, bargaining, and analytical approaches were used to evaluate alternatives. *Judgment* was evidenced by decision makers in applying their intuition to select among courses of action without explaining the reasoning or rationale. *Bargaining* was said to occur when parties to the decision negotiated to reach an agreement. *Analysis* was used to produce factual evaluation. Mintzberg and fellow researchers found that judgment was the method used most frequently and that analysis was the method applied least frequently. Bargaining was used when opposition arose.

Who Should Be Involved in Decision Making?

Groupthink Remodeled

A major area of decision making addresses the question of who should be involved in the decision process. In this regard, there are three basic methods of decision making: (1) **Authoritative decisions** are those an individual makes alone or on behalf of the group. (2) **Consultative decisions** also are decisions an individual makes, but in this case they are made after seeking input from or consulting with members of the group. (3) **Group decisions** are those all members of the group make, ideally through consensus. Naturally there are advantages and disadvantages to each approach. As noted earlier, involving many people in the process may result in a better decision because many will have had the opportunity to think of the pros and cons and therefore will be more likely to support a decision in which they have been involved. On the other hand, involving many also may sacrifice efficiency given that the more people who are involved, the more time-consuming the decision-making process becomes. In group decision making, the process is slower than if an individual were to make the decision.

Involving the Group to Prevent Poor Decisions

Moreover, there is the possibility of **Groupthink**, a mode of thinking that occurs when people are deeply involved in a cohesive group and their desire for unanimity offsets their motivation to appraise alternative courses of action. The individual's mental efficiency, reality testing, and moral judgment deteriorate as a result of group pressures.[62] In 1971, Janis wrote, "My belief is that we can best understand the various symptoms of groupthink as a mental effort among group members to maintain . . . emotional equanimity by providing social support to each other."[63] For example, imagine that you are part of a software company's sales team that has a number of sales calls to make on a daily basis. You have a staff meeting to determine the redesign of the office to allow for more open space. You prefer the current configuration that allows for more privacy. Your coworkers are sold on the open configuration and you do not want to be seen as the non-team player so you vote to go along with the redesign.

Authoritative decisions: those an individual makes alone or on behalf of the group

Consultative decisions: decisions an individual makes with input from others

Group decisions: made by members of the group, ideally through consensus

Groupthink: a mode of thinking that occurs when people are deeply involved in a cohesive group and their desire for unanimity offsets their motivation to appraise alternative courses of action

Managers can take several steps to prevent Groupthink (see Table 8.4). It requires critical thinking on the part of individuals and groups to avoid contamination of the process or goal displacement. Contamination of the process or goal displacement is encountered when the cohesion of the group overcomes the process for decision making or the goal for the assignment. Figure 8.4 presents the antecedents, symptoms, and consequences of Groupthink and may be utilized by the manager to diagnose and be aware that Groupthink is occurring in the team or organization.

TABLE 8.4 PREVENTING GROUPTHINK

The Leader	Stay out of deliberations
	Assign everyone the role of critical evaluator
	Assign the devil's advocate role to at least one of the group members
The Organization	Set up independent groups to study the same issue
	Train managers and group leaders in recognizing symptoms of Groupthink and its prevention techniques
	Assign outsiders to review group decisions and processes
The Individual	Take responsibility to speak out
	Be a critical thinker
	Review and discuss group deliberation with trusted outsiders; report back to the group
Overall Process	Break the group into subgroups
	Study external factors
	Hold "second-chance" meetings to rethink issues before making a commitment

Source: Adapted from Janis, I. L. (1982). *Groupthink: Psychological studies of decisions and policy decisions and fiascoes.* Boston, MA: Houghton Mifflin.

FIGURE 8.4 ANTECEDENTS, SYMPTOMS, AND CONSEQUENCES OF GROUPTHINK

ANTECEDENT CONDITIONS
1. High cohesion
2. Complex situation
3. Directive leader
4. Insulation from outside
5. Lack of procedures to consider alternatives

SYMPTOMS OF GROUPTHINK
1. Illusion of invulnerability
2. Belief in the morality of the group
3. Collective rationalizations
4. Stereotypes of out-groups
5. Self-censorship
6. Illusion of unanimity
7. Direct pressure
8. Self-appointed mind guards

CONSEQUENCES: POOR DECISION MAKING
1. Poor information gathering
2. Selective information processing
3. Development of few alternatives
4. Failure to fully consider risk
5. Failure to reevaluate decision and alternatives
6. Failure to develop contingency plans

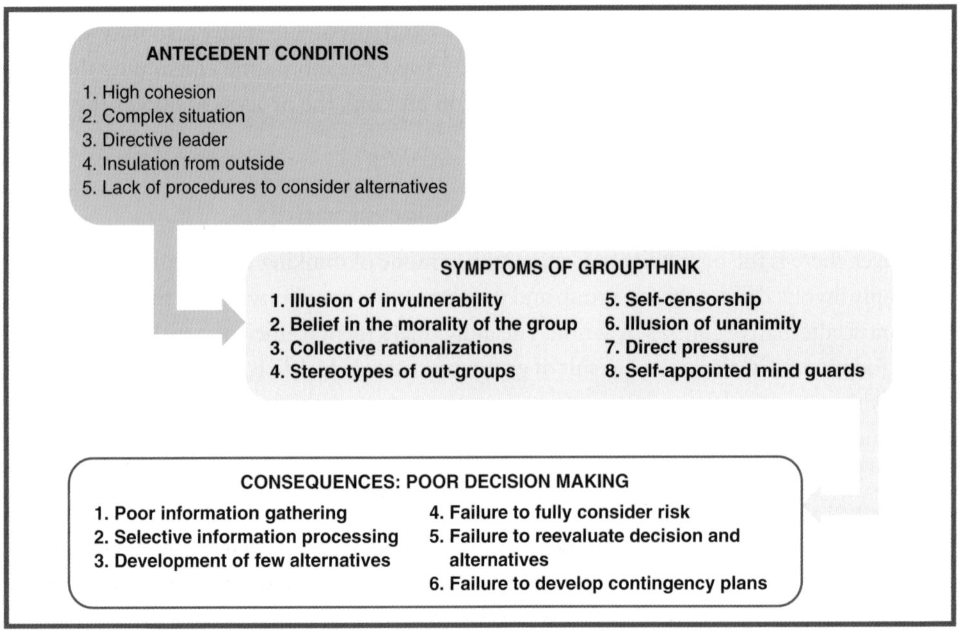

Levels of Participation and Styles of Decision Making

Vroom and Yetton[64] provide a detailed formulation of the issue of participation called the Normative Decision Model. The model focuses on the question of when or under what circumstances managers should involve others in decision making. In this model, the matter of participation is viewed as more complex than simply having subordinates participate. Five different levels of participation or style of decision making are presented in Table 8.5.

How Presidents Make Big Decisions

TABLE 8.5 STYLES OF DECISION MAKING

Decision Style	Description
AI	Autocratic I: Leader makes the decision alone, without input, based on information he or she has.
AII	Autocratic II: Leader obtains any necessary information from subordinates and then decides on a solution to the problem.
CI	Consultative I: Leader shares the problem with the relevant subordinates individually, getting their ideas and suggestions, then makes the decision, which may or may not reflect their input.
CII	Consultative II: Leader shares the problem with subordinates in a group meeting to obtain their ideas and suggestions, then makes the decision, which may or may not reflect their input.
GII	Group II: Leader shares the problem with subordinates as a group. Together they generate and evaluate alternatives and attempt to reach agreement (consensus) on a solution. The leader will accept and implement the solution proposed by the group.

Source: Based on Vroom, V. H., & Yetton, P. W. (1973). *Leadership and decision making.* Pittsburgh, PA: University of Pittsburgh Press.

To answer this question, the manager is advised to work through the decision tree presented in Figure 8.5. The decision tree initially appears complex but, in fact, is easy to use. One begins under Point A by asking Question A. (All questions must be answered with a *yes* or *no*. Answers of *maybe* or *sometimes* are not allowed.) Depending on the answer, one proceeds to either Question B (for a *yes* response to Question A) or Question D (for a *no* response to Question A). One continues answering questions as indicated on the decision tree until reaching an endpoint. Each endpoint is numbered and is followed by a listed set of participation levels. (These refer to the participation levels listed in Figure 8.5.) This is a "feasible set," meaning that each of the levels listed in the set is likely to result in a successful outcome.

But this does not mean that there is no reason to pick one style over another within the set, for the styles are ordered in terms of the amount of time it will take to reach a decision. The fastest approach is listed first, the next fastest is listed second, and so on. Again, the model takes into account the type of decision being made (a process aided by the decision tree) and then offers a level of participation that is most likely to be successful.

There is one more question to consider when reviewing who should be involved: Are the decisions that we are making representative of the demographics of stakeholders? Let's examine why diversity should be considered in decision making.

FIGURE 8.5 DECISION TREE FOR DETERMINING LEVELS OF PARTICIPATION

A. Does the problem possess a quality requirement?
B. Do you have sufficient information to make a high-quality decision?
C. Is the problem structured?
D. Is acceptance of the decision by subordinates important to effective implementation?
E. If you were to make the decision by yourself, is it reasonably certain that it would be accepted by your subordinates?
F. Do subordinates share the organizational goals to be attained in solving the problem?
G. Is there likely to be conflict among subordinates over preferred solutions?

Source: Adaptation of Table 2.1 from Vroom, V. H., & Yetton, P. W. (1973). *Leadership and decision-making.* Pittsburgh, PA: University of Pittsburgh. © 1973. Reprinted by permission of the University of Pittsburgh Press.

Diversity: Opportunities and Challenges for Decision Making

Diversity in
Decision Making

As we discussed in Chapter 2, the current focus on diversity in the workplace results in part from demographic shifts of racial and ethnic minorities, women, and older workers in the domestic workforce, and pressures of globalization.[65] The thought of diversity as being crucial for decision making has been around a long time: "Persons drawn from diverse groups . . . will bring to bear upon decisions and activities different perspectives, knowledge, values, and abilities. And the products of their interaction will very likely differ from the products where they are all of a single genre."[66] This enhances the organization, as a diverse work environment provides an increased awareness of global opportunities, a more cogent approach to problem identification and solution, and a check on the insidious effects of Groupthink.[67]

More recent research has found that women managers are significantly more participative than their male counterparts. In general, participation is valued by direct reports, but this is truer for women than for men. Moreover, participative men and women are equally valued, but autocratic males are strongly preferred to autocratic females.[68]

Management of diversity may be seen as a new organizational paradigm where differences are recognized, valued, and engaged.[69] The goal of managing diversity is to increase awareness of ethical questions related to difference in the workplace and to help managers engage in dialogue to solve complex moral issues.[70] Effectively managing diversity increases creativity in decision making, reduces diversity-related conflict, improves cross-cultural understanding, and provides more functional interpretation of pluralistic differences.[71] Europeans, Africans, Native Americans, Asians, and other racial groups possess unique cultural norms and values that affect their decisions.[72]

Diversity also provides challenges for decision making. For example, cultural differences create deviations from the rational model as we will see using the example of Indonesia. In the United States we emphasize rationality and problem solving, while in Indonesia, the focus is on accepting the situation as it is. Yet we do not, nor does the bulk of the literature on decision making, recognize that the cultural background of a decision maker can significantly influence the selection of problems, the tools used for analysis, the importance of logic and rationality, or whether the decision should be made individually or collectively.[73] Cultures differ in their time orientation, the importance of rationality, their belief on individual problem solving, and their preference for collective decision making.

Cultural diversity is not the only cause of challenges for decision making. You may recall in earlier chapters that some of these differences not only affect culture, but may also be influenced by personality, gender, and individual preferences. For example, a male manager may charge his largely female workforce with the responsibility of selecting the venue of the firm's next retreat. Yet he becomes extremely frustrated with how long the group takes to make the decision. From your readings in Chapter 2, what personal preferences may be having an impact on this situation?

Techniques for Making Decisions

There are a variety of techniques to assist you in various aspects of the decision-making process. In this section, we examine two popular techniques for securing more information and then discuss several others for choosing from among alternatives. Let's start by providing a framework for the process of decision making, or assigning clear and specific roles for the decision maker(s).

The Decision-Making Primer

You may recall earlier in the chapter the bottlenecks that can occur when employees do not feel accountable for the decision or when many are involved in the decision-making process. Rogers and Blenko[74] have designed a process they refer to as RAPID for assigning clear roles and responsibilities. The elements of the process are as follows:

Recommend. The responsibility of the person in this role is to make a proposal by gathering input and providing the right evidence and analysis to make a timely decision. Recommenders must have analytical skills, common sense, and organizational smarts.

Agree. The Recommender has veto power over recommendations. In the event that agreement or consensus cannot be reached, the Recommender may need to go to the Decider.

Input. People that are involved in the implementation are sought for recommendations. Successful implementation requires Input, although the Recommender is not bound by the recommendations.

Participants make collages during a focus group for Suave conducted by Spark, a company that uses art and play in its focus groups to glean consumer's opinions.

Decide. The Decider has responsibility for the ultimate decision and will ultimately be held accountable for the decision. The Decider may also resolve any impasse and commit the organization to implementation.

Perform. A person or group of people, which may or may not include the decision makers, is now responsible for the implementation.

We would add *Feedback* as a step to allow for review and adjustments as needed.

Focus Groups

Focus groups are a popular method for receiving input from a large number of individuals, serving as "group interviews."[75] A typical focus group consists of 10 to 12 people brought together to discuss a particular topic, usually with the help of a trained facilitator. Focus groups may be used for problem identification, planning, implementation, or assessment. Managers then use the data gathered from these meetings to make decisions.

Focus groups require careful planning. Indeed, Morgan recommended that the planning occur throughout the whole project. He described the focus group process as consisting of four basic steps:

1. *Planning.* This step requires the anticipation of major decisions that will need to be made.

2. *Recruiting.* Having well-targeted participants is as important as asking good questions or using a skilled facilitator. "Problems with recruitment are the single most common reason why things go wrong in focus group projects."[76]

3. *Moderating.* Effective recruiting and good questions will greatly aid the facilitator or moderator in the focus group endeavor.

4. *Analysis and reporting.* The information gathered during the focus group is finally analyzed and reported so that it can be used in the decision-making process.

Focus groups can be used in many ways. For example, a nationwide gym owner wanted to know why its national campaign to promote membership among women had not increased membership. Focus groups indicated that the message in existing marketing, although welcoming of this population, did not mention availability of day care or programs for children. The focus groups resulted in including the availability of these resources in the advertising. Similarly, a large business wanted to increase sales to the African American community. Through a nationwide series of focus groups, the organization learned that it was virtually unknown to that community despite an advertising campaign that was geared to African Americans. Finally, a corporation facing major cutbacks wanted to provide a job counseling program that would be of practical use to its former employees. Focus groups revealed the need for different programs for those who wanted jobs in a similar industry as opposed to those who wanted to pursue new careers.

Brainstorming

Originally developed during the 1930s in the advertising industry, brainstorming is a method of generating a large number of ideas in a short period of time.[77] More specifically, brainstorming typically is used to create ideas and generate alternatives. Brainstorming is one of the most widely used and, unfortunately, misused techniques for fostering creativity. The key concept behind brainstorming is to increase thinking creatively and generating solutions by prohibiting criticism. Its misuse most commonly takes the form of participants failing to understand or adhere to its ground rules. Brainstorming works best when the following guidelines are followed:

1. *State the problem clearly and neutrally.* It can be helpful to restate the problem using the phrase, "How can I/we . . . ?" Post the stated problem where it can be easily seen.

2. *Generate ideas using ground rules.* Rules may include the following: There is no judgment made about the ideas as they are being generated, the objective is to generate the greatest quantity (not quality) of ideas, all ideas (even wild ones) are welcomed, and it is appropriate to embellish, or "piggyback," on ideas.

Group brainstorming sessions tend to work best when someone takes on the role of facilitator. The facilitator reminds the group of the ground rules and helps the group to enforce them, for example, by stopping participants who might begin evaluating other people's ideas. These ground rules are so important to successful brainstorming that they always should be put on display during the brainstorming session. Wycoff[78] suggested a number of additional ways of enhancing group brainstorming sessions:

1. *Allow time for individual idea generation.* Allow 3 to 5 minutes of silent individual brainstorming before beginning the group brainstorming session. This can reduce anxiety and prevent a "follow the leader" type of thought process.

2. *Alternate between small groups and large groups.* Groups of three or four can make it easier for people who are too shy or reticent to participate in larger groups. Larger groups can provide greater diversity and generate more laughter, which can serve as a catalyst for creativity.

3. *Realign groups frequently.* This can help groups to equalize participation and avoid the development of rigid roles.

4. *Use activities and humor.* Movement, participation, and humor can help to break down barriers to communication and creativity.

When used appropriately, brainstorming can be a highly useful technique for generating a large volume of ideas and triggering creative solutions to problems. Brainstorming also can be used effectively in conjunction with other techniques such as focus groups.

Cost-Benefit and Cost-Effectiveness Analysis

After gathering facts and suggestions, the decision maker should begin assessing the various alternatives. A variety of analytical tools are available for decisions that require this level of analysis. Here we provide a quick overview of **cost-benefit analysis** and **cost-effectiveness analysis**, techniques that focus on financial value–added cost-benefit analysis. Organizations use this technique to plan programs, allocate resources, evaluate outcomes, and assess the efficiency of organizational processes. This is used for example in capital

Ideas Versus Vision

Cost-benefit analysis: a technique used to determine the efficiency of a program requiring that all costs and benefits are expressed in monetary terms

Cost-effectiveness analysis: a technique used to compare the program's output to the costs encountered; the outputs may be in qualitative terms

requests. "The general approach is to identify and quantify both negative impacts (costs) and positive impacts (benefits) of a proposed project and then to subtract one from the other to determine the net benefit."[79] All costs and benefits must be expressed in monetary terms, so this technique is useful if we are interested in the efficiency of a program. However, we also can consider tangible and intangible items as well as direct and indirect benefits and costs. These sometimes are fuzzy, requiring the analyst to pass judgment. An example of an intangible benefit is the prestige that a company might gain by its location in a major city. To measure the effectiveness of a program that includes nonmonetary items, the analyst must use cost-effectiveness analysis.

Cost-effectiveness analysis. This technique is used to compare the program's output to the costs encountered. Costs consist of expenditures of money and other resources (e.g., personnel, facilities, equipment) to maintain a program. (Again, some of the "cost" measures might be qualitative.) The costs are then compared with how the program is meeting the goals and objectives that have been established. The steps for cost-effectiveness analysis include the following:[80]

1. Identify the objectives of the work activity and corresponding criteria to assess whether the objectives are being met.

2. Examine the current cost and level of quality of the service activity.

3. Based on this evidence and on observations of the way in which the current activity is performed, identify alternative ways of doing the activity. Consider ways of eliminating unnecessary tasks and new procedures.

4. Assess the cost and service quality effects of each alternative.

Nominal Group Technique

This technique was developed to ensure that every group member has equal input in the process.[81] The process for the **nominal group technique** is as follows:

- First, each participant, working alone, writes down his or her ideas on the problem to be discussed. These ideas usually are suggestions for a solution.

- Second, the group conducts a round-robin in which each group member presents his or her ideas to the group. A group member writes the ideas down on a blackboard for all of the participants to see. No discussion of the ideas occurs until every person's ideas have been presented and written down for general viewing.

- Third, after all ideas have been presented, there is an open discussion of the ideas for the purpose of clarification only; evaluative comments are not allowed. This part of the discussion tends to be spontaneous and unstructured.

- Fourth, after the discussion, a secret ballot is taken in which each group member votes for preferred solutions. This results in a rank ordering of alternatives in terms of priority. As desired, the third and fourth steps can be repeated to add further clarification to the process.

Nominal group technique: a technique developed to ensure that every member of the group has an equal chance of participating

Evidence-Based Management

When used systematically, a practice close to performance management is **evidenced-based management**. The term is adopted from the health care industry and is gaining popularity in management decision making. With the use of evidence-based management, practicing managers make organizational decisions informed by organizational research and practice. Evidence-based practice includes the following:

Evidence-Based
Management

- Learning about cause–effect connections in professional practices: Using crime statistics, we would be able to tell where crime has increased or decreased. We would then examine the data to see if the number of arrests has made a difference in the increase or decrease of crime in the areas. If there is no change, we may infer that arrests do not necessarily decrease crime rate and move on to testing another theory.

- Isolating the variations that affect desired outcomes: Using the example above and testing a variety of theories in crime prevention, we may be able to isolate interventions that affect crime prevention.

- Creating a culture of evidence-based decision making and research participation: In order to be effective, the organization needs to provide opportunities for professional development.

- Using information-sharing communities to reduce overuse, underuse, and misuse of specific practices: The best example of this is found in the health care industry through the Cochrane Collaboration at www .cochrane.org/.

- Building decision supports to promote practices the evidence validates, along with techniques and artifacts that make the decision easier to execute or perform (e.g., checklists, protocols, or policies): As students, we might have received checklists of what is necessary in order to complete our program of study. The provision of similar documents encourages and validates the process.

- Having individual, organizational, and institutional factors promote access to knowledge and its use: It is important to create ways to make sure information is broadly distributed and employed in decision making.[82]

To summarize, we can think in terms of building blocks for effective decision making.[83] Building Block 1 is to *smoke out the issue*. Ask yourself *why* a decision is necessary. Recognizing and defining a problem is an important first step in problem solving and decision making. The answer to this first step not only provides you with a definition for the problem at hand but also clarifies whether there is a problem at all. If there is a problem, then keep asking why until all issues have been determined. It is possible to deceive yourself with superficial answers. By asking why repeatedly and verifying the answers, you are able to expose the real issue, which aids in making the correct decision.

What *is* or *is not* the problem? This question helps to define the problem as precisely as possible by separating the mere symptoms from the root cause. Asking what the problem is not, through the process of elimination might help to uncover a truth or eliminate barriers to a problem. Sometimes we believe that the restraints are greater than they really are.

What is, should be, or could be happening? This question is a supplement or may serve as a substitute to what is or is not the problem. Asking what is, what should be, or what

Evidence-based
management:
managers make
organizational
decisions informed by
organizational research
and practice

could be requires that we examine the differences among reality, expectation, and desire or conceivability.

Building Block 2 is to *state your purpose*. The statement of purpose is the most critical step in the decision-making process, yet it is a step that often is neglected. The neglect comes from not wanting to waste time on examining purpose when time could be spent on solutions. Unexamined statements of purpose frequently mask the real problems. For example, a new assistant professor at a research institution might enjoy teaching so much that she neglects her requirements to contribute to knowledge through research and publication. Examining her purpose at these institutions, she might learn not only that research is a requirement of the position but that it would enhance her teaching as well.

Building Block 3 is to *set your criteria*. Setting criteria requires answers to the following three questions, which will be used to judge possible solutions: (1) What do you want to *achieve* by any decision you make? (2) What do you want to *preserve* by any decision you make? (3) What do you want to *avoid* by any decision you make? To illustrate the point using the example discussed in the preceding paragraph, we could say that the assistant professor wants to achieve the following: to provide the best education possible to students, to contribute to knowledge so as to meet the tenure and promotion requirements, and to provide service to the community. She wants to preserve a job at a university she really likes and to remain in a field for which she has prepared. And she wants to avoid having to look for another position.

Building Block 4 is to *establish your priorities*. This step requires that you refine your criteria by setting your priorities. In most decisions, not all criteria are of equal importance. Starting with the list of things you want to achieve, preserve, and avoid, you begin by separating the items into categories of relative importance (e.g., very high, high, medium, and low). This will help you to decide which ones are absolute requirements and which ones are desirable objectives. Assigning the values to the criteria is not easy. Some of the criteria might not be as important to you as you originally had thought, or you might discover that you have not stated them correctly or completely. Now is the time to restate, refine, and reevaluate the criteria. When restating the criteria, be as specific as possible.

Implications for
Leadership and
Organizations

Building Block 5 is to *search for solutions*. After determining your purpose and defining your criteria and priorities, you begin your search for solutions by asking the following questions: How can you meet the criteria you have set? What are the possible courses of action? Answering these questions requires brainstorming. You do not want to limit yourself to the obvious alternatives. Let your criteria generate your alternatives; this will facilitate fresh solutions and provide several alternatives. The alternatives might then need to be combined or modified to fit your criteria and priorities.

What Do You Think?

▶ You consider your boss's proposal for a new outlet in eastern Kentucky to be ridiculous, but you know she feels strongly about it. A friend advises you to just lay low and let it pass. What do you think? Would you be able to just let it pass? Or will you feel that it is your responsibility to gather information to help her make an informed decision?

Building Block 6 is to *test the alternatives*. Testing the alternatives requires answering the question, How well do the alternatives meet each criterion? Each alternative is matched against the criteria, and a choice is made.

Building Block 7 is to *troubleshoot your decision*. This final building block is perhaps the most critical and the least practiced. This step helps you to take action to prevent, minimize, or overcome the possible adverse consequences by asking the question, What could go wrong with the solution that I have chosen? Make a list of all the possible problems, and then make a rough calculation of the likelihood of each problem occurring and the likely impact if it did occur. Finally, take preventive action to cope with each potential problem.

▶ Summary and Applications for Managers

In this chapter, we learned that there are different types of decisions that we will be faced with in the workplace and that different decisions call for different strategies and actors. We also discussed the difference between decision making and problem solving and learned that there are times when we can rely on previous patterns for decision making and other times when the problem requires new and perhaps innovative solutions. In addition, we learned several models that may help us frame the problems, develop alternatives, and ultimately formulate solutions. We also looked at the question of who should be involved in organizational decisions. Finally, we discussed techniques that are available to the decision maker in examining alternatives. The following behavioral guidelines might help in implementing these various methods correctly.

1. *Define and verify the problem fully and accurately.* You must overcome the temptation as a group or an individual to try to define the problem too quickly. Problem definition is difficult. Problems are not always clear. For example, you might initially attribute turnover in the workplace to a lack of opportunity for promotion. Interviews with those who have left the organization, and with those who have remained, might suggest instead that turnover is due to the lack of resources available to complete the work required.

2. *Use the problem to generate solutions.* You might find that well-defined problems have implied solutions. For example, if the problem is dissatisfaction in the workplace and the problem includes inadequate facilities, then the alternative solutions will begin with how to improve the inadequate facilities.

3. *Prevent premature evaluations of solutions.* Continue brainstorming until all possible alternatives have been generated. When alternatives are evaluated, the idea generation for possible solutions typically ceases.

4. *Provide a climate that values disagreement.* As we will see in Chapter 11, healthy conflict is helpful in generating ideas. Make sure that you seek input from those who disagree with you as well as those who agree with you. Consider all alternatives equally.

5. *Provide a climate that values diversity.* Valued and well-managed diverse environments enhance creativity in decision making and divert Groupthink.

6. *When possible, gain consensus from all of those affected while avoiding premature consensus building.* Solutions will be much more likely to be accepted if all of those affected have been involved in the decision-making process. For example, you might find that the solution to the facilities problem requires moving to a new location. Employees will be more satisfied with the move if they have been kept informed of the options and have contributed to the decision.

▶ Key Terms

Authoritative decisions   251

Choice opportunities   249

Collaborative decision-making model   249

Consultative decisions   251

Cost-benefit analysis   257

Cost-effectiveness analysis   257

Decisions   237

Evidence-based management   259

Garbage can model   249

Group decisions   251

Groupthink   251

High-risk decisions   237

Incrementalism   248

Low-risk decisions   238

Nominal group technique   258

Nonprogrammed decisions   237

Organizational decision making   236

Organizational process model   247

Problem   238

Programmed decisions   237

Rational model   245

▶ Exercise 8.1 Package Delivery: Exercising Moral Imagination

You work for a delivery service and have been delivering packages to the same urban neighborhood for the last 5 years. One of the older adult homeowners where you deliver is not at home and she has asked you to leave packages on the front step to avoid having to make a trip to your central office. This is the first package that she has received while not at home. It is the policy of your local office not to leave packages unattended. Let's examine and answer questions you will need to consider in exercising moral imagination:

1. What is the values dilemma presented in this short case study? What values seem at issue as you define the problem?

2. Who are the stakeholders and how would they define the problem? What are the values of greatest importance to these stakeholders?

3. What is at stake for you? What are your values? Are there motives that may be persuading you in one direction instead of another?

4. What are the facts that need to be considered? What assumptions are you making?

5. Are there values in conflict now that you have a better understanding of the problem?

6. Are there assumptions that should be tested prior to making the decision?

7. How might you go about testing these assumptions?

Identify Options

1. Who is responsible for resolving this dilemma?

2. How would you define success in this situation? How would other stakeholders define success?

3. What are the options available to you? List the positive and negative for each of these options.

Make and Implement a Decision

1. What options best satisfy your core values while acknowledging and faithfully considering the values of other stakeholders?

2. How will you implement your chosen option and mitigate negative impact?

Source: Adapted from Newell, T. (2008). Value-Based Leadership for a Democratic society. In T. Newell, G. Reeher, & P. Ronayne (Eds.), *The Trusted Leader* (pp. 19–48). Washington, DC: CQ Press, p. 31.

▶ Exercise 8.2 A Decision-Making Framework

Using your business experience, a community service project, an internship, or other experience, use the following framework adapted from Philip[84] to analyze the process of decision making.

1. Clarify your objectives.

   o Describe the situation on which you are working. State your precise objective.

2. Consider the factors that will influence your choice of action.

   o List the factors that are important to you and to those affected by the decision.

   o Extend the factors into statements that specify the results expected, resources available, or constraints that might exist.

   o Classify the statements that will have to be regarded as essential.

   o Assess the importance of the remaining factors and list them in descending order of importance.

   o Generate the options that could be compared with your specifications. Do not forget to include the status quo and inaction as options.

   o Compare your options with your essential factors.

3. Collect information with regard to the benefit and risk factors for the remaining options and assess the degree of satisfaction that each option provides.

   o Identify the benefit–risk area for each option to be considered.

   o Describe your best-balanced choice.

Case 8.1 Using Focus Groups for New Coffee Shop on Main Street

Jannell Adami is the new manager of a recently opened coffee shop. She has many challenges ahead of her given that she is working in a community with a large number of coffee shop chains. Her owners have given her a series of priorities to implement during her first year, and she has promised to deliver exceptional quality and customer service at a fair price. Her first priority is to find a niche that is not being addressed by the other coffee shops, but she recognizes that she cannot address the unmet niche without getting to know the customers and the community better. Because she has limited funds, she would like to maximize her resources by determining the most critical and prevalent interests of coffee drinkers in this community. Before the end of the month, she will identify coffee drinkers to participate in a focus group. She would like to ask participants

what they are interested in receiving from a coffee shop that is not currently delivered by those available before making decisions on programs to implement. Through a variety of sources, she is able to identify 20 individuals who would serve as a starting point for the discussion. She likes the idea of using focus groups to generate ideas. She has asked you for advice.

1. What recommendations would you give her for collecting the information?

2. Is the focus group the ideal way to collect the information? Why or why not?

3. What would you expect the focus group to come up with?

4. How much of this would depend on the composition of the group?

Case 8.2 Using Decision Tree for Levels of Participation

Max Herbert heads a large transportation consulting firm charged with developing a new traffic flow design for the busiest intersection in the largest city in the state. Max earned an MBA and had several years' experience in the firm before moving to a management level. His staff consists primarily of traffic engineers and planners, most of whom are considerably older than Max and have far more experience in transportation than he does. Max recognizes their expertise, although he believes that his staff members have become a bit tradition bound, tending toward "safe" solutions to traffic problems. He recognizes that different staff members are likely to have different approaches to solving the problem they face, although he also believes that in the end they will arrive at an acceptable compromise and probably one that is "safe."

Delays and bottlenecks caused by the current traffic pattern have made the issue of a new design a fairly high-profile issue, so Max is concerned about his

group producing a high-quality product, one that will be technically sound as well as acceptable to his superiors. Although he is not a traffic engineer, Max has done his homework and learned a lot about transportation issues during his time in the firm. Following a recent conference in London, Max went on a study tour of several European cities, during which he developed some ideas that he considers forward-looking and certainly workable in this particular city. Although he is not prepared to do the technical details and drawings necessary to support his idea, he has a concept in mind that he thinks will work. At the same time, he is concerned that if he forces his idea on his staff, they will "rebel" and not do as good a job as they might otherwise do in completing the follow-up details and drawings.

1. Using the Vroom-Yetton diagram in Figure 8.5, discuss how Max should approach the question of developing the overall concept for the city's new traffic pattern.

Case 8.3 Relocating Regional Offices Overseas

Ann Hess is the vice president in charge of sales for a manufacturing company in the Northeast. She has noticed that other U.S. companies have been seeking

opportunities in China and South Africa, and most have opened offices in those countries. She is being encouraged by the company's president to seek those opportunities by closing down some of the U.S. regional offices. The overseas offices will be staffed by citizens of those countries and will be under her leadership. She has several decisions to make.

1. Which U.S. regional offices should she close?

2. Where in the two countries should she place the new offices?

3. How will she staff the offices?

4. Knowing what you know about decision making, how should she go about making the decisions?

5. What decision-making model would you advocate?

6. What data will she need?

7. What traps should she avoid?

▶ Case 8.4 Choosing Your College

Whether we are aware of it or not, we make decisions every day. You are sitting in this class because you chose to attend this particular college or university. A young person you know (sibling, neighbor, family member) has asked for your help in deciding what college or university to attend and begins by asking you how you went about deciding where to go. Think back to the day when you had to select the place that you would attend.

1. How did you go about your selection?

2. Did you have many choices or were there constraints that narrowed your selection?

3. Did you seek anyone's advice?

4. Did you rethink your decision?

5. How courageous was your decision?

6. What advice would you give the young college applicant?

$SAGE edge™

Sharpen your skills with SAGE edge at edge.sagepub.com/nahavandi

SAGE edge for students provides a personalized approach to help you accomplish your coursework goals in an easy-to-use learning environment.

▶ Endnotes

1. Nocera, J. (2011). Steve Jobs broke every leadership rule. Don't try it yourself. *Forbes*, August 27. Retrieved from http://www.forbes.com/sites/frederickallen/2011/08/27/steve-jobs-broke-every-leadership-rule-don't-try-that-yourself on July 11, 2013.

2. Jobs, S. (2005). *Stanford commencement address*. Retrieved from http://news.stanford.edu/news/2005/june15/jobs-061505.html on July 11, 2013.

3. Lashinsky, A. (2011). How Apple works: Inside the world's biggest startup. *CNN Money*, August 25. Retrieved from http://tech.fortune.cnn.com/2011/08/25/how-apple-works-inside-the-worlds-biggest-startup/ on July 11, 2013.

4. Lashinsky, 2011.

5. Lashinsky, 2011.

6. Hall, R. H. (1999). *Organizations: Structures, processes, and outcomes*. Upper Saddle River, NJ: Prentice Hall.

7. Nutt, P. C. (2005). Decision aiding search during decision making. *European Journal of Operational Research, 160,* 852–876.

8. Bryson, J. M., Broiley, P., & Jung, V. S. (1990). The influences of context and process on project planning success. *Journal of Planning Education and Research, 9*(3), 183–195; Eisenhardt, K., & Zbaracki, M. T. (1992). Strategic decision making. *Strategic Management Journal, 13,* 27–37; Mintzberg, H., Raisinghani, D., & Theoret, A. (1976). The structure of unstructured decisions. *Administrative Science Quarterly, 21*(2), 246–275; and Witte, E. (1972). Field research on complex decision making process—the phase theory. *International Studies of Management and Organization, 56,* 156–182.

9. Simon, H. A. (1977). *The new science of management decision* (2nd ed.). Englewood Cliffs, NJ: Prentice Hall.

10. Buchanan, L., & O'Connell, A. (2006). A brief history of decision making. *Harvard Business Review, 84*(1), 32–41.

11. Eisenhardt & Zbaracki, 1992; Harrison, M., & Phillips, B. (1991). Strategic decision making: An integrated explanation. *Research in the Sociology of Organizations, 9,* 319–358; and March, J. G. (1994). *A primer on decision making: How decisions happen.* New York, NY: Free Press.

12. Morehead, G., & Griffin, R. W. (1992). *Organizational behavior.* Boston, MA: Houghton Mifflin.

13. Buchanan & O'Connell, 2006, p. 31.

14. Rogers, P., & Blenko, M. (2006). Who has the D?: How clear decision roles enhance organizational performance. *Harvard Business Review, 84*(1), 52–61.

15. Nutt, P. C. (1997). Better decision-making: A field study. *Business Strategy Review, 8*(4), 45–52; Nutt, P. C. (1999). Surprising but true: Half of the decisions in organizations fail. *Academy of Management Executive, 13*(4), 75–90; Nutt, P. C. (2002). *Why decisions fail: The blunders and traps that lead to decision debacles.* San Francisco: Berrett-Koehler.

16. Snyder, S. (2013). What J.C. Penney's Ron Johnson must do now. *CNN Money,* March 5. Retrieved from http://management.fortune.cnn.com/2013/03/05/jc-penney-ron-johnson-2/?iid=SF_F_River on March 7, 2013).

17. Nutt, P. C. (2001). Decision debacles and how to avoid them. *Business Strategy Review, 12*(2), 1–14.

18. Bazerman, M. H., & Tenbrunsel, A. E. (2011). Ethical breakdowns: Good people often let bad things happen. Why? (Failure: understand it). *Harvard Business Review, 89*(4), 58–65.

19. Newell, T. (2008). Value-based leadership for a democratic society. In T. Newell, G. Reeher, & P. Ronayne (Eds.), *The trusted leader* (pp. 19–48). Washington, DC: CQ Press.

20. Adapted from Arnold, J. D. (1978). *Make up your mind.* New York, NY: AMACOM.

21. Schermerhorn, J. R., Hunt, J. G., & Osborn, R. N. (1994). *Managing organizational behavior* (5th ed.). New York, NY: Wiley.

22. Nutt, 2002.

23. Nutt, 2001.

24. Allison, G. T. (1971). *The essence of decision: Explaining the Cuban missile crisis.* Boston, MA: Little, Brown, p. 7.

25. Murray, M. (1986). *Decisions: A comparative critique.* Marshfield, MA: Pitman, p. 10.

26. Elbing, A. (1970). *Behavioral dimensions in organizations: A framework for decision making.* Glenview, IL: Scott, Foresman; Harrison, E. F. (1975). *The managerial decision-making process.* Boston, MA: Houghton Mifflin; and Pressman, J. (1973). *Implementation.* Berkeley: University of California Press.

27. Allison, 1971.

28. Simon, H. A. (1976). *Administrative behavior.* New York, NY: Free Press.

29. Allison, G. & Zelikow, P. (1999). *Essence of decision: Explaining the Cuban missile crisis* (2nd ed.). New York, NY: Longman.

30. Nutt, 2005.

31. Glaser, M. A., Aristigueta, M. P., & Payton, S. (2000). Harnessing the resources of community: The ultimate performance agenda. *Public Productivity and Management Review, 23*(4), 428–448.

32. Nutt, 2001.

33. Etzioni, A. (1988). Normative affective factors: Toward a new decision-making model. *Journal of Economic Psychology, 9*, 125–150.

34. Camic, C. (1985). The matter of habit. *American Journal of Sociology, 91*, 481–510.

35. Fenton-O'Creevy, M., Soane, E., Nicholson, N., & Willman, P. (2011). Thinking, feeling and deciding: The influence of emotions on the decision making and performance of traders. *Journal of Organizational Behavior, 32*(8), 1044–1061.

36. Janis, I. L., & Mann, L. (1977). *Decision making*. New York, NY: Free Press.

37. Allison & Zelikow, 1999.

38. Allison & Zelikow, 1999, p. 146.

39. Simon, 1976, p. xix.

40. Beach, L. R. (1990). *Image theory: Decision making in personal and organizational context*. Chichester, UK: Wiley.

41. As cited in Shafritz, J. M., & Russell, E. W. (2000). *Introducing public administration* (2nd ed.). New York, NY: Addison Wesley Longman, p. 52.

42. Fligstein, N. (1992). The social construction of efficiency. In M. Zey (Ed.), *Decision making: Alternatives to rational choice models*. Newbury Park, CA: Sage.

43. Goodrich, E., & Salancik, G. (1996). Organizational discretion in responding to institutional practices: Hospitals and cesarean births. *Administrative Science Quarterly, 41*, 1–28.

44. Murray, 1986.

45. Cooper, P. J. (1996). Understanding what the law says about administrative responsibility. In J. L. Perry (Ed.), *Handbook of public administration* (2nd ed.). San Francisco, CA: Jossey-Bass, p. 134.

46. Allison & Zelikow, 1999.

47. Snyder, 2013.

48. Cohen, M. D., March, J. G., & Olsen, J. P. (1972). A garbage can model of organizational choice. *Administrative Science Quarterly, 17*, 1–25.

49. Takahashi, N. (1997). A single garbage can model and the degree of anarchy in Japanese firms. *Human Relations, 50*, 91–109, p. 92.

50. Meredith, R. (2008). Sailing from old to new Asia. *Forbes.com*, August 8. Retrieved from http://www.forbes.com/global/2008/0915/088.html on April 11, 2013; and *Bloomberg*. Retrieved from http://www.bloomberg.com/quote/JM:SP on April 11, 2013.

51. Matheson-Connell, C. (2004). A business in risk: Jardine Matheson and the Hong Kong Trading Industry. Westport, CT: Praeger; and Studwell, J. (2007). *Asian godfathers: Money and power in Hong Kong and Southeast Asia*. New York, NY: Grove Press.

52. Jardine Mindset. (2013). *Jardine's*. Retrieved from http://www.jardines.com/community/mindset.html on April 11, 2013.

53. Chan, S. (2009, October). Managing diverse talents from the nucleus. *China Staff*, 2–5.

54. *Jardine executive training scheme*. (2013). Retrieved from http://jardines.com/careers/career-opportunities-for-graduates/jardine-executive-trainee-scheme.html on April 11, 2013.

55. Takahashi, 1997, p. 92.

56. Takahashi, 1997, p. 106.

57. Takahashi, 1997, p. 106.

58. March, J. G., & Simon, H. A. (1958). *Organizations*. New York, NY: Wiley; also Simon, 1976.

59. Starbuck, W. H. (1983). Organizations as action generators. *American Sociological Review, 48,* 91–102.

60. Anderson, P. A. (1983). Decision making by objectives and the Cuban missile crisis. *Administrative Science Quarterly, 28,* 201–222.

61. Mintzberg, Raisinghani, & Theoret, 1976.

62. Janis, I. L. (1982). *Groupthink.* Boston, MA: Houghton Mifflin.

63. Janis, I. L. (1971, November). Groupthink. *Psychology Today,* p. 174.

64. Vroom, V. H., & Yetton, P. W. (1973). *Leadership and decision making.* Pittsburgh, PA: University of Pittsburgh Press.

65. Wentling, R. M., & Palma-Rivas, N. (2000). Current status of diversity initiatives in selected multinational corporations. *Human Resources Development Quarterly, 11,* 35–60.

66. Mosher, F. C. (1968). *Democracy and the public service* (2nd ed.). New York, NY: Oxford University Press.

67. Dunphy, S. M. (2004). Demonstrating the value of diversity for improved decision making: The "wuzzle-puzzle" exercise. *Journal of Business Ethics, 53,* 325–331; Esser, J. K. (1998). Alive and well after 25 years: A review of groupthink research. *Organizational Behavior and Human Decision Processes, 73*(2/3), 116–141; Larkey, L. (1996). Toward a theory of communicative interactions in culturally diverse workgroups. *Academy of Management Review, 2*(2), 402–433; Milliken, F. J., & Martins, L. J. (1996). Searching for common threads: Understanding the multiple effects of diversity in organizational groups. *Academy of Management Review, 21*(2), 402–433; Morehead, G., Neck, C., & West, M. (1998). The tendency toward defective decision making within self-managing teams: The relevance of groupthink for the 21st century. *Organizational Behavior and Human Decision Processes, 73*(2/3), 327–351; and Watson, W., Johnson, L., & Merritt, D. (1998). Team orientation, self-orientation, and diversity in task groups. *Group and Organization Management, 23*(2), 161–188.

68. Vroom, V. (2000). Leadership and the decision-making process. *Organizational Dynamics, 28*(4), 82–94.

69. Gilbert, J. A., Stead, B. A., & Ivancevich, J. M. (1999). Diversity management: A new organizational paradigm. *Journal of Business Ethics, 21*(1), 61–76; and Pless, N. M., & Maak, T. (2004). Building an inclusive diversity culture: Principles, processes, and practice. *Journal of Business Ethics, 54*(2), 129–147.

70. Kujala, J., & Pietilainen, T. (2007). Developing moral principles and scenarios in the light of diversity: An extension to the multidimensional ethics scale. *Journal of Business Ethics, 70*(2), 141–150.

71. Combs, G. M., & Luthans, F. (2007). Diversity training: Analysis of the impact of self-efficacy. *Human Resource Development Quarterly, 18*(1), 91–120; Cox, T. H. (2000). *Creating the multicultural organization: A strategy for capturing the power of diversity.* San Francisco, CA: Jossey-Bass; Cox, T. H., & Beale, R. L. (1997). *Developing competency to manage diversity.* San Francisco, CA: Berrett-Koehler; Dass, P., & Parker, D. (1996). Diversity, a strategic issue. In E. E. Kossek & S. A. Lobel (Eds.), *Managing diversity: Human resource strategies for transforming the workplace.* Cambridge, MA: Blackwell Business.

72. White, H. L., & Rice, M. (2005). The multiple dimensions of diversity and culture. In M. F. Rice (Ed.), *Diversity and public administration: Theory issues and perspectives.* New York. NY: M. E. Sharpe.

73. Adler, N. J. (2002). *International dimensions of organizational behavior* (4th ed.). Cincinnati, OH: South Western Publishing.

74. Rogers & Blenko, 2006, p. 55.

75. Morgan, D. L. (1997). *The focus group guidebook.* Thousand Oaks, CA: Sage.

76. Morgan, D. L. (1998). *Planning focus groups.* Thousand Oaks, CA: Sage, p. 4.

77. Rawlinson, J. G. (1981). *Creative thinking and brainstorming*. New York, NY: Wiley.

78. Wycoff, J. (1995). *Transformation thinking*. New York, NY: Berkley Books.

79. Sylvia, R. D., Sylvia, K. M., & Gunn, E. M. (1997). *Program planning and evaluation for the public manager*. Prospect Heights, IL: Waveland.

80. Hatry, H. P., Blair, L., Fisk, D., & Kimmel, W. (1987). *Program analysis for state and local governments*. Washington, DC: Urban Institute Press.

81. Guzzo, R. A. (1982). *Improving group decision making in organizations*. New York, NY: Academic Press, pp. 95–126.

82. Rousseau, D. M. (2006). Is there such a thing as "evidence-based management"? *Academy of Management Review, 31*(2), 256–269.

83. Arnold, 1978.

84. Philip, T. (1985). *Improving your decision-making skills*. Maidenhead, UK: McGraw-Hill, pp. 84–91.

9 Communicating Effectively With Others

LEARNING OUTCOMES

After studying this chapter, you should be able to:

1. Analyze the dynamics of interpersonal communications in organizational settings

2. Discuss some of the limits on effective communications

3. Improve your skills in basic communications, both speaking and listening

4. Build your skills in special communications areas, such as effective listening and persuasive communications

5. Evaluate the impact of new technologies on patterns of communications both internally to the organization and externally

6. Plan new approaches to conducting effective meetings

7. Clarify your written communications, such as proposals and reports

A Failure to Communicate ▶

Mary Lou Cooper, head of the management services division in a large manufacturing firm, sees signs of fatigue in John Carter, one of her best employees. Being concerned about his health, she suggests that he take some time off. John, on edge because of an illness in his family, is already worried that he is not doing his job as well as he can and takes Mary's suggestion as an effort to get him out of the way. Concerned that he might lose his job, he does not follow Mary's advice and instead works even harder—at some risk to his health and well-being. Meanwhile, Steve Jackson and Phil Dexter, two very close friends, hear rumors of a new and very attractive management position for which they both would be eligible. In a lunchroom conversation, Steve happens to comment on a recent mistake Phil made in an important project. Phil hears of the comment from someone else, takes offense at Steve's "negative campaigning" for the new job, and isolates himself from Steve. The two friends soon become intense rivals or even enemies. Then they hear that John has been working especially hard recently. They assume that he also wants the new job, so they both begin to shape their conversations to disparage John. Suddenly the organization is in chaos. People are hurt, friendships are damaged, and the actual work of the organization is pushed to a back burner.

Obviously, clear and constructive communication is essential not only for people to accomplish their tasks but also for people to live happier and more satisfying lives. However, communicating effectively with others is not easy. What would seem to be a simple process of speaking, listening, and understanding actually is enormously complex. Moreover, there are a number of important barriers to effective communication in organizations, many of which we examine in this chapter. There also are some lessons we can learn about communication that will enable us to communicate more effectively with others.

To learn through listening, practice it naively and actively. Naively means that you listen openly, ready to learn something, as opposed to listening defensively, ready to rebut. Listening actively means you acknowledge what you heard and act accordingly.

—Betsy Sanders, Former Senior Vice President & General Manager, Nordstrom

What Is
Communication?

Defining Communication

Communication can be defined most simply as the transmission of information from one party to another. In its classic formulation, communication appears to be quite straightforward. One person sends a message that others receive. In practice, however, communication is much more complicated. For example, Anne Nordahl, the dean of the School of Business at a major Midwestern university, wants to encourage her faculty to contribute to the college's endowment fund, especially because this would provide a model for those outside who might be asked to give. The first problem that Anne faces is how to formulate the message. Anne knows what she wants and what she means to communicate, but she also knows that faculty might resent her request. For this reason, she wants to choose just the right words to express her meaning. She also must make a decision about what channel to use to communicate her message. In the best of all possible worlds, she would like to talk with each faculty member individually so that she could gauge each individual's response and shape her message to that reaction, but time limitations make that impossible. She is left with other alternatives, such as making an announcement in a meeting of the school faculty or sending an e-mail to everyone in the school. Whatever her choice, when the message is received it will be interpreted differently by different faculty members. Some might recognize the importance of having solid internal contributions from those in the organization prior to undertaking an external fund-raising campaign. Others might believe that the university's recent raises have been so small that for someone to ask faculty and staff for money is simply ludicrous. In response to Anne's message, some faculty members might send contributions. Others might send back sharply worded letters complaining about the dean's cruel and ruthless arm-twisting tactics.

As this example shows, what is critical in any communication is what the sender meant and what the receiver understood. When Anne began to think about her communication issue, she knew what she meant, but she also recognized the difficulty of putting that meaning into words. Obviously, the receivers of the message will interpret the message differently based on their own perceptions (of the situation, of the dean, and even of themselves). They will translate the message into terms meaningful to them. Communication, then, not only is concerned with transmitting information but also is concerned with establishing common meanings.

If we are to fully understand the communication process, we need to understand the enormous complexity of what is involved in communicating human meaning. A more complete understanding of the communication process recognizes that communication is not merely a mechanical exercise in transmitting information but also an effort to establish shared meaning. This raises a number of important issues for us to keep in mind as we explore the communication process.

Communication: the transmission of information from one party to another

1. Some messages are *unintentionally* ambiguous with respect to their meaning. The sender believes that the appropriate meaning has been expressed, and the receiver thinks that he or she understands what has been said, but both of them are wrong. The sender meant one thing, and the receiver heard another.

How would you respond to the following statements? Choose one of the alternative responses or just fill in the blanks. Then discuss your responses with classmates.

1. [From the head of your division] "I've heard some disturbing rumors about the way you treat our customers."

    a. "That's ridiculous."
    b. "You can't believe everything you hear."
    c. "Could you please be more specific?"
    d. _____

2. [From a coworker] "I'm terribly afraid that the mistake I made on the Harris contract means that the boss is going to transfer me to the end of the world."

    a. "That's stupid. He hates Harris."
    b. "You shouldn't be so worried. He'll get over it."
    c. "So you're worried that your position may be in jeopardy?"
    d. _____

3. [From your subordinates] "We really think that we deserve more money for doing this job."

    a. "That's silly. You're really not worth what we're paying you now."
    b. "You know that the company won't give us any more money."
    c. "Why don't we sit down and think through our salary structure together?"
    d. _____

4. [From a member of the executive board] "I want to see all the information we have on the new construction project, and I want it in my office in one hour."

    a. "That's none of your business."
    b. "That's impossible. I'll need at least three hours to get it together."
    c. "It will be very difficult for me to get it together that quickly. But could we set an appointment for later this afternoon?"
    d. _____

5. [From a citizen] "Can you tell me who to talk with about a junk car that I'd like to have removed from the vacant lot next door?"

    a. "That's not my department."
    b. "Ask the secretary over there."
    c. "That would be the public works department. Let me show you where they are located."
    d. _____

2. Other messages, especially in organizations, are *intentionally* ambiguous. Managers may be *strategically ambiguous* for several reasons.[1] They may face multiple and conflicting goals; they may be in fast changing situations; have difficult and complicated relationships; or be threatened. In cases like these, some degree of ambiguity might be necessary because of the particular circumstances of the communicator.

3. Meaningful communication, or communication that carries meaning, is not merely rational; it also is laden with emotions. We often ask about a person's intentions in his or her communication: "What did you mean by that?" Or we sometimes believe that it is important to explain our own intentions to others: "That's really not what I meant to say." Although our intentions are important, communication does not operate only at that rational level. We communicate emotions as well as words, and often do so through facial expressions and body language as much as through words. Often the emotional content that others perceive in our communications is not those that we intend.

4. Power shapes communication in organizations as elsewhere. That is, we tend to shape our conversations depending on the people with whom we are talking. We talk with our friends in a different way than we talk with our boss. In such situations, there are four things to consider.[2] First, what you would really like to say if you were completely free to do so. For example, you agree with your boss, instead of telling her she really does not understand the problem. Second, what you decide you should say. For example, you can very carefully suggest that there are flaws in the plan. Third, what you actually do say. For example, you might say that the idea has lots of potential. Finally, what the message means to the receiver. In the example we have been using, your boss might be offended and upset that you did not whole-heartedly support her idea.

The Communication Process

Communication
Defined

Encoding: the process by which a sender puts the message in a certain format

We are constantly communicating; we cannot help but communicate. We communicate verbally through words, and nonverbally through our body language, our expressions, and our tone of voice. By some estimates, we spend about 70% to 80% of our waking hours engaged in communication, with about 40% of that time spent sending messages and 60% of the time receiving them. Managers spend even a higher percentage of their time receiving messages.[3] If communication plays such an important role in organizations, then it is important to understand ways in which communication can be improved. Fortunately, there are some specific guidelines that can be used that will help considerably in the transmission not only of information, but also of meaning among those in business and other organizations.

What Would You Do?

▶ Your boss likes to delegate tasks to you (and others), but typically is not very specific regarding what she wants. You bring back the answer only to find that she had something much more precise in mind. It's like, "Bring me a rock." You bring her a rock only to hear, "That's not the right rock. I was looking for purple and blue pebbles." What would you do? What's the communication problem here?

The basic communication process[4] is presented in Figure 9.1. First, the sender, or the one who initiates the communication, sends some type of message. That message is transmitted through various means—speech, body language, e-mail, all of which are the methods of communication. The message goes to the receiver, who then may or may not provide feedback. Communication is successful when the receiver understands what the sender intended. In many cases, the receiver does not fully understand the message, partly because of interference or noise that has the potential to change or garble the message throughout the whole process.

However, the process of establishing common meaning raises several other issues. First, as we already have seen, the sender has to encode the intended meaning into a certain format, and the receiver has to **decode** the meaning by translating the sender's message. Communication involves creating meaning, transmitting meaning, and deciphering meaning. But the different parties involved in the process do so in terms of their own particular **frames of reference**. As we saw in our chapter on perception, we view the world through different lenses shaped by our accumulated attitudes, beliefs, and interpretations. Using different lenses, we see (or hear) different things.

This topic has recently been popularized in discussions of women seeking executive-level positions in businesses and other organizations. Sheryl Sandberg, COO of Facebook, in a popular TED Talk, and later in her book, *Lean In*,[5] argues that women who aspire to the highest level jobs often undermine themselves by being less assertive and less confident than men. Some of the problem is related to body language. For example, Sandberg encourages women to "sit at the table," not off to the side. While they are at the table, both men and women are likely to be more successful if they sit up straight, project interest in the discussion, speak with confidence and a firm voice, and avoid rambling.

Facebook Chief Operating Officer Sheryl Sandberg's book *Lean In* raised a number of important questions about women seeking executive positions, including issues such as pay, work-family balance, and how to get promoted. But the book also explored how women (and men) can be more effective communicators, especially through careful attention to body language. Thus, the title of the book is also one piece of advice to those in meetings—show your interest and engagement by "leaning in."

FIGURE 9.1 THE COMMUNICATION PROCESS

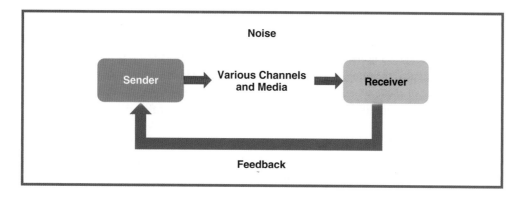

Seven Communication Mistakes

Improving Interpersonal Communication

As we know too well, even though we spend so much time "practicing" communication, there often are breakdowns that threaten the work of the organization and even endanger people's lives. In this section, we examine the various ways in which communication fails and some specific methods we can implement to improve our capacity for effective and responsible communication, both in speaking and in listening. Table 9.1 presents some examples of communication breakdowns. Each line indicates a sample conversation. In all

Decoding: the process by which the receiver interprets and translates the meaning of the sender's message

Frames of reference: the personal context we each bring to communications with others

these examples, what the sender communicates is not what he really intends; the receiver gets yet another meaning that neither matches what the sender said nor what he intended. So why are such miscommunications so common?

TABLE 9.1 EXAMPLES OF COMMUNICATION BREAKDOWNS

What the Manager Said	What the Manager Meant	What the Employee Heard
There is a position open in the finance department that might give you valuable experience in understanding our financial situation.	This would be a good opportunity for someone from our office to learn about the insides of the company's finances and then come back and really help us out.	I'm being pushed out!
You've met the standards for satisfactory work performance this year.	You are barely getting by, and you really need to improve your work.	Wow! I'm doing great.
I'd like you to get the new personnel classification report ready as soon as possible.	I need the report for a meeting in 10 days.	I'd better drop everything and get that report to him today.
You sure have been putting in a lot of hours lately.	I'm worried about your health; you might be getting overloaded.	Sounds like a hint. I'd better get to work.
The CEO is considering eliminating our division.	I think we can counter this move if we build an effective case for our division to be continued.	I'd better polish my résumé.

Barriers to Effective Communication

In the simple model of communication in Figure 9.1, there are several obvious places where communication might break down and distortion might occur. **Distortion** refers to the difference between the meaning that the sender intends and the meaning that the receiver decodes (see Figure 9.2 for barriers to communication). First, the sender must express the intended meaning in symbols, usually words. There are many words available, but only a few of these words can be used in any statement, meaning that almost any communication is incomplete. For example, think of a 10-second segment of a television show that you recently watched. Chances are good that you could describe that segment in 25 words or less. But a skilled novelist, intent on conveying the incident as completely as possible, might write several pages. In many conversations, listeners might think that they heard what was intended, but they actually "hear" only an abbreviated version of the meaning that was intended. (You know, of course, the classic difference between "listening" and actually "hearing.")

There is also the question of **semantics**, which is the study of meaning. The sender must encode the message in words. But most words mean many different things. Indeed, according to a study of word meanings, the *Oxford English Dictionary* gives an average of 28 different definitions for each of the 500 most used words in the English language.[6] In addition, all organizations seem to depend heavily on **jargon**, a specialized "shorthand" language often composed of terminology and acronyms known to insiders but often mystifying to others. Relying excessively on jargon may serve to further obscure one's communication. In any case, a poor choice of symbols or words can distort the intended message.

Distortion: the difference between the meaning that the sender intends and the meaning that the receiver decodes

Semantics: the study of the meaning conveyed by words or symbols

Jargon: shorthand language or terminology known to insiders but mystifying to others

One's intended meaning also can be subject to **filtering**. Filtering involves manipulating the information that is being sent so that it will be received more favorably by the receiver. Filtering is especially prevalent where one party to the conversation has more power than the other, as in cases where lower-level employees send information to upper-level employees. Many executives have complained that they often receive the answers that people think they want rather than the answers that are most honest and, typically, most helpful.

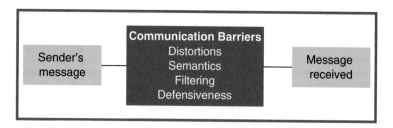

FIGURE 9.2 BARRIERS TO EFFECTIVE COMMUNICATION

Communication Barriers
Distortions
Semantics
Filtering
Defensiveness

Sender's message

Message received

Second, the sender must choose the correct channel or medium to send the message. Although oral communication allows the possibility for feedback and interaction, a message transmitted orally also might be misinterpreted as words pass by quickly and soon are forgotten as people move on to other things. Oral communication also is particularly susceptible to "noise"—either *actual noise* or *social noise*. The possible interference from actual noise is obvious. If you are trying to talk with someone while others are talking nearby or while a fire engine is passing by outside, then both you and the other person might be distracted and the message might not be heard clearly. Social noise refers to the way in which individuals involved in more complex communications may alter their messages as they transmit them to others.

Administrative Jargon as a Barrier

Written communication, on the other hand, has the advantage of permanence. But the formal character of written communication might be considered inappropriate for many types of messages. One way of deciding whether to use written communication is to think about the purpose of the communication. A formal memo might be necessary if the purpose is to establish procedures or regulations. But if the purpose is merely to inform people of new developments, then conversations, staff meetings, or even e-mail might provide a better mode of communicating. Of course, as we note later in this chapter, electronic communication is rapidly changing the way in which we communicate in organizations. One of the biggest challenges for managers is to know when to use e-mail and other electronic forms of communication and when to rely on more traditional channels of communication.

Third, as the receiver decodes the message, there is an additional possibility for breakdown. As we noted earlier, the receiver will understand, or at least seek to understand, the message through the lens of his or her biases and perceptions. Different people perceive the world in different ways, and the differences in their perceptions make an important difference in the ways in which they interpret messages that they receive. This phenomenon often occurs in problem-solving situations, where the accountant will see the problem as an accounting problem, the economist will see it as an economic problem, and so on. Those who receive messages also might project their expectations of others into what they hear. If an interviewer expects a female applicant to put family before work, then that interviewer might hear such a preference even if the interviewee tries very hard to communicate the opposite. The various perceptual biases that we reviewed in Chapter 3 all can impact and distort communication.

Filtering: manipulating the information that is being sent so that it will be received more favorably by the receiver

Defensiveness: defensive behavior occurs when people feel or anticipate some sort of threat and rush to defend themselves

Another factor that affects communication, is **defensiveness**. Defensive behavior occurs when a person feels or anticipates some sort of threat.[7] The content of the message can cause defensiveness, or the message can touch a particularly sensitive nerve in the receiver and trigger a reaction. For example, messages that appear to judge other people, those that are used to control others, those that appear to be based on hidden agendas, those that convey an attitude of superiority or disdain, and those that seem lacking in concern for others might provoke defensiveness on the part of recipients. If Mary starts a conversation by saying, "I know this isn't all your fault . . . ," Jack may immediately anticipate criticism and prepare to defend his actions.

In sum, even if we all speak the same language, we often do not really speak the same language. Our use of certain words varies as is the case between Americans and the British, we filter what we say based on what we think others want to hear, we use the wrong channels of communication, and we misinterpret the intent of others. Although we tend to assume that all of our communications are clear and effective, that assumption is not always correct. But there are ways in which we can improve the process of communication so that, as individuals and as members of business and other organizations, we can be more effective and more responsible in our communication.

Oral Communication

Despite the recent dramatic increase in electronic communication, much of the manager's communication time is spent in face-to-face oral communication, either one-on-one, in relatively small groups, or in presentations to larger audiences. There are several helpful guidelines to keep in mind when you speak with others. Conversational speaking is particularly useful in situations where immediate feedback is important or where those engaged in the conversation need to brainstorm or build on the ideas of others. However, where the content of the communication is very lengthy, technical, or complex, using written communication or at least following up a conversation by putting matters in writing may be helpful.

In thinking about oral communication, remember that when you speak, you transmit both rational and emotional messages (see Figure 9.3). For example, regardless of the substance of your message, your tone of voice will send an emotional message to the receiver. If you speak loudly or with the slightest hint of sarcasm, then your message might seem to be angry, regardless of how neutral the actual words you use might be. Similarly, a highly formal or stilted tone will convey a far different emotional message from one delivered in a friendly and good-natured way. The trick is to pick the right tone of voice to communicate what you wish to communicate in a particular situation.

Making sure that your content, tone, and approach fit the situation is aided by being fully attentive to yourself and to others. Often, and especially when we are very busy, we speak carelessly, with little concern for the context of the communication. But to the extent that we can become sensitive to the thoughts and feelings of others, as well as to our own thoughts and feelings, we will communicate more effectively. Sensitivity to others involves understanding "where they are coming from"; it requires empathy, or the capacity to put yourself in the place of others.

FIGURE 9.3 ORAL COMMUNICATION

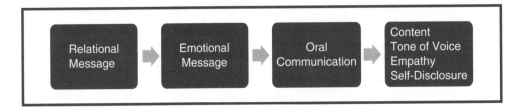

Avon, the cosmetics company, has been on the cutting edge of many issues during its 200-year history. It was global before business became global; it hired women before any one else did; it served diverse populations before others did; and it has always focused on its customers. And it finally appointed a female CEO in 2001. Andrea Jung was appointed CEO and chairman in 2001.[8] Jung has reinvented the old door-to-door sales company to become a high-tech responsive organization by focusing on research and development and jazzy marketing that often involves celebrities such as Salma Hayek. Aside from improving the company's financial performance, Jung has also made Avon a responsible corporate citizen, raising millions of dollars for causes such as the children affected by September 11, 2001, "Race for the Cure," and most recently the campaign against breast cancer with Reese Witherspoon as its global ambassador.[9]

Jung was able to achieve impressive results through dogged determination and unwavering confidence in her strategy, which involved the slow introduction of the Internet and other retail sales and a gradual blending of new retail methods with the traditional direct sales. The company has become one of the world's biggest online retailers.[10] Jung is described as "the rock star of Avon," while also being friendly and dedicated to the company.[11]

Born into a highly educated Chinese immigrant family—her father is an architect and her mother was Canada's first female chemical engineer—Jung always was expected to succeed. She received a Princeton education, graduated magna cum laude, and speaks fluent Mandarin and Cantonese as well as some French. Her parents did not initially approve of her choice of a lowly retail career at Bloomingdale's and Neiman Marcus, although they are now satisfied with their daughter's success.[12] Jung believes that she had to learn to shed her cultural Asian submissiveness and become tougher for the corporate world by adopting a tactful aggression that was more compatible with her cultural roots.[13] One of her strengths is building consensus among her team and making sure everyone's voice is heard. She makes an extra effort to listen to her team members' suggestions and ideas and believes that communication is one of the most important things she does.[14] When her global marketing team was having difficulty finding an appealing name for a new facial cream, she engaged everyone in the discussion. Joking about integrating everyone's ideas, she states, "It was like naming a child after your mother, your husband's mother, your grandmother, and your great aunt."[15]

Her constant smile and upbeat approach and attitude set the tone for her company and sent a message of confidence and success. Discussing leadership, Jung says, "I think there is a big and significant difference between being a leader and being a manager—leaders lead from the heart. Flexibility is one of the key ingredients to being successful. If you feel like it's difficult to change, you will probably have a harder time succeeding."[16]

Andrea Jung became Avon's chief executive officer in 2001 and began a reinvention of the company, emphasizing more responsive technologies, more contemporary advertising, and a new commitment to social responsibility. Jung is pictured here with U.S. secretary of state Hillary Rodham Clinton, Avon's global ambassador Reese Witherspoon, and First Lady Michelle Obama at the 2010 International Women of Courage Awards.

1. How do various levels of culture impact Jung's behavior and management style?

2. How important is communication to Avon's success?

One way to contribute to an organizational culture where people are more willing to reveal their deeper feelings and emotions is through **self-disclosure**. Disclosing to others what you think and how you feel about deep-seated personal matters—those things you like and those you hate, those things that appeal to you and those that scare you, and so on—may help to establish a situation in which others are willing to do the same, thereby making communication easier for all. But there are dangers in self-disclosure. If you try to engage in self-disclosure in a hostile work environment, then your efforts might be seen as inappropriate or even manipulative, causing others to react defensively. Self-disclosure is far easier in a trusting work environment where it may act to extend trust even further.

Active Listening

Listening is the single most important communication skill, consuming more time than any other aspect of communication. Indeed, as we saw earlier, managers spend as much as 30% to 40% of their time listening. Moreover, listening clearly affects the success of managers. Not only are managers who listen well able to pick up more and better information; they are also likely to encourage and motivate employees, most of whom appreciate managers "who really listen." Yet despite the obvious benefits of listening more carefully, listening has been called the neglected skill of management because it is the least practiced and least understood. Most people are passive listeners who simply listen without fully engaging with and understanding the message. Lee Iacocca, former CEO of Chrysler Corporation, commented, "Business people need to listen at least as much as they need to talk. Too many people fail to realize that real communication goes in both directions."

Active listening involves the listener consciously engaging in a series of actions intended to clarify and confirm the meaning of the message he or she is receiving.[17] The active listener shows empathy and understanding for the other person and confirms his or her

FIGURE 9.4 ELEMENTS OF ACTIVE LISTENING

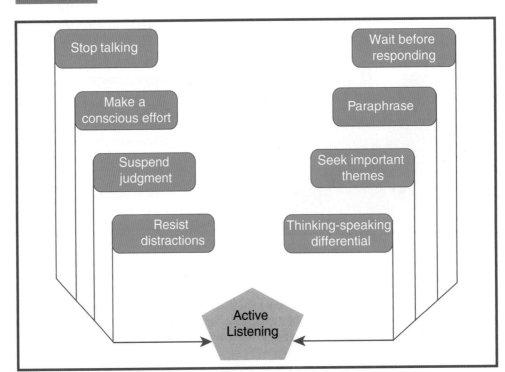

Self-disclosure: disclosing to others what you think and how you feel about deep-seated personal matters

Active listening: listening that involves the listener consciously engaging in a series of actions intended to clarify and confirm the meaning of the message he or she is receiving

own comprehension of the message by restating what has been said, summarizing major points, and listening not only to the words being said but also to the emotional tone and the accompanying nonverbal cues being transmitted.[18] Active listening can be a central element in an effort to improve your listening skills, an effort that might include the basics summarized in Figure 9.4.

The first and most basic element of active listening is to actually listen, which means you have to stop talking. Additionally, other factors include:

- *Make a conscious effort and have a reason or purpose for listening.* To listen most effectively, you must be motivated to listen; it does not just happen. Think carefully about why it is important that you listen effectively in a classroom situation, for example. Is it because the information will be on the next test? Is it because the material will help you on the job? At first, the reason or purpose might not be at all clear. If you cannot immediately think of a reason to listen, then search for one. Ask yourself, "How can this information help me be more effective?" or "How can I use this information in some way, either on the job or elsewhere?"

- *Suspend judgment initially.* In order to improve communication, we should try to listen with empathetic understanding—that is, understanding *with* a person rather than *about* the person.[19] This means seeing the matter from the other person's point of view. Of course, at some point, you might need to evaluate the material that you listen to, but you should first understand the complete message.

- *Resist distractions.* As we noted earlier, there are many things that can distract us as we try to communicate with others, but those distractions can be resisted. Some distractions are a part of the environment, for example, a noise outside the window. But the distraction might be closer to home, as in the case of trying to listen to someone who has mustard on his coat. Similarly, there might be something unusual about the way in which the speaker talks; the speaker might have a particularly raspy voice or speak with an unfamiliar accent. Regardless of the source of the distraction, the answer is to try to increase your concentration. By increasing your concentration, you can resist distractions that you would have thought were impossible to overcome.

- *Wait before responding.* There is a strong tendency to respond to someone's statement before she is finished, especially if you believe that you already have received the gist of the person's message. This can occur in a couple of ways. First, even while the person is still talking, you begin to formulate your response. Second, you may simply interrupt the other person and state your opinion. When you are overly eager to contribute to a conversation, you become so excited about your own anticipated contribution that you tune out the other person. The "response" principle suggests that, in either case, you relax and wait for the natural opportunity to speak instead of jumping into the conversation immediately.

- *Paraphrase what you hear.* **Paraphrasing** means restating what you hear in your own words. This is an essential process that shows the other person that you are not only listening, but that you also understand what the other person said before making your own contribution. You might say, "What I understand you to be saying is that the budget projections are incorrect because the initial information was compromised." By restating the other person's comments without evaluation, you almost have to enter into the person's frame of reference and to understand the context of her comments. Moreover, if your understanding of these comments is inconsistent with the person's

Sound From Silence

Paraphrasing: restating what you hear in your own words

intended meaning, then she will have a chance to try to clarify that meaning. Finally, taking time to clarify the meaning of communication in this way tends to reduce the emotional level of the conversation and allows more reasoned communication. Obviously, to restate or paraphrase every statement in a conversation produces a very stilted and awkward conversation, although it is an extremely good exercise. But if used judiciously and accompanied by comments that let the other person know exactly what you are doing (e.g., "Just so I'm sure I understand your position, let me try to state my understanding"), this aspect of active listening can be extremely helpful.

- *Seek the important themes.* Listening for the main ideas in a message is more important than listening for specific facts. Understanding the major themes of the message gives you a framework for organizing the facts, thereby making the facts themselves easier to remember. For example, research has shown that students who listen for the main ideas in a lecture are more likely to receive better grades than those who merely listen for the facts. Generally, it is much easier to fit specifics into the "big picture" than to construct the big picture based only on a few facts.

Thinking-speaking differential: the lag of time between our thinking and our speech

- *Use the* **thinking-speaking differential.** This differential refers to the lag of time between our thinking and our speech. People think much faster than they speak. Although the rates vary by region, people in the United States speak at a rate of about 150 words per minute. But they think at a rate of about 500 words a minute, more than three times as fast as they speak. This differential can offer a temptation to do things that interfere with effective listening, such as daydreaming, thinking about something completely apart from the conversation, and practicing your response in advance. But it also can provide an opportunity to listen more effectively. Most important, it provides the opportunity to reflect on what the other person is saying and to try to find the major themes or meanings in his or her comments.

In spite of the importance of listening in effective interpersonal communication, we know that managers differ widely in their listening abilities.[20] Generally, women are perceived as better listeners than men, younger managers are considered better listeners than older managers, and managers who are new to their current positions are perceived to be better listeners than managers who have been in their positions for longer periods of time. Most important for our purposes, managers who have had training in listening skills and managers who try harder to listen well seem to be perceived as better listeners. This means that there is a good chance that you can improve your listening skills by learning new techniques of listening and by consciously practicing these skills from day to day.

Supportive Communication

Effective communication in organizations, as elsewhere, aims at transmitting information accurately, honestly, and in such a way that the receiver will understand, accept, and use

Listening is considered one of the most important skills of today's leaders and managers. It is also a skill that can be improved upon by careful attention to what is being said, by rephrasing what you are hearing, and by being attentive to the emotional tone as well as the words that are being spoken.

that information. But effective communication also must help to develop and maintain interpersonal relationships, specifically by enabling people to express and accept differences in how they feel. **Supportive communication** refers to an approach to communicating with others that recognizes both of these purposes of communication: to convey needed information *and* to enhance interpersonal relationships in the group or organization. Engaging in supportive communication probably will engender a happier and more pleasant work environment, and it also probably will lead to greater productivity. Supportive communication has the characteristics shown in Figure 9.5.

Communicate
Better at Work

FIGURE 9.5 SUPPORTIVE COMMUNICATION

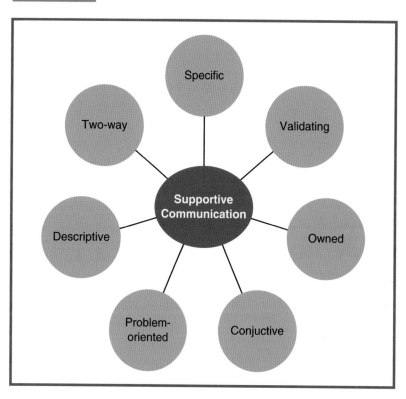

1. *Supportive communication is problem oriented, not person oriented.* It focuses on problems and their solutions rather than on the individual. For example, a manager practicing supportive communication would say, "Let's work together to improve our work" rather than "Your laziness is really the problem." The reason for this approach is that people rarely change their personalities, but they can change their behavior. Focusing on the problem rather than on the person opens opportunities for positive and constructive change.

2. *Supportive communication encourages being descriptive, not evaluative.* Similarly, providing information that is descriptive rather than evaluative avoids making a judgment or placing a "label" on the other person and is, therefore, less likely to be met with a defensive reaction. For example, a manager practicing supportive communication might say, "You have been late to work three days this week" rather than "You really messed up this time." To engage in descriptive communication does not mean that you ignore the issue at hand; rather, it means that you approach it in a more positive, action-oriented way.

Understand
Supportive
Communication

3. *Supportive communication is specific, not general.* The more specific a statement is, the more helpful it will be. For example, a manager practicing supportive communication might say, "There were three factual errors and five grammatical mistakes in your report" rather than "You are really sloppy." General statements often are extreme and might make the person feel incompetent or insignificant. Under these conditions, there is little reason to expect anything to change. Similarly, it is important to avoid *either/or* statements (e.g., "Either improve your writing or you'll be assigned less important work"). Both extreme statements and either/or statements reduce the range of possible actions that might be taken to correct the problem and, therefore, reduce the likelihood that anything positive will be done.

Supportive
communication:
an approach to
communicating that
recognizes both the
need to transmit
information and to
enhance interpersonal
relationships

4. *Supportive communication is conjunctive, not disjunctive.* Conjunctive statements clearly relate to what was said previously and move the conversation forward. Disjunctive statements are not connected and often create a roadblock interfering with effective communication. They tend to be final. For example, a manager practicing supportive communication might say, "Let me try to build on what you just said" rather than "That's not important. Let's move on." Effective communicators recognize that it is important for people to take turns speaking and do not dominate conversations; they want to listen to others, not just to themselves. And they recognize that all parties must agree to move to a new topic (at least implicitly) or else someone might get lost. The shift should not occur too abruptly or appear to be an exercise of control.

5. *Supportive communication is validating, not demeaning.* Supportive communication helps people to feel recognized, understood, accepted, and valued, whereas negative or demeaning comments make people feel inadequate, incompetent, and insecure. A demeaning message or a message expressed in a demeaning tone, even if unintended, can cause serious damage to effective interpersonal relationships. A supportive communicator might say something like, "I understand your position even if mine is slightly different" rather than "You simply aren't making any sense." There are various types of communications that people consider demeaning. One is taking a superior attitude or giving others the impression that you think you know everything and that they know very little. This may occur through put-downs (where the communicator tries to make himself or herself look good by making others look bad) or through one-upmanship (where the communicator tries to elevate herself in the eyes of others). Validating communication, on the other hand, acknowledges the importance of others, including their feelings and values, and is characterized by respect and flexibility.

6. *Supportive communication is owned, not disowned.* Supportive communication also is owned in the sense that the speaker takes responsibility for what is being said. Someone communicating supportively might say, "I have decided to deny your application" rather than "They have decided to deny your application." Communication that is not owned puts the person receiving the message at a psychological distance from the speaker and inhibits building a strong interpersonal relationship. Communication that is attributed to another person or that is ambiguous with respect to the source of the information also makes it difficult for the receiver to pursue the issue further, and that can be very frustrating.

7. *Supportive communication is two-way, not one-way.* Supportive communication also involves listening carefully and receiving feedback from the other person. A manager practicing supportive communication might say, "That's my understanding of the issue. What's yours?" rather than "Here's my position." Effective listening is essential to receiving accurate feedback, which in turn is essential to supportive communication.

What Do You Think?

▶ Some people say that most of what managers say is inherently manipulative, seeking to get people to do things they would not otherwise do. What do you think?

Dialogue

A great deal of attention has been given to the idea of dialogue as a special case of group and intergroup communications. Dialogic processes have been tried in a variety of settings, from schools to businesses to public and nonprofit organizations. To get a clearer understanding of what makes dialogue special, we can contrast dialogue with debate and discussion.[21] In debate, people counter arguments with other arguments in order to win points. Each claims his or her view of the world is right and the other's is wrong. In dialogue, participants work toward a mutual understanding. They listen carefully and try to explore the special meanings that others bring to the table. Discussion also tends to emphasize differences rather than commonalities, while dialogue reverses these tendencies. Trust can occur only where participants feel equal and not coerced, where they listen empathetically, and where they probe assumptions.

We can also distinguish solving problems by competitive strategies, authoritative strategies, or collaborative strategies.[22] The most complex problems we face today are characterized by the fact that we not only can't agree on a solution. We can't even agree on what the problem is. Subsequently, we can compete, we can submit to authority, or we can collaborate. The process of dialogue is intended to achieve collaboration. Through a series of carefully guided (facilitated) phases, participants in the dialogue are encouraged to listen and really hear, to try to understand differences rather than magnify them, and to build relationships of trust and respect. Dialogue, then, is "the co-creation of new meaning through mutual understanding and reciprocal communications between two or more parties."[23]

In this photo, President Barack Obama and Governor Mitt Romney are engaged in one of their three presidential debates in the Fall of 2012. Many felt that President Obama was lackluster at best in the first debate, but his ability to rebound in the second and third debates was one important factor in his reelection.

Dialogue Theories

While there are many ways in which dialogues can be structured, ranging from small to very large groups, from situations that are strictly conversational to those mediated by technology, there are some typical patterns to dialogues:

1. Dialogue is a process, not an event.

2. Dialogue is about relationship building and thoughtful engagement about difficult issues.

3. Dialogue requires an extensive commitment.

4. Dialogue takes place face to face.

5. Dialogue takes place best in an atmosphere of confidentiality, and issues of sponsorship and context are important to its success.

6. Dialogues often focus on race, but they also address multiple issues of social identity that extend beyond race.

7. Dialogue focuses on both intergroup conflict and community building.

8. Dialogue is led by a skilled facilitator.

9. Dialogue is about inquiry and understanding and the integration of content and process.

Cut Off E-mail

10. Dialogue involves talking, but taking action often leads to good talking, and dialogue often leads to action.[24]

THREE LESSONS IN CONTEMPORARY COMMUNICATIONS

There is no doubt that both business and personal communications are moving more rapidly and over greater distances than ever before. We are daily bombarded with faxes and e-mails that come to control our days. News from around the world flows instantaneously into our iPads and television sets. One result is that many of our communications take place under greater pressure and time-sensitivity than ever before. That opens the door for greater distortions in communications, something that several recent commentators have explored.

The Power of the Pause

Maria Shriver delivered a commencement address on Friday, May 11, 2012, at the University of Southern California's Annenberg School Commencement Ceremony. In that speech, she acknowledged the benefits of modern communications but also spoke of the potential dangers. Her solution was to slow down the pace of communications just enough to be clear about what is being said.

> But today, I have one wish for you. Before you go out and press that fast forward button, I'm hoping—I'm praying—that you'll have the courage to first press the pause button. That's right: the *pause* button. I hope if you learn anything from me today, you learn and remember—The Power of the Pause. I'm asking you to learn how to pause, because I believe the state of our communication is out of control. And you? I believe you have the incredible opportunity to fix it.[25]

Anthony K. Tjan makes a related case for "slow" conversations, those that put aside the quantity of communications (made possible by modern communications technology) to place more emphasis on the quality of communications (optimized in face-to-face interactions). As examples, he notes that building relationships and mediating interpersonal conflicts are simply better done in person, in real-time, than through electronic media.[26]

The Power of Storytelling

In an effort to bring greater clarity to organizational communications, a number of recent writers have extolled the virtue of storytelling as a way of connecting with others. In business, a good story can help solidify an idea, a brand, or a product. Peter Guber, movie producer and sports entertainment guru, argues in his book *Tell to Win*[27] that people are not moved by appeals just to the "head," for example, massive data dumps or detailed PowerPoint presentations; rather, they are moved by appeals to the "heart," the emotions. And one avenue for making that appeal is through conversations that begin with "once upon a time."

Rita Paskowitz elaborates by pointing out that storytelling allows the listener to have a better opportunity to internalize a concept and remember it. It is also a more entertaining way to deliver a message. One powerful element in mastering storytelling lies in the ability to present a specific message in a broad enough way to allow listeners to claim ownership of the meaning on their own.[28]

In her message to graduates of the Annenberg School for Communication and Journalism at the University of Southern California, Maria Shriver argued that, in this world of instant and widespread communications through a variety of new media, sometimes it's important to pause for a moment to consider the social and ethical impact of the message you are sending.

Electronic Communication

Obviously, forms of electronic communication have dramatically affected communication in business (as elsewhere). E-mail, texting, voice mail, fax, videoconferencing, group decisions support systems, and local and wide-area networks, have revolutionized organizational communication. These forms of communication have certain advantages over other forms. They typically are much faster, they allow communication among geographically dispersed people, and they permit information to be broadcast to many people at once. They have much greater capacities for memory, storage, and retrieval. They also permit asynchronous communication—that is, communication that occurs at different points in time.

Electronic
Paper Trail

There are, however, a number of questions about how these technologies affect human communication in organizations. We examine several potential problem areas:

1. *A decrease in opportunities for face-to-face contact and nonverbal cues* that reduce the opportunity for spontaneous information sharing.

2. *More exchange of informal messages that bypass the organizational hierarchy.* The informal exchange often redefines organizational structure and formal information flow.

3. *Messages of affect and value decrease.* Ambiguity in interpreting information increases and managers seek new ways of communicating the affective component of messages.

4. *Electronic communication reduces trust* that usually develops with shared experience, values, give-and-take, and the result of human communication.

5. *Technology imposes a discipline of linear thinking* that requires organizations to find ways to encourage and protect nonlinear thinking and communicating.

6. *Technology can dehumanize the workplace* and create unrealistic work expectations.

Certainly, electronic forms of communication create the possibility of flattening organizations. In the past, a line employee wishing to make a proposal to a high-level manager would have to go through several levels of the organization (and numerous secretaries and administrative assistants) just to get an appointment. Today, that same employee can simply send an e-mail to the manager and attach the proposal. Not only does this process avoid the delays and confusion of messages that move up the hierarchy, but it also establishes a record of accountability.

Texting at Work

One other question that continues to arise about electronic communication is where such communication fits into the array of channels available to managers to communicate with

▶ E-mail and the use of social media have become prevalent forms of business communication. But some say that only face-to-face communication allows you to capture the nuances of a conversation. Others argue that, in today's organizations, you have to move at the speed of light and that only the new forms of communication allow that speed. What do you think?

Internet Makes
Us Overshare

their employees. That is, which channel of communication is best for reminding employees of a meeting as opposed to, say, settling a dispute between members of a group? Some have described communications that are personal, natural, and allow instant feedback as rich media, whereas those that have few of these characteristics are called lean media. On a continuum of media richness, face-to-face communication would be considered most rich, and impersonal media (e.g., flyers, computer-generated reports) would be considered most lean. Between these endpoints, from rich to lean, would be telephone, e-mail, and text messages. Generally, managers facing a highly ambiguous issue would choose the richest possible medium and vice versa.

Others have pointed out that messages contain both data and symbols, and managers must consider both aspects in selecting communication channels. For example, the manager who needs to remind employees of a meeting faces a relatively unambiguous task and might choose e-mail for the reminder. However, the manager might believe that daily interpersonal contact is important because of the strong symbolic value of face-to-face communication.[29] Generally, you should not simply choose electronic media because they carry information quickly and easily; you need to keep in mind the symbolic importance of other, more traditional forms of communication as well.

Specialized Forms of Communication

There are several specialized forms of communication that you should also master. In this section we will review several of these: persuasive communication, personal counseling, conducting effective meetings, and writing memos, reports, and proposals.

Persuasive Communication

The key to effective persuasion is the *credibility* of the source. A sender with strong credibility is more effective in changing the beliefs and attitudes of others than a sender with low credibility.[30] Credibility, in turn, is aided by two characteristics: *expertise* and *trustworthiness*. Someone who is considered an expert will be taken more seriously than someone who is thought to know little about a subject. For example, a research scientist who has extensively studied the effects of tobacco on smokers' health is presumed to know more about that issue than the average person on the street. But the question of trustworthiness may cut in a different direction. In some situations, a person who actually has experienced lung cancer as the result of smoking might be far more persuasive. In general, if the issue is one of facts (e.g., how many smokers die from lung cancer each year), then expertise will be the more important factor in persuasion; if the issue is one of values (e.g., whether people feel better after they stop smoking or even whether they should stop smoking), then the most effective communicator might be one who shares characteristics or experiences with the intended audience.

The character of the message also can affect how persuasive it is. Although we think of persuasive messages as involving rationality and objectivity, there also are emotional elements that enter into the process of persuasion, and these elements can be addressed through either a "hard-sell" approach or a "soft-sell" approach.[31] The approach that is chosen may depend on several factors. For example, people frequently rely on soft tactics—flattery, praise, acting humble, and so on—when they want something from another person, especially from a supervisor. But when they want to persuade the supervisor or to endorse a request for a new piece of equipment, then they are likely to be more rational. Finally, people use different approaches based on their expectations about whether they will be successful. When they believe that their requests will be granted, they are likely to use softer tactics; when they anticipate resistance (and when they have power), they use hard tactics.

Coaching and Personal Counseling

Occasionally, you may find it necessary to discuss work problems with individual employees. You might notice a decrease in an employee's performance or productivity. The employee might be in violation of a rule or policy. There might be conflict with other employees. Or the employee might be exhibiting increased tardiness, absenteeism, increased use of sick days, irritability, increased or decreased talkativeness, depression, or signs of substance abuse.[32] These types of cases call for employee counseling or coaching.

Career Coaches
Help Minorities

The primary purpose of both coaching and counseling is to address work-related issues at an early stage so as to prevent their growing and further affecting the work of the organization. While coaching is focused on work-related behaviors, counseling tends to involve assisting an employee in addressing outside problems that might be affecting his work. In any case, the hope is that through both the employee's behavior will be changed so that he once again becomes a productive member of the organization. Coaching and counseling have several goals: (1) correct performance problems before they escalate, (2) motivate employees toward more effective performance, (3) provide guidance in areas such as career counseling and retirement planning, and (4) provide assistance or, better yet, referrals to employees who reveal personal concerns affecting their work. Importantly, counseling should address problems as early as possible[33] (see Figure 9.6).

Before conducting a coaching or counseling session with the employee, collect all the facts so that you are clear on the specific problem, who is involved, when, where, and so on. You may even want to prepare notes so that you can keep the details straight and keep the conversation focused. You should meet with the employee as soon as possible after the problem has been identified, but do not rush through the meeting and do not hold the meeting if you are angry. During the conversation, try to keep the discussion focused on the specific problem with which you are concerned. The employee, quite naturally, might want to deflect the blame or shift the focus of attention to someone else. If a personal problem is revealed, then do not let it shift the focus of the meeting. Stay work centered.

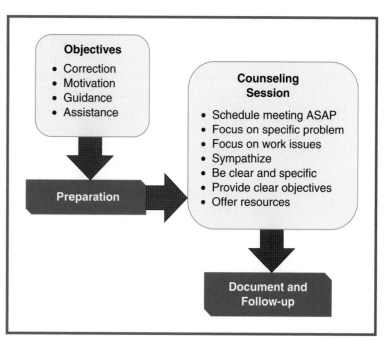

FIGURE 9.6 COACHING AND COUNSELING

Objectives
- Correction
- Motivation
- Guidance
- Assistance

Preparation

Counseling Session
- Schedule meeting ASAP
- Focus on specific problem
- Focus on work issues
- Sympathize
- Be clear and specific
- Provide clear objectives
- Offer resources

Document and Follow-up

Coaching in the Workplace

What an employee does or is involved in outside of work is—legally—none of the supervisor's business. The only aspect that does become the supervisor's business is the effect the outside circumstances have on performance; that is, the supervisor must deal exclusively with the job performance issues and stay clear of inquiring into whatever difficulty the employee may be experiencing external to the organization.[34]

In dealing with personal concerns that do arise, you certainly should be sympathetic, but not so sympathetic that the work issues are ignored. Where it is necessary and appropriate, you should provide referrals to the employee assistance program or other sources of help. But remember that it is the employee's responsibility to take care of whatever personal issues are affecting his or her performance.[35]

In any case, be as specific and clear as possible. For example, state the problem in explicit and factual terms. Instead of just saying, "You've been abusing the sick leave policy," you might say, "You left work early last Monday because you said you hurt your back, but you were later seen dancing at Club Tango." Specify exactly what is expected of the employee and what actions will result if the employee does not meet expectations. Naturally, you should be consistent, applying the same approach and expectations to each employee. Establish a follow-up meeting or plan, and then summarize what was accomplished and agreed on. After the meeting, you might want to document in writing what occurred in the meeting and what was agreed on.

Conducting Effective Meetings

Managing Meetings to Build Consensus

Meetings have developed an awful reputation. People see most meetings as dragging on endlessly and accomplishing little (if anything). By some estimates, the average manager spends the equivalent of about 20 weeks a year in meetings—and 6 weeks worth are a complete waste of time.[36] Think about the typical meeting. The meeting is set for 9 A.M., but people drift in slowly and nothing begins until about 10 or 15 minutes later. The person conducting the meeting, who we will call Belinda, makes a short speech about how she knows that everyone is busy but reminds everyone that having meetings like this is very important. Then she starts through a list of loosely connected bits and pieces of information, often interrupted by silly questions and unrelated comments.

Soon the conversation begins to drift as people try to work their own "agendas." There are frequent disagreements, some of which get a little personal, but nothing ever seems to be resolved. Finally, Belinda gets a message from her secretary and leaves the room to return a call. By the time she returns, most of those in attendance have slipped away, and most who have remained are deeply involved in conversations about topics ranging from the lottery, to cable television, to the latest online auction. Belinda, feeling frustrated about the whole thing, throws up her hands and says, "Well, that's all for today." Those in the room think to themselves, "It's about time."

Fortunately, meetings actually can be productive, and even inspiring, although it takes a person with great skill to move a group successfully through the many pitfalls of "meeting behavior." It helps, at the outset, to have a good idea of what meetings actually are all about—information to be transmitted, problems to be solved, assignments to be worked out, and so on. Meeting these *functional* purposes can build the competence of the group. But meetings also serve *symbolic* purposes. The way in which the meetings are run help to establish norms and values, as well as communication patterns that continue to develop even after the meetings are over.[37] If the people conducting meetings are attentive to both the functional and symbolic purposes of the meetings, then great things can be accomplished and people can leave with an even greater commitment to the organization and its work.

There actually are some specific steps that you can take to make a meeting both more productive and more meaningful (see Figure 9.7). First, you should decide whether the meeting is even necessary. If a memo or an e-mail would accomplish the same or better results, then you should choose one of those avenues. You should exhaust all other methods for communication before calling a meeting.[38] Second, if you decide to hold the meeting, then develop a clear purpose for the meeting and communicate that purpose to those who will attend. Keep the purpose of the meeting clear and do not try to accomplish more than should be expected in the time allocated for the meeting. Keep the meeting focused on a few key objectives and be clear in advance about how long the meeting will take or, better yet, exactly when it will end. Third, develop an agenda, seeking suggestions from others about what should be on the agenda. (Sometimes it is helpful to rank items in terms of importance so that you are sure you will have time for the most important items.) Be clear with individuals about what they will be expected to bring to the meeting or to do in the meeting.

How to Conduct
Meetings

When the meeting time arrives, you already should be there and should start on time. Waiting for latecomers rewards that behavior and imposes a cost on those who have been punctual. As you go through the meeting, you should stick to the agenda and keep the focus of the conversations on the topics at hand. You should also control interruptions and side conversations and prevent any one person from monopolizing the meeting. Another key behavior is to specifically solicit comments from everyone in attendance. Remember that people who are asked to participate in decision making are likely to feel better about the meeting and also are more likely to help implement the resulting decisions. Although meetings often must focus on very serious topics, if the situation allows, try to maintain some informality. Some social conversations and informal discussions can be helpful in building the spirit of the group. And, of course, give people the chance to be funny. "The ability to identify the humor or absurdity of a situation is a wonderful way to maintain energy and build group camaraderie. Sharing funny stories and anecdotes about work-related subjects is a terrific way to build bridges of understanding among meeting participants."[39]

When you have accomplished the objectives of the meeting or if you reach the time to close, you should end the meeting. Summarize the progress you have made, remind participants of assignments they have received and (if appropriate) tell people when the next meeting will be. After the meeting, prepare and distribute the minutes as soon as possible so that people will be reminded of what they are supposed to do next. Hopefully, people will look back on the meeting with a feeling of accomplishment and pride and will give you credit for conducting a good meeting.

Writing Memos, Reports, and Proposals

Managers often are called on to produce memos, reports, and other forms of written communication ranging from proposals to personnel evaluations. You might be called on to develop a written analysis of a new business proposal. You might be asked to write an annual report for your division. Or you might be asked to develop a lengthy memo laying out the circumstances under which an employee received disciplinary action. In any of these cases, your ability to write clearly and communicate effectively will be key.

Seven Quick Tips

FIGURE 9.7 STEPS TO EFFECTIVE MEETINGS

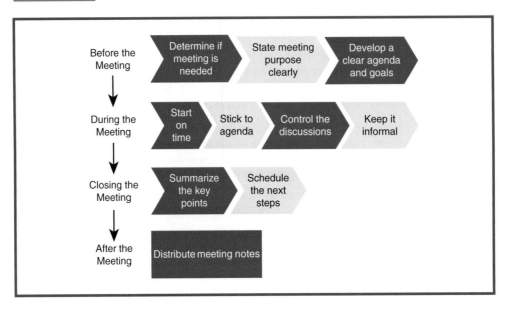

Writing Effective
Memos

Writing memos or reports is different from oral communication for several reasons. Obviously, in written communications, you cannot use gestures or a special tone of voice to convey your intent, and the audience cannot ask questions of you (at least initially). For these reasons, written communication may be more difficult. On the other hand, as we noted earlier, written communication has the advantage of greater permanence. What you write will remain "on the record" for a longer period of time than oral comments, so people can come back to your writing to check what you said. Written documents can be saved, duplicated, distributed, filed, retained, and referred to later.

Writing requires several basic steps. You must know exactly who your audience is and be clear about the purpose of what you are writing. Are you trying to communicate the facts in an objective fashion, or are you trying to persuade someone to adopt your position? Also, you must research the topic thoroughly and gather all of the information needed to meet your purpose. What do you need to know to communicate your message? Then you must organize your material into an outline that can keep you focused and ensure that you cover all that you need to. Once you have carefully organized your material, you are ready to begin writing.

Effective writing takes years of study and practice, but there are a number of guidelines that you can follow to improve your writing. The six rules of effective managerial writing are presented in Table 9.2.

In addition to following the six C rules, you also should be attentive to creating a neat and orderly final product. No matter how well your report or proposal is written, if it is presented in a sloppy manner, then it will not communicate effectively. Keep your paragraphs relatively short, typically between four and eight sentences. Avoid excessive use of italics and capital letters that may clutter your presentation. Be careful in your use of graphics and visuals. Use visuals only when they will enhance readers' understanding of the material. Choose the appropriate visual (e.g., graph, table) and place it close to the text that corresponds to it.

TABLE 9.2 THE RULES OF EFFECTIVE MANAGERIAL WRITING: THE SIX Cs

Rule	Description
Clarity	Put yourself in the reader's position. Write in the active voice (e.g., "Dave painted the house") rather than the passive voice (e.g., "The house was painted by Dave"). Use the positive form rather than the negative form (e.g., "Lucy is happy" rather than "Lucy isn't sad").
Courtesy	Courtesy involves knowing your readers, adapting to their mood, and writing at their level, providing neither too much nor too little information.
Conciseness	Be short and to the point. Think of it this way: Which are you more likely to read, a 50-word memo or a 10-page report?
Confidence	Write with confidence. Confidence really is a matter of judgment, but you should avoid the extremes: being overbearing (too confident) or being wishy-washy (not confident enough).
Correctness	Use correct grammar and composition—the technical rules of writing that include spelling and punctuation. Proofread carefully for proper spelling, grammar, and punctuation.
Conversational tone	Write in the same way as you talk and try to imagine one specific person to whom you are writing. It is much easier to write to John Jones than to "all economics professors."

Source: Sussman, L., & Deep, S. (1984). *COMEX: The communication experience in human relations.* Cincinnati, OH: South-Western.

One final consideration is to avoid bias in the language that you are using.[40] First, do not mention race, gender, age, or disability unless it is pertinent. Second, avoid stereotypes and labels that reveal bias. Third, give parallel treatment (e.g., "Mr. Waxman and Ms. Stone," not "Mr. Waxman and Linda"). Fourth, find substitutes for words that may be considered insensitive or confusing, such as masculine pronouns. You can use "he or she" or alternate "he" and "she"—as we have done in this book. Again, being sensitive to the needs and concerns of those who constitute your audience is the key to effective writing.

► Summary and Applications for Managers

We have discussed a variety of approaches to communicating more effectively, but remember that understanding communication skills and putting them into practice are two different things. It is easy enough to learn the skills of effective communication intellectually, but under the pressures of the moment in the real world, it is easy to revert to old and less effective communication techniques. As in many areas of organizational behavior, it is not just what you *know* that counts but also what you can *do*. In any case, the following guidelines might be helpful as you seek to improve your communication skills.

1. *Remember that effective communication involves creating meaning, transmitting meaning, and deciphering meaning.* At any of these points, the communication process can break down. We see the world in different ways, and we shape our own communication and respond to the communication of others based on the way in which we see the world. Many messages are ambiguous, in part because some communication serves different functions. We communicate both our ideas and our feelings, and both must be appreciated for others to fully understand our meanings.

2. *Recognize the many barriers that inhibit effective communication.* There are obvious distortions through semantic differences and through mechanisms such as filtering. But there also is the question of which medium or channel of communication is the best for a particular situation. For various reasons, some may be "noisier" than others. Finally, the psychological state of the recipient of any message will affect what is heard.

3. *Practice supportive communication.* Strive to focus on problems and solutions rather than people. Try to resist immediate evaluation. Be as specific as possible. Try to relate to what has been said before. Help others feel accepted and validated through your communication. Take responsibility for what you are saying. Finally, listen carefully to the other person and encourage feedback in both directions.

4. *When speaking, consider your audience and make sure that your content, tone, and approach fit the situation.* Think about what other people need to know and what they want to know. Be empathetic to the feelings and dispositions of others. Engage in appropriate self-disclosure.

5. *When you wish to persuade someone to accept your position, consider your credibility and work to improve it.* If the issue is one of facts, then expertise will be important; if the issue is one of values, then you will be more effective if you share similar experiences with those you are trying to persuade. Choose the communication strategy that best fits the situation.

6. *Listen, listen, listen!* Practice active listening. Have a reason or purpose for listening. Suspend immediate judgments or evaluations. Resist distractions, whether the distraction is a part of the environment or a characteristic of the one with whom you are talking. Wait before responding; let the other person finish before you start making your response. Rephrase what you hear in your own words; let the other person know you understand, and if you do not, then give him a chance to clarify. Listen for themes rather than details or specifics. Use the thinking-speaking differential to reflect on what the other person is saying and to look for themes.

7. *Remember that body language communicates as much as, or more than, what we actually say.* For example, there are 55 muscles in the face that communicate tons of information. However, you need to be careful in interpreting body positions. A person with arms crossed may not be closed off from what's happening; he may just be most comfortable sitting that way. You should also be especially sensitive to the differences that exist across various cultures in nonverbal communication. In all cases, know your audience and consider any differences that might affect your message.

8. *Take advantage of electronic communication, but use electronic channels only when they are appropriate.* When the issue is clear

and straightforward, you can use a lean medium such as e-mail. But when the issue is complex or ambiguous, use a richer medium such as face-to-face conversation. This will increase the opportunities for feedback and clarification.

9. *In specialized forms of communication, always consider the receiver or audience and the norms and expectations embedded in the situation.* In counseling employees, be specific and stay on target. Do not advise with respect to personal problems, but do refer employees to other sources of help. In conducting meetings, clarify your purposes and keep the meetings on track with respect to those purposes. In preparing written reports, know your topics, know your audiences, plan your papers, and then be attentive to the six Cs of effective writing.

10. *Remember to consider the ethics of communication.* Your ethics and integrity are most clearly on display when you communicate with others. The truth of what you say obviously is important, but the way in which you communicate is important as well. Many people will measure your credibility by how you communicate. An honest, open, and straightforward way of communicating will significantly enhance your credibility.

▶ Key Terms

Active listening   280

Communication   272

Decoding   275

Defensiveness   277

Distortion   276

Encoding   274

Filtering   277

Frames of reference   275

Jargon   276

Paraphrasing   281

Semantics   276

Self-disclosure   280

Supportive communication   283

Thinking-speaking differential   282

▶ Exercise 9.1 Supportive Communication

Read the following portion of a conversation between Frank Banks, head of a small internal audit unit in a grocery chain, and Mary Ann Burke, one of his employees.

Frank: I've asked you to come in because we've had some serious complaints about your work from some of the store managers. Generally, they say that you are rude and abrasive in your conversations with them. I'd like an explanation.

Mary Ann: I really don't know what you are talking about, but it sounds like the old rumor mill has been working overtime and that you've gotten caught up in it.

Frank: Don't try to deny that there's a problem. You can't get out of it that easily.

Mary Ann: There's *not* a problem—except that you don't trust your employees. And you're too blind to see the way some of the managers perceive our office—and your leadership—or rather the lack thereof.

Frank: Mary Ann, you won't get anywhere with personal attacks on me. I'm not the one who's on trial here.

Mary Ann: Frank, give me a break. This isn't a trial. Except that you're really trying my patience. Good-bye.

Analyze this conversation in terms of the principles of supportive communication presented in this chapter. Show examples of how Frank and Mary Ann violated each of the principles. Then create groups of three individuals. Let one person play

Frank and another play Mary Ann, with the third person acting as an observer. Try to demonstrate how the same conversation might go if both Frank and Mary Ann made an effort to use supportive communication. How would the conversation differ? How might the outcome differ?

▶ Exercise 9.2: Turmoil in a Chemical Lab

Read the following conversation fragments, and then pick up and role-play the conversation that is beginning between Bob and Patti. Try to use the principles of effective communication discussed in this chapter.

Robert Gentry is director of the research and development lab in a large chemical company. Patti Lazard recently joined the lab as associate director. Freddie King and Linda Graham both are chemists in the lab.

One day, as Robert is walking down the hall, Freddie and Linda pull him aside. Freddie begins the conversation:

> Bob, we wanted to talk with you about your new associate. I know she has some impressive degrees and all, but I'm not sure she really knows what we're all about in this lab. You know, this is hard work, and we have to be very careful to get everything just right. We also have to make sure that our clients are being brought along. But Patti seems to be concerned that we are moving too slow. In fact, a couple of times, she's actually come into my work area and pushed me out so she could show me how to do the job faster. Frankly, it's really getting on my nerves.

Linda continues:

> There's no question that Patti knows what she's talking about technically, but she just doesn't understand the culture of this organization. Maybe it's because she previously worked in a small lab where it didn't matter whether she talked with anyone else. But if we get too far out in front of our clients, we're in big trouble. Sometimes we have to sacrifice a little efficiency in order to be responsive to what people around the country are thinking and saying. And that takes time. Bob, I really think you need to rein her in—or maybe just put her out. She's trouble.

Robert is taken aback by the conversation. He was terribly impressed with Patti when she was hired and has not heard anything negative about her prior to this conversation. After giving the matter some thought, he walks over to Patti's office and asks to come in. He closes the door behind him and begins to speak:

> Patti, I've heard a couple of concerns expressed about your approach to the work we're doing and wanted to talk about it a little. Specifically, some people seem to feel that you want to move too fast and are neglecting the time it takes to work with customers. Also, there seems to be some concern that you are pushing them aside and showing them how to do their work.

Patti replies as follows:

> That's silly. We have some people in this office who just don't understand what efficiency means. They take forever doing things that can be done in a matter of a few hours. When I've been asked how the job could be done more quickly, I've shown them. But I certainly haven't pushed anyone aside to do that. I'm afraid there are just some people working here who are too lazy to keep around.

Source: Adapted from Schoem, S. H., Sevis, T., Chester, M., & Sumida, S. H. (2001). Intergroup dialogue: Democracy at work in theory and practice. In D. Schoem & S. H. Schoem (Eds.), *Intergroup dialogue* (pp. 1–21). Ann Arbor: University of Michigan Press.

▶ Exercise 9.3 Trends in Electronic Communication

Earlier in this chapter, we listed several possible limitations of electronic communications. Review the list (on page 287) and then discuss which of these issues most concern you as you think ahead about the work you will soon be doing. Are there other limitations you can think of? Do any of these offset the benefits of electronic communications?

▶ Case 9.1 A Dispersed Workplace

Your nonprofit organization, one concerned with stimulating and communicating innovations in local government, is headquartered in the western United States. But you have long recognized the importance of having a number of regional representatives in various parts of the country, people who can help identify innovations, share information about local government practices, and, perhaps most important, stimulate new memberships among local governments in their areas. While you communicate with the regional representatives regularly by phone and e-mail, and see them in person two or three times a year, for the most part they are out there "on their own." Your board is highly supportive of the idea of having regional representatives, but wants to be sure (1) that the regional representatives are getting what they need from the organization in terms of support, encouragement, and a sense of belonging to the organization, and (2) that the regional representatives are being properly "managed" and held accountable for their work.

1. What considerations would you take into account in developing a strategy for managing these remote employees?

2. How would you take lessons from the literature on leadership and management, such as the importance of involving employees in organizational decision making, and apply them in this kind of situation?

3. How, for example, can you incorporate dialogue into your communication and be effective in supportive communications at a distance?

4. How would the fact that your organization is multigenerational be likely to affect its operation?

⑤SAGE edge™

Sharpen your skills with SAGE edge at edge.sagepub.com/nahavandi

SAGE edge for students provides a personalized approach to help you accomplish your coursework goals in an easy-to-use learning environment.

▶ Endnotes

1. Eisenberg, E. M. (1984). Ambiguity as a strategy in organizational communication. *Communication Monographs, 51,* 227–242.

2. Stohl, C. (1995). *Organizational communication.* Thousand Oaks, CA: Sage.

3. Tracey, W. R. (1988). *Critical skills.* New York, NY: American Management Association.

4. Schramm, W. (1964). *Mass media and national development.* Stanford, CA: Stanford University Press.

5. Sandberg, S. (2013). *Lean in.* New York, NY: Knopf.

6. David, K., & Newstrom, J. W. (1985). *Human behavior at work.* New York, NY: McGraw-Hill, p. 431.

7. Gibb, J. R. (1961). Defensive communication. *Journal of Communication, 11*(3), 121–128.

8. Avon board of directors. (2103) Retrieved from http://www.avoncompany.com/aboutavon/

boardofdirectors/index.html on December 15, 2012.

9. Avon media center. Retrieved from http://media.avoncompany.com/index .php?s=10922&item=126180 on December 15, 2012.

10. Tedeschi, B. (2007). When beauty is more than a click deep. *The New York Times,* October 1. Retrieved from http://www.nytimes .com/2007/10/01/technology/01ecom.html?_ r=1 on April 6, 2010.

11. Chandra, S. (2004). Avon's Andrea Jung Pins Hopes on China as Sales in U.S. Fade. *Bloomberg.com,* December 27. Retrieved from http://www.bloomberg.com/apps/news?pid=1 0000080&sid=aBrmvGQAml1c&_refer=asia# on January 31, 2005.

12. Executive sweet. (2013). *Goldsea: Asian American.* Retrieved from http://goldsea.com/WW/ Jungandrea/jungandrea.html on December 15, 2012.

13. Executive sweet, 2013.

14. Jones, D. (2009). Avon's Andrea Jung: CEOs need to reinvent themselves. *USAToday,* June 15. Retrieved from http://www.usatoday.com/money/ companies/management/advice/2009-6-14-jung-ceo-avon_N.htm on December 15, 2012.

15. Morris, B. (2004, July 21). If women ran the world it would look a lot like Avon. *Fortune,* p. 79.

16. Executive sweet, 2013, p. 3.

17. Rogers, C. R., & Farson, R. E. (1976). *Active listening.* Chicago, IL: University of Chicago Press.

18. Knippen, J. T., & Green, T. B. (1994). How the manager can use active listening. *Public Personnel Management, 23*(2), 357–359.

19. Rogers, C. R. (1991, November–December). Barriers and gateways to communication. *Harvard Business Review,* 105–107.

20. Brownell, J. (1990). Perceptions of effective listeners: A management study. *Journal of Business Communication, 27*(4), 401–415.

21. Daniel Yankelovich, as cited in Roberts, N. C. (2002). Calls for dialogue. In N. C. Roberts (Ed.), *The transformative power of dialogue* (pp. 3–26). Amsterdam: JAI Press, p. 7.

22. Roberts, 2002.

23. Roberts, 2002, p. 6.

24. Schoem, S. H., Sevis, T., Chester, M., & Sumida, S. H. (2001). Intergroup dialogue: Democracy at work in theory and practice. In D. Schoem & S. H. Schoem (Eds.), *Intergroup dialogue* (pp. 1–21). Ann Arbor: University of Michigan Press; see pp. 6–14.

25. This material is drawn from remarks by Maria Shriver delivered on Friday, May 11, 2012, at the University of Southern California's Annenberg School Commencement Ceremony.

26. Tjan, A. K. (2013, January 9). It's time for a "slow" conversation movement. HBR Blogs. Retrieved from http://blogs.hbr.org/2013/01/its-time-for-a-slow-conversation-m.

27. Guber, P. (2011). *Tell to win.* New York, NY: Crown Publishers.

28. Paskowitz, R. (2013, September 13). Authentic communications. Presentation to the University of Southern California Executive Master of Leadership. (Summarized by Tony Rivera.)

29. Miller, K. (1999). *Organizational communication.* Belmont, CA: Wadsworth, p. 285.

30. Cherrington, D. J. (1994). *Organizational behavior.* Boston, MA: Allyn & Bacon, pp. 537–542; see also Kouzes, J. M., & Posner, B. Z. (2012). *The leadership challenge* (5th ed.). San Francisco, CA: Jossey-Bass.

31. Kipnis, D., & Schmidt, S. (1985, April). The language of persuasion: Hard, soft, or rational. *Psychology Today,* 40–46.

32. DeVoe, D. (1999, March). Employers can help workers with personal problems. *Info World, 29,* 92.

33. McConnell, C. R. (1997). Effective employee counseling for the first-line

supervisor. *Health Care Supervisor, 16*(1), 77–86; see p. 82.

34. McConnell, 1997, p. 80.

35. Cook, G. D. (1989, August). Employee counseling session. *Supervision,* 3–5; see p. 5.

36. Sandwith, P. (1992). Better meetings for better communication. *Training and Development, 46*(1), 29–31; see p. 29.

37. Sandwith, 1992, p. 30.

38. Petty, A. (2012). At least 11 more ideas to help you run effective meetings. *Management Excellence by Art Petty.* Retrieved from http://artpetty.com/2012/11/20/at-least-11-more-ideas-to-help-you-run-effective-meetings/ on April 2, 2013.

39. Hawkins, C. (1999). The "F" words for effective meetings. *Journal for Quality and Participation, 22*(5), 56–57.

40. Venolia, J. (1998). *Write right.* Berkeley, CA: Ten Speed Press.

10 Working in Groups and Teams

Whole Foods ▶

Whole Foods, the natural food grocery chain, provides a rich and exceptional selection of products and outstanding service to its customers while it also provides a unique workplace for its employees. The company founder and CEO, John Mackey, considers his over 50,000 employees to be his children. Mackey says: "We're trying to do good. And we're trying to make money. The more money we make, the more good we can do."[1]

John Mackey started the company in 1980 in Austin, Texas, with the first organic food store; it now numbers close to 350 stores and is becoming a global company with stores in the United Kingdom. Although Mackey is known for some of his very vocal, and sometimes controversial, political stances, he is also known for having created a distinctive organization based on cooperation and democracy with a team-based culture that empowers employees and involves them in all aspects of decision making while demanding performance and customer service.

The basic decision-making power at Whole Foods rests with the teams that run each department (e.g., bakery, produce, seafood) in each store. The teams decide whom to hire, whether to retain members, what products to carry, how to allocate raises, and so forth. All teams together also make strategic decisions, such as the type of health insurance the company will offer. The National Leadership Team of the company makes the overall decision based on majority vote. Mackey says, "I don't overrule the National Leadership Team. . . . I've done it maybe once or twice in all these years."[2] He admits making some top-down decisions, but only when time to consult is not available.

Whole Foods has a "Declaration of Interdependence" that affirms the interdependence of all stakeholders and clearly states the goals of satisfying and delighting customers and of team-member happiness and excellence.[3] Building healthy relationships with team

The strength of the team is each individual member. The strength of each member is the team.

—Phil Jackson

members, getting rid of the "us versus them" management mentality, and a deep-seated belief in employee participation are also highlighted. The core values regarding working at Whole Foods include having self-directed teams, open books, profit sharing, continuous learning, and promotion from within.[4] Although the positive work culture, fun, and friendship are key to the company's ongoing success, competition and focus on performance are not lost. Because individuals' raises are tied to their team's performance, team members want good workers on their team.

Questions related to teams and teamwork permeate our lives these days. No matter where you are, on the athletic field, in a classroom, or in other organizations, and no matter who you are, a manager, an employee, or a student, it is almost impossible to avoid being part of a group. Increasingly, and for various reasons, organizations are using either groups or teams to accomplish tasks that used to be assigned to individuals. Additionally, many organizations are moving to team-based structures by organizing around various types of teams as opposed to organizing around the traditional organizational hierarchies and horizontal divisions of labor. Our discussion of groups and teams in this chapter is applicable to many settings outside of the workplace. We'll define groups and teams, discuss their key elements, the role of culture in teams, how teams are formed and develop over time, what types of teams there are, and finally how teams can be implemented effectively.

Defining Groups and Teams

Difference Between Groups and Teams

Groups are two or more people who interact in an organized manner to perform a task or activity to achieve a common goal. This definition has several elements. First, a group involves two or more people who have the opportunity to interact. The group members must also have some common purpose that requires each member to perform a specific role or task, and groups members must be interdependent to some extent. Finally, the group members have to perceive that they are part of a group. Based on that definition, you are part of many formal and informal groups in your community and your organization. Not all groups are teams, however. **Teams** are mature groups with a high degree of interdependence geared toward the achievement of a goal or the completion of a task. As opposed to groups, teams have a strong common purpose, complementary skills, and mutual accountability regarding their work. Teams also often have some degree of self-management and authority to assess their own work processes and outcomes.[5] While we often use the word *team* when talking about people working together, for example when we form "teams" in classes, these are more often groups rather than teams. Table 10.1 summarizes the differences between groups and teams.

The current interest in teams and teamwork began during the 1980s with the idea of quality circles that were used successfully in Japanese organizations. W. Edward

Groups: two or more people who interact in an organized manner to perform a task or activity to achieve a common goal

Teams: mature groups with a high degree of interdependence geared toward the achievement of a goal or the completion of a task

ASSESSING TEAM PERFORMANCE

Think of a group of which you are (or were) a part, whether in a classroom, personal, or workplace setting. How do (or did) members of your team address the following issues?

1. Purpose of team
   a. What is the purpose of the team?
   b. What are its goals and objectives?

2. How does the team fit into the overall management structure of the organization, classroom, and so on?

_____

_____

_____

3. Membership
   a. How were members selected to join the team?
   b. Will new members be welcomed?
   c. How will members be allowed to rotate out of the team if they so desire?

4. What is the role of the leader?
   a. How will the leader be selected?
   b. Will there be one assigned leader?
   c. Will leaders rotate periodically?

5. How will the members be held accountable?

6. Do you currently have a "team agreement"?

7. Do you generate agendas with the dates, places, and times for the next meetings?

8. Trust
   a. Do team members trust each other?
   b. Does senior management trust the team?
   c. How is trust demonstrated?
   d. How will lack of trust be handled?

TABLE 10.1 FROM GROUPS TO TEAMS

Groups	Teams
Limited interdependence	Highly interdependent members
Assigned leadership	Shared leadership
Individual accountability or accountability to the leader	Individual and mutual accountability
Goals assigned by the organization	Goals determined by the team members
Focused on efficiency	Focused on quality and creativity, as well as efficiency
Effectiveness measured by others	Measure own quality and effectiveness

Source: Partially based on Katzenbach, J. R., & Smith, D. K. (1993). _The wisdom of teams: Creating the high-performance organization._ Boston, MA: Harvard Business School Press; and Hackman, J. R. (1990). _Groups that work (and those that don't): Creating conditions for effective teamwork._ San Francisco, CA: Jossey-Bass.

Toyota has changed the assembly line by relying on teams as the cornerstone of its quality management.

Deming, one of the founders of the quality movement, stated, "Isn't it logical? If you work together, you should end up with something better than if you work apart."[6] More recently, the idea of total quality management has raised the awareness of managers and executives about the strategic value of teams in continuous improvement. Consequently, researchers found a well-documented growth rate in the number of teams in organizations as early as the mid-1990s.[7] It is becoming clear that, with increasing complexity and the growing influence of technology, the importance of innovation, and the new focus on the stakeholders, teams are becoming more and more popular. However, there still is some resistance to moving beyond individual roles and individual accountability in our culture. Studies have demonstrated that in individual cultures such as the United States, people believe that they can be more effective as individuals than as groups.[8] This mindset may present a challenge during an era when team building, diversity, and use of teams have escalated to meet new demands on managers. However, groups and teams can also pose a management challenge and they are not a cure-all.

Good Teams and
Bad Teams

In some cases, the failure to engage in team-based solutions to problems can be disastrous. Donald Straus, former president of the American Arbitration Association, illustrated that point in telling of his involvement in the acid rain controversy. Straus believed that our ability to collaborate effectively in developing and implementing concrete responses to the problems of acid rain lagged far behind our technical ability to detect the environmental damage and document the increasing severity of the problem.[9] In other words, technical solutions might mean little if we lack the capacity to act together, in teams and other organized groups, to implement those solutions.

Groups and teams are used for a variety of reasons (see Figure 10.1). They can outperform individuals acting alone or in larger organizational groupings, particularly when the task is complex and performance requires multiple skills, judgments, and experiences; when there is time to work through a group or team; and when there is a need for member commitment to implement the solutions. Teams have the potential to be more effective than individuals for five reasons:[10]

- Teams produce a greater number of ideas and pieces of information.

- Teams improve understanding and acceptance among individuals involved in problem solving and decision making due to the participation of each team member in the process.

- Teams have higher levels of motivation and performance than individuals acting alone due to the effects of "social facilitation"—that is, the reinforcing effect of each member "pushing" the others in the groups.

- Teams offset personal biases and blind spots that inhibit effective problem analysis and implementation but that individuals might overlook.

- Team members are more likely to entertain risky alternatives and take innovative action than individuals working alone.

When teams are well managed and effective, team members tend to be more motivated and creative and learn faster. Teams also seem to perform better under some circumstances than larger organizational groupings. Teamwork also has proved to be a powerful tool for shifting social values, including racism. During the 1970s, several research projects demonstrated that the least prejudiced students were those who participated in sports teams and school bands with members of other races.[11] Thomas Kolditz, a consultant who specializes in leader development and the founder of West Point's Leadership Academy, suggests that working in teams even when there are weak members can be helpful to an organization. When weaker performers were part of the team, Kolditz says: "We became better—not in spite of the weakest performers, but because of them. Their performance focused us on organizational vulnerabilities and areas where we could make changes to strengthen our processes."[12] However, groups and teams are not ideal in all situations. They clearly have the potential for creativity and higher commitment and can be very supportive of learning. Individuals who work in groups may experience **social facilitation**, which occurs when individuals work harder in the presence of others. For example, a recent study found that the slowest athletes go faster in team relays.[13] However, as many of you have probably experienced, groups and even teams can be inefficient, waste time, and face major obstacles such as Groupthink, which we discuss in the chapter on decision making. Additionally, individual team members can be subject to **social loafing**, which involves working less when your individual contributions cannot be measured.[14] Social loafing may be prevented by holding individual team members accountable for their performance. Research has found that it decreases with the potential of performance monitoring and evaluation.[15]

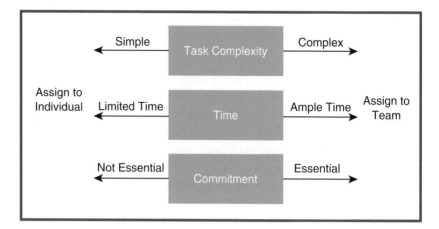

FIGURE 10.1 FACTORS IN THE USE OF TEAMS

Interpersonal Logic

Structural Issues in Groups and Teams

Long before groups and teams were used in business organizations, social scientists studied group processes and dynamics and identified a number of factors in the performance of groups.[16] These factors include group size and composition, roles and norms, cohesion and conformity, and deviance.

Group Size and Composition

Determining the size and composition of a group or team is one of the first decisions managers make when forming a group. How many people should be included and who should the members be? While there is no ideal group size, groups larger than 10 to 12 members are less likely to function smoothly. Additionally, having an odd number of members may protect against deadlocks in case of disagreement. Generally, as size increases, individuals do not have the opportunity to participate and are less likely to take responsibility for their actions and the team outcomes. Smaller groups provide the opportunity for extensive

Social facilitation: individuals work harder in the presence of others

Social loafing: people work less when their individual contributions cannot be measured

interaction among members and a chance for all members to have input. Moreover, as groups get larger, subgroups form to deal with different issues or to take on different parts of the task. While the formation of subgroups is not, in and of itself, a negative factor, subgroups have the potential to lose touch with one another and the result can lead to poor coordination of activities.

In addition to size, managers must also pay close attention to the group's composition. Many factors affect how group members are selected. Managers often base their choice on the requirements of the task. A job may require a certain technical expertise such as accounting or marketing. Or a certain level or type of experience, for example international experience, or status within the organization may be important. Generally, **homogeneous groups**, with members who are similar to one another in a number of different ways, are able to get along better.[17] People who are similar tend to like each other and have easier interactions. **Heterogeneous groups**, with members of different backgrounds, style, and so forth, are more likely to face conflict and disagreement.

Before you decide that group members should be similar because they can work more easily together, consider three issues that affect creative decision making. First, the more similar the group members the less creative they are likely to be. People with similar backgrounds tend to think the same way. Accordingly, they may not look at issues from different points of view. Second, conflict is necessary for good decision making. If everyone always agreed, few new ideas would be considered. Finally, consider diversity. If managers chose team members based on their ability to get along and have few conflicts, they would most likely exclude any diversity. Diversity can take many forms. A group could include a male in an all female group; a marketer in a group of engineers; an Asian in a predominantly Hispanic group; or a Southern European in a Scandinavian group. Note that the goal of diversity is not diversity for its own sake. Rather, it is to bring in new points of view and ideas to the team when the task could benefit from it. For instance, a culturally diverse group that designs a marketing campaign for a new product can help develop better plans for reaching different cultural market segments. Managers need to balance the need for easy, comfortable interaction with the importance of creative and productive group processes.

Roles and Norms

One of the defining elements of a group or team is the presence of hierarchy or structure. All groups develop some type of structure. Different members take on different tasks and fulfill different functions. Some members become leaders; others are followers. Similarly, most groups quickly establish rules regarding how members should behave and how they get activities done.

As people take on different aspects of a group's activities and perform different functions, and based on their own personalities, expertise, and styles, people perform different roles. Roles are specific formal or informal activities that each person performs in the group or team. Formal roles include titles and other status symbols. For example, groups have leaders, treasurers, secretaries, and so forth. Informal roles are not as clearly defined but nonetheless are known to group members. The types of roles in groups fall into three general categories of task, relationship, and self-oriented roles.[18] Task roles relate to the job or task the group is performing. Relationship roles, also called maintenance roles, relate to the social interaction among group members. Self-oriented roles are roles that people take on to satisfy their own

Homogeneous groups: groups with members who have a number of similarities

Heterogeneous groups: groups with members who have many differences

Roles: specific formal or informal patterns of behavior that an individual performs in a team

What Do You Think?

▶ Do you think it's OK for a manager to select only women and minorities to join a high-profile group charged with reviewing the company's diversity practices? Why or why not?

rather than the group's needs. The first two types are necessary for the group's effectiveness; the third often detracts from team performance (see Figure 10.2). It also is important to understand that individuals bring their own personality styles to the team. That is, different people react to and engage in the team experience in different ways. There are four primary styles or roles of team players:[19]

1. *Contributor.* This is a task-oriented member who enjoys providing the team with good technical information and data, does his or her homework, and pushes the team to set high performance standards and to use its resources wisely. As a team member, the contributor is viewed as dependable.

2. *Collaborator.* This is a flexible, both task- and relationship-oriented member who sees the vision, mission, or goal of the team as paramount but who is flexible and open to new ideas. He or she is willing to share the limelight with others and is viewed as a person who sees the big picture.

3. *Communicator.* This is a relationship- and process-oriented individual with good listening and facilitative skills. He or she is viewed as a good people person who is able to resolve conflict and build informal relaxed relationships.

4. *Challenger.* This person openly questions the goals and methods of the team and is willing to disagree with the leader. This person encourages risk taking and is appreciated for his or her candor and openness.

FIGURE 10.2 ROLES IN GROUPS AND TEAMS

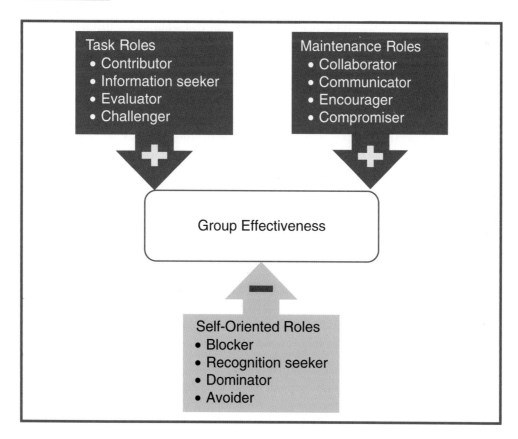

▶ One of your employees does not follow the team's well-established informal norms about proper business attire. How far should you go, as a manager, to enforce those norms? What is and is not acceptable behavior on your part and on the part of other group members to bring that member in line?

Don't Let
Coworkers
Sour Your Job

Group
Cohesiveness

Norms: shared rules and expectations about group members' behaviors

Central norms: rules of behavior that are essential to the group's identity, goals, and survival

Peripheral norms: rules of behavior that support central norms but are not central to the group's identity

Cohesion: the degree to which members of the group are attracted to the group and to one another

Conformity: the process of abiding by the group norms

As groups develop and members take on different roles, they develop rules regarding how the group should function. **Norms are shared rules and expectations about group members' behaviors.** They develop early and continue evolving as the group matures into a team, so teams often have many formal and informal norms. Having norms allows a group to bring order and control to the members' interaction. They regulate social interaction and the way the group achieves its goals. They also set the group apart from other groups, thus helping provide the group with its identity.

Many norms are not formally stated, but they often become obvious when a member or an outsider violates them. For example, a group norm about avoiding sexual jokes can be implicit and not discussed but may become a topic of discussion when a new member tells an off-color joke. At that point, the group verbalizes its norm to educate the new member. Some norms are key to the group's identity, goals, and survival; these are **central norms.** Others are less important, although they support the central norms; they are called **peripheral norms.** Doing quality work and respecting others are examples of central norms, whereas being on time and friendly may be peripheral. Central norms in mature teams are part of the deep cultural assumptions or the third level of culture, whereas peripheral norms are part of the first and second levels of cultures (see Chapter 2). Central norms are hard to change and difficult to challenge; peripheral norms change more easily as different behaviors are needed to achieve goals at different points in time. Groups can afford to be lenient in the enforcement of peripheral norms. However, not enforcing central norms threatens the group's existence and reason for being, and therefore cannot be tolerated.

Cohesion, Conformity, and Deviance

One of the most desirable qualities of a team is cohesion. **Cohesion,** also called cohesiveness, is the degree to which members of the group are attracted to the group and to one another. Cohesive groups and teams are tight and supportive. Members perceive less inter-group conflict.[20] They share deeply the central and peripheral norms of the team and they want to be in the group and work to support group goals and one another. One of the characteristics of a mature team is its cohesion. In cohesive groups, members voluntarily conform to the norms. **Conformity** refers to the extent to which people adhere to group norms. For instance, among the employees of Harley-Davidson, manufacturer of the famous motorcycles in Milwaukee, Wisconsin, many employees tattoo the company name on their bodies with pride as a way to conform to this group norm.[21]

Although cohesive teams have many benefits, managers must also watch for some potential drawbacks (see Table 10.2). People who are part of a cohesive team are generally more satisfied and happier because they feel supported and valued.[22] They will be more motivated to achieve the group's goals. However, increased satisfaction and motivation does not always lead to better performance. If the group norms include high productivity and performance, then members of such a cohesive group will be more productive. But, as was found during the Hawthorne experiments (see Chapter 1), cohesive groups can also impede productivity if the norms are focused on other factors.

One of the key benefits of a cohesive team is that it provides a supportive climate for learning. Members can safely experiment without fear of ridicule, a factor that can help in training. Many police organizations, for example, take advantage of unit cohesion and pair up new officers with veterans to socialize and train them. The same cohesion can be a problem if the group norm goes against the organization. In the police example, a cohesive but corrupt unit can perpetuate corruption by enforcing its own norms. Cohesive groups can also lose some of their creativity, even fall prey to Groupthink (see Chapter 8), if the members are more worried about not rocking the boat than about being innovative. Managers can reap many of the benefits of a cohesive team with proper monitoring and management of their teams. Particularly, they can take many actions to build cohesion. These include:

- Increasing work and social interaction
- Rewarding cooperation rather than competition inside the group
- Keeping the team size small
- Providing resources to team members
- Building progressive challenges into their tasks so that they have early successes
- Limiting hierarchy within the group
- Providing competition with outside groups

By implementing these strategies, managers can increase their team's cohesion and provide members with a supportive environment that leads to productivity and satisfaction. However, consider this challenge. If everyone always conformed to group norms, how would new ideas ever develop? Additionally, what happens to team members who are not willing to conform to the norms?

Assembly line worker Jonathan Hueton shows off his tattoo that he got to commemorate the one-year anniversary of his employment at the Harley-Davidson plant in Kansas City, Missouri. The tattoo is a cultural ritual that builds cohesion at Harley-Davidson.

Deviants in groups are those individuals who do not conform to norms. While they can threaten a team's cohesion and effectiveness, they can also be a source of creativity and innovation. The reaction of the team will differ greatly based on whether the deviant rejects central or peripheral norms. Figure 10.3 presents four options for how deviants are managed. Well-managed teams encourage *creative individualism* rather than always enforcing conformity. Team members must be aware of individuals who appear to conform, but practice *subversive rebellion*. They can be bigger threats to the team's effectiveness than those who openly challenge the norms. Typically, team members will pressure deviants and increase interaction with them to remind them of the norms.[23] If coaxing and direct pressure do not work, the deviant group member may be threatened with

Deviants: individuals who do not conform to the group norms

TABLE 10.2 BENEFITS AND DISADVANTAGES OF COHESION

Group or Team Cohesion	
Advantages	**Disadvantages**
• Increased satisfaction	• Focus on team rather than organization
• Increased motivation	• Loss of creativity
• Goals assigned by the organization	• Goals determined by the team members
• Supportive learning environment	• Groupthink
• Strong norms and culture	

punishment. Eventually, if the team member continues to deviate and the team does not benefit from the deviance in any way, the deviant may be isolated, ostracized, and finally expelled from the group. It is essential for managers to manage deviance well, rather than always try to eliminate it. The creative individuals are one of the primary sources of innovation and creativity in cohesive teams.

FIGURE 10.3 FOUR TYPES OF DEVIANCE

	Central Norms	
	Accept	**Reject**
Peripheral Norms — Accept	**Conformity** The individual is happy; fully conforms to all norms and is an accepted team member	**Subversive Rebellion** The individual accepts peripheral norms but not central ones; appears to conform; team may not be aware of challenge
Peripheral Norms — Reject	**Creative Individualism** The individual accepts central norms; team tolerates the member	**Open Revolution** The individual does not accept any team norms and is likely not accepted by other members; harsh treatment from team; likely to leave

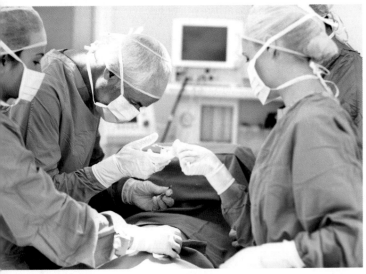

Teamwork is prevalent in the health care industry where multiple individuals are often working on the same patient. In this example, people's well-being and lives depend on extensive teamwork, highlighting the importance of team communication, cohesion, and trust.

Although groups and teams exist in most organizations and cultures, they are not equally prevalent, valued, or successful in all cultures or organizations. Organizational culture affects how groups are used and perceived. Some organizations stress individual performance almost exclusively; in others, groups play a central role. In some cases, the industry determines the organizational culture and the degree of group orientation. For instance, investment banking and brokers tend to be individualistic. They compete with one another and focus on personal rewards. At Morgan Stanley-Smith Barney, individual brokers are rewarded for the value of their clients' portfolios. In contrast with investment banking, health care requires extensive collaboration and interaction, so the organizational culture of health care organizations tends to be more group oriented.

GLOBAL SOCIETY

MANAGEMENT WITH TRADITIONAL ROOTS

On November 26, 2008, the Taj Mahal Palace Hotel in Mumbai, India, came under terrorist attack. What ensued was unimaginable bloodshed that left dozens dead and hundred of others wounded. The attack brought to light the exemplary and uniquely selfless conduct of the hotel's staff members who remained and helped many guests escape at great risk to their own safety. The Taj is part of the Tata group, the $100 billion family-owned Indian industrial giant that includes anything from information systems, steel, energy, cars, consumer goods, and hotels with operations in over 80 countries, and ownership in international brands such as Jaguar, Land Rover, and Daewoo Motors.[24] Aside from financial success, the Tata group has been recognized for its unique management and leadership style that blends ancient traditional and religious-based beliefs with modern capitalism. That management style permeates throughout the organization. Tata leadership has been labeled "Responsible, authentic and integral" with commitment to a triple bottom line of profits, people, and the planet.[25]

The key to Tata's success and unique management style are deep cultural values of integrity, hospitality,

humility, kindness, and selflessness—all ideals from the family's Parsi religious background and their rural roots.[26] As a family-owned and run business, Tata benefited from the leadership of Ratan Tata for 21 years until he handed the reins to Cyrus Mistry, also a family member, in December 2012. An executive who worked with Ratan Tata says:

The chairmanship did not change him or his manner of arriving at the most appropriate course of action. . . . Ratan Tata is not the type of boss who is given to thumping the table. He softly mandates, and those to whom the message is addressed get the point very clearly. He thinks big and encourages others to do likewise. He does not discourage those who occasionally fail to deliver."[27] Tata is reputed to be a good listener while also able to express his own view convincingly.

While many executives around the world develop arrogance and hubris and seek attention as international superstars, Ratan Tata has remained a private, self-effacing, and humble man who advocated the importance of globalization ahead of his time.[28] The company also promotes broad cultural diversity. Alan Rosling, executive director at Tata Sons, says: "The successful organization of tomorrow will diffuse geographically, and draw its competitive edge from a creative intermingling of people from all over."[29] He believes that India has a unique advantage in promoting diversity because the country itself is one of the most diverse in the world. Although cultural misunderstandings and tension are bound to happen, Rosling believes that: "Only by exposing people to colleagues internationally can these issues be tackled, and the potential for consequent value turned to real competitive edge."[30]

1. How does culture influence Tata's management?

2. To what extent would their management work elsewhere?

Cyrus Mistry (*left*) with Ratan Tata (*right*)

FIGURE 10.4 STAGES OF TEAM DEVELOPMENT

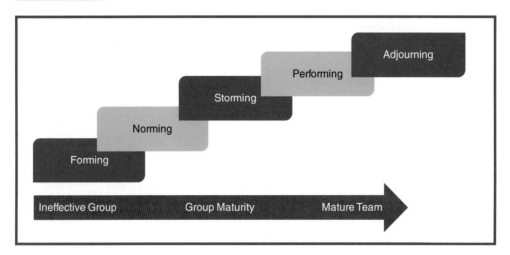

Developing Teams

Remember
the Titans

You have been part of many groups in your classes or at work that either never seem to get anything done, spend too much time socializing, or get bogged down in conflict that they cannot resolve. These events are an inherent part of the development of teams.[31] In order to reach maturity, most teams go through the steps of forming, norming, storming, and finally performing, depicted in Figure 10.4. Effective teams get to the final step; ineffective ones get stuck at earlier stages.

The Forming Stage

You might recall that on first entering a team as a potential member, you asked questions such as the following: Who are these people? What are their expectations of me? How do I fit in? Will everyone be a "team player"? How much work will this involve? If one or all of these questions surfaced in your mind, then you are not alone. Our first questions when forming a team have to do with establishing a sense of security and direction, getting oriented, and becoming comfortable with the new situation. Sometimes team members articulate these questions, and other times team members fail to articulate these feelings but still experience them as a vague sense of discomfort and disconnectedness.

In the Forming stage, groups face the following issues:[32]

Group
Development

- *Team charter.* Are overall objectives, resources, and constraints defined and clear to all team members?

- *Goals.* What are the measurable team outputs and related milestones?

- *Team norms.* What standards of behavior do team members agree to? How will they handle routine issues, such as how work is divided or how disagreements are to be resolved? Team norms also help members address unexpected or complex situations.

- *Task performance strategy.* What is the overall approach the team will take and what key actions are needed to achieve goals?

- *Shared understanding.* Do team members have a common perspective? What key assumptions may affect performance? Teams can be easily tripped up by different beliefs about the challenges the team faces, the tools or resources available, or the desired working relationships among team members, for example.

- *Team memory.* What relevant knowledge, information, and skills do team members have or can access? What gaps exist?

The Norming Stage

Once the issues of the forming stage have been resolved, team members enter a new stage of development, the norming stage. When a team begins to function as a unit and team members become comfortable in their setting, they experience pressure to conform to the emerging norms. The concern of team members shifts from overcoming uncertainty and increasing clarity during the forming stage to becoming unified and identifying roles that can be played by each member during the norming stage. Typical questions in the minds of team members during this stage include the following: What role will I be allowed to perform? Will I have the support of my team members and management? How much time and commitment should I give to this team? What are the norms and expectations of team members? During the norming stage, team members become content with team membership and begin to value the team's goals more than their personal goals. This is facilitated if the team has reached a team agreement during the forming stage. But as we saw, the reactions of different types of individuals will vary during the forming stage.

When teams are in action and engaged in activities that directly lead to goal accomplishment, they are likely to benefit from considering the following:[33]

- *Monitoring output.* How does the team track and communicate progress?

- *Monitoring systems.* What methods or resources are available for tracking people, budgets, and information—and for keeping up with stakeholders, markets, or other external factors?

- *Coordination.* How does the team prioritize and sequence key activities and events?

- *Communication.* Do team members communicate openly with each other? Does the team experience a high-quality exchange of ideas and information?

- *Monitoring team behavior.* How is feedback given to team members?

- *Maintaining boundaries.* How and when does information flow with other groups or units?

The Storming Stage

The differentiation that begins to occur during the norming stage often leads to conflict in the team. During this stage, members question the legitimacy of the team, the leader, the roles and actions of the other members, and the team's objectives. The long-term success of the team will depend on how well it manages this storming stage of development. Team members must learn to cope with conflict, differences, and disruptions. If they do not, then the team might disintegrate. Typical questions that arise during this stage include the following: Do I want to remain a team member? How can we make decisions amid disagreements? Is there someone else who would be a better leader? Can this team make the necessary changes? During this stage, the team must learn to deal with adversity, especially adversity produced by its own members. If it is to be effective, then the team's focus must not be simply on maintaining harmony at all costs. Rather, the differences that emerge must be confronted directly and openly. Team members must make efforts to solve problems and accomplish tasks so as to be effective in the long run. This is a natural phase of development in the team, and again, team members play different roles and develop different perspectives.

The Performing Stage

At the performing stage of development, the team is able to function as a highly effective and efficient unit. It has been able to work through issues of lack of trust, uncertainty, unclear expectations, lack of participation, and self-centeredness—issues characteristic of the forming stage. It has clarified a mission, team members' roles, the degree of personal commitment to the team, and the leader's direction—questions characteristic of the conforming stage. The team also has overcome tendencies toward conflict, polarization, and disharmony—questions typical of the storming stage. The questions that team members have at this stage include the following: What further improvement may be made to our processes? How can we continuously improve? What do we need to do to continue to be creative and innovative? How do we maintain this level of energy? A team during this stage of development relies less on strong directive leadership and begins to function more like a self-managing team.

Having knowledge of the stages of group development can help managers move a group to maturity and to becoming an effective team. Managers need to know that no group can become cohesive immediately. They all need time to develop norms, goals, and a functional culture. Second, conflict is an integral part of groups and teams. All groups need to face conflict and resolve it as part of their maturation. Finally, you need to keep in mind that even mature teams do not stay in the performing stage. New challenges, new members, new leadership, and difficult conflicts all can push the team to face conflicts of earlier stages. Managers can play a key role in helping teams become and stay effective.

Characteristics of Effective Teams

Building Effective Teams

Once a group of people successfully goes through the stages of development and become a performing team, they typically have the following characteristics:[34]

- They have a sense of urgency, demanding performance standards, and direction.

- Members are selected for skills and skill potential, not personality.

- Attention is paid to first meetings and actions. Initial impressions always mean a great deal.

- Rules of conduct are developed at the outset to help teams achieve their purpose and performance goals.

- Teams set and seize upon a few immediate performance-oriented tasks and goals.

- The group is challenged regularly with fresh facts and information.

- The members spend lots of time together to develop trust and form into a team.

- Team members are provided positive feedback, recognition, and reward.

Types of Teams

Now that we have established the difference between teams and groups, what do we need to know before we implement a team in our organization? First, we should recognize that there are many different types of teams that may operate even within a single organization. Indeed, in organizations that emphasize the team concept, we might find up to six different types of teams: (1) top management teams, (2) project teams, (3) cross-functional teams, (4) process-improvement teams, (5) self-directed work teams, and (6) virtual teams. Even though we make distinctions among these types of teams, all teams use similar approaches for organizing, decision making, and continual improvement. Each team distinguishes itself by fulfilling a specific purpose.

Top Management Teams

A top management team is responsible for establishing the overall mission of the organization and for selecting the management system. The top management team sets the course for the organization, but it rarely is involved in the day-to-day operations of the organization. Members of this type of team tend to be visionaries and try to keep their eyes on the "big picture." In team-based organizations, the top management team becomes a process-improvement team concentrating on the needs of the whole system as opposed to a particular process.

Project Teams

A project team typically is formed by management and given a specific mission. Membership in the team is based on individual expertise and experience. A project team functions only as long as is needed to solve the assigned problem and is discontinued once the problem is resolved. Project teams often must work within a time frame with a primary goal to advise managers of alternatives rather than to implement any decisions. They are some of the most common teams used in organizations.

Process-Improvement Teams

A process-improvement team is a small group of individuals who interact with each other for the purpose of improving those work processes in which they engage. In contrast to the other types of teams we have already discussed, these teams are responsible for implementation of decisions, not only providing recommendations. For example, a process-improvement team might explore the way in which checks sent to a company are processed and deposited. By speeding up that process, the team might significantly increase the interest that the company earns on those funds. Table 10.3 presents the key issues for process teams.

Cross-Functional Teams

A cross-functional team is similar to a project team but serves the purpose of breaking down the barriers or "silos" that exist in many organizations. The cross-functional team may bring together representatives from several divisions to improve a specific process such as how vacations are assigned, or have a more complex task such as revamping job classifications and salary structures for a whole organization. As is the case with project teams, cross-functional teams make recommendations to management and do not typically implement decisions.

What Do You Think?

▶ Some unions are leery of the use of teams based on the fact that team members take on many managerial functions without an increase in compensation. What do you think? Should there be additional compensation for the work of teams? Why or why not?

Top management team: responsible for establishing the overall mission of the organization and for selecting the management system

Project team: formed by management based on expertise of its members

Process-improvement team: individuals who interact with each other for the purpose of improving work processes in which they engage

Cross-functional team: similar to a project team but serves the purpose of breaking down barriers by bringing together members from different divisions to work on a common goal

TABLE 10.3 ISSUES FOR PROCESS-IMPROVEMENT TEAMS

Issue	Description
Organize the team around organizational processes	The team must be formed around the organizational processes, keeping in mind that many of these processes will include members from several programs.
Control the process, not the team	Managers must focus on helping the team define its processes. Once the process is clearly defined, it should be the responsibility of the team to control the process.
Maintain process partnerships	The team must accept the responsibility to develop and maintain partnerships with those affected by the process.
Continually improve the process	The focus of each team meeting should be to improve the process that the team has been charged with examining.
Require team participation	All team members must participate actively to achieve quality outcomes that include perspectives from all represented groups.
Base decisions on data	The team must be data-driven and collect and analyze data to improve the process.
Empower teams	Managers must provide the team with authority to make the changes necessary to improve the process.
Develop and train team members	Each employee should be trained and educated for the betterment of the organization.

Source: Koehler, J. W., & Pankowski, J. M. (1996). *Teams in government: A handbook for team-based organizations.* Delray Beach, FL: St. Lucie.

Self-Directed Teams

Self-directed teams: self-managed teams that decide themselves how and when work is going to be done

Organizations are increasingly using self-managed or **self-directed teams**. In fact, any of the previously mentioned teams may function as a self-directed team. Within the boundaries of its obligations to the organization, including agreed-on deadlines, productivity goals, and quality standards, the self-directed team itself decides how and when work is going to be done. If the team has to wait for supervisory direction of its tasks, then it is not a self-directed team. There are several misconceptions about self-directed teams.[35] They are presented in Table 10.4.

TABLE 10.4 MISCONCEPTIONS ABOUT SELF-DIRECTED TEAMS

Misconception	Reality
Self-directed teams do not need leaders	There is a definite need for leaders to serve the function of coaches or facilitators so as to transfer what traditionally has been left to management to these team members.
Leaders lose power in the transition to teams	Power is not a zero-sum game; rather, it is an expandable and flexible resource.
Newly formed teams are automatically self-directing	Team development takes considerable time and effort. Describing new teams as self-directed might establish unrealistic expectations.
All employees welcome the opportunity to be empowered	Not everyone will welcome the empowering effect of self-directed teams. With empowerment comes responsibility, and some will not want more responsibility than they already have.

THE CHILEAN MINE DISASTER

On August 5, 2010, 33 Chilean miners drilling for copper and gold almost a half mile beneath the surface were trapped by a massive cave-in. Within hours of the accident, the miners found one another, all alive and unharmed, and began to organize for what was sure to be a long stay underground, but also for a possible rescue attempt.

For the next 17 days, the miners were cut off completely from the outside world, living in what they called their "refuge," and carefully monitoring food, water, and sanitation. And though the miners rarely talked about those first days after they were finally removed from the cavern, there were serious meltdowns among some of the younger members and strong hints of friction—as you might imagine. Then a drill operator on the surface felt some vibrations, a drill came back up with red paint, and another with a note, saying, "We are fine in the refuge, the 33."

With that, hope of rescue was ignited beneath the ground while the rescue effort above became even more focused. The country's president, for example, promised to use all available resources to extract the miners. While the intensity of the rescue effort above ground was difficult and stressful, the courage and skill of the miners underground in managing their situation became legendary to people around the world.

Health officials were initially concerned about the emotional state of several of the miners, but the miners developed their own team or "society" including roles to care for their fellow captives. Some were assigned to make a space for exercise, others were assigned to make a plan for allocating resources.

The shift leader, Luis Urzua, 54, became the leader of the group, acting through democratic processes on major decisions, but also bringing order to the group through his calm and unflustered manner. Another miner commented, "We had a boss who every day said we must stay strong." It was he who also insisted that everyone wait to eat until all had been served through the tiny shaft that first connected the miners with the surface.

Another veteran of the mines, 65-year old Mario Gomez, became the spiritual leader of the group, urging prayers and helping to counsel members of the group who were most susceptible to distress. (In this, he often communicated with a group of psychologists on the surface.)

Finally, Yonny Barrios, 50, who took a 6-month nursing course many years ago, became the group's medical "doctor," administering shots and vaccinations, as well as dispensing medicines sent from the surface.

After 69 days in the mine, a record, the group emerged one by one through a narrow tube that had been constructed. As you can imagine, the stress of the event took a toll, with many of the miners suffering post-traumatic stress disorder and others showing signs of alcoholism. But, by staying together, and building a team with a culture of confidence and resilience and resolve, they emerged alive, something few thought would ever happen.

1. What were the elements of teamwork that proved so important in this situation?

2. How were various roles filled?

3. Would you say that effective teamwork saved their lives?

Several conditions are crucial to allowing self-directed teams to be effective:[36]

1. Management wants to give employees greater emotional ownership for the tasks they perform

2. Management is willing to relinquish control and to trust the team to make decisions

3. The team must have the resources it needs to meet expectations

4. The team members are trained to function without direct supervision

5. Members are highly motivated to take control of their work

Team of Rivals

6. Team members respect and trust each other

7. Team members are equally committed to the success of the team and to the success of the larger organization

Virtual Teams

Making Virtual Teams Work

Virtual teams are a recent phenomenon aiming to deal with the issue of communicating with team members who might be a distance away. Any of the teams we discussed above can be virtual. Alternative worksites, long-distance work, telecommuting, and regional or branch offices are now mainstream arrangements. The virtual team makes use of ever-increasing information technology, including videoconferencing, satellite television, and the Internet. Four key factors make these teams unique:[37]

1. *Electronic dependence.* Technology alone does not make a virtual team. It is the degree of reliance on electronic communication that increases virtuality. Technology continues to improve with the availability of chat rooms, private websites, virtual team buildings, and video teleconferences.

2. *Geographic dispersion.* Members must not take for granted that other members share their contextual knowledge, culture, and common values. Effective virtual teams need to share more information about context and in much greater detail than they would if working in the same location.[38]

3. *Cultural diversity.* In highly virtual teams, it is often necessary to create a hybrid culture, structure, and set of operating policies that represent a compromise among the various alternatives preferred by different team members.

4. *Dynamic structure.* Due to the nature of the teams, the team structure is dynamic and evolving.

Virtual teams: a mature group that functions through the use of information technology including videoconferencing, satellite television, and the Internet

Studies show that over time the outputs of virtual teams lag behind those that meet face-to-face. Pure virtual teams develop lower levels of participative decision making and higher levels of conflict than their face-to-face counterparts. While virtual teams evolve better processes over time, teams reported lower level of participation, lower satisfaction, and worse cost performance. These findings suggest that mixed-media, or teams that include both face-to-face meeting and computer-mediated teams, report similar participative decision making, performance, and satisfaction to pure face-to-face team meetings. To address these concerns, (1) teams set the stage for future processes and outputs at their first session; (2) processes evolve over time, so a shorter time frame results from participants knowing each other; and (3) a face-to-face meeting before a computer-mediated session can lead to better processes and outputs over time (Figure 10.5).[39]

Virtual teams require skills that are not simply different from those needed for running colocated teams; they are often the exact opposite.[40] In order to ensure a virtual team's success, you must be aware of the following:

Many teams in today's organizations are connected virtually.

1. Virtual teams need a manager who provides clearly defined direction and removes all ambiguity from the process.

2. Teams arrive at decisions differently in different countries; understanding those differences improves effectiveness. In the United States, managers are trained to solicit input from a team, choose a direction quickly, and make adjustments as the project moves forward. It works, but then so do other methods. In Sweden teams learn to make decisions through lengthy consensus building, which can span many meetings but eventually leads to strong buy-in and rapid implementation.

3. Trust in virtual teams is measured almost exclusively in terms of reliability.

4. Managers of global virtual teams who sit rigidly at their desks, glued to Skype or videoconference screens, tend to lose their interpersonal or persuasive edge. Walking around or simply moving their arms is just one of many simple but effective communication tricks that managers can use to improve the sound of their message.

FIGURE 10.5 VIRTUAL TEAMS

1	Teams set the stage for future processes and outputs at their first session
2	Processes evolve over time, so a shorter time frame results from participants knowing each other
3	Beginning with a face-to-face meeting before a computer-mediated session can lead to better processes and outputs over time.

Source: Kennedy, D., Vozdolska, R., & McComb, S. (2010). Team Decision Making in Computer-Supported Cooperative Work: How Initial Computer-Mediated or Face-to-Face Meetings Set the Stage for Later Outcomes. *Decision Sciences Journal*, *41*(4), 933–954.

Helping Teams Become Effective

While most organizations use groups and teams to some extent, not all use a full team structure. The use of team-based structures can be seen as a continuum (see Figure 10.6). On the one end are organizations with traditional structures and departments that use groups to perform various tasks under centralized management control. On the other end are organizations that are fully based on teams that have considerable autonomy and control. Implementing a team concept in any organization requires careful advance planning and starting with a clear commitment to the team concept on the part of senior management. In considering the implementation of work teams, managers should consider the long-term needs and goals that they wish to achieve through the use of teams and carefully determine the role and importance of the teams within the larger organization. Typically, organizations that are successful in implementing teams have top management and employees who are ready for active participation and empowerment. They depend on genuine commitment to participation, values based on fairness and equity, training directed at teams, and time and opportunity to experiment.

How can a manager be sure that implementing a team concept will be effective? Successfully implementing a team requires changes to how the organization runs. Among the issues to consider are the following:

Team Building Retreat

FIGURE 10.6 FROM TRADITIONAL HIERARCHIES TO TEAM-BASED ORGANIZATIONS

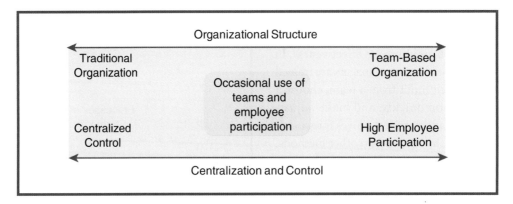

Organizational Structure

Traditional Organization

Team-Based Organization

Occasional use of teams and employee participation

Centralized Control

High Employee Participation

Centralization and Control

Clear Goals

Effective teams are committed to common goals. Unless the team has clear, well-developed goals accepted by all members, goal commitment and achievement are not possible. Goals must be specific, measurable, achievable, and reasonable, and also have a time frame. These elements are essential to teams. Without a clear sense of direction, team members flounder. Their efforts do not lead to clear performance and they are bound to lose their motivation. The importance of clear goals cannot be over emphasized. The managers who create the teams must take sufficient time to explain the reasons the team was created and clarify their vision. In some cases, managers set the team goals, allowing the team input and participation. In the case of self-directed teams, organizational leaders provide general vision and direction; the team then sets its goals.

For example, Whole Foods, the natural foods grocery chain, is a team-based organization. While the founder and CEO, John Mackey, has a strong vision for the company, each department and team sets its own goals based on the company's philosophy and mission, which are clearly described in its "Declaration of Interdependence."[41]

Building Cohesion and Managing Diversity

Helping a group become mature and cohesive is the first step toward team success. That means that managers must select members with care and provide them with opportunities for interaction and, in some cases, competition with outside groups, all elements of building cohesion that we reviewed earlier in this chapter. Groups also need time to develop their norms and become teams. Once a group reaches maturity, managers need additional steps to develop high-performing teams.

Another factor that managers and team members must pay attention to is the composition of the team. Membership in effective teams is based on expertise in various areas that are necessary for task accomplishment. Teams that face diverse and complex tasks can be more effective if they maintain a flexible, fluid membership, a factor that is particularly important in U.S. organizations and other heterogeneous cultures. Without conscious effort and active management, teams often drive out individuals who are different from other team members.[42]

Group Processes in Diverse Teams

Today, U.S. and Western businesses understand that they must preserve an individual focus yet still encourage collaboration and cooperation. To be successful, U.S. teams need to value individual differences and capitalize on the benefits of diverse members who have different values, goals, and skills. Steps to handle diversity in teams in U.S. and other individualist cultures include:

- *Preserve and reward individual contributions.* This means combining team and individual rewards.

- *Encourage and manage positive and constructive conflict.* Rather than aiming for harmony and quick consensus, diverse teams should focus on capitalizing on conflict that results from diversity. Members should then be trained to manage conflict well.

- *Focus on short-term as well as long-term results.* Given the U.S. short-term and proactive orientations, teams must focus both on short-term and long-term goals to avoid losing member interest and motivation.

Developing Trust

Teams must commit to a common goal, develop mutual accountability, and learn to collaborate. These actions cannot occur without trust. Trust is defined as each team member's faith in the others' intentions and behaviors. Having gone through the various stages of development together, team members should, if the challenges are well managed, have developed some trust in one another. In addition, trust can be built through the elements presented in Figure 10.7. Integrity is the starting point of developing trust in any interpersonal relationship. Additionally, individual members must commit to respect and support one another and to demonstrate competence and hard work. Managers can further build trust through open communication, rewarding cooperation rather than competition, and practicing fairness and equity. All of these are hallmarks of good leadership and management and are particularly important in building a strong team.

Leadership and Ethics

Team Leadership

Team leaders, whether appointed by the organization or chosen by the team members, must be aware of their role as facilitators and avoid over-controlling and over-directing their teams.[43] As facilitators, their role is to help define goals, provide assistance and support, and remove internal and organizational obstacles so the team members can perform their tasks. Additionally, as opposed to traditional models of management in which a manager's role is primarily to supervise others, team leaders must continue to contribute as team members.

FIGURE 10.7 BUILDING TRUST

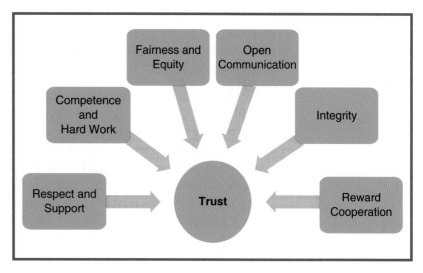

Self-leadership is particularly appropriate for the diffused leadership in effective teams.[44] Self-leadership suggests that instead of leaders who rely on fear (the "strong man"), focus on narrow exchange relationships (the "transactor"), or inspire commitment while discouraging thinking (the "visionary hero"), leaders and followers must focus on leading themselves. As a result, team members must be taught and encouraged to make their own decisions and to accept responsibility to the point where they no longer need leaders. Self-leadership within teams means that all team members set goals and observe, evaluate, critique, reinforce, and reward one another and themselves. In such an environment, the need for one leader is reduced; team members set goals and decide how to achieve them. Increased use of technology, the information revolution, and the preponderance of knowledge workers all support the need for self-leadership, which involves a focus on behaviors, providing natural rewards, and engaging in constructive thought patterns.[45] Specifically, self-leaders:

- *Develop positive and motivating thought patterns.* Individuals and teams seek and develop environments that provide positive cues and a supportive and motivating environment.

- *Set personal goals.* Individuals and teams set their own performance goals and performance expectations.

- *Observe their behavior and self-evaluate.* Team members observe their own and other team members' behaviors and provide feedback and critique and evaluate their own and one another's performance.

- *Self-reinforce.* Team members provide rewards and support to one another.

In addition, the success of a team greatly depends on its external leader. External leaders who struggle with their role usually exert too much control, undermining the ability of the team to do its work.[46] If the leader does not sincerely believe in the team's ability to address its task, such a message will get communicated to the team members either directly or through subtle actions and messages.

Training

One of the factors that can contribute to the effectiveness of teams is proper training. In addition to providing individual team members technical training to develop their expertise, team members need specific team skills related to managing relationships and team processes. The focus is to help members manage interpersonal relationships better so that they can create a trusting and collaborative climate in which commitment to a common goal is possible.

Many organizations have a series of courses for their team members. Successful training, particularly for more self-directed teams, depends on allowing team members to select the type of training they need. This ability to choose is part of enabling the team to make its own decisions and allows team members to focus on their needs. For example, one team may need more help in basic communication, listening, and providing feedback; another may need training in time management and running meetings. For example, the Art Petty Group, a leadership development consulting firm, recommends various steps to having effective meetings including making sure a meeting is needed, preparation, and using creativity tools.[47]

Managing Team Conflict

The type of conflict teams encounter is partly determined by their stage of development. Typically, in the very early stages conflict is low and builds up as roles and norms develop. One study suggests that most high-performing teams have a low level of task conflict at the beginning and end of the project, with a moderate level of conflict in the middle.[48] One could assume that there is usually a high degree of agreement on the group goal at the outset, a healthy disagreement over the pros and cons of alternatives for achieving the goal in the middle phase, and a high degree of agreement on the team's output and its implementation at the conclusion of the project.[49] In an effective team, the behavior of team members is interdependent and personal goals are subservient to the accomplishment of the team goals.

A team can only be effective if all members are engaged and participating fully. One disengaged or distracted member can be the source of much conflict.

The creativity and performance of teams depends on some level of healthy conflict. Managers need to know how to create teams that feel psychologically safe enough for conflicting opinions to be aired and the benefits of diversity exploited. Teams should encourage creative individualism. Even the most effective teams will feel conflict-prone at times. And there are good reasons for this. Teams composed of high-performing individuals are naturally subject to contradictory tensions, like cooperation and rivalry, trust and vigilance. These tensions should not be managed away—they are productive and can help teams perform better.[50] At any stage in the development of teams, conflict may occur, and the causes of the conflict must be known before it can be resolved. The sources of team conflict might include the following:[51]

Is Conflict Good?

- *Intrapersonal, or conflict from within oneself.* In this case, the team member's internal conflicts often influence his or her working relationships with other team members. For example, consider the young employee who does not feel that he is in the right profession and participates without interest in the team assignments.

- *Interpersonal, or conflicts that occur between two or more people on the team.* For example, consider a team of six where five of the six team members work hard to collect data for their assigned project by conducting interviews, yet one fails to do any of the interviews assigned, reducing the sample size considerably.

- *Structural, or conflicts that are innate to the organizational structure or the work.* For example, consider a team at a school that is told that they are not to address curriculum issues because those can be handled only at the district level.

- *Values/beliefs, or differences attached to deep-seated emotions.* Consider a team member who values collectivism and is explicit about this being a priority in his decision-making style. However, this person is in a team with members who value individualism and do not believe that the good of the whole should be prioritized over the good of the individual.

HOW WELL DOES YOUR TEAM DEAL WITH CONFLICT?

1. Have two observers witness the team in action as members debate important agenda items or strategies. Write detailed notes on who said what, to whom, what the reaction was, and so forth. Once you have enough information, discuss between the two of you, in front of the group, what you observed. Mention contributions, strengths, and weaknesses of team members, including the leader. Keep comments as factual as possible, quoting team members and reporting specific reactions from the group.

2. Have the team members identify the potential sources for the conflict.

3. What are potential solutions?

4. Do the observers agree or disagree with the potential sources and solutions identified by the team members? Why or why not?

- *Personality differences in style and behavior.* For example, consider the team member who always completes assignments on a timely basis and has a colleague on the team who treats deadlines as suggestions and on time is when she gets around to it.

Resolving Team Conflict

- *Perceptions or differences in view or perspective of the situation or issue.* Consider the team that attributes a lack of time for the project as the reason for delay when the leader views the lack of progress as a lack of dedication on the part of the team members.

- *Work methods or disagreements about solving problems.* For example, consider the team member who believes the best solution to the problem will require a systematic evaluation, yet another team member believes that an intuitive solution will suffice.

Solutions to the conflict include "creative collaboration, giving in, controlling, workable compromise, and avoiding."[52] All are valuable and can be highly effective depending on the situation.

To become more comfortable with team conflict:

- Be careful not to confuse what things *feel* like with what they really *are* like. What feels dysfunctional may, for all practical purposes, be perfectly effective.

- Be creative in engaging team members.

Remind your team that these differences of opinion are both inevitable and useful.

Reward Structure

As managers introduce the team concept in the workplace, they must consider adjusting the reward structure. Obviously, reward systems that are based only on individual performance will work against the goals of the team. For this reason, the traditional style of performance evaluations, which focuses on the individual, is not well suited to the evaluation of a team. Although it is difficult to implement, finding a way of focusing on the team's performance is important. One way of doing this is to involve the team itself in establishing the performance appraisal system that eventually will be used to evaluate its work. Involving the team in the performance appraisal not only can lead to effective ways of measuring team performance but also models the value of teamwork in the organization.

EMOTIONAL INTELLIGENCE IN TEAMS

Consider each of the statements below to determine your own self-awareness as a team member, management of your own emotions, awareness of others, and management of their emotions.

Awareness of Own Emotions

1. I can explain the emotions I feel to team members.
2. I can discuss the emotions I feel with other team members.
3. If I feel down, I can tell team members what will make me feel better.
4. I can talk to other members of the team about the emotions I experience.

Management of Own Emotions

1. I respect the opinion of team members even if I think they are wrong.
2. When frustrated with fellow team members, I can overcome my frustration.
3. When deciding on a dispute, I try to see all sides of a disagreement before I come to a conclusion.
4. I give a fair hearing to fellow members' ideas.

Awareness of Others' Emotions

1. I can read fellow team members "true" feelings, even if they try to hide them.
2. I am able to describe accurately the way others in the team are feeling.
3. When I talk to team members, I can gauge their true feelings from their body language.
4. I can tell when team members don't mean what they say.

Management of Others' Emotions

1. My enthusiasm can be contagious for members of a team.
2. I am able to cheer up team members when they are feeling down.
3. I can get fellow team members to share my keenness for a project.
4. I can provide the "spark" to get a fellow team member enthusiastic.

Source: From Jordan, P. J., & Lawrence, S. A. (2009). Emotional intelligence in teams: Development and initial validation of short version of the Workgroup Emotional Intelligence Profile (WEIP-S). *Journal of Management and Organization, 5,* 452–469.

Diane Scott, Executive Vice President, Western Union Ventures, states:

> Recognizing individual contributions in a team environment is essential in this day and age. When you think about it, we are all very human. And what people really want is to be recognized—not just for a project, but the role they played in a project, whether it is big or small. And one of the best ways to do that, the thing I found to be helpful, is to help people be recognized by others. . . . Those are big opportunities to help people feel really motivated and part of the team.[53]

Organizational Structure

When managers use process teams to improve customer service or put together a project team to recommend purchase of a database, they change the way people organize to work. The result is some degree of change to their organization's structure. Teams are one way to organize the human resources of an organization. A team-based structure focuses on groups of people rather than on individuals. Various teams can work parallel to traditional structures of departments and divisions. However, implementing a team-based organization involves a wholesale change in the structure of an organization. The hierarchy, the span of control, how people are grouped, allocation of responsibilities, and finally how activities are coordinated and integrated are significantly different in a traditional compared to a team-based organization (you will learn more about structure in Chapter 14).

The structure of a true team-based organization includes few, if any, vertical lines and boxes with one person's name in them. W. L. Gore and Associates, a company well known for its outdoor equipment, boasts of not having a traditional chart, a chain of command, or predetermined communication channels.[54] There are no managers and employees; everyone is called an associate. Their CEO, yes, they do have one, Terri Kelly, says: "We don't want to operate in a hierarchy, where decisions have to make their way up to the top and then back down. We're a lattice or a network, not a hierarchy, and associates can go directly to anyone in the organization to get what they need to be successful."[55] She suggests that their leaders draw their power and authority from being followers and experts respected by their coworkers.

Building an Ethical and Collaborative Culture

Building a
Teamwork Culture

Teams cannot be effective unless the organizational culture accepts their value. The organization must recognize or, better yet, embrace the importance of teams. Organizations and their leaders must create an ethical culture of trust and teamwork or what some call a collaborative community.[56] In these communities, people are encouraged to continually apply their unique talents to group projects, "and to become motivated by a collective mission, not just personal gain or the intrinsic pleasures of autonomous creativity."[57] Such communities are used in organizations such as IBM, NASA, Citibank, and Kaiser Permanente. The characteristics of these communities or cultures are:[58]

1. *They define and build a shared purpose through trust and organizational cohesion.* For example, when managers in one organization were asked why they worked on a given project, "They did not answer because that's my job or that's where the money is. They talked instead about how the project would advance the shared purpose."[59]

2. *They cultivate an ethic of contribution.* This means going beyond one's formal responsibilities to solve broader problems, not just apply greater effort or do a good job. An analogy that may be considered is that of street ball versus professional football. In playing street football, you play for yourself, for the love of the game, rather than the team. In professional football, you're part of a team that practices and plays together. You are not playing just for yourself or even the team, as there are others involved—managers, agents, advertisers, lawyers.

3. *They develop scalable processes for coordinating people's efforts.* Interdependent process management needs to be explicit, flexible, and interactive. It has the potential to intrude on employees' autonomy and requires people to adapt to others' needs.

For example, employees at Johnson & Johnson found that the key was to review and update their process document as they had conversations.

4. *They create an infrastructure that values and rewards collaboration.* "If work is organized in teams and workers increasingly serve on more than one team, the need for a new type of authority structure arises—one that involves overlapping spheres of influence. We call this participative centralization."[60]

Developing an inclusive, collaborative, ethical community is a long-term investment. Yet it provides the opportunity to be innovative and efficient, agile and scalable, all of which are necessary in a service, knowledge-based economy. For today's economy, organizations need employees who are ethical and equipped to adapt—those who are collaborative, communicative, creative, and flexible.

Why eBay Failed
in China

▶ Summary and Applications for Managers

In this chapter, we have learned that teams often are used in organizations to achieve important assignments. The performance of a team can be greater than what an individual can accomplish. In addition, the team provides a supportive environment for learning and may help weak performers and the organization address shortcomings. Individuals bring different personalities to the group, and those personality differences will affect their concerns during different stages of team development, and conflicts may occur at any of the stages. When they work at their best, teams can add significantly to the quality and productivity of the organization. And, of course, the team experience can create positive bonds among individuals.

We also have seen that a successful team needs the commitment of the organization as reflected in a culture that allows for interdependence, allows for group decision making, and rewards teamwork. Overall, this chapter should help you in determining a team's stage of development, in becoming familiar with the attributes of high-performing teams and incorporating these into your own team, in understanding the different roles that team members play during each stage of team development, and in helping your team to progress through the different stages of development by managing challenges and issues that predominate at particular stages. As a review, it might be useful to return to the exercise that you completed at the beginning of the chapter. You might then try to design an effective and specific action plan for use by the individual members of your team to improve the team's overall performance. Here are some things you can do to help groups and teams get started on the right path.

1. *Be purposeful about using groups and teams.* Teams are not a cure-all, but they have the potential to greatly increase effectiveness if appropriately implemented. Use them well and only when needed.

2. *Provide your groups and teams with clear goals.* While effective and mature teams may develop their own goals, be clear about why the members have been brought together. A clear mission and goals helps focus the members and avoids wasting time.

3. *Clearly define roles in groups and teams.* Start by having formally designated roles so that each team member knows what is expected. When roles are shared, be clear about how the shared roles are assigned and used. Use each member's talents and involve everyone in the team's activities so that no one feels under-used, left out, or taken advantage of.

4. *Set high performance expectations, but don't expect miracles.* Groups and teams have the potential to deliver great performance, but they need time and resources to become effective.

5. *Trust your teams.* The leader has to be sincere in his or her expectations and belief in the team's ability to accomplish its tasks. If you do not trust the teams to do the job, don't assign them the task. Once you do, trust them; don't hover.

6. *Monitor your teams.* Even self-directed teams need to stay connected to the rest of the organization. Trust does not mean complete laissez-faire. Having a group or any kind of team, and empowering its members, also requires that you stay in touch, get progress reports, and communicate with them actively.

7. *Use and manage constructive conflict.* Help your teams manage conflict well to ensure both continued cohesion and creativity. Balancing both is possible, but it may require your facilitation and specialized training to achieve the right balance.

8. *Revisit norms occasionally.* An effective team has strong norms, but it also needs to have some flexibility about how to do things. Discuss which norms are central and important and which norms can be changed.

9. *Encourage the right type of deviance.* Not all disagreements are bad. Team members should be encouraged to find a balance between conforming and being creative. As the leader, you can set the right tone and encourage constructive dissent.

10. *Be mindful of culture—at all levels.* Team members come in with their own culture that may or may not make it easy to work in a group. The organization also has a culture that either encourages or discourages teams. Being aware of these cultures can help you prevent problems and take the right type of action.

▶ Key Terms

Central norms 308

Cohesion 308

Conformity 308

Cross-functional
team 315

Deviants 309

Groups 302

Heterogeneous
groups 306

Homogeneous
groups 306

Norms 307

Peripheral norms 308

Process-improvement
team 315

Project team 315

Roles 306

Self-directed teams 316

Social facilitation 305

Social loafing 305

Teams 302

Top management
team 315

Virtual teams 318

▶ Exercise 10.1 Assessing Team Development

Use the following exercise, adapted from Amachi and Wade,[61] to get to know your team better and to assess your team's development.

Assess the Team

- How effective is the current team?

Interview Team Members

- What is the perception that members have of the team?

- Gather feedback from the team's designated leaders. Do their views differ from those of the team members?

- Interview any other key members of the organization. For example, who organized the team originally? Who is getting feedback on the team's work? How are the team's recommendations being used in the organization?

Help the Team Define Its Mission, Values, and Roles

- How do members envision the "ideal team"?

- Compare the current team to the "ideal team."

- Have ground rules been established for the team?

- Are these ground rules written?

- Are the rules readily available?

- Have issues been prioritized?

- Has the team been empowered to prioritize the issues?

- Has the priority order been provided by someone else?

- Have roles been defined and assigned?

- How are members held accountable for serving in the assigned roles?

Communication and Conflict Management

- Is "how things are said" consistent with "what is said"?

- Is what is spoken or communicated in writing consistent with the actions of the team?

- Are conflict management processes implemented in the event of conflict among members?

Analysis and Feedback

After completing this chapter, design an effective and specific action plan for use by individual team members to improve overall team performance.

▶ Exercise 10.2 Creating Team Agreements

If you do not currently have a "team agreement," then you might want to create one. Team agreements are formulated around the issues of values, norms, and team processes. These should be developed early in the process of team development. For example, an Internal Revenue Service virtual team agreed on the following values, norms, and processes for operating as a team.[62] Look at each set and then ask which values, norms, and processes you would like to see as part of your team's agreement.

Values

- Integrity

- Trust/respect

- Freedom/autonomy

- Challenging/stimulating work

- Professional/personal balance

- Personal/team excellence

- Experiment/risk taking

What values would you include in your team agreement?

Norms

- Work as partners together

- Own our perspectives

- Take personal responsibility

- Provide feedback on task/behavior

- Practice respectful confrontation

- Expect contributions by everyone

- Have fun

What norms would you include in your team agreement?

Process approach

- Collaborative teamwork

- Building on past successes

- Participative decision making

- Mutual agreement and discussion

- What am I supposed to do?

- Self/peer assessment

- Learning organization—on the leading edge

What process approach would you include in your team agreement?

▶ Exercise 10.3 A Team-Building Exercise

The most successful team-building activities will be explicitly linked back to participants' jobs, and they'll understand how skills developed can translate into workplace habits. To make that happen, each teambuilding experience must be strategically designed with specific goals in mind. See more at: http://www.entrepreneur.com/article/201322#sthash.7PovSFWX.dpuf. The following exercise, with students in mind, is used to improve the relationships among team members.[63]

Divide into teams of seven or eight who eventually will be asked to make recommendations to the dean of your college about improving student services. In your teams:

1. Come up with a team name and perhaps even a song or logo that represents you as a team.

2. Take time to understand the jobs of all team members. The team also might wish to discuss life outside of the workplace. You may share what you do for entertainment, information about your families, and so on with the goal of getting to know each other better and helping all members to feel part of the team.

3. For the assignment, come up with three major recommendations to improve the services offered to the students in your college. Each team member should take a few minutes and list what he or she would do. Then each member should read his or her top three recommendations to the group. One team member should list all the recommendations on an easel pad or whiteboard. The team's charge is to develop one list with consensus reached on the recommendations.

▶ Case 10.1 Relocating a Manufacturing Plant

The manager of a manufacturing plant in a northeastern state has decided that the plant is grossly inadequate and a dangerous firetrap. After some struggle, the president of the company has appropriated funds for a new manufacturing plant. The department wishes to build the plant in what is now a state forest and the governor and legislature have agreed to the sale. Such a location would provide attractive surroundings, isolation from cities, and low cost of land. Besides, the property is owned by the state, but has been left unattended for years.

Recently, conservation groups have issued vehement protests and threatened court action to block the move. They also have started a public campaign to force the governor and the state legislature to reverse the decision. The community where the present manufacturing plant is located has organized a committee to keep it in their community as they fear loss of revenue to nearby businesses if the plant is moved.

The plant manager wants to form a team to develop a marketing campaign strategy. She has asked for your recommendations on what type of team to use and how to organize it.

Respond to the following questions:

1. What factors would determine what type of team is appropriate to look into the situation?

2. What type of team would you recommend?

3. Who would the members be? What benefits may be gained from including women?

4. Who would lead the group?

5. What information would the team members need?

▶ Case 10.2 A Team Exercise: Branch Closure

Scenario: The bank headquarter's vice president of human resources has informed the branch managers that one of the six branches will need to close by the end of the year. The branch managers have been instructed that human resources will establish self-directed, cross-functional, virtual teams to study and identify the branch most fitting for closure. The vice president will ask the teams to make formal presentations of their findings.

Instructions: This can be structured as an in-class or virtual multiple team assignment. Experts should be identified to assess team performance.

Team members: Drawing on discussion and reading materials on communication, decision making, interpersonal skills, and teams: (1) Establish an agenda for the meeting, (2) select a team leader, (3) discuss team agreement, (4) establish a goal for the team, (5) determine information that you will

need in order to make the decision, and (6) prepare your findings to be presented to the vice president of human resources.

Experts: Please use the form for "Assessing Team Performance" in this chapter to evaluate the performance and be ready to assist the team as needed.

Respond to the following questions:

1. What were the issues and solutions proposed by each team?

2. Which team criteria for closure is more likely to be pursued and why?

3. Did the groups function as teams?

4. Were members encouraged to participate?

5. What was the role of the team leader? How was he or she selected?

▶ Endnotes

1. Paumgarten, N. (2010, January 4). The food fighter. *The New Yorker*, January 4. Retrieved from http://www.newyorker.com/reporting/2010/01/04/100104fa_fact_paumgarten on July 13, 2013.

2. Fishman, C. (2004). The anarchist's cookbook. *Fast Company*, July, 70–78.

3. Whole Foods declaration of interdependence. (2013). Retrieved from http://www.wholefoodsmarket.com/mission-values/core-values/declaration-interdependence on July 13, 2013.

4. Whole Foods, 2013.

5. Katzenbach, J. R., & Smith, D. K. (1993). *The wisdom of teams*. New York, NY: Harper Business; and Kinlaw, D. C. (1998). *Superior teams*. Brookfield, VT: Gower.

6. Cited in Koehler, J. W., & Pankowski, J. M. (1996). *Teams in government: A handbook for team-based organizations*. Delray Beach, FL: St. Lucie, p. 17.

7. Lawler, E. E., III, Mohrman, S. A., & Ledford, G. E. (1995). *Creating high performance organizations: Practices and results of employee involvement and total quality management in Fortune 1000 companies*. San Francisco, CA: Jossey-Bass.

8. Earley, P. C. (1993). East meets West meets Mideast: Further explorations of collectivistic and individualistic work groups. *Academy of Management Journal, 36*, 319–348; Earley, P. C. (1994). Self or group? Cultural effects of training on self-efficacy and performance. *Administrative Science Quarterly, 39*, 89–117; and Lawson, R. B., & Ventriss, C. L. (1992). Organizational change: The role of organizational culture and organizational learning. *Psychological Record, 42*(2), 205–220.

9. Larson, C. E., & LaFasto, F. M. (1989). *Teamwork*. Newbury Park, CA: Sage.

10. Maier, N. R. (1967). Assets and liabilities of group problem solving: The need for an integrative function. *Psychological Review, 74*, 239–249.

11. Parker, G. M. (1990). Listen to the interview with **Anita Woolley**. Retrieved from http://hbr.org/2011/06/defend-your-research-what-makes-a-team-smarter-more-women/ar/1.

12. Kolditz, T. (2012). How to turn your worst employee into a top asset. *Inc.*, March 26. Retrieved from http://www.inc.com/tom-kolditz/why-your-worst-performer-is-a-gift.html on April 2, 2013.

13. Cody, J., & Feitz, D. (2012). Weakest links show greatest gain in relay races. *MSU Today*, July 24. Retrieved from http://msutoday.msu.edu/news/2012/-2/ on April 2, 2013.

14. Watch social loafing defined on YouTube: Retrieved from http://www.youtube.com/watch?feature=player_detailpage&v=Chj2F3Ao_gw on June 11, 2013.

15. Karau, S. J., & Williams, K. D. (1993). Social loafing: A meta-analytic review and theoretical integration. *Journal of Personality and Social Psychology, 65*, 681–706.

16. For classic studies of groups see Cartright, D., & Zander, A. (1953). *Group dynamics: Research and theory*. Evanston, IL: Row, Peterson.

17. Jackson, S. E., Brett, J. F., Sessa, V. I., Cooper, D. M., Julin, J. A., & Peryonin, K. (1991). Some differences make a difference: Individual dissimilarity and group heterogeneity as correlates of recruitment, promotion, and turnover. *Journal of Applied Psychology, 76*, 675–689; for a review see Milliken, F., & Martins, L. L. (1996). Searching for common threads: Understanding the multiple effect of diversity in organizational groups. *Academy of Management Review, 21*, 402–422.

18. The issue of roles in groups was first discussed by K. D. Benne & P. Sheats. (1948). Functional roles of group members. *Journal of Social Issues*, 41–49.

19. Parker, 1990.

20. Labiance, G., Brass, D. J., & Gray, B. (1998). Social networks and perception of intergroup conflict: The role of negative relationship and

third parties. *Academy of Management Journal, 41,* 55–67.

21. Levering, R., & Moskowitz, M. (1998, January 12). The 100 best companies to work for in America. *Fortune, 137,* 86.

22. Research by Alvin Zander supports the common belief that members of cohesive groups are generally more satisfied and happier; see Zander, A. (1982). *Making groups effective.* San Francisco, CA: Jossey-Bass.

23. Lauderdale, P. (1967). Deviance and moral boundaries. *American Sociological Review, 41,* 660–676.

24. For information about the Tata group: What Cyrus Mistry inherits from Ratan Tata. (2013). *Business Today,* January 28. Retrieved from http://businesstoday.intoday.in/story/what-cyrus-mistry-inherits-from-ratan-tata/1/191081.html on April 1, 2013.

25. Babu, S. (2012). Why Ratan Tata is a role model for India Inc. *Yahoo Finance,* December 27. Retrieved from http://in.finance.yahoo.com/news/why-ratan-tata-is-a-role-model-for-india-inc-101918923.html on April 1, 2013.

26. For a case of about the Taj's attack and management practices see Deshpandre, R., & Raina, A. (2011). The ordinary heroes of the Taj. *Harvard Business Review,* December. Retrieved from http://hbr.org/2011/12/the-ordinary-heroes-of-the-taj/ar/1 on April 1, 2013.

27. Irani, J. (2013). He would never thump the table. *Business Today,* January 20. Retrieved from http://businesstoday.intoday.in/story/j.j.-irani-on-ratan-tata-leadership-style/1/191230.html on April 1, 2013.

28. Anand, M. (2007). Globalization: The Ratan Tata way. *Business Outlook India.* Retrieved from http://business.outlookindia.com/printarticle.aspx?100345 on April 2, 2013.

29. Rosling, A. (2009). Business blooms in diversity. *Tata—Leadership with trust.* Retrieved from http://www.tata.com/careers/articles/inside.aspx?artid=IAECTN1VmjM= on April 2, 2013.

30. Rosling, 2009.

31. Banker, R. D., Field, J. M., Schroeder, R. G., & Sinha, K. K. (1996). Impact of work teams on manufacturing performance: A longitudinal study. *Academy of Management Journal, 39,* 867–890.

32. Morgeson, F. P., Lindoerfer, D., & Loring, D. (2010). Developing team leadership capability. In E. Van Velsor, C. McCauley, & M. Ruderman (Eds.), *The Center for Creative Leadership handbook of leadership development* (3rd ed.). San Francisco, CA: Jossey-Bass.

33. Morgeson, Lindoerfer, & Loring, 2010.

34. Katzenbach, J. R., & Smith, D. K. (2005, July). The discipline of teams. *Harvard Business Review.* Retrieved from http://hbr.org/2005/07/the-discipline-of-teams/ar/1 on September 12, 2013.

35. Caudron, S. (1993, December). Are self-directed teams right for your company? *Personnel Journal,* 76–84.

36. Deep, S., & Sussman, L. (2000). *Act on it! Solving 101 of the toughest management challenges.* Cambridge, MA: Perseus.

37. Gibson, C. B. (2005). Virtuality and collaboration in teams. In J. S. Osland, M. E. Turner, D. A. Kolb, & I. M. Rubin (Eds.), *The organizational behavior reader* (pp. 325–337). Upper Saddle River, NJ: Pearson/Prentice Hall; and Gibson, C. B., & Gibbs, J. (2005). *Unpacking the effects of virtuality on team innovation* [Working paper]. University of California, Irvine.

38. Cramton, D. C., & Orvis, K. L. (2003). Overcoming barriers to information sharing in virtual teams. In C. B. Gibson & C. G. Cohen (Eds.), *Virtual teams that work: Creating conditions for virtual team effectiveness* (pp. 214–230). San Francisco, CA: Jossey-Bass.

39. Kennedy, D., Vozdolska, R., & McComb, S. (2010). Team decision making in computer-supported cooperative work: How initial computer-mediated or face-to-face meetings set the stage for later outcomes. *Decision Sciences Journal, 41*(4), 933–954.

40. Meyer, E. (2010). The four keys to success with virtual teams. *Forbes.com.* Retrieved

from http://www.forbes.com/2010/08/19/virtual-teams-meetings-leadership-managing-cooperation.html on June 11, 2013).

41. Whole Foods Market—Declaration of interdependence, 2013.

42. Milliken & Martins, 1996.

43. Katzenbach & Smith, 1993.

44. Manz, C. C., & Sims, H. P. (2001). *The new superleadership: Leading others to lead themselves.* San Francisco, CA: Berrett-Koehler; for a recent review, see Neck, C. P., & Houghton, J. D. (2006). Two decades of self-leadership theory and research: Past developments, present trends, and future possibilities. *Journal of Managerial Psychology, 21,* 270-295.

45. Manz, C. C., & Neck, C. (2004). *Mastering self-leadership: Empowering yourself for personal excellence* (3rd ed.). Upper Saddle River, NJ: Prentice Hall.

46. Urch Druskat, V., & Wheeler, J. V. (2007). How to lead a self-managing team. In J. S. Osland, M. E. Turner, D. A. Kolb, & I. M. Rubin (Eds.), *The organizational behavior reader* (pp. 338–348). Upper Saddle River, NJ: Pearson/ Prentice Hall.

47. Petty, A. (2012). At least 11 more ideas to help you run effective meetings. *Management Excellence by Art Petty.* Retrieved from http://artpetty.com/2012/11/20/at-least-11-more-ideas-to-help-you-run-effective-meetings/ on April 2, 2013.

48. Jehn, K. A., & Mannix, E. A. (2001). The dynamic nature of conflict: A longitudinal study of intragroup conflict and group performance. *Academy of Management Journal, 44,* 238–251.

49. Levasseur, R. E. (2011). People skills: Optimizing team development and performance. *Interfaces, 41*(2), 204–208.

50. De Rond, M. (2012). Conflict keeps teams at the top of their game. *HBR Blog Network.* Retrieved from http://blogs.hbr.org/cs/2012/07/conflict_keeps_teams_at_the_to.html on February 28, 2012.

51. Topchik, G. S. (2007). *The first time manager's guide to team-building.* New York, NY: AMACOM.

52. Topchik, 2007, p. 107.

53. Scott, D. (2012, March 23). How do you acknowledge individual achievement in a collaborative environment? [Video]. *30-second MBA.* Retrieved from http://www.fastcompany.com/mba/video/mba2016/diane-scott-how-do-you-acknowledge-individual-achievement-collaborative-environment on March 31, 2013.

54. W. L. Gore and Associates. (2013). A team-based, flat lattice organization. *Our Culture.* Retrieved from http://www.gore.com/en_xx/aboutus/culture/index.html on March 31, 2013.

55. Hamel, G. (2010). W. L. Gore: Lessons from a management revolutionary. *The Wall Street Journal,* March 18. Retrieved from http://blogs.wsj.com/management/2010/03/18/wl-gore-lessons-from-a-management-revolutionary/ on March 31, 2013.

56. Adler, P., Heckscher, C., & Prusak, L. (2011). Building a collaborative enterprise: Four keys to creating a culture of trust and teamwork. *Harvard Business Review, 89*(7–8), 95–101.

57. Adler, Heckscher, & Prusak, 2011, p. 96.

58. Adler, Heckscher, & Prusak, 2011.

59. Adler, Heckscher, & Prusak, 2011, p. 97.

60. Adler, Heckscher, & Prusak, 2011, p. 100.

61. Adapted from Amachi, R. N., & Wade, L. (1996, September). Government employees learn to work in sync. *Personnel Journal,* 91–95.

62. Ferrero, M. J., & Lewis, D. (1998). Reach out and touch your team: Development of a high-performing virtual team. In S. D. Jones & M. M. Beyerlein (Eds.), *Developing high-performance work teams.* Alexandria, VA: American Society for Training and Development, p. 183.

63. Adapted from Koehler & Pankowski, 1996, pp. 70–71.

11 Managing Conflict and Negotiation

LEARNING OUTCOMES

After studying the material in this chapter, you will be able to:

1. Define conflict and its consequences

2. Demonstrate an understanding of the types and levels of conflict

3. Explain the role of culture in conflict

4. Analyze various sources of conflict

5. Apply the appropriate methods to manage conflict

6. Apply the appropriate methods to prevent and reduce conflict

7. Demonstrate knowledge of the negotiation process and the key approaches to negotiation

8. Identify non-effective negotiation strategies and their causes

9. Evaluate the consequences of conflict

Conflict at Yahoo ▶

What happens when a successful 37-year-old working mom and CEO bans flexible work for her employees? Aside from many disgruntled employees, she becomes the center of national controversy about women in the workplace.[1] This is what happened to Marissa Mayer, CEO of Yahoo, when she declared that employees would lose their telecommuting option and had to show up for work every day. Mayer who left Google to join Yahoo with high expectations for improved performance at Yahoo, joined the company when she was 5 months pregnant. She returned to work after a 2-week maternity leave after the birth of her son, who gets to stay in the nursery she built at her own expense next to her office so that she can work the long hours that have earned her the reputation of being a workaholic—all of which received extensive media coverage. As she was looking for ways to improve performance, Mayer noticed that the Yahoo parking lot was too empty in the early and late hours during which she was at the office.

As one of the youngest female CEOs and few women leading a Fortune 500 company, Mayer was considered by many to be a role model for young women.[2] Her actions triggered a deluge of e-mails, tweets, and commentary about the role of women in the workplace and her lack of support for other women. Mayer has not lived up to expectations of being a role model female CEO, but she has lived up to the promise of improving the company's bottom line and performance with a 50% increase in share prices.[3] The decision to ban telecommuting came suddenly and with a simple explanation from Mayer: "We need to be one Yahoo, and that starts with physically being together."[4] Jackie Reese, Yahoo's HR chief said: "To become the absolute best place to work, communication and collaboration will be important, so we need to be working."[5] Interestingly, just about the same time as Mayer

Creativity comes from a conflict of ideas.

—Donatella Versace

banned telecommuting, another company, Best Buy—headed by a male CEO—ended its own pioneering flexible work-from-home program.[6] Little controversy ensued in that case. Also released around the same time were several reports about the benefits of telecommuting to both employees and company bottom lines.

Conflict

When people with different goals and interests work together, the potential for disagreement is always present. This disagreement or **conflict** may be about personal preferences, political differences, or organizational policies and procedures. It may reside largely below the surface, but it also may break into the open—sometimes at the oddest times—and, on occasion, latent conflict may explode into sheer nastiness. Similarly, negotiating with others to reach a deal or to resolve conflict is also part of all relationships inside and outside organizations. You may experience conflict with a friend, a classmate, a coworker, a supervisor, or a subordinate. In organizations, as in personal relationships, managing conflict constructively and negotiating well are essential.

Most students of organizations view conflict as inevitable.[7] Negotiating to resolve such conflict or to make deals is an inherent part of a manager's job. In addition, the current trends toward workforce diversity, globalization, and partnerships with other organizations are making increasingly important the way in which managers from different organizations and cultures deal with conflict and negotiate.

Defining Conflict

Conflict is a process in which people disagree over significant issues, thereby creating friction. For conflict to exist, several factors must be present:

Workplace Conflict

- People must have opposing interests, thoughts, perceptions, and feelings.

- Those involved must recognize the existence of different points of view.

- The disagreement must be ongoing rather than a singular occurrence.

- People with opposing views must try to prevent one another from accomplishing their goals.

Conflict can be a destructive force. However, it can also be beneficial when used as a source of renewal and creativity. Before we look at views, sources, consequences, and ways to manage conflict, note that we often use the terms *conflict* and *competition* interchangeably, although the two differ. **Competition** is the rivalry between individuals or groups over an outcome and always has a winner and a loser. While competition can be one of the sources of conflict, conflict does not necessarily involve winners and loser; we can have conflict over issues, but cooperate so that no one loses or wins.

Conflict: a process in which people disagree over significant issues, thereby creating friction

Competition: rivalry between individuals or groups over an outcome; always has a winner and a loser

Views of Conflict

There are two general views of conflict. First, conflict can be considered a negative force and dysfunctional—that it makes people feel uncomfortable and, consequently, makes

HOW DO YOU BEHAVE DURING CONFLICT?

The following questions provide additional insight into how you behave in conflict situations.[8] Answer each question as to the extent that you think or believe that the statement is true.

	Never	Seldom	Occasionally	Usually	Always
1. Do you believe that in every conflict situation, mutually acceptable solutions exist or are available?	1	2	3	4	5
2. Do you believe that in each conflict situation, mutually acceptable solutions are a desirable thing?	1	2	3	4	5
3. Do you favor cooperation with all others in your everyday activities and disfavor competition with them?	1	2	3	4	5
4. Do you believe that all people are of equal value regardless of age, race, religion, culture, or gender?	1	2	3	4	5
5. Do you believe that the views of others are legitimate (i.e., genuine, accurate, true) expressions of their positions?	1	2	3	4	5
6. Do you believe that differences of opinion are helpful and beneficial?	1	2	3	4	5
7. Do you believe that others are worthy of your trust?	1	2	3	4	5
8. Do you believe that others can compete but that they also can choose to cooperate?	1	2	3	4	5
9. Do you believe that how one thinks and how one feels are factors in deciding how one behaves?	1	2	3	4	5

After answering these questions, go back and reflect on your answers. For example, are you more likely to accommodate or avoid confrontations? What else did you learn? You should revisit these questions after you have finished reading this chapter.

Source: Lulofs, S., & Cahn, D. D. (2000). *Conflict: From theory to action* (2nd ed.). Boston, MA: Allyn & Bacon, p. 36.

them less productive. Second, conflict can be viewed as a natural part of organizational life and beneficial to the workplace.[9]

Early views of management considered conflict to be dysfunctional. For example, one of the fathers of management, Frederick Taylor (see Chapter 1), viewed conflict as a threat to managerial authority and as a waste of time. According to his view, conflict can cause unnecessary stress, reduce communication and group cohesion, and prevent employees from focusing on their task. Many of you have experienced the negative impact of conflict when infighting and personality conflicts create intense animosity that made it hard to

What Makes Conflict?

Globalization has increased the frequency of cross-cultural communication, conflict, and negotiations.

work cooperatively with coworkers. Organizational psychologist David Javich suggests that many people hold inaccurate beliefs about conflict, what he calls conflict myths.[10] These include the belief that conflict will destroy team cohesion, make cooperation impossible, and that it will cause an unmanageable chain reaction in organizations.

We already have noted that the environment in which today's organizations operate is highly turbulent and often chaotic. Actually, organizations in which there is a little disagreement and well-managed conflict are more likely to do well in such environments. As a matter of fact, some researchers suggest that too much agreement can lead to complacency and can be destructive.[11] Members are either so homogeneous that they are ill equipped to adapt to changing environmental conditions, or so complacent that they see no need to improve the status quo. Indeed, a positive view of conflict argues that it is the very lifeblood of vibrant, progressive, and stimulating organizations because it sparks creativity, fosters innovation, and encourages personal improvement.[12]

As with most organizational processes we have discussed so far, conflict is neither all good nor all bad. Some levels and types of conflict are healthy; others are not. Figure 11.1 shows how moderate levels of conflict stimulate creative decision making and prevent groupthink and apathy. Very low conflict levels lead to complacency and stagnation. Very high levels, especially if based on individual and personality differences rather than issues related to organizational goals and processes, are detrimental to the organization, and cause dysfunctional behavior. The level and type of conflict and how it is managed determine whether it is beneficial or detrimental to the organization.

FIGURE 11.1 CONFLICT AND PERFORMANCE

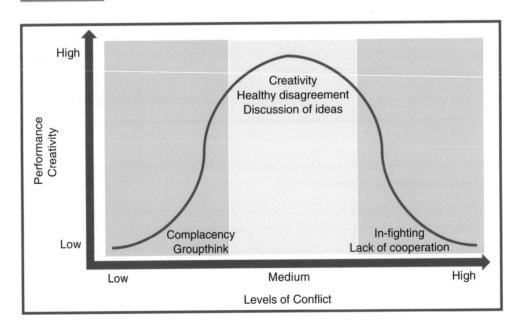

Managers should expect intelligent, well-trained, and motivated employees to disagree over a variety of issues. In fact, employees agreeing easily on how to approach any issue of importance to a company may signal trouble. By the same token, constant disagreements over every issue, or personal conflict, are dysfunctional and destructive. The ability to generate disagreement might be a hallmark of the effective decision maker, but we should note that generating conflict requires considerable maturity and self-confidence on the part of the manager; many managers feel too insecure to stir up conflict among their subordinates. By managing conflict properly, a manager can mobilize disparate pieces of information and diverse perspectives into productive solutions. For this reason, conflict presents opportunities for mobilizing ideas and approaches in the organization and can promote increased creativity, innovation, flexibility, and responsiveness as well as generally improve the overall effectiveness of the organization. Conflict forces people to test and assess themselves and, as a result, stimulates interest and curiosity in others, promoting productive change.

Consequences of Conflict

Clearly, conflict has both positive and negative consequences, as we see in Figure 11.2. On the positive side, all of us have experienced the exhilaration and energy that come from competition. Competition and conflict can motivate people and inspire them to focus on the task. Involvement in competition brings group members closer together and leads to increased discussions of various issues and alternatives. When outside conflict or competition occurs, groups members band together and brainstorm to find creative solutions. This process increases group cohesion and effectiveness.

Companies can use competition with other companies as a way of reducing internal conflict and focusing the employees' energies on outside competitors. Although conflict is inevitable and desirable in organizations, a high level of unresolved conflict can be destructive. Individuals, teams, or departments that are engaged in high conflict may lose sight of the common goals and focus on winning at all costs. They could withhold important information from others, or even actively sabotage others' work. When conflict leads to winners and loser, losers may be demoralized and become demotivated. Consider an organization that sets up a competition among four teams for the design of a new service. The team that wins receives accolades and rewards; the losers are ignored or even punished. At the outset of the competition, all teams may be strongly motivated to win, so they work hard on their task and creativity is likely to be high. However, when the manager announces the winner, the remaining three teams lose their motivation to contribute. This *loser effect* harms long-term relationships and overall organizational performance.

Ideally, managers are proactive in creating an environment in which the likelihood of dysfunctional conflicts is minimized as the diversity of contributions and talents of others are appreciated.[13] When conflict is not resolved or reaches levels that are too high, managers risk letting differing perspectives go undirected, often resulting in tension and dysfunction rather than creative and progressive change.

FIGURE 11.2 CONSEQUENCES OF CONFLICT

BENEFITS	DISADVANTAGES
• High energy	• Focus on conflict
• Focus on the task	• Concern with winning at all costs
• Stimulate innovation	• Distorted judgment
• Increased in-group communication	• Lack of cooperation
• In-group cohesion	• Loser effect
• Discussion of issues	

Interpersonal
Conflict

Types and Levels of Conflict

Table 11.1 summarizes the four types of conflict that managers encounter. **Intrapersonal conflict** is a person's internal conflict. For example, a father who wants to be heavily involved in his young children's school activities *and* to be on the corporate fast track may experience intrapersonal conflict. His goals and values regarding family conflict with his goals as a manager. **Interpersonal conflict** refers to conflict that arises between two or more people who are required to interact and who have different goals, values, or styles. This is the type of conflict we often call "personality conflict." Because such conflict typically revolves around personal differences rather than organizational goals, the potential for negative impact is high and it can be problematic for managers.

TABLE 11.1   TYPES OF CONFLICT

Type of Conflict	Description
Intrapersonal	Within a person, because he or she is motivated to engage in two or more activities that are incompatible
Interpersonal	Between two or more people who interact and have incompatible goals, styles, or values
Intragroup	Within a group when members disagree over group goals, activities, leadership, or processes
Intergroup	Between different groups, departments, or divisions that disagree over task, processes, resources, or information

Intrapersonal conflict: a person's internal conflict

Interpersonal conflict: conflict that arises because two or more people who are required to interact have different goals, values, or styles

Intragroup conflict: conflict within a work group over goals or work procedures

Intergroup conflict: when groups within and outside an organization disagree over various topics

Horizontal conflict: between departments or groups at the same level of the organization

Vertical conflict: between groups at different levels of the hierarchy

Intragroup conflict refers to conflict within a work group over goals or work procedures. While some level of intragroup conflict is healthy and helps prevent problems such as groupthink, this type of conflict, if not well managed, can be extremely detrimental to group cohesion and productivity. As you read in Chapter 10, all groups and teams face some conflicts, particularly in the early stages of development. Navigating these conflicts successfully is an important aspect of a group's maturity and a predictor of its success.

Finally, **intergroup conflict** occurs when groups within and outside an organization disagree over various topics. Intergroup conflict is usually about broad organizational issues such as resource allocation, access to information, and system-related processes. For instance, departments in most organizations face conflict over the allocation of resources during budget negotiations, each vying for a larger share of the pie. Or key departments may disagree as to how a product should be designed or marketed. Intergroup conflict occurs at different organizational levels. **Horizontal conflict** takes place between departments or groups at the same level of the organization. As departments work together to achieve organizational goals, they may disagree over schedules, quality, efficiency, and so forth. Sales and production departments often conflict over production and delivery schedules. Sales people promise customers certain delivery dates without double-checking the production schedule. When the sales team learns of product delays, conflict results. As you will learn in Chapter 14, proper management of horizontal conflict is essential for integration of activities within an organization.

Vertical conflict occurs between groups at different levels of the hierarchy. It typically involves broad organizational issues of control and power. A department may have a conflict with top executives over the allocation of resources for raises. Another vertical conflict may arise because managers want autonomy to stay flexible and responsive to local customers' needs but headquarters wants to control and standardize procedures to monitor costs. Understanding the type and level of conflict is the first step for managers to manage conflict well.

Culture and Conflict

Culture is one factor that determines how people handle and view conflict. Individuals' dispositions are rooted in their early social and cultural experiences, and, because conflict is an interpretive behavior, culture shapes people's interpretation of behavior and their style of interaction with others. Therefore, cultural values create a social environment that encourages members to select some behaviors over others.

Multicultural
Organization
Conflict

Some cultures are more tolerant and accepting of conflict than others who tend to view it as a sign of trouble. Any cross-cultural contact has the potential for conflict because people from different cultures often have different values and goals. Any differences in goals or values can lead to conflict, so we cannot identify all those differences here. It thus is not surprising that research has also found that strategies for negotiating conflict vary according to one's cultural background and cultural values.[14] Collectivist cultures such as those of Asian, Middle Eastern, and Latin American countries tend to adopt a harmony perspective on conflict.[15] Individualistic cultures in English-speaking countries are more likely to use a confrontational approach.[16] Eastern European and Hispanic countries are likely to adopt a regulative model of conflict, which relies on bureaucracy and organizational structure to contain conflict.[17] A study of businesspeople in Japan, Germany, and the United States found that the Japanese used power strategies more than Germans, who used more power than Americans.[18] Generally, people in individualistic cultures, such as that of the United States, value and encourage competition. In collectivist cultures, characteristic of many Asian and Latin American countries for example, people focus on the community and consensus. Thus, in collectivistic cultures, managers are more likely to discourage competition to reduce conflict.

Social status and gender, group-level cultural factors, will also influence individuals' choice of conflict management strategies.[19] For example, avoiding disputes or refraining from direct confrontation with conflict issues in a formal or public sphere has been found to be a prevailing mode of conflict management by low-status individuals and members of minorities.[20] Additionally, research on gender and conflict resolution found that femininity was significantly related to the use of an accommodative style in conflict resolution, while masculinity was related to the competitive style.[21]

The culture of an organization can also act in much the same way as national or group culture. An organization based on individual achievement and competition will encourage conflict, whereas one based on cooperation and group consensus is likely to discourage conflict. Furthermore, because of the leader's impact on culture, a leader's conflict management style, which we discuss later in this chapter, can affect how the organization as a whole views and manages conflict.

Sources of Conflict

Conflict can arise because of both personal and organizational sources (see Figure 11.3). While it is not always easy to separate the two, some conflicts are more directly related to individuals having incompatible goals or values while others are related to the way the organization is structured or managed.

FIGURE 11.3   SOURCES OF CONFLICT

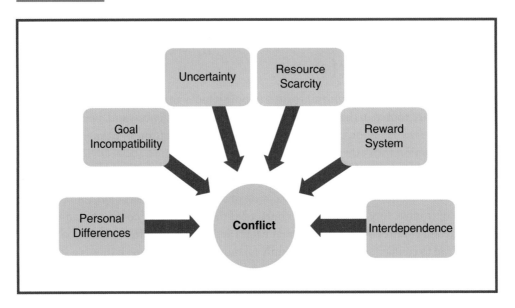

Personal Sources of Conflict

Managing Conflict
Relationships

Personal sources of conflict are often interpersonal in nature and cover many different grounds.[22] For example, two coworkers may have different work styles, or an employee may want more autonomy than her manager is willing to give her. These sources of conflict often involve individual perceptions and expectations about how the work should be done and what is important in the work environment. They are influenced by the personality, style, and culture of the individual. Because they involve individual values, conflicts based on personal differences tend to be highly emotional and difficult to resolve. For example, a devout Catholic business owner might have difficulties locating his business near a Planned Parenthood clinic where abortions are performed. A disagreement about location may turn into a bitter argument about who is morally correct.

Perception may also lead to personal differences. Differing perceptions alone may be enough to invite conflict. An employee may perceive that he is not valued by his supervisor because he does not receive regular praise for his efforts. The supervisor values his work and believes he is making excellent contributions in a tough financial environment. However, she is internally motivated, does not personally have the need for constant praise, and does not see the point of praising her employee often. The conflict is caused by how each person perceives the situation.

What Do You Think?

▶ Some managers try to control conflict to maintain smooth operations. Others stimulate disagreements, hoping to get all sides of the issue. Both strategies make some sense. What do you think? Which strategy are you most comfortable using? Why?

Many conflicts caused by cross-cultural differences are further related to differences both in values and in perception. Since culture influences what people value, it is not surprising that culture can be a factor in personal sources of conflict in organizations. A Mexican manager may perceive his North American employee who calls him by his first name and interrupts him in meetings to disagree with him to be rude and disrespectful. The employee is simply behaving according to his cultural values that suggest openness and participation. Similarly, a Thai employee who comes from a culture that values indirectness and avoiding conflict may find her European manager's honest and direct performance review or her North American team members' open disagreement offensive, causing conflict and leading to lack of motivation.

Organizational Sources of Conflict

Sometimes we attribute conflict to personal factors, where organizational structures and processes may really be the source. For example, we may think a coworker is uncooperative and unhelpful by nature while the organization's reward system that encourages competition may be to blame. We consider five organizational sources of conflict (see Figure 11.3).

Managers from masculine cultures are likely to be more assertive and independent, a potential cause of conflict when working with those from cultures that value indirectness or cooperation.

Goal Incompatibility

Goal incompatibility is the source of many conflicts. Because different departments in organizations are focused on different tasks and functions, conflict among them is inevitable. The manufacturing department may be focused on efficiency and cost cutting while the designers aim at creating the most innovative product. The goal of the human resources manager is likely to include ensuring that all employment laws are followed in the hiring of new employees, causing delays and additional steps, while managers throughout the organization may be seeking to fill their vacancies quickly. Legal departments focus on risk management and documentation; good management may contradict those goals.

Uncertainty

Today's rapidly changing work environment further contributes to conflict.[23] Uncertainty makes it difficult for managers to set a clear direction. Because they lack information, they either have to change course often or remain flexible. Managers are increasingly forced to adapt to rapidly shifting environmental constraints and are under pressure to "do more with less," contributing to conflict as departments and individuals deal with shifting goals. Additionally, uncertainty puts in question accepted practices and procedures, opening the door for disagreement related to both goals and processes. We will review the impact of uncertainty on organizations in more detail in Chapter 14.

Resource Scarcity

When resources are scarce, employees and departments have to compete to get their share of those resources. Such competition increases the likelihood of conflict. Cost-cutting activities are an example of the effect of resource scarcity. As resources dwindle and the organization has to make do with less, individuals, work teams, and departments compete over those limited resources. Such competition leads to higher conflict.

Reward Systems

The fourth organizational source of conflict is the reward system.[24] If managers reward competition and set up a win-lose environment for their employees, they will increase

HELPING RELATIONSHIPS

The dynamics of helping relationships have been explored in great detail by Edgar Schein in his book, *Helping*.[25] A helping relationship can be informal (as when we seek help from a friend, a spouse, or a coworker), semiformal (as when we go to a computer consultant), or formal (as when we hire a management consultant), but all of these involvements bear certain features in common. Most important, helping involves a relationship between people and that relationship must be understood for effective helping to occur.

Initially, the helping relationship must be based on conditions of mutual trust. "Trusting another person means, in this context, that no matter what we choose to reveal about our thoughts, feelings, or intentions, the other person will not belittle us, make us look bad, or take advantage of what we have said in confidence."[26] Trust equates to emotional safety. Beyond that, building an effective relationship requires that both parties get something out of it and it feels "fair." Over time, we learn the different roles we play and the expectations associated with those roles. But we also recognize that confusing these roles can be detrimental to an effective relationship. For example, though we may be a parent, if we act in a parental way toward others at work, we may appear patronizing, and trust in the relationship will be undermined.

The helping relationship, while potentially beneficial for both parties, can also be riddled with tension and ambiguity. When people ask for help, they expose a certain dependency, which in many cultures and in many situations are seen as self-degrading. On the other hand, the person being asked for help is elevated in the relationship. But if that person is in any way dismissive, the status difference is accentuated and trust is eroded. And if, after help has been given, the one being helped doesn't express appreciation, another type of tension arises. In either case, the tension in the relationship must be dealt with.

Anyone attempting to help another must be mindful of the emotional state of the "client." For example, the client may be cautious about initially stating the full problem. The helper, in this case, must be careful not to jump too quickly to presenting advice or possible solutions. There may be more to the story than is being initially revealed. Similarly, the client may ask for help but really be seeking attention or recognition for what he has already done. The helper who provides a quick solution may be missing the point. In any case, the helper must be sensitive to the emotional state of the client.

1. Leaders and managers learn to give help and to get help. What are some of the ways in which they get really good advice?

2. How does the leader or manager know that people are not just saying what she wants to hear?

3. Explain why understanding the emotional state of the other is essential to the helping relationship.

Thinking Through Interdependence

conflict in their organizations. For example, most organizations give raises and promotions on a competitive basis. Many set up a system whereby only a certain percentage of their employees can get the top rankings regardless of performance. Such a reward system may motivate employees to do their best, but it also encourages competition for limited spots and thus creates conflict among employees. Other examples of factors that may produce conflict include common practices such as employee of the month or major awards that are given on a competitive basis. Similarly, rewards based on individual, rather than team, performance are likely to increase intragroup competition and conflict. While such practices are not inherently wrong and often are designed to motivate employees, managers must be aware of their consequences.

Interdependence

The final source of organizational conflict is **interdependence**, which is defined as the extent to which employees depend on others to get their work done. As long as people with different goals can stay away from one another, there is little conflict. The conflict arises when interdependence is high. Consider, for example, three shifts of workers, each of which picks up where the previous one leaves off. Each group's actions affect the others. Their disagreements over work procedures, cleanup, documentation, organization of their common workplace, and so forth will lead to conflict because of their interdependence.

Many of you have experienced conflict related to interdependence in the group and team projects for your classes. You may like the company of your fellow students and not really care about how they work or what grade they pursue in their class. But once you have to work with them on a paper or project, your grade depends on them having the same focus and goal as you. Such interdependence often leads to conflict.

Managers cannot avoid either the personal or the organizational sources of conflict. Based on our earlier discussions, there really is no reason to avoid them. Moderate conflict can be beneficial to the organization. The key is for managers to learn to manage conflict effectively. In some cases, they will need to reduce conflict; in others they may need to encourage conflict.

Rewards given to a single individual, such as an employee of the month, can motivate employees but also increase intragroup competition and conflict.

Managing Conflict

Managers and leaders are no longer interested in eliminating conflict completely. Instead, they are interested in finding ways to *manage* conflict effectively. Managers must consider several factors before deciding how to manage a conflict. These are presented in Figure 11.4. Managers must consider how complex the source and issues involved in the conflict are, whether they are seeking quick relief or a long-term solution, how much time they have to spend on conflict management, how important the conflict and issues are, and how much power the conflicting parties have.

Two General Approaches

To manage conflict effectively, the organization should maintain a moderate level of conflict through prevention and reduction or through an increase or stimulation of conflict. Table 11.2 presents two general approaches to conflict management. Managers may target behaviors or attitudes to manage conflict.[27] The behavioral approach is aimed at simply stopping the behaviors that are causing the conflict. It does not delve into the roots of the conflict or analyze its sources. The results are often quick, short-term, and are useful if the conflicting parties are not interdependent so that they can limit or avoid interaction. The attitudinal approach addresses the roots of the conflict by focusing on emotions, beliefs, and behaviors. It is more time-consuming than the behavioral approach, but has the potential for a long-term resolution of the conflict. Managers should use the attitudinal approach when conflicting parties have to work together—such as in a

Interdependence: the extent to which employees depend on others to get their work done

FIGURE 11.4 FACTORS TO CONSIDER IN CONFLICT MANAGEMENT

The Good Fight

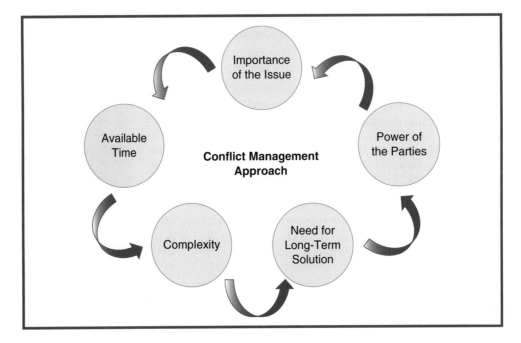

self-managed team or between members of two departments that are highly interdependent. They should rely on behavioral approaches to address more simple conflicts where a quick resolution is needed.

TABLE 11.2 GENERAL APPROACHES TO CONFLICT

	Behavioral Approach	Attitudinal Approach
Focus	Changing individuals' behaviors	Changing individuals' attitudes, beliefs, feelings, and behaviors
Impact	Quick and short term	Slow and long term
Time needed	Can be implemented quickly	Time-consuming
Examples	*Keeping parties on separate floors; enforcing policies; establishing rules that limit interaction; assigning a go-between*	*Team building; rotating conflicting employees to each others' teams; counseling*

Individual Conflict Management Styles

In addition to various methods managers can use to manage conflict, their individual conflict management style also plays a role. Because of the importance and consequences of conflict, researchers have developed several models for understanding how different individuals handle conflict.[28] Two dimensions are used to identify different conflict management styles. The first is concern for self or *assertiveness*; the second is concern for others, or *cooperativeness*.[29] Assertiveness is defined as taking action to satisfy

Assertiveness: taking action to satisfy one's own needs and concerns

one's own needs and concerns. Cooperativeness is defined as taking action to satisfy the other party's needs and concerns. Figure 11.5 depicts how the combination of these two dimensions creates five conflict management styles: collaboration, competition, accommodation, avoidance, and compromise. You can identify your dominant styles from the self-assessment at the beginning of this chapter (see Self-Assessment 11.1). Each style has benefits and disadvantages and should be used in different situations.[30]

- *Collaboration* involves high concern for satisfying both your own needs and the needs of others. People with this style focus on openness, cooperation, and exchange of information. They focus on a win-win style and on finding a solution that is in both parties' best interest. This style typically takes more time, but can deliver long-term gains.

- *Competition* is a style that is high on assertiveness and low on cooperation. Individuals who consistently use this style are interested in their own positions, ignore the needs of others, and view the world as a zero-sum game with winners and losers. They view conflict as competition and their goal is to win. Although this is a common way of handling conflict, it is not viewed as beneficial to individuals or groups that have repeated interaction. But it might be appropriate when an unpopular action needs to be implemented for the greater good of the organization.

- *Accommodation* is a style that is low on assertiveness but high on cooperation. The person who relies on accommodation is willing to sacrifice his own needs to satisfy the needs of others. The individual doing the accommodating is able to build credibility for the next conflict. Accommodation may be useful in the short run but harmful in the long run. If one party continuously accommodates while the other party has its needs and concerns met, then the accommodating party eventually will begin to resent the other party.

- *Avoidance* is a style that is low on assertiveness and low on cooperation. The person using it to manage conflict does not satisfy her needs or the needs of the other person. Instead, she avoids the issues and does not want to explore the sources or solutions to the conflict. People can avoid conflict by withdrawing or creating a physical separation so that they do not have to engage in the conflict. Avoidance may be useful for trivial issues or in the short run in that it allows individuals time to cool off and regain perspective, but it can be quite harmful in the long run. Individuals might resent having to suppress their feelings about the conflict, and they might find other dysfunctional ways of dealing with the issues.

FIGURE 11.5 INDIVIDUAL CONFLICT MANAGEMENT STYLES

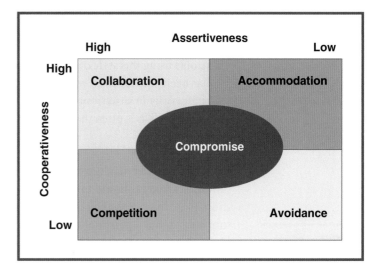

Cooperativeness: taking action to satisfy the other party's needs and concerns

What Would You Do?

▶ You are director of a purchasing department. The two division directors who report to you have been feuding for years. They even built a wall separating what was once a completely open space where people needing help from the other side could simply walk over and ask. Now they have to go out the door, down the hall, to the person's desk, and back. Employees on both sides of the wall think the feud is silly. You do too. What would you do? Are you able to identify sources of the conflict?

- *Compromise* falls in the middle of both assertiveness and cooperation. People using this style take the middle ground. They explore issues to some extent and move to a give-and-take position where there are no clear winners or losers. Everybody ends up with something, though not everything he wanted. This style focuses on negotiation and diplomacy. Although it may appear to be ideal and it allows parties to work together, it focuses on satisficing—finding an acceptable solution that everyone can minimally accept—rather than taking the time to find optimal solutions. Additionally, people using this style often will focus on what they have given up rather than on what has been gained. Even with these disadvantages, *compromising* may be the only style that works in situations where the parties have equal power and strongly opposing views, such as is often the case in diplomatic negotiations.

When Should the Different Styles Be Used?

So which conflict management style works best? Most would say it depends on the situation. Managers should take a contingency approach and match the style to the situation. Note that although conflict management style may have a basis in personality, it is not considered a personality trait. Rather, it is a behavior related to managing conflict. As such, people can practice and learn new styles, thereby expanding their ability to handle different conflict situations. Table 11.3 summarizes the situations in which each style should and should not be used.

Satisficing: making a satisfactory, but not optimal decision

TABLE 11.3 USING CONFLICT MANAGEMENT STYLES

Style	When to Use	When Not to Use
Collaboration	• When issues are complex and require input and information from others • When commitment is needed • When dealing with strategic issues • When long-term solutions are needed • When there is time	• When there is no time • When others are not interested and do not have the skills • When conflict occurs because of different value systems
Competition	• When there is no time • When issues are trivial • When all solutions are unpopular • When others lack expertise • When issues are important to you	• When issues are complex and require input and information from others • When working with powerful others • When long-term solutions and commitment are needed
Accommodation	• When the issues are not important to you • When your knowledge is limited • When there is a long-term give and take • When you have no power	• When others are unethical or wrong • When you are certain you are correct • When there is no chance of future give and take
Avoidance	• When issues are trivial • When conflict is too high and parties need to cool off	• When a long-term solution is needed • When you are responsible for resolving the conflict
Compromise	• When goals are clearly incompatible • When parties have equal power • When a quick solution is needed	• Where there is an imbalance in power • When the problem is complex • When long-term solutions are needed • When conflict is rooted in different value systems

Source: Based on Rahim, M. A. (1983, June). A measure of styles of handling interpersonal conflict. *Academy of Management Journal*, 368–376; Rahim, M. A. (1992). *Managing conflict* (2nd ed.). Westport, CT: Praeger.

All of the styles of managing conflict are valid; what is appropriate depends on the situation and the factors that we presented in Figure 11.4 and how important it is for you to satisfy your own needs and those of others.

Preventing and Reducing Conflict

Table 11.4 summarizes the different methods of conflict prevention and reduction. As the table shows, the prevention and reduction methods can use either the behavioral or the attitudinal approach.

What Would You Do?

▶ You feel that your team has become complacent and uncreative. The members are just too cozy and comfortable. So you take action. You pick several of the most complacent members and pair them with aggressive go-getters that you know will push them. You hear that conflict is intense and stressful. Should you intervene?

TABLE 11.4 CONFLICT PREVENTION AND REDUCTION METHODS

Method (B = Behavioral; A = Attitudinal)	Appropriate When . . .	Consequences
Enforcing rules (B)	• Issues are trivial • Immediate relief is needed	• Quick results • Causes of conflict not addressed • No long-term change • Conflict likely to reemerge
Separation (B)	• Parties are not interdependent	• Quick results • May increase conflict • No long-term change • Conflict likely to reemerge
Clear tasks (B)	• Ambiguity and uncertainty are the cause of conflict • Tasks can be clarified	• Quick results • No long-term effects
Find common enemy or encourage competition with outside group (B or A)	• When competition with outside is part of organizational goals	• Increased in-group cohesion • Source of conflict not addressed • Conflict can re-occur when outside threat is gone
Member rotation (A)	• When there is interdepartmental conflict	• Increased empathy for others • Flexibility in work assignment • Short-term increase in training costs • Long-term impact • Time-consuming
Increasing resources or rewarding cooperation (B or A)	• When resources are available • When conflict is caused by too much competition	• Works as long as resources are available • Source of conflict not addressed • Possible long-term impact
Team building; organizational development (A)	• Conflict is complex with major impact • When there is time • When long-term solution is essential	• Long-term change and impact • Addresses sources of conflict • Skill development • Requires considerable commitment, time, and resources

Behavioral Methods of Conflict Prevention and Reduction

What should a manager do if her employees are in constant conflict, often over trivial issues? First, she can refer to the professional conduct section in the company policies and procedures manual. Say that she finds several statements about cooperation and respect for others, or vague reference to professional conduct. In a department meeting, she can bring up these statements with her employees and tell them that the company policy requires them to work cooperatively. She may also move several employees' offices away from one another or transfer others to another department. Finally, she may make threats about the consequences of not following her directions and violating company policy.

The manager is using *enforcement of rules and policies* and *separation* as *methods of resolving conflict*. The source of the conflict is not addressed and employees do not develop the skills to address their differences. The manager has not presented a long-term solution; the conflict is simply suppressed. These tactics are appropriate when the individuals or groups do not have to work together. They also can be used successfully if the conflict is over trivial issues and when "time off" can give a chance for cooler heads to prevail. In addition to rules and separation, *clarifying tasks* can help reduce conflict. This behavioral method is effective when the conflict is caused by a lack of clarity concerning work procedures or goals.

Attitudinal Methods of Conflict Prevention and Reduction

Compared to the behavioral approaches, attitudinal methods of conflict resolution aim not only at changing people's behavior, but also at changing how they think (cognition) and feel (emotion) about the conflict and one another. Attitudinal approaches focus on finding and resolving the root causes of the conflict. This approach tends to result in longer-term resolution compared to the behavioral approach.

One attitudinal method of conflict reduction is to find a *common enemy* or to compete with another group outside the organization. The focus on an outside enemy or group can help pull conflicting parties together. For instance, two departments that are fighting may join forces to ensure that their new product gets to the market before their competitors' products. In the process, they come to think, feel, and behave differently. Similarly, two companies engaged in intense domestic competition may join forces to fight a global competitor.

The presence of an outside enemy does not fully address the source of a conflict, but it increases interaction and cohesion, eases internal tensions, and provides an opportunity for the conflicting parties to work productively together and focus on common goals rather than on their differences.

Rotating members among departments achieves a similar goal. Employees who rotate to other departments learn to look at conflict from varying points of view. This new perspective and the increased interaction with other employees provide opportunities for the conflicting parties to discuss and resolve their differences. Rotation has the added benefit of increasing an organization's flexibility in work assignments. As employees learn different skills, they can fill in for one another as needed.

Managers can further resolve conflict by *increasing resources* so that individuals and departments do not have to compete for them. A related approach is to allocate resources in a manner that precludes pitting one individual or department against another. For example, managers can fund any project that merits funding regardless of which department proposed the project.

A More Engaged
Workforce

Another attitudinal method of conflict resolution is full-scale intervention through *team building*. The various methods of team building that we discussed in Chapter 9 can be used to resolve conflict. Through building trust, respect, and support; clarifying goals; and similar methods, managers can help increase group cohesion and reduce conflict. Similarly, teaching individuals and groups problem-solving skills can help them manage conflict. They can discuss seemingly incompatible goals by relying on rational decision-making models, brainstorming, or other methods presented in Chapter 7. Team building and problem solving both focus on long-term solutions and can be time-consuming.

Along with team building, managers can use organizational development (OD), which involves making wholesale changes in organizations by addressing issues at the individual, group, and organizational levels. As you will discover in Chapter 15, OD uses various team-building techniques in addition to numerous diagnostic and problem-solving tools that analyze a broad range of organizational problems. For the purpose of this discussion, you need to know that the methods are appropriate for dealing with complex and deep-rooted conflict. They require a considerable investment of time and resources, but they have the potential for long-term change, skills development, and long-lasting impact.

Conflict Styles

Increasing or Stimulating Conflict

Remember that very low conflict can be unproductive, so managers may face situations in which they must stimulate conflict to prevent employee complacency and groupthink, and to encourage creativity.[31] The four methods for stimulating conflict are presented in Table 11.5. They are: introducing change, increasing task ambiguity, creating interdependence, and introducing competition. The key to successfully stimulating conflict is to focus on organizational issues rather than personal issues and to closely monitor the situation.

TABLE 11.5 METHODS FOR STIMULATING CONFLICT

Method	Examples
Introduce change	Assign new, less routine task; bring in new members; change processes; change structure and reporting lines; change leadership
Increase task ambiguity	Assign unknown or new task without providing clear guidelines or training to force group members to figure it out on their own
Create interdependence	Bring together groups that do not typically work together on a task force to address a specific organizational issue; assign tasks where people need others to get their job done
Introduce internal competition	Set up a competition between individuals or groups for best new product, for reaching a target or goal, or for a promotion or bonus

First, managers can stimulate conflict by *introducing change* to a team or department. Change requires reevaluating procedures and relationships with fresh perspectives and, as a result, can lead to varying degrees of conflict. Second, managers can *increase ambiguity*. This method is closely related to introducing change. Just as clarifying tasks prevents and reduces conflict, uncertainty stimulates it. Managers can assign tasks for which there are no clear requirements, instructions, or procedures so that employees need to discuss and debate such issues. Not having a clear path or well-established procedures generally leads to disagreement, creates conflict, and increases creativity. Another method

What Do You Think?

▶ Some people consider conflict, courage, and creativity together as central to the capacity of an organization to respond to rapid environmental change. They say you can't have one without the other—and still be successful. What do you think? Are you comfortable with stimulating conflict?

of stimulating conflict is *creating interdependence among employees and departments*. Depending on others to perform tasks requires interaction, a consideration of other perspectives, and negotiation of incompatible goals and approaches.

The simplest and probably most commonly used method of conflict stimulation is *internal competition*. Competing to achieve a goal or to get a promotion, bonus, or a prize stimulates creativity and motivates individuals and groups, particularly in more individualistic cultures. While simple, this method has the potential to get out of hand, especially if there are clear winners and losers. Competition decreases interaction and may be hard to manage, even after the contest ends. Regardless of which method a manager uses, he must monitor the situation carefully to keep conflict at a constructive level by using a combination of conflict resolution and conflict stimulation. Part of managing any conflict involves negotiating with the various parties who are involved, a topic we consider next.

Negotiating

Conflict Resolution and Negotiation

Whether you manage a small department, own your own business, head a major corporation, or hold an entry-level sales position, you must know how to negotiate. **Negotiation** is a process whereby two or more parties reach a mutually agreeable arrangement. It is one of the most commonly used and beneficial skills managers can develop. The global business environment, the diverse workforce, rapid pace of change, and shift toward teams and empowerment all require managers to hone their negotiation skills.

The Negotiation Process

All negotiations share four common elements:[32]

- The parties involved are in some way interdependent

- The parties are in conflict over goals and processes

- The parties involved are motivated and capable of influencing one another

- The parties believe they can reach an agreement

These four elements come into play at different stages of the negotiation process presented in Figure 11.6. While most of us think of the third and fourth stages—bargaining and agreement—as the heart of negotiation, most experts emphasize the importance of both careful and thorough preparation and presentation in negotiating well and successfully.[33] As we will discuss in the next section, culture plays a significant role in all phases of negotiation.

Negotiating Isn't the Reason

The first or *preparation* phase includes gathering factual information about the issues and alternatives and acquiring "softer" information about the other party's interests, positions, personality, and style. Intense preparation not only leads to a better outcome, but also reduces the anxiety of negotiation. The second phase is the *presentation* of initial offers and demands, either orally or in writing. Careful choices of words and self-presentation to project the right image through effective verbal and nonverbal communication are essential in this phase. The third phase is the actual *bargaining* in which

Negotiation: a process whereby two or more parties reach a mutually agreeable arrangement managers use various negotiating strategies to reach an agreement. Their preparation concerning facts and people can strengthen their position. Active listening, feedback, persuasion, and the various communication techniques and barriers we reviewed in Chapter 9 all come into play in this phase. The final phase is the *agreement* that closes the negotiation process. The agreement is finalized and put into a format that is acceptable to both parties.

As indicated in Figure 11.6, the process of negotiation is continuous. Once an agreement is reached, negotiation over clarification and implementation are likely to continue. Additionally, one party can stop the negotiation process at any time, forcing all to restart the process.

Overcoming Obstacles

Ethics and Negotiation

Negotiating to get what you need raises a number of ethical dilemmas. Should you always tell the truth? Should you be up front and reveal your game plan? What can you ethically not tell? These are difficult questions that arise regularly in all formal and informal negotiations. Below are some typical ethical violations to avoid; they are progressively more serious:[34]

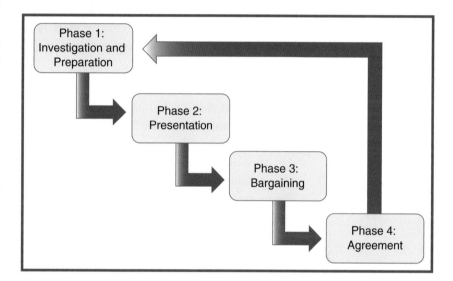

FIGURE 11.6 PHASES OF NEGOTIATION

- *Selective disclosure:* Negotiators highlight positive information and downplay or fail to mention negative information

- *Misrepresentation:* Negotiators misstate facts or their position; for example, they misrepresent the lowest price they are willing to accept

- *Deception and lying:* Negotiators give the other party factually incorrect information or information that leads to incorrect assumptions or conclusions

- *False threat and false promises:* Negotiators provide misinformation about actions that they may take and concessions they may be willing to make

- *Inflict direct or indirect harm:* Negotiators intentionally sabotage the other party's chance of success

What Would You Do?

▶ During your company's negotiations with a supplier, you inadvertently stumble upon information the other team left on a table. It contains their negotiation strategy and pricing information. What should you do with the information? How would that fit with the guidelines on this page?

Any of these violations is likely to occur in negotiations. The last two, giving false information and inflicting harms, are the most severe violations, although how a negotiator ranks the others depends on his values and morals, and in some cases, his culture. Table 11.6 provides some guidelines for monitoring your own ethical behavior.

Men's Morals Malleable

TABLE 11.6 TIPS FOR MONITORING YOUR OWN ETHICS

Advice	Description
Learn from your mistakes	We all have committed ethical violations; learn from them and do not repeat them
Do you like what you see?	Evaluate your own behavior and strategies. Can you look at yourself in the mirror? Are you proud of yourself?
What does the other person see?	Consider how you appear to the other party or to an observer. Are you projecting an image you like?

Culture and Negotiation

Negotiating
Intractable
Conflict

Globalization has increased the frequency of cross-cultural negotiations. Given that negotiation involves exchange, interaction, and communication, culture's impact on this process is significant. Knowing how culture affects negotiations and having information about another party's culture allow for more focused preparation, clearer presentation, better bargaining, and more effective agreement.

The various cultural dimensions we discussed in Chapter 2 all affect the process of negotiation. Managers from masculine cultures are likely to be more assertive and independent, see negotiation as a competition, and focus on winning at all costs. Managers who value uncertainty avoidance (e.g., from China or Japan) will rely on bureaucratic rules and established procedures and rituals when negotiating, whereas those from cultures that are more comfortable with ambiguity, such as North Americans or Scandinavians, will be comfortable with free flowing discussions that may yield more creative solutions. The power distance and individuality-collectivism dimensions further affect the negotiation process. Low power distance will likely lead to open sharing of ideas and cooperative behaviors during negotiation, whereas individualism will emphasize self-interests. Managers from collectivistic cultures are likely to consider building relationships essential before bargaining. Negotiators from individualistic cultures will often have the authority to make the decision on their own while those from collectivistic cultures will tend to seek their group's input, a factor that may slow down the process.[35]

High and low context is another cultural dimension that influences negotiations. Negotiators from high-context cultures rely on the context, various nonverbal cues, and situational factors to communicate with others and understand the world around them.[36] Those from low-context cultures, such as Germany or Canada, pay attention to what is said and written and want clear, formal written documentation of all agreements. Those from high-context cultures, such as Korea or Vietnam, will look for subtle cues, read between the lines, and operate on trust and implicit agreements.

Negotiators from cultures where display of emotions is accepted, such as Italy or Brazil, may upset their British, low emotion counterparts, with an outburst or show of emotion. Additionally, those who are focused on the present and have a short-term orientation, for example the United States, may be confused when their Egyptian counterparts keep referring to events that happened in the past and consider them an integral part of their discussion. According to a recent survey that compared 2,500 professionals from eight countries on their reactions to negotiation, 39% of Americans report being anxious about negotiating, the highest percentage, while Germans are the most positive, and Indians are most confident.[37]

While none of these culturally based negotiation styles is either right or wrong, they add considerable complexity, subtlety, and confusion to an already difficult process. In addition to national

GLOBAL SOCIETY · CROSS-CULTURAL NEGOTIATIONS

Western businessmen have been accused of focusing too much on the financial aspects of a deal. They often believe that as long as a proposal is financially attractive, it will succeed.[38] Many experts in global negotiations warn against taking such a position. Horatio Falcao, a professor in the world-renowned INSEAD business school in Paris, believes that we both over and underestimate the impact of culture in negotiations but that we should also consider every negotiation a cross-cultural exercise. Falcao has worked with hundreds of global managers on how to negotiate across cultures. He says: "People come to me normally and ask 'how do I negotiate with the Chinese?' And I would say which Chinese exactly do they want to talk to? Do you want to talk to the Chinese from Beijing or in Shanghai? The one who came from the countryside and moved to the city, or the one who was born and raised in the city?"[39] Falcao believes that you can't look just at national culture; you also have to consider many other factors such as education, social class, and religious culture. Similarly, we often overestimate the impact of culture for people who are similar to us. Just because an American is negotiating with an Australian, and they think they speak the same language, does not mean that cultural factors are not relevant.

Consultant Richard Lewis believes that people fall back on their culture in times of crisis or challenge or when they are under pressure, so it is very important that any negotiator does not fall back on his simple intuition. He states: "We feel that our unwritten behavioural codes for persuasion and negotiation are universal and innate. In fact, they are largely acquired and culturally-bound."[40] So what is the solution? Do we always judge people by their culture and put culture first? Or do we look at the person? The answer is to achieve a balance and push back your assumptions. Falcao recommends: "start with the assumption maybe, at the very 'get-go,' of zero: I don't know. And why does that help me? That helps me to approach you from a learning perspective; I'll start to try to learn as fast as I can about you to know if you're friend or foe."

In cross-cultural negotiations, as in other aspects of management, the key to success, according to global practitioners and experts, is to get the know the individual you are dealing with.

1. Which aspect of negotiation is most influenced by culture?

2. What are some steps managers can take to avoid cultural conflict during negotiation?

culture, many ethnic, gender, or other group-based values affect how people negotiate. For example, women often shy away from making clear demands during negotiations, a factor that has been found to work against them. As a matter of fact, the cross-national survey about negotiation indicates that women in all the surveyed countries feel less comfortable than men about negotiating (26% vs. 41%, respectively). Selena Rezvani, author of *Pushback: How Smart Women Ask—And Stand Up—For What They Want* believes that women, more than men, forgo their own demands to ensure that the relationship is maintained. She says: "A big part of that problem for women is the belief that relationships should trump agenda."[41]

Savvy and effective managers include culture in their preparation and in other phases of negotiation to ensure that they meet their goals and those of the other person. Knowledge of culture at all levels, including organizational culture, can help in negotiation.

Common Mistakes in Negotiation

Even skilled negotiators make mistakes. Table 11.7 presents common mistakes and their causes. One of the most common is the fear that we may be conceding too much either because we appear to give in too easily or because we make a major blunder. While we worry

Negotiate, Don't Argue

As secretary of state, Hillary Rodham Clinton often engaged in cross-cultural negotiations. Here she meets with former Egyptian president Mohammed Morsi.

about how we look, many of us simultaneously believe that we are more reasonable and rational than others. These fears distort our judgment and add to a number of other mistakes we make while negotiating. The perceptual biases that we discussed in Chapter 3 play a particular role in negotiation because the process heavily depends on social perception. Selective attention and other perceptual filters and biases, such as stereotyping and halo effects, affect our perception of others and ourselves.

The *Winner's Curse* and *Overconfidence* stem from lack of information and misperceptions concerning the correctness of our position. Considerable research indicates that we tend to underestimate our chances of being wrong.[42] We tend to not rely on experts and end up making mistakes that can be avoided. Careful preparation and awareness of biases can help avoid many of these common mistakes. Bill Richardson, former governor of New Mexico, Ambassador to the United Nations, and 2008 U.S. presidential candidate, has skillfully negotiated with foreign countries on behalf of the United States. He suggests: "You have to be a good listener. You have to respect the other side's point of view. Certainly you want to have a goal. You want to come out of a meeting with something, even if it's only a second meeting. And basically you have to use every single negotiation technique you know—bluster, reverence, humor."[43] He also emphasizes his preparation: "I talk to the people who know the guy I'll be negotiating with. I talk to scholars . . . experts, journalists."[44]

TABLE 11.7 COMMON MISTAKES IN NEGOTIATION

Mistake	Description	Causes
Irrational escalation of commitment	Continuing a selected course of action beyond what is considered rational, and in spite of contrary information	• Wanting to win at all costs • Impression management (ego) • Perceptual biases
Mythical fixed pie	There is a set amount on the table and one party has to win and the other lose	• Lack of creativity in problem solving
Winner's curse	Making a quick high offer and feeling cheated when the offer is accepted	• Lack of preparation • Lack of expertise • One party having more information than the other
Overconfidence	Overestimating your ability to be correct	• Lack of information • Arrogance • Distorted perception

Source: Based on information in Bazerman, M. H., & Neale, M. A. (1992). *Negotiating rationally*. New York, NY: Free Press.

Negotiation Strategies

In addition to preparing carefully and avoiding mistakes, skillful negotiators need to be ready to use a variety of skills, strategies, and qualities.

FBI Hostage
Negotiator

- *Creativity* allows for developing novel solutions and seeking win-win solutions.

- *Flexibility* allows both parties to consider alternatives and change course when needed.

- *Keeping the climate positive* even when strong conflict and disagreement exist increases the chances of success.

- Being aware of how much *control* one does and does not have is essential. No one can control all aspects of the negotiation process; instead, good negotiators identify the issues they can control and focus on them.

- Managing the *balance of power* and using appropriate sources of power to persuade and influence the other parties allows negotiators to address needed issues.

- Knowing your *goals* and your own motives is also essential to keeping a focus on what matters to you most. Success depends on focusing on the real issue and not getting side-tracked by irrelevant and unimportant factors.

- Finally, every negotiator should be able to *say no* to deals that do not match her goals and be prepared to walk away.

Specific negotiation strategies are basically focused on either a win-win or a win-lose approach. The traditional view of negotiation (which corresponds with the traditional view of conflict we discussed at the beginning of the chapter) considers negotiation a zero-sum game in which one party's gain always leads to the other's loss. This view is called **distributive negotiation** because the rewards and outcomes are divided among the parties. Another approach, called **integrative negotiation,** offers a win-win scenario whereby parties try to reach an agreement that benefits them both by focusing on creating new options and solutions. Although integrative strategies create a positive climate by eliminating winners and losers, they are not easily achieved.

When selecting a negotiating strategy, managers must consider two factors. First, they must determine the importance of the relationship with the other party. Does the manager want to establish a positive, long-term relationship with the other party? Do the other party's thoughts and feelings matter? Is it important that the other party leave the negotiation satisfied and happy? Remember from our earlier discussion that women, for example, are often too focused on this aspect of negotiation. If the answer to these questions is yes, the relationship with the other negotiating party is important and must be preserved.

Second, managers must ascertain the importance of the outcome.[45] Is this an important deal? Does this agreement affect organizational performance? Does it affect the manager's career success and chances for promotion? If the answer to these questions is positive, then the outcome of the negotiation is important. The manager must therefore ensure that she achieves her goals. The combination of these two factors leads to the four negotiation strategies illustrated in Figure 11.7.

Trusting collaboration involves cooperation, give and take and compromise, and collaborative problem solving to achieve a win-win outcome. Negotiators use this strategy when both the relationship and the task outcomes are important.[46] Parties can share motives, ideals, and goals openly as they want to reach a mutually acceptable agreement that promotes long-term relationships and continued cooperation. Using trusting collaboration in teams or within organizations where people are mutually interdependent is essential. When using trusting collaboration, managers must do the following:

- Use a neutral setting where both parties are comfortable

- Take turns making offers

Distributive negotiation: a zero-sum negotiation in which one party's gain always leads to the other party's loss

Integrative negotiation: parties try to reach an agreement that benefits them both by focusing on creating new options and solutions

FIGURE 11.7 FOUR NEGOTIATION STRATEGIES

Is the Substantive Outcome Important?

	Yes	No
Yes Is the Relationship Outcome Important?	**Trusting Collaboration** • Openness • Cooperation • Win-win • Problem solving	**Open Subordination** • Openness • Yielding • Yield-win • One-way acceptance
No	**Firm Competition** • Aggressive • Forcing issues • Win-lose • Imposing a solution	**Active Avoidance** • No interaction • Refusal to negotiate • No win • No solution

- Explain and clarify their reasons and motives

- Offer an honest consideration and appraisal of their own and the other party's position

- Be willing to yield on some issues

Firm competition is appropriate when you do not care about the long-term relationship with the other party but the outcome is important. It is an aggressive win-lose strategy in which managers concentrate on imposing their own solution. Using firm competition as a negotiating strategy requires access to power, organizational support, and the willingness to forgo future relationships. Tactics of firm competition include:

- Impose the negotiation location

- Present your own offers and demands first

- Refuse to discuss the other party's issues

- Exaggerate your own positions and the extent to which you have made concessions

- Yield little

Open Subordination should be used when the task or substance of the negotiation is not as important as the relationship. It involves yielding to the other party on all or most points and openly accepting the other's solutions. Open subordination may be the only option when managers do not have much power or leverage to negotiate. However, they can also use this strategy when they have power but want to create goodwill or reduce hostilities when conflict is high. For instance, it is important for many start-up operations and small businesses to have well-known clients, however unreasonable they may be, to gain access to other high-profile customers. Tactics of open subordinate include:

- Let the other party present all offers and demands

- Make high offers and low demands

- Magnify the other party's concessions and downplay your own

- Concede on as many demands as possible

Active Avoidance involves refusing to negotiate, as the negotiator does not care about either the task or the relationship. In this case, one neither seeks to win nor to lose. The individual is simply not party to the exchange and interaction. Often managers avoid negotiating because they have no stake in the results.

To determine which of the four strategies to use, managers must consider the situation. Their conflict management style and personality may also influence their selection of strategies. For example, if your primary conflict management style is competition (see Figure 11.5), you are likely to feel most comfortable with firm competition as a negotiating strategy. Similarly, a person with a **collaborative style** of conflict management (Figure 11.5) is more likely to use trusting collaboration. Personal style and preferences notwithstanding, managers should evaluate the situation and apply the strategy that will most likely achieve the relationship and task outcomes that they seek.

When using trusting collaboration, the setting is important. Negotiators may select a neutral setting where both parties are comfortable and neither has the home turf advantage.

A very popular approach to negotiating presented by authors Roger Fisher, William Ury, and Bruce Patton in their book, *Getting to Yes*, offers four key points to negotiating effectively:[47]

1. *Focus on People* and separate the people from the problem. A basic fact about negotiations, yet not one easily remembered, is that we are dealing with human beings who have emotions, deeply held values, and different backgrounds and viewpoints. Fisher and his colleagues suggest: "A working relationship where trust, understanding, respect, and friendship are built up over time can make each new negotiation smoother and more efficient."[48]

2. *Pay attention to people's interests, not their positions or demands.* One of the basic problems in negotiation lies not in conflicting positions, but rather in the conflict between each side's needs, desires, concerns, and fears. You need to ask the *why* and the *why not* questions. In addition to eliciting information about the other party's interests, you need to communicate information about your own. By identifying where these interests overlap or are compatible, you can overcome apparently conflicting demands and begin to move to the next stage.

3. *Generate many options* before deciding what to do. Brainstorming (discussed in Chapter 7) is a good technique to arrive at as many options as possible. Decisions should not be made until all options have been exhausted. Fisher and colleagues suggest that you can convert ideas into options by using different perspectives or "invent[ing] agreement of different strengths."[49] Look for mutual gains in the options.

4. *Use standards and criteria* based on some objective standards that have been established by neutral experts. Once the objective criteria and procedures have been identified, frame each issue as a joint search for objective criteria. Ask others what objective standards would be most appropriate for dealing with the issue.

By accurately identifying individual needs as well as the sources of conflict, the principled approach can result in positive growth of the individuals involved and the organization as a whole.

Performance in Negotiations

Collaborative style: seeks a win-win solution for all parties

▶ Summary and Applications for Managers

Let's begin by reemphasizing the importance of viewing both conflict and negotiation as natural parts of life for individuals and organizations. Managers often worry about conflict in their organizations and are afraid that any sign of trouble will undermine performance. Their response is likely to be to ignore or avoid the conflict, or try to impose a solution without getting to the root of the problem. While this strategy may be appropriate when conflict is trivial, it is not always the best solution.[50]

Here are some ways you can apply the material you learned in this chapter.

1. Take time to evaluate and understand the conflict you are facing. Some level of conflict is necessary and healthy, so use it to your benefit.

2. Focus on actively managing, not just reducing, conflict. This may mean that sometimes you will reduce it, and sometimes you may want to stimulate it. The goal is not to suppress conflict at all costs.

3. Step outside of the conflict you are facing. Sometimes we get pulled into conflict with a coworker or boss. Attack brings counterattack. The spiral begins. Nine times out of ten, if you step away from the conflict for a few moments/hours/days, you'll see how small and petty the issue being fought over likely is. Without regaining this perspective, you're doomed to get involved in a battle that's not worth fighting. On top of that, you might miss an easy solution to the problem because you're too busy attacking.

4. Develop self-awareness about your most preferred style of conflict management and practice the other ones. Chances are that you will find the style that is diagonally across from your preferred style (see Figure 11.5) most challenging. Practice all of them in safe and low-cost settings.

5. You may not be able to control the other party, but you do have control over your own behavior and reaction. Your enemy may take shots at you. The defining moment comes in how you react to them. You either attack back or you try to take the high road. You can ignore the insult or laugh off the verbal slight. You can kill them with kindness. Those around you will take note of how each of the combatants is behaving and of your professionalism; it will be hard for you to look bad.

6. Pick your conflicts. Not everything is worth fighting over and you cannot win every fight. Use your energy to address things that are important to you and your organization. This is one more reason for you to know your own values and priorities.

7. Extend the olive branch. When it costs nothing, be kind (even if it costs you something—be kind). The best way to be the bigger person is to set differences aside and create a positive environment. If your enemy continues the conflict, he is not going to be the one to reach out to end hostilities. That leaves the task to you. Take him out to lunch. Tell him you'd like to work with him more productively and end the conflict. Ask what you can do to change the way you communicate and LISTEN when he tells you what's wrong.

8. Negotiation is a skill. Practice it any chance you get and become comfortable with the different strategies.

9. While the task and the outcome are often important, conflict and negotiation are about people. Deal with the people. You can be kind without giving in on the outcome you need. Fisher and his colleagues call this being "soft on people and hard on issues."

▶ Key Terms

▶ Exercise 11.1   How Do Relationships Affect Conflict?

Think back over the past 5 years and recall conflicts that you had with three different people: (1) a personal friend, (2) a coworker, and (3) a roommate. Respond to the following questions.

1. What happens to conflicts as relationships become closer, more personal, and more interdependent?

2. Did you find that as relationships become closer and more interdependent, there are more opportunities for conflict, the more trivial complaints become significant ones, and feelings become more intense?

What type of resistance are you encountering during conflict or have you experienced in the past?

1. "I don't get it."

○ Do you see people's eyes glaze over, eyebrows furrow, or head tip slightly to one side when you are proposing an idea?

2. "I don't like it."

○ Does someone encounter fear of, for example, a loss of job with your idea? These fears are not always aired, so it may require that you ask questions.

3. "I don't like you."

○ Are ideas that you propose shut down simply because you proposed them?

Source: Adapted from Maurer, R. (2002). Why don't you want what I want: The three faces of resistance. *Manage Online, 1*(2). Retrieved from http://nma1.org/Communications/Manage/.

▶ Exercise 11.2   Asking Questions

The most basic method for promoting mutual understanding is to ask questions. Sometimes others are hesitant to ask questions because they might be perceived as criticism. By providing structure, this exercise will help you to understand that questions are not intended as attacks.

1. Ask for a volunteer to be the "focus person" and another to be the facilitator. The focus person in the group is invited to speak on any controversial problem facing the country. This person starts with, "Here is the point I want to make" and is given 3 minutes to speak.

2. When the speaker is done, the facilitator asks the group, "Can you explain why?" or "What did he [or she] mean by that?"

3. The group answers the questions.

4. If the answers are clear to all participants, then go to Step 5. If they are not, then ask those who

are unclear about what was said and exactly what they still find to be unclear. For example, someone might say, "I heard the person say that we should all share the assignment equally. But I am not sure why he feels so strongly about it. In my view, if we divide up the tasks according to skill, the work may not be equally divided, but the product may be more effective." Give the focus person a chance to respond.

5. When both the group and the speaker feel understood, ask for someone else in the group to take a turn as the focus person.

The goal of this exercise is to promote understanding, not to resolve differences. This should be emphasized beforehand and throughout the activity.

Source: Adapted from Kaner, S. (1996). *Facilitator's guide to participatory decision-making.* Gabriola Island, British Columbia: New Society, pp. 173, 175.

Exercise 11.3 Individual Needs

Have you ever been in a situation where the arguing just kept going around in circles? It will be helpful if the parties can stop arguing over the proposed solution and start talking about their individual interests instead. For an example of a situation that might cause this type of discussion, look at Case Study 11.1 about emergency evacuation at the end of this chapter, where a family is interested in staying in the town in spite of the mandatory evacuation. It will become easier to develop proposals that meet a broader range of needs when those needs have been made explicit and understandable to all. Assume the role of the business owner trying to protect the employee and his family. Allow each group to make a case for its viewpoint.

1. Make sure that group members understand the difference between their proposed solutions and what the family in the case study needs. For example, evacuating is a proposed solution, whereas staying home with family is a need or an interest. Take time, if necessary, to clarify this distinction among group members.

2. Ask everyone to answer the question, "What are the needs and interests in this situation?"

3. Continue until everyone is satisfied that his or her own needs and interests have been stated clearly, then ask the group to generate new proposals that seek to incorporate a broader range of everyone's needs.

Exercise 11.4 When Is Conflict Healthy?

Not all issues in organizations are worth conflict. Use any of the earlier case studies, and apply the following three principles to decide if the issue merits conflict:

1. Are the stakes high enough to motivate employees? If so, what is at stake?

2. Does the challenge reflect a larger cause that is central to the program or organization's mission? Explain.

3. Is there opportunity to improve current circumstances? How so?

4. If the situation merits the conflict, what would need to change to avoid the conflict?

Case 11.1 Conflict in an Emergency Evacuation

You are a small business owner on the Jersey shore. In 2012, Hurricane Sandy hit the Northeast. The Northeast has had very little experience with hurricanes, and this one hit the most highly populated areas. In order to evacuate the beaches, state public health was coordinating with the National Guard, the Federal Emergency Management Agency, and local governments. They had planned and scheduled all evacuation to occur before the storm hit on Saturday evening. On Saturday morning, a member of the National Guard calls to inform you that one of your employees, along with his family, has decided that he would not be evacuated. The governor of New Jersey had stated the evening before that if anyone stayed behind in the areas under evacuation, they would not be receiving services. The member of the National Guard had tried to encourage the family to go; the family refused. The National Guard had called on the state social worker to speak with the family. The family was infuriated that the state would impose their values on their family. This family had weathered many storms as they had moved to the northeast from Puerto Rico. Their feeling was that they should be together as a family and protect their property. If Sandy were to take them, at least they would be together. As Mr. Ortega's employer, you are viewed as the last resource to try to talk some sense into this family. The National Guard calls you later in the morning and tells you that they are not wasting their time with Mr. Ortega, and the family can do what they choose. You become terribly upset, as you believe that their lives are being placed at risk and you ask the National Guard to let you speak with Mr. Ortega and his family.

1. Identify the sources for this conflict?

2. How will you, as Mr. Ortega's employer, try to resolve this situation?

3. Are there cultural issues that may be at play in this scenario?

4. What negotiation methods would you find most useful in trying to deal with the conflict?

► Case 11.2 A Group Project

You have been assigned to work on a Marketing group project with randomly selected classmates. When you discover who will be your coworkers, you realize that the group is made up of students who do not take their work as seriously as you do. You are given until the end of the semester to complete the project, so you have plenty of time. You decide to take the lead and assign people to specific components of the project. When you meet with the group the first time, you assign the tasks only to find much discontent. Your classmates want to know what made you think you could just tell them what to do. You now need to exercise damage control in order to avoid a very long semester.

1. What will you do?

2. What techniques might you employ to negotiate with your classmates?

► Case 11.3 Executive Compensation

On the same day in March that a large manufacturer warned that the sequester could lead to thousands of employee furloughs and layoffs, the nation's largest federal contractor disclosed that it had just boosted the compensation of its former CEO by more than $2 million, according to Securities and Exchange Commission (SEC) forms.

You work in the organization's human resources department and will be designated as the person people may contact if they have questions. Since the release of the CEO's compensation was made, your voice mail and e-mail boxes have been filled by disgruntled employees wanting explanations. You share some of their same concerns, but are conflicted with the role that you have been asked to play in the organization.

1. How will you respond to your colleagues?

2. How will you respond to management?

3. What methods would you find most useful in trying to deal with the conflict?

4. How will you apply the materials you learned in this chapter?

► Endnotes

1. For some examples see Bonk, A. (2012). New Yahoo CEO Marissa Mayer & the war on women. *Philly2Philly,* August 5. Retrieved from http://www.philly2philly.com/politics_community/politics_community_articles/2012/8/5/49172/new_yahoo_ceo_marissa_mayer_the_war_wo on July 11, 2013.

2. Guynn, J. (2013). Yahoo CEO Marissa Mayer causes uproar with telecommuting ban. *The Los Angeles Times,* February 26. Retrieved from http://articles.latimes.com/2013/feb/26/business/la-fi-yahoo-telecommuting-20130226 on July 13, 2013.

3. Erickson, J. (2013). Marissa Mayer backlash reveals double standard for women CEOs. *Huffington Post,* March 19. Retrieved from http://www.huffingtonpost.com/jennifer-erickson/marissa-mayer-backlash-re_b_2908194.html on July 13, 2013.

4. Erickson, 2013.

5. Guynn, 2013.

6. Nisen, M. (2013). End of working from home: Best Buy kills flexible work program. *Business Insider,* March 5. Retrieved from http://www.businessinsider.com/best-buy-ending-work-from-home-2013-3 on July 13, 2013.

7. DeVoe, D. (1999, August 9). Don't let conflict get you off course. *Info World,* 69–72.

8. Lulofs, S., & Cahn, D. D. (2000). *Conflict: From theory to action* (2nd ed.). Boston, MA: Allyn & Bacon, p. 36.

9. Caudron, S. (1999). Productive conflict has value. *Workforce, 78*(2), 25–28.

10. Javich, D. (2010). Positive steps for managing conflict. *Entrepreneur,* March 11. Retrieved from http://www.entrepreneur.com/article/205490#ixzz2RV5peyVC on April 29, 2013.

11. Joni, S., & Beyer, D. (2009). How to pick a good fight. *Harvard Business Review, 87*(12), 48–57.

12. Gruber, H. E. (2006). Creativity and conflict resolution. In M. Deutsch, P. T. Coleman, & E. C. Marcus (Eds.), *The handbook of conflict resolution.*

San Francisco, CA: Jossey-Bass; Pascale, R. T. (1990). *Managing on the edge: How the smartest companies use conflict to stay ahead.* New York, NY: Simon & Schuster; and Wanous, J. P., & Youtz, M. A. (1986). Solution diversity and the quality of group decisions. *Academy of Management Journal, 29*(1), 149–159.

13. Van Wart, M. (2005). *Dynamics of leadership in public service: Theory and practice.* Armonk, NY: M. E. Sharpe.

14. Tinsley, C. (2001). How negotiators get to yes: Predicting the constellation of strategies across cultures to negotiate conflict. *Journal of Applied Psychology, 86*(4), 583–593; and Triandis, H. C. (1994). Cross-cultural industrial and organizational psychology. In H. C. Triandis (Ed.), *Culture and social behavior.* New York, NY: McGraw-Hill.

15. Kamil, K. M. (1997). Culture and conflict management: A theoretical framework. *International Journal of Conflict Management, 8,* 338–360.

16. Ayoko, O. B., & Hartel, C. E. J. (2006). Cultural diversity and leadership: A conceptual model of leader intervention in conflict events in culturally heterogeneous workgroups. *Cross Cultural Management: An International Journal, 13*(4), 345–360.

17. Kamil, 1997.

18. Tinsley, 2001.

19. Tinsley, 2001.

20. Desivilya, H. S., & Yagil, D. (2005). The role of emotions in conflict management: The case of work teams. *International Journal of Conflict Management, 16*(1), 55–69.

21. Korabik, K. (1992). Sex-role orientation and leadership style. *International Journal of Women's Studies, 5,* 328–336.

22. Whetten, D. A., & Cameron, K. S. (1998). *Developing management skills* (4th ed.). Reading, MA: Addison-Wesley.

23. Susskind, L. E., & Cruikshank, J. L. (2006). *Breaking Robert's rules: The new way to run*

your meeting, build consensus, and get results. New York, NY: Oxford University Press.

24. Deutsch, M. (1968). The effects of cooperation and compensation upon group process. In D. Cartwright & A. Zander (Eds.), *Group dynamics* (pp. 461–482). New York, NY: Harper & Row.

25. Schein, E. H. (2009). *Helping: How to offer, give, and receive help.* San Francisco, CA: Berrett-Koehler.

26. Schein, 2009, p. 18.

27. Neilson, F. (1972). Understanding and managing intergroup conflict. In J. W. Lorsch & P. R. Lawrence (Eds.), *Managing group and intergroup relations* (pp. 329–342). Homewood, IL: Irwin & Dorsey.

28. Thomas, K. W. (1976). Conflict and conflict management. In M. D. Dunnette (Ed.), *Handbook of industrial and organizational psychology.* Chicago, IL: Rand McNally.

29. Joni & Beyer, 2009.

30. Faerman, S. R. (1996). Managing conflict creatively. In J. Perry (Ed.), *Handbook of public administration.* San Francisco, CA: Jossey-Bass.

31. Cosier, R. A., & Schwenk, C. R. (1990, February). Agreement and thinking alike: Ingredients for poor decisions. *Academy of Management Executive,* p. 119.

32. Lax, D. A., & Sebenius, J. K. (1986). *The manager as negotiator.* New York, NY: Free Press.

33. Fisher, R., Ury, W., & Patton, B. (1991). *Getting to yes: Negotiating agreements without giving in.* New York, NY: Penguin.

34. Lewicki, R. J. (1983). Lying and deception: A behavioral model. In M. H. Bazerman & R. J. Lewicki (Eds.), *Negotiating in organizations.* Beverly Hill, CA: Sage.

35. Hendon, D. W., Hendon, R. A., & Herbig, P. (1996). *Cross-cultural business negotiations.* Westport, CT: Quorum.

36. See Munter, M. (1993, May–June). Cross-cultural communication for managers. *Business Horizons,* 69–78.

37. Casserly, M. (2012). Why American women lose at negotiation—and what we can do about it. *Forbes,* April 3. Retrieved from http://www.forbes.com/sites/meghancasserly/2012/04/03/why-american-women-lose-negotiation-linked-in-career/ on May 2, 2013.

38. Kwintessential: Cross cultural negotiation. (2013). Retrieved from http://www.kwintessential.co.uk/cultural-services/articles/cross-cultural-negotiation.html on May 4, 2013.

39. Falcao, H. (2008). *Cross-cultural negotiation: Avoiding the pitfalls.* Retrieved from http://knowledge.insead.edu/leadership-management/organisational-behaviour/cross-cultural-negotiations-avoiding-the-pitfalls-1928 on May 4, 2013.

40. Lewis, R. (2013). Negotiating across cultures. Retrieved from http://www.crossculture.com/services/negotiating-across-cultures/ on May 4, 2013.

41. Casserly, 2012.

42. For example, Taylor, S. E., & Brown, J. D. (1988). Illusion and well-being: A social psychological perspective. *Psychology Bulletin, 103,* 193–210.

43. Martin, J. (1997). How to negotiate with really tough guys. *Fortune Advisor 1997,* 110–113.

44. Martin, 1997.

45. Savage, G. T., Blari, J. D., & Sorenson, R. L. (1989, February). Consider both relationships and substance when negotiating strategically. *Academy of Management Executive,* 37–47.

46. See Lulofs, R. S., & Cahn, D. D. (2000). *Conflict: From theory to action* (2nd ed.). Boston, MA: Allyn & Bacon.

47. Fisher, Ury, & Patton, 1991.

48. Fisher et al., 1991, p. 19.

49. Fisher et al., 1991, p. 7.

50. Edmondson, A. C., & Roloff, K. S. (2009). *Leveraging diversity through psychological safety.* Retrieved from http://hbr.org/product/leveraging-diversity-through-psychological-safety/an/ROT093-PDF-ENG?Ntt=psychological+safety&Nao=0 on May 1, 2013.

12 Leadership

Classic to Contemporary

37Signals Experimental Leadership ▶

Jason Fried is the cofounder and CEO of 37signals, a software firm based in Chicago, and one known for its innovative leadership and workplace experimentation. The firm's website heralds the company's products, such as Basecamp and Highrise, but also lays out the company's values and some of its most innovative practices. For example, the first value is: "Useful is forever: Bells and whistles wear off, but usefulness never does. We build useful software that does just what you need and nothing you don't." Another is: "Clarity is king: Buzzwords, lingo, and sensationalized sales-and-marketing-speak have no place at 37signals. We communicate clearly and honestly."[1] But in addition to its values, the company's homepage also emphasizes 37signals's fresh approach to business.

In a recent interview, Fried discussed one of his company's experiments, requiring employees to work no more than 4 days a week during the summer. In response to a question about whether people felt uncomfortable working only 4 days a week, Fried admitted that some did, but soon got used to the idea that most things could wait from Thursday to Monday. Asked whether it's rational to not allow people to work 5 days a week if they wish to do so, he commented, "If you're a short-term thinker you'd think so, but we're long-term thinkers. We're about being in business for the long haul and keeping the team together over the long haul. I would never trade a short-term burst for a long-term decline in morale. That happens a lot in the tech business: They burn people out and get someone else. I like the people who work here too much. I don't want them to burn out."[2]

Fried is also a proponent of slow, careful, methodical growth. Many companies, he argues, especially in the high-tech field, seem to want to grow for growth's sake. Often that leads to companies "crashing and burning." 37signals, on the other hand, has only about 35 employees (though its revenue and profit figures could support many more than that) and

A leader is best when people barely know that he exists, Not so good when people obey and acclaim him, Worst when they despise him. "Fail to honor people, they fail to honor you"; But of a good leader, who talks little, when his work is done, his aim fulfilled, they will all say, "We did this ourselves."

—Lao-tzu, circa 600 BC

has a long-term commitment to those employees. Fried contends that many high-tech firms are cutthroat in their approach to their competitors. Many have multiple rounds of financing in the millions of dollars and still are not making money.[3]

In their book, *Rework*, Fried and his cofounder David Heinemeier Hansson take on some of the sacred cows of business leadership. For example, they ridicule the unquestioned development of business, financial, and strategic plans, arguing that each of these are at best guesses about what the future will bring. Moreover, they argue, plans let the past drive the future. They say, "Here's where we're going, because that is where we said we were going." Such an approach prevents leaders and managers from adapting to changing conditions. The key is to improvise appropriately as conditions change. "You have to be able to pick up opportunities that come along. Sometimes you need to say, "We're going in a new direction because that's what makes sense today."[4]

Leadership is one of the most important and widely debated but least clearly understood concepts in organizational behavior. There are frequent calls for better leadership at all levels and in organizations of all types. Yet no one seems to know exactly what constitutes leadership, where it comes from, or how it might be developed. Certainly there is agreement that the traditional top-down models of leadership that we associate with groups such as the military are outdated and unworkable in modern society—even in the military. For this reason, many people now argue that a new approach to leadership is needed.

First, in today's world and certainly in tomorrow's world, more and more people are going to want to participate in the decisions that affect them. Increasingly, those in organizations want to be involved; they want a piece of the action. Various constituents, including customers and clients, also want to participate, as well they should.

Leadership Theory

Second, leadership is increasingly being thought of not as a position in a hierarchy but rather as a process that occurs throughout organizations (and beyond). In the past, a leader was considered the person who held a formal position of power in an organization or a society. But today we would say that leadership is not just something reserved for presidents, governors, mayors, CEO's, and department heads. Everyone should lead from time to time.

What Do You Think?

▶ We have said that most organizations are moving toward shared, group-centric leadership. Others say that there are still circumstances where top-down leadership is appropriate? What do you think?

Third, it is safe to predict that, over the coming years, we will see more and more instances of what we term *shared leadership*, both within organizations and as leaders and managers relate to their many external constituencies. Leaders in the future will be found "not only among those at the top, the 'lead horses,' but also among those who constitute what in the industrial era we called the rank and file."[5] In the new *group-centric* leadership, leaders and managers will need to develop and employ new skills that include important elements of empathy, consideration, facilitation, negotiation, and brokering.

Fourth, we should understand that leadership is not just about doing things right; it is about doing the right things.[6] In other words, leadership inevitably is associated with important human values, including the most fundamental values of our society. Through the process of leadership, people working together make choices about the directions they want to take; they make fundamental decisions about their futures. Such choices cannot be made simply on the basis of a rational calculation of costs and benefits. They require a careful balancing of human values. Leadership, as we will see, can play a transformational role in this process, helping people to confront important values and, indeed, helping them to grow and develop individually and collectively.

In this chapter, we consider these important and evolving issues, but we will also consider how these ideas will affect the way in which you go about trying to improve your own leadership capabilities. To get to that point, however, we need to understand first how leadership has been studied and practiced in the past; this will enable us to understand the context in which modern discussions of leadership are taking place. We will then explore the implications of these ideas for your own leadership development.

SELF-ASSESSMENT 12.1

WHAT MAKES A GOOD LEADER?

Think of a person who you think is an excellent leader. This could be someone you know personally, someone you have watched from afar, or someone you have only read about or otherwise studied. It could be someone living today or someone from another time and place. What are the 10 qualities that make you think highly of that person's leadership?

1. _____
2. _____
3. _____
4. _____
5. _____
6. _____
7. _____
8. _____
9. _____
10. _____

Consider a specific incident in which you thought this person exercised exceptional leadership skills. Which of the preceding characteristics (or others) were most important in this particular case of leadership? Why?

_____

_____

_____

(Continued)

Your Experience as a Leader

Now consider your own experiences as a leader. Don't restrict yourself to times in which you were in a position of formal leadership, such as president of a student organization. Instead, consider leadership as something that everyone engages in from time to time. Think of a situation in which you *led*, even if only for a short period. Write down the circumstances in which you led:

What was it you did in this situation that caused others to follow you?

What five characteristics do you consider your best leadership qualities or traits?

1. _____

2. _____

3. _____

4. _____

5. _____

If we asked your friends to list your best leadership qualities, what do you think they would say?

1. _____

2. _____

3. _____

4. _____

5. _____

Thinking About Leadership

To begin, think for a moment about what we mean by the term *leadership*. One review of major studies in leadership pointed out that there are nearly as many definitions of leadership as there are people trying to define it and that many of the definitions are ambiguous.[7] Moreover, as we noted earlier, the way in which we think about leadership is changing, meaning that the way in which we should define leadership is changing as well.[8] In the past, leaders were thought of as people in positions of power and authority and people who used their power and authority, as well as other forms of influence, to direct others toward goals and objectives that they had established in advance. Put simply, the leader's role was to (1) come up with good ideas about the direction that the group should take, (2) decide on a course of action or a goal to be accomplished, and (3) exert his or her influence or control in moving the group in that direction.

As the head coach of Penn State's women's basketball team, Coquese Washington is focused on leading her team to win on the court but also mentoring her players off the court. Washington said, "Mentoring them and helping them learn to become powerful, dynamic women—that's the thing I love best of all."

As we have noted, the way in which we think about leadership is changing. Leadership no longer is simply what those in leadership positions do. Rather, it refers to a process by which one or more people influence others to pursue a commonly held objective. We might define leadership in this way: *Leadership occurs where one or more members of a group or organization stimulate others to more clearly recognize their previously latent needs, desires, and potentialities and to work together toward their fulfillment.*

The Biggest Mistake for a Leader

Whether leadership comes from someone in a formal position of "leadership" or from someone else, we can say that leadership has occurred only when the group has been stimulated to move in a new direction. To move a group in this way, a person does not necessarily need to exercise power or control. Indeed, power actually can be destructive to leadership in the long term. Rather, the potential leader must understand the group or organization and find ways of stimulating, moving, or, in a word, *energizing* it.

What Do You Think?

▶ Many argue that our traditional theories of management and leadership are based on masculine traits. Do you find this to be the case? How well would that serve women? In fact, how well would that serve men?

Traditional Approaches to Leadership

The Trait Approach

The **trait approach** to leadership addresses the question of what constitutes effective leadership based on personal characteristics or traits associated with successful leaders, whose lives and careers are studied to try to determine what qualities set leaders apart from others. Are leaders smarter than others? Do they have more highly developed verbal skills? Are they taller or more masculine? Note that most of the subjects of these discussions, as well as the subjects of the earliest formal studies of leadership during the early 1900s, were men, a fact that many have suggested might have biased the early study of leadership toward a particular model of leadership behavior.

Trait approach: addresses the question of what constitutes effective leadership based on personal characteristics or traits associated with successful leaders

In an early review of leadership traits, Stogdill (1974) argued that leaders are characterized by (1) a strong drive for responsibility and task completion, (2) considerable vigor and persistence in the pursuit of goals, (3) creativity and originality in problem solving, (4) the exercise of initiative in social situations, (5) self-confidence and a strong sense of personal identity, (6) a willingness to accept the consequences of their decisions and actions, (7) a capacity for absorbing stress, (8) a willingness to tolerate frustration and delay, (9) the ability to influence the behavior of others, and (10) a capacity to organize groups to achieve the purpose at hand.[9] However, while certain traits are associated with leadership, traits alone cannot predict who will be a leader, let alone whether a person with certain traits will be an *effective* leader.

The Behavior Approach

As a result of the limitations of the trait approach, researchers turned their attention from *who* leaders are to *what* leaders do, focusing on leader behaviors. This is called the **behavior approach**. During the late 1940s, a group of researchers at The Ohio State University undertook a series of studies of leadership behavior, largely basing their work on a questionnaire that asked people about the behavior that their leaders exhibited.[10] Two factors emerged: what they called "consideration" and "the initiation of structure." Consideration describes the extent to which the leader is concerned for the welfare of those in the group. The idea of consideration is primarily focused on *relationships*. Initiation of structure, on the other hand, describes the extent to which the leader initiates activity in the group, organizes the group, and defines the way in which the work is to be done. The idea of initiation is primarily focused on tasks.

While task and relationship are well accepted as two key leadership behaviors, the focus on behaviors is not able to consistently predict whether task or relationship is related to effective leadership. Meanwhile, we know that leadership may be the result of the interaction of leaders and situations, not simply as a set of traits or behaviors.

The Contingency Approach

The **contingency approach** to leadership assumes that understanding requires consideration of both leadership characteristics—either traits or behaviors or a combination—and the leadership situation.[11] Theories such as "the Managerial Grid"[12] and Situational Leadership®[13] suggest that different situations require different styles of leadership and, correspondingly, that leaders need to be able to understand the key characteristics of the organizations they lead and then adapt their own behavior to fit the situation.

This same basic premise underlies several other approaches. For example, Fiedler's[14] contingency model of leadership suggests that effective group performance is based on the match between the leader's style of leadership and the degree to which the situation enables the leader to exert influence. This theory considers the leader's style in terms of task and relationships while key situational factors include the relationship with follower, the degree of the task, and the power of the leader. Fiedler's contingency model assumes that task-oriented leaders will be most effective when they can exert more influence and control. Relationship-oriented leaders will be most effective when the situation provides less control.

Another approach suggesting that a leader needs to select a behavior meeting the needs of subordinates and the degree of the structure and clarity of the task is called path–goal theory.[15] The theory proposes that a directive behavior will be most effective in situations

Behavior approach:
leadership approach that focuses on behaviors of leaders

Contingency approach:
understanding leadership requires consideration of both leadership characteristics—either traits or behaviors or a combination—and the leadership situation

WHAT IS YOUR LEADERSHIP STYLE?

The following questionnaire will help you to assess your leadership style. Read each item and think about how often you engage in the described behavior. Indicate your response to each item by circling one of the five numbers to the right of each item (1 = *never*, 2 = *seldom*, 3 = *occasionally*, 4 = *often*, 5 = *always*). We will discuss the results of the questionnaire later in the chapter.

	Never	Seldom	Occasionally	Often	Always
1. Tells group members what they are supposed to do	1	2	3	4	5
2. Acts friendly with members of the group	1	2	3	4	5
3. Sets standards of performance for group members	1	2	3	4	5
4. Helps others to feel comfortable in the group	1	2	3	4	5
5. Makes suggestions about how to solve problems	1	2	3	4	5
6. Responds favorably to suggestions made by others	1	2	3	4	5
7. Makes his or her perspective clear to others	1	2	3	4	5
8. Treats others fairly	1	2	3	4	5
9. Develops a plan of action for the group	1	2	3	4	5
10. Behaves in a predictable manner toward group members	1	2	3	4	5
11. Defines role responsibilities for each group member	1	2	3	4	5
12. Communicates actively with group members	1	2	3	4	5
13. Clarifies his or her own role within the group	1	2	3	4	5
14. Shows concern for the personal well-being of others	1	2	3	4	5
15. Provides a plan for how the work is to be done	1	2	3	4	5
16. Shows flexibility in making decisions	1	2	3	4	5
17. Provides criteria for what is expected of the group	1	2	3	4	5
18. Discloses thoughts and feelings to group members	1	2	3	4	5
19. Encourages group members to do quality work	1	2	3	4	5
20. Helps group members to get along	1	2	3	4	5

Scoring

The style questionnaire is designed to measure two major types of leadership behavior: task orientation and relationship orientation. Score the questionnaire by first summing the responses on the odd-numbered items; this is your task score. Then sum the responses on the even-numbered items; this is your relationship score. We discuss the question of leadership style later in the chapter.

Total scores: Task _____ Relationship _____

Interpretation

45–50 Very high

40–44 High

35–39 Moderately high

30–34 Moderately low

25–29 Low

10–24 Very low

Source: From Northouse, P. G. (2013). *Leadership: Theory and practice* (6th ed.). Thousand Oaks, CA: Sage, pp. 93–94. Used by permission.

where employees themselves are somewhat dogmatic, where the demands of the task are ambiguous, and where rules and procedures are unclear. A supportive leadership behavior, on the other hand, will be most effective in situations where subordinates are engaged in work that is stressful, frustrating, or unsatisfying. In these cases, the supportive leader can provide necessary encouragement and help to the subordinates.

When compared to either the trait or the behavior approaches to leadership, the contingency theories provide a more complex view of leadership by taking into account both the leader and the situation in which she finds herself. Figure 12.1 summarizes the early approaches to understanding leadership. Contemporary theories of leadership build on all the previous approaches and provide a richer view of leadership.

FIGURE 12.1 EARLY LEADERSHIP APPROACHES

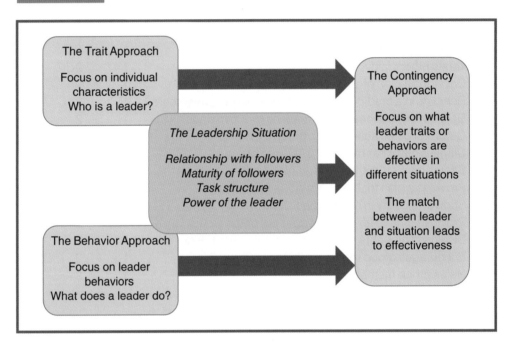

Contemporary Approaches to Leadership

From Traits to Skills and Competencies

Even today, there continues to be considerable interest in defining the characteristics that are associated with successful leadership. But there has been an interesting recent twist in this approach. Increasingly, in addition to describing traits of leaders, scholars are now focusing on the skills, competencies, and strategies associated with leadership. Various writers have developed different lists of traits, competencies, or skills required of leaders.[16]

While there are many such lists, certain traits or competencies seem to stand out. Among these, we would suggest the following (Figure 12.2).

1. *Intelligence and self-understanding.* Intellectual ability seems to be positively associated with leadership success. Leaders need a strong capacity for conceiving possibilities that might be hidden within a situation, the ability to articulate their ideas clearly and persuasively, and the intelligence to understand the context in which those ideas are to be played out. Leaders

must be engaged with the outside world, but they also must be adept at self-understanding (as well as what we have called emotional intelligence). Indeed, many see the process of leadership development as merely one aspect of personal development. "The process of becoming a leader is much the same as the process of becoming an integrated human being."[17]

What Do You Think?

▶ Before reading further, think about some of the limitations of the traditional approaches we have examined to this point. What are they missing? What would you like to see addressed? What environmental circumstances have changed since these ideas were proposed? How would those affect the theory and practice of leadership?

2. *Self-confidence and self-esteem.* Obviously, those who aspire to leadership must have a certain degree of confidence that they will succeed. They must feel sure of their own abilities as well as the abilities of their followers. Indeed, leaders who have high expectations for themselves are likely to inspire high expectations in subordinates as well.[18] Self-confidence is important, but it also is tricky. Too little self-confidence might cause a potential leader to be indecisive and vague, whereas too much self-confidence, an inflated ego, might cause the person to be arrogant and intolerant of criticism.

3. *High energy and determination to succeed.* Leaders have been shown to have greater energy, physical stamina, and tolerance for stress than do others. Leadership is hard, demanding work, so physical vitality and emotional resilience are quite helpful characteristics for leaders to possess.[19] In addition, leaders need to exhibit high degrees of initiative and drive to get things done. They not only must be willing to commit to putting in long hours but also must make a deep psychological commitment to the task at hand. For example, in his well-known book, *Good to Great,* Jim Collins described "Level Five Leaders" as ambitious for the cause and the work—but not ambitious themselves. "The Level Five Leader displays a paradoxical blend of personal humility and professional will."[20]

4. *Creativity.* The 2010 IBM Global CEO Study concluded that the single most important attribute of future leaders will be creativity. "Creative leaders invite disruptive innovation, encourage others to drop outdated approaches and take balanced risks. They are open-minded and inventive in expanding their management and communication styles, particularly to engage with a new generation of employees, partners, and customers."[21]

5. *Sociability (interpersonal awareness).* Generally speaking, leaders like to interact with others and tend to be warm, friendly, outgoing, and diplomatic in their relations with others. They have good interpersonal skills and generally are able to achieve cooperative relationships with others. In any case, leaders need to be sensitive to the social and psychological needs of those around them; they need to exhibit interpersonal awareness.

6. *Integrity.* Integrity refers not only to knowing the right course of action but also to being able to pursue that course, even under pressure not to do so. Leaders with integrity are honest, principled, and ethical in their dealings with others. They can be trusted to do what they say they will do and to follow up on promises made. They will keep their commitments. In acting with integrity, they command the respect of others who recognize their sense of responsibility.[22] Most important, their actions will match their words; they will act in accord with their principles and will "walk the walk."

Moving from a discussion of traits and skills to a discussion of what leaders do, how they act, and what strategies they employ, we examine one popular approach to the question

FIGURE 12.2 NEW LEADERSHIP CHARACTERISTICS

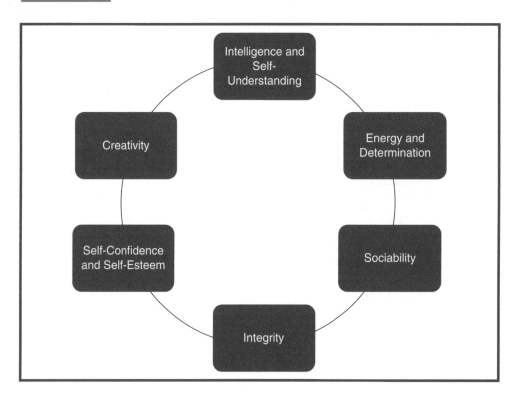

Personal Business at Work

of leadership practices—an approach developed by Kouzes and Posner in their book *The Leadership Challenge*.[23] Kouzes and Posner began their work by surveying thousands of managers in the United States, asking the question, "What values (personal traits or characteristics) do you look for and admire in your superiors?" The most frequent responses were that superiors be honest, competent, forward-looking, and inspiring. Kouzes and Posner noted that these categories were surprisingly similar to those communication experts use in assessing the believability of sources of communications such as newscasters and salespeople. In such studies, qualities such as trustworthiness, expertise, and dynamism were associated with greater credibility. Kouzes and Posner (2007) concluded that, more than anything else, we want leaders who are *credible*: "Above all, we must be able to believe in our leaders. We must believe that their word can be trusted, that they will do what they say, that they have the knowledge and skill to lead, and that they are personally excited and enthusiastic about the direction in which we are headed."[24]

If credibility is the foundation of all leadership, then what are the things leaders do that enhance their credibility? Kouzes and Posner[25] answered that leaders establish their credibility through five "practices" that they engage in when they are at their best. These include the following:

1. *Challenging the process*. Leaders accept the challenge of change. The specific challenge may come in a number of ways—from trying to introduce a new product line, to implementing a new program, to turning a struggling organization around. Leaders are willing to step out into the unknown and explore new ideas and approaches. They encourage risk and innovation—in themselves and in others. And they learn from both their successes and their failures.

2. *Inspiring a shared vision.* Leaders look into the future, explore its possibilities, and dream about what the future might be like. This vision or mission represents an important change—a desire to make something happen that is new, different, and hopefully better. But leaders not only have to articulate the vision; they also have to inspire others to buy into that vision.

3. *Enabling others to act.* Leaders cannot carry forward important projects on their own. They need the help and assistance of people throughout the organization. Successful leaders encourage, empower, and enable others to act. They promote teamwork and collaboration throughout the organization, and they model the importance of teamwork in their own behavior.

4. *Modeling the way.* The most successful leaders are those who "practice what they preach." These are the leaders who have a clear awareness of their beliefs and values and who constantly sharpen their understanding of those beliefs and values. They are people who have a clear sense of their own behavior—what they are doing and how it is affecting the group.

5. *Encouraging the heart.* The most successful leaders encourage others to do their very best and then recognize and celebrate their successes. Leaders are in part cheerleaders, boosting the spirits of those with whom they work and cheering them on to greater accomplishments.

Deborah Ancona, director of the MIT Leadership Center in the Sloan School of Management, has provided an interesting summary of some of these lessons for leaders. First, she suggests, leadership is personal. There is no one best way to lead and each leader needs to call forth her most important qualities and adapt them to the situation she finds herself in. "Each person needs to figure out his or her own unique leadership signature—one that draws on his or her own strengths."[26] Second, Ancona suggests that all leadership is based on four specific capabilities: "*sensemaking* (in other words, making sense of the business environment in which your company operates); *visioning*; *relating* to others; and *inventing* new ways to get things done."[27] Third, leaders need the capacity to understand complex environments. You must be able to make sense out of complexity and to draw out the most relevant lessons for the future of the organization. Fourth, Ancona argues, leadership is not a solo performance, but involves bringing many people together to engage in group leadership, what she calls distributed leadership.[28]

The Transformational Approach

One of the most powerful formulations of leadership in the modern era—the idea of transformational leadership—is the key concept in a classic study by Harvard University political scientist James MacGregor Burns titled simply *Leadership*.[29] In this monumental work, Burns did not merely try to understand the dynamics of leadership in terms of getting things done or meeting organizational objectives. Rather he sought to understand leadership as a relationship between leaders and followers—a mutual interaction that ultimately changes both.

Burns started by noting that although historically we have been preoccupied with power in organizations and in society, there is an important difference between power and leadership. Typically, power is thought of as carrying out one's own will despite resistance. But such a conception of power neglects the important fact that power involves a relationship between leaders and followers and that a central value in that relationship is *purpose*—what is being sought, or what is intended, by both the one who is exercising power and the one who is on the receiving end. In most situations, the recipient has some flexibility

Avoid Leadership
Derailment

Nelson Mandela, former president of South Africa and a leader in the anti-apartheid movement in that country, is an example of a transformational leader. His strong moral posture attracted the respect and even adoration of those in his home country as well as people around the world. It's hard to say whether many leaders really transformed their country or their organization, but there is no question that Mandela did.

in his or her response to an attempted exercise of power, so the power that one can exercise is dependent on the way in which both parties view the situation. Leadership, according to Burns, is an aspect of power, but it is a separate process. Power is exercised when potential power wielders, acting to achieve goals of their own, gather resources that enable them to influence others. Power is exercised to realize the purposes of the power wielders, whether or not those purposes also are the purposes of the respondents. Leadership, on the other hand, is exercised "when persons with certain motives and purposes mobilize, in competition or conflict with others, institutional, political, psychological, and other resources so as to arouse, engage, and satisfy the motives of the followers."[30] The difference between power and leadership is that power serves the interests of the power wielder, whereas leadership serves both the leader's interests *and* those of the followers.

There actually are two types of leadership, Burns argues. The first is **transactional leadership**, which involves an exchange of valued things (e.g., economic, political, psychological) between initiators and respondents. For example, a political leader might agree to support a particular policy in exchange for votes in the next election, or a student might write a superb paper in exchange for an A grade. In the case of transactional leadership, the two parties come together in a relationship that advances the interests of both, but there is no deep or enduring link between them.

Transactional leadership: involves an exchange of valued things (e.g., economic, political, psychological) between initiators and respondents

Transformational leadership: occurs when leaders and followers engage with one another in such a way that they raise one another to higher levels of morality and motivation

Moral leadership: a form of leadership that raises the level of moral aspiration and moral conduct of both leaders and followers

Transformational leadership, on the other hand, occurs when leaders and followers engage with one another in such a way that they raise one another to higher levels of morality and motivation. Although the leaders and followers initially might come together out of the pursuit of their own interests or because the leader recognized some special potential in the followers, as the relationship evolves their interests become fused into mutual support for common purposes. The relationship between leaders and followers becomes one in which both parties become mobilized, inspired, and uplifted. In some cases, transformational leadership even evolves into **moral leadership** as leadership raises the level of moral aspiration and moral conduct of both leaders and followers. Moral leadership results in actions that are consistent with the needs, interests, and aspirations of the followers but that fundamentally change moral understandings and social conditions.

A narrower approach to transformational leadership, proposed by Bernard Bass and his associates, focuses more closely on the *relationship* of leaders and subordinates in complex organizations with a particular application to business organizations.[31] In this view, the transactional leader exchanges rewards for services rendered so as to improve subordinates' job performance. Based on this view, the early leadership theories such as Fiedler's model or path-goal theory are primarily focused on such transactional relationships. The transformational leader, rather than focusing on how the current needs of subordinates might be met, concentrates on arousing or altering their needs. This narrower view of transformational leadership does not imply a moral element. Instead it focuses on large-scale change that results from three elements that are presented in Figure 12.3. Based on this view of transformational leadership, even destructive unethical leaders such as Hitler are considered effective because they are able to dramatically change their organization or society.

An Irresistible Leader

FIGURE 12.3 BASS'S MODEL OF TRANSFORMATIONAL LEADERSHIP

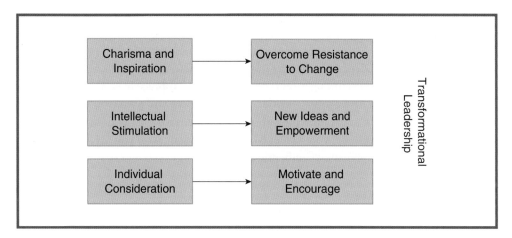

Value-Based Leadership

The importance of morality and values in defining leadership has been central in several more recent studies. Robert K. Greenleaf,[32] a longtime AT&T management development specialist turned consultant and writer, emphasized the role of the spirit and the spiritual in his concept of **servant leadership**. The idea is that leadership begins with a commitment on the part of the potential leader to serve others. The leader does not pursue his or her self-interest but rather is primarily concerned with serving others. In this view, the organizational "bottom line" is less important than the leader's capacity for honesty, integrity, character, or spirit. Although there is the implication that, in the long run, the servant-leader will help the organization accomplish its work more effectively, the first priority is service to others—clients, customers, citizens, or the community.

The idea of approaching leadership from the standpoint of values has been echoed in several other works. O'Toole (1995) contrasted values-based leadership with contingency or situational approaches, arguing that all such approaches ultimately involve an effort on the part of the leader to impose his or her will on followers without regard to their own needs or interests and often without even consulting them, something that O'Toole called "the ultimate in disrespect for individuals."[33] By contrast, the leader must understand why people resist change and make the personal investment required to overcome this resistance, typically by offering a new system of beliefs that resonates with followers so that they come to adopt it as their own. O'Toole suggested that to develop a theory of leadership that has more substance than "it depends," values and morality need to be at the center. "If the goal is to bring about constructive change, values-based leadership is, yes, always more effective."[34]

Servant leadership: a type of leadership that begins with a commitment on the part of the potential leader to serve others

Authentic Leadership

A relatively recent addition to the field of leadership is called authentic leadership. The **authentic leader** is one who remains true to his or her values, preferences, hopes, and aspirations, and acts in a way that is consistent with those values and beliefs. Authentic leaders are both self-reflective and empathetic, establishing a basis for clear and trusting communications in both directions. They are aware of their own strengths and weaknesses, aware of the environment within which they operate, and they are confident, hopeful, and resilient. Padmasree Warrior, chief technology officer at Cisco Systems, says: "To be a great leader, you need to be yourself."[35] Hatim Tyabji, a world-renowned innovation expert and an executive at Bytemobile Inc., a wireless infrastructure provider, agrees, "The first principle of leadership is authenticity: Watch what I do, not what I say. Leadership requires moral authority. You can't have moral authority if you behave differently from your people."[36]

Leadership
in Teams

The key to authentic leadership is understanding your personal strengths and developing them. Consistent with our emphasis on a strengths-based approach, consultant Marcus Buckingham suggests, "To become a leader, identify where you are strongest and most confident, and then work to expand those areas. If you want to be a better leader, don't try to be all things to all people . . . you will lead best by following who you are."[37] Table 12.1 summarizes the key components of authentic leadership.

TABLE 12.1 COMPONENTS OF AUTHENTIC LEADERSHIP

Components	Description
Self-awareness	Being aware of your emotions, motives, and traits
Unbiased or balanced processing	Being able to consider multiple perspectives and inputs and assess information in a balanced manner
Being true to self and motivated by personal convictions	Being focused by your convictions and guided by personal values
Relational authenticity or transparency	Being able to disclose and share information about self appropriately

Source: Based on information in Avolio, B. J., & Gardner, W. L. (2005). Authentic leadership development: Getting to the root of positive forms of leadership. *The Leadership Quarterly, 16,* 315–338; Kernis, M. H. (2003). Toward a conceptualization of optimal self-esteem. *Psychological Inquiry, 14,* 1–26.

Shared Leadership

As we have seen, the traditional model of leadership revolves around a single individual (the lonely hero) wielding power and influence in a unilateral and largely downward fashion. Newer approaches emphasize *shared leadership* and *group-centric leadership*. Shared or group-centric leadership may be described as "a dynamic interactive influence process among individuals in groups in which the objective is to lead one another to their achievement of group or organizational goals."[38] As such, shared leadership at some times involves peer or lateral influence, and at other times involves upward or downward influence. In any case, leadership is broadly distributed among members of the group, the organization, or the society.[39] For those seeking to assert leadership in

Authentic leader:
one who remains true to his or her values, preferences, hopes, and aspirations, and acts in a way that is consistent with those values and beliefs

situations involving many groups and interests, the traditional skills of organizational management—motivating, delegating, and so on—are less applicable than a new set of skills that includes negotiating, brokering, and resolving conflict. One writer has called this shift a move from chief executive to chief influencer.[40]

What Do You Think?

▶ Some say leadership is a science. Others say leadership is an art. What do you think?

Collaborative Leadership

Obviously, the key to shared or group-centric leadership is the capacity to collaborate with others. Salesforce.com, for example, was experimenting with Chatter, a social media offshoot of Facebook. As people throughout the company voiced their thoughts and ideas, CEO Marc Benioff realized that many of the best ideas being discussed were coming from people throughout the organization, not just the people at the top who he knew best. At the next company retreat he invited not only the top executives but all 5,000 employees, some in the room but most connected virtually. The session began with regular presentations, but then opened up to Chatter. Initially, ideas came in slowly, but soon ideas were pouring in and those who were there felt a real sense of empowerment. The conversation continued long after the meeting itself was concluded, and the result was the creation of a more open and empowered culture in the organization.[41]

Marc Benioff, founder and CEO of Salesforce.com, is persuaded that securing input from people throughout the organization is essential to good business practice.

Several scholars have elaborated on such an approach. In *Connective Leadership*, Jean Lipman-Blumen (2000) stresses the need for greater collaboration in a diverse society, arguing that the role of a leader is to "transform interdependence and diversity from opposing into symbiotic forces."[42] Connective leaders are trusting, social, and personal; they are motivated by maximizing the interaction and collaboration among diverse people to achieve a particular end. Similarly, Sally Helgesen argues in *The Web of Inclusion*[43] that since change is the only constant in modern life and modern organizations, leaders must insist on change at a manageable rate, provide an environment for adaptive work, and empower the front-line employees with the capacity to innovate. She compares the modern organization to a web: a flat, flexible structure with permeable edges susceptible to external influences and multiple lines of communication that weave together and create an intricate network of interconnected and diverse people and organizations. The goal of the organization is to satisfy the needs of its constituency and this can only happen if the constituents themselves are regarded as participants in the evolution of the organization.

Other scholars have focused even more specifically on the *relationship* between leaders and followers as the key to understanding leadership. (In some variations, this view is called leader–member exchange theory, in others, relational leadership.) This approach does not use the terms *manager* and *leaders* interchangeably, but focuses specifically on acts of leading that can occur in many circumstances. It also moves well beyond hierarchical forms of leader control. In relational leadership, it is not the attributes or behaviors of either leaders or followers that are most important, but what happens *between* leaders and followers—how the exchange between the two produces relationships that can lead to change. The focus is not on either party to the exchange but on the "space" between leaders and followers and how shared meaning is constructed in that space.[44] The leadership relation is seen as a dynamic process based on the interactions of leaders and followers and how they negotiate or create a social order.

Positive Leadership

The Crucial Skills

Writing from the perspective of positive organizational scholarship, Kim Cameron has developed an approach he calls positive leadership.[45] Positive leadership is primarily concerned with facilitating extraordinary performance, affirming human potential, and facilitating the best of the human condition. It focuses on how leaders can develop virtuousness and positive energy in their organizations. Characteristics of positive leaders are presented in Table 12.2.

TABLE 12.2 POSITIVE LEADERSHIP

Characteristic	Description
Being Optimistic	Seeing the glass half full
Encouraging positive deviance	Promoting outstanding results regardless of approach
Focusing on strengths	Having an affirmative bias that promotes what is going well instead of only correcting what is wrong
Creating a positive climate	Giving people the benefit of the doubt; fostering compassion, forgiveness, and gratitude while celebrating success
Maintaining positive relationships	Establishing positive relationships with followers based on cooperation, support, and kindness
Providing positive communications	Using affirmative language; open and honest feedback aimed at building and supporting strengths
Dealing with negativity	Addressing negative behavior and people quickly to maintain positive energy in followers

Source: Based on Cameron, K. S. (2008). *Positive leadership: Strategies for extraordinary performance.* San Francisco, CA: Berrett-Koehler; and Lopez, S. J., & Snyder, C. R. (Eds.). (2009). *Oxford handbook of positive psychology* (2nd ed.). Oxford, UK: Oxford University Press.

Consistent with the positive psychology approach, positive leadership suggests that we shift our focus away from weakness and problems in the organizations (though it does not say they should be ignored), and instead focus on strengths and opportunities. The result should be an improvement in both individual and organizational performance and an improvement in personal and interpersonal relationships.

Emotions and Leadership

Complementary to the authentic and positive leadership are approaches that focus on the connection between leadership and the emotions, then suggest that there is indeed an *art* of leadership. In *Primal Leadership,* Daniel Goleman and his colleagues Richard Boyatzis and Annie McKee (2002) apply the notion of emotional intelligence (see Chapter 2 in

CREATIVITY AND CHANGE — FULLY HUMAN LEADERSHIP

Robert Chapman is chairman and CEO of Barry-Wehmiller Companies, Inc., a $1.5 billion global manufacturer of capital equipment and provider of engineering consulting. Robert Denhardt interviewed CEO Robert Chapman in the spring of 2013.

Q Bob, I've heard you say that we have a crisis in this country, a crisis of leadership. How would you describe that?

A We have over 130 million people in our workforce who go home every day feeling they work for a company that doesn't care about them. That's seven out of eight people in the workforce. Our goal is to create an environment where everybody matters. We can create a leadership process that values people, one where everybody matters.

Q What do you mean by the idea of "Fully-Human Leadership"?

A Our idea of leadership is that our responsibility is to create an environment where people can discover their gifts, develop their gifts, share their gifts, and—this is extremely important—be recognized and appreciated for doing so. It creates an opportunity for them to go home each night to their families and have a more meaningful life, a life of purpose where they feel valued and where they get a chance to be who they want to be and become all that they can be.

Q And how did you implement these ideas in your company?

A We created The Guiding Principles of Leadership, the articulation of our beliefs about how we should treat each other. For instance, the first principle is "We measure success by the way we touch the lives of others." And how do we sustain and build that culture? We created a university to teach people-centric leadership—the profound responsibility for the lives they have the privilege of leading. We tried to convert managers into leaders, people who understand the significance of their everyday actions. We don't teach management, we teach leadership.

If organizations would embrace the responsibility to send people home with a sense of fulfillment, a sense that what they do matters, they will be better husbands, better wives, and have a better chance in dealing with the issues of marriage, raising a family, and getting along in this world. And if we can do that, many of the problems we have in this nation will dissipate. We can change the world—we don't need the government or politicians or any organization—it's up to us—the way we treat each other every day and the profound impact that makes on our lives.

Q What would you say to students aspiring to be leaders, not managers?

A Simply that you have an amazing opportunity to change the world by the way in which you see the people that join you in that journey and that you have a chance to influence. From your family to the organization, they're all precious human beings who deserve to be respected. You are going to have an opportunity to impact lives. Live your values in harmony with your leadership skills and to impact your people's lives. That is the responsibility of leadership.

1. How does the culture and leadership style Chapman is trying to instill in his organization compare to that in those with which you are familiar?

2. Is this just an ideal that can never be realized? Or can it be implemented across a broad range of organizations?

3. Should it be?

this volume) to the study of leadership, arguing that "great leadership works through the emotions."[46] That is, a leader needs to be fully attuned to the emotional as well as intellectual impact of what he or she is saying and doing. People will react to the emotional "signals" the leader gives off, and where those signals "connect," individuals resonate with the leader. As opposed to dissonance, which is created when there is a lack of harmony between potential leaders and followers, the successful leader stimulates resonance among those who follow. The leader and the followers are on the same "wavelength," they are "in sync," and there is less "noise" in the system. People get along better and work together more effectively. Most of all, the leader's skill in understanding his or her own values and emotions as well as those of others leaves people feeling encouraged, excited, and uplifted, even in difficult times.[47]

Max De Pree,[48] chairman emeritus of Herman Miller, Inc., in *Leadership Jazz*, drew an analogy between the leader of a jazz group and leaders in industry, an analogy that Robert Denhardt also explored in *The Pursuit of Significance*.[49] Denhardt argued that leaders are rarely able to write and conduct a "symphony" that others play; more often they are called on to be fully integrated into the performance themselves, to play along with others, like the leader of a jazz ensemble improvising a tune. Finally, Barrett,[50] analyzing leadership from the perspective of jazz, uses the term *provocative competence* to describe the process by which leaders see the potential in others even though their level of performance is not up to the quality desired.

Robert and Janet Denhardt[51] took the idea of leadership as an art in a more practical direction in their book *The Dance of Leadership*. Since most leaders would say that leadership is an art rather than a science, the Denhardts decided to take seriously the notion that leadership is an art. They began by interviewing artists, musicians, and especially dancers—not about their leadership, but about how they approach their art. Armed with lessons about how people approach art, the authors then interviewed prominent leaders in the world of business, politics, the military, higher education, and even sports to see if they approach leadership in the same way. From these interviews, they confirmed that leaders do in fact approach their work using categories very similar to those in art—rhythm and timing; communicating in images, symbols, and metaphors; improvisation; and focus and concentration. In this sense, art, music, and dance are not just metaphors for leadership, but instead leadership itself is an art, better associated with the aesthetic tradition than the mechanical. Again, leadership is not only *like* art, it is an art.[52]

Stimulated by findings such as these, many businesses and business schools have sought to incorporate emotional intelligence and artistic creativity into their curricula. In a recent interview, Robert Redford, actor turned businessman, endorsed this view. He pointed out that when he moved into business in the 1980s, he found that he needed to speak an entirely new language. His artistic language was a little too abstract. But at the same time it brought a new dimension to business discussions. "The creative aspects of art applied to business have enormous value and are just beginning to be touched on. Some amazing things could happen; it's a whole area to expand," he said.[53]

The Ethics of Leadership

Parker Palmer (2002) has written,

> A leader is someone with the power to project either shadow or light upon some part of the world, and upon the lives of the people who dwell there. A leader shapes the ethos in which others must live, an ethos as light-filled as heaven or as shadowy as

Organizational Ethics

LEADING THE GLOBAL FUND FOR WOMEN

"For me, what I do at the Global Fund is so deeply connected to my sense of who I am and what I can give back to this world and what my responsibilities are to this world. It's a deep sense of commitment. It's not a 9–5 job"[54] are the words of Kavita Ramdas, former president and chief executive officer, and current senior advisor to the Global Fund for Women. The Global Fund for Women provides grants to women's groups around the world with the goal of supporting equality and social justice focused on helping women achieve full equality and participation.[55] The organization was founded in 1987 to raise funds to support women-led enterprises and activities that promote better health, economic, education, and social welfare for women. It prides itself on being accessible, providing global expertise, having flexible grants, and on utilizing and building local philanthropies. Since its creation, the organization has provided over $80 million of grants to 4,300 organizations in over 170 countries.[56] It has funded programs such as a movement against the killing of women in Mexico, a Buddhist orphanage in Sri Lanka, health and reproductive rights in South America, empowering women in Nepal, legal aid for women in China, and women's rights organization in Guatemala.[57]

The work of the Global Fund is certainly aimed at transforming the world, and Ramdas has received numerous awards for her leadership and been recognized as one of the world's top 20 entrepreneurs in 2002. "Kavita is one of the very few people who, when she enters a room, you know there's a presence. It's important in this work that we do to have that type of presence and grace—to hold people's attention," says one of her colleagues.[58]

Ramdas believes that there is an undeclared "war" against women around the world through increases in abuse, health crises, silence in case of abuse and neglect, a crisis that she is changing one person and one organization at a time.[59] Her personal background prepared her for this role. She was born into a prominent secular Hindu family in Mumbai, India. Her father is a retired former head of the Indian navy turned peace and antinuclear activist and her mother is highly active in social causes.[60] At 18, Ramdas volunteered to work in a small farm in India until a village elder told her to use her education and compassion to tell the world about them. Ramdas's passion for what she does allows her to lead her organization to make changes to improve women's lives one step at a time.

Kavita Ramdas is the founder and former CEO of the Global Fund for Women. The organization was founded to support women's activities in reducing poverty, increasing housing, and advancing women's rights in the workplace. She is known as a creative and passionate leader as well as one who achieves results.

1. What are some of Ramdas's key leadership abilities?

2. To what extent do you think culture has impacted her?

hell. A *good* leader has high awareness of the interplay of inner shadow and light, lest the act of leadership do more harm than good.[61] (sec. 2, para. 1)

Certainly James MacGregor Burns (1978) made just that point in his classic *Leadership*.[62] As we noted earlier, Burns argued that leadership involves a relationship between leaders and followers, who engage with one another in a process of determining what is to be sought. Leaders act on their own motives and interests, but these must be connected to the motives and interests of followers. In order for moral leadership to occur, the values of both the leader and the followers must be represented.

The Follower

A series of more recent publications has argued that studies of the leader–follower relationship have tended to put too much emphasis on the leader and not enough on the follower.[63] For some, studies of followership seek to identify the circumstances under which the follower might be most readily convinced to comply with the wishes of the leader, but for others the follower is seen as possessing power and resources that can be judiciously used to help guide the organization in new directions—the follower can lead!

In such a relationship, the views of the followers should be freely expressed and fully entertained. Leaders and followers should engage in a dialogue, not a monologue, and it should be structured so that fundamentally new ideas and relationships emerge. This suggests that the leader should above all aid in creating an open and visible process through which members of the group can express their needs and interests. Lacking that orientation, the leader may be tempted not only to rule with excessive power, but also to make decisions based on his or her personal interests rather than those of the group. And, the leader may be tempted to lie to followers to protect the organization, or at least "spin" the truth to conceal what is actually happening.

Leadership, Morality, and Globalization

In a global society, there is the additional challenge of confronting the different moral perspectives that exist within various cultures. The German scholar Silke Astrid Eisenbeiss[64] has explored this challenging question and suggests that the world's great religions and philosophies actually agree on many central points and that these can form the basis for a cross-cultural or integrative approach to the ethics of leadership. The four elements are presented in Figure 12.4.

In other writings, however, we can find significant questions being raised about the universality of ethics. For example, philosopher Zygmunt Bauman, who takes an explicitly postmodernist stance, argues that finding absolutes or universal truths is extremely difficult. In today's "fractured society," one in which the moral standards of any group or culture reflect its own circumstances and cannot be generalized to others, there is no basis for giving preference to one version of the truth over another. "The choice is not between following the rules and breaking them, as there is no one set of rules to be obeyed or breached. The choice is, rather, between different sets of rules and different authorities preaching them."[65]

Ethical Issues

The ethical issues facing the leader are significant, but there are no easy guides for the leader. Moral leadership is not based on a set of principles or rules that a leader can choose to follow or ignore. As much as we have tried over the past several hundred years to construct rules or codes of conduct, the ethical choices we face are always too difficult for those codes to readily fit. (Note that even the Eisenweiss material fails to draw a unified moral code, only suggesting perspectives that managers bring to their work.) And, besides, most moral lapses are not based on a conscious choice to "break a rule" or, more generally,

Why Do
Whistleblowers
Act?

Tim Cook on
Ethical Leadership

FIGURE 12.4 FOUR ELEMENTS OF ETHICAL LEADERSHIP

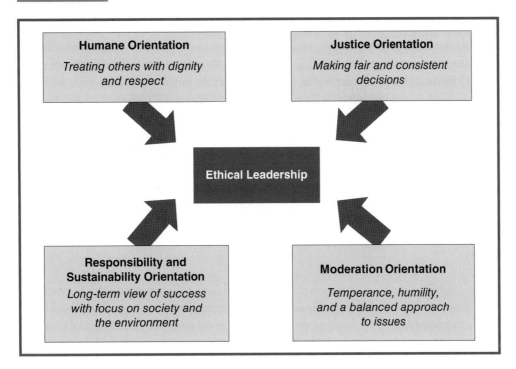

to promote evil rather than good. Most leaders don't make ethical mistakes based solely on greed or callousness—though some do. Rather, most fail to see moral issues that are inherent in a situation but lie just beneath the surface.

Unfortunately, many leaders uncritically accept an organization's culture and fail to recognize the ethical traps it could hold for them. They neglect low-probability events, they miscalculate risks, they fail to consider all the parties that might be involved, and they downplay long-term consequences. They allow themselves to be blinded by opportunity and don't see the negatives. They arrive at a point when they say, we've gotten ourselves into a situation that we can't get out of. We have to do whatever we can to save the organization—and save ourselves.[66]

Identifying and resolving moral issues requires moral imagination—a good sense of ethical awareness but also the imagination to promote a moral process and result. Moral imagination involves not just heightened attention to moral concerns, but rather carefully and thoughtfully understanding and evaluating various options from a moral point of view. Acting with moral imagination requires expanding our capacity for moral reasoning and charting new directions for moral action. Having that kind of vision today is a moral imperative.[67]

Ethical, Fair, and Lawful

Creative Leadership

As a future leader, you will need to exhibit creative leadership. You will need to improve your own creative capacities and you will need to encourage others in the organization to unleash their creative powers. But, as a creative leader, you must also exhibit creativity in your own leadership. Fortunately, there are many leaders who are already modeling

Developing
Creative
Leadership

Madness and
Leadership

creative leadership and from whom we can learn a great deal. Interestingly, what we learn first is that these creative leaders "lead from the inside." That is, they have or have developed personal qualities or "aspects of character" that support their creative leadership.

As individual leaders grow, mature, and evolve, their impact on their organizations grows as well. The Greek historian Plutarch once said, "**What we achieve inwardly will change outer reality.**" By changing your inner world, you will impact the outer world. Hintendra Wadhwa of the Columbia Business School writes that, to be an exceptional leader, you "need to be both flexible and at the same time, centered and grounded—anchored in a sense of direction and purpose. . . . Great leaders need to have the capacity to be both adaptive and resilient and to surround this ability around a stable core, an inner anchor."[68] Angela Blanchard, CEO of Houston's Neighborhood Centers, puts it this way: "You must move through this chaotic, fast-changing world with an eye for an opportunity—focusing on what works and what is strong, using what's available to build something better, faster, more effective. It is not about choosing to be either flexible or consistent; it's about being flexible and consistent at the same time."[69]

Certainly we are witnessing the emergence of new generation leaders (of which you will be a part) who are willing to move beyond the structural and cultural limitations of their group, organization, or society to encounter new problems and opportunities and to address these with courage and creativity. These leaders are not only able to "think outside the box," but to "act outside the box," that is, to detach themselves from the constraints of tradition and structure and act more creatively. But the capacity for such creativity, as we said, comes from inside; it seems based in a set of qualities, some rational, some intuitive, some defying description. Among these, we will highlight purpose and passion, learning agility, courage, empathy, love and compassion, and a skillful understanding of the interaction between personal energy and social or organizational energy (Figure 12.5).

FIGURE 12.5 COMPONENTS OF CREATIVE LEADERSHIP

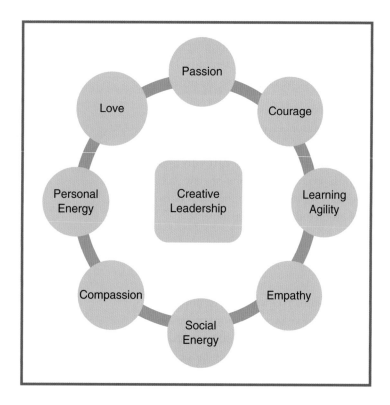

First, to be creative, leaders need a sense of *purpose*, or even passion that drives them in a singular direction. This is quite different from the goal setting that managers do, for example, to exceed last year's productivity and profit by 10%. The purpose here might instead be stated in terms of the leader's relationship with others in the organization, the leader's capacity to act artfully in bringing people together, or the leader's success in "getting out of the way" so the organization can thrive.

Second, creative leaders display *learning agility*—the capacity to learn from their experiences, to engage in self-reflection and self-critique, and to apply their learning and personal competencies to future problems. Learning agility requires self-awareness, mental agility, people agility, change agility, and results agility. It also requires a strong commitment to self-reflection and self-critique, the ability to learn from one's experiences, including intellectual, emotional, and spiritual experiences. Few employees, managers, and leaders today consistently demonstrate this capacity.[70] But, we suspect, those who do possess it will be more and more valued for their skills and insight, their creative leadership.

Third, creative leadership is aided by *courage*. As we have seen before, courage is a prerequisite to creativity, a prerequisite to innovation, and a prerequisite to forward-thinking action. In other words, courage underlies positive efforts toward organizational change and development. But, becoming an integrated human being also requires courage—it pushes the individual to the edge of what is considered safe and then says, "you need to take another step." Dr. Detlief Reis of Mahidol University in Thailand writes, "Building an independent, unique self that expresses who you are and what you believe and value requires real courage. And living a life full of passion and purpose, striving to realise your potential in the face of possible failure requires real courage. To achieve much, you need to aim high."[71]

Fourth, creative leadership is also associated with *love and compassion*, factors rarely found in the traditional literature on leadership, but two that have now been demonstrated to have significant influence on organizational productivity—as well as being simply the right thing to do. An Australian study of 5,600 people at all levels in 77 different organizations has shown that the largest single influence on productivity and profitability was the leaders' willingness to take time to engage with employees, to talk with them about their own growth and development, and to freely exchange helpful criticism—in both directions."[72] According to Christina Boedker, leader of the study, compassion has to do with the leader's ability "to understand people's motivators, hopes and difficulties and to create the right support mechanism to allow people to be as good as they can be. . . . It's about valuing people and being receptive and responsive to criticism."[73]

Fifth, a related idea is one's capacity for *empathy*, identifying with or vicariously experiencing the feelings of another. To empathize with another is to not only understand that person's experience at a deep level, but literally to put oneself in the other's shoes. Empathy requires careful listening, deep sensing, and thoughtful reflection.

Finally, the experience of creative leadership rests on the leader's *energy* and his or her capacity to *energize* others. "Leading involves drawing energy forward, organizing that energy, and stimulating its movement through time and space in a rhythmic way—that is, in a smooth and coordinated fashion characterized by ease and efficiency."[74] Leaders who are able to develop a strong reservoir of personal energy will be better able to energize those with whom they work.

The most creative leaders understand the energy that sustains them personally and are able to shape the energy that resides in individuals, groups, and organization. The act of energizing the group or organization can come not just from the top, but from anywhere in the group or organization. Indeed, the most creative leaders excel in developing other creative leaders. Their bringing special energy to bear on the problems and opportunities facing the organization stimulates more energy, and that spreads throughout the organization. The creative leader models the energizing force of leadership and stimulates a contagion of creativity.

What Would You Do?

▶ Your boss encourages you to come up with creative ideas to improve the quality and productivity of your company. But every time you come up with such an idea, he assigns you to work on it. You are getting overloaded and now hesitant to bring up any new ideas for fear you'll just get more work. What would you do?

▶ Summary and Applications for Managers

One remaining question is how leadership skills can be developed. Although there is general agreement that leadership skills can be built or at least improved on, there are differences in how one might seek improvements. We offer the following suggestions.

1. *Examine the traits, skills, and commitments associated with leadership and try to assess your own strengths and weaknesses.* As we have seen, the lists of traits and skills vary, but there are some areas of agreement (see Figure 7.3). There also are a variety of assessment surveys (a couple of which are included at the end of this chapter) that will give you some idea of the traits and skills that you value most. You also might ask others who know you and perhaps work with you to complete an assessment form *about you*. This will give you some extra feedback and might point to some areas that you did not recognize as areas in need of work. With this information about your leadership style and your skill levels, you can then begin a program to develop those areas that seem most important.

2. *Learn about leadership by observation; study examples of leadership excellence.* Identify people whom you think are excellent leaders. Talk with them about how they approach their leadership activities or simply watch them carefully as they interact with others. How do their actions reflect some of the ideas that we have talked about in this chapter? How would you describe their leadership styles? Look especially carefully for the role of values in their leadership activities. What are the deep-seated commitments that seem to underlie their work? Look also for the ways in which these leaders enter into psychological or emotional relationships with followers. What can you say about the complex dynamics that might underlie the leader–follower relationship? In addition to identifying leaders whom you actually can observe, you might read the biographies or autobiographies of well-known leaders. Look especially for information about those influences that shaped their approaches to leadership. What is it about their backgrounds or experiences that might help to explain their approaches? Novels are another good source of leadership lessons. You also might watch films such as *Patton*, *The Caine Mutiny*, *Norma Rae*, *Twelve Angry Men*, and *Bagger Vance* to look for leadership lessons. Take notes as you watch the films and then discuss the leadership lessons they contain.

3. *Experiment with your own behavior.* As in other areas discussed in this book, such as motivation and communication, you should use the classroom to try out alternative ways of approaching leadership situations. Some students already will have had extensive leadership experience in businesses, in schools, in churches, on sports teams, and so on. Others will have had relatively little. In either case, the classroom provides a safe place in which you can try out various approaches to leadership. Perhaps you would like to see what would happen if you were a little more assertive or even aggressive than usual, or perhaps you would like to see what would happen if you were less demanding and more supportive. Classroom exercises can give you an opportunity to try out different behaviors and practice those that are most effective.

4. *Model important values.* As we have seen, values play an important role in leadership at all levels and in all organizations. Leadership involves change and change involves shifting values. For this reason leaders must be attentive not only to matters of personal integrity, but also sensitive to value implications of the strategies and policies they pursue. Both those in the organization and those outside will be affected by decisions made by organizational leaders. For example, building an organizational culture based on openness, transparency, and inclusion demonstrates quite different values from one based on the top-down, hierarchical exercise of authority. Similarly, policies that reflect a strong commitment to sustainability model basic values quite different from those in companies that are inattentive to such issues. And, of course, the leader must not only hold strong values, but demonstrate and model those values. Be aware that people are watching what you do as well as

listening to what you say. And develop habits of self-reflection and self-critique with respect to the value positions you hold.

5. *Assume leadership.* One of the best ways to develop as a leader is through engaging in a leadership experience. In addition to direct work experience, you can gain leadership experience by becoming involved in clubs and other organizations, by engaging in service projects in your community, or by accepting internships or other related experience. The experience itself will teach you important lessons about leadership, but you will get much more out of your experience if you take time to reflect critically on what occurs in your group or organization. For example, you might want to keep a journal of leadership experiences—your own as well as those of others. What seemed to make a difference in your capacity to energize others? What approaches to persuasion or communication did you use in conjunction with your efforts to lead? When were you most successful? When were you least successful? What specific lessons about leadership can you use in future situations?

▶ Key Terms

Authentic leader 382

Behavior approach 374

Contingency approach 374

Moral leadership 380

Servant leadership 381

Trait approach 373

Transactional leadership 380

Transformational leadership 380

▶ Exercise 12.1 Practicing the Ethics of Leadership

As a topic for discussion, consider instances in which you have seen leaders act in a way you consider unethical. What about those situations made them unethical? What choices did the leader have that might have led in a different direction? And what about you? As a leader, how can you be sure to consider the ethical implications of your actions? How can you bring the same creativity to addressing moral questions that you bring to addressing questions of cost, performance, or results? How can you expose your own faulty assumptions about yourself, about other people, and about the world in general, assumptions that may lead you to minimize the moral consequences of your actions? How can you be creative in your leadership, yet at the same time be sure that your creativity is not used to develop faulty justifications for your actions?

▶ Exercise 12.2 Developing a Leadership Autobiography

Trace the history of your personal development as a leader. In a 10-page essay, consider the major influences on your understanding of what it means to be a leader. You might consider questions such as the following to guide your writing: What were your most influential models of leadership? What were your earliest leadership experiences like? What qualities of leadership do you find most attractive? Why do you think you chose these particular qualities? How would you rate yourself in terms of these qualities? What other leadership traits might you develop? What leadership styles or strategies do you employ most frequently? What were the influences that led you to use these approaches as opposed to others? How would you like to grow in terms of your capacity for leadership? How do you think you will? What will be necessary for this to occur? What are the issues that you believe leaders of the future will have to confront? What is your philosophy of leadership?

▶ Exercise 12.3   A Debate Topic

James McGregor Burns would say that Hitler's leadership was not transformational because it did not further good in the society. However, Bernard Bass contends that Germany still was transformed by Hitler's leadership and that Hitler's influence still is felt today. Because Germany was transformed, according to Bass, Hitler was a transformational leader.

Based on what you have learned about transformational leadership in this chapter and in your view, should Hitler be called a transformational leader? Would it even be proper to call Hitler a leader? Develop a classroom debate on this question, with half of the class taking one position and the other half taking the other.

▶ Exercise 12.4   Transactional Versus Transformational Leadership

Instructions. For each of the following 10 pairs of statements, divide 5 points between the two according to your beliefs and perceptions of yourself or according to which of the two statements characterizes you better. The 5 points may be divided between the *a* and *b* statements in any one of the following ways: 5 for *a*, 0 for *b*; 4 for *a*, 1 for *b*; 3 for *a*, 2 for *b*; 1 for *a*, 4 for *b*; and 0 for *a*, 5 for *b*. They cannot be divided equally (2.5 for each) between the two. Weigh your choices between the two according to the one that better characterizes you or your beliefs.

1. a. As a leader, I have a primary mission of maintaining stability.
   b. As a leader, I have a primary mission of change.

2. a. As a leader, I must cause events.
   b. As a leader, I must facilitate events.

3. a. I am concerned that my followers are rewarded equitably for their work.
   b. I am concerned about what my followers want in life.

4. a. My preference is to think long range—what might be.
   b. My preference is to think short range—what is realistic.

5. a. As a leader, I spend considerable energy in managing separate but related goals.
   b. As a leader, I spend considerable energy in arousing hopes, expectations, and aspirations among my followers.

6. a. Although not in a formal classroom sense, I believe that a significant part of my leadership is that of teacher.
   b. I believe that a significant part of my leadership is that of facilitator.

7. a. As a leader, I must engage with followers at an equal level of morality.
   b. As a leader, I must represent a higher morality.

8. a. I enjoy stimulating followers to want to do more.
   b. I enjoy rewarding followers for a job well done.

9. a. Leadership should be practical.
   b. Leadership should be inspirational.

10. a. What power I have to influence others comes primarily from my ability to get people to identify with me and my ideas.
    b. What power I have to influence others comes primarily from my status and position.

Scoring. Circle your points for Items 1b, 2a, 3b, 4a, 5b, 6a, 7b, 8a, 9b, and 10a and add up the total points you allocated to these items; enter the score here: Tf = _____. Next, add up the total points given to the uncircled Items 1a, 2b, 3a, 4b, 5a, 6b, 7a, 8b, 9a, and 10b; enter the score here: Ta =_____.

Interpretation. This instrument gives an impression of your tendencies toward *transformational* leadership (your Tf score) and *transactional* leadership (your Ta score). Refer to the chapter's discussion of transactional and transformational leadership to interpret your scores.

Source: From Northouse, P. G. (2001). *Leadership: Theory and practice* (2nd ed.). Thousand Oaks, CA: Sage. Used by permission.

▶ Exercise 12.5 Assessing Your Leadership Style

David Campbell, the H. Smith Richardson Senior Fellow at the Center for Creative Leadership (CCL), produced an interesting assessment device. CCL, a nonprofit educational institution founded in 1970, develops models of effective managerial practice and applies them as guides for assessment and development. Following are the categories that Campbell uses for assessing leadership capacities, categories that you can use in your own informal examination of your leadership capacities. Rate yourself, and have others rate you, on a scale of 1 to 5 for each category. Try to think of specific examples of how you have displayed each characteristic.

- Leadership
  - Ambitious: Determined to make progress, likes to compete
  - Daring: Willing to try new experiences, is risk oriented
  - Dynamic: Takes charge, inspires others, is seen as a leader
  - Enterprising: Works well with the complexities of change
  - Experienced: Has a good background
  - Farsighted: Looks ahead, plans, is a visionary
  - Original: Sees the world differently, has many new ideas
  - Persuasive: Articulate and persuasive in influencing others

- Energy/Affability
  - Affectionate: Acts close, warm, and nurturing
  - Considerate: Thoughtful, is willing to work with others
  - Empowering: Motivates others and helps them to achieve
  - Entertaining: Clever and amusing, enjoys people
  - Friendly: Pleasant to be around, smiles easily

- Dependability
  - Credible: Open and honest, inspires trust
  - Organized: Plans ahead and follows through
  - Productive: Uses time and resources well
  - Thrifty: Uses and manages money wisely

- Resilience
  - Calm: Has an unhurried and unruffled manner
  - Flexible: Easily adjusts to changes
  - Optimistic: Positive, handles personal challenges well
  - Trusting: Trusts and believes in others

Source: Campbell Leadership Index (CLI), Center for Creative Leadership (CCL). Reprinted by permission of NCS London House.

▶ Case 12.1 Leadership When No One Is in Charge

Read and discuss the following case:

A small work team consisting of Eddie, Cyndi, Gina, Jennifer, and Ralph was asked to meet after work to come up with a theme for the company picnic, to be held the third of July at a park on the outskirts of town. No one had a great deal of enthusiasm for this project—or the idea of staying after work.

All were silent for the first few minutes, each probably hoping someone else would come up with an idea that would make this chore go away. When it was apparent that no one was going to take the lead, Gina said, "None of us wants to be here. Let's just make it a Fourth of July party and be done with it."

A couple of heads nodded, but Ralph responded, "I'd love to get out of here, too, but couldn't we come up with something a little more inventive than that? You know, the boss will be paying attention to this."

"Well, Mr. Brown-nose," Cyndi laughed, "still after that raise you didn't get last quarter?" Several members of the group smiled, although they could sense an underlying tension between Ralph and Cyndi.

Eddie came to the rescue: "We'd all like that raise, wouldn't we? What about giving this just a few more minutes and see if we can come up with something?"

Jennifer stood up, opened her cell phone, and walked out of the room. Gina mumbled, "Fourth of July."

"Let me try once again," Ralph said. "What about a Fourth of July party?"

"That was Gina's idea," Cyndi reminded the group, unnecessarily.

"And it was a good idea, too," said Eddie. "But what about building on that idea by thinking about a different kind of celebration—maybe something like a circus?"

"That's not bad," said Gina. "We could do costumes and have a parade . . ."

"I like clowns," said Ralph.

"You *are* a clown," said Cyndi.

"No, really," Ralph said. "We could have a parade with clowns, and animals, and all that stuff."

"Sure," said Eddie, "circus in July!"

Suddenly energized, the group started making plans in earnest and even assigned responsibilities for carrying the idea forward.

Analysis. Think through the pattern of leadership exhibited in this case. There was no formal leader, but several people exercised leadership—some effectively, some not so effectively.

1. Who was the leader of the group? What made this person the leader?

2. What behaviors were most helpful to the group? Which were least helpful?

3. In the context of "leadership energizes," what happened to energize this group? How much involved rational intelligence? How much involved emotional intelligence?

4. What does your experience tell you about leadership in groups when no one is in charge?

⑤SAGE edge™

Sharpen your skills with SAGE edge at edge.sagepub.com/nahavandi

SAGE edge for students provides a personalized approach to help you accomplish your coursework goals in an easy-to-use learning environment.

▶ Endnotes

1. 37signals.com. (2013). Retrieved from http://37signals.com on September 10, 2013.

2. Zax, D. (2012). 37signals earns millions each year. Its CEO's model? His cleaning lady. *Fast Company,* August 29. Retrieved from http://www.fastcompany.com/3000852/37signals-earns-millions-each-year-its-ceo%E2%80%99s-model-his-cleaning-lady on September 10, 2013.

3. Zax, 2012.

4. Fried, J., & Hansson, D. H. (2010). *Rework.* New York, NY: Crown Business.

5. Helgesen, S. (1996). Leading from the grassroots. In F. Hesselbein, M. Goldsmith, & R. Beckhard (Eds.), *The leader of the future.* Francisco, CA: Jossey-Bass, p. 21.

6. Bennis, W., & Nanus, B. (1985). *Leaders: The strategies for taking charge.* New York, NY: Harper & Row.

7. Bass, B. M. (1990). *Handbook of leadership.* New York, NY: Free Press, p. 11.

8. Northouse, P. G. (2012). *Introduction to leadership: Concepts and practice.* Thousand Oaks, CA: Sage.

9. Stogdill, R. M. (1974). *Handbook of leadership.* New York, NY: Free Press, p. 81.

10. Bass, 1990, pp. 511–543.

11. Cartwright, D., & Zander, A. (Eds.). (1960). *Group dynamics.* Evanston, IL: Row & Peterson; Katz, D., & Kahn, R. L. (1966). *The social psychology of organizations.* New York, NY: Wiley; Likert, R. (1961). *New patterns of management.* New York, NY: McGraw-Hill.

12. Blake, R. R., & McCanse, A. A. (1991). *Leadership dilemmas: Grid solutions.* Houston, TX: Gulf Publishing; Blake, R. R., & Mouton, J. (1964). *The managerial grid.* Houston, TX: Gulf Publishing.

13. Hersey, P., & Blanchard, K. H. (1988). *Management of organizational behavior* (5th ed.). Englewood Cliffs, NJ: Prentice Hall, chap. 8.

14. Fiedler, F. (1967). *A theory of leadership effectiveness.* New York, NY: McGraw-Hill.

15. House, R. J., & Mitchell, T. R. (1974). Path-goal theory of leadership. *Journal of Contemporary Business, 3,* 81–97.

16. Bennis, W. (1997). *Managing people is like herding cats.* Provo, UT: Executive Excellence Publishing; Bennis & Nanus, 1985; Hitt, M. D. (1993). *The model leader.* Columbus, OH: Battelle Press; Northouse, P. G. (2001). *Leadership: Theory and practice* (2nd ed., pp. 51–52). Thousand Oaks, CA: Sage; also Yukl, G. (1998). *Leadership in organizations* (4th ed.). Upper Saddle River, NJ: Prentice Hall.

17. Bennis, as cited in Hitt, M. D. (1993). *The model leader.* Columbus, OH: Battelle Press, p. iii.

18. Kouzes, J. M., & Posner, B. Z. (2012). *The leadership challenge* (5th ed.). San Francisco, CA: Jossey-Bass, chap. 9.

19. Yukl, 1998, p. 244.

20. Collins, J. (2005). *Good to great and the social sector, a monograph to accompany* Good to great. New York, NY: HarperCollins, p. 34.

21. IBM. (2010). IBM 2010 Global CEO Study: Creativity selected as most crucial factor for future success. *IBM News Releases.* Retrieved from http://www-03.ibm.com/press/us/en/pressrelease/31670.wss on December 16, 2012; see sec. 2.

22. Barendsen, L., & Gardner, H. (2007). Three elements of good leadership in rapidly changing times. In J. C. Knapp (Ed.), *For the common good* (pp. 21–32). Westport, CT: Praeger, p. 21.

23. Kouzes & Posner, 2012.

24. Kouzes, J. M., & Posner, B. Z. (2007). *The leadership challenge: How to get extraordinary things done in organizations* (4th ed.). San Francisco, CA: Jossey-Bass, p. 23.

25. Kouzes & Posner, 2012.

26. Manglesdorf, M. (2012). The elements of good leadership (Interview with Deborah Ancona). *MITSloan Management Review,* July 27. Retrieved from http://sloanreview.mit.edu/article/the-elements-of-good-leadership/#.UBlKRLRDx8E on September 20, 2013.

27. Manglesdorf, 2012.

28. Manglesdorf, 2012.

29. Burns, J. M. (1978). *Leadership.* New York, NY: Harper & Row.

30. Burns, 1978, p. 18.

31. Bass, 1985; Bass, B. M., & Avolio, B. J. (Eds.). (1994). *Improving organizational effectiveness through transformational leadership.* Thousand Oaks, CA: Sage.

32. Greenleaf, R. K. (1998). *The power of servant leadership* (L. C. Spears, Ed.). San Francisco, CA: Berrett-Koehler; also Greenleaf, R. K. (2002). *Servant leadership, anniversary edition.* New York, NY: Paulist Press.

33. O'Toole, J. (1995). *Leading change.* San Francisco, CA: Jossey-Bass, p. 12.

34. O'Toole, 1995, p. 15.

35. Warrior, P. (2010). Cisco's CTO's tips for a top career. *Fortune-Postcards,* March 8. Retrieved from http://postcards.blogs.fortune.cnn .com/2010/03/08/cisco-ctos-tips-for-a-top-career/ on April 4, 2010.

36. Tyabji, H. (1997, February–March). What it means to lead. *Fast Company,* p. 98.

37. Buckingham, M. (2005). What great managers do. *Harvard Business Review,* March. Retrieved from http://hbr.org/2005/03/what-great-managers-do/ar/1, pp. 1–7.

38. Pearce, C. L., & Conger, J. A. (2003). *Shared leadership.* Thousand Oaks, CA: Sage, p. 1.

39. Bennis, W. G., & Townsend, R. (2005). *Reinventing leadership: Strategies to empower the organization.* New York, NY: Collins Business Essentials; and Crosby, B., & Bryson, J. (2005). *Leadership for the common good* (2nd ed.). San Francisco, CA: Jossey-Bass.

40. Moreland, J. (2012). The shift from chief executive to chief influencer. *Fast Company,* July 2012. Retrieved from http://www.fastcompany .com/3001612/shift-chief-executive-chief-influencer on September 10, 2013.

41. Ibarra, H., & Hansen, M. T. (2011). Are you a collaborative leader? *Harvard Business Review,* July. Retrieved from http://hbr.org/2011/07/are-you-a-collaborative-leader/ on September 10, 2013.

42. Lipman-Blumen, J. (2000). *Connective leadership: Managing in a changing world.* New York, NY: Oxford University Press, p. 107.

43. Helgesen, S. (2005). *The web of inclusion: A new architecture for building great organizations.* New York, NY: Currency/ Doubleday.

44. Uhl-Bien, M. (2006). Relational leadership theory: Exploring the social processes of leadership and organizing. *The Leadership Quarterly, 17*(6), 654–676; see also Ladkin,

D. M. (2010). *Rethinking leadership: A new look at old leadership questions.* Northampton, MA: Edward Elgar.

45. Cameron, K. S. (2008). *Positive leadership: Strategies for extraordinary performance.* San Francisco, CA: Berrett-Koehler.

46. Goleman, D., Boyatzis, R. E., & McKee, A. (2002). *Primal leadership: Realizing the power of emotional intelligence.* Cambridge, MA: Harvard Business School Press, p. 3.

47. Goleman, Boyatzis, & McKee, 2002, p. 20; see also Pescosolido, A. T. (2002). Emergent leaders and managers of group emotion. *Leadership Quarterly, 13*(5), 583–599.

48. De Pree, M. (1992). *Leadership jazz.* New York, NY: Currency/Doubleday.

49. Denhardt, R. B. (2000). *The pursuit of significance: Strategies for managerial success in public organizations.* Long Grove, IL: Waveland Press.

50. Barrett is discussed in McKinney, M. (2012). Leadership as provocative competence. *Fast Company,* August 24. Retrieved from http:// www.leadershipnow.com/leadingblog/2012/08/ leadership_as_provocative_comp.html on September 10, 2013.

51. Denhardt, R. B., & Denhardt, J. V. (2005). *The dance of leadership.* Armonk, NY: M. E. Sharpe.

52. Hansen, H., Ropo, A., & Sauer, E. (2007). Aesthetic leadership. *The Leadership Quarterly, 18*(6), 544–560; Guillet de Monthoux, P., Gustafsson, C., & Sjöstrand, S.-E. (2008). Aesthetic leadership: Managing fields of flow in art and business. *Scandinavian Journal of Management* [London], 74–75; and Ladkin, 2010.

53. Hammer, A. K. (2010). Sundance: Synthesizing art and business. *Entrepreneur,* July 20. Retrieved from http://www.entrepreneur.com/ article/207606 on December 16, 2012; p. 1.

54. Curiel, J. (2002). A woman's work. *San Francisco Chronicle,* November 10. Retrieved from http://www.sfgate.com/cgi-bin/article. cgi?f=/chronicle/archive/2002/11/10/

CM148265.DTL&type=news on December 16, 2012.

55. *Global Fund for Women: Social capitalists.* (2010). Retrieved from http://www.globalfundforwomen.org/cms/ on December 16, 2012.

56. *Global Fund for Women: Impact* (2012). Retrieved from http://www.globalfundforwomen.org/impact on December 16, 2012.

57. See *Global Fund for Women—Success stories.* (2013). Retrieved from http://www.globalfundforwomen.org/impact/success-stories; and Patel, P. (2007). Money makers: Five questions for Kavita Ramdas. *Houston Chronicle,* June 12. Retrieved from http://www.chron.com/disp/story.mpl/business/4884490.html April 8, 2010.

58. Curiel, 2002.

59. *Now* with Bill Moyers. (2004). *Women and the world: Kavita Ramdas biography.* Retrieved from http://www.pbs.org/now/politics/ramdas.html# on December 16, 2012.

60. Curiel, 2002.

61. Palmer, P. (2002). Learning from within. From *Let your life speak.* Retrieved from http://www.couragerenewal.org/parker/writings/leading-from-within, sec. 2, para. 1.

62. Burns, 1978.

63. Kellerman, B. (2008). *Followership: How followers are creating change and changing leaders.* Boston, MA: Harvard Business School Press; Maccoby, M. (2007). *The leaders we need: And what makes us follow.* Boston, MA: Harvard Business School Press; and Riggio, R. E., Chaleff, I., Lipman-Blumen, J. (2008). *The art of followership: How great followers create great leaders and organizations.* San Francisco, CA: Jossey-Bass.

64. Eisenbeiss, S. A. (2012). Re-thinking ethical leadership. *Leadership Quarterly,* 791–808.

65. Bauman, Z. (1997). *Postmodernity and its discontents.* New York, NY: New York University Press, p. 20.

66. Ciulla, J. B. (2004). *Ethics, the heart of leadership.* Westport, CT: Praeger; Johnson, C. E. (2005). *Meeting the ethical challenges of leadership: Casting light or shadow.* Thousand Oaks, CA: Sage; Price, T. L. (2009). *Leadership ethics: An introduction.* New York, NY: Cambridge University Press; Rhode, D. L. (2006). *Moral leadership: The theory and practice of power, judgment, and policy.* San Francisco, CA: Jossey-Bass.

67. Brown, M. E., & Treviño, L. K. (2006). Ethical leadership: A review and future directions. *Leadership Quarterly, 17,* 595–616; also Gardner, H. (2006). *Five minds for the future.* Boston, MA: Harvard Business School Press.

68. Wadhwa, H. (2012). A practical path to leadership greatness. *IEDP Blog,* July 30. Retrieved from http://www.iedp.com/Blog/LeadershipGreatness, p. 1, on December 16, 2012.

69. Mulanny, A. (2012). Generation flux salon. *Fast Company,* November 5. Retrieved from http://www.fastcompany.com/3002714/generation-flux-salon-how-do-you-dodge-constant-distractions-and-stay-course on December 16, 2012.

70. Swisher, V. V. (2012). *Becoming an agile leader.* Los Angeles, CA: Korn/Ferry Lominger International.

71. Reis, D. (2012.) Creative leadership requires courage. *Bangkok Post,* August 30. Retrieved from http://www.bangkokpost.com/print/309950/ on December 16, 2012.

72. The rise of the compassionate leader: Should you be cruel to be kind? (2012). Knowledge@ *Australian School of Business [UNSW],* August 21. Retrieved from http://knowledge.asb.unsw.edu.au/article.cfm?articleid=1671 September 20, 2013.

73. Rise of the compassionate leader, 2012.

74. Denhardt & Denhardt, 2005, p. 77.

ORGANIZATIONAL CONTEXT ◄

PART

4

13 Organizational Power and Politics

Learning Power and Politics on the Job ▶

Ken Welch was a summer intern in the management services division of NASA. During his 3-month assignment, Ken was to undertake a variety of projects related to management concerns in the various laboratories at the center. The management services division was part of the personnel department, but personnel in the division often acted as troubleshooters for top management, so Ken's unit enjoyed considerable prestige.

A couple of weeks into his internship, Ken was asked to come to Jim Pierson's office. While others had been quite friendly, inviting Ken to parties and asking him to join the personnel department's softball team, Jim had seemed somewhat aloof. But then Ken and Jim had very little contact on the job, so maybe, Ken reasoned, it was not so strange after all. Ken saw the meeting as a friendly gesture on Jim's part and looked forward to getting better acquainted. Any hope of a friendly conversation, however, was immediately dispelled; as soon as Ken arrived, Jim began a lecture on how to manage one's time, specifically pointing out that taking on too many projects meant that none would be done well.

Ken was stunned by the meeting. No one had in any way questioned the quality of his work. There were no time conflicts between his two projects. And even if there had been, Ken wondered why Jim would take it on himself to deliver such a reprimand. Ken hinted at the controversy the next day in a conversation with his immediate supervisor but received only a casual remark about the "out-of-date" members of the division. Ken began to feel that he was a pawn in some sort of office power struggle and immediately resolved to try to get out of the middle. As soon as he had an opportunity to see the division chief, he explained the whole situation, including his feeling that no real problems existed and that he was being used. The chief listened carefully but offered no real suggestions.

Later in the week, at a beer-drinking session after a softball game, the director of the department of personnel asked how the internship was going. In the ensuing conversation,

Power is America's last dirty word. It is easier to talk about money—and much easier to talk about sex—than it is to talk about power.

—Rosabeth Moss Kanter, management scholar

Ken told him what had happened. The director launched into a long discourse on the difficulties he had experienced in reorganizing units within his department. But he also pointed out how the combination of the two units into the division had decreased his span of control and made the operation of the department considerably easier.

In part, he said that the reorganization had buried one of his main problems, or, Ken thought later, maybe he said it would do so soon.

As Ken found out the hard way, power and politics are an inescapable part of organizations. All types of organizations involve people using power and politics to influence others. People form coalitions and alliances, bargain and strategize, and engage in other forms of politics to influence decision making and organizational outcomes. The problem, of course, is that sometimes power and politics are used for things that we support or need, whereas other times they are used for things that we judge to be less desirable. They may even thwart organizational objectives.

Historic Hunger Strike

An awareness and understanding of how power and politics influence behavior can contribute to our success in groups and organizations. People who acquire and use power appropriately can be persuasive, can influence others, and are able to obtain necessary support for their programs, people, and priorities. While there might be a seamy side to power, power can also be a positive and necessary force as well. "Education in the politics of organizations in the positive sense of the word, reciprocal obligations, is crucial to the personal development of any successful manager and absolutely central to the long-term success of any senior executive."[1]

SELF-ASSESSMENT 13.1

YOUR UNDERSTANDING OF POLITICS AND POWER

How do you currently think about and use power? Indicate for each of the following whether you think the statement is true or false.

1. It is important to get along with everyone in organizations, even people you do not like.

2. Organizational politics should have no role in the management of organizations.

3. You can gain power by making others feel important.

4. The simplest and best long-term strategy for getting others to do what you want is to let them know that you are the boss.

5. It often is a good idea to make others dependent on you for your expertise and knowledge.

6. To maintain power, you should not compromise, even when an issue is of minor importance to you.

7. It is advisable to do favors for people whenever possible.

8. Empowerment requires delegation; if your boss does not give it to you, then it is not possible to make it happen.

9. Power and politics can be destructive forces in organizations.

10. If you have good relationships with the people in your unit, then it is not necessary to have good relationships with people in other parts and levels of the organization.

11. As a manager, it is necessary to have organizational power just to do a good job with the tasks assigned to you.

12. It is advisable to always tell people everything you know about a situation.

13. You always should try to make a good first impression.

14. Reaching organizational goals requires that organizational politics and power be avoided whenever possible.

15. On very controversial issues, it often is best to delay or avoid your involvement as long as possible.

16. If you have very little power in an organization, then there is basically nothing you can or should do about it.

17. Gaining power often involves making friends rather than making enemies in the organization.

18. If you have power, then people will dislike and fear you.

19. It is not a good idea to become dependent on one person in an organization.

20. The best way of handling power and organizational politics is to stay away from them.

Scoring. Give yourself 1 point for every odd-numbered statement you marked *true* and every even-numbered statement you marked *false.* You can interpret your scores based on the following scale:

17–20: You have an excellent grasp on power and politics in organizations. You appreciate that power and politics can be both constructive and destructive. You have a strong grasp of some of the tactics and strategies of politics, and you understand how they can be used in a positive manner.

13–16: You have a good sense of power and politics. You have an appreciation for some of the aspects of power and politics in organizations but perhaps do not yet fully understand some of its manifestations.

9–12: Your success in organizations might be enhanced by gaining a greater appreciation for power and organizational politics in their many forms. You might want to think about how your power can be enhanced and used constructively in organizations.

8 or less: You might be uncomfortable with notions of power and politics. Enhancing your understanding of how power and politics work in organizations might be important in your career development, and it might give you some important insights into organizational behavior.

Regardless of your score, as you read this chapter, think about your own experiences with power and organizational politics. How can you gain and use power in your organization in a manner that benefits you, the people you work with, your organization, and the people you serve? How can you respond to organizational politics constructively? How can you become an organizational politician in the best sense of the word?

Thinking About Power and Politics

Power and organizational politics are closely related concepts, and for the purposes of this chapter, they are considered together. **Power** is the ability to influence others. **Politics** generally refers to the use of power and authority to influence organizational outcomes.

These appear to be relatively straightforward definitions. But power and politics have been the subject of debate for many hundreds of years. Although at one time workers might have willingly accepted the use of power and force by their supervisors, society has undergone a significant change in how we view power. Questions have been raised about who has a right to power and how that power should be used. In today's organizations, simply ordering or openly coercing someone to do something is rarely the best strategy. Power and organizational politics in the contemporary environment often are more subtle and are exercised in relationships that are more egalitarian and involve the use of shared power. The following subsections trace these changes, beginning with three early voices.

Early Voices

Much of our understanding of the nature of power and politics in organizations is derived, to a greater or lesser extent, from the early literature on governmental politics and political rulers. Machiavelli's *The Prince,* written during the early 16th century,[2] is still used when discussing the use of power. In Machiavelli's view, the strength of a leader's power is measured by the degree to which he or she is independent of others and maintains domination. Machiavelli argued that because the survival of the state (or country) is paramount, whatever means are necessary to perpetuate the power of the state must be undertaken by the leader. The leader should be ruthless if necessary. "A prince should care nothing for the accusation of cruelty so long as he keeps his subjects united and loyal."[3] Accordingly, Machiavelli's work is perhaps most commonly known for the philosophy of "the end justifies the means."

We still talk of some people who use power in organizations as being "Machiavellian," meaning that they are power hungry and self-serving. Machiavelli's view of power hinges on the assumption that people are typically ungrateful, fickle, and deceitful—assumptions that most students of organizational behavior and modern management would reject. Yet, Machiavelli might have some useful lessons for us, particularly the idea that leaders often need power to do their jobs. He pointed out that during his day (as well as now) powerless leaders could do little to ensure the protection and well-being of the people for whom they were responsible. This view points to one of the key issues related to power. *Power is necessary* for leaders and managers; without power, they cannot get anything done.

But what type of power and how much of it is needed, and how should it be used? Early organizational theorists such as Max Weber who first wrote about bureaucracy, struggled with fundamental questions about power. Weber was particularly concerned about the nature of power and the question of why people obey others or are willing to be controlled by them. He proposed three types of power or domination:

1. *Charismatic:* where power and control are derived from the personal magnetism of the power wielder. You remember this concept from our discussions of charismatic and transformational leadership

2. *Traditional:* where power is granted through family lineage from one generation to the next

3. *Legal–rational:* where laws and constitutional processes create legitimate authority

Power: the ability to influence others

Politics: the use of power and authority to influence organizational outcomes

Weber argued that the last of these, the *legal–rational* (or bureaucratic) form of authority, was superior to other forms of power because in bureaucracies, authority was based on the position a person held and the person's power was controlled by rules, hierarchy, and reporting relationships.[4]

Although Weber argued that these bureaucratic organizations were technically superior, he also worried about their effect on people. He predicted that people would become trapped by the legalistic and rule-bound structure. He was also concerned that the focus on expertise and efficiency would make organizations difficult to control. Despite his ambivalence, he still thought that power based on position in the organization was better than alternatives such as charisma or inheritance.

Certainly, we still can see the influence of Weber's perspectives today. Many of us might believe that power in organizations ought to reside with the position held, rather than with the person, and that the power that is exercised should be within that person's official authority to act. In other words, we may readily accept the power and influence of a CEO or manager, but we question or feel uncomfortable with power derived from personal magnetism, deal making, or family position. When people in particular positions use power, it may be seen as good and necessary; when others exercise power, it may be viewed as unfair and inappropriate. We are ambivalent about power.

Changing Perspectives on Power

Our perspectives on power and organizational politics continue to evolve. A key idea that has guided how we understand power in organizations is the recognition that it is latent. The word *latent* means that something is present, but hidden. In the case of power, this means that power is the perceived *potential* to influence, rather than the actual *act* of influencing. When used, it becomes visible as authority, persuasion, force, or coercion.

During his presidency, Bill Clinton used both legal-rational and charismatic power.

Because power is latent, from a practical point of view, how much power you have depends in large measure on how much power people think you have. Most people have an intuitive sense of power as based on a relationship between people where "A has power over B to the extent that he can get B to do something that B would not otherwise do."[5] Although you can compare how much power different people have, the comparison should be based on how others react rather than how much power someone has.[6] Again, the idea is that power is a latent potential or *capacity* to influence or control, not just the act of coercing or influencing someone else. In fact, as we will see later in this chapter, sometimes acts of coercion or force can actually lessen the power held by an individual.

▶ At a dinner party, a new acquaintance happens to mention that one of your employees, whom she knew from a previous assignment, was suspected there of mishandling financial accounts to the point that an internal investigation was undertaken. The investigation couldn't confirm that funds were mishandled but everyone in the office felt that this employee was guilty of embezzlement. The investigation is still open but this never came up when you interviewed and hired this person. What would you do?

Power Influence
in Organizations

Questioning Power and Authority

The 1960s were not only a period of political unrest in the United States but also an era that called into question the nature of power and authority and who should have the "right" to tell people what they could or could not do. In organizations, attitudes about the types of power that individuals were willing to grant their "superiors" underwent a marked shift. The human relations movement (see Chapter 1) during the 1960s and 1970s challenged the idea that the job of management was to manipulate workers for the benefit of organizations. Instead, it was felt that organizations should meet both individual and collective needs. During the early stages of the organizational development movement, the nature and desirability of traditional hierarchical authority relationships came under particularly heavy fire. In short, people began to openly question authority and the power that accompanied it.

When writers during the 1960s asked the same question that Weber had asked decades earlier—"Why do people do what they are told?"—they came up with very different answers. Executive authority traditionally had been based on ownership of the company; the owners of factories had the right to use power to control the people who worked in them. Although ownership became increasing separated from organizational management, the assumption that power and authority are an inherent right of management had remained largely unchanged through the 1950s. But in the 1960s, researchers were urging us to change our conceptions about management and the nature of people. Instead of being inherently lazy, people might exhibit these behaviors because of outmoded organizational forms and authority relationships. If we embrace a more optimistic view of people, and authority in organizations can be made more participative, power will become more equalized and people will behave in a positive and productive way.[7]

Our views of organizations themselves had also evolved. Instead of seeing organizations as economically rational in their decision-making process, the idea that organizations were also political entities and that the people in them act politically became more accepted.[8] Some argued that organizations always seek to reduce uncertainty and dependency. Because power is the opposite of dependency, organizations will try to minimize their dependency on external entities and people by maintaining alternatives, seeking prestige, engaging in cooperative strategies, contracting, and co-opting those who impose threats. Individuals behave in much the same way as organizations by seeking to minimize dependence, forming coalitions, and attempting to acquire power. Accordingly, the traditional idea that one person could hold absolute authority had ceased to make a lot of sense. "An individual can be powerful . . . and can exercise significant leadership . . . only with the consent and approval of the dominant coalition."[9] In this view, the power of individuals was not derived, nor should it be derived, solely from their positions.

In the global context, it becomes increasingly important to recognize that people of different cultures may view power and authority differently. In Chapter 2, we examined differences in national culture. Among those differences were the concepts of power distance, which refers to how power is distributed, and uncertainty avoidance, which indicates how comfortable people are with uncertainty. In countries that score low on power distance (the United States, Canada, the Netherlands, Great Britain, Australia, Luxembourg, Germany, Norway, Sweden, Costa Rica), subordinates are more likely to disagree with their bosses and expect a consultative style of management. Employees in the countries that score high on power distance (Malaysia, Venezuela, Guatemala, Arab countries, Russia, Romania, Panama, Serbia, Slovenia) are willing to accept more autocratic bosses, and they rarely disagree with their managers (see Figure 13.1). Similarly, in cultures where people are comfortable with uncertainty, for example in the United States, power is less centralized whereas when people avoid uncertainty, they also assign more power to managers.

These cultural differences become very important, of course, in multinational corporations. In such cases, there is often conflict over what are considered legitimate behaviors, and developing a common view will be a matter of negotiation. When the political and other norms of the headquarters and host country are at odds, it is not necessary for the headquarters to completely adopt the norms of the host culture, but some adjustments will invariably need to occur. A knowledge of politics and organizational influence tactics, and an understanding of the influence of societal-level culture on organizational culture is particularly essential to success in these settings.[10]

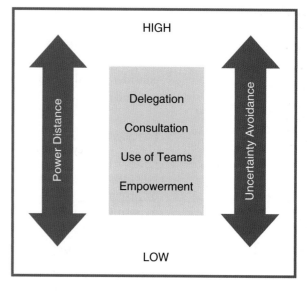

FIGURE 13.1 POWER AND CULTURE

Sources of Power for Individuals

How do people in organizations get power? The idea that you will have sufficient power to shape the organization because of your title, span of control, and/or the size of your budget is no longer true. "Now, power can also come from social collaboration. If Kickstarter, TEDx, and Wikipedia and other related platforms have taught us nothing else, it's that people can become powerful without first being picked or vetted, through what we create together."[11] While it is true that having a particular position may make it easier to gain access or an audience, your capacity to exercise leadership is based on your ability to shape, champion, and frame ideas. Collaboration does not mean a loss of power; in fact, it can enhance your power to lead.

While this may be truer today than it has ever been, the idea that power can be acquired through a variety of sources is not a new one. The bases proposed by French and Raven are still accepted as the primary sources of individual power in organizations.[12] They are presented in Table 13.1.

Intergroup Relations and Power

TABLE 13.1 SOURCE OF INDIVIDUAL POWER

Source	Description
Legitimate	Power based on accepted authority such as title or official position
Reward	Power based on access to resources and the ability to reward others
Coercive	Power based on force and ability to punish others
Expert	Power based on expertise or access to information others need
Referent	Power based on respect and being a role model

Source: Based on French, J. R., Jr., & Raven, B. (1989). The bases of social power. In J. S. Ott (Ed.), *Classic readings in organizational behavior*. Belmont, CA: Wadsworth. (Original work published 1959)

Legitimate Power

Legitimate power arises from people's values and beliefs that someone has the right to exert influence over them and that they have an obligation to comply. In organizations, this type of power often is derived from people's positions or job titles. Although most organizations use position titles to designate levels of authority, some organizations rely on position power more than do others. For example, military and police organizations use symbols (e.g., uniforms) to convey differences in position. But even in these organizations, power is derived from other sources as well. Not all people with the title of "director" have the same amount of power—even within the same organization.

Nonetheless, legitimate power is important. We are influenced by the positions or titles that people hold in organizations, particularly with regard to the legitimacy that others will be likely to accord those people in the use of power. As a practical matter, then, it makes sense to pay attention not only to other people's titles, but to our own as well. Although there can be limited flexibility in changing position titles, it is worthwhile to consider the title of your position as one of the factors that can influence how others will respond to you.

Reward Power

Reward power is just what the label implies—power arising from our ability to reward other people for behaving as we want them to. Reward power involves influencing others by providing positive outcomes and preventing negative ones. Reward power is similar to positive reinforcement. When managers recommend promotions, give positive performance evaluations, give desirable assignments, provide recognition, offer support, and so on, they gain power. Effective managers use reward power to highlight good work and to reinforce behavior that advances organizational values. We might not think of rewarding others as giving us power. But if we provide rewards that people want, then it makes sense that we can influence their behavior. If used appropriately, this can help employees to learn and grow and can help organizations to attain their objectives.

You don't have to be a manager to use reward power. By sincerely praising others, bringing the good work of coworkers to your supervisor's attention, or providing positive feedback to others, you not only are being a "good person" but also are creating a situation in which you are likely to be able to influence those people in the future. The use of reward power typically engenders cooperation and minimizes resistance. Furthermore, its use can be supportive of others, enhance the organizational environment, and reflect positively on you.

Coercive Power

Coercive power is the opposite of reward power. Coercive power is based on our ability to apply sanctions or punishments for the failure of others to behave as we want them to. Using coercive power involves exerting influence through the use of punishments or the threat of punishments. Supervisors can use coercive power by reducing pay, controlling assignments, initiating transfers, giving poor performance evaluations, oversupervising, or providing criticism. Punishments can go in the other direction as well. You can "punish" supervisors by refusing to work hard, ignoring them, or making them look bad by withholding information or embarrassing them.

Coercive power can have its pitfalls. Particularly if punishments are dispensed without also offering rewards, negative consequences can result. For example, coercive power typically produces more resistance than does reward power. Nonetheless, coercive power has

Legitimate power: power based on accepted authority

Reward power: power based on access to resources and rewards

Coercive power: power based on force and the ability to punish

its place in organizations. If an employee is not performing, is behaving inappropriately with coworkers or customers, or has engaged in wrongdoing, then negative consequences are appropriate. If other employees see negative behavior as having no consequences, then this can, in turn, affect their behavior in an undesirable manner. But the use of coercive behavior by itself as the sole means of influencing others is not recommended.

Expert Power

French and Raven[13] defined **expert power** as power based on our knowledge and expertise. Expert power is drawn from having a special expertise that is needed or valued in an organization. It is also related to having information that is needed by others. This may take the form of technical expertise (e.g., computer skills), may be grounded in a person's insights with regard to the market, or may even be based on someone's connection with an influential person. If you know or understand something important that other people in the organization do not, then this gives you expert power.

The problem with coercion is that it produces more resistance than other types of power.

What Do You Think?

▶ Someone said, "Power corrupts!" What do you think?

This suggests, from a practical standpoint, that you should "do your homework," so to speak. Whether you are a line-level employee or an executive, having expertise in your area of work gives you an edge. If you work in the accounting office, then learn all you can about accounting. If you work in personnel, then study personnel systems and become knowledgeable about innovative practices. Becoming knowledgeable in a manner that helps your organization to function better and to serve customers more effectively and makes you more powerful.

In a recently published "guide" to acquiring power, Pfeffer states that people with power seem to have a number of personal qualities including ambition, energy, focus, self-knowledge, confidence, empathy with others, and capacity to tolerate conflict.[14] He also argues that we ought to seek power because it is not only essential to organizational survival, it is necessary in order to exercise influence and leadership. He even goes so far as to suggest having power may be more important than good performance. You may agree or disagree with this statement, but your ability to use and acquire influence is not wholly dependent on your successful performance of your assigned duties. Also, power is a double-edged sword. Organizational politics can result in winners and losers, and whether you view politics positively or negatively may have a lot to do with which category you find yourself in at a particular time. Even so, researchers have consistently found that the perception of politics and political behavior by others in an organization is related to lower job satisfaction, performance, and organizational commitment.[15]

Referent Power

Referent power is based on the psychological identification between people. Its strength depends on the degree to which others desire to have a relationship or identify with us. Put simply, we are influenced by people we like or admire. When we admire other people,

Expert power: power based on expertise

Referent power: power based on respect

we are apt to see what they do in a favorable light, de-emphasize their mistakes, and seek their approval. We want to do what they want because we want to please them and have them continue to like us. Simply having the positive regard and respect of others, then, is a potential source of power. It is interesting to note that French and Raven,[16] in distinguishing between reward power and coercive power, pointed out that the use of reward power tends to increase referent power, whereas the use of coercive power tends to diminish referent power. Although this might appear to be just good sense, remember that rewarding people will increase their positive regard, thereby giving you more capacity to positively influence them in the future. Conversely, if you coerce others to comply, then your referent power will diminish, leaving you with fewer tools for positive influence.

In practical terms, we gain influence through referent power by being liked, admired, and respected. Research shows that our ability to influence is first based on how friendly and warm we are perceived to be, and secondarily, on how strong and competent people think we are.[17] If you focus on strength and competency you may undermine leadership because people might comply without fully adopting the deep values and culture of the organization. They further may become defensive about their own values and interests. When people evaluate us, they judge warmth first, and then evaluate our strength in that context. For that reason, the best way to influence people is by being genuinely likable, admirable, and respectable. Warmth cannot just be something we "turn on" when convenient. We have to actually earn people's respect and admiration the hard way—by consistently treating them well. Behaving in a manner that is professional, kind, respectful, caring, and interested is desirable in its own right, but it also gives you the power to influence others to our own benefit, to their benefit, and to the organization's benefit.

Why Some Have It

Balancing Power

Power in today's organizations is not unidirectional. Most people in contemporary settings do not unquestioningly accept the power of their superiors. People have different reactions to power based on the source of the power (see Figure 13.2). If a manager relied primarily on coercion as a way of influencing others, chances are his employees would resist either openly or passively. When managers rely on their title or rewards as a way of influencing others, employees will comply, but they may not fully buy into the manager's decisions. Finally, when a leader's power is based on expertise or respect, his reports are more likely to be committed to his decisions.

People often will attempt to balance power relationships. That is, individuals' power may be confined to certain spheres and balanced by the influence of others in different spheres.[18] Politics, then, involves efforts both to gain power and to limit or balance the power of others.

People with less power use four different ways to equalize or balance power in a relationship, all based on the idea that dependence reduces

FIGURE 13.2 POTENTIAL REACTIONS TO INDIVIDUAL SOURCES OF POWER

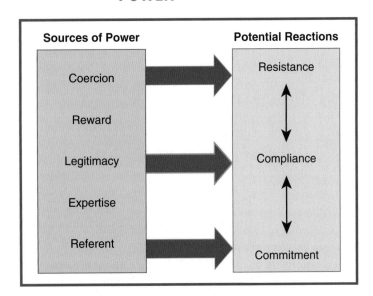

power and independence increases it. To increase power, people can:[19]

1. *Decrease their needs* or demands (need less or be less dependent)

2. *Increase their alternative* sources of getting what they want, thereby gaining independence

3. *Increase other people's needs* thereby making the others more dependent

4. *Decrease other people's alternative* sources, again making them more dependent

These power-balancing operations, then, either decrease dependence, in the first two cases, or increase the dependence of other people. Decreasing our dependence on the organization can be less desirable for an organization as it may reduce our engagement with the organization. On the other hand, increasing the dependence of other people while not decreasing our dependence on the organization can result in increasing our involvement in the organization and, at the same time, make us more valuable to it.

For example, consider the following example. You very much want praise and positive feedback from your supervisor, but it is not forthcoming. As a result, she has potential power over you by denying something that you want. If you do nothing, then you might end up being resentful, unhappy, and unproductive. There are several ways to change or balance the effect of this potential power. First, you could decide to rely on your own self-assessment of your performance and not to make your professional self-image so dependent on feedback from your supervisor. This decreases your dependence by changing what you want from her. Second, you could look for other sources of positive feedback, thereby increasing your alternatives and decreasing your dependency. Third, you could work to make your work more central to the unit's success, thereby increasing your supervisor's dependence on you. When you ask for more positive feedback, her dependency on your performance would make her more likely to provide it. Fourth, you could gain special expertise that no one else in the unit has, again making yourself less dependent on the supervisor and making her more dependent on you. The first and second options might result in a sort of psychological distancing from your supervisor and the organization, whereas the third and fourth options might result in a stronger commitment on your part.

You might ask yourself, isn't what has been described really just a matter of manipulating your supervisor to get something you want? The answer is yes, it is, at least in some sense. But it is important to remember three things. First, relationships are becoming more egalitarian in organizations, with positive consequences for individuals and the organizations themselves. You are more valuable to your organization if you have the power to influence others, act independently, and be self-reliant than if you are powerless and dependent. But at the same time, creating psychological distance between yourself and your organization might be detrimental to both. Second, gaining expertise and knowledge that are critical to organizational success not only is helpful to you but also can help the organization to better accomplish its mission. Third, as a manager, it is important for you to recognize that although you might have organizational authority and other sources of power at your disposal, your employees have a number of sources of power as well. Recognizing your mutual dependency with others can foster mutual respect and cooperation.

Structural Aspects of Power

Power and organizational politics are not just an individual phenomenon, they are also a function of organizational structure.[20] There is a degree of power that goes along with one's position in the organizational structure. Beyond this position power, the farther up the organizational ladder you go, the better access you have to information, people, and resources. Once this structure is established, it resists change because it is in the interest of those in power to keep the structure that gave them power in the first place. After all, why change a structure that reinforces your power and political influence?

The structure of power touches many aspects of organizational life. One of the major issues of the past several decades has been the representativeness of the workplace and the assimilation of new groups into organizational life. This assimilation can be seen, at least in part, as an issue of structural power. Rosabeth Moss Kanter,[21] for example, argued that the behavior of members of certain groups (particularly women and minorities) can be explained by structural factors in the organization rather than by the stereotypical attributes of those groups. More specifically, she suggested that powerlessness, and structural characteristics of organizations that perpetuate such powerlessness, result in counterproductive behavior. She indicated that as leaders change the structure of rewards and opportunities, feelings of powerlessness will diminish and the negative behavior associated with these groups will decrease.

Men and women may behave differently in organizations not so much because of gender differences but rather because of the structural characteristics of their roles. Women tend to be clustered in low-power, dependent, and low-mobility positions. Furthermore, those women and minorities who are placed in other roles find that their lack of numerical representation and their inability to command resources make them powerless. This powerlessness leads to ineffective management behavior (e.g., refusal to delegate, lack of concern for tasks and goals). Incidentally, white men behave similarly when placed in low-power, dependent, and low-mobility jobs.[22]

In short, structural determinants—opportunity, mobility, perceived political power, dependency, influence in garnering resources and rewards for subordinates, and numerical representation—are critical to understanding the influence of power in organizational behavior. In order to correct these imbalances, organizations must seek to expand opportunity and mobility, empower people, and balance numerical representation.

Positive and Negative Power

People at lower ranks of organizations, such as secretaries or receptionists, do not have power that comes from titles, but they often have expertise and information and control access to powerful others, factors that can give them some power.

Is Power a Positive Force or a Destructive Force?

So far, we have talked about changing attitudes toward power and authority, sources of power, balancing power and empowerment, the structural aspects of power, and power and organizational learning, but we have not fully explored the question of whether power is a positive and

GLOBAL SOCIETY

LUXOTTICA AND THE POWER OF CONTROLLING RESOURCES

Did you have a sticker shock the last time you bought glasses? If you did, you are not alone. Even if you were not seeking the latest designer eyewear—they are no longer called eyeglasses—and stopped by one of the mass retailers to get your prescription, you most likely paid well over $150, no matter how hard you tried. Add a designer label and the

brand such as Chanel, Prada, or Versace, or are insured by the second largest eye insurer, Eye Med Vision Care—all owned by Luxottica.[24] Andrea Guerra estimates that half a billion people around the world own their product.[25]

This is no small feat for a company with a little over 60,000 employees, founded in 1961 by Leonardo Del Vecchio, an orphan who has become one of the 100 richest men in the world.[26] Located in a small town in the Italian Alps, Luxottica has seen steady growth, first in its home country, and eventually world wide through an aggressive campaign of acquisitions of brands such as Ray Ban and Oakley, licensing agreements with some of the most prestigious fashion houses such as Armani and Tiffany,[27] and the purchase of distribution outlets such as Sunglass Hut and Lens Crafters. Luxottica has been accused of using strong-arm tactics to achieve this dominance. For example, it prevented Oakley, maker of specialized sport-oriented eyewear, from selling its glasses in Luxottica Sunglass Hut outlets, causing a drop in stock prices and forcing Oakley into a merger. However, Andrea Guerra responds that they convinced Oakley that "life is better together."[28] In response to why eyewear costs so much, he says: "Everything is worth what people are ready to pay."[29] Some say that Luxottica has too much control of the market and too much power. Brett Arends, business reporter says: "One company has excessive dominance in the eyewear market. The appearance of variety is an optical illusion."[30] But Luxottica continues to provide, or maybe determine, what consumers want and the company's dominance and power continue to grow.

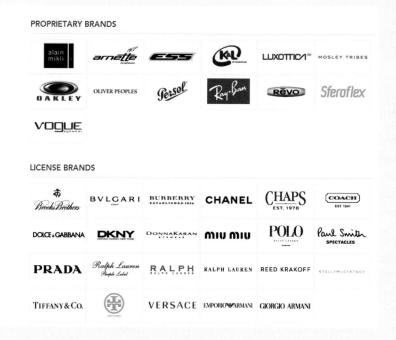

Luxottica has been able to exert considerable power and control over the eyewear industry because they own many of the brands and many of the outlets. Although Luxottica owns a wide variety of brands, each brand retains its own unique signature look and style. How do these logos reflect the diversity of Luxottica's offerings?

cost easily tops $300. Eyeglasses are no longer an unattractive staple for nerds; eyewear has become face jewelry that is used to make a fashion statement. Luxottica has had a major hand in that transformation.

Luxottica controls 80% of the eyewear market, worldwide. Through that dominance it also controls and dictates the price of eyewear; it has the power to be what is called a "price maker."[23] Even if you have never heard of Luxottica, and the company seems to prefer it that way, you have bought their product if you have shopped at Sunglass Hut, Sears Optical, Target, Lens Crafters, Pearle Vision, or bought Ray Bans, Oakleys, or Persols, or almost any luxury

1. How does Luxottica gain and maintain power?

2. How does the company address cultural challenges?

3. How does the perception of power differ from culture to culture?

constructive force in organizations or a negative and destructive one. Unfortunately, as with many other facets of human behavior, there is not a clear answer. Table 13.2 presents the two sides of power.

TABLE 13.2 BENEFITS AND DISADVANTAGES OF POWER

Advantages	Disadvantages
Essential to survival	Self-serving
Essential to conflict resolution	Potential for destructive outcome
Critical to leadership	Subject to abuse
Critical for buy-in	Can decrease engagement
Necessary for learning	Can decrease involvement

Power Influences
Creativity

Positive Aspects of Power

First, on the positive side, although political power in organizations often is considered an unfair, unjust, and generally undesirable phenomenon, political processes are essential to resolving conflicts and to organizational effectiveness.[31] From this perspective, power is not only necessary for positive organizational functioning but also a vital and critical force in ensuring organizational survival. Power and politics can help organizations to adapt to and interact appropriately with their environments.

Power can be seen as a positive force because those organizational subunits "most able to cope with the organization's critical problems and uncertainties acquire power."[32] In this "strategic-contingency" theory of power the reason subunits or persons who deal with critical problems acquire power is because these subunits or persons play a critical role in organizational success. Accordingly, the power of these units is functional and positive in terms of organizational goal attainment. Moreover, power appropriately plays a role in the selection of executives. Power, in this view, helps to ensure that organizations will protect the survival of their most critical components and select executives best able to deal with environmental contingencies.

In addition, power is a necessary and healthy aspect of organizational functioning because it is a critical component of leadership.[33] Some even say that the problem in most situations is not the use of power but rather powerlessness. Powerlessness leads us to say "I don't know what to do," "I don't have the power to get it done," or "I can't really stomach the struggle that might be involved." As such, it is "a prescription for both organizational and personal failure."[34] Without power, we are forced to rely on solely hierarchical authority, an approach that is fraught with difficulties. Not only are people likely to resist it, but such an approach ignores the need for cooperation, participation, persuasion, and other influence processes. Attention to organizational politics is absolutely necessary to effectively lead organizational change. Attention to the question of power is needed to establish and get buy-in on goals, to identify dependencies and strengths, to identify key actors who support or oppose implementation, and to choose approaches and strategies that will increase one's influence over the outcome.

Finally, power and organizational politics are necessary components of organizational learning. "Organizational learning is a multilevel process that begins with individual learning, that leads to group learning, and that then leads to organizational learning,"[35] and this sequence involves the use of different types of power. Organizational learning involves four processes, or 4Is: "intuiting, interpreting, integrating, and institutionalizing."[36] Intuiting happens when individuals develop new ideas, and interpreting occurs when these ideas are communicated or explained to others. Integrating involves translating the new ideas into coordinated actions. The last phase, institutionalizing, refers to the incorporation of new ideas and insights into organizational practice.

The types of power and tactics used will vary based on the phase of organizational learning: intuition is linked with discipline, interpretation with influence, integration with force, and institutionalization with domination. For instance, in the interpreting phase, an individual's actions to influence or persuade others will affect how an idea is received. Integration, on the other hand, may involve the use of force more than persuasion. "This might involve restricting the consideration of alternative practices, restricting issues for discussion on formal and informal agendas, and removing/transferring opponents of the innovation."[37] The politics of institutionalization almost often involves the use of systemic power, such as changing procedures or rules, to overcome resistance.[38] Most important, "Having smart employees with great ideas is not enough. Managers who want to foster learning require a slate of employees with appropriate political skills and resources." Without political behavior, "new ideas may be generated by individuals, but organizations will never learn"[39] (see also Figure 13.3).

Negative Aspects of Power

In contrast to these positive views on the role of power in organizations, others urge caution in advocating power and politics in organizations. The dark or selfish side of power should not and cannot be ignored. Political activities are, by definition, not formally sanctioned by organizations.[40] In other words, power and politics in organizations are, by their nature, self-serving processes.

When Power Goes to Your Head

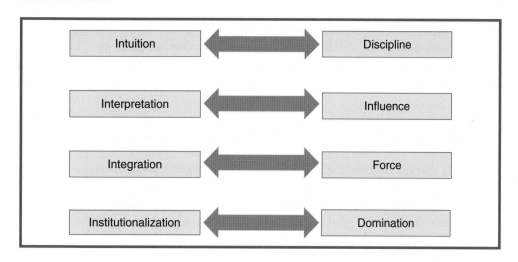

FIGURE 13.3 ORGANIZATIONAL LEARNING AND POWER

Intuition	⟷	Discipline
Interpretation	⟷	Influence
Integration	⟷	Force
Institutionalization	⟷	Domination

Organizational politics is both an individual phenomenon and a group phenomenon that is undertaken to influence others in the direction of the actor's or group's goals. In political situations, these goals are either not sanctioned or unofficially sanctioned by the organization. "A group's or [an] individual's goals or means are political to the extent that they are not positively sanctioned by an organization's formal design or to the degree [that] they are positively sanctioned by unofficial political norms."[41] This makes organizational politics more likely to result in destructive outcomes than in positive ones.

We also need to remember that power can be abused in organizations and that hierarchical, interpersonal abuse of power is a danger to both the individuals hurt by it and the organization itself. Power can be used in a manner that negatively affects others' sense of dignity and self-respect in both style and substance. Such abusive power interferes with employee job performance, interferes with goal attainments, and can block deserved rewards.[42] From this perspective, power politics aren't just potentially harmful to individuals. Members of organizations may invest a significant amount of time in trying to influence decisions in which they have personal stakes. While this might be rational for individuals, these attempts to influence impose costs on organizations.[43] For example, individuals might find it in their interest to manipulate or distort information so as to influence decision makers in a manner that benefits their interests. When that happens, decisions are made based on imperfect and incomplete information. This decreases the quality of the resulting decisions and diverts time and energy away from more productive pursuits. If this is the case, then organizations should employ strategies to discourage organizational members from engaging in such activities by (1) limiting access to decision makers, (2) altering the decision criteria to favor good performers, and (3) offering financial incentives to discourage political activity.[44]

Finally, as noted earlier, the perception of workplace politics has been shown to have negative consequences for employees, including decreases in job involvement, commitment, and satisfaction, and increases in stress, turnover, absenteeism, and perceived inequity.[45] While there are various factors that may mediate these negative effects—including age, culture, emotional intelligence, and supervisor communication—it is clear that many people are troubled when they perceive high levels of political behavior in their organization.[46] This may be particularly true for those who have few political skills themselves and feel victimized.

In the end, we are left with no clear answer. Politics and power are organizational facts of life, and they can have both positive and negative consequences. If we manage our dependencies and are sensitive to political issues, then we can go a long way toward avoiding the negative aspects of power. But there are other things we can do as well. There are a number of practical tools for and approaches to managing power that may be helpful to consider.

Managing Organizational Politics and Being Influential

Remember that organizational politics are most likely to occur when the stakes are high, resources are limited, or goals and processes are unclear. Although there might be relatively few things that we can do to change the importance of an issue, or the uncertainty and resource scarcity that might surround it, goal ambiguity is something that we can influence. By seeking clarification of goals, or by developing a shared sense of direction and purpose through dialogue and interaction, some of the negative consequences of

Any discussion of power should acknowledge that power sometimes "corrupts" and people in positions of power often use their power for their personal ends. Among the things that businesses can do to promote ethical fitness is to establish clear values and standards of behavior, frequently contained in a specific code of ethics. (We should note that this alone is not enough; Enron had a much lauded code of ethics that consisted of 64 pages of details.) Even if a code of ethics is in place, the culture of the organization has to reflect that perspective and make it easier for people to do the right thing rather than the wrong thing.

Managers and others must be sensitive to the behavior of their coworkers and willing to step in when potential ethical violations occur. Managers should base hiring decisions in part on the character and ethical sensitivity of prospective employees and take matters such as ethics and responsibility into account in annual reviews, pay raises, and promotions.

Finally, regular training programs in ethics should emphasize matters of individual responsibility and educate employees with respect to the basic steps in ethical deliberation—to carefully define the problem, to identify the ethical values that are at play, to develop several courses of action that might be pursued, and to compare each of these with the values you have identified. Then, and often most importantly, you have to act in a way that is consistent with the ethical choice that you have made, recognizing that coming to a solution in your head is often far less difficult than putting that solution into practice. James P. Hackett, president and chief executive of Steelcase, notes that "people tend to double down and do bad things under the most extreme pressure."[47] But that's really what integrity is all about, that is, the capacity to "integrate" your values and your actions, even under pressures not to do so.

1. Where do our ethics and values come from? Where does our approach to power come from?

2. Why does the accumulation of power seem to color our ethical reasoning?

3. Why do seemingly good people do such bad things when they reach positions of power?

power and politics can be moderated. At a minimum, when there is greater agreement on goals, it is easier to distinguish organizational politics that are primarily focused on organizational and shared goal achievement from organizational politics that are largely self-serving. When goals are unclear and conflicting, it is much easier for individuals to claim and to convince others that their agenda is the "right" one for the organization.

Human Nature

In addition to clarifying goals, people who are successful and influential in organizations use various tactics and strategies to gain power, exercise influence, and balance the power of others. Rather than focusing directly on power, we can look to behavior that is more or less likely to influence others. **Influence tactics** are used intentionally to influence or change the attitude or behavior of someone else.[48] One kind of influence tactic is termed **proactive influence** because it has an immediate task objective to get a person to complete a task, change methods, or agree to something.

Table 13.3 shows some of the proactive influence tactics commonly used in organizations and their relative effectiveness.

In general, different tactics work better, sometimes depending on whether we are trying to influence "upward" to our managers, "laterally" to our peers, or "downward" to our subordinates. Inspiration, consultation, and rational persuasion all work moderately well and are socially acceptable in any direction. On the other hand, pressure, coalition building,

Influence tactics: actions used intentionally to influence or change the attitude or behavior of someone else

Proactive influence: tactics used to accomplish an immediate purpose or task

TABLE 13.3 PROACTIVE INFLUENCE TACTICS

Tactic	Description	General Effectiveness
Rational Persuasion	Logical arguments and factual evidence	High
Inspirational Appeal	Request based on values and ideals	High
Consultation	Seek others' participation in a decision	High
Collaboration	Offer to provide resources or assistance in exchange for agreement	High
Ingratiation	Get someone to feel favorable toward you before asking them something	Moderate
Exchange Tactics	Make a reciprocal or quid pro quo agreement that benefits both	Moderate
Personal Appeal	Asking a favor based on friendship or loyalty	Moderate
Apprising	Convince people that what you want will actually benefit them	Moderate
Coalition Building	Getting help from other people to influence a target or key decision maker	Low to moderate
Legitimating	Establishing your authority to make a decision or request	Low
Pressure	Demands, threats, and warnings	Low

Source: Based on Yukl, G., & Tracey, J. B. (1992). Consequences of influence tactics used with subordinates, peers, and the boss. *Journal of Applied Psychology, 77*(4), 525; Yukl, G., Chavez, C., & Seifert, C. F. (2005). Assessing the construct validity and utility of two new influence tactics. *Journal of Organizational Behavior, 26*(6), 705–725.

Abuse of Power

and legitimating are usually ineffective, may be seen as socially undesirable, and can result in resistance. Ingratiation and exchange work moderately well with subordinates and peers, but not as well with superiors. Apprising can be useful with subordinates.[49]

The challenge in managing politics, of course, is to choose strategies and tactics that are both legitimate and effective in a given circumstance. "The manager of political conflict will be more effective if his or her responses and strategies fit the problems in his or her environment."[50] To do so, managers need to assess their resources, diagnose the situation, and find the desired fit between strategies and the environment. Managers possess a range of resources including "authority, force, persuasion, symbolic rewards, personal style, bargaining techniques, negotiating and mediating skills, coalition-building approaches, and allocations of benefits."[51] In choosing the appropriate approach, managers consider the nature of the problem and the organizational environment. For example, if there is conflict between two people with equal power, then negotiating makes more sense than using force. Conversely, if there is a yes/no conflict between you and someone who works for you, then the use of authority might be more effective than engaging in a long negotiation. But power is a scarce resource. The use of power involves time, energy, and the depletion of the amount of power available over time. In other words, we need to choose our battles carefully and not expend political resources when it is unnecessary to do so.

YOUR POWER POTENTIAL

How powerful and influential are you? Think about the sources of power outlined by French and Raven and the power-balancing techniques described in this chapter. Are there specific areas where you feel less powerful than you would like to be? What specifically might you do to increase your capacity to influence others and create more balanced power relationships at work? Most important, how will you use that power constructively to benefit your company and the customers you serve?

Fostering a positive organizational climate requires not only eliminating negative political behavior, but also developing positive ethical political behavior such as collaboration and constructive conflict management. Organizations can foster a positive organizational climate by focusing on the following:

- A shared view of power based on partnership, collaboration, and empowerment

- Inclusiveness based on respect and dignity

- Connectedness based on valuing differences and communication

- Excellence based on ideals, goals, and values

- An encompassing value system grounded in kindness, humility, and trust

- Participation, accountability, and fairness[52]

Gaining Positive Political Skills

Most of us are not born with the skills necessary to manage and use politics in a positive manner in organizations, but those skills can be developed through training, mentoring, and practice.[53] Gaining political savvy makes it more likely that you will not only be able to influence others in a positive manner, but also gives you the ability to "recognize and stop deception, destructive politics, and selfish agendas."[54] Political skill can be defined as "the ability to effectively understand others at work, and to use such knowledge to influence others to act in ways that enhance one's personal and/or organizational goals."[55] Having political skills, particularly networking skills, is very important to professional success. Political skills have been shown to be associated with getting more promotions, higher perceived career success, and perceived organizational mobility.[56]

Positive Office
Politics

While we may think of someone having well-developed political skills in a negative light, positive organizational scholars highlight the constructive and useful skills involved in successfully navigating organizational politics. As noted earlier in this chapter, a big part of being politically skilled and influential is to be an emotionally healthy, likeable person. "It is not sufficient to know a lot, work hard . . . you have to make yourself liked."[57] While this may seem a little simplistic, politically skilled people have well-developed social skills, and the ability to adjust their behavior to different situations and to act in ways that others perceive as sincere and trustworthy. This could cause us to think that our "real" motives are less important than what others believe them to be, and all we have to do is *appear* to be sincere. But the converse is also true; it doesn't matter if your intentions are good if your behavior is not perceived to be well intentioned.

Powerful Yet Despised

Stop Avoiding Office Politics

Part of being politically savvy is recognizing how you present yourself to others or **impression management.**[58] You may choose to take the position that "my work will speak for itself," but the truth is that too many talented people are passed over for promotions and other opportunities because they have failed to authentically, accurately, and responsibly promote themselves and their team. You might begin by asking yourself: What do I (we) know that can be shared? What have I (we) achieved? How can I (we) contribute to organizational effectiveness? Authentic, positive self-promotion is not about making yourself feel important, it is aimed at sharing your talents and skills in order to accomplish organizational objectives and do the very best you can for the people you work with.

There are at least four additional dimensions of political skill: (1) social astuteness, (2) interpersonal influence, (3) networking ability, and (4) apparent or perceived sincerity.[59] They are presented in Figure 13.4. Social astuteness, or emotional intelligence, helps people to understand and manage their own emotional responses as well as understand and positively influence the emotions of others. In fact, while the perception of organizational politics has been found to have a negative effect on employee commitment, emotional intelligence minimizes this negative effect.[60] Emotional intelligence can be seen as a way to personally gain perspective on and manage the emotional effects of organizational politics; it can also be considered a political skill in and of itself. Interpersonal influence requires the ability to read and respond to changing situations, and also to communicate this ability to others as sincere and genuine, which results in trust. Seen in this way, political skills actually lead to the development of other positive characteristics such as "a calm sense of self-confidence, personal security and control."[61] Political skills also positively relate to job performance and leadership effectiveness, serve as an antidote to stress, and enhance career success and reputation.[62] *Positive organizational politics, then, is less about self-interest and manipulation, and more about authenticity, sincerity, and emotional health and intelligence.*

FIGURE 13.4 POLITICAL SKILLS

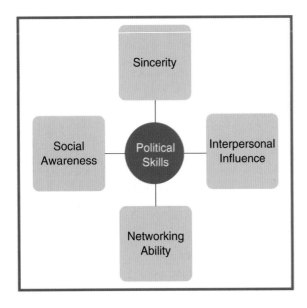

Empowerment: More Than Delegation

As we have seen, recent scholars and practitioners have suggested that, as a manager or leader, you should focus on creating conditions that foster the development of personal power and the empowerment of others to accomplish their goals. Although the word **empowerment** has been used widely, there is some confusion and lack of clarity regarding what empowerment actually is.[63] The idea of empowerment is often oversimplified and treated primarily as a management technique. The root construct of empowerment is based on a different view of power than is suggested in most of the literature on organizational politics. Existing views on power can be divided into two categories: relational constructs (where power is a function of the relative dependence or interdependence of the actors, a view reflected in much of the literature reviewed in this chapter) and motivational constructs (which are found primarily in the psychology literature and based on the idea that "power and control are used as motivational and/or expectancy belief states that are internal to individuals."[64] In *relational constructs,* the empowerment process becomes one of delegation or sharing of power. In other words, managers empower workers by delegating to them. By contrast, in *motivational*

Impression management: the act of consciously and carefully monitoring and managing the impression we make on others

Empowerment: either delegating or sharing power OR creating conditions that increase feelings of power or personal efficacy in others

constructs, empowerment is an enabling process aimed at creating conditions that increase motivation and the development of personal efficacy feelings.

Creating conditions that foster empowerment requires us to consider our assumptions about power in organizations and the behavioral consequences of these assumptions. For instance, managers can view power in organizations as either "fixed sum" or "expandable."[65] If power is perceived as "fixed sum," managers will believe that when employees gain power, they do so at the manager's expense. Managers will likely behave in ways that thwart the empowerment of others, because they believe that doing so protects their own power. In more empowering environments, power is viewed as "expandable." Managers who see power as expandable will act on the belief that their power will increase if their employees' performance is high, or in other words, "the success of employees can make them successful."[66] These managers are more apt to empower, encourage, help, and support their employees. There are a number of things that we can do to foster people's willingness to empower themselves. When we encourage workers to participate in decision making, treat workers with respect, provide opportunities for growth and development, and reward initiative and responsibility, we can foster empowerment. Equally important is how we treat mistakes and failure. If someone who works for us takes appropriate responsibility and initiative to solve a problem or address an issue and it does not work, then we need to gauge our response carefully. (It might be helpful to first ask ourselves whether anything we have ever tried has failed to work out as planned.) Some of the key questions we should ask ourselves in responding to mistakes or even flat-out failures include the following:

Empowerment

- Did the person take the initiative to understand the issue and gather needed information?

- Was the person thoughtful about the alternatives, and did he or she make a reasonable and appropriate choice given the information available?

- Was there an effort to involve the appropriate people?

- Is the person willing to deal with the consequences?

- Are there lessons that can be learned from the experience that will inform future practice in a positive manner?

If the answer to most of these questions is yes, then it would be a mistake to respond punitively by seizing control of the situation. It would be more constructive to sit down with the person and try to understand what went wrong and determine how you will proceed, both individually and collectively. Imagine, for example, that an employee identifies a problem with the automated customer support function in your company, resulting in a significant number of customers hanging up without getting answers to their questions. With your buy-in, this employee looked into options by examining practices in other organizations and consulting with staff from other units in your organization. When this employee came to you with a proposal to revamp the system, the proposal seemed well thought out, and the potential benefits seemed worth the risk and expense. You told the employee to implement the idea. Unfortunately, after implementation, customer complaints about the system increased significantly.

Employee Empowerment

What will happen if you respond in a manner that communicates that the employee has done a bad thing, that you no longer trust him or her, and that you will now take over? The most likely result will be that the person will not take responsibility and initiative in the future. The person may well withdraw or even leave the organization. As a result, others may be hesitant to bring ideas forward, and insights that might be gained about the

Members of the Toms Shoe team deliver shoes in the first "Shoe Drop 2006" at a Buenos Aires soup kitchen, "Los Piletones," in 2006. Toms Shoe Company uses their market position to help those in need around the world.

nature of the problems with customer service may well be lost. On the other hand, if you provide support and allow the person and the organization to learn from the experience, then everyone concerned is likely to benefit.

In other words, if we don't foster empowerment, it can lead to feelings of powerlessness and a dampening of initiative. On some level, however, empowerment is up to each individual. Although empowerment can be encouraged by organizational conditions, it is primarily achieved through the decisions of individuals to change their self-image and belief systems. Empowerment, in this view, is not something granted from the outside but rather something we give ourselves. In fact, it can be argued that "the process of organizational politics as we know it works against people taking responsibility."[67] Traditionally, organizations have fostered a bureaucratic management mentality that emphasizes caution, compliance, patriarchal supervisory styles, and narrow self-interest. A more desirable management style, which has been called "entrepreneurial," can be fostered through the use of political processes in organizations. From this perspective, empowerment is grounded in enlightened self-interest based on service and contribution to the organization. The empowered manager is a "Theory Y" individual—creative, committed to organizational goals, and willing to take risks and shoulder the responsibility for consequences. Power, in this view, is acquired through the alteration of a person's state of mind.

Three Empowerment Lessons

As a part of this self-empowerment process, managers model this behavior for others. This modeling can be defined as political in that it is intended to create, and therefore redistribute, power in organizations. In modeling self-empowerment, managers adopt the belief that they are their own authority (rather than looking to their superiors), engage in and encourage self-expression in others, and make personal commitments to achieving results.[68]

What Would You Do?

▶ You have just discovered a piece of information that would make your boss very uncomfortable if it were revealed. You realize that you have just gained considerable leverage. What would you do?

To make this empowerment and enlightened self-interest possible, organizations reflect and express values about work, achievement, and community that organizational members can affirm. This sense of organizational values is expressed as visions for the future. Once successful managers work with others to create these visions, they engage in political processes, such as negotiating for support and building coalitions. From there, they recognize and build on healthy interdependencies balanced with autonomy. In short, they avoid sticking their heads in the proverbial sand about organizational politics. Understanding the need for power and influence, and taking action based on that knowledge, is a path that sometimes requires courage and conviction. But the alternative—to use their dependence on others as a manipulative tool or to simply throw their hands in the air and claim to be powerless to make things better—might be worse.

As the subject of power has been debated throughout history, notions of the role and rightness of power have evolved and changed. In general, although there has been a growing acceptance and recognition of power as a facet of organizational behavior, Americans are ambivalent about its exercise in the absence of authority and standards of legitimacy. As Burns[69] asserted, the world lacks moral leaders, not power holders. Power alone, without moral purpose and reasoned values, will not satisfy the need for compelling and creative leadership. In short, whereas power can be explored empirically and debated pragmatically, it appropriately remains a philosophical and moral issue as well.

► Summary and Applications for Managers

1. *Enhance your personal power by considering all of its possible sources.* Just because you lack the title of a person in authority does not mean that you do not need or cannot gain power and influence. Power is derived from many sources—expertise, admiration and respect for others, doing things for other people, giving rewards and recognition, and so on. Anything that makes people more dependent on you, or that makes you less dependent on them, increases your capacity to influence people. Such dependencies can be highly positive for both parties and the organization. Even if you are in a position of authority, relying solely on position power is not advisable. To get things done in an organization, you need to be able to engender cooperation, persuade others, and negotiate solutions to problems. These are political skills that are needed at all levels of the organization, regardless of position.

2. *Make yourself visible and indispensable.* It is important to remember that being highly skilled and competent in your job and taking on responsibilities that are critical to your unit make for a positive political strategy. Again, power is in part a matter of dependency. If the people at work learn that you are knowledgeable about and skilled in matters that are critical to your organization's success, then they are more likely to listen to and be influenced by you. But in addition to being an expert on key matters, you must make yourself visible enough so that people know that to be the case. This suggests that taking on visible assignments, speaking at meetings, and being clear and accurate about your contributions to key projects not only can help you career-wise but also can help you to be more influential in your present position.

3. *Take charge of your own empowerment.* Claiming to be powerless sometimes is an excuse for not taking responsibility. Empowerment is more about changing the way you think than a formal delegation of authority from your boss. Although empowerment can be fostered by management behavior or organizational conditions, it is primarily a matter of deciding to change your self-image and belief system. You can empower yourself to be creative, be committed to organizational goals, take calculated risks, and shoulder the responsibility for consequences. Doing so requires that you ask yourself how you can take initiative and responsibility when confronted with problems. For example, when you encounter a difficulty or problem, do not simply take it to your supervisor for his or her resolution. Instead, take responsibility for formulating some potential strategies for solution. When you see your supervisor, explain the problem, briefly describe the alternative solutions, and recommend the one you judge to be the best. Or, if you have the authority to act, simply solve the problem.

4. *Use power constructively and effectively.* Remember that not all sources of power and political strategies are created equal in terms of their effect on individuals and the organization. Leadership at all levels of the organization should be fundamentally based on respecting the dignity and worth of people, a commitment to organizational goals, and sound ethics. When you acquire power and use it to serve your own needs and agendas, or simply for the thrill of feeling as though you are in control, you are not using power constructively. Doing so is destructive to the organization, the people you interact with, and ultimately yourself. Power and political acumen are necessary ingredients for personal and organizational success. But each of us needs to be self-aware and self-reflective about how we are using power and for what purpose. Developing your employees, or what Wilson[70] called "uplifting" others (i.e., fostering their participation, listening carefully to their values and interests, and building and supporting their confidence and skills), is a constructive use of power. Doing so also enhances your reserve of referent power. In using that power to secure needed information, to obtain necessary resources, or to bargain with other organizational actors, you increase the likelihood of being successful in attaining organizational goals. That is not to say that other

strategies such as using hierarchical authority, punishment, secrecy, and so on are not sometimes appropriate. But they often are less effective in the long run because they tend to result in resistance and do not build the positive regard of others.

5. *Devote time and energy to clarifying goals.* In one sense, political behavior occurs because different people have different goals. People try to gain power and use their influence to have their goals take precedence over competing goals. Remember that political behavior is most likely to occur when goals are unclear and resources are scarce. It also should be kept in mind that one of the key differences between the constructive and destructive aspects of power in organizations is whether the power is used in pursuit of organizational or personal goals. Accordingly, clarifying and building shared goals reduces the likelihood of political behavior that does not positively contribute to the organization or, at a minimum, makes that political behavior easier to recognize as negative. If no one agrees on the goals, then it is difficult (if not impossible) to sort out what is positive influence and what is self-serving manipulation.

6. *Support and foster the empowerment of others.* Although empowerment is principally something you can do for yourself, there are several things that management and the organization can do to foster people's willingness to empower others. By providing opportunities to become involved in decision making, showing respect, giving trust, and allowing people to grow, you can enhance people's development and reward their efforts in taking responsibility. Equally important as these steps is how

you treat mistakes and failure. If someone who works for you takes appropriate responsibility and initiative to solve a problem or address an issue and the approach does not work, then you need to gauge your response carefully.

7. *Think about, plan for, and maintain your awareness of political issues in management and in the implementation process.* Being successful in organizations is not always about being "right." Effective management and leadership are accomplished through the dedication, hard work, and cooperation of people. It is sometimes difficult to accept that your perception of what is right is not going to be the same as everyone else's. So, the idea that effective organizational politics is about forcing others to conform and bend to your will is both ineffective and inconsistent with society's values, even if you are absolutely convinced that you have discovered the "one best way."

8. *Whenever possible, be nice.* This final way of acting flows from everything else that we have discussed. Being nice is not about being mealymouthed, weak, or ineffectual. In fact, when we talk about being nice, we are trying to reinforce the idea that being kind, considerate, and respectful toward others builds mutual trust and respect. It enhances your influence, power, and persuasiveness. It helps you to accomplish your objectives. It models the sort of treatment that you want your employees to emulate in their dealings with customers. It fosters the empowerment of others. And it makes organizational life a more pleasant experience for everyone involved. Being nice not only is the good and right thing to do for its own sake but also is a good political strategy.

▶ Key Terms

Coercive power 410	Impression management 422	Politics 406	Referent power 411
Empowerment 422		Power 406	Reward power 410
Expert power 411	Influence tactics 419	Proactive	
	Legitimate power 410	influence 419	

► Exercise 13.1 Observing Organizational Politics

1. Think of the most effective and successful organizational politician you know. From what sources of power does this person draw?

2. What strategies does this person employ? What strategies have been the most effective and why?

3. Are these strategies used constructively to enhance organizational goal attainment? Are these strategies used for self-serving purposes? Explain.

4. Do you have power relative to this person? Why or why not? Do you need or want more power in this case? If yes, then what are some of the ways in which you might increase your influence and power?

5. What can you learn from this person that will help you to gain power and use it constructively for your own benefit and for the organization's benefit? (In some cases, this might involve learning from behavior and strategies that you want to avoid rather than emulate.)

► Exercise 13.2 It's Not What You Know; It's Who You Know?

We have all heard the cliché, "It's not what you know; it's who you know." While most of us would argue that both are important, networking and building relationships are important parts of organizational and career success. Some people may have more networking savvy than others, and there may be ethical issues involved as well. Consider the following questions:

1. On balance, do you think networking is best thought of as a way to meet interesting people or a way of using people to get what you want?

2. Have you ever been offended by someone seeking to network with you? If so, what was it about the interaction that bothered you?

3. Have you ever felt good or been flattered by someone seeking to network with you? What did the person do to make you feel good about the interaction?

4. How comfortable are you with introducing yourself to people? What kind of impression do you think you give others? (You may want to check your self-assessment by asking a trusted friend or colleague what kind of first impression you made on him or her.)

5. Under what circumstances is introducing yourself to someone you don't know a good idea? When is introducing yourself not such a good idea?

6. What are some of the ethical principles that ought to guide your efforts in networking with others?

► Case 13.1 Annie's Dilemma

Annie has worked for a website design company for 6 years as sales representative. One year ago, when Annie completed her master's degree in business administration, she was thrilled when the director of sales and marketing, Esther, offered her a promotion to one of four regional sales manager positions. Esther had told Annie, "You have really proved yourself to be invaluable to our organization, and I hope this promotion signals our belief in your leadership potential." Annie was understandably flattered, and despite other opportunities, accepted the new position.

A few months later, Annie was wondering if she had done the right thing. While Esther was the director of sales and marketing, her assistant director, Peter, managed day-to-day operations. When Annie had first joined the organization, Peter had been her mentor, helping her learn the policies and routines, and kindly encouraging her when her confidence flagged.

Unfortunately, now that Annie was a supervisor, Peter was continuing to treat her as his young protégé, and markedly different than the other three supervisors in the office. He would routinely go to other supervisors, even when the issue at hand primarily involved Annie's area of responsibility. When she made recommendations and suggestions in meetings, he would smile at her, but engage in serious discussion only with others who were present. When she tried to get an entirely justifiable pay increase for one of her employees, Peter dismissed her without listening to her argument. Her employees have started to increasingly question her effectiveness, and have largely stopped coming to her with issues, choosing instead to go to people outside the unit with their problems and questions, or even directly to Peter. Yesterday, Peter reassigned one of her employees to a project without consulting her.

Now, Annie is angry, frustrated, and very much wanting to be treated equally with others at her rank. She is concerned that, as the situation stands, she lacks the power and political clout to accomplish her new responsibilities effectively and well.

1. What do you think is going on here? What are the elements of organizational politics that may be operating here? Power dynamics?

2. While this case clearly involves power relationships, is there anything else that might be going on? If you think other factors are contributing to Annie's problems, which of these factors can Annie successfully change or influence? Which can she not?

3. How would you advise Annie to proceed if she wants to stay in the organization and be successful? How can she increase her influence and power in the organization?

▶ Case 13.2 The Politics of Measurement

John was thrilled when, after completing his MBA degree, he was hired to work as a financial analyst for HeathStat, a major health care corporation. During his first year on the job, John impressed his supervisor and coworkers with his excellent analytical skills, initiative, and attitude. Even though his time on the job was short, at his 1-year performance review, he received an "excellent" overall rating. He was young, ambitious, and felt ready to make his mark on the business world.

Shortly after his 1-year anniversary on the job, a new president and CEO of the company was hired. She had many innovative ideas and changes that she wanted implemented to improve the efficiency and effectiveness of HeathStat. One of the key changes she wanted to implement was the introduction of an internal productivity measurement and tracking system throughout the organization. John was thrilled. This was exactly the sort of management approach that he had studied in school; he was anxious to share his expertise and knowledge to make sure the system was implemented successfully. He approached the CEO with a proposal for the type of system he was familiar with and asked if he could be assigned to work on the project. Although John was relatively inexperienced, the CEO believed that his excellent work and fresh outlook qualified him to serve as the point person for the implementation of measurement and tracking system. John was moved into the president's office and given charge of having the system up and running in one year.

It was John's job to help the various divisions to develop goals and objectives and set up data collection strategies to obtain information on performance against those goals. He was to personally advise the president and CEO on a periodic basis and to make a formal presentation to the vice presidents each quarter on progress toward productivity targets. John quickly learned that achieving cooperation from all the divisions was going to be very difficult. Two of the division directors he worked with were openly hostile to the idea of collecting new data on performance, did not complete reports on time, and were generally uncooperative with the effort. These division heads viewed John as an inexperienced, naive, and intense young man who presented an organizational annoyance that probably would disappear in time. Although they were publicly supportive of the program, John was finding it nearly impossible to work with them.

In response, John attempted to coerce the division heads to cooperate, threatening to "expose" them and punish them (and their divisions) for their lack of support and involvement. When he had his first meeting with the CEO, he expressed his outrage at how difficult and obstinate some of the division heads were as well as anger at his mistreatment and the lack of respect he was being shown. He told the CEO that these individuals were simply "deadwood" and should be fired in order to bring the business into the future. "My loyalty is to you, this is the right approach to take, and if they aren't going to cooperate, I say they should be fired," he said. Shortly thereafter, John was reassigned to an internal, lower priority project.

1. How would you analyze this case in terms of power and politics?

$SAGE edge™

Sharpen your skills with SAGE edge at edge.sagepub.com/nahavandi

SAGE edge for students provides a personalized approach to help you accomplish your coursework goals in an easy-to-use learning environment.

▶ Endnotes

1. Coates, J. (1994). Organizational politics: A key to personal success. *Employment Relations Today, 21*(3), 259–262; see p. 261.

2. Machiavelli, N. (1947). *The prince* (T. G. Bergin, Ed.). New York, NY: Appleton-Century-Crofts.

3. Machiavelli, 1947, p. 47.

4. As cited in Gerth, H. H., & Mills, C. W. (1946). *From Max Weber: Essays in sociology.* New York, NY: Oxford University Press.

5. Dahl, R. (1957). The concept of power. *Behavioral Science, 2,* 201–215; see pp. 202–203.

6. Dahl, 1957, p. 206.

7. Haire, M. (1989). The concept of power and the concept of man. In J. S. Ott (Ed.), *Classic readings in organizational behavior.* Belmont, CA: Wadsworth. (Original work published 1962); and McGregor, D. (1960). *The human side of the enterprise.* New York, NY: McGraw-Hill.

8. Cyert, R., & March, J. (1963). *A behavioral theory of the firm.* Englewood Cliffs, NJ: Prentice Hall.

9. Thompson, J. D. (1967). *Organizations in action.* New York, NY: McGraw-Hill, p. 142.

10. Morgan, G. (2011). Reflections on the macro-politics of micro-politics. In C. Dorrenbacher & M. Geppert (Eds.), *Power and politics in the multinational corporation.* New York, NY: Cambridge University Press.

11. Merchant, N. (2012, December 14). Are you giving up power? *Harvard Business Review.* Retrieved from http://blogs.hbr.org/cs/2012/12/are_you_giving_up_power.html on September 10, 2013.

12. French, J. R., Jr., & Raven, B. (1989). The bases of social power. In J. S. Ott (Ed.), *Classic readings in organizational behavior.* Belmont, CA: Wadsworth. (Original work published 1959)

13. French & Raven, 1959/1989.

14. Pfeffer, J. (2010). *Power: Why some people have it—and others don't.* New York, NY: HarperCollins.

15. Miller, B., Rutherford, M., & Kolodinsky, R. (2008). Perceptions of organizational politics: A meta-analysis of outcomes. *Journal of Business Psychology, 22,* 209–222.

16. French & Raven, 1959/1989.

17. Cuddy, A., Kohut, M., & Neffinger, J. (2013, July/August). Connect, then lead. *Harvard Business Review*, 54–61.

18. Wrong, D. (1968). Some problems in defining social power. *American Journal of Sociology, 73*, 673–681.

19. Emerson, R. (1962). Power-dependence relations. *American Sociological Review, 27*, 31–41.

20. Pfeffer, J. (1981). *Power in organizations.* Cambridge, MA: Ballinger.

21. Kanter, R. M. (1977). *Men and women of the corporation.* New York, NY: Basic Books.

22. Kanter, 1977.

23. Sticker shock: Why are glasses so expensive. (2012). *60 Minutes.* October 7. Retrieved from http://www.cbsnews.com/video/watch/?id=7424700n on April 18, 2013.

24. Crutchfield, D. (2012). Luxottica sees itself as king, raising questions about brand authenticity. *Forbes*, November 27. Retrieved from http://www.forbes.com/sites/deancrutchfield/2012/11/27/luxottica-sees-itself-as-king-raising-questions-about-brand-authenticity/ on April 18, 2013.

25. Sticker shock, 2012.

26. Leonardo Del Vecchio, Luxottica founder, went from orphan to eyewear Titan. (2012). *Huff Post*, October 8. Retrieved from http://www.huffingtonpost.com/2012/10/08/leonardo-del-vecchio-luxx_n_1948324.html on April 18, 2013.

27. Luxottica—History. (2013). Retrieved from http://www.luxottica.com/en/company/history/timeline/ on April 18, 2013.

28. Sticker shock, 2012.

29. Sticker shock, 2012.

30. Fleming, O. (2012). Why do designer glasses cost more than an iPad? *Daily Mail Online*, October 9. Retrieved from http://www. dailymail.co.uk/femail/article-2215287/Luxottica-The-eyewear-company-total-domination-setting-astronomical-prices.html on April 18, 2013.

31. Salancik, G., & Pfeffer, J. (1989). Who gets power—and how they hold onto it: A strategic-contingency model of power. In J. S. Ott (Ed.), *Classic readings in organizational behavior.* Belmont, CA: Wadsworth. (Original work published 1977).

32. Salancik & Pfeffer, 1989, p. 471.

33. Pfeffer, J. (1992). Understanding power in organizations. *California Management Review, 34*(2), 29–50.

34. Pfeffer, 1992, p. 49.

35. Lawrence, T., Mauws, M., Dyck, B., & Kleysen, R. (2005). The politics of organizational learning. *Academy of Management Review, 30*(1), 180–191.

36. Lawrence et al., 2005, p. 181.

37. Lawrence et al., 2005, p. 186.

38. Lawrence et al., 2005, p. 186.

39. Lawrence et al., 2005, p. 190.

40. Vrendenburgh, D. J., & Maurer, J. G. (1984). A process framework of organizational politics. *Human Relations, 37*(1), 47–66.

41. Vrendenburgh & Maurer, 1984, p. 50.

42. Vrendenburgh, D., & Brender, Y. (1998). The hierarchical abuse of power in work organizations. *Journal of Business Ethics, 17*, 1337–1347.

43. Milgrom, P., & Roberts, J. (1988). An economic approach to influence activities in organizations. *American Journal of Sociology, 94*(Suppl.), S154–S179.

44. Milgrom & Roberts, 1988.

45. Ferris, G., Frink, D., Galang, M., Zhou, J., Kacmar, K. M., & Howard, J. (1996). Perceptions of organizational politics: Prediction, stress-related implications, and outcomes. *Human Relations, 49*(2), 233–266; Kacmar, K., Bozeman, D., Carlson, D., &

Anthony, W. (1999). An examination of the perceptions of organizational politics model. *Human Relations, 52*, 383–416; Miller, Rutherford, & Kolodinsky, 2008; and Vigoda, E. (2002). Stress related aftermaths to workplace politics. *Journal of Organizational Behavior, 23*, 571–591.

46. Harris, K., & Harris, R. (2009). Relationships between politics, supervisor communication, and job outcomes. *Journal of Applied Social Psychology, 39*(11), 2669–2688; and Miller, Rutherford, & Kolodinsky, 2008.

47. Bryant, A. (2012). Leadership never looks prepackaged. *New York Times,* August 19, p. 1. Retrieved from http://www.nytimes.com/chrome/#/Business//www.nytimes.com/2012/08/19/business/james-hackett-of-steelcase-on-authentic-leadership.html April 18, 2013.

48. Yukl, G., Chavez, C., & Seifert, C. F. (2005). Assessing the construct validity and utility of two new influence tactics. *Journal of Organizational Behavior, 26*(6), 705–725.

49. Yukl, G., & Tracey, J. B. (1992). Consequences of influence tactics used with subordinates, peers, and the boss. *Journal of Applied Psychology, 77*(4), 525; and Yukl, G., Chavez, C., & Seifert, C. F. (2005). Assessing the construct validity and utility of two new influence tactics. *Journal of Organizational Behavior, 26*(6), 705–725.

50. Yates, D. (1985). *The politics of management.* San Francisco, CA: Jossey-Bass, p. 91.

51. Yates, 1985, p. 91.

52. Gotsis, G., & Kortezi, Z. (2009). Ethical considerations in organizational politics. *Journal of Business Ethics, 93*, 497–517; see p. 509.

53. Ferris, G., Treadway, D., Perrewe, P., Brouer, R., & Douglas, C. (2007). Political skill in organizations. *Journal of Management, 33*, 290–320.

54. Horan, J. (2012). *I wish I'd known that earlier in my career.* Hoboken, NJ: Wiley.

55. Perrewe, P., Ferris, G., Stoner, J., & Brouer, R. (2007). The positive role of political skill in organizations. In D. Nelson & C. Cooper (Eds.), *Positive organizational behavior.* Thousand Oaks, CA: Sage.

56. Todd, S., Harris, K., Harris, R., & Wheeler, A. (2009). Career success implications of political skill. *The Journal of Social Psychology, 149*(3), 179–204.

57. Levine, M. (2005). *Ready or not: Here life comes.* New York, NY: Simon & Schuster, p. 118.

58. Yukl, G. (2006). *Leadership in organizations.* Upper Saddle River, NJ: Pearson.

59. Perrewe et al., 2007.

60. Vigoda-Gadot, E., & Meisler, G. (2010). Emotions in management and the management of emotions. *Public Administration Review, 70*(1), 72–85.

61. Perrewe et al., 2007, p. 120.

62. Perrewe et al., 2007.

63. Conger, J., & Kanungo, R. (1988). The empowerment process: Integrating theory and practice. *Academy of Management Review, 13*(3), 471–482.

64. Conger & Kanungo, 1988, p. 473.

65. Tjosvold, D., & Sun, H. (2006). Effects of power concepts and employee performance on managers' empowering. *Leadership & Organization Development Journal, 27*(3), 217–234.

66. Tjosvold & Sun, 2006, p. 219.

67. Block, P. (1987). *The empowered manager: Positive political skills at work.* San Francisco, CA: Jossey-Bass, p. xiii.

68. Block, 1987.

69. Burns, J. M. (1978). *Leadership.* New York, NY: Harper & Row.

70. Wilson, P. (1995). The effects of politics and power on the organizational commitment of federal executives. *Journal of Management, 21*(1), 101–118.

14

Organizational Strategy and Structure

LEARNING OUTCOMES

After reading this chapter you should be able to:

1. Explain the five contextual strategic elements that influence organizations

2. Identify the different levels of an organization's external environment and define the components of environmental uncertainty

3. Define technology and how it impacts organizations

4. Discuss the relationship among mission, goals, and strategy, and outline the steps in the strategic management process

5. Describe the basic components of structure and some typical organizational structures

6. Highlight how to manage organizations strategically

McCormick: Extracting Flavor and Profits ▶

"Make the best—someone will buy it" has long been the motto of McCormick, the global spice maker that calls itself the "global supplier of value added flavor solutions."[1] The company was started by Willoughby McCormick in 1889 in a one-room basement and is now a close-to $4 billion global company. It has seen its share of ups and downs and has sailed through many changes successfully. Consumer lifestyles and tastes across the United States and the world have changed; two-career families spend less time in the kitchen; more people are eating out; increased cultural diversity and globalization constantly fuel demand for new spices and flavorings; and expanding global markets and geo-political changes create considerable challenge for the company. In the 1990s, McCormick redefined itself from an herb and spice maker to a "flavoring company" and addressed the needs of time-pressed working families by introducing seasoning mixes, trying to capture the market for gourmet cooking, and marketed more aggressively to industrial customers.[2] It also undertook a series of mergers and acquisitions to strengthen its global footing and grow its offerings, most recently by expanding into other brands such as Lawry's Zatarain, Old Bay, and Thai Kitchen and purchasing Ducros, the largest spice and herbs company in France. The company also opened its first retail store to inspire customers and it has been giving a flavor forecast since 2000 to both predict and influence trends it can then address with new products.

As we have seen, just like McCormick, leaders of most modern organizations face a fast-changing environment and are having to adjust their goals and internal structures to address them. You may think that the strategic issues of organizations are the domain of top managers and therefore not related to what you do. However, there are several reasons why understanding the context and strategic issues may be important to you.[3] First,

Strategy 101 is about choices: You can't be all things to all people.

—*Michael Porter*

> *The biggest risk is not taking any risk. . . . In a world that is changing really quickly, the only strategy that is guaranteed to fail is not taking risks.*
>
> —Mark Zuckerberg
>
> *However beautiful the strategy, you should occasionally look at the results.*
>
> —Winston Churchill

a strategic perspective may allow you to evaluate the strategies of the business where you might work so that you can make a more informed decision. Second, even if you do not deal with strategic issues on a day-to-day basis, having strategic knowledge can give you a wider perspective and allow you to be a more effective manager. Finally, if you work for a small business with few employees, or if you plan to start one yourself, the strategic issues are everyone's business. Today's managers at all levels must not only understand how to motivate and manage people, they must be aware of the context of their organization and how to create a fit between the context and internal organizational elements. In this chapter, we focus on the key external and internal contextual elements that affect organizations and on how managers must manage to create a fit between their environment and their organization.

SELF-ASSESSMENT 14.1

IDENTIFYING YOUR STRATEGIC MANAGEMENT TYPE

This exercise helps you identify your strategic leadership style. You can also use the scale to rate your organizational leaders. For each of the items listed, please rate yourself using the following scale.

0 = Never

1 = Sometimes

2 = Often

3 = Always

_____ 1. I enjoy working on routine tasks that I know how to do well.

_____ 2. I am always looking for new ways of doing things.

_____ 3. I have trouble delegating tasks to my subordinates.

_____ 4. I like my subordinates to share the same values and beliefs as me.

_____ 5. Change makes me uncomfortable.

_____ 6. I encourage my subordinates to participate in decision making.

_____ 7. It is difficult for me to get things done in situations with many contrasting opinions.

_____ 8. I enjoy working on new tasks.

_____ 9. I feel comfortable giving power away to my subordinates.

_____10. I consider myself to be a risk taker.

Scoring: Reverse scores for items 1, 5, 6, 7, and 9 (0 = 3, 1 = 2, 2 = 1, 3 = 0).

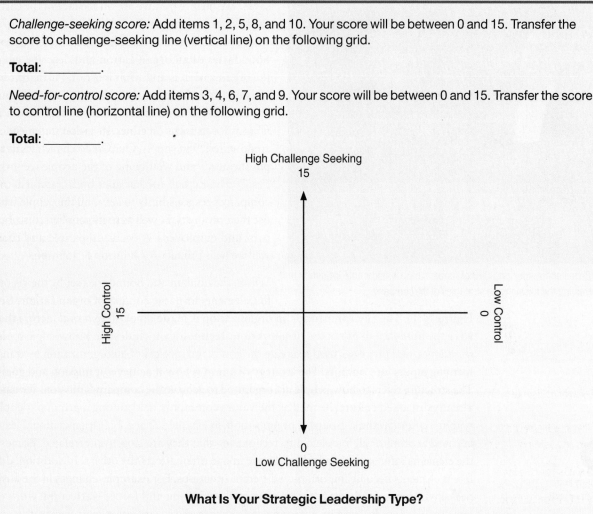
The Organizational Context

At a very basic and broad level, the starting point for any organization is a **vision** that describes where the firm wants to be and its purpose and values. The vision is focused on the future. People working in an organization need to know where they are headed. As the saying goes, if you don't know where you are going, any road can get you there or you will end up somewhere else. Without a vision, the organization cannot focus. The vision provides the general framework in which all other activities take place; it sets the direction. Bill Gates, Microsoft's founder, remembers the starting point of his company: "We talked about a computer on every desk and in every home. It's been amazing to see so much of that dream become a reality and touch so many lives. I never imagined what an incredible and important company would spring from those original ideas."[4] For Amazon, the vision statement is: "to be earth's most customer centric company; to build a place where people can come to find and discover anything they might want to buy online."[5] Apple's new CEO

Marissa Mayer's Strategy

Vision: describes where the firm wants to be and its purpose and values

Jeff Bezos as founder and CEO of Amazon has considerable influence in determining the mission and strategies of the company.

says: "We believe that we are on the face of the earth to make great products and that's not changing."[6] These vision statements define the domain or the boundaries of an organization and describe what the organization is and what it is not. Furthermore, a vision often describes the values and ethical principles of the organization. Johnson & Johnson is famous for its focus on ethics. Its vision statement or credo states: "Put simply, Our Credo challenges us to put the needs and well-being of the people we serve *first*."[7] Their credo further goes on to establish the company's responsibility to serve all the people who use their products, as well as to its suppliers, distributors, and employees. A focus on people and their well-being is primary for Johnson & Johnson.

Within the domain and boundaries set by the vision, five elements form the context of organizations (see Figure 14.1). The environment of an organization is made up of all *external* factors that have the *potential* to affect the organization. Technology includes the knowledge, tools, techniques, and processes used to create the goods and services of an organization by transforming inputs into outputs. The strategy of a firm is how it achieves it mission and goals. The structure refers to how people are organized to achieve the company's mission. We have already discussed culture, defined as the values commonly held among a group of people within a country, ethnic group, or organization, in Chapters 2 and 12. Organizational leaders need to monitor all five elements, recognizing that they are closely interrelated. Because the elements influence one another, change in one often affects the others. In addition, different elements become important in different situations. For example, changes in the business environment and competition—external environmental forces—affect the work of any organization. Because of environmental changes, the organization may change its strategy and may have to restructure itself. It may also initiate a cultural change to ensure that employees can adapt to the change. In order to manage effectively, managers must understand how each contextual element affects their organization. The simultaneous management of these elements is essential.

Strategy and
Implementation

The Organizational Environment

Organizations like McCormick do not function in a vacuum. They interact with their environment by taking inputs, changing their internal processes and technologies because of the environmental requirements, and giving outputs to the environment. The environment, then, is a key factor in understanding organizations. But what constitutes the environment?

Recall that an organization's **environment** consists of all the factors outside the organization that have the *potential* to affect it. For example, the presence of competition and changes in consumer tastes and lifestyles are major environmental factors that have a significant impact on McCormick. The environment does not consist of every external factor—only those that can affect the organization. Accordingly, an airline and a restaurant franchise will not have identical environments even though they may operate in the same city and cater to similar customers. The airline's environment includes factors such as aircraft and part suppliers, pilot, flight attendant and ground crew unions, other airlines, regulatory agencies, and

Environment: all the external factors that have the potential to affect the organization

FIGURE 14.1 THE FIVE STRATEGIC FORCES

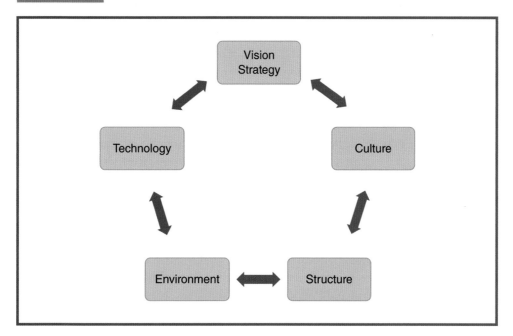

fuel suppliers. These factors do not affect a restaurant franchise and are therefore not part of its environment. The range of environmental sectors that businesses may have to consider is presented in Figure 14.2. Note, however, that although all organizations have society, national culture, and the economic situation as part of their environment, elements such as organized labor or certain demographic groups are not relevant for all organizations. In addition, even when the sectors are the same, the importance an organization gives to each varies and depends on the organization's mission and strategy.

Strategy Formation
Patterns

FIGURE 14.2 SECTORS OF THE EXTERNAL ENVIRONMENT

The environment can be classified into two categories. The first is the **general environment**. It consists of the broad context within which an organization operates and includes sectors such as social, demographic, and cultural trends; the political climate; and the global business environment. These interrelated sectors affect how organizations are run at a broad, general level. Two particularly important sectors of the general environment deserve attention. These are the national and ethnic cultures. As we discussed in depth in Chapter 2, managers must develop a cultural mindset to function in today's global environment, and organizations benefit from becoming diverse and multicultural. The McCormick case, for example, shows how cultural, social, and demographic trends of women working outside the home can affect a firm. Additionally, increasing diversity in the United States and extensive globalization have changed food tastes, which affects what the company makes and how it markets its products.

The second category in the environment is the **business environment**, which consists of specific sectors such as customers, competitors, human resources, suppliers, financial institutions, governmental regulations, the economy, and technology. Typically, managers interact with their business environment on a day-to-day basis. For example, changes in interest rates affect all businesses directly because they change managers' ability to obtain loans and their short-term and long-term costs. Similarly, when a competitor declares bankruptcy, or introduces a new successful product or service, its actions impact other firms in that industry. In our opening case, in addition to demographic changes, competition affected McCormick and at the same time gave the company the opportunity to expand its market.

Similarly, technological change has an ever-growing impact on all organizations. In addition to the growth of firms that deal specifically with technology, many others directly see its impact. For example, the music industry continues to feel the impact of technology on how people listen to music, where they purchase it, and how they store it. We now buy music on the Internet with a click and listen to what we specifically choose on sites such as Slacker, Pandora, and Spotify. Artists can connect directly with fans and market their music on social media, bypassing the large labels and radio stations. Radio stations, which were traditionally the primary way to reach potential fans, and used advertising as their income source, are affected; music producers are affected; as are fans and artists and the developers of hardware and software.

Not all aspects of the general or business environment affect all organizations at one time or to the same extent. Even firms within the same industry can have different environments. For example, although Estée Lauder and Urban Decay are both cosmetics companies and have many common environmental sectors, because they have different visions, missions, size, markets, and product lines, each has to deal with different aspects of the environment. Estée Lauder has an extensive line of skin care products, targets an older market, and has a strong global presence. In contrast, Urban Decay targets younger customers and focuses on color cosmetics and trendy products. In spite of being in the same industry, the two companies have defined or enacted different environments.

Other organizations may focus on one sector more than others. For example, when Walmart, the world's biggest retailer, started its global expansion, it made plenty of mistakes, such as stocking American footballs in soccer-obsessed Brazil, selling 110-voltage electrical appliances in countries that use 220 voltage, and underestimating the power of giant retailers such as Carrefour.[8] But, once it learned to read its environment and competition correctly, the global business sector quickly became one of Walmart's most successful areas of growth.[9]

General environment: social, demographic, and cultural trends; the political climates; and historical and religious influences

Business environment: customers, competitors, human resources, suppliers, financial institutions, governmental regulations, the economy, and technology that managers typically deal with on a day-to-day basis

Enacting the Environment

Once managers understand how the general and business environments impact them, they must identify which aspects are relevant to their organization. This important process, known as **enactment**, clarifies the environment of the organization.[10] Managers, based on the vision and mission, decide which developments need their attention and which can be on hold. In an ideal situation, and in highly effective organizations, managers continuously and mindfully keep track of events, successes, and failures and continuously adjust their views and organizational structures to fit the environment.[11] So why does this matter?

The U.S. postmaster general, Patrick Donahoe, is aware of how important this process can be. He has the challenging task of leading an organization that is one of the biggest employers in the United States and that must keep itself relevant in the age of e-mail and with powerful competitors such as FedEx and UPS. Having grown up in Pittsburgh, Pennsylvania, a city that was affected by the demise of the U.S. steel industry, he says: "**In the '80s, we lost the steel industry. Gone! Well, I witnessed 100,000 people lose their jobs because people did not pay attention to what was going on in the economy.**"[12] He does not want the U.S. mail to make the same mistake. The United States Postal Service faces challenges from a combination of technological, demographic, and economic changes, and poor management, not to mention a changing political climate and powerful unions with high pension costs. Donahoe has to read his environment correctly and devise strategies that will allow the USPS to survive and thrive.

Consider also an auto manufacturer that decides that global competition is not a concern. It decides that it is too big and too powerful to worry about foreign manufacturers. Such a decision may seem ludicrous to you, since Toyota is now the world's largest car manufacturer, but that is exactly what the U.S. automakers did in the 1970s and 1980s. They did not pay attention to the fast-rising global competition. They did not pay attention to their Japanese competitors, ignored their customers' demands for smaller, cheaper, more reliable cars, and overlooked the economic and global political signals that pointed to an increase in gas prices. Either because of arrogance that comes from market dominance or by mistake, they misread their environment and enacted it poorly. As a result, hundreds of dealership went out of business, and the Japanese auto industry was able to establish itself as the dominant automaker in the world.

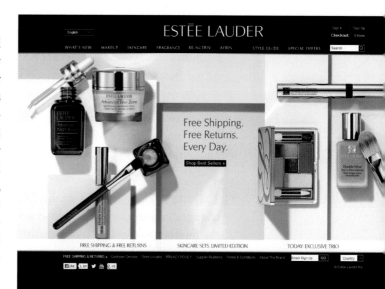

Estée Lauder has defined its environment as global and targets an older customer base. Urban Decay is in the same industry as Estée Lauder, but it targets a younger and trendier group. The two cosmetic companies have enacted their environments differently. Notice how Estée Lauder's home page uses much more subtle, sophisticated colors whereas Urban Decay's home page is decidedly colorful, bold, and more youthful.

Enactment: the process of identifying relevant environmental elements to define the environment of the organization

Correct enactment is a process that is part art, part science, part luck. It requires careful gathering and interpretation of information and sound judgment. Education and experience can help business leaders develop such skills, but in today's world they cannot guarantee success.

Environmental Uncertainty

It Gets Worse

Why is enacting and defining the environment so difficult? The major reason is environmental uncertainty.[13] Most organizations must cope with uncertainty in both their general and business environments. Two factors make the environment uncertain. First is the rate of change and second is the complexity of the environment.[14]

The rate of change refers to the speed at which various elements in the environment change. It addresses the degree to which the environment is stable. Complexity refers to the number of sectors an organization has to consider in the enactment process. Organizations that have a simple environment deal with only a few sectors at any one time. Organizations that have a complex environment must either juggle many different sectors at once, or the many sectors are highly interdependent. For example, consider how the decisions and actions of Walmart affect its suppliers, competitors, and their customers. Whether you shop at the store or not, what it does and how it sells its products affects you.[15] Many of the company's suppliers such as Procter & Gamble (P&G) decide which products to manufacture based on what Walmart decides to sell. The retail industry environment is changing fast and is complex because of high interdependence.

Generally, the more complex the environment, the more complicated the manager's job is. The rate of change and complexity, which includes interdependence, combine to create different levels of environmental uncertainty. Table 14.1 shows four general levels of environmental uncertainty. If the environment has few elements that do not change frequently, then uncertainty is low. High uncertainty results from many elements that are interdependent and change often; moderate uncertainty is the result of either few elements that change often, or many elements that are relatively stable and independent.

Environmental uncertainty: unpredictability in the environment

Rate of change: the speed at which various elements in the environment change

Complexity: The number of elements an organization has to consider in the enactment process

TABLE 14.1 LEVELS OF ENVIRONMENTAL UNCERTAINTY

		Level of Complexity (Number of Elements)	
		Low (few elements)	High (many elements)
Rate of Change	Low	*STABLE + SIMPLE = LOW UNCERTAINTY* Small number of external factors that change slowly. *Example: Packaging industry*	*STABLE + COMPLEX = LOW/ MODERATE UNCERTAINTY* Large number of external factors that change slowly. *Example: Refrigeration and trucking industries*
	High	*HIGH CHANGE + SIMPLE = MODERATE/LOW UNCERTAINTY* Small number of external factors that change quickly. *Example: Toy and fashion industries*	*HIGH CHANGE + COMPLEX = HIGH UNCERTAINTY* Large number of external factors that change quickly. *Example: Computer and airline industries*

Source: Based on Duncan, R. B. (1972). Characteristics of organizational environments and perceived environmental uncertainty. *Administrative Science Quarterly, 17,* 313–327.

Many of today's organizations face an uncertain environment that they can neither predict nor control. So what are the effects of uncertainty?

- It creates stress for managers who rarely have complete and accurate information for making decisions.

- It makes planning difficult because there are many unstable factors to consider.

- The chances of error and the risks associated with a bad decision increase.

For example, as the environment changes, competitors change their organizational structure. Investors become edgy, so managers feel compelled to restructure their organization to keep up. The decision to restructure the organization in an uncertain environment is risky because there are no guarantees that managers have selected the appropriate structure.

The U.S. Supreme Court's decision to strike down DOMA is a political and social change in the environment that creates opportunities for many businesses to address the needs of new customers.

However, changes in the environment can also provide considerable opportunity for organizations. New technologies open opportunities; changing demographics demand new products; and political and legal changes create new markets. For example, the recent U.S. Supreme Court decisions regarding marriage equality have triggered growth and new markets for event and wedding planners. Scott Stevens, owner of Iowa's Gay Wedding planners, a business that helps gay and lesbian couples with everything from finding a caterer to applying for a marriage license, says he started getting increased business as soon as the Supreme Court decisions were announced: "They said we were just waiting for DOMA [Defense of Marriage Act] to fall."[16]

Managers can define the environment for their organization by assessing environmental uncertainty and evaluating its effects on the organization. The next step is to manage that environment. We have already addressed the importance of culture and the cultural mindset in Chapters 2 and 12. In the remainder of this chapter, we examine the ways managers use technology and how they design strategies and structures to address the changes in their environment.

The Organization and Technology

Technology includes the knowledge, tools, techniques, and processes that organizations use to create goods and services.[17] As such, it includes computers, machines, and hardware used in production. However, it also includes work processes and procedures. Because technology changes rapidly and is central to the organization, it is a contextual strategic element that managers must be aware of and manage well.

Technology: the knowledge, tools, techniques, and processes used to create the goods and services of an organization by transforming inputs into outputs

INDRA NOOYI: THE INDIAN-BORN CEO OF PEPSI

Being one of only two women CEOs of a Fortune 100 company and rated one of the most powerful women in business is no small accomplishment. Indra Nooyi, known for having a keen business sense and an irreverent personal style, is perfect for the job. Whereas female CEOs continue to be relatively rare, female CEOs of color are even rarer. She is firmly at the helm of PepsiCo, in spite of the company not meeting expectations in recent years.[18] Born and educated in South India before attending Yale University for her graduate degree, Nooyi joined PepsiCo in 1994, after working for Motorola and the Boston Consulting Group. She became chief financial officer of PepsiCo in 2001 and its first female CEO in 2006.

Indra Nooyi of Pepsi Co is one of the few women CEOs of top global companies. Her style reflects her cultural and educational roots, and she has focused on diversity as a priority for her company.

She is known as a "master of substance" and she takes her responsibility as a role model very seriously.[19] "Brilliant," "supertalented," and able to think several steps ahead of everyone else are just some of the terms people use to describe her. The former company president, Enrico, states, "Indra can drive as deep and hard as anyone I've ever met, but she can do it with a sense of heart and fun."[20]

Many celebrate Nooyi's leadership at Pepsi as a victory for diversity. PepsiCo, however, has been at the forefront of promoting diversity, with actress Joan Crawford, widow of the company's president, replacing her husband on the board of directors in 1959 and Brenda Barnes heading the North American divisions for many years (before leaving in 1989 with a much publicized statement that she wanted to spend more time with her family). In the 1940s, the company was one of the first to create an all-Black sales team to market to African American consumers and it continues to be at the forefront of cultural diversity, something Nooyi is very proud of.[21] Nooyi's predecessor, Steven Reinemund, is recognized as a champion of diversity who stated, "I often refer to our diversity and inclusion as a marathon. . . . The challenge comes in creating an environment in which every associate—regardless of ethnicity, sexual orientation, gender, or physical ability—feels valued and wants to be part of our growth."[22] Nooyi is sending a very strong message about what she calls "talent sustainability." She states: "By valuing our employees, we are ensuring that PepsiCo is the kind of company where talented people of all backgrounds want to work. . . . We foster an inclusive workplace by increasing female and minority representation in management ranks, creating rewarding opportunities for people with disabilities and recognizing our employees for their contributions."[23]

Her formula for success is relatively simple; she suggests that success comes from five "Cs": competence, confidence, communication skills, having a moral compass and integrity, and being the conscience for the organization.[24] She continues to practice what she preaches. She admits to being consumed with PepsiCo; the company is her passion.

1. What is the strategic benefit of diversity for PepsiCo?

2. What are the strategic contextual elements that Nooyi emphasizes?

Types of Technology

Types of technology differ according to the type of organization. **Manufacturing firms** produce an actual product, such as shoes, steel pipes, cosmetics, spices, or computers. Their output is tangible. **Service firms** deliver a service rather than a tangible product. The service sector accounts for 68% and four out of five jobs of the U.S. economy and one of the biggest exports.[25] The technology of service firms includes the processes and knowledge involved in the creation and delivery of the service. These outputs are intangible: Service providers deliver the service directly to the customer and customers use the service as it is delivered. For instance, a financial consultant offers advice to clients directly and the customer receives the advice at the moment the provider offers it. Examples of service organizations include banks, consulting firms, health care providers, the hospitality industry, and governments.

Technology is the main link between the organization and its environment whether the business is a manufacturing or a service organization. For example, consider Amazon. It does not manufacture anything; it sells other companies' products. One could argue that Amazon's primary technology is the Internet. However, the core of the company's technology is its well-honed distribution system that gets products to customers in record time and with consistent reliability.

Managers can either buy the technology they need to produce their products and services or develop it internally through research and development. **Research and development (R & D)** is the process by which organizations search for information and create techniques to improve their products and services. For example, a company that needs new computer software for its accounting department can either buy that technology from another firm, or develop the software internally.

Technological changes force organizations to reconsider how they transform their inputs into outputs. We consider next some major technological changes and their effects on organizations.

High technology (high tech) refers to the latest and newest technological developments and has become a whole industry in its own right. Almost all businesses today rely on some high-tech tools to deliver quality products and services. In order to keep up with rapid change in high tech, managers must monitor their environments and provide continual innovation to their customers and training to their employees. Chances are that many of you are getting your e-mail and working from a smart phone or a tablet computer. You also may be reading this book online.

Apple's creative technologies and designs have revolutionized the personal high-tech industry and have forced other manufacturers to redefine what they produce and how they serve their customers. The extent to which others have tried to follow or copy Apple has been the subject of lawsuits. For example, Samsung was found guilty of infringing on Apple's designs in 2012 by copying the Apple "pinch and zoom" (a term, by the way, that was meaningless just a few years ago), and other technologies.[26] Apple's innovative technologies push all its competitors to search for equally creative products.

While the fast-changing technologies may stress employees and organizational resources, they often can lead to increased profits. Shoppers at Nordstrom Rack, Nordstrom's discount store, have seen much faster service with sales people being able to check them out all around the store using a high-tech hand-held mobile check-out system. Long lines are cut short, customers are happy, and sales increase.[27]

Manufacturing firms: produce an actual product or tangible output

Service firms: deliver a service rather than a tangible product

Research and development (R & D): the process by which organizations search for information and create techniques to improve their products and services

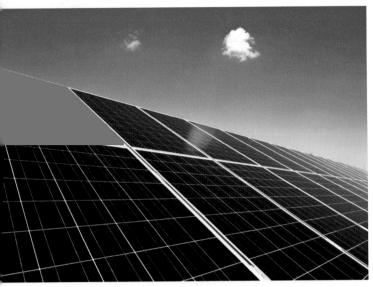

Solar panels and solar energy are examples of new products and services that result from the public interest in sustainability and fast-changing technologies.

Data mining is an interdisciplinary field that uses complex computational methods, technology, artificial intelligence, statistics, research methods, and databases to obtain information from very large, sometimes seemingly unrelated data sets. While businesses have always used data to make strategic decisions, advances in technology now allow them to track considerably more information and connect information in highly complex ways. Amazon and Google track what you search for and market deals and ideas to you based on your searches. In a recent case, the retailer Target was able to find out who was pregnant even before their family did by tracking their purchases.[28]

Managers can also use data mining to address the needs of their employees and make their organizations more effective. Google, which is well known for tracking everything, also tracks its employees' reactions, satisfaction, health, turnover, and productivity and relates them to managers' actions, such as greeting employees, the set-up of the work environment, the perks and amenities it provides, and the foods it offers in its cafeteria.[29] All the data Google collects are used "to create the happiest, most productive workplace in the world," according to a Google spokesman, Jordan Newman.[30]

Director Denies
Data Mining

Green Technology. A special case of changing technology is the green movement.[31] The push for sustainability has opened up opportunities for new businesses through renewable energy and green technology. While some suggest that the green movement has not lived up to its promises, we are increasingly seeing its impact on organizations.[32] Consider how Walmart's decision to go green has impacted many other organizations and may have social benefits in the long run. The company's decision is a business one; going green can help it eliminate waste and save money.[33] However, the same way Walmart pushes its suppliers to cut costs, its decision to go green is challenging its suppliers, from component makers to manufacturers to shippers, to look for sustainable technologies. Walmart CEO Lee Scott, says: **"Our goal is for supplier factories to meet or exceed all social and environmental laws and regulations."**[34] Scott considers meeting environmental standards and goals a requirement rather than an option. Changes in sustainable technology both make such a business decision possible and, further, engender more technological changes.

Effects of Changing Technology

Real About
Analytics

How do these fast-changing technologies affect people in organizations? They change the way we work, manage people, and view organizations (see Figure 14.3). They can help businesses become much more productive and efficient. They also create more options for organizing people. For example, telecommuting changes how people work, allowing employees more flexibility, increasing satisfaction, and creating challenges for management. While some suggest that telecommuting employees are more productive and many companies have adopted this structure, others worry about loss of interaction and employees slacking off when not in the office.[35] Yahoo!'s now famous decision to stop telecommuting was prompted by such concerns. Yahoo used its own technological capabilities to check to see that employees were not plugged into the company system often enough, indicating abuse of the telecommuting option.[36] On the other hand, technology can be used to enhance interaction capabilities through videoconferencing and data sharing tools that allow individuals across the globe to work together.

FIGURE 14.3 EFFECTS OF CHANGING TECHNOLOGIES

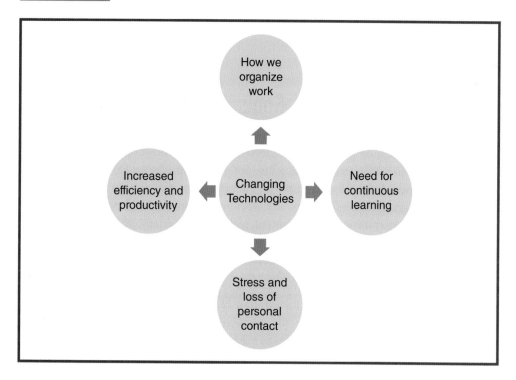

Third, changing technologies require that managers and employees continuously keep their skills current. On the one hand, this pressure allows managers to keep up with, use, and be prepared to train others to use changing technology to function effectively. In fact, the pace of change is so rapid that many organizations create their own universities that teach employees new processes. On the other hand, although employees are developing new skills, they often feel the pressure of always having to stay ahead of the curve. Similarly, organizations benefit from well-trained employees, but they have to shoulder the high cost of training.

Changes in technology can also have negative effects. First, the pressure to keep up can lead to stress when employees and managers can't keep pace and struggle as a result. Second, high-tech often replaces personal contact with other employees and managers. Though people are connected electronically, they interact less with others, feeling isolated and potentially losing the benefit of creativity that can occur through informal interaction. Yahoo!'s CEO Marissa Meyer cited wanting to encourage collaboration as one of the reasons for changing the company's telecommuting policy.[37]

Managers must carefully weigh the potential advantages of new technologies against their potential disadvantages. If technology suits the business and is well managed and well implemented, it can reduce costs, free workers of repetitive and menial tasks, put them in touch with managers and others across the world, and open up new opportunities to do business. However, many organizations can continue to operate successfully by using low-tech tools and practices that fit their culture and strategy. Shayne Hughes, CEO of Learning Leadership, tried to make this point when he banned all internal e-mails for a week. Shayne believes that e-mail often prevents people from dealing with complex issues. He states: "Buried beneath our collective e-mail dysfunction are the important conversations our organizations and relationships need to move forward. E-mail is the worst forum for tackling these."[38] Whether the changing technologies excite or threaten you, they are a fact of business. Managers consider the environment and technology as they set the direction for their organization. Both have considerable impact on strategy, the next contextual element we examine.

Strategic Basics: Mission, Goals, and Strategy

Designing
for Impact

No two organizations are alike. As we have seen, each organization responds to its environment and uses technology differently. Moreover, each organization has a different purpose and accomplishes that purpose in a distinct manner. Businesses also structure their employees in a special way. Finally, employees in each organization have varying skill levels, backgrounds, cultural perspectives, and working relationships. The choices managers make about their organization's environment, technology, strategy, structure, and culture are the essence of the strategic management process. In the following section, we define *strategy*, the third contextual strategic element, and examine its various components.

Mission is a statement of the organization's purpose and reason for existence. The mission provides the general direction for the organization and keeps all managers and employees in sync. To achieve its mission, a company sets **goals**—objectives that specify what needs to be achieved and when. The organization tries to achieve short-term goals typically within one year. Long-term goals are those that extend beyond one year. A firm's **strategy** is a comprehensive road map that states how a firm can reach its goals and achieve its mission within a set time frame. Figure 14.4 illustrates the relationships among mission, goals, and strategy.

FIGURE 14.4 RELATIONSHIPS AMONG MISSION, GOALS, AND STRATEGY

Mission: a statement of the organization's purpose and reason for existence

Goals: objectives that specify what needs to be achieved and when

Strategy: how a firm achieves it mission and goals

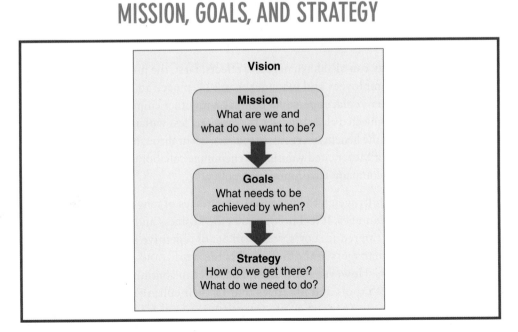

Each organization has a unique mission. Some missions are comprehensive, formal, and frequently mentioned. Others may be informal and brief. Regardless of their format, mission statements provide a sense of direction for the organization. McCormick's vision is: "**McCormick will be the leading global supplier of value-added flavor solutions. Building on strong brands and innovative products, we will provide superior quality and service to customers and consumers around the world.**"[39] Tom's of Maine and Procter & Gamble (P&G) are in similar industries, personal care products. Tom's mission states: "To serve our customers' personal care needs with imaginative science from plants and minerals; To inspire all those we serve with a mission of responsibility and goodness; To empower others by sharing our knowledge, time, talents, and profits; and To help create a better world by exchanging our faith, experience, and hope."[40] P&G's mission is: "We will provide branded products and services of superior quality and value that improve the lives of the world's consumers, now and for generations to come. As a result, consumers will reward us with leadership sales, profit and value creation, allowing our people, our shareholders, and the communities in which we live and work to prosper."[41] Through their mission statement, each of these companies defines what it is and also enacts its environment by identifying important stakeholders. The mission gives priority to one group over others. Tom's of Maine identifies natural products as a target and provides a more spiritual focus. P&G serves a different, broader, and more traditional market.

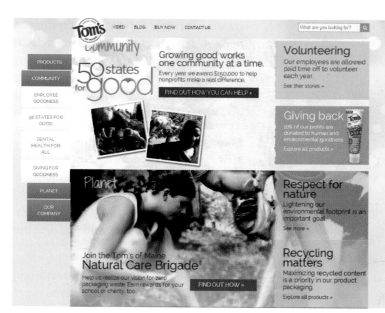

Tom's of Maine is a consumer goods company that has defined its mission and strategy based on natural and eco-friendly products, differentiating itself from other companies in that industry. The greens used on their home page as well as the links highlighting their commitment to volunteering, giving back, and recycling all signal the core mission and strategy to the customer.

Vision and Mission

Mission statements should ideally create a sense of excitement for the organization's employees and stakeholders. When you walk into an organization with a well-defined and broadly accepted mission, you get a sense that everyone working there knows what the mission is, believes in it, takes pride in it, and practices it. Such an organization has a better chance of being successful than one with a poorly defined mission. Although having a well-defined and broadly accepted mission is not a guarantee of success, it helps employees work toward the same goals. For example, employees at Medtronic, a medical product company located in Minneapolis, Minnesota, are inspired by the mission of their organization: "to alleviate pain, restore health, and extend life." One senior manager hands every new employee a medallion engraved with the mission. CEO Bill Hawkins states: "It is an honor, a privilege, and a duty to have a purpose that calls us to save and improve people's lives."[42]

Organizational goals, based on the mission, can be both financial, for example related to profit, growth, or efficiency, or nonfinancial, for example related to increasing the number of employees or improving morale and satisfaction. One of Google's goals, as we saw, is to have happy employees. Organizations set goals for every possible activity, then measure their performance against those goals. The challenge for organizational leaders is to ensure that goals support the mission and vision statement. For instance, if the mission statement refers to developing natural products, managers must seek new products that are derived from nature. Similarly, if affordability is part of the mission, as it is for Walmart ("Saving people money to help them live better"[43]), then every decision managers make should consider that mission and focus on cost-cutting. In Walmart's case, part of their success can be attributed to their single-minded focus on that mission. Everything they do is related to cost-cutting and providing cheaper products.

Managers can choose from many different strategies to achieve goals. Their strategy, however, must support the company's mission and goals. If the goal is to keep the cost of the products affordable, then managers might select a strategy to produce a limited array of products with just a few options. That way, they minimize production costs. If quality is the aim, then organizational leaders could choose a strategy of manufacturing a wide array of products with multiple options and instituting additional quality control programs.

While setting mission, goals, and strategies are typically the domain of top level leaders, increasingly everyone in a successful organization takes ownership of them. This participation increases the sense of ownership and makes more people accountable and responsible for the goals and strategies. However, specific goals and strategies are assigned to specific people or groups to ensure that the necessary work is done.

Managing Strategy

Closing the Chasm

Managers evaluate the contextual strategic elements and then design strategies to take advantage of business opportunities. **Strategic formulation** is the process of forging a cohesive integrated set of strategies designed to deal with the environment and achieve the business mission and goals. **Strategy implementation** is the actions the organization takes to execute the strategy it has formulated. The **strategic management process** consists of strategy formulation and implementation (see Figure 14.5).

To formulate strategy, managers analyze the strengths and weaknesses of their organization and examine opportunities and threats in their environment.[44] This analysis is called a SWOT analysis (strengths, weaknesses, opportunities, threats). A SWOT analysis is an evaluation of the organization's environment for opportunities and threats, often called environmental scan, and a consideration of how those match with the company's internal strengths and weaknesses. It is the first step in the strategic management process. A SWOT analysis is typically used in strategic management, but it is a very useful method to aid any decision-making process. Typically, strengths are internal factors and opportunities are external ones. Table 14.2 provides the typical SWOT matrix. Once a company conducts a SWOT analysis, its managers can design specific strategies to match strengths to opportunities and minimize weaknesses to avoid threats to achieve the mission and goals.

Strategic formulation: the process of forging a cohesive integrated set of strategies designed to deal with the environment and achieve the business mission and goals

Strategy implementation: the actions the organization takes to execute the strategy it has formulated

Strategic management process: the combination of strategy formulation and implementation

FIGURE 14.5 THE STRATEGIC MANAGEMENT PROCESS

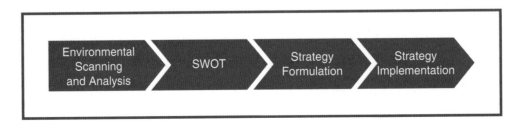

TABLE 14.2 TYPICAL SWOT MATRIX

		Internal	
		Strengths	**Weaknesses**
External	Opportunities	*Easy/Obvious Path* Internal strengths match external opportunity Easy implementation High likelihood of success	*Potential Future Path* Likely to produce growth Identify and address internal issues Internal improvement Good risk
	Threats	*Easy to Defend* Awareness of external factors needed Internal capabilities are present Should be easy to address	*High Risk* Awareness and monitoring are crucial High risk of failure

Assume that you want to open a bookstore. First you should analyze the business and general environment of bookstores. You will quickly find a highly competitive industry dominated by Amazon. After doing a SWOT analysis and considering the hefty resources needed to compete with Amazon, you decide that your bookstore's strengths are its small size and ability to address the specific needs of your community. The opportunity you see in the environment is the presence of many educated families and retired people who may be drawn to a family bookstore and the fact that the large chain bookstores in the area have gone out of business. Your weakness is lack of resources, and the major threat is the presence of a powerful and successful competitor. Based on this SWOT, you need to formulate your strategy—how will I establish my store and make sure it survives the first year and makes a profit in 2 years—and decide what you need to implement the strategy (budget, programs, people, and procedures). The formulation and implementation of strategy are not fully sequential. They often occur simultaneously as managers modify and reformulate strategies as they are trying to implement them.

Formulating the right strategy for the organization is as much art as it is science. Consider the case of Honda. When Soichiro Honda created the strategy to start exporting small Honda motorcycles to the United States in 1959 to achieve the company's goal of growth, the Japanese government advised him not to do so. According to Japanese analysts, the U.S. environment was not suitable for small bikes since it was dominated by manufacturers such as Harley Davidson who produced powerful bikes. They perceived the American motorcycle customers as leather-jacket-wearing riders interested only in large motorcycles. Mr. Honda disagreed. He envisioned millions of young Americans riding small bikes for fun around their neighborhoods.

After some initial setbacks, Honda's strategy of focusing on young people paid off. Its logo of "You meet the nicest people on a Honda," and ads showing casually dressed young couples riding Honda Scooters contributed to the phenomenal success that Honda motorcycles became. With low prices and a clear image that set it apart from the big bikes, the company established a strong foothold in the U.S. market. This success eventually let to the export of small Honda cars to the United States, with the Accord becoming one of the best-selling cars in the United States and the world.

Five Forces

Low-Cost Strategies Versus Differentiation

One of the most well-known classifications of various strategic options was developed by Harvard Professor Michael Porter.[45] He identified two types of strategies: low cost and differentiation. **Low-cost strategies** are based on designing, producing, marketing, and delivering a product or service more efficiently than competitors. For example, Walmart has consistently and successfully pursued such a strategy. **Differentiation** is based on providing unique and different products of superior quality with special features. Those of you using newer Gillette razors have seen the benefits of such a strategy. Their razors are highly specialized and relatively expensive. Similarly, companies delivering luxury goods and services follow such a strategy.

In addition, Porter identified the scope of strategy for various businesses.[46] **Scope** refers to whether a business is setting a wide or broad net, or whether it has a narrower focus. Consider the examples of Sony and of Bang and Olufsen. Both sell high-quality consumer electronics; both have a differentiation strategy. However, Sony has a broad scope and markets its products to many different consumers while Bang and Olufsen targets customers interested in very high-end design.

None of these strategies is better or worse than the other. The key is for the firm and its manager(s) to formulate a strategy that fits its environment and implement it through the proper technology, structure, and organizational culture and management systems. It is also essential for managers and employees at all levels to be aware of their organization's strategy so that they can focus on the proper implementation.

Organizational Structure

Organizational Structure

The structure of an organization refers to the way human resources are organized to achieve the company's mission. Structure addresses questions such as who is responsible for what; who reports to whom; and how information moves up, down, and across the organization. The simplest way to assess the structure of an organization is to look at its **organizational chart**, a diagram of how people are organized and of the organization's skeletal structure.

Structure is central to an organization's effectiveness. It must fit the environment, the use of technology, and support the strategy and culture. Designing the structure or changing an existing structure is often a way strategy is implemented. An organization that does not have the appropriate structure is unlikely to achieve its mission and goals easily. We stress the word *appropriate* because there is no best way to structure the human resources of an organization. What works depends on many factors, such as the environment, technology, culture, and size. For instance, larger businesses tend to organize their employees in much more complex ways than smaller organizations because an increase in size means that it's harder for people to interact.

Basic Components of Structure

What makes up the structure of an organization? Table 14.3 presents the six basic components of structure. These are combined in a variety of ways to allow a firm to organize its human resources. Some of these components tend to be related. For example, typically, a formal organization is also centralized and standardized; however, there are a wide number of possible combinations that make every organization unique. Employees in an organization such as the Union Pacific Railway, which has a tall hierarchy with centralized

---

Low-cost strategies: based on designing, producing, marketing, and delivering a product or service more efficiently than competitors

Differentiation: based on providing a unique and different product of superior quality with special features

Scope of strategy: whether a business is a setting wide or broad net, or whether it has a narrower focus

Organizational chart: a diagram of how people are organized and of the organization's skeletal structure

decision making and a high degree of specialization, formalization, and standardization, will behave and feel differently from those in an organization such as Southwest Airlines, which has few levels in the hierarchy, decentralized decision making, and a low degree of specialization and formalization. While there are formal titles, all employees do whatever is needed to get the planes off on time in an informal and cooperative atmosphere.[47]

TABLE 14.3 COMPONENTS OF STRUCTURE

Component	Description
Formalization	The number of formal, written documentation relating to organizational procedures, activities, and behaviors. A formal organization clearly describes all activities in writing.
Specialization	The degree to which each individual, department, or team performs special, narrow tasks as compared to a broad set of tasks. High specialization means that individuals perform specific limited tasks.
Standardization	The degree to which similar activities are performed in a standardized, similar way. In a standardized organization, all individuals performing a similar task perform it the same way.
Centralization	The extent to which decisions are made at either the top or at the other levels of the organization. In a centralized organization a few people at the top make most decisions.
Span of Control	The number of reporting relationships and the span of control of managers. Managers with a wide or large span of control have many employees reporting to them.
Departmentation	How the organization is divided into divisions, departments, groups, and/or teams.

In designing their organizations managers must also consider one more important factor. They must plan how people from different departments will coordinate their activities and how they will integrate their work to achieve the goals of the organization. Particularly, it is important for employees who are staff and those who are line to work well together. **Line employees** are the people directly involved in production or service delivery. They are on the "front lines" and directly involved with the output of the organization. Examples are managers and employees in manufacturing, operations, marketing, and sales. **Staff** employees are those employees and managers who support the line employees through a variety of functions. They include such departments as human resources, information technology, accounting, and legal services. There have traditionally been many conflicts between line and staff employees and managers regarding who is most important and valuable to the organization, but both are essential to the organization achieving its goals. Indeed, the quality of cooperation and integration within the organization and between the two groups is essential to the organization's effectiveness. The key challenge of designing the structure of an organization is the use of integration tools that allow employees to do their job well and allow access to the information they need when they need it.[48]

Consider the case of W. L. Gore and Associates and its unusual and highly effective structure. The company makes all types of outdoor, campus, medical, and other products based on the Gore-Tex membrane, a flexible, water-resistant material. Most outdoor enthusiasts own some of the company's camping gear and numerous health care professionals use their supplies. The unique structure of W. L. Gore & Associates is called a lattice

Team Takes Charge

Line employees: people directly involved in production or service delivery

Staff: employees and managers who support the line employees through a variety of functions

organization.[49] Each of the company's plants has only about 200 employees, a number that founders Bill and Vieve Gore feel encourages a sense of belonging and flexibility. No one has a formal title; employees are simply called associates. The company does not establish clear lines of hierarchy or assign authority to specific people. There are no bosses, only "sponsors" who help others learn new tasks. Associates often change positions through what the company calls natural leadership and followership.

The organization does not have differentiated departments. Instead, the structure integrates various activities and encourages person-to-person communication and participatory decision making. It doesn't assign tasks and functions to formal departments. Rather, teams and committees that operate in a non-hierarchical structure accomplish tasks and functions. The owners encourage experimentation, realize that mistakes will happen, expect associates to ask questions and experiment with new ideas, but do not tolerate poor performance. Through the unique combination of informal processes, low specialization, low standardization, decentralized decision making, and well-integrated teams, W. L. Gore has created a structure that supports the company's mission of innovation, world-class quality, and customer satisfaction. It has also been consistently ranked as one of the 100 best U.S. companies to work for.

Organic and Mechanistic Organizations

In Praise of Bureaucracy

When managers combine the basic components and elements of structure, the resulting structure has certain characteristics. One method of understanding these characteristics is through the concepts of organic and mechanistic organizations. **Organic organizations** are informal, they have low degrees of specialization and standardization, decentralized decision making, and well integrated activities. Organic organizations are most appropriate when the environment is uncertain.[50] Loose structures, decentralized decision making, and good integration give organizations the flexibility to deal with fast-paced environmental change and many different elements.

Organizations that have centralized decision making and formal, standardized control systems are mechanistic. Such organizations work well in stable, simple environments. Managers integrate the activities of clearly differentiated departments through formal channels in formal meetings. An example of a mechanistic organization is a *bureaucracy*—an organization that has a highly formalized, specialized, standardized, centralized structure with many layers and a focus on hierarchical reporting relationships. General Motors (GM) is an example of a bureaucracy. For an example, look in your wallet or purse for your driver's license. With some difference in each state and country, getting a driver's license involves interaction with a bureaucracy

Organic organizations: have a low degree of formality, specialization, and standardization, decentralized decision making, and well integrated activities

What Would You Do?

▶ You are working in a department that has many rules and regulations and lots of red tape. You find that almost anything you want to do takes much longer than it should. You have some ideas about how to improve the processes to make them more efficient. What information do you need and how should you approach your manager?

that will make you move through a formal and standardized process. You need to check in, someone verifies your identity, charges you a fee, and hands you a standard written exam. If you pass that exam, you take a standardized driving test that makes you work through a series of formal driving-related activities. Again, if you pass, you get a vision test, and your picture is taken. Several hours after entering the office, you may have a driver's license or hope that one will be mailed to you. Every step of this process is standardized, formalized, specialized, centralized, hierarchical, differentiated, and integrated. Everyone who wants a driver's license goes through the same process; everyone in that office has a clear and specific job that they perform the same way. After 9/11, the process for getting a driver's license became even more onerous, a change that was aimed at addressing the new security concerns.

Charles Merrill is particularly known today for founding the iconic investment firm Merrill-Lynch in 1940. But his influence on the business world and the world of personal finance goes far beyond the founding of his company. And it marks Merrill as a master strategist.

For example, Merrill was the first investment banker to realize the potential of chain stores to dominate retail activity. Consequently he provided underwriting for such companies as S.S. Kresge (now K Mart) and the Safeway grocery chain.[51]

Merrill was also the first major Wall Street executive to predict the Great Crash of 1929. By February of that year, he liquidated his firm's stock portfolio. He sent out a market letter that read:

"Now is the time to get out of debt. We think you should know that with a few exceptions all the larger companies financed by us today have no funded debt. This is not the result of luck but of carefully considered plans on the part of their managements and ourselves to place these companies in an impregnable position. The advice that we have given important corporations can be followed to advantage by all classes of investors. We do not urge you to sell securities indiscriminately, but we advise you in no uncertain terms that you take advantage of present high prices and put your own financial house in order. We recommend that you sell enough securities to lighten your obligations, or better yet, pay them entirely." He was right, of course, and many, many others were wrong.[52]

But Merrill is especially remembered for his democratization of the market, that is, bring new entrants to the market who significantly broadened the base of the market. And the results: "Half of America's households now invest, compared with only 16% in 1945, and mutual funds alone hold more of America's financial assets than banks do."[53] Merrill focused on the small investor and, as a result, many Americans now rely on stocks to fund college for their kids, to provide a sound basis for their retirement, and support a middle-class lifestyle. Moreover, he began to provide a wider variety of services that were geared toward middle-class investors. All changes brought about by a master strategist.

1. What do you think set Merrill apart as a master strategist?

2. How does strategy interconnect with organizational behavior?

3. How do good ideas, such as those Merrill came up with, reach consumers?

As irritating as the process may be, this bureaucratic structure ensures that everyone who wants a driver's license is treated the same way and goes through the same checks and balances. Would you have it any other way? The mission of the driver's license bureau is to ensure that every person who gets a license can drive safely at some basic level and is fit to do so. The mechanistic structure of the bureaucracy supports that mission well.

Most organizations fall somewhere in between the two extremes of organic and mechanistic. Table 14.4 highlights the differences between the two. Although they provide some clear advantages, mechanistic organizations are also inflexible and slow to change. An organic organization such as W. L. Gore can respond to change quickly by reassigning employees, whereas a bureaucracy cannot. However, some employees may be confused with the lack of clarity and some efforts may be duplicated. As long as the structure supports the mission and fits with other contextual factors, particularly with the degree of environmental uncertainty, the structure is appropriate and the organization has a chance of being effective.

TABLE 14.4   MECHANISTIC AND ORGANIC ORGANIZATIONS

Mechanistic Organizations	Organic Organizations
Specialized tasks	General tasks
Well-defined departments with clear hierarchy	Loosely defined departments with loosely defined hierarchy
Centralized decision making by few people	Decentralized decision making by many individuals
Integration achieved by relying on formal meetings and communication among managers	Integration achieved by employees and managers interacting and exchanging information as needed
Clear and efficient reporting relationships	Flexible and adaptable
Appropriate in low-uncertainty environments	Appropriate in high-uncertainty environments

Influence of Structure

Traditional Structural Options

The four traditional structural options are the functional, product/divisional, hybrid, and matrix structures. As managers organize their employees to accomplish the organizational mission and goals, these traditional structures can offer a starting point. Each has certain advantages and disadvantages and each fits a certain organizational size and mix of contextual factors.

Functional Structures

The simplest form of structure is to group employees by their functional specialization. In a functional structure, people who perform the same function are in the same groups, teams, or departments. Such an organization would, for example, have accounting, marketing, production, and human resources departments (see Figure 14.6). The functional structure is one of the most commonly used designs and is usually the starting point for most organizations. Large firms such as American Airlines, Kellogg, and P&G all started with a functional structure.

The functional structure is generally appropriate in low-uncertainty environments and for a small to medium-size organization that focuses on control and efficiency. The biggest challenge for a functional structure is how to encourage different functional departments to interact and coordinate their activities to achieve the goals of the organization, rather than each department focusing on how it can get the resources it needs to achieve its own goals.

FIGURE 14.6   THE FUNCTIONAL STRUCTURE

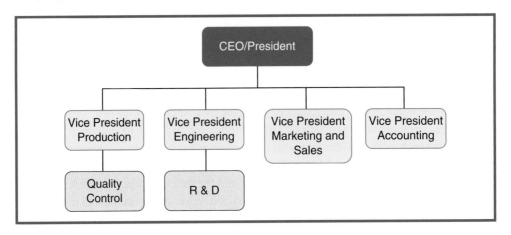

Product/Divisional Structures

The second traditional structure, presented in Figure 14.7, is the product or divisional structure. It groups people by the product or services they work on, or according to the geographic region. For example, employees working on shampoos or cereals or in the Northeastern United States or in Central America are part of one division. The product structure is appropriate for large organizations that face a complex and uncertain environment, have demands for quick response to customers, and command considerable resources. For example PepsiCo has a number of both product (e.g., Quaker Foods, American Beverage) and regional divisions (e.g., Europe, Asia–Middle East–Africa).[54]

Such organizations typically have decentralized leadership with a mission of customer satisfaction and flexibility. Although integration among departments tends to be good, organizations with this type of structure can lose sight of overall organizational goals and the latest development in the environment. Why? Because each product group or division becomes a kingdom unto itself. The challenge in the product/divisional structure, then, is to integrate the various goals and activities of the divisions in a meaningful way.

GM used a product structure for many years. The original five divisions of GM competed with one another and lost sight of the external environment and their foreign competition. The whole corporation suffered until the 1980s when the structure was redesigned to focus on the external market and a specific group of customers. The structure the company adopted in the 1980s reduced the competition among divisions, although it did not solve all the challenges GM faced.

FIGURE 14.7 THE PRODUCT/DIVISIONAL STRUCTURE

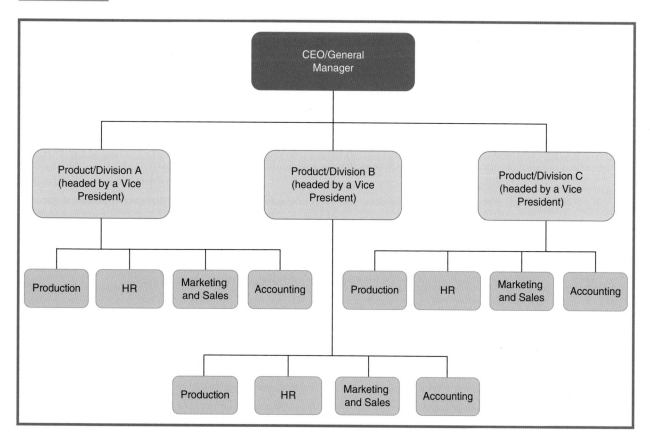

FIGURE 14.8 THE HYBRID STRUCTURE

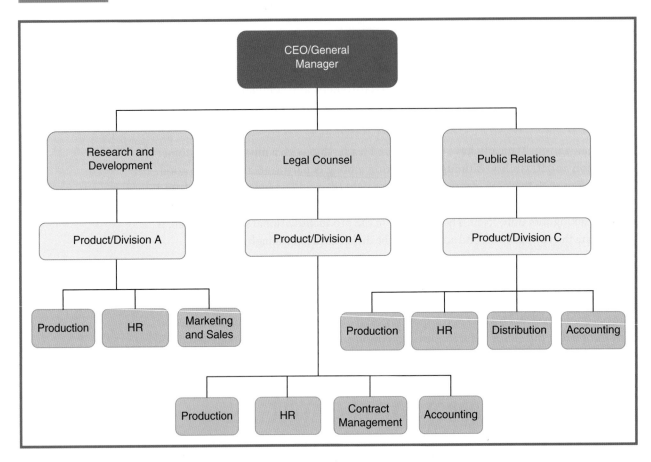

Hybrid Structures

As organizations grow and neither the functional nor the product structure allows them to be effective, they look for other structural options. One option available to very large organizations that operate in many different locations is to combine the functional and product structures to form a hybrid structure, as we see in Figure 14.8. The hybrid organization has headquarters that provide several functions to all divisions. The divisions then specialize either by product or by region. Because the hybrid structure can work for large organizations in many locations, many multinational organizations such as Exxon and Procter & Gamble (P&G) use it. At P&G, Global Business Services are centralized for efficiency with six global hubs to address local needs.[55]

The hybrid generally has both the disadvantages and the advantages of the functional and product structures. It provides many potential benefits such as flexibility, greater ability to deal with an uncertain environment, and responsiveness to customers.

Matrix Structures

The final traditional form of organizations is the matrix. It was originally developed to address the problems associated with the other three structures and to respond to environmental uncertainty and customer demands for efficiency, flexibility, and high quality. As you see is Figure 14.9, the matrix uses project teams in a flexible manner that includes both functional specialists and product or project specialists. The goal of the matrix is to provide a high level of integration between function and product and to do so without extensive resources.

FIGURE 14.9 THE MATRIX STRUCTURE

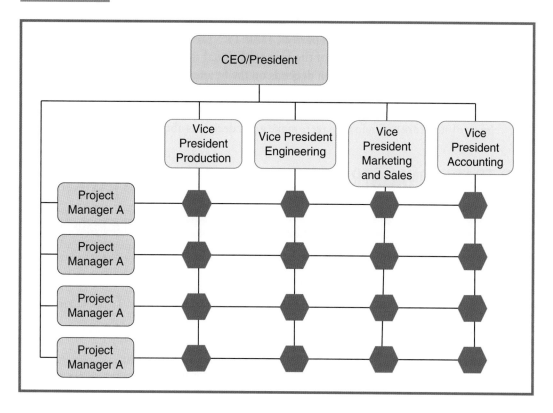

The matrix is appropriate for organizations that face a highly uncertain environment and are under pressure both to be efficient and to respond to their customers quickly. The organization creates and disbands project teams as needed to address customer needs and environmental changes. In fact, if an organization constantly creates teams of people from different departments, also referred to as cross-functional teams, and those teams either never seem to disband or are continuously recreated, moving formally to a matrix may be the next step.

Matrix Managing

Many project-based businesses such as high-tech companies, consulting firms, defense contractors, and research and development firms use matrix structures. By pulling experts from their functional departments and putting them, temporarily, on certain projects, the organization uses their expertise efficiently and effectively and the project teams can be responsive to customer needs. The matrix can address integration problems better than any other form of structure. Since employees and managers from different functions work together on projects, they can easily coordinate their activities. For example, Boeing produces new airplanes using a matrix structure. When the company designed its newest 787 Dreamliner, managers, engineers, designers, marketers, and hundreds of other specialists were pulled from their functional departments and put on the 787 team. Team members were able to coordinate their activities relatively easily.

Before you decide that the matrix is the best structure and wonder why all organizations do not use this structure, consider the potential problems. First, organizations need considerable expertise in managing teams before they implement this structure effectively. Second, the matrix puts a lot of pressure on project managers to make sure that jobs are done on time and within budget. Third, people from different functional areas often have difficulty working together. Fourth, project teams spend considerable time and resources coordinating and integrating their activities and training people to work in teams. Finally, individuals who work on teams often end up reporting to two or more managers, namely their functional manager and project leaders for each team. This multiple reporting is often highly stressful and difficult to manage.

None of the structural options is perfect. Table 14.5 presents a summary analysis of the advantages and disadvantages of the four traditional structures. Whether a structural option works for an organization depends on the fit among the contextual strategic elements of environment, technology, strategy, and culture. Knowing the advantages and disadvantages of each structure and being aware of the effect of the contextual factors on the choice of structure can help managers make good decisions about how to organize people.

TABLE 14.5 FOUR TRADITIONAL STRUCTURAL OPTIONS

	When Appropriate	Advantages	Disadvantages
Functional	• Environment is certain • Organization is small • Focus is on efficiency • Few goals	• Is efficient • Provides functional specialization	• Poor integration across functional departments • Inflexible • Can't handle multiple goals • Slow to change
Product/Divisional	• Environment is uncertain • Organization is large • Focus is on customer satisfaction • Business has multiple goals	• Good integration inside divisions • Can handle multiple goals and demands	• Requires considerable resources • Duplication of effort • Fosters competition among divisions within the company
Hybrid	• Environment is uncertain • Very large organization • Multiple goals	• Can help manage large and complex organizations • Can address multiple goals	• Requires considerable resources • Can lead to duplication • Poor coordination across the organization
Matrix	• Environment is uncertain • Customers demand quality, flexibility, and efficiency • Project-type business	• Good integration of department • Can handle multiple goals and projects • Uses limited resources efficiently	• Requires considerable coordination • High stress due to multiple demands • Can be inefficient because of time spent on coordination

Most organizations use a combination of structural designs and many create their own structures to fit their contextual elements. For example, Gore uses a flat team-based lattice structure where there are no charts, no formal chain of command, and no predetermined communication channels. Employees are encouraged to communicate as needed and coordinate their activities with anyone they think can help them be effective.[56] Additionally, organizations often restructure how they work in response to competitive pressures, change in leadership, or to address a performance gap. Another factor that is forcing changes in the structure of organizations is the reliance on temporary workers at all levels. While these types of "contract" employees used to be employed primarily at lower levels of organizations, many professional-level jobs are now often filled by contract, temporary, or so-called independent workers.[57]

Restructuring efforts and new structural forms have become standard in today's organizations and more often than not, come with some pain for employees and communities since many jobs are eliminated and departments and divisions are shut down in search of efficiencies. For example, when Yahoo! changed leadership in 2010, new CEO Scott Thompson announced a restructuring that was to cause job loss for potentially thousands of employees.[58]

Managing in an Uncertain Environment

To keep their organizations competitive, managers need to monitor the contextual strategic elements of environment, technology, strategy, structure, and culture and the ways in which they influence one another. The fit among the contextual strategic elements is key to an effective organization. Monitoring the environment is the starting point because environmental changes dictate the type of adjustments the organization must make to stay competitive. Managers can respond to environmental changes through a number of activities such as using new technology, designing a new strategy, or altering the structure. Most of these changes eventually may require a cultural change as well. Managers can respond to environmental changes in three general ways that we consider next; most organizations use these in combination.

Managing in Uncertain Times

Gathering Information

Information is vital. Managers need complete, reliable information to conduct a SWOT analysis, formulate and implement strategy, assess technological needs, and ensure that their culture and structure are responsive enough to environmental changes, including customers' and other stakeholders' demands. There are two methods managers can use to gather information.

1. *Environmental scanning* is the systematic gathering of information about the environment, its elements and characteristics. Examples include market research and competitive analyses or searching for new technologies.

2. *Boundary spanning* is the process of interaction with the environment to accomplish the twin goals of gathering information and informing the environment about the organization's activities. A *boundary spanner* is the person or department with the responsibility for interacting with the environment to gather and disseminate information.[59] Spanners often conduct environmental scanning. Salespeople and public relations departments who exchange information with the environment are examples. Similarly, employees involved in research and development look for and design new technologies and products to make the organization more effective and efficient.

The information that organizations gather from their environment through various methods is used to make decisions regarding the other contextual elements. For example, environmental scanning allows managers to identify upcoming technological advances, set goals for using those or developing their own, and devising strategies to achieve those goals. Their strategies may include the creation of new departments, hiring new people, or restructuring existing departments to achieve those goals. The process of gathering information is essential to SWOT analysis.

Adapting Internal Culture and Structure

The second action managers can take to manage uncertainty is to adapt internal organizational culture and structure. We discussed organizational culture in Chapter 12. Earlier in this chapter we mentioned that there are no perfect structures. The structure, and the culture, must fit with the other contextual elements. For example, an uncertain environment that is fast changing and complex will require a more organic structure, whereas a mechanistic structure will most likely work in a simple and stable environment. Similarly, a functional structure is appropriate for a low-uncertainty environment when the organization is focused on efficiency, whereas the matrix can address the needs of multiple constituents and is appropriate for organizations with limited resources. Organizations experiment with new structures to respond to global competitive pressures for quality and efficiency. In general, uncertain environments create the need for high levels of integration and flexibility.

Changing the Environment

In addition to gathering information and changing internal structures and cultures to respond to environmental pressures, many organizations take the further step of changing or controlling their environment.

Alliances Across Boundaries

Lobbying

Lobbying involves active interaction and exchange with government officials with the goal of influencing their decisions and thereby creating a more favorable environment for the organization. Large organizations either have their own lobbyists or rely on industry lobbyists hired by several companies in the same industry. Alternatively, businesses join trade organizations that provide strong lobbying representations for a group of organizations with similar objectives. For instance, small U.S. manufacturers can join the National Association of Manufacturers and be represented to advance U.S. manufacturing interests politically.

The primary goal of lobbying is to reduce uncertainty by changing various elements of the environment to provide more control to the organization and its managers. For example, internet giants Google, Facebook, EBay, and Amazon are founding members of a new lobbying group called the Internet Association that aims at protecting and promoting an open, innovative, and free Internet.[60] Similarly, coal-mining companies have strong lobbying efforts to limit environmental regulations that may increase their costs. As a matter of fact, both coal mining and other utility companies were major contributors to the 2012 presidential election in the United States hoping to sway the election.[61]

Strategic Alliances

Managers can reduce uncertainty and change their environment by entering into alliances with other organizations so that they can control suppliers, competitors, and customers. There are three types of alliances:

1. *Joint contracts* are temporary agreements organizations make with others for specific tasks or resources. By joint contracting with a supplier, a company reduces its risk of resource shortage. By controlling its resources, it reduces uncertainty.

2. *Joint ventures* involve two or more companies that join to create a subsidiary company. Managers create joint ventures by each partner investing a certain amount of resources for a specific purpose, such as sharing of technologies. These joint ventures are either spun off into separate businesses or dismantled after a certain period of time.

3. *Mergers and acquisitions* are legal processes in which one company purchases or combines with another to become one entity. For example, 2013 saw a rash of mega mergers such as one between American and U.S. Airlines, one between Liberty Global and Virgin Media, and a proposed merger between US Airways and American Airlines that has faced opposition from the U.S. Department of Justice.[62]

The goal of all of these strategic alliances is to gain access to resources, reduce risk, share costs, and overall change the complexity or the rate of change of the environment.

► Summary and Applications for Managers

Strategic contextual elements are typically the domain of leaders at the higher levels of organizations. However, in today's dynamic environment, every manager at every level needs to have an understanding of these elements and how they affect the behavior of people in organizations. Particularly, all managers must take part in reducing environmental uncertainty. Many also are involved in formulating strategy while all managers must set goals and implement strategies to achieve those goals, often by making structural and cultural changes inside their department or team. So while strategic issues may appear to be "too big" or "too strategic" for the middle manager, everyone in an effective organization is aware of them. Here are strategic actions you can take to help you and your organization become more effective:

1. *Gather information* from outside your organization any chance you get. Talk to suppliers, customers, and competitors; actively listen and ask questions about what is going on outside of your organization that may affect you.

2. *Track business and economic trends* by keeping up with news, pertinent government reports, and industry and trade journals.

3. *Stay informed about managerial trends and innovation* by reading practitioner or academic journals, attending lectures and seminars, or taking courses.

4. *Stay close to your community* by getting to know all the people who have a stake in your organization. Shareholders and customers are important, but many others also have a stake in what you do.

5. *Join a trade organization* that has political or economic relevance for your business. They are a great source of information.

6. *Actively network* with people inside and outside your industry.

7. *Demonstrate and maintain your expertise and competence.* Changing environments affect everyone's job. Being valued by your company is essential.

8. *Move to different positions* within your organization whenever you can. The broad perspective and new skills make you more valuable and allow you to have a strategic view of the organization.

9. *Gain international experience.* All organizations are global at some level. The more you understand and know the global and cultural environment, the more information and skills you will have to think strategically.

10. *Take care of people.* While strategic issues may appear abstract, implementation of any of them depends on good leadership and the connections you have with people inside your organization.

► Key Terms

Business environment 440	Line employees 453	Research and development (R & D) 445	Strategy implementation 450
Complexity 442	Low-cost strategies 452	Scope (of strategy) 452	Strategic management process 450
Differentiation 452	Manufacturing firms 445	Service firms 445	Technology 443
Enactment 441	Mission 448	Staff 453	Vision 437
Environment 438	Organic organizations 454	Strategy 448	
Environmental uncertainty 442	Organizational chart 452	Strategic formulation 450	
General environment 440	Rate of Change 442		
Goals 448			

Exercise 14.1 SWOT Analysis

You are part of the leadership of your student government and your university is undergoing a lengthy strategic planning process. Student government has been asked to participate in the process and you have suggested using a SWOT analysis. Your task is to conduct a SWOT analysis for your university based on the information you and your team members have.

1. What are the strengths of your university? Consider academic programs, student services, financial resources, facilities, locations, and so forth.

2. What are some weaknesses? What things could use improvement or are ongoing problems?

3. What are some opportunities? Consider new programs, new markets (for older students, or online programs), special student services, and so forth.

4. What are some threats? Consider other universities, lack of resources from the state or declining enrollments, demographic factors, and so forth.

5. Summarize your SWOT and use Table 14.2 to determine where your university stands.

6. What do you recommend?

Exercise 14.2 Understanding Strategic Elements

This exercise is designed to help you understand the role of leaders in managing the six strategic elements of environment, strategy, culture, structure, technology, and leadership presented in the chapter.

The Scenario

You are a member of a school board for a medium-sized middle (junior high) school in a major western city. The city has experienced tremendous growth in the past 5 years, and as a result, the student body increased by 20% without much change in facilities and relatively limited increases in funding. The classrooms are overcrowded, much of the equipment is old, teachers have limited resources to enrich the curriculum, and the sense of direction is unclear. During the same time period, the school slowly developed one of the poorest records for student academic performance and drop-out rate.

Before the past few years, however, the school held a well-established reputation as one of the most creative and academically sound schools in the city. Traditionally, parent involvement and interest in the school varied greatly. Similarly, the faculty are diverse in their approach, tenure, and backgrounds, but the majority demonstrate dedication to their students and are committed to the improvement of the school.

Because of a number of recent threats of lawsuits from parents over equal opportunity issues, several violent incidents among the students, and the poor academic performance, the principal was asked to resign. Many parents, teachers, and board members blame her for a laissez-faire attitude and what appears to be a total lack of direction and focus. Problems and complaints were simply not addressed and no plan articulated for dealing with the changes that the school was experiencing.

After a 2-month multistate regional search and interviews with a number of finalists, the school board narrowed its search for the new principal to two candidates.

The Candidates

J. B. Davison is 55 years old, with a doctorate in education administration and bachelor's and master's degrees in education. He previously served as principal at two other schools where he was successful in focusing on basic academic skills, traditional approaches, discipline, and encouragement of success. Before moving to school administration, he was a history and social studies teacher. The board is impressed with his clear-headedness and no-nonsense approach to education. He readily admits that he is conservative and traditional and considers himself to be a father figure to the students. He runs a tight ship and is involved in every aspect of his school.

Jerri Popovich is 40 years old. She holds M.A. and Ph.D. degrees in education administration with an undergraduate degree in computer science. She worked in the computer industry several years before teaching science and math. She worked as assistant principal in one other school and is currently the principal of an urban middle school on the West Coast. She successfully involved many business and community members in her current school. The board is impressed with her creativity and her ability to find novel approaches. She considers one of her major strengths to be the ability to involve many constituents in decision making. She describes herself as a facilitator in the education process.

Understanding Strategic Elements Worksheet: Comparing the Candidates

In helping you decide which person to recommend, consider how each would handle and balance the five strategic management elements of environment, strategy, culture, structure, technology, and leadership.

Discussion Items

1. How are the two candidates different?

2. What explains the differences between them?

Your Choice

Who would you recommend for the job? Why?

Source: Nahavandi, A. (2011). *The art and science of leadership* (6th ed.). Upper Saddle River, NJ: Pearson-Prentice Hall. Reprinted with permission.

Strategic Elements	J. B. Davison	Jerri Popovich
Environment		
Technology		
Strategy		
Structure		
Culture		

▶ Exercise 14.3   Changing the Structure of Your Organization

The structure of an organization should follow from the mission and strategies. Often, a structure that is already in place impacts the ability of managers to implement new strategies. Changing the structure starts with identifying core business processes and the most important technologies. Once that is completed, you can start with a blank sheet of paper and ask the question: "*What is the best way to do what you want to do?*" The answer to this question should be the basis of any restructuring process. Obviously, few organizations have the luxury of starting from scratch. However, thinking about what is important and the ideal way to accomplish the mission is highly beneficial. The goal of this exercise is to get you to that process for your organization or team.

1. Select and describe the target organization or team.

   o In your group, discuss each member's work experiences.

   o Select one organization, team, or job to be restructured. It could be a whole organization or just one team or department. You should select a job that you understand well and that currently faces some problems and inefficiencies. In other words, do not pick a department that is running well or one about which you have limited information.

   o Fully describe the current structure and processes in your target organization/department so that all your group members understand them well. To achieve this, informally interview the person whose organization was selected.

2. Once you have completed the first step, ask and answer the following questions:

   o What is the mission?
   o Who are the primary customers?

- What is the current structure (how are people organized to get their job done)?
- What are the current problems and challenges?

3. The next step is to ask the key question: "If you had total freedom and resources and could start from scratch, what would be the best way to achieve the mission of the organization/team?" Your goal is to develop a number of alternatives to the current work processes and structure.

4. Once your team has developed a number of alternatives, examine and evaluate each carefully by addressing the following questions:

- What are the benefits and disadvantages of each alternative?

- Who will be affected? Consider people inside and outside the organization—all stakeholders.
- What are the obstacles to implementing each alternative?

5. Based on your analysis in the previous step, select one alternative as your new design. Explain why it is the best one and make sure it can address the mission and goals of the organization.

Source: Nahavandi, A. (2011). *The art and science of leadership* (6th ed.). Upper Saddle River, NJ: Pearson-Prentice Hall. Reprinted with permission.

▶ Case 14.1 Bound by the Structure

Eloise joined Events Are Us with 5 years of excellent experience working for a small events planning company. She had had the opportunity to see and do all parts of the business and now needed more and bigger challenges. The family-owned business where she used to work was great, turned on a dime, and served many private events and small companies, but it provided no promotion opportunity. Events Are Us was located in Southern California and had grown considerably in the past few years with branches in six Western and Southwestern states. The company had contracts with major companies and sports organizations for their big events and provided a complete menu of services from expert event planners to catering and facilities, photographers, and even decorators and architects as well as a variety of other services. They also still served some private customers with events such as weddings. Most of their large clients had a predetermined set of events every year, often complicated and big affairs, and needed consistency and reliability with a hint of adventure, things Events Are Us provided very well. Eloise signed on! There was lots to do and lots to learn and, with close to 1,000 employees, lots of room to grow.

Eloise was the creative type and loved to work with clients from the ground up, and because of her broad experience, she was quickly assigned to the Event Planning department to report to the assistant case manager, Jeremy, who reported to the case manager, Melina, who reported to the VP of events, Ms. Bellizzi. She went through 3 days of training with HR, most of which was focused on learning the policies and procedures, as well as the extensive benefits employees had. Once she completed orientation, she was put on a team of four planners who all reported to Jeremy and who handled several big clients. Each planner did a part of each project. The most senior one, Adam, worked directly with the clients to help them with their planning once Jeremy had signed the contracts. Jeff took the work from Adam and organized the catering and facilities and worked with Sarah who handled the entertainment along with Kim. Eloise's job was to handle the paperwork, all the accounts from the client and suppliers, and work with the billing department. The team met every day for 1 hour to review cases, and Eloise met with her manager once a week to report on her work.

Her team members were great; they all really knew their stuff. After just a couple of weeks, Eloise had many ideas that she brought up during the daily meetings. Her team members said it all sounded great and told her to share them with her manager, which she did. Jeremy thanked her and said he would pass them on as appropriate. After several attempts at making suggestions that did not seem to go anywhere, Eloise put them in writing and sent them to Adam in a memo. He forwarded them to Jeremy who reminded Eloise that she needed to go through him since Adam was not her supervisor. Eloise was getting both confused and frustrated. She knew her ideas were good; her colleagues were all telling her so. She did not understand why she had to go through all these steps.

Although Eloise rarely met with clients directly or face to face (just lots of phone call and e-mails), she happened to go with Adam to one of his client meetings. The clients had a lot of repeat business with Events Are Us, and Eloise suggested several changes to what had already been proposed regarding their big company retreat. She was very excited; finally a chance to do some creative work and talk to people again! The client loved her ideas and asked for her e-mail so she could get more details. Adam looked very uncomfortable and cut the meeting short. He was very quiet during the drive back to the office.

As soon as she got back to the office, Eloise put her ideas in an e-mail and made sure she copied Adam and Jeremy. The client was still very interested. The next day, Jeremy's assistant called Eloise in for a meeting with him. Jeremy told Eloise that she had overstepped her bounds, that she should not have contacted the client, and should not have embarrassed Adam in front of her. Eloise was confused: "The client loved the ideas, right? And they actually will increase our billing? I did this with Adam; he was right there. I didn't go over his head or behind his back. I don't understand what the problem is?" Jeremy reminded her it is very important that she follows the procedures and respects the authority of more senior people and asked her not to do this again.

At the next morning's team meeting, Adam did not seem upset. Jeremy had convinced the client to go back to the original plans and all was back on track and on schedule. He encouraged Eloise to continue to suggest ideas in the meetings, but make sure that she stayed "in her box" when it came to the work. He told her: "We all have a job to do. I can't do yours and you can't do mine. It confuses the clients and our suppliers, messes up the schedules, and makes it hard for us to finish our projects when things are disorganized. We need to know who is responsible for what."

Eloise was doing well at her job and except for being told that she needs to "stay in her box" several more times by her teammates and her boss, she was getting good reviews. The work was not very exciting, but there was the distinct possibility of a promotion soon to lead another team. She missed the excitement of the small company she used to work for where everything was done quickly and everyone jumped in to do whatever was needed when it was needed. Yet, at Events Are Us, she had the chance to move up . . . if she could just stay in her box.

1. Using the structural elements you learned in this chapter, compare the structure of Events Are Us and Eloise's first job.

2. What are some of the strategic contextual elements for Events Are Us?

3. How well does the structure fit the other elements?

4. What is the impact of the structure on Eloise?

5. What do you think Eloise should do?

Endnotes

1. McCormick vision and values. (2013). Retrieved from http://www .mccormickcorporation.com/OurCompany/ CorporateMissionVision.aspx on March 13, 2013.

2. Hayes, C. L. (1998, February 20). Trouble in spice world. *New York Times*, pp. C1–C5.

3. Barney, J. B., & Hersterly, W. S. (2010). *Strategic management and competitive advantage: Concepts.* Upper Saddle River, NJ: Pearson-Prentice Hall.

4. Beaumont, C. (2008). Bill Gates's dream: A computer in every home. *The Telegraph*, June 27. Retrieved from http://www.telegraph .co.uk/technology/3357701/Bill-Gatess-dream-A-computer-in-every-home.html on June 26, 2013.

5. Hull, P. (2012). Be visionary. Think big. *Forbes*, December 19. Retrieved from http://www .forbes.com/sites/patrickhull/2012/12/19/ be-visionary-think-big/ on June 26, 2013.

6. Hull, 2012.

7. Johnson & Johnson. (2013). *Our credo values.* Retrieved from http://www.jnj.com/about-jnj/ jnj-credo on June 26, 2013.

8. Friedland, J., & Lee, L. (1997). Going tough for Wal-mart in South America. *Lakeland Ledger*, October 12. Retrieved from http:// news.google.com/newspapers?nid=1346&da t=19971012&id=kposAAAAIBAJ&sjid=vfw DAAAAIBAJ&pg=3412,1613922 on June 26, 2013.

9. Loeb, W. (2013). Successful global growers: What we can learn from Walmart, Carrefour, Tesco, Metro. *Forbes*, March 7. Retrieved from http:// www.forbes.com/sites/walterloeb/2013/03/07/ walmart-carrefour-tesco-metro-successful-global-growers-what-can-we-learn-from-them/ on June 26, 2013.

10. Weick, K. E. (1988). Enacted sensemaking in crisis situations. *Journal of Management Studies*, 24(4).

11. Weick, K., & Sutcliffe, K. (2007). *Managing the unexpected: Resilient performance in an age of uncertainty.* San Francisco, CA: Jossey Bass.

12. Noguchi, Y. (2013). Being postmaster general isn't what it used to be. *NPR-All Things Considered*, June 25. Retrieved from http:// www.npr.org/2013/06/26/195936587/being-postmaster-general-isnt-what-it-used-to-be on June 26, 2013.

13. Duncan, R. B. (1972). Characteristics of organizational environments and perceived environmental uncertainty. *Administrative Science Quarterly, 17,* 313–327.

14. Aldrich, H. (1979). *Organizations and Environments.* Englewood Cliffs, NJ.: Prentice Hall.

15. Hopkins, J. (2013). Wal-Mart's influence grows. *USA Today*, January 28. Retrieved from http:// usatoday.printthis.clickability.com/pt/cpt?actio n=cpt&expire&urlID=5243978&fb=Y&partn erID=1661 on April 2, 2013.

16. McCammon, S. (2013). Same-sex wedding planners get a boost from Supreme Court. *Marketplace-Business*, June 26. Retrieved from http://www.marketplace.org/topics/ business/same-sex-wedding-planners-get-boost-supreme-court on June 27, 2013.

17. Colvin, S. (2012). Indra Nooyi's Pepsi challenge. *CNN Money,* May 29. Retrieved from http:// management.fortune.cnn.com/2002/05/29/ pepsi-indra-nooyi-2 on June 25, 2013.

18. Pappas, C. (2013). Indra Nooyi of PepsiCo is a symbolic leader of culture. *People Priority.* Retrieved from http://peoplepriority.com/blog/ indra-nooyi-pepsico-symbolic-leader-culture on June 25, 2013.

19. Brady, D. (2007, June 11). Indra Nooyi: Keeping cool in hot water. *Business Week*, p. 49.

20. Nooyi, I. (2011). PepsiCo diversity and inclusion awards. Retrieved from http://www.pepsico.com/ assets/speeches/IndraNooyiDIAwardsFINAL. pdf on June 25, 2013.

21. Ortiz, P. (2006). Historic change: Indra Nooyi to be CEO of PepsiCo. *Diversity Inc.* May.

22. Letter from Indra Nooyi. (2010). *PepsiCo India*. Retrieved from http://pepsicoindia.co.in/purpose/performance-with-purpose/letter-from-indra-nooyi.html on September 15, 2010.

23. Indra Nooyi's 5-C formula for global success. (2006). *The Times of India,* August 16. Retrieved from http://timesofindia.indiatimes.com/business/international-business/indra-nooyis-5-c-formula-for-global-success/articleshow/1898674.cms on June 25, 2013.

24. Perrow, C. (1967). A framework for the comparative analysis of organizations. *American Sociological Review, 32,* 194–208.

25. Services. (2013). *Office of the United States Trade Representative.* Retrieved from http://www.ustr.gov/trade-topics/services-investment/services on June 26, 2013.

26. Bosker, B., & Grandoni, D. (2012). Apple-Samsung lawsuit: What you need to know about the verdict. *The Huffington Post,* Retrieved from http://www.huffingtonpost.com/2012/08/24/apple-samsung-lawsuit-verdict_n_1829268.html on March 13, 2013.

27. Greene, J. (2012). Nordstrom Rack listened. *Forbes,* August 30. Retrieved from http://www.forbes.com/sites/chicceo/2012/08/30/nordstrom-rack-listened/ on April 2, 2013.

28. Hill, K. (2012). How Target figured out a teen girl was pregnant before her father did. Retrieved from http://www.forbes.com/sites/kashmirhill/2012/02/16/how-target-figured-out-a-teen-girl-was-pregnant-before-her-father-did/ on April 2, 2013.

29. Inside Google workplaces, from perks to nap pods. (2012). *NBC This Morning,* January 22. Retrieved from http://www.cbsnews.com/8301-505266_162-57565097/inside-google-workplaces-from-perks-to-nap-pods/ on April 2, 2013.

30. Stewart, J. B. (2013). Looking for a lesson in Google's perks. *The New York Times,* March 15. Retrieved from http://www.nytimes.com/2013/03/16/business/at-google-a-place-to-work-and-play.html?pagewanted=all on April 2, 2013.

31. Mark, J. (2013). The green movement isn't fringe. *Salon.com,* March 5. Retrieved from http://www.salon.com/2013/03/05/michael_grunwald_im_a_respectable_environmentalist_partner/ on April 2, 2013.

32. Montague, P. (2012). Why the environmental movement is not winning. *The Huffington Post,* February 29. Retrieved from http://www.huffingtonpost.com/peter-montague/green-initiatives_b_1301418.html on April 2, 2013

33. Hsu, T. (2011). Wal-Mart's motive is no secret: Going green saves it money. *Los Angeles Times,* June 4. Retrieved from http://articles.latimes.com/2011/jun/04/business/la-fi-walmart-green-20110604 on April 2, 2013; and Humes, E. (2011). *Force of nature: The unlikely story of Wal-Mart's green revolution.* New York, NY: HarperCollins.

34. Aston, A. (2009). Wal-Mart: Making its suppliers go green. *Bloomberg Business Week,* May 14. Accesses at http://www.businessweek.com/magazine/content/09_21/b4132044814736.htm on April 2, 2013.

35. Lopez. R. (2013). Unlike Yahoo, most firms to keep telecommute option survey says. *LA Times.* Retrieved from http://www.latimes.com/business/money/la-fi-mo-telecommuting-yahoo-resource-managers-20130311,0,4373450.story on March 13, 2013.

36. Molina, B. (2013). VPN logs led to Yahoo telecommute ban. *USA Today.* Retrieved from http://www.usatoday.com/story/tech/2013/03/06/report-vpn-yahoo-mayer/1967957/ on March 13, 2013.

37. Cain Miller, C., & Perlroth, N. (2013). Yahoo says new policy is meant to raise morale. *New York Times,* March 5. Retrieved from http://www.nytimes.com/2013/03/06/technology/yahoos-in-office-policy-aims-to-bolster-morale.html?pagewanted=all&_r=1& on March 13, 2013.

38. Hughes, S. (2012). I banned all internal emails at my company for a week. *Forbes,* October 10. Retrieved from http://www.forbes.com/sites/

forbesleadershipforum/2012/10/25/i-banned-all-internal-e-mails-at-my-company-for-a-week/ on April 2, 2013.

39. McCormick vision and values, 2013.

40. Tom's of Maine—Our reason for being. (2013). Retrieved from http://www.tomsofmaine.com/company/overlay/Our-Reason-For-Being on September 15, 2013.

41. P&G—The power of purpose. (2013). Retrieved from http://www.pg.com/en_US/company/purpose_people/index.shtml on March 13, 2012.

42. Medtronic—Careers. (2013). Retrieved from http://www.medtronic.com/careers/mission-culture/index.htm on March 13, 2013.

43. Walmart annual report. (2013). Retrieved from http://www.walmartstores.com/sites/annualreport/2011/mission.aspx on March 13, 2013.

44. Barney, J. B. (1977). *Gaining and sustaining competitive advantage*. Reading, MA: Addison-Wesley.

45. Porter, M. E. (1990). *The competitive advantage of nations*. New York, NY: Free Press.

46. Porter, 1990.

47. Smith, G. (2004). An evaluation of the corporate culture of Southwest Airlines. *Measuring Business Excellence, 8*(4), 26–33.

48. Mintzberg, H. (1983). *Structure in five's: Designing effective organizations*. Englewood Cliffs, NJ: Prentice Hall.

49. W. L. Gore and Associates—our culture. (2013). *A team-based, flat lattice organization*. Retrieved from http://www.gore.com/en_xx/aboutus/culture/index.html on March 31, 2013.

50. Burns, T., & Stalker, G. M. (1961). *The management of innovation*. London: Tavistock.

51. Nocera, J. (1998). Main Street broker. *Time Magazine*, December 7. Retrieved from http://content.time.com/time/magazine/article/0,9171,989774-3,00.html

52. Charles Merrill, broker, dies; founder of Merrill Lynch firm. (2010). *NY Times*, 2010. Retrieved from: http://www.nytimes.com/learning/general/onthisday/bday/1019.html

53. Nocera, 1998, p. 2.

54. Pepsico—Our business and brands. (2013). Retrieved from http://www.pepsico.com/Purpose/Performance-with-Purpose/Our-Business-and-Brands.html on April 2, 2013.

55. P&G—Strength in structure. (2013). Retrieved from http://www.pg.com/en_US/company/global_structure_operations/corporate_structure.shtml on April 2, 2013.

56. Gore—Our culture, (2013). Retrieved from http://www.gore.com/en_xx/aboutus/culture/index.html on March 21, 2013.

57. For an interesting perspective on the challenges of contract workers, see S. Greenhouse (2013). Tackling concerns of independent workers. *The New York Times*. March 23. Retrieved from http://www.nytimes.com/2013/03/24/business/freelancers-union-tackles-concerns-of-independent-workers.html?pagewanted=all&_r=0 on April 2, 2013.

58. Yahoo reportedly preparing big restructuring, layoffs. (2010). *NBC.com-Business*, October 14. Retrieved from http://www.nbcnews.com/business/yahoo-reportedly-preparing-big-restructuring-layoffs-322355 on March 21, 2013.

59. Jemison, D. (1984). The importance of boundary spanning roles in strategic decision making. *Journal of Management Studies, 21*, 131–152.

60. Sasso, B. (2012). Silicon Valley web giants go their own way with a new lobbying startup. *The Hill*, July 13. Retrieved from http://thehill.com/business-a-lobbying/241149-web-firms-go-their-own-way-with-new-lobbying-startup- on March 25, 2013.

61. Quinones, M. (2011). Coal industry deploys donations, lobbying as its issues gain prominence. *The New York Times*, October 13. Retrieved from http://www.nytimes.com/gwire/2011/10/13/13greenwire-coal-industry-

deploys-donations-lobbying-as-it-45582.
html?pagewanted=all on March 25, 2013.

62. For information about several big mergers see
Farrell, M. (2013). M&A making a comeback.
CNN Money, February 14. Retrieved from
http://money.cnn.com/2013/02/12/investing/
merger-acquisition/index.html on March
25, 2013; for information about the U.S.

Airways and American Airlines merger and
the Department of Justice opposition, see
Koenig, D. (2013). Proposed US Airways,
American Airlines merger challenged by Justice
Department, states. *The Huffington Post*, August
13. Retrieved from http://www.huffingtonpost.
com/2013/08/13/us-airways-american-airlines-
merger_n_3748865.html on August 31, 2013.

15 Organizational Culture and Change

LEARNING OUTCOMES

After reading this chapter you should be able to:

1. Discuss and evaluate the concept of organizational culture

2. Interpret the forces compelling change as well as those resisting change

3. Critique classic approaches to understanding organizational change

4. Evaluate the role of culture in organizational change

5. Contrast contemporary approaches to bringing about organizational change

6. Analyze some of the ethical and personal issues in changing organizations

Burberry: A "Young Old Company" ▶

Burberry is a historic company known first for outfitting military and global explorers then evolving into a luxury clothing firm known for its "check" pattern. But when Angela Ahrendts became CEO of the company in 2006, it was struggling financially. (Sales the year before were up about 2% vs. the luxury retail average of 13%.[1]) One of the first things Ahrendts did was to bring together the top managers, some 60 in all. They flew in from around the world into typically damp and misty London—but not one of the 60 was wearing a Burberry trench coat. Ahrendts quickly decided that the company had lost its focus and the enthusiasm of its workforce, and was in need of a drastic change.[2]

Part of the approach was to recognize the company's history, particularly its iconic trench coat and the Burberry check, and to center the company's activities on a "global, high-growth . . . luxury brand with a very British sensibility."[3] The idea was to focus on the brand and be sure that everything else—product lines, public relations, and social media—was consistent with the brand identity. The new focus on the heritage of the company was balanced by the idea of creating a "young old company," one that would embrace its history while appealing to younger customers reachable more by social media than traditional retail outlets. This idea also included a commitment to "democratize luxury,"[4] that is, to broaden the appeal of the product to those who might not think of themselves as luxury shoppers.

But, Ahrendts reasoned, if democratic luxury is an external strategy, then democracy should be promoted internally as well. Ahrendts comments: "When I started, only 10% of our employees were in on a bonus scheme or had any shares in the company. If you're going to be democratic, then you have to get that out to everyone and by doing that it unites the culture."[5] Beyond that, Ahrendts sought a company more socially conscious as well as more socially connected. For example, the company now sponsors emerging acoustic musicians in its shows and on its website.[6]

[
Where there is no vision, the people perish.

—*Proverbs 29:18*
]

But the biggest move was to establish a culture of creativity. Ahrendts named designer Christopher Bailey as Burberry's "brand czar"[7] and told the company that anything that the customer would eventually see would go through his office. Ahrendts also created a Strategic Innovation Council, chaired by Bailey, and comprised of the younger generation of great thinkers in the company, and a Senior Executive Council, chaired by Ahrendts, and charged with executing the "young vision."[8] As Ahrendts puts it, "We actually flipped the traditional hierarchy, and the way we communicated these councils to the entire company showed that we were serious about being creatively led."[9]

The result: Annual sales in 2012 were $3 billion, or double the 2007 levels, and the stock has returned nearly 300% over the last six years.[10]

It's obvious—change is all around us. The environment is rapidly changing, bringing new requirements and demands almost daily. The economy is in constant flux, governments change, society evolves, and populations shift. Technology is moving so quickly that today's work practices become outdated almost overnight. Similarly, there are changes in the workforce and the expectations of workers, leading to thoughtful consideration of previously radical ideas such as family medical leave, telecommuting, and job sharing. There is also the impact of the new global economy and the constant pressure on institutions to do more with less. In addition to external pressures, organizations face many internal pressures for change. Low performance, new leadership, new mission, and employee demands all require major or minor changes in organizations (see Figure 15.1). As you enter your career, you'd better be prepared to embrace change—because it will be all around you.

Those organizations that develop the creativity and flexibility to adapt to changing circumstances will be those that thrive during the coming decades. However, studies have shown that most change efforts are reactive and ad hoc, and that 70% fail.[11] Of course, one reason is that change is very difficult for most people. When new ideas come forward about how the organization might improve, especially when those ideas fundamentally challenge the existing culture, people are very naturally apprehensive and cling to the status quo. Some of this resistance to change is probably based on objective reasoning. That

FIGURE 15.1 FORCES FOR CHANGE

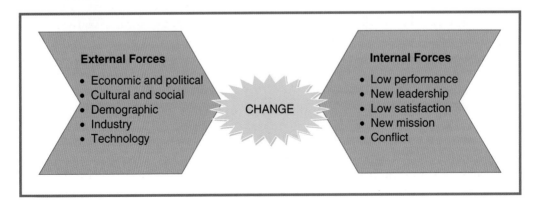

is, people truly believe that the proposed changes will not work or that they will undermine an important part of the organization's mission. But much of the resistance will be based on more emotional and psychological reactions. People develop standard ways of coping with their environments, and new ideas may be seen as undermining the security that past practices afforded. Situations that are well known and comfortable will be seen as giving way to something that is less clear and therefore scary.

The Relationship Between Culture and Change

Change takes place within the context of an organization's culture. As we have seen, culture is generally taken to embrace those norms, beliefs, and values expressed by members of a particular group and manifest in their typical behaviors and in the artifacts they produce. The term is used in a similar fashion in studies of complex organizations. The idea is that members of an organization share certain ideas about everything from the appearance of their offices, to the overall values they hold, to the basic assumptions they have about the work they do.

Culture acts both as a force to restrain change and a way to bring about change. Since organizational culture is basically a set of existing values, beliefs, and practices, it is an inevitably conservative notion. Established practices are highly resistant to change. "That's the way we've always done things around here." On the other hand, many managers, seeking to bring about changes in their organizations, have focused on changing the organization's culture as a way of changing the organization. As we have said, cultures are highly resistant to change, but, once changed, they are likely to be maintained for a significant period of time.

There are, however, several ways in which people's normal resistance to change may be overcome and in which cultural change may be implemented more successfully. Four "hurdles" to executing effective change are[12]

1. The cognitive hurdle—that people are wedded to the status quo

2. A resource hurdle—that there are limited resources

3. The motivational hurdle—that people must be motivated to change

4. The political hurdle—some groups may oppose the change

Change Processes in Organizations

Overcoming these hurdles requires a keen understanding of organizational culture and of the change process in organizations. We should first recognize that there are several different types of change that occur. For example, we can distinguish between incremental change and discontinuous change. Even during periods of relative calm, every organization is constantly changing. Managers and others make improvements in work processes, they experiment with new reporting relationships, and they modify the organization's strategies and approaches to meet changing demands. However, these changes take place within the context of the organization's existing framework; they involve solving problems or tinkering with or fine-tuning operations. Each effort builds on the existing work of the organization and occurs in relatively small increments. These changes are called *incremental*.[13]

On the other hand, managers increasingly are finding it necessary to make more fundamental and dramatic changes in their organizations. In cases such as these, the organization will not just be trying to adjust its relation to the environment; it also will be seeking

Organizational Change Management

Incremental change: change that occurs within the existing framework of the organization

Discontinuous change: change that seeks a whole new strategy or configuration for the organization

YOUR ORIENTATION TOWARD CHANGE

Choose the endings to the following questions that best represent your preferences.

1. Do you prefer _____
   a. doing a job that you are comfortable with and know well?
   b. doing a job that presents a new challenge every day?

2. Do you find change _____
   a. invigorating?
   b. stressful?

3. In terms of your career, do you think you are or will mostly be _____
   a. fixed in place?
   b. always moving?

4. Do you consider yourself _____
   a. mostly focused on the future?
   b. mostly focused on the present?

5. Would you prefer a job that _____
   a. is pretty much the same from day to day?
   b. changes constantly?

6. When change occurs, are you _____
   a. typically out in front leading the way?
   b. typically holding back and waiting to see what will happen?

7. Do you like to _____
   a. go with the flow?
   b. make things happen?

8. Do you tend to see _____
   a. the possibilities in a situation?
   b. the realities of a situation?

9. In terms of style, are you _____
   a. solid and mainstream?
   b. always on the cutting edge?

10. Are you _____
    a. a leader?
    b. a follower?

Total your scores by giving yourself one point for each "a" answer on questions 2, 4, 6, 8, and 10 and for each "b" answer on questions 1, 3, 5, 7, and 9. The total score represents your orientation toward change, with higher scores a more favorable orientation toward change. Discuss the results with others in your class. Does the result sound like you? Are there particular questions that you found troublesome? Does this scale really measure an orientation toward change, or is it just a trigger for discussion?

a whole new strategy or configuration. Changes of this type will involve a complete break with the past and a major reconstruction of every element of the organization's work. These changes are called *discontinuous*.[14]

Similarly, we might differentiate between **strategic change** and **grassroots change**.[15] Strategic change refers to efforts that are both broad range (typically organization-wide) and long term. Strategic changes are often developed in the course of a planning process that considers the mission, vision, and values of the organization; those forces acting on the organization from the environment; the strengths and weaknesses of the existing organization; desired future states or "scenarios of the future"; and tactics that might be employed to move the organization in the desired direction. These efforts often aim at broad cultural change. Grassroots changes, on the other hand, are those that take place at the local or street level and involve middle-level and supervisory-level managers as well as workers on the front line of the organization. These changes are concerned with implementing and sustaining the changes envisioned at the strategic level.

Another way to look at change in organizations is to consider the dynamic rhythms of organizational change: dramatic, systematic, and organic change.[16] Dramatic change is initiated in times of crisis, systematic change is slower and less ambitious (and is often promoted by staff groups and consultants), and organic change usually arises from the ranks without being formally managed. While each change considered separately can be chaotic, there is an advantage in creating a rhythm of change, where these three changes are functioning in a "dynamic symbiosis."[17]

Finally, there is disagreement about the scope of change. There is an alternative to the kind of dramatic—and often traumatic—large-scale cultural change initiatives that are often undertaken but generate few long-term positive results. Some advocate a more moderate approach that involves engaging the company's employees in looking for disconnects between how work is done—and how it could be done better. Similarly, some argue that instead of trying to change the entire culture of the organization at once, leaders and managers would be better advised to start with one or a very few projects and see how that brings change about or suggest alternative approaches to bring change about.[18]

Organizational Culture

Organizational Culture

One more contemporary way of understanding organizational change relies on a concept borrowed from anthropology—the concept of culture. Although anthropologists themselves disagree on the exact meaning of culture, the term generally is taken to embrace those norms, beliefs, and values expressed by members of a particular group and manifest in their typical behaviors and in the artifacts they produce. The term is used in a similar fashion in studies of management and organizations. The idea is that members of an organization share certain ideas about everything from the appearance of their offices, to the overall values they hold, to the basic assumptions they have about the work they do.

Edgar Schein (1985), whose early work on organizational culture was groundbreaking, actually distinguished among three levels of organizational culture.[19] First, there are *artifacts and creations* of the culture, the social and physical environment, things such as physical layout, technological preferences, typical language patterns, and the day-to-day operating routines that guide people's behavior. Second, there are the *values* of the organization, ideas about the way in which the organization *ought* to be. Presumably, if the

Strategic change: change efforts that are both broad range (typically organization-wide) and long term

Grassroots change: changes at lower levels of the organization that are concerned with implementing and sustaining the changes envisioned at the strategic level

values of the organization are fully accepted by the organization's members, then their behavior will reflect those values. But as Argyris and Schön[20] pointed out, many times certain values will be "espoused" by those in the organization but will not actually guide the behavior of members in real-life situations. Third, there are the *basic underlying assumptions* of the organization, those patterns of believing or acting that are taken for granted to the point where they are not even questioned. For example, someone from a Western culture might place an emphasis on problem solving, whereas someone from an Eastern culture might emphasize saving face. In either case, the belief is so basic that, although it affects behavior daily, it is not even a subject of conscious discussion. Schein (1985) ultimately took this latter category to be the core definition of culture: a pattern of basic assumptions—invented, discovered, or developed by a given group as it learns to cope with its problems—that has worked well enough to be considered valid and, therefore, to be taught to new members as the correct way to perceive, think, and feel in relation to those problems.[21]

In a somewhat more direct fashion, another writer outlined six elements of the notion of organizational culture on which he found general consensus:[22]

1. Organizational culture is the culture that exists in an organization; it is similar to national culture.

2. It is made up values, beliefs, assumptions, perceptions, behavioral norms, artifacts, and patterns of behavior.

3. It is often an unseen and unobservable force behind organizational activities.

4. It is a force and energy that moves organization members to act.

5. It is a unifying theme that provides meaning, direction, and mobilization for organization members.

6. It allows the organization to control the behavior of its members informally by setting norms.

In a competitive organizational culture, employees may feel pressured to check e-mail constantly, even at home. How do you think such a culture impacts the productivity of the company's employees? Do you think that many organizations would benefit from less e-mail rather than more?

The much-talked-about financial institution Goldman Sachs is known as a highly competitive organization. One of the company's chief accountants Sarah Smith says, "It's a 24/7 culture. When you're needed, you're here. And if you're needed and you're not answering your phone, you won't be needed very long."[23] Another former employee describes the culture, "completely money-obsessed. I was like a donkey driven forward by the biggest, juiciest carrot I could imagine. Money is the way you define your success."[24]

Another unique organizational culture that focuses on employee concerns and needs is that of the Atlanta-based consulting firm North Highland, which employs 250. The company prides itself at providing consultants who live where their clients are.[25] The company established a "no-fly zone" when CEO David Peterson grew tired of being constantly on the road and missing out on his family life; so he created a company to serve local clients.[26]

Peterson considers 50 miles to be the maximum distance people should have to travel for work. His company allows employees to balance their work life and home life and provides its clients with consultants who are part of their community.

Richard Tuck, cofounder and CEO of Lander International, a company based in El Cerrito, California, similarly encourages his employees to spend less time at work.[27]

When Jon Westberg, the company's executive recruiter, hit a performance slump and sought Tuck's advice; Tuck suggested that "maybe he was spending too much time at work that he needed to devote more time to his art."[28] Tuck wants his employees to have outside hobbies and commitments. He hates rules. As a result, the company's culture is loose, with an emphasis on "anything goes." Office manager Helen Winters notes, "I kept waiting for policies to be firmed up, but he just wouldn't do it."[29]

Elements of Organizational Culture

These different organizational cultures have different models of what is considered effective. At North Highland, work-life balance is key to effectiveness; at Lander's, the leader is supportive and almost spiritual; at Goldman's, the leader pushes for performance and outcomes. Let's apply the model of organizational culture described above to a particular organization, Medtronics. Remember that there are at least three elements of an organization's culture:[30]

Facebook's Innovative Culture

- First, there are *artifacts and creations* of the culture, the social and physical environment, things such as physical layout, technological preferences, typical language patterns, and the day-to-day operating routines that guide people's behavior.

- Second, there are the *values* of the organization, ideas about the way in which the organization *ought* to be. Presumably, if the values of the organization are fully accepted by the organization's members, then their behavior will reflect those values.

- Third, there are the *basic underlying assumptions* of the organization; those patterns of believing or acting that are taken for granted to the point where they are not even questioned.

Among the artifacts and creations of an organization are its rituals and ceremonies. Medtronic, the Minneapolis-based medical products organization, is a company with a ritual that clearly reflects its culture. Every December the company gives a holiday party and invites not only all its employees but also patients and their families. During the party, patients whose lives were saved because of Medtronic's various devices get up and thank the employees. "I remember going to my first holiday party, and someone asked me if I had brought my Kleenex. I assumed I'd be fine, but then these parents got up with their daughter who was alive because of our product. Even the surgeons who see this stuff all the time were crying,"[31] explains Art Collins, Medtronic's president.

The second component of culture includes the core values and beliefs shared by members of the organization about what is important and what is not. At Medtronic, every new employee is given a medallion inscribed with the mission statement: "to alleviate pain, restore health, and extend life." The organization makes sure its employees are reminded of these values. In time, these values become an integral component of the culture of the organization.

Finally, organizational culture also includes basic assumptions that are often unstated and hard to observe. These assumptions are the root of values and behaviors shared by organizational members and deal with general philosophical issues that are not always directly related to business. For example, the culture of Starbucks, the global coffee house, emphasizes fairness, not leaving anyone behind, and taking care of employees. This assumption about the importance of employees stems from the CEO's personal experiences as a child when his father got hurt, did not have insurance, and could not work, resulting in considerable hardship for his family.

Individual Behavior and Organizational Culture

Company Culture
at Zappos

Culture can have a strong influence on the behavior of organizational members, especially in times of change. But before we explore that issue, we should say a word about how organizational culture comes into being and is transmitted throughout organizations. Within organizations, many important aspects of a specific organization's culture are derived from the larger societal culture, specifically its standards and expectations concerning the role of business organizations in the social and economic systems. But in addition, the cultures of organizations are likely to be affected by their charters, by public sentiment concerning their work, and by the imprint of early and important leaders within the organizations. Whatever their derivation, the cultures of private organizations, like those of other organizations, are likely to be transmitted overtly to members through the processes of hiring, orientation, performance appraisal, and promotion as well as more subtly through conversations and communications concerning "the way things are done around here." The result may be organizations with widely varying norms, beliefs, and values. For example, some organizations place a high value on stability and permanence, whereas others emphasize change and innovation.

What might this image reveal to you about Zappos' organizational culture? Think especially about terms like fun, weirdness, and WOW! Do you think an organization with this culture can still get things done? Would you be comfortable working in such an environment?

With respect to organizational change, of course, the key idea is that the culture of an organization will shape the values and attitudes and, in turn, the *actions* of the organization's members. If this is the case, then changing the organization's culture may be a key step in changing the behavior of the organization's employees. For example, many organizations recently have sought, with considerable success, to create a "culture of innovation" in which members will discard their traditional aversion to risk and innovation in favor of experimentation and change. When asked about their new orientation, they might respond, "That's just the way we do things around here"—a sure indicator that new beliefs and assumptions have become fully embedded in the culture of the organization.

Various corporations have created statements that articulate the vision and values of the organization. These can help frame change in an organizational culture. For example, The Barry-Wehmiller Company has created a set of guiding principles of leadership as shown in Figure 15.2. Consideration of a set of principles was initiated by the company's CEO, Bob Chapman, but the process involved people throughout the organization. The result is an impressive statement of leadership guidelines.

There are some practical issues in achieving cultural change by focusing on behavior that can be approached, according to author Gary P. Latham, through a five-step process to behavior change.[32] The first step is establishing a superordinate goal, the purpose of which is "to capture the imagination, hence to galvanize people to take action."[33] The primary effect of the superordinate goal is affecting people's emotion (e.g., Martin Luther King: "I have a dream.")[34] The second phase is goal setting, establishing goals, which will make the superordinate goal concrete. Latham pointed out that the goal must be SMART: "specific, measurable, attainable, relevant, and have a time-frame."[35] The importance of the SMART goal for the organization is to "obtain goal commitment" by the employees.[36] The next two steps, ensuring integrity and accessibility of the managers in the organization, are especially important for overall performance and reaching goals as a result. Latham argued that leaders have to make sure that their words match the organizational superordinate and SMART goals. "Leaders need to take a look in the mirror to see whether their words are consistent with the superordinate and SMART goals."[37] And, he also pointed out that leaders' accessibility is key to achieving the goals successfully. "It is difficult to be an effective leader when you are inaccessible to the people who are on your team."[38]

Cultural Change

But at best an organization's culture is far from simple, and there are disagreements in the literature on organizational change about how successful managers can be in employing a cultural approach to change. Because the organization's culture is socially constituted (i.e., the result of a constant stream of interactions and negotiations among people at all levels), there might be actors scattered throughout the organization who are strong enough to resist the planned changes that management would like to see in the organization's culture. On the other hand, situations do occur in which managers can decisively influence the core beliefs and values of organizational members and, consequently, reorient the entire organization. When thinking about seeking cultural change, managers should at least recognize several possible limitations to this approach. First, cultural norms are deep-seated and people may be quite resistant to change. Second, successful changes in an organization's culture typically occur over a long period—5 to 15 years, according to some estimates.[39] Third, important ethical questions may arise as managers attempt to "manipulate" the norms and values of those in the organization, a question we will return to later in this chapter. Schein (1997) recognized the limitations of efforts to change culture in writing that managers seeking to change an organization's culture must "build on and evolve the culture one has rather than wishing for some dramatic changes or some other cultural forms."[40]

FIGURE 15.2 BARRY-WEHMILLER COMPANY'S GUIDING PRINCIPLES OF LEADERSHIP

Barry-Wehmiller

GUIDING PRINCIPLES OF LEADERSHIP

We measure success by the way we touch the lives of people.

A clear and compelling *vision*, embodied within a sustainable business model, which fosters personal growth

Leadership creates a dynamic environment that:
- Is based on *trust*
- Brings out and *celebrates* the best in each individual
- Allows for teams and individuals to have a *meaningful role*
- Inspires a sense of *pride*
- *Challenges* individuals and teams
- *Liberates* everyone to realize "true success"

Positive, insightful communication empowers individuals and teams along the journey.

Measurables allow individuals and teams to relate their contribution to the realization of the vision.

Treat people *superbly* and compensate them fairly.

Leaders are called to be visionaries, coaches, mentors, teachers, and students.

As your sphere of influence grows, so grows your responsibility for *stewardship* of the Guiding Principles.

We are committed to our employees' personal growth.

WE BUILD GREAT PEOPLE WHO DO EXTRAORDINARY THINGS

Spark Culture Clash

Corporate Culture

Heart of Change

Driving forces: those that support the direction of a proposed change

Restraining forces: those that oppose the direction of the proposed change

In any case, the cultural perspective provides important insights into the operation of complex organizations. And new cultures can clash with old cultures in dramatic ways, as illustrated in an extended public/private sector case study of the Washington State ferry system.[41] The ferry system began as a private family-owned business but eventually fell on hard times and was bought by the state of Washington and assigned to the highways department and eventually the U.S. Department of Transportation (DOT). During its early days, the culture of the ferry system was much like that of a large, extended, and quite happy family. People joked, socialized, and celebrated together. Their interactions were guided by friendship and family ties as much as by managerial systems and detailed accounting standards.

But the DOT prided itself on the strength of its management systems and eventually found it necessary to recommend "the establishment of a mission statement, development of means to measure the achievement of objectives consonant with the mission, and the creation of a performance monitoring and reporting system" as well as to move toward more automated technical systems.[42] Although the approaches the DOT put forth certainly were consistent with images of high-performing public organizations held by the larger culture, they clearly were at odds with the traditional culture of the ferry system, and indeed, there were grave difficulties brought about by the resulting clash of cultures. Certainly, the meanings that people hold, or those beliefs and values that are deeply embedded in their ideals and practices, constitute important sources of stability and resistance to change. But acknowledging their importance may cause managers to recognize the need to take culture into account in attempting to bring about organizational changes.

Approaches to Understanding Change

Classic Approaches to Managing Change

Most contemporary approaches to understanding organizational change have their roots in the early work of social psychologist Kurt Lewin. Lewin wrote, "Group life is never without change, merely differences in the amount and type of change exist."[43] Whether in an organization, a social group, or a family, there are both forces trying to bring about change and forces trying to resist change. To use a football analogy, at any given point in the game, the position of the ball on the field actually is the result of many plays by each team and many moves by individual players. There is an offensive team, whose players employ force to try to bring about change in the position of the ball, and there is a defensive team, whose members try to resist or restrict change. Although at any point prior to a new play the ball appears to be at rest, its resting place really is the balance of fiercely contending forces moving back and forth on the field.

Consider an organization moving to a new accounting system. The situation "on the field" at any time (with respect to this issue) is determined by some forces that seek to bring about change and others that resist or restrict change (see Figure 15.3). Lewin called these driving forces and restraining forces. For example, one force driving change might be the additional information that will become available if the new system is implemented. On the other hand, a restraining force might be that conversion to the new system will be costly. Similarly, another driving force might be that the new system will be easier to use. On the other hand, another restraining force might be that people understand the old system and are accustomed to using it. At any given point, the driving and restraining forces may appear to be in equilibrium. One way of using this understanding in real-life situations is to conduct a force field analysis—that is, listing in one column the driving forces at play in a particular change opportunity and in a second column the restraining forces. Once these are apparent, it might be easier to see what strategies, affecting what forces, are most likely to be successful.[44]

FIGURE 15.3　LEWIN'S FORCE FIELD

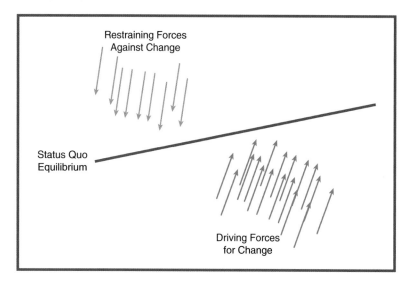

Restraining Forces
Against Change

Status Quo
Equilibrium

Driving Forces
for Change

For change to occur there must be a shift in the balance of forces at play on any given organizational "field." Either those forces propelling change must be increased or those forces restricting change must be lessened. (Interestingly, in many cases, the latter is easier to accomplish than the former.)

In either case, the first step is *unfreezing* (see Figure 15.4) the existing situation or shaking loose the current condition of equilibrium. For example, people must come to recognize the need for change and begin to loosen their normal resistance to change. In order words, people must be prepared for change, a step that is not often fully implemented in organizations.

The second step is the *change* itself. The new program—say, the new accounting system—is implemented, and the new knowledge and behaviors that are required to make it work are learned.

The third step is *refreezing* the situation. Here an effort is made to institutionalize the change, or make it part of the organization's routine way of operating, something that may be accomplished through training, encouragement, and new reward systems.

Organizational Learning

Another way of viewing organizational change, one closely related to and often overlapping with the cultural approach, is called organizational learning and is sometimes described as building a *learning organization*. Organizational learning starts with individual learning; organizations cannot really learn, but individuals within them can. Organizations clearly have an interest in encouraging individuals to learn as much as they can about their work, the social and economic context within which it occurs,

Getting Beyond
the "Like" Stage

Force field analysis: listing in one column the driving forces at play in a particular change opportunity and in a second column the restraining forces

Organizational learning: learning that builds on individual learning and permeates the organization as a way of doing business

FIGURE 15.4　STEPS IN THE CHANGE PROCESS

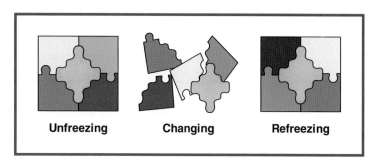

Unfreezing　　**Changing**　　**Refreezing**

CREATIVITY AND CHANGE   A CULTURE OF RESPONSIBILITY

Suzanne Fallender, Director of Corporate Social Responsibility, Strategy and Communications at Intel, was interviewed by Robert Denhardt of the University of Southern California in the Spring of 2013.

Q   How do you define Corporate Social Responsibility? And how long has Intel engaged in CSR?

A   I define CSR as a management approach—CSR is about looking at the full range of environmental, social, and governance impacts related to your business and effectively managing the risks and taking advantage of the opportunities that arise. Intel's history of CSR goes back to the company's founding. Intel co-founder Gordon Moore has long been a strong advocate of environmental stewardship, and he instilled a commitment to the environment that continues today. When I reflect on how Intel's commitment to and actions around CSR have evolved, I believe the main development has been one of integration. Particularly over the past five years—we have continued to embed CSR even further into the company's culture and governance structures. We have integrated CSR directly into our new vision and strategy, developed programs to engage our employees on CSR issues, and even linked a portion of every employee's compensation (from front line employees up to the CEO) to CSR factors.

Q   What are the factors that have gone into the most successful CSR efforts?

A   There are many different examples—at large and small companies. I think the keys to success are integration, collaboration, and scale and sustainability.

- *Integration:* Successful companies have taken steps to effectively integrate CSR into their business—it's not just done by a separate CSR department—they have engaged multiple parts of the business (such as supply chain, finance, IT) and have the support of senior management.

- *Collaboration:* On collaboration, success stories involve companies working with multiple partners (sometimes including other companies)—but forming partnerships with NGOs, governments, and development agencies to develop solutions that meet the needs of multiple stakeholders.

- *Scale and Sustainability:* Successful initiatives are ones that have a longer time horizon—they are not one-off projects or programs that are announced for a PR benefit. They have a plan for sustained investment and how the impact will be scaled.

Q   One important element of CSR is environmental sustainability. How would you describe Intel's performance in this area?

A   Intel's approach to environmental sustainability covers three main areas: reducing the impact of our manufacturing operations, improving the energy efficiency of our products, and applying our technology to help solve global challenges. In terms of products, we estimate that Intel technology will enable the billion PCs and servers installed between 2007 and 2014 to consume half the energy and deliver 17 times the computing capacity of the first billion PCs and servers (installed between 1980 and 2007).

Q   But CSR is more than environmental sustainability. How would you describe your other efforts to create a culture of social responsibility and community engagement?

A   In terms of social responsibility, Intel has also adopted a comprehensive approach to transforming educational access and quality through technology. We believe our approach benefits not only society but also our business since our future success rests on the availability of skilled workers, a healthy technology ecosystem, and knowledgeable customers.

and their own energies and ambitions. Although individual learning is essential, it is not enough. "An organization may be staffed by authentic, well-informed, capable, self-knowing, and self-developing individuals. But unless it takes steps to allow individual insights and perceptions to blossom outward into a greater whole, no true organizational learning may emerge."[45]

Contemporary approaches to organizational learning derive from several sources, but most notably early work on organizational learning, particularly the work of Chris Argyris and Donald Schön. In 1974, Argyris and Schön began by noting how the ideas or "theories" that people hold shape the way in which they actually behave. In terms of guiding action, a theory offers a set of guidelines for practice that will lead to the results the person desires. But there are different types of theories of action. For example, Argyris and Schön pointed to a distinction, which we already have noted, between **espoused theories** and **theories-in-use**.[46] An espoused theory is one to which we give conscious allegiance; it is the one we describe when people ask us what ideas govern our actions. But the theory that *actually* governs our actions is called the theory-in-use. Obviously, there may be differences between those ideas or approaches we espouse and those we actually follow. We might not do what we say; we might not "walk the walk."

In either case, there are two ways in which we can learn. We can first learn new strategies that will lead to our desired goals, whether those goals are objective and achievable (e.g., greater productivity) or more personal (e.g., achieving a more integrated personality). Or we can learn to change our goals. Learning new strategies is called **single-loop learning**; learning new goals is called **double-loop learning**. Both types of learning are required in organizations, although single-loop learning is by far the more common type. Where organizational members face routine or repetitive issues, and where the desired end states are clear, single-loop learning is appropriate. Where members face decisions that are more complex and "nonprogrammable," double-loop learning is more appropriate.

A closely related approach, called **systems theory**, emerged in the social and organizational sciences during the 1960s and 1970s after enjoying success in areas such as biology and cybernetics before that. In all cases, the basic systems model showed the system (whether biological, political, or organizational) first receiving various inputs from the environment either in the form of resources (e.g., human or financial resources, information, technology) or demands (e.g., legal or political mandates, customer or citizen expectations). These inputs pass through the system and are converted into outputs (e.g., products, services, regulations, ideas). These outputs flow into the environment, where they may affect customers, clients, citizens, families, other organizations, or society in general. The response of these individuals and groups to the organization's outputs becomes feedback to the organization (e.g., requesting more or fewer services, requesting more or fewer regulations). The system then takes this information into account along with other new inputs, and the cycle begins again (Figure 15.5).

Basically, systems theory (as applied to an organization) emphasizes (1) the relation between an organization and its environment and (2) the way all the elements of an organization connect to one another. In this way, systems theory guards against our natural tendency to see immediate problems as being independent of the setting in which they reside. The systems approach can be applied to a wide variety of groups, including organizations, subunits, or sets of organizations, any one of which can be analyzed in

Learning
Organization

Espoused theories: theories to which we give conscious allegiance; the ones we describe when people ask us what ideas govern our actions

Theories-in-use: theories that actually govern our actions

Single-loop learning: learning new strategies

Double-loop learning: learning new goals

Systems theory: an approach to understanding human, physical, or biological processes involving an examination of inputs, conversion processes, outputs, and feedback

FIGURE 15.5 THE SYSTEM MODEL

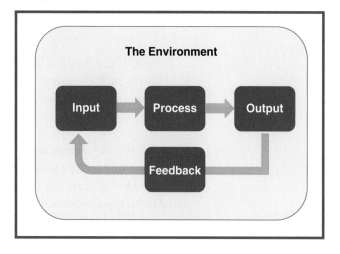

terms of the flow of inputs, the processing of these, and the production of goods or services that are the outputs of the system. This approach also helps to clarify the relationships between the focal organization and actors in the environment as well as the relationships among various organizational components such as technology, behavior, and culture. The systems approach is therefore seen as a way of ensuring attention to the big picture.

SELF-ASSESSMENT 15.2

DISCUSSING YOUR EXPERIENCES WITH CHANGE

Be prepared to talk about your answers to the following questions. Think of a specific change, preferably in a group or organization of which you are a part; if necessary, it can be a change in your personal life. How did the change come about? Who were the people that triggered the change? How did they bring the change forward? What did they do? What did they say? Did they force the change on others, or were others involved in the change and agreeable to it? How did others in the group or organization react to the proposed change? Which members of the group or organization were most resistant to the change? What were the reasons for their resistance? How was their resistance overcome? How did you feel about the change? Were you an early convert to the new way of operating or one of the last to give in? What were the reasons for your conversion or resistance? Was your reaction in this case typical of your reactions in situations involving change? If the change has been in place for a while, how is it working out? If you had been the one managing the change process, how would you have done things differently?

Large Systems Change

More recently, Peter Senge and his colleagues[47] have explored large systems change from the perspective of learning and what they call *presence*.[48] The notion is that change doesn't come about through the accumulation of individually controlled changes, but systemically through a focus on the whole. For example, no single individual or group could have created global warming, yet globalized institutions have caused a worldwide phenomenon seemingly beyond the reach of individuals to affect in any significant way. If this is the case, then it makes more sense to speak of change not in terms of what one individual or leader can do, but rather how the species can learn and grow. But there are constraints in how this growth can occur.

> As long as our thinking is governed by habit—notably by industrial, "machine age" concepts such as control, predictability, standardization, "faster is better"—we will continue to re-create institutions as they have been, despite their disharmony with the larger world, and the need of all living systems to evolve.[49]

Deeper levels of learning can occur, Senge and others argue, as we develop the capacity to increase our awareness of the whole and to develop actions that are part of creating a future. The core capacity to create large systems change comes from within and is captured in the term *presence*. Presence starts with being immediately and fully aware of one's circumstances, but there is more:

We began to appreciate presence as deep listening, of being open beyond one's pre-conceptions and historical ways of making sense. We came to see the importance of letting go of old identities and the need to control and . . . making choices to serve the evolution of life.[50]

In this way, how we engage the world shifts and large-scale change is possible. But change comes first from within, with how we see ourselves and our relation to the larger community—the larger world.

Otto Scharmer has elaborated on this perspective in *Theory U*. Scharmer, using the notion of presence as a way of understanding learning and change, argues that the key task of anyone bringing about change is to enable others to see the whole. "The primary job of leadership . . . is to enhance the individual and systemic capacity to see, to deeply attend to the reality that people face and enact. Thus the leader's real work is to help people discover 'the power of seeing and seeing together.'"[51] The key ingredient in successful change is to shift the way in which people see the field in which they operate, moving away from the world of habits and routines to enter contexts that matter, then connecting with the source of the highest future possibilities and bringing them into the present. Only at this point can we begin to undertake actions that will allow us to connect with the future and the new institutional ecologies. Scharmer described seven inflection points that are arrayed in a U pattern: (1) downloading, (2) saying, (3) sensing, (4) presence, (5) crystallizing, (6) prototyping, and (7) performing. In order to make transformative change possible, we must move through a threshold at the bottom of the U. As we move through this threshold, we encounter our best future selves, either as individuals or as a collective. To do so we need not only an open mind to envision new possibilities, but an open heart to embrace them, and an open will to move them forward.

Others have explored a similar approach to large systems change using the concept of emergence.[52] They argue that large systems change rarely comes about as a result of top-down or control strategies and is rarely the result of one person or one dominant group imposing their will on others. Instead, change in social organizations and social systems follows a pattern similar to that of change in nature, where several small actions come together to create a new dynamic.

Retire Massey's Legacy

Change begins when active and thoughtful people start to connect with one another in networks where knowledge and practices can be exchanged and improved upon. (There is a tendency to think of networks in terms of how they might be used or controlled; however, much more important, networks enable creative communication in the generation of innovative ideas.) At some point, networks evolve into communities of practice (CoPs). In communities of practice, individuals realize the benefit that they and others can receive through their interaction and make a commitment "to share what they know, to support one another, and to intentionally create new knowledge for their field of practice."[53]

From these communities of practice, new patterns of thinking and new systems of influence can emerge. These systems represent a fundamental departure from previous patterns; they actually come into being through the interaction of individuals with others, representing something new and fundamentally different. "When separate, local efforts connect with each other as networks, then strengthen as communities of practice, suddenly and surprisingly a new system emerges at a greater level of scale. This system of influence possesses qualities and capacities that were unknown in the individuals."[54] This is the process of emergence.

Emergence: the idea that change in social systems follows a pattern similar to that of change in nature, where several small actions come together to create a new dynamic

Parmalat SpA, a multinational Italian corporation, has first hand experienced the impact of change triggered by both internal and external forces. The company was the leading producer of ultra high temperature milk (UHT), dairy products, and other food products when it collapsed in 2003 and became Europe's biggest bankruptcy and one of its most talked about business scandals, earning it the dubious nickname of Europe's Enron.[55] With over 150 factories and close to 40,000 employees at its peak, the company sponsored many sporting and racing events all over Europe, including Formula One races.

While pursuing an aggressive global expansion in the 1990s, Parmalat started posting losses in 2001 under the financial leadership of CFO Fausto Tonna who was forced to resign while planning a 500-million-euro bond issue. After the discovery of suspicious financial deals and the statement in 2003 by the Bank of America that the company was inaccurately reporting its holdings, several of its officers were forced to resign. The company set up several shell companies to generate fake profits that executives supported with forged documents. The CEO, Calisto Tanzi, who initially claimed no knowledge of the shady dealings, finally admitted that the company could not account for 8 billion euros and that he had siphoned 500 million euros to family-owned accounts.[56] He was convicted of fraud and money laundering and convicted to an 18-year sentence in 2010.[57]

The Parmalat financial scandal has involved lawsuits and counter-lawsuits and accusations and counter-accusations from companies and institutions from all over the world including Bank of America Citigroup, Morgan Stanley, Deutsche Bank, Credit Suisse First Boston, companies in the Cayman Islands, the U.S. District Court in Manhattan, British pension funds, and Italian courts. The close to 10-year-long litigations have seen the collapse of companies, disgrace of one of Italy's most prominent industrial families, and continued questions about the complex management of global companies. In addition to simple greed, some attribute the false reporting and creation of shell companies to market pressure for profits.

While Parmalat, now owned by the French dairy group Lactalis, is showing profit and strong performance in many countries, the case continues to draw attention with some suggesting that the company and Italy's corporate structure are trying to maintain a status quo to prevent changes in governance and regulations.[58]

Newer Approaches to Bringing About Change

Change Through Management Action or Reorganization

Historically, most organizational changes have been brought about by unilateral action on the part of leaders and managers, and indeed, many organizational changes continue to occur in this way. Certainly such an approach is consistent with centuries of organizational practice, especially the hierarchical practices of traditional military and industrial organizations. In this model, orders contained in memos, policy declarations, or verbal commands flow downward through the hierarchy, with the expectation that they will be obeyed. Change of this type tends to be formal, impersonal, and task oriented. Although contemporary thinking has cast doubt on this approach to organizational change in favor of approaches that are characterized by openness, involvement, and shared decision making, many managers continue to use this approach, especially in situations where tasks are somewhat routine, highly structured, and easily programmed.

Many leaders and managers also seek to bring about changes in their organizations through restructuring or redesigning their organizations' structures, their basic work processes, and their core systems. Such efforts are deeply rooted in the history of organizational change; reorganization is a familiar refrain in most organizations. But there are more contemporary approaches that suggest greater flexibility on the one hand and greater attention to detail on the other. In either case, organizational structure—the arrangement of the organization's human resources so as to best meet its objectives—is considered closely connected to the behavior of individuals within the organization. Presumably, all else being equal, people operating under one structure will behave differently from those operating under a different structure. Moreover, many believe that changes in the basic strategy of the organization must be reflected in the structure of the organization.

Those interested in structural change must ask other questions such as the following. Who will report to whom? What is the appropriate span of control (i.e., how many people can reasonably report to one manager)? How will the assignment of duties and responsibilities for each task or functional area be determined? How will the various units of the organization interact with one another? In any case, long-term structural change must be attentive to scale (the change affects all or most of the organization), magnitude (it involves significant alterations of the status quo), duration (it lasts for months, if not years), and strategic importance.[59]

Most managers seeking structural change even today answer these questions merely on the basis of the advice of other practitioners and on sheer intuition. But recently scholars and practitioners have begun to investigate the question of organizational structure more systematically and have identified a much wider range of structural possibilities. For example, a distinction sometimes is made between **mechanistic** and **organic structures**. Mechanistic structures are highly formalized, specialized, standardized, and centralized. They rely primarily on traditional top-down hierarchical authority. Organic structures, on the other hand, emphasize horizontal rather than vertical relationships and are much "looser"—more flexible, adaptable, and responsive. Such organizations, which are becoming more and more common, are especially well suited to dealing with rapidly changing environments and to promoting change and innovation.

There are a variety of other organizational approaches that are being tried today as organizations seek greater flexibility and adaptiveness. Many organizations are becoming flatter—that is, having fewer levels from top to bottom. Others are seeking to overlay the traditional organizational structure with self-managed work teams or other such groups that are empowered to come up with solutions to organizational problems independent of their place in the organizational hierarchy. As one example, the *matrix* organization superimposes a project structure on a traditional functional structure, in some cases establishing permanent project teams. John Kotter suggests another approach, which he calls a dual operating system: "a management-driven hierarchy working in concert with a strategy network."[60] The idea here is that the traditional hierarchy can maintain the core business while an innovative group leads the change process.

Many managers believe that they can come up with plans for reorganization by locking themselves in their offices and experimenting with assorted organizational charts drawn on their walls. Unfortunately, that approach often spells disaster. More recent explorations of how to bring about organizational change through organizational redesign recognize the greater complexity of the issue. That is, the degree to which the organization's

Mechanistic structures: structures that are highly formalized, specialized, standardized, and centralized

Organic structures: structures that emphasize horizontal rather than vertical relationships and are much more flexible, adaptable, and responsive

strategy, its work processes, its people (and their capabilities), its structure, and its culture are aligned will determine the organization's effectiveness (Nadler and Tushman).[61] The key is to engage in a careful and systematic analysis of these various components with an eye toward their *congruence*.

Interestingly, some have argued that the design of organizational arrangements should not be limited to questions of organizational structure—those decisions reflected in that standard organizational chart. Rather, there are three categories:[62]

1. Structures (the formal patterns of relationships between groups and individuals)

2. Processes (specifically designed sequences of steps, activities, and operational methods)

3. Systems (applications of either physical or social technologies that enable the performance of work such as human resources systems or information systems)

Despite these advancements, we should note that many recent writers have called into question changes in the organizational structure as a way to improve performance. They argue that organizational communication and performance management no longer depend heavily on the organizational hierarchy. They emphasize that new technologies (e-mail, voice mail, text messages) make communications across levels much easier. They further point out that the increasing knowledge and competitiveness of the employees together with project-by-project evaluations and individual project consolidation make less significant the levels in the organizational hierarchy.[63] They suggest focusing on "non-structural issues such as *people, process,* and *rewards*" in order to achieve flexibility in the organization.[64] "Flexibility is trumping structure as the governing principle behind organization design."[65]

Change Through Organization Development

Another approach to organizational change that has received widespread attention and application over the past several decades is organization development (OD). OD is based on science and is data-driven. It further focuses on people and processes and improving the system, not just specific and separate parts of organizations. Finally, OD often requires facilitation from outside the organization. In a classic portrayal of the interventionist's role in OD, Argyris[66] suggested the importance of having solutions generated from within the organization rather than imposed from outside of the organization. In keeping with this approach, he recommended that the consultant's role be to generate valid and useful information, to promote free and informed choice on the part of the client group, and to help build internal commitment to the choice that is made. Argyris explained each point as follows.

Past, Present, and Future

What Would You Do?

▶ As head of the marketing department in a large entertainment company, you recognize that your efforts are failing to "get more bodies in the seats." Your job is on the line unless things change quickly. Your first thought is to reorganize the department. What would you do?

- *Valid and useful information.* "Valid information is that which describes the factors, plus their interrelationships, that create the problem for the client system."[67] Such information not only must be valid but also the client group must be able to use it to change the system.

- *Free choice.* "Free choice places the focus of decision making in the client system. . . . Through free choice, the clients can maintain the autonomy of their system."[68]

- *Internal commitment.* "Internal commitment means the course of action or choice that has been internalized by each member so that he experiences a high degree of ownership and has a feeling of responsibility about the choice and its implications."[69]

Where the OD consultant aids the client system in exploring problems and in designing solutions to those problems, the consultant is, in this view, largely neutral with respect to the solutions chosen so long as the group is committed to those solutions. Figure 15.6 presents the major objectives of OD.

Future of
Organization
Development

FIGURE 15.6 ORGANIZATIONAL DEVELOPMENT PRINCIPLES

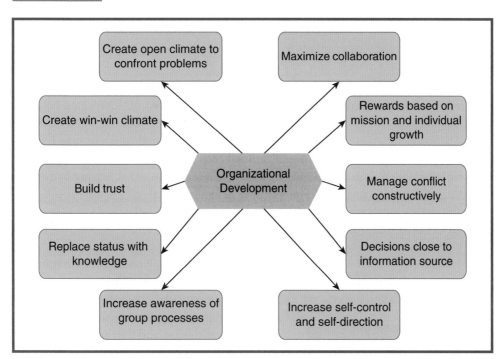

Whatever their philosophies, OD practitioners typically employ a variety of strategies and techniques to help facilitate organizational change. These include the following.

T-groups. The earliest (and still most controversial) OD interventions evolved from the T-group (with *T* standing for *training*) or sensitivity group movement of the 1960s. T-groups involve 10 to 12 members and a facilitator brought together for an extended period in an unstructured group situation where the group must create its own agenda, its own norms and expectations, and its own models for appropriate behavior. Advocates of T-group training suggest that such training can increase members' sensitivity to and competence in dealing with behavioral issues, their understanding of group and intergroup dynamics, and their skills in dealing with uncertainty and ambiguity.

Process consultation. As mentioned earlier, process consultation is concerned with helping a client or client group understand more clearly and act on those process issues that arise in organizational settings. These process issues include but are not limited to communications, the roles and functions of group members, group problem solving and decision making, the development and maintenance of group norms and expectations, and the roles of leadership, power, and authority in groups and organizations.

Third-party interventions. Conflict or competition occasionally arises in groups and organizations. Third-party interventions are designed to bring the parties together in the presence of a facilitator to identify problems and begin to develop ways of dealing with them in a constructive way, often reaching solutions that are consistent with the basic interests of both parties to the conflict.

Survey feedback. Perhaps the most widely used OD technique, survey feedback involves the consultant collecting data from a broad cross-section of the organization (or its entire population) through questionnaires, interviews, or focus groups and then analyzing the resulting data and feeding back the data to the members so that they can work together to interpret the information and design corrective actions. Typically, members of the organization hold a great deal more information about the organization and its problems than is apparent in their day-to-day interactions. Having such information collected and presented to them often helps members to assume ownership not only of existing problems but for their solutions as well.

Quality of work life. Traditionally, quality of work life programs alternated between improving the social and psychological conditions of work for individuals and involving lower-level participants in organizational decision making, both of which seem to contribute at least indirectly to enhanced organizational performance.[70] Among the approaches that might be undertaken in a quality of work life intervention are creating flatter and leaner organizational structures, developing job designs that provide employees with high levels of discretion and involve them in a variety of tasks, and opening communications throughout the organizations.

Team building. Much of the work of the modern organization is done in groups or teams, so it is not surprising that OD practitioners have been especially attentive to building effective teams. Again, a facilitator may work with a specific team to identify elements of individual behavior and group dynamics that might impede the group's functioning and then to develop strategies for overcoming those problems. The content of such sessions probably will include attention to the purpose of the group, how comfortable members are with one another, how open the pattern of communication within the group is, how various members play different and important roles in the group, and how leadership in the group is shared among members.[71]

Change Through Appreciative Inquiry

A more recent variant of the organization development approach is called *appreciative inquiry,* sometimes abbreviated AI (Table 15.1).[72] This approach, consistent with the positive organizational behavior movement, focuses on emphasizing the strengths in an organization rather than focusing on weaknesses or "deficits." Proponents of this approach feel that traditional approaches to change management place too much emphasis on the weaknesses of the

A GE Capital Solutions employee (*right*) rolls dough for an hors d'oeuvres that he and his team are making for a team-building cooking class. Note the expressions of the participants, from serious to all smiles. What do you think of this approach to building teamwork and team effectiveness?

organization and on solving problems, and not enough on building upon positive things that are happening in an organization. Appreciative Inquiry seeks to reverse this process and emphasize the organization's strengths in meeting the needs of customers and stakeholders, building resilience and adaptive management, enhancing revenue and productivity, and fully engaging those throughout the organization. "Appreciative Inquiry is the cooperative, co-evolutionary search for the best in people, their organizations, and the world around them. It involves systematic discovery of what gives life to an organization or community when it is most effective and most capable in economic, ecological, and human terms."[73]

TABLE 15.1 THE PHASES OF APPRECIATIVE INQUIRY

Phase	Description
Discovery	Mobilize the whole system by engaging all stakeholders in the articulation of strengths and best practices. It entails identifying "the best of what has been and what is."
Dream	Create a clear results-oriented vision in relation to discovered potential and in relation to questions of higher purpose, such as, "What is the world calling us to become?"
Design	Create possibility propositions of the ideal organization, articulating an organization design that people feel is capable of drawing upon and magnifying the positive core to realize the newly expressed dream.
Destiny	Strengthen the affirmative capability of the whole system, enabling it to build and sustain momentum for ongoing positive change and high performance.

Appreciative Inquiry creates conversations within an organization about what the organization does best and how it might build on its successes to better meet the future. It focuses on key organizational issues, not from the perspective of what is wrong, but from the perspective of what the organization is doing right. This enables members of the organization to share best practices (sometimes called the "positive core") and to develop a shared commitment to excellence across the board. This new knowledge and commitment is then linked to the strategic direction of the organization. Underlying this approach is a belief that positive organizational change requires positive affect and social bonding, and that these features are prerequisites for generative or emergent change.

Angela Blanchard is president and CEO of Neighborhood Center, Inc., in Houston. Among her many projects is Promise Community Schools, which have been especially recognized for raising levels of student achievement while at the same time maintaining fiscal integrity. At the Promise Schools, students are lifelong learners—for good.

Steps in Organizational Transformations

Managers often are called on to bring about modest change in their agencies. But leaders are called on to bring about large-scale transformations. Angela Blanchard, CEO of Houston-based Neighborhood Centers, points out the paradoxical nature of the change

CREATIVITY AND CHANGE   HYUNDAI SOARS

John Krafcik, CEO of Hyundai Motor America, has steered his company through an amazing period of growth since his appointment in 2008. But still he can't seem to get free of a story from the early 1990s when he was a middle level executive at Ford Motor Company. He was barreling down Interstate 94 near Detroit in his Ford Taurus SHO, when Bob Lutz, the leader of Chrysler, went by him in a Dodge Spirit R/T. Krafcik stepped on the gas and he and Lutz engaged in a triple-digit race. They passed each other several times, which Krafcik later described as "ridiculous." But, he added, "I hate being passed."[74] And, guess what, today nobody is passing Hyundai.

When Krafcik joined the company in 2004 in a product planning role, Hyundai cars were unattractive and unreliable. They were considered a joke. Indeed, Jay Leno once said that you could double the Hyundai's value by filling up with gas. But since that time Hyundai has made remarkable strides.[75] Sales are up more than 60% since 2008, and quality has improved dramatically. J. D. Power, the automobile quality rating company, measures the number of reported problems per hundred vehicles in the first 90 days of ownership. In 2001 Hyundai was 32nd out of 37 manufacturers. In 2011, they were 10th. On other measures of quality, Hyundai has now passed Toyota as the highest ranked mass-market automobile and stands behind only Lexus, Porsche, and Cadillac.

There is no question that Hyundai has the hot hand in the industry today. While the rest of the auto industry was in free-fall in 2009, off more than 20%, Hyundai's sales were up 8% and it moved past Ford to become the number four car maker in the world.[76] That same year, the Hyundai Genesis was named the North American Car of the Year.

Under Krafcik's leadership, Hyundai is being transformed from a low-quality, low-reliability brand, to a high-quality, high-reliability brand. In addition, Hyundai now boasts much sharper designs in contrast to other car manufacturers that treat midrange cars as comfortable boxes. Hyundai has also moved dramatically into the luxury car market, with a new entry called the Equus. If you want to test drive an Equus, the dealer will bring the car to your home; if you buy an Equus, you will find the owner's manual preloaded on a free iPad. Again, this is a far cry from the company's reputation of a dozen years ago.

In addition to improvements in the quality and reliability of its cars, Hyundai has developed several clever marketing ploys. First, the company offered America's Best Warranty, a 10-year, 100,000-mile powertrain warranty, which was huge for the company, as it produced about 90,000 units per year in the late 1990s and moved to 300,000 to 400,000 within 4 or 5 years. When asked whether the warranty was a "bet the company" move, Krafcik replied "it was an absolute bet the company move. If we had gotten that one wrong then the company would have failed. And rather quickly, too, as the warranty expense and exposure are significant when you're taking a bath that big."[77] As the economic downturn threatened, and people were worried about unemployment, Hyundai offered people the opportunity to return their new car risk free if they lost their jobs. (Incidentally, Hyundai announced this program in a blitz of nine Super Bowl ads narrated by actor Jeff Bridges.)

Krafcik has been preaching a message of quality and trust since he arrived at Hyundai. Hyundai is now a hyper aggressive company, marked by ambition and lofty goals. Whereas other companies, including other car manufacturers, set targets that they are confident of achieving, Krafcik prefers to set bold targets, and then see if they can be reached. The idea is that bold targets drive great things. According to Krafcik, "(It) stretches your boundaries, and your mind and your team in ways that you wouldn't otherwise have stretched and achieved." When asked about his own management style, Krafcik answered, "My job is to set some aspirational targets and continually communicate those targets. I believe in repetition of message."[78]

process: "You must move through this chaotic, fast-changing world with an eye for an opportunity—focusing on what works and what is strong, using what's available to build something better, faster, more effective. It is not about choosing to be either flexible or consistent; it's about being flexible and consistent at the same time."[79] We already have examined some of the approaches and strategies that managers might employ in specific situations, but we also should ask how leaders might bring about system-wide improvements in quality and productivity in their organizations.

What Do You Think?

▶ Some efforts at organizational change focus on structure, others on behavior. Which makes the most sense to you? Can you have one without the other?

Based on a series of case studies, Denhardt and Denhardt[80] developed a model of leadership for change that posits a series of five steps that those wishing to successfully bring about change in their companies must undertake. Managers hoping to lead change must

1. Assess the organizations' environment and ascertain the need for change

2. Plan for change both strategically and pragmatically

3. Build support for the change process both through conversation and through modeling the change process in the managers' own behavior

4. Implement specific changes while at the same time encouraging a broader positive attitude toward change and innovation

5. Institutionalize the changes

Successful Change Management

Cutting across these issues, Denhardt and Denhardt also pointed out the importance of the leaders' own learning capacities, especially with respect to knowing themselves and their values, knowing their organization's capacities, and understanding external constituencies or stakeholders. Finally, the form of leadership these leaders exhibited differs significantly from the traditional top-down, internally focused approach frequently employed. It is more open, free-flowing, engaging, and collaborative.

Similarly, Nadler and colleagues[81] suggested five phases in the change process.

1. *Diagnosis.* This first phase is a thoughtful assessment of the current state—its strengths, weaknesses, and goals. Diagnosis should not be complex or cumbersome; rather its primary purpose is to identify the resources available for developing the new organization. Therefore, the focus is on clarity, simplicity, and communicability.

2. *Clarification and coalition building.* The objectives during this phase are to refine and clarify the vision of the future state and to recruit key change agents and interventions. Here activity picks up; staff members are involved in articulating the future state and describing the specific changes to take place.

3. *Action.* The major changes are launched, and the organizational identity and architecture are communicated. At the end of this phase, the major pillars of the new organization should be in place.

4. *Consolidation and refinement.* During this phase, there are several activities ranging from assessment and checking to moving people who are not working out. The key output at the end of this phase is the broad-based implementation and acceptance of change.

5. *Sustainability.* During this phase, the challenge is to reflect on how the organization is working and what refinements, if any, are required to achieve the original design intent. Typically, the executive team collects data and uses them to evaluate the new organization's strengths and weaknesses. In fact, one of the outputs of this phase might be to launch incremental change or refinements to the now current state. The purpose is to build the new organization into a high-performance mode.

John Kotter's classic work *Leading Change* added an interesting dimension to the transformational process, suggesting that too much complacency is the death knell of organizational change. He argued that leaders often overestimate their own influence in organizations and underestimate how difficult it is to get people to change. According to Kotter, "Without a sense of urgency, people won't give that extra effort that is often essential."[82] He even recommended that managers create crises by allowing financial losses to occur or allowing errors to blow up instead of being corrected. Although such tactics seem questionable, they at least emphasize Kotter's recommendation that managers begin the change process by creating (or at least communicating) a sense of urgency.

Change Management Failure

The Ethics of Managing Change

Although many consider management to be a fairly technical endeavor, there are important value questions that affect almost everything that leaders and managers do. Obviously, most efforts at organizational change involve attempts to maximize efficiency, effectiveness, and productivity in the organization. But these values are the values of those at the top and might not necessarily be those of employees. For this reason, most organizational changes require changing the value system of the organization and its members in some way. "It has become received wisdom that high levels of commitment and performance require employees to espouse values that are aligned with the managerial vision."[83] In this view, the question becomes one of how the leader or manager can persuade, entice, or co-opt others into following his or her vision of the organization and its future.

Payday Lenders

Some say that most organizational change efforts actually serve to increase the power of those at the top relative to others in the organization.[84] This occurs for several reasons.

First, planned change, especially strategic change, typically is initiated by top management and implicitly bears the message that top management not only is in control but also has a right to be in control.

Second, as we have discussed, planned change creates uncertainty and ambiguity in the organization. Under these conditions, employees might seek stability through conformity to the wishes and desires of those who appear to be in charge.

Third, efforts at organizational change involve management defining a new reality for the organization's members. "It reaffirms the right of management to define the 'order' of the organization."[85]

Obviously, at some point, change can become coercion, and influence can become manipulation. Being aware of some of the potential ethical dilemmas that are inherent in management and especially organizational change can help the manager to be more sensitive to the concerns of others in the organization and to be more likely to act in a consistently ethical manner. There are two areas that deserve our attention. First, who determines the need for change, the intended outcomes, and the organization's values? Second, how can leaders and managers bring about change in a way that is both effective and ethical?

The first question—who determines the need for change—may be addressed by thinking through the various obligations that managers have. Obviously, a manager who pursues organizational change for his or her own self-interest would be acting in an unethical manner. We typically assume that by involving ourselves in organizations, we give up some of our decision-making autonomy. But we also recognize that there are limits on the extent to which those in positions of power and authority can impose their will on us.

Resistance
to Change

This goes to the second question—how managers can bring about change in a way that is both effective and ethical. We can begin to address this issue by noting when leaders' or managers' activities would be unethical. For example, we generally would label as unethical actions that would coerce employees into certain behaviors. "Coercion takes place when one person or group forces another person or group to act or refrain from acting under threat of severe deprivation," such as the loss of one's life, job, or well-being.[86] Obviously, we would find overt acts of coercion to be objectionable, but in fact coercion is not always overt.

Again, although most contemporary approaches to change favor openness and involvement, there still are situations in which employees are told essentially to "shape up or ship out." Whether these actions are unethical is perhaps only possible to judge within the context of particular activities, but they certainly raise not just technical issues but ethical ones as well. (We should, of course, point out that in addition to the ethical question that coercion raises, in the long run, coercion is not likely to be effective anyway. At a minimum, it generates resentment, but beyond that it can lead to strikes, employee turnover, or even sabotage.)

Many of the same issues that we associate with coercion also can be raised with respect to manipulation. Although manipulation is a somewhat vaguer concept, it generally is taken to mean a type of interpersonal influence in which the manipulator intentionally deceives the target. "Manipulation operates by robbing the victim of autonomy . . . for the sole purpose of advancing the perpetrator's objective."[87] The results are actions that are not freely undertaken.

We can easily think of examples of manipulation in organizations—fooling someone into doing something by the use of flattery or lies, playing on the emotions of someone to get one's own way, making the target think that the agent's way was his or her own idea, and so on. In any case, as with coercion, manipulative tactics that involve deception, threats, fear, secrecy, and dishonesty should be considered unethical. As with coercion, there may be practical negative consequences as well in that manipulation is likely to breed anger, fear, resentment, and hostility.

The question of autonomy leads to a final consideration—that organizational change efforts can become dehumanizing and therefore ethically questionable. Basically, this argument holds that efforts at organizational change that suppress human development or limit an individual's pursuit of meaning and autonomy. Many, of course, have argued that modern organizations, by their very nature, have tendencies toward dehumanization. Individual members of the organization are not valued per se but only as means to given ends. The individual is viewed in an instrumental fashion—valued only as a contributor to the organization's objectives. As with coercion and manipulation, dehumanization raises not only important ethical issues but also practical ones—dissatisfaction, lack of innovation, groupthink, and the creation of an overly conformist culture in which productive conflict cannot be found.

Reviewing the ethics of organizational behavior leads us to ask how managers can bring about change while still maintaining a sense of responsibility and whether efforts at organizational change can be carried out in a way that avoids coercion, manipulation, or dehumanization. In either case, an appropriate response is to suggest that doing those things that promote the autonomy and independent involvement of individual employees provides the best possible ethical response. Indeed, one of the most significant ethical issues facing leaders and managers is how they can fully involve all of those individuals both within and outside of the organization who should play a role in decisions concerning the work of the organization.[88]

► Summary and Applications for Managers

The following guidelines for action may help you to use the information contained in this chapter in your day-to-day work as a leader or manager:

1. *Expect resistance.* If you are seeking to lead change, consider carefully the emotional and psychological components of resistance to change, both your own and those of others. People may oppose change for rational and objective reasons, but resistance also may indicate the play of emotional and psychological forces. People generally are more comfortable with patterns of behavior that are familiar to them. Changing those patterns requires a psychological adaptation, which often is quite difficult. In part, people must become accustomed to the new situation; in part, they must learn to accommodate the loss of what they had before. In either case, they need time to work through the important issues that often accompany change.

2. *Communicate often.* If you are seeking to lead change, try to clarify and communicate throughout the organization the problems associated with the current way of operating and what benefits might accrue if you tried something else. When people operate in one way for a long period of time, they come to think that is the only way of operating. That is why people justify keeping things as they are by saying, "We've always done it that way." That might be true, but there also might be other ways of operating that would be far more effective.

3. *If you are seeking to lead change, try to involve people throughout the organization in the change process.* People are more likely to accept changes if they fully understand what is going on and if they feel a sense of "ownership" of the changes that are being made. Even more important, in most cases, people who are closest to the actual work and do it on a day-to-day basis know best how to improve it. For this reason, involving a wide range of people in the change process is likely to yield better ideas for how to improve the system.

4. *Think about the forces that are driving change as well as those that are resisting change.* A careful analysis of these factors often will indicate ways in which change can be introduced more effectively. Be especially careful to consider not just how to increase the pressure to change but also—and often even more important—how to reduce resistance to change. Be sure to match your approach to change—whether OD or Six Sigma or so forth—to the particular environment in which the changes will occur.

5. *Consider the culture of the organization.* Understanding the existing norms, beliefs, and values of those in the organization is an important first step in bringing about change. Cultural attributes typically are deep-seated in any organization (or any culture) and will represent substantial forces restraining change. On the other hand, by exposing the existing norms of the organization and by carefully developing a new statement of the organization's vision and values (hopefully with broad participation from those in the organization), you might be able to set a course for a new culture. Just remember that it will take a long time before any new culture becomes fully accepted as part of the very fabric of the organization.

6. *Listen, listen, listen.* The first step in bringing about change is to fully understand the organization and its stakeholders. Take time to listen to employees, customers, and other constituent groups and those in various interest groups. Find out what they think about the organization and how it might be improved. Heed the advice of an analyst for a major national bank, who said, "If our manager comes up with ten ideas a year, that's good. But if a thousand people in the organization each come up with one, that's even better. And besides, he probably won't come up with ten anyway" (Ben Vinzant, personal communication, spring 2013). You might be that manager. Listen to the advice of those throughout the organization.

7. *Think of building a capacity for learning in the organization.* Although only individuals, and not organizations, are capable of learning, it is possible for you to affect the conditions under which learning that is helpful to the organization might occur. Individual insights and perceptions must

be allowed to flow out into the larger organization where their impact will be greatest.

8. *Remember the difference between single-loop and double-loop learning* (learning new strategies vs. learning new basic assumptions). Where those in the organization are facing decisions that are routine or repetitive, single-loop learning probably will be sufficient; where they are facing more complex and "nonprogrammable" decisions, double-loop learning will be required.

9. *If changes in the organization's structure appear necessary, think twice.* Make sure that the real issues are structural and not behavioral. If they still appear to be structural, then make sure that they require changes in the organization's structure as opposed to work processes or core systems (e.g., technology). If structural changes still appear necessary, then proceed with caution and with the involvement of those affected.

10. *Remember that today's organizations reside in a complex world of diverse networks.* This means that for organizational changes to be effective, they often must involve employees, customers, stakeholders of the organization, and other organizations. Consider ways of involving all the relevant players in the design and execution of organizational changes, especially those that will affect other participants in the network.

11. *To encourage change and innovation throughout the organization, consider employing a more organic, democratic, or participatory way of operating.* Creating a culture in which people throughout the organization feel comfortable in proposing changes and feel confident that they will not be "killed" if well-considered risks do not pan out eventually will pay great benefits in terms of innovation. A key to innovation is to create spaces for innovation to occur. That is, give people the freedom, authority, and responsibility to propose and carry out needed changes. Encourage and reward innovation. Let people know that calculated risks sometimes are necessary for positive change to occur. Share leadership.

12. *Be attentive to the politics of change.* Remember that no matter what changes you make in an organization, there will be social and political implications. The existing system is the way it is because others—often managers of some consequence—thought that it should be that way. Recognize that changing something that others have invested political capital in has political ramifications.

▶ Key Terms

Discontinuous change 475

Double-loop learning 485

Driving forces 482

Emergence 487

Espoused theories 485

Force field analysis 483

Grassroots change 477

Incremental change 475

Mechanistic structures 489

Organic structures 489

Organizational learning 483

Restraining forces 482

Single-loop learning 485

Strategic change 477

Systems theory 485

Theories-in-use 485

▶ Exercise 15.1 Reasoning Processes in Organizational Change

Imagine a conversation in which Gina Leonard, the supervisor, called her employee Peter Brown into her office to talk about Peter's recent performance. Gina had observed several recent lapses in Peter's performance and had received complaints from others who were concerned as well. Moreover, she was concerned that Peter's disdain for others was affecting the performance of the work group as a whole. Gina really wanted to keep Peter in the organization because he was a highly skilled technician. But she also recognized that if things did not change, then she would have to build a case for his dismissal.

Among the things Gina said in the conversation were the following:

Peter, your performance simply hasn't been at the level we expect here.

People at your level have to set an example for others.

You seem to have a chip on your shoulder.

I don't want to talk about what happened in the past that has led to these problems. That's history. We have to deal with the future.

Let's clear the air once and for all.

We need to be clear about your work and your impact on others.

I've heard several people describe you as "disruptive," "uncaring," and "detached."

Others have even complained that you have been downright rude to them.

What is your reaction to Gina's approach and her language? How would you diagnose what was happening here? What advice would you give to Gina in handling situations like this?

Assume that you met Gina in the hall later and that she asked what you thought of her approach as she explained it in a memo about her meeting with Peter. Write out a conversation between Gina and you using the right-hand side of several sheets of paper.

On the left-hand side, write any thoughts or feelings that you might have during the conversation that you would not, for whatever reason, want to communicate to Gina. Following is an example:

Let Gina commit herself first so I can see what she thinks happened.

Gina: Did you read my memo on meeting with Peter?

You: Yes, I saw it. Must have been tough.

Gina: I just don't know how to get through to a guy like Peter.

"A guy like Peter." There's a clue.

Write out your version of the conservation from here on. Trade your written conversations with another class member and analyze the hidden assumptions that person made in talking with Gina. Did that person consider Gina effective? If not, then why not? How close were the inferences that person made to the actual observable data? What actions might flow from such inferences? Is it necessary to create more abstract inferences to deal with the problem? If so, then how does the process of inference affect that of organizational change? How does all this connect to the idea of double-loop learning?

Source: This exercise is adapted from Argyris, C. (1999). *Organizational Learning* (2nd ed.). Oxford, UK: Blackwell. See pages 71–87 for a detailed examination of the factors at play here and their connection to the question of double-loop learning.

▶ Case 15.1 Rethinking Change: Leadership and Meaning

This interview of Michael Mathieu, C.E.O. of YuMe, an online video advertising firm in Redwood City, CA, was conducted by Adam Bryant.

Q What about leadership lessons from particularly good or bad bosses?

A You're a collection of all your experiences, good, bad, indifferent, and great leaders you've worked with. Actually, you learn a lot from the worst managers you've had. You learn probably more than from the great managers.

Q Did you?

A Absolutely. I think my worst bosses were hyper-controlling. I've learned that leaders actually do

the opposite, which is to give their best people complete freedom to do the job. The worst managers come in and believe, "O.K., I'm going to control this." They're very structured. And what I've learned is that actually stifles high performers.

People who are really good at what they do want freedom. They want to be able to be innovative. So I try to hire the best people and give them the freedom and flexibility to do the job they were hired to do. But they have to sign up for things to get that freedom.

Q What are those things?

A One is, make people feel like they're part of the team. To do that, you've got to make people feel like they can come in and talk about anything with absolutely no fear of, "O.K., this could be stupid." They need to feel like their voice is heard, and feel completely fearless to have those conversations with me.

Two, they have to be clear on what our goals and vision are. This is the mountain we're trying to go after, and let's be clear on what we have to do. And if you do sign up for that, you're going to be accountable. If you give good people clear goals, you can let them be accountable and go after it in their own way. And then reward and recognize.

1. What elements of the classic views of organizational culture are expressed here?

2. What elements of more contemporary views of culture and change are expressed here?

3. How would this philosophy fit in your organization?

Source: Bryant, A. (2010, June 19). Want the job? Tell him the meaning of life. *New York Times.* Accessed at http://www.nytimes.com/2010/06/20/business/20corner.html?_r=0

▶ Case 15.2 An Approach to Leading Change

In April of 2007, Michael Gold was asked to present his Jazz Impact program to a gathering of IBM's thought leaders at their world headquarters in Armonk, New York. They were gathering to explore the relationship between transformational leadership, creativity, risk, and innovation; and seeking a touchstone experience for their discussions.

Jazz Impact held appeal for a number of reasons. First, jazz is an art form based in the essentials of collaborative transformation: generative growth, integrating change, and the ability to sustain innovation. Second, jazz musicians know how to work with ambiguity, how take action despite uncertainty, and how to challenge the status quo. Finally, the Jazz Impact group promised a collaborative-style learning experience tied to the challenges of complexity and accelerated change.

When the executives entered the meeting space, they were, of course, surprised to see a jazz ensemble—piano, upright bass, small drum kit, and alto saxophone. Before any words were spoken, the musicians engaged them with their music, prompting their minds in a way entirely unexpected. Incoming information in the form of music was captured and stored as *somatic experience*, coded into the body's senses and feeling states with the result of intensifying its capacity for recall. Longer recall would also facilitate the possibility of integrating this new experience with deeply seated existing knowledge. But no one in the audience was aware of this at the time. They were fascinated just listening and this was good.

When the piece ended, Gold engaged the 25 participants in a simple polyrhythmic exercise of clapping opposing rhythms and singing a simple melody. The intent was to push their processing away from the rubric of handouts, PowerPoint, and analytic monologue. Bit by bit, they got into it. Over the next 2 hours, the model of the jazz ensemble would push them further still, helping them to frame discussions of organizational dynamics difficult to address in ordinary language. Jazz provided the perfect vehicle because it was made of the same "stuff."

Gold placed the executives in what he likes to call "liminal" situations and challenged them to work creatively and collaboratively. The term *liminal* refers to the threshold between what we *do* and *do not* understand. In jazz, as in life, we are constantly moving back and forth across that threshold. Just so, we discover new knowledge, and via the cognitive process known as transfer, we integrate our new knowledge with our existing knowledge. The most useful integrations (those actually facilitating transformational change) take place only when our new knowledge has been retained in a deep and meaningful way—and for long enough periods—to allow transfer to happen.

1. How would you assess the value of an approach like this?

2. How would using this approach compare to using appreciative inquiry?

3. When would you use one approach and when would you use another?

Source: Adapted from Cimino, J. J., Jr., & Denhardt, R. B. (2012). Music, leadership, and the inner work of art. In C. S. Pearson (Ed.), *Being the change: 21st century thinking for transformational leaders* (pp. 201–210). San Francisco, CA: Berrett-Koehler.

▶ Endnotes

1. Ahrendts, A. (2013). Turning an aging British icon into a global luxury brand. *Harvard Business Review*, January–February, Reprint. Retrieved from http://hbr.org/2013/01/burberrys-ceo-on-turning-an-aging-british-icon-into-a-global-luxury-brand/ar/1, p. 1.

2. Ahrendts, 2013, p.1.

3. N.A. (2008). Checked growth. *Knowledge@Wharton*, November 20, 1–4. Retrieved from http://knowledge.wharton.upenn.edu/article.cfm?articleid=2094

4. Gilchrist, S. (2012). The democratic republic of Burberry. *Brunswick Review*, (6), 62. Retrieved from http://www.brunswickgroup.com/files/html/brunswickreviewIssue6/burberry.html

5. Gilchrist, 2012, p. 63.

6. Kowitt, B. (2012). Burberry's Angela Ahrendts. *CNN Money*, June 5, 1–7. Retrieved from http://tech.fortune.cnn.com/2012/06/05/burberry-angela-ahrendts, p. 1.

7. Ahrendts, 2013, p. 3.

8. Gilchrist, 2012, p. 64.

9. Gilchrist, 2012, p. 64.

10. Ahrendts, 2013, p. 3.

11. By, R. T. (2005). Organisational change management: A critical review. *Journal of Change Management*, 5(4), 370.

12. Kim, W. C., & Mauborgne, R. (2005). *Blue ocean strategy*. Boston: Harvard Business Review Press.

13. Nadler, D. A., Shaw, R. B., Walton, A. E., & Associates. (1995). *Discontinuous change*. San Francisco: Jossey-Bass, p. 22.

14. Nadler et al., 1995, pp. 22–23.

15. Galpin, T. J. (1996). *The human side of change*. San Francisco: Jossey-Bass, pp. 1–13.

16. Huy, Q. N., & Mintzberg, H. (2003, Summer). The rhythm of change. *MIT Sloan Management Review*, 80–84.

17. Huy & Mintzberg, 2003, p. 80.

18. Shaffer, R. H. (2012, December 12). Retrieved from http://blogs.hbr.org/cs/2012/12/to_change_the_culture_stop_try.html

19. Schein, E. H. (1985). *Organizational culture and leadership*. San Francisco: Jossey-Bass, pp. 14–21.

20. Argyris, C., & Schön, D. A. (1974). *Theory in practice: Increasing professional effectiveness*. San Francisco: Jossey-Bass.

21. Argyris & Schön, 1974, p. 9.

22. Ott, J. S. (1989). *The organizational culture perspective*. Pacific Grove, CA: Brooks/Cole, p. 50.

23. Arlidge, J. (2009). I'm doing "God's work." Meet Mr. Goldman Sachs. *Timesonline* November 8, http://www.timesonline.co.uk/tol/news/world/us_and_americas/article6907681.ece (accessed on March 24, 2010).

24. Arlidge, 2009.

25. North Highland—Working here. (2010). http://www.northhighland.com/working_here/index.html (accessed January 8, 2010).

26. Canabou, C. (2001). Have kid, won't travel. *Fast Company*, October, 48.

27. Fromartz, S. (2000). The right staff. *Inc.* Retrieved from http://www.inc.com/magazine/19981015/1106_pagen_2.html on January 8, 2010.

28. Fromartz, 2000.

29. Fromartz, 2000, p. 126.

30. Schein, 1985, pp. 14–21.

31. R. B. Lieber (1998). Why employees love these companies. *Fortune*, 137(1), 74.

32. Latham, G. P. (2003). A five-step approach to behavior change. *Organizational Dynamics*, 32(3), 309–315.

33. Latham, 2003, p. 309.

34. Latham, 2003, p. 309.

35. Latham, 2003, p. 311.

36. Latham, 2003, p. 311.

37. Latham, 2003, p. 314.

38. Latham, 2003, p. 314.

39. Bluedorn, A., & Lundgren, E. (1993). A culture-match perspective for strategic change. *Research in Organizational Change and Development*, 7, 137–179.

40. Schein, E. H. (1997). *Organizational culture and leadership* (3rd ed.). San Francisco: Jossey-Bass, p. 243.

41. Ingersoll, V. H., & Adams, G. B. (1992). *The tacit organization*. Greenwich, CT: JAI.

42. Ingersoll & Adams, 1992, p. 228.

43. Lewin, K. (1951). *Field theory in social science*. Westport, CT: Greenwood, p. 199.

44. Bruce, R., & Wyman, S. (1998). *Changing organizations*. Thousand Oaks, CA: Sage, p. 125.

45. Canadian Centre for Management Development. (1994). *Continuous learning*. Ottawa: Minister of Supply and Services Canada, p. 58.

46. Argyris & Schön, 1974.

47. Senge, P., Scharmer, C. O., Jaworski, J., & Flowers, B. S. (2005). Presence: Human purpose and the field of the future. New York, NY: Crown Business.

48. Jaworski, J., & Flowers, B. S. (1996). *Synchronicity: The inner path of leadership*. San Francisco: Berrett-Koehler.

49. Senge et al., 2005, p. 9.

50. Senge et al., 2005, p. 13.

51. Scharmer, C. O. (2007). *Theory U: Leading from the future as it emerges*. Cambridge, MA: Society for Organizational Learning, p. 136.

52. Wheatley, M., & Frieze, D. (2008). *Using emergence to take social innovation to scale*. Retrieved from http://www.margaretwheatley.com/articles/using-emergence.pdf

53. Wheatley & Frieze, 2008, p. 5.

54. Wheatley & Frieze, 2008, p. 1.

55. The Parmalat scandal. (2011). *World Finance*, June 24. Accessed at http://www.worldfinance.com/home/special-reports-home/the-parmalat-scandal on April 9, 2013.

56. Sverige, C. (2004). The Parmalat scandal: Europe's ten-billion euro black hole. *World Socialist Web Site*, January 6. Accessed at http://www.wsws.org/en/articles/2004/01/parm-j06.html on April 9, 2013.

57. Dinmore, G. (2010) Ex-head of Parmalat jailed for 18 years. *Financial Times*, December 10. Accessed at http://www.ft.com/intl/cms/s/0/319fbaa4-03d6-11e0-8c3f-00144feabdc0.html#axzz2Q5jVaSwq on April 9, 2013.

58. Sanderson, R. (2013). Amber chief urges reforms in Italy. April 1. Accessed at http://www.ft.com/intl/cms/s/0/d9c2d640-8f15-11e2-a39b-00144feabdc0.html#axzz2Q5jVaSwq on April 10, 2013.

59. Jones, J., Aguirre, D., & Calderon, M. (2004). 10 principles of change management: Tools and techniques to help companies transform quickly. *Strategy+Business*. Accessed at http://www.strategy-business.com/article/rr00006?gko=643d0 on September 7, 2013.

60. Kotter, J. (2012). Accelerate! *Harvard Business Review*, (November), 1–7. Retrieved from http://hbr.org/2012/11/accelerate/ar/1

61. Nadler, D. A., & Tushman, M. L. (1997). *Competing by design*. New York: Oxford University Press.

62. Nadler & Tushman, 1997, pp. 47–48.

63. Oxman, J. A., & Smith, B. D. (2003, Fall). The limits of structural change. *MIT Sloan Management Review*, 78–80.

64. Oxman & Smith, 2003, p. 79.

65. Oxman & Smith, 2003, p. 80.

66. Argyris, C. (1970). *Intervention theory and method*. Reading, MA: Addison-Wesley.

67. Argyris, 1970, p. 17.

68. Argyris, 1970, p. 19.

69. Argyris, 1970, p. 20.

70. Cummings, T. G., & Huse, E. F. (1989). *Organization development and change* (4th ed.). St. Paul, MN: West, chap. 11.

71. Parker, G. M. (1990). *Team players and teamwork: The new competitive business strategy*. San Francisco: Jossey-Bass, p. 33.

72. Cooperrider, D. L., & Whitney, D. K. (2005). *Appreciative inquiry: A positive revolution in change*. San Francisco: Berrett-Koehler; Whitney, D. K., & Trosten-Bloom, A. (2003). *The power of appreciative inquiry: A practical guide to positive change*. San Francisco: Berrett-Koehler.

73. Cooperrider & Whitney, 2005, p. 8.

74. Woodyard, C. (2012). Hyundai's John Krafcik isn't your typical chief executive. *USA Today*, February 9. Retrieved from http://usatoday30.usatoday.com/money/autos/2010-08-23-ceockrafcik23_CV_N.htm

75. Hyundai CEO interview. (2012). *MLive*, April 12. Retrieved from http://www.mlive.com/auto/index.ssf/2012/04/hyundai_ceo_how_korean_automak.html on December 16, 2012.

76. Hyundai: Driven to success. (2010). *CBS News*, February 28. Retrieved from http://www.cbsnews.com/8301-3445_162-6252476.html on December 16, 2012.

77. Hyundai CEO interview, 2012.

78. Hyundai CEO interview, 2012.

79. Blanchard, A. (2012). How do you dodge constant distractions and stay on course? *Fast Company*, November 5. Retrieved from http://www.fastcompany.com/3002714/generation-flux-salon-how-do-you-dodge-constant-distractions-and-stay-course on December 16, 2012.

80. Denhardt, R. B., & Denhardt, J. V. (1999). *Leadership for change: Case studies in American local government*. Arlington, VA: PricewaterhouseCoopers Endowment for the Business of Government.

81. Nadler, D. A., Shaw, R. B., Walton, A. E., & Associates. (1995). *Discontinuous change*. San Francisco: Jossey-Bass, chap. 6.

82. Kotter, J. P. (1996). *Leading change*. Boston: Harvard Business School Press, p. 5.

83. Woodall, J. (1996). Managing culture change: Can it ever be ethical? *Personnel Review*, 25(6), 26–40; see p. 28.

84. McKendall, M. (1993). The tyranny of change: Organization development revisited. *Journal of Business Ethics, 12*, 93–104.

85. McKendall, 1993, p. 99.

86. Warwick, D. P., & Kelman, H. C. (1973). Ethical issues in social intervention. In G. Zaltman (Ed.), *Processes and phenomena of social change*. New York: Wiley, p. 377.

87. Seabright, M. A., & Moberg, D. J. (1998). Interpersonal manipulation. In M. Schminke (Ed.), *Managerial ethics*. Mahwah, NJ: Erlbaum, p. 167.

88. Svara, J. H. (2006). *Ethics primer for public administrators in government and nonprofit organizations*. Sudbury, MA: Jones and Bartlett.

Glossary

Abilities: natural talents to do something mental or physical

Active listening: listening that involves the listener consciously engaging in a series of actions intended to clarify and confirm the meaning of the message he or she is receiving

Actor-observer difference: the tendency to rely more on external attributions when explaining our own actions

Affirmative Action: aims at correcting past injustice and imbalance through direct action aimed at increasing the number of members of minority groups or women

Alarm: the first GAS stage; includes the initial physical reaction to stressors

Assertiveness: taking action to satisfy one's own needs and concerns

Attention stage of perception: the selection of stimuli, cues, and signals to which we will pay attention

Attribution process: the process of assigning or attributing a cause to a behavior or event

Authentic leader: one who remains true to his or her values, preferences, hopes, and aspirations, and acts in a way that is consistent with those values and beliefs

Authoritative decisions: those an individual makes alone or on behalf of the group

Behavior approach: leadership approach that focuses on behaviors of leaders

Bureaucracy: a form of organization exhibiting hierarchy, division of labor, impersonal rules, and top-down authority (Weber, 1947)

Business environment: customers, competitors, human resources, suppliers, financial institutions, governmental regulations, the economy, and technology that managers typically deal with on a day-to-day basis

Central norms: rules of behavior that are essential to the group's identity, goals, and survival

Channeling or confirmatory hypothesis testing: the process by which we limit people's interactions with us so their behavior supports our expectations

Chaordic: chaotic and orderly at the same time

Choice opportunities: occasions when organizations are expected to produce decisions

Closure: the process of filling in missing information to understand a stimulus

Coercive power: power based on force and the ability to punish

Cognitive knowledge: intellectual understanding of the task

Cohesion: the degree to which members of the group are attracted to the group and to one another

Collaborative decision-making model: decisions in organizations are made through a collaborative process that bears little resemblance to a single executive making a rational choice

Collaborative style: seeks a win-win solution for all parties

Communication: the transmission of information from one party to another

Competition: rivalry between individuals or groups over an outcome; always has a winner and a loser

Complexity: The number of elements an organization has to consider in the enactment process

Conceptual skills: knowledge of problem solving, logical thinking, decision making, creativity, and reasoning in general

Conflict: a process in which people disagree over significant issues, thereby creating friction

Conformity: the process of abiding by the group norms

Consultative decisions: decisions an individual makes with input from others

Contingency approach: understanding leadership requires consideration of both leadership characteristics—either traits or behaviors or a combination—and the leadership situation

Cooperativeness: taking action to satisfy the other party's needs and concerns

Corporate social responsibility: companies going beyond their bottom-line economic interests and engaging in activities that promote social well-being and environmental sustainability

Cost-benefit analysis: a technique used to determine the efficiency of a program requiring that all costs and benefits are expressed in monetary terms

Cost-effectiveness analysis: a technique used to compare the program's output to the costs encountered; the outputs may be in qualitative terms

Creativity: the generation of new and useful ideas

Cross-functional team: similar to a project team but serves the purpose of breaking down barriers by bringing together members from different divisions to work on a common goal

Cultural diversity: refers to such differences at the national level as well as the differences in race, ethnicity, language, religion, gender, or generations among various groups within a community or nation

Cultural iceberg: what we see and can observe from culture is only a small part of what culture is

Culture: a set of beliefs and values shared by members of a given group

Decisions: choices made from two or more alternatives

Decoding: the process by which the receiver interprets and translates the meaning of the sender's message

Defensiveness: defensive behavior occurs when people feel or anticipate some sort of threat and rush to defend themselves

Design thinking: an approach to creativity that incorporates graphic and industrial design methods which involves brainstorming and rapid prototyping to test ideas

Deviants: individuals who do not conform to the group norms

Differentiation: based on providing a unique and different product of superior quality with special features

Discontinuous change: change that seeks a whole new strategy or configuration for the organization

Discrimination: organizations making personnel decisions based on other than job-relevant factors or performance

Distortion: the difference between the meaning that the sender intends and the meaning that the receiver decodes

Distributive justice: the fairness of the outcome or decision

Distributive negotiation: a zero-sum negotiation in which one party's gain always leads to the other party's loss

Diversity: achieving a workforce generally reflective of the social environment surrounding the organization, with special attention to race, gender, sexual orientation, and so on, as well as cultural differences

Double-loop learning: learning new goals

Driving forces: those that support the direction of a proposed change

Emergence: the idea that change in social systems follows a pattern similar to that of change in nature, where several small actions come together to create a new dynamic

Emotional challenge: any real or perceived threat to our security, self-image, or sense of self-worth

Emotional dissonance: projecting one emotion while feeling another

Emotional intelligence: the social and interpersonal aspect of intelligence

Emotional labor: the act of expressing organizationally desired emotions during service transactions

Emotions: provide information about our reactions to situations and reveal our needs, concerns, and motives

Employee Assistance Programs (EAP): programs in organizations that offer employees help in managing challenges and problems in both work and non-work-related issues

Employee engagement: the rational and emotional attachment and commitment employees have to their work and their organizations or the involvement, satisfaction, and enthusiasm employees have for their work

Empowerment: either delegating or sharing power OR creating conditions that increase feelings of power or personal efficacy in others

Enactment: the process of identifying relevant environmental elements to define the environment of the organization

Encoding: the process by which a sender puts the message in a certain format

Environment: all the external factors that have the potential to affect the organization

Environmental uncertainty: unpredictability in the environment

Equal employment opportunity (EEO): forbids discrimination on the basis of race, color, national origin, sex, religion, age, disability, political beliefs, and marital or familial status; the goal of EEO is to be proactive and encourage diversity in the workplace

Espoused theories: theories to which we give conscious allegiance; the ones we describe when people ask us what ideas govern our actions

Ethnic or group culture: the second level of culture; a set of values and beliefs shared by people within a group

Evidence-based management: managers make organizational decisions informed by organizational research and practice

Exhaustion: the third GAS stage; results from long-term exposure to stressors

Expectancy theory: a motivation theory that holds that people will be motivated when they expect that their efforts will result in desirable outcomes

Expert power: power based on expertise

External or situational attribution: the process of assigning a cause to a behavior that is related to factors external to the person

Feelings: indicators of our implicit or unconscious judgments of the significance of events

Filtering: manipulating the information that is being sent so that it will be received more favorably by the receiver

Force field analysis: listing in one column the driving forces at play in a particular change opportunity and in a second column the restraining forces

Formal organization: a system of consciously coordinated activities or forces of two or more persons

Frames of reference: the personal context we each bring to communications with others

Fundamental attribution error: the tendency to underestimate situational factors and overestimate personal factors when making attributions about others' actions

Garbage can model: decision processes are affected by the timing of problems, solutions, participants, and choice opportunities, all of which are assumed to be independent

General adaptation syndrome (GAS): the three stages that individuals go through when they respond to stressors and try to adapt to them

General environment: social, demographic, and cultural trends; the political climates; and historical and religious influences

Glass ceiling: invisible barriers and obstacles that prevent individuals from moving to the highest levels of organizations

Globalization: the extent to which cultures, societies, and economies are interconnected and integrated

GLOBE: Global Leadership and Organizational Behavior Effectiveness; cross-cultural differences and leadership study conducted in 62 countries

Goals: objectives that specify what needs to be achieved and when

Grassroots change: changes at lower levels of the organization that are concerned with implementing and sustaining the changes envisioned at the strategic level

Group decisions: made by members of the group, ideally through consensus

Groups: two or more people who interact in an organized manner to perform a task or activity to achieve a common goal

Groupthink: a mode of thinking that occurs when people are deeply involved in a cohesive group and their desire for unanimity offsets their motivation to appraise alternative courses of action

Halo effect: a bias that occurs when a general impression or evaluation of one characteristic of a person or situation creates a positive impression that becomes the central factor around which all other information is selected, organized, and interpreted

Hawthorne effect: the finding that people change their behavior when they know they are being observed

Heterogeneous cultures: include many different cultural groups

Heterogeneous groups: groups with members who have many differences

Hierarchy of needs: Maslow's theory that different levels of human needs are aroused in a specific sequence, and as each lower-level need is substantially satisfied, the person is motivated to seek to satisfy the next higher level of need

High-context culture: a culture in which people rely heavily on nonverbal cues and situational factors to communicate with each other and understand situations

High-risk decisions: decisions that take place at the top of the organization and are often strategic

Homogeneous cultures: include one or few cultural groups

Homogeneous groups: groups with members who have a number of similarities

Horizontal conflict: between departments or groups at the same level of the organization

Impression management: the act of consciously and carefully monitoring and managing the impression we make on others

Incremental change: change that occurs within the existing framework of the organization

Incrementalism: decisions are dependent on small incremental choices made in response to short-term conditions

Influence tactics: actions used intentionally to influence or change the attitude or behavior of someone else

Innovation: the successful implementation of creative ideas

Instrumental values: desirable conduct or methods for attaining an end

Integrative negotiation: parties try to reach an agreement that benefits them both by focusing on creating new options and solutions

Interactional justice: the nature of communication and how a person is treated

Interactionist view: suggests that heredity and the environment interact to influence the development of individual differences

Interdependence: the extent to which employees depend on others to get their work done

Intergroup conflict: when groups within and outside an organization disagree over various topics

Internal or personal attribution: the process of assigning a cause to a behavior that is related to internal factors within a person

Interpersonal conflict: conflict that arises because two or more people who are required to interact have different goals, values, or styles

Interpersonal skills: knowledge of interpersonal relationships including communication, conflict management

Interpretation and judgment stage: the clarification and translation of organized information to allow for the attribution of meaning

Intragroup conflict: conflict within a work group over goals or work procedures

Intrapersonal conflict: a person's internal conflict

Jargon: shorthand language or terminology known to insiders but mystifying to others

Job burnout: characterized by exhaustion, sense of powerlessness, cynicism, and disengagement

Knowledge workers: those whose primary contribution to the organization is not physical but mental

Law of effect: people repeat behaviors that bring them satisfaction and pleasure, and stop those that bring them dissatisfaction or pain

Leadership: occurs where one or more members of a group or organization stimulate others to more clearly recognize their previously latent needs, desires, and potentialities and to work together toward their fulfillment.

Legitimate power: power based on accepted authority

Line employees: people directly involved in production or service delivery

Liquid Modernity: the tendency for modern societies to exhibit more liquid or fluid tendencies

Low-context culture: a culture in which people rely on explicit, specific cues such as verbal or written messages to communicate with each other and understand situations

Low-cost strategies: based on designing, producing, marketing, and delivering a product or service more efficiently than competitors

Low-risk decisions: decisions that involve little uncertainty

Manufacturing firms: produce an actual product or tangible output

Mechanistic structures: structures that are highly formalized, specialized, standardized, and centralized

Micromanaging: when employees are closely monitored, allowed few choices, denied opportunities to participate in decisions, and pressured to act in particular ways

Mindmapping: a specific technique to aid visually and spatially thinking about issues and problems

Mission: a statement of the organization's purpose and reason for existence

Moral leadership: a form of leadership that raises the level of moral aspiration and moral conduct of both leaders and followers

Motivation: a state of mind, desire, energy, or interest that translates into action

Multicultural mindset: a way of thinking where culture is taken into consideration in deliberations, decisions, and behaviors

National culture: the first level of culture; a set of values and beliefs shared by people within a nation

National organizational heritage: a particular organizational management style largely based on national culture

Needs: based on personality and values and related to things that are lacking and are desired

Negative reinforcer: an unpleasant outcome aimed at encouraging a certain behavior

Negotiation: a process whereby two or more parties reach a mutually agreeable arrangement

Nominal group technique: a technique developed to ensure that every member of the group has an equal chance of participating

Nonprogrammed decisions: decisions for which there is no apparent decision rule, and managers are required to engage in difficult problem solving

Norms: shared rules and expectations about group members' behaviors

Organic organizations: have a low degree of formality, specialization, and standardization, decentralized decision making, and well integrated activities

Organic structures: structures that emphasize horizontal rather than vertical relationships and are much more flexible, adaptable, and responsive

Organization stage of perception: the organization of information that the perceptual filter has allowed through during the attention stage

Organizational behavior: the study and practice of how to manage individual and group behavior in business, government, and nonprofit settings

Organizational chart: a diagram of how people are organized and of the organization's skeletal structure

Organizational culture: the set of values, norms, and beliefs shared by members of an organization

Organizational decision making: when a person in authority identifies an important issue and carries out a process to make a choice that produces outcomes with consequences

Organizational learning: learning that builds on individual learning and permeates the organization as a way of doing business

Organizational process model: relies on incrementalism for decision making

Organizational rewards: positive outcomes that organizations provide to individuals

Overjustification: the tendency to make external attributions about our own behavior when an external reward is given

Paraphrasing: restating what you hear in your own words

Perception: the mental process we use to pay attention selectively to some stimuli and cues and not to others

Perceptual biases: distortions in perception, often caused by cognitive shortcuts, and that lead to mistakes

Perceptual filter: the process of letting some information in while keeping out the rest

Peripheral norms: rules of behavior that support central norms but are not central to the group's identity

PERMA: Positive emotion; Engagement; positive Relationships; Meaning; Accomplishment

Personality: a set of psychological characteristics that makes each person unique

Politics: the use of power and authority to influence organizational outcomes

Positive organizational behavior: an approach to organizational behavior based on positive psychology and emphasizing strengths rather than weaknesses

Positive reinforcer: a pleasant outcome that follows a desired behavior and is aimed at encouraging the behavior

Power: the ability to influence others

Primacy effect: a tendency to overemphasize early information

Primary dimensions of diversity: the visible and stable aspects of a group or person

Proactive influence: tactics used to accomplish an immediate purpose or task

Proactive personality: people who are action-oriented, tend to identify opportunities and take advantage of them, and generally persevere in the face of obstacles and change

Problem: a discrepancy between what is actually occurring and the ideal or desired

Procedural justice: the fairness of the process used in making the decision

Process-improvement team: individuals who interact with each other for the purpose of improving work processes in which they engage

Programmed decisions: Decisions that are repetitive and routine and for which a procedure or decision rule has been established or may be easily specified

Project team: formed by management based on expertise of its members

Punishment: a negative event that occurs after an undesirable behavior and is aimed at stopping that behavior

Pygmalion effect or self-fulfilling prophecy: the process by which one's expectations and perceptions becoming reality because of the strength of the original expectation

Rate of change: the speed at which various elements in the environment change

Rational model: phases for decision making are performed deliberately and consciously, relying on the rationality of the decision maker's thoughts and behaviors

Recency effect: a tendency to overemphasize the most recent information rather than earlier data

Referent power: power based on respect

Reinforcement theory: recommends providing an organizational environment and response patterns that reward and encourage desirable behaviors while discouraging or punishing undesirable ones

Reinforcement: an outcome or event that increases the likelihood that a behavior will occur again

Research and development (R & D): the process by which organizations search for information and create techniques to improve their products and services

Resistance: the second GAS stage; occurs when one fights the threat

Restraining forces: those that oppose the direction of the proposed change

Reward power: power based on access to resources and rewards

Role ambiguity: a lack of clarity about the role one is playing

Role conflict: when compliance with one role makes it impossible to comply with another role or when individual needs conflict with role demands

Roles: specific formal or informal patterns of behavior that an individual performs in a team

Salient cues: those cues that are somehow so striking that they stand out

Satisficing: making a satisfactory, but not optimal decision

Schemas: mental patterns that people apply to understand and explain certain situations and events

Scientific management: the application of scientific techniques to work processes, as advocated by Frederick Taylor

Scope of strategy: whether a business is a setting wide or broad net, or whether it has a narrower focus

Secondary dimensions of diversity: the less visible or more dynamic aspects of a group or person

Selective attention: the process of paying attention to some, but not all, physical and social cues

Self-awareness: ability to recognize and understand your moods, emotions, and drives as well as their effect on others

Self-directed teams: self-managed teams that decide themselves how and when work is going to be done

Self-disclosure: disclosing to others what you think and how you feel about deep-seated personal matters

Self-efficacy: people's judgments of their capabilities; in other words, it is our assessment of what we can do with the skills we possess

Self-management: ability to control or redirect disruptive impulses and moods and regulate your own behavior

Self-perception theory: a theory suggesting that people make attributions about themselves by looking at their behavior

Self-serving bias: the tendency to accept credit for our success and reject blame for failures

Semantics: the study of the meaning conveyed by words or symbols

Servant leadership: a type of leadership that begins with a commitment on the part of the potential leader to serve others

Service firms: deliver a service rather than a tangible product

Sexual harassment: unwelcome sexual advances, requests for sexual favors, and other verbal or physical conduct of a sexual nature that tends to create a hostile or offensive work environment

Similar-to-me: developing a liking for a person that we perceive is similar to us and disliking those who are different

Single-loop learning: learning new strategies

Skills: acquired talents that a person develops related to specific tasks

Social facilitation: individuals work harder in the presence of others

Social loafing: people work less when their individual contributions cannot be measured

Social perception: the process of gathering, selecting, and interpreting information about how we view ourselves and others

Social skills: proficiency in managing relationships and building networks

Sophisticated stereotypes: generalizations about people based on valid and reliable research rather than opinion or personal experience

Staff: employees and managers who support the line employees through a variety of functions

Stereotype: a generalization about an individual based on the group to which the person belongs

Strategic change: change efforts that are both broad range (typically organization-wide) and long term

Strategic formulation: the process of forging a cohesive integrated set of strategies designed to deal with the environment and achieve the business mission and goals

Strategic management process: the combination of strategy formulation and implementation

Strategy implementation: the actions the organization takes to execute the strategy it has formulated

Strategy: how a firm achieves it mission and goals

Stress: an individual physiological, behavioral, and psychological response to perceived challenges and threats in the environment

Stressors: environmental threats perceived by an individual

Supportive communication: an approach to communicating that recognizes both the need to transmit information and to enhance interpersonal relationships

Sustainability: meeting the needs of the present generation in a way that doesn't compromise the capacity of future generations to meet their needs

Synectics: joining together different and apparently unconnected or irrelevant elements

Systems theory: an approach to understanding human, physical, or biological processes involving an examination of inputs, conversion processes, outputs, and feedback

Teams: mature groups with a high degree of interdependence geared toward the achievement of a goal or the completion of a task

Technical skills: knowledge of job processes, methods, tools, and techniques

Technology: the knowledge, tools, techniques, and processes used to create the goods and services of an organization by transforming inputs into outputs

Terminal values: desired states or end goals

Theories-in-use: theories that actually govern our actions

Theory X: the traditional command-and-control approach based on assumptions of people as lazy, uninvolved, and motivated solely by money

Theory Y: more humanistic form of management based on assumptions of people as active and involved in their work

Thinking-speaking differential: the lag of time between our thinking and our speech

Top management team: responsible for establishing the overall mission of the organization and for selecting the management system

Trait approach: addresses the question of what constitutes effective leadership based on personal characteristics or traits associated with successful leaders

Transactional leadership: involves an exchange of valued things (e.g., economic, political, psychological) between initiators and respondents

Transformational leadership: occurs when leaders and followers engage with one another in such a way that they raise one another to higher levels of morality and motivation

Type A individuals: those who are hard driving and have a high need for control

Values: stable long-lasting beliefs and preferences about what is worthwhile and desirable

Vertical conflict: between groups at different levels of the hierarchy

Vertical thinking: when a problem is defined in a single way until the solution is reached

Virtual teams: a mature group that functions through the use of information technology including videoconferencing, satellite television, and the Internet

Vision: describes where the firm wants to be and its purpose and values

Photo Credits

Chapter 1

p. 3, Chapter 1 opening photo: Daly and Newton/OJO Images/Getty Images

p. 4, Facebook: AP Photo/Jeff Chiu, File

p. 7, Western Electric: Factory Cabling Department, ca. 1925. Western Electric Company photograph album. Baker Library Historical Collections, Harvard Business school (olvwork278799).

p. 9, Working together: © iStockphoto.com/laflor

p. 15, Howard Schultz: AP Photo/Koji Sasahara

p. 21, Connectedness: © iStockphoto.com/Erikona

p. 23, International McDonalds: AP Photo/Achmad Ibrahim

p. 25, Lisa Jackson: AP Photo/Toby Talbot

Chapter 2

p. 33, Chapter 2 opening photo: © iStockphoto.com/Yuri

p. 36 (Figure 2.1): (a) Thomas Northcut/Photodisc/Thinkstock; (b) Martin Poole/Lifesize/Thinkstock; (c) © iStockphoto.com/fotostorm

p. 37, Hand gestures: George Doyle/Stockbyte/Thinkstock

p. 38, Indira Gandhi: Bundesarchiv, Bild 183-R0703-026/Koard, Peter/CC-BY-SA

p. 40 (Figure 2.3): Jupiterimages/liquidlibrary/Thinkstock

p. 46, Ursula Burns: © EDUARDO MUNOZ/Reuters/Corbis

p. 50, Frank Brincho: © Paul Bersebach/ZUMA Press/Corbis

p. 54, Greeting rituals: (a) © iStockphoto.com/skynesher; (b) Ryan McVay/Digital Vision/Thinkstock

Chapter 3

p. 71, Chapter 3 opening photo: Stephane Cardinale/People Avenue/Corbis

p. 75, Children from an Indian village: (c)iStockphoto.com/hadynyah

p. 77, David Henderson: AP Photo/Luis M Garza

p. 81, Ken Chenault: Taylor Hill/Getty Images Entertainment/Getty Images

p. 82, Waiting tables: © iStockphoto.com/kali9

p. 86, Susan Cain: AP Photo/Geoffrey Swaine/Rex Features

p. 93, Receiving feedback: © iStockphoto.com/Alina55

Chapter 4

p. 111, Chapter 4 opening photo: ADRIAN DENNIS/AFP/Getty Images

p. 118, Perceptions: © iStockphoto.com/alvarez

p. 122, Lindsey Bailey: AP Photo/Lara Solt

p. 127, Trayvon Martin: © Splash News/Corbis

p. 130, Sheryl Sanberg: CC BY-SA 2.0; Author: World Economic Forum

Chapter 5

p. 141, Chapter 5 opening photo: Jupiterimages/Brand X Pictures/Thinkstock

p. 146, Circuit City: © iStockphoto.com/nazdravie

p. 148, Richard Semler: © James Leynse/Corbis

p. 149, Expectancy theory: AP Photo/Kathy Willens

p. 155, Life stages: © iStockphoto.com/GlobalStock

p. 158, McChrystal: Pete Souza (Public Domain) via Wikimedia Commons

Chapter 6

p. 171, Chapter 6 opening photo: KAREN BLEIER/AFP/Getty Images

p. 175, Too much stress: BananaStock/Thinkstock

p. 177, Candlelight vigil: AP Photo/Mark Crosse

p. 184, Working conditions: © iStockphoto.com/Yuri

p. 190, Twitter employees: AP Photo/Ole Spata

p. 193, Amanda Camp: AP Photo/Ted S. Warren

Chapter 7

p. 203, Chapter 7 opening photo: Kimberly White/Corbis

p. 211, Preparation phase of creativity: © iStockphoto.com/GlobalStock

p. 212, Tim Cook: CC-BY 2.0; Author: Mike Deerkoski

p. 216, Costco: © iStockphoto.com/diane39

p. 217, Citigroup: T. Nergaard

Author Index

Ackerman, L. P., 156(n30), 156(n31)
Adair, W. L., 121(n23)
Adams, G. B., 482(n41), 482(n42)
Adams, J. S., 151(n24)
Adler, N. J., 255(n73)
Adler, P., 326(n56), 326(n57), 326(n58),
    326(n59), 327(n60)
Aguirre, D., 489(n59)
Ahrendts, A., 472(n1), 472(n2),
    474(n7), 474(n10)
Alarcon, G., 180(n25)
Aldrich, H., 442(n14)
Alinsky, S., 93(n56)
Allen, K. J., 120b(n20)
Allison, G., 214, 245–246, 247, 249(n46)
Allison, G. T., 244
Amabile, T. M., 163(n56), 205(n3), 209(n18),
    209(n21), 209(n23), 215(n41), 215(n42),
    217(n48), 217(n49), 218(n59), 220(n70),
    220(n74), 221(n78)
Amachi, R. N., 329(n61)
Amanatullah, E. T., 46(n54)
Amble, B., 44(n39)
Amidi, A., 72(n7)
Anand, M., 311b(n28)
Anderson, C., 86(n36)
Anderson, N. R., 218(n60)
Anderson, P. A., 251(n60)
Andrews, F. M., 220(n71)
Angelo, B., 110(n2), 112(n4)
Anthony, W., 418(n45)
Arfken, D. E., 46(n59)
Argyris, C., 485, 490–491
Aristigueta, M. P., 77(n14), 246(n31)
Arlidge, J., 478(n23), 478(n24)
Armstrong, M., 78(n16)
Armstrong, P. I., 46(n54)
Arnold, J. D., 241(n20), 259(n83)
Arroba, T., 184(n43)
Ashforth, B. E., 82(n28)
Asplund, J., 15(n37), 157(n39)
Aston, A., 446(n34)
Atkins, A., 161(n49)
Avruch, K., 90(n48)
Ayoko, O. B., 343(n16)

Babu, S., 311b(n25)
Bain, P., 78(n15)
Baldes, J. J., 150(n20)
Banaji, M. R., 23(n55)
Bandura, A., 150(n23)

Banker, R. D., 312(n31)
Barbulescu, R., 92(n53)
Barendsen, L., 377(n22)
Barnard, C., 7
Barney, J. B., 434(n3), 450(n44)
Barrick, M. R., 85(n34)
Barron, F. B., 208(n17)
Barsade, S. G., 220(n74)
Bartels, L. K., 80(n18)
Bartlett, C. A., 52(n79)
Bass, B. M., 373(n7), 374(n10), 380, 381f
Batemam, T. S., 180(n24)
Bauman, Z., 19
Bazerman, M. H., 240(n18)
Bazron, B. J., 59(n89)
Beach, L. R., 248(n40)
Beale, R. L., 255(n71)
Beauchamp, M. R., 43(n28)
Beaumont, C., 437(n4)
Becherer, R. C., 89(n44)
Bechger, T. M., 128(n41)
Beck, M., 183(n33)
Beckman, H., 190(n60)
Beehr, T., 178(n17), 190(n59)
Bellar, S. L., 46(n59)
Benne, K. D., 306(n18)
Bennis, W., 371(n6), 376(n16), 377(n17)
Bennis, W. G., 51(n77), 51(n78), 382(n39)
Bern, S., 124(n31)
Beyer, D., 340(n11), 348(n29)
Bianchi, S. M., 46(n50)
Bird, A., 40(n19)
Bisoux, T., 45(n48)
Blacksmith, N., 15(n37), 157(n39)
Blair, L., 258(n80)
Blake, R. R., 374(n12)
Blanchard, A., 495(n79)
Blanchard, K. H., 374(n13)
Blari, J. D., 359(n45)
Blenko, M., 239(n14), 255, (n74)
Block, P., 424(n67), 424(n68)
Bluedorn, A., 481(n39)
Bommer, W. H., 80(n18)
Bongiorna, R., 127(n38)
Bonk, A., 336(n1)
Boone, L., 206(n9), 210(n25)
Borden, M., 70(n2)
Bosch, K., 24(n63)
Bosker, B., 445(n26)
Bouchard, T. J., Jr., 75(n8)
Bowling, N., 180(n25)

Risavy, S. D., 129(n46)
Ritti, R. R., 150(n16)
Rizzo, J. R., 84(n32), 84(n33)
Roberts, J., 418(n43), 418(n44)
Roberts, N. C., 284(n21), 285(n22), 285(n23)
Robinson, M., 120b(n21)
Robison, J., 160(n46)
Roddy, D. J., 17(n43)
Rodriguez, C., 117(n13)
Roethlisberger, F. J., 7
Rogers, C. R., 280(n17), 281(n19)
Rogers, M., 239(n14), 255, (n74)
Roloff, K. S., 362(n50)
Romero, E., 190(n62), 190(n63)
Ropo, A., 386(n52)
Rosenthal, R., 131(n52)
Rosett, A., 90(n47)
Rosling, A., 311b
Ross, L., 123(n28), 126(n33)
Ross, M., 129(n44)
Rossey, G. L., 23(n56)
Rost, K., 147, 155(n29)
Rothstein, H., 193(n73)
Rounds, J., 46(n54)
Rousseau, D. M., 259(n82)
Rozelle, R. M., 43(n28)
Rubin, R. S., 80(n18)
Ruckes, M. E., 43(n29)
Rusch, C., 48(n73), 156(n37)
Rushton, K., 110(n3), 112(n8), 112(n9), 188b(n51)
Russell, E. W., 248(n41)
Rutherford, M., 411(n15), 418(n45), 418(n46)
Ryan, M. K., 127(n38)
Ryan, R., 217(n51), 218(n56), 218(n58)

Sacks, D., 202(n1), 202(n2)
Sadler, P., 37(n13)
Safian, R., 158b(n43), 158b(n44)
Salancik, G., 248, 416(n31), 416(n32)
Sandberg, S., 45, 46, 130, 133b, 275, 275(n5)
Sanderson, R., 488b(n58)
Sandwith, P., 290(n36), 290(n37)
Sasso, B., 462(n60)
Satterstrom, P., 217(n47)
Sauer, E., 386(n52)
Savage, G. T., 359(n45)
Sawyer, J., 209(n22), 217(n53)
Scharmer, C. O., 486(n47), 487(n49), 487(n50), 487(n51)
Schein, E. H., 8, 39(n15), 40(n18), 346, 479(n30)
Schermerhorn, J. R., 242(n21)
Schmidt, S., 288(n31)
Schneider, S. C., 39(n16)
Schoem, D., 285(n24)
Schoem, S. H., 285(n24)
Schon, D. A., 90(n52), 478, 485
Schramm, J., 175(n8)

Schramm, W., 274(n4)
Schroeder, R. G., 312(n31)
Schuler, R., 183(n32)
Schwartz, N. D., 81(n25)
Schweizer, K., 110(n1)
Schwenk, C. R., 353(n31)
Scott, D., 325
Scott-Elliot, R., 130(n47)
Seabright, M. A., 497(n87)
Sebenius, J. K., 354(n32)
Seifert, C. F., 419(n48)
Seligman, M., 189(n54)
Seligman, M. E. P., 9, 75(n9), 75(n10), 187–190
Seller, P., 45(n49)
Selma, R., 148b(n9)
Senge, P., 8, 486(n47), 487(n49), 487(n50)
Serafeim, G., 25(n65)
Sessa, V. I., 306(n17)
Sevis, T., 285(n24)
Seyle, H., 163, 178
Shaffer, R. H., 477(n18)
Shafritz, J. M., 248(n41)
Shalley, C. E., 213(n33), 213(n34), 213(n35)
Shaw, R. B., 475(n13), 477(n14), 495(n81)
Sheats, P., 306(n18)
Shepherd, C., 220(n77)
Shepherd, D. A., 130(n50)
Shinn, S., 148b(n11)
Sidebotham, B., 90(n47)
Simon, H., 245
Simon, H. A., 237(n9), 247(n39), 251(n58)
Simpson, J., 219b(n68)
Sims, H. P., 322(n44)
Sims, J., 1610(n48)
Singer, J., 175(n7)
Singh, P., 206(n11)
Sinha, K. K., 312(n31)
Skinner, B. F., 153(n27)
Slancik, G., 416(n32), 416(n33)
Slaughter, A. M., 44
Smith, B. D., 490(n63), 490(n64), 490(n65)
Smith, C. G., 150(n16)
Smith, D. K., 304(n6), 314(n34), 321(n43)
Smith, G., 453(n47)
Smith, M. J., 184(n38)
Smith, P. B., 45(n45)
Snider, M., 70(n1)
Snipes, J., 150(n16)
Snyder, M., 130(n49)
Soane, E., 247(n35)
Solomon, N., 61(n94)
Sorenson, R. L., 359(n45)
Spataro, S. E., 86(n36)
Spiegel, A., 131(n53)
Strack, F., 130(n48)
Stadler, D. R., 126(n33)
Stalker, G. M., 454(n50)
Stanley, D. J., 129(n46)
Starbuck, W. H., 251(n59)

Wexley, K. N., 128(n42)

Wheatley, M., 8

Wheeler, A., 421(n56)

Wheeler, J. V., 322(n46)

Whetten, D. A., 344(n22)

White, H. L., 255(n72)

Whiteford, H., 177(n10)

Whitney, D. K., 492(n72), 493(n73)

Williams, K. D., 305(n15)

Williams, R., 10(n23)

Willman, P., 247(n35)

Wilson, D. C., 60(n91)

Wilson, P., 426(n70)

Wilson, T. D., 124(n30)

Winters, M. F., 60(n92)

Wiscombe, J., 61(n93)

Wolfson, P. J., 44(n43)

Woodall, J., 496(n83)

Woodman, R., 209(n22), 217(n53)

Woodyard, C., 494b(n74)

Woolliams, P., 116(n12)

Wright, T. A., 193(n70), 193(n71)

Wrong, D., 412(n18)

Wurtzel, A., 146(n5)

Wycoff, J., 206(n10), 223(n83), 256

Wyman, S., 483(n44)

Xie, J. L., 183(n35)

Yagil, D., 343(n20)

Yankelovich, D., 284(n21)

Yates, D., 420(n50), 420(n51)

Yetton, P. W., 253

Young, J., 190(n60)

Youtz, M. A., 340(n12)

Yu, M., 193(n72)

Yukl, G., 377(n19), 419(n48), 420(n49), 422(n58)

Zaccaro, S., 182(n28), 184(n40)

Zaleznik, A., 10

Zander, A., 305(n16), 308(n22), 374(n11)

Zax, D., 368(n2), 370(n3)

Zbaracki, M. T., 237(n11)

Zeevi, G., 217(n49)

Zelikow, P., 246, 247, 249(n46)

Zemke, R., 48(n72)

Zenger, J, 16(n41)

Zhang, H., 90(n48)

Zheng, W., 90(n48)

Zhou, J., 184(n42), 418(n45)

Zolli, A., 48(n69), 48(n70)

Subject Index

Note: Page numbers followed by "b" indicate boxed text, by "f," a figure, and by "t," a table.

teams for, 322
T-group, 491
Trait approach, 207, 208f, 373–374, 376f
Traits/skills for leadership, 376–379, 378f
Transactional leadership, 380
Transformational leadership, 218, 379–381, 381f
Tranter, Gary, 160
Tree map, 223
Trends
   in business, 463
   in organizational behavior, 9–10
   See also Environment
Trust
   collaboration and, 359–360, 360f
   conflict and, 346b
   engagement and, 165
   negotiations and, 361
   power and politics and, 427
   teams building, 321, 321f, 326, 328
Tuck, Richard, 479
Twitter, 220
Two-factor approach to motivation, 146–147
Two-way communication, 284
Type A individuals, 179–180

Ulrich, Bob, 79–80b
Uncertainty
   conflict and, 345
   environmental, 442–443, 442t
   organizational strategy/structure for, 461–462
Uncertainty avoidance, 52–53, 52f, 408–409
Unintentional ambiguity, 272
Union Pacific Railway, 452–453
United States Postal Service, 224, 441
Universality of ethics, 388
Urban Decay example, 440, 441
Urgency of change, 496
Ury, William, 338

Valid information, 490
Validation of communication, 284
Value-based leadership, 381
Values
   changing, 496
   creativity and, 225
   cultural, 479

defining, 56
importance of, 89–91
organizational, 477
Reddin's Personal Values Inventory, 90, 91t, 96–103
team conflict and, 323
Veneman, Ann, 20b
Verification stage of creativity, 211
Versace, Donatello, 337
Vertical conflict, 342–343
Vertical thinking, 214
Violence at work, 177
Virtual teams, 318–319, 319f
Visibility of leaders, 426
Vision, 225, 379, 437–438, 448–450, 448f
Visuals in communications, 292
Vital Voices, 20b
Vocabulary and creativity, 226

Wadhwa, H., 390
Walmart, 440, 442, 446, 450, 452
Washington, Coquese, 373
Washington State ferry system, 482
Watson, Thomas J., 4
The Web of Inclusion (Helgesen), 383
Weber, Max, 406–407, 408
Welch, Jack, 142
Wellness commitment, 185–186b
Western Union, 23–24
Wheatley, Margaret, 204
Whole Foods, 300–302, 320
Win-lose approach, 359
Winner's curse, 358
Win-win scenario, 359
Women in leadership, 20b, 133b. *See also* Gender differences; Gender diversity
Work tasks for creativity, 217, 218
Working conditions, 184
Work-life balance, 148b, 187, 194
Workload pressures, 183, 220
Written communications, 291–293, 293t
Wurtzel, Sam, 146

Yahoo!, 170, 336–338, 446–447

Zander, Ed, 60
Zappo's, 480
Zuckerberg, Mark, 436